Encyclopaedia of

COMPUTERS APPLICATIONS IN MANAGEMENT

Encyclopaedia of
COMPUTERS APPLICATIONS IN MANAGEMENT

Volume 1

Sumit Sethi

ANMOL PUBLICATIONS PVT. LTD.
NEW DELHI - 110 002 (INDIA)

ANMOL PUBLICATIONS PVT. LTD.
H.O.: 4374/4B, Ansari Road, Daryaganj,
New Delhi-110 002 (India)
Ph.: 23278000, 23261597
B.O.: No. 1015, Ist Main Road, BSK IIIrd Stage
IIIrd Phase, IIIrd Block,
Bangalore - 560 085 (India)
Visit us at: www.anmolpublications.com

Encyclopaedia of Computers Applications in Management

First Edition, 2009

ISBN 978-81-261-3912-5 (Set)

PRINTED IN INDIA

Printed at Mehra Offset Press, Delhi.

Contents

Contents

Preface

This Encyclopaedia is designed to provide a comprehensive introduction to the design and analysis of computer algorithms and data structures. In terms of the computer science and Computer Application, this encyclopaedia to be primarily focused on the Junior-Senior level Algorithms course.

This Encycloparedia owes its existence to the collaboration made possible by the Internet and the free software movement. Its author — a college professor, have yet to meet face to face, but we have been able to work closely together and have been aided by many wonderful folks who have donated their time and energy to helping make this encyclopaedia better.

Author

Chapter 1

Computers and the Behavioral Scientist

The behavioral scientist–by definition—studies and evaluates the com-plex interactions of men as individuals, within societies, and within environments. Why then should he be concerned with computers, which belong to the realm of the physical sciences? Although all the material in this book is designed to answer the question comprehensively, even the most cursory consideration must recognize the challenge to the social scientist implicit in the impact of computer technology on science and civilization.

The behavioral scientist studies man-machine relations in order to define the role of man in the control and use of the machine and thus to op-timize system interactions. In the growth of computer technology, man is assigning increasingly complex tasks to the machine and, in turn, is freeing himself to assume increasingly more complex tasks. From subjects as basic as perception, learning, and thinking, through analysis of spe-cialized social organizations, man is harnessing the capabilities of the computer as a powerful research tool. The researcher in behavioral sci-ence must learn to use this tool or risk being left behind as his discipline advances. But the computer is more than a research device; it is a production tool. As such, it is being used to automate manufacturing processes, warehousing and office procedures. The applied behavioral scientist must be aware of the effects of this new technology upon industrial management, labour, and the other forces in our society.

IMPLICATIONS OF THE COMPUTER FOR THE RESEARCH SCIENTIST

As a research tool, the computer may contribute in three principal functions:

- Organization and reduction of statistical data
- Hypothesis seeking, by finding relationships
- Hypothesis testing, through modeling and simulation

Research involves the accumulation of data and their eventual analysis and reduction. As our research capabilities expand, more and more data are accumulated and analysis becomes increasingly complex and time consuming. The statistical techniques are themselves becoming more sophisticated. If behavioral science remains chained to the desk calculator, it will stagnate. High-speed electronic data processing provides a means for rigorously, analyzing masses of data. While analyzing and reducing these data, special computer programs can search for patterns and relationships which, because of the number and quality of variables, might remain obscured and undiscovered. From these patterns, the researcher can develop new and significant hypotheses.

Testing hypotheses can also be facilitated through the use of automatic data processing technology, by using a computer to simulate and study human behaviour. But why study simulation models rather than human beings? The physiological psychologist will immediately recognize the similarity of this question to the older, more common query: "Why do you study rats if you are primarily interested in human behaviour?" And the answer is very much the same: By simulating behaviour on a computer, and studying its operation in detail, we can, by analogy, make inferences about the more complex human activities. These inferences must then be validated before being applied.

By way of illustration, consider the temperature control mechanism of warm blooded animals, or more specifically of man. Normal temperature is 9.6°. The body temperature must remain constant within approximately five degrees. Yet the temperature of the environment changes from 110° or more in the heat of summer to below freezing in winter. The organism's life depends upon accurate control of heat production and heat loss. As scientists, we are interested in studying the homeostatic mechanisms in temperature control; as computer-oriented researchers, we consider simulating this process. In fact, such a model already exists, for a thermostat operates in a fashion analogous to the hypothalamus.

In a low ambient temperature, the body temperature tends to fall. The skin, which has in it receptors for heat and cold, responds to the change. Messages are sent along nerve fibers to the hypothalamus, and the organism takes action to conserve body heat—action such as shivering and/or the constriction of blood vessels near the skin. Alternately, responding to a high ambient temperature, the message sent to the hypothalamus initiates action to dissipate body heat.

The thermostat works analogously. A desired room temperature is set. A thermometer is the sensing device or receptor. Detecting that the room is too cold, the thermometer creates a message, sent along an electrical conductor, that controls and starts the furnace. When the temperature exceeds the optimal limit, the furnace is stopped. The simulation model, i.e., the thermostat, operates on a feedback principle. The similarity between the operation of the thermostat and the observable control of body heat leads to the conclusion that the human organism uses a similar principle. The hypothesis is, at the very least, worthy of additional study and testing. In the course of these interactions, the computer specialist learns to design more sophisticated machines, and the behavioral scientist achieves greater understanding of the human organism—the most complex of all machines.

Through the data organization capabilities of the computer, far more complicated relationships can be defined and enormous masses of information processed in terms of those relationships. Thus the computer becomes analogous to organizations such as those comprising another machine, a natural resource, an industry, or a social community. The computer programed to model an industry, for example, responds to controlled fluctuations in variables such as production, sales, inventory, etc., and provides a basis for generalized conclusions about the parameters and their relationships.

The analogy of the organization of the computer itself to that of the human nervous system is even more pertinent to the behavioral scientist. It has been suggested that experience leaves a permanent mark on the brain—possibly by changing the configuration of protein molecules in the brain cells. The existing memory trace permits recall of the experience. Computer memory is somewhat similar. Information is recorded by magnetizing a certain small area of core memory. The computer can recall this information by checking to determine whether the part is or is not magnetized.

During the past few year, much effort has gone into the development of a formal theory of thought and memory. Cybernetics has this basic concept: the brain is a control and communication system which can be described mathematically in the form of logical nets composed of elements and connections. Although man-made communication nets may become extremely complex, then do not approach the magnitude of complexity existing in the human organism. Certainly, if we were able to describe thought, memory, and other human processes in mathematical terms—John von Neumann has pointed out that self-reproduction is also a mathematical problem—we could achieve a much better understanding of these functions. But the development of a theoretical model is not sufficient in itself. The model must be checked and verified under various operating conditions. For testing, the use of the computer is a necessity.

Hand calculation would be infinitely laborious if not outright impossible. In research, the computer can be used:

- To simulate a system of complex interacting variables, in order to facilitate control of the elements under investigation
- To simulate the environment in which the system must operate, again to permit a study of the system under various environmental conditions
- To record, reduce, and aid in the mathematical analysis of experimental observations

Yet, as versatile as it is, the computer is only a tool. By itself it can accomplish nothing, but in the hands of an imaginative scientist, its potentials are almost limitless.

IMPLICATIONS OF THE COMPUTER FOR THE APPLIED SCIENTIST

The computer has ushered in the age of self-regulating devices and automatic control. As more extensive use is made of the computer potentialities, man will receive new benefits and face new problems. Research involving these new applications is already under way, and some of the studies are reported in Part 3 of this book. Ward, Fruchter, and Koons discuss some of the recent advances in statistical techniques made possible by the electronic computer. Silberman studies the effects of automation on the teaching techniques employed in elementary schools and in universities, and Ledley applies automation to medical science. Sprowls shows how the technique could be used to study business decision making; Benson studies international diplomacy. Whether the behavioral scientist is interested in pure or applied research, he will be using the electronic computer. In addition, the applied scientist will be concerned with automation and its effects.

The trend or direction in which automation is leading us is obvious, for it is simply an extrapolation of our present practices. Just as mechanization has been a continuing process, so one can predict that automation will find ever wider applications throughout the economy. Production, the gross national product, and our standard of living will all continue to rise. New products that are the result of automated manufacturing techniques will appear on the market. Fewer people will be employed in routine factory and office jobs, but employment will increase in those concerns manufacturing automated equipment. This is the trend. It is obvious, definite and inescapable. Attempts to dismiss it or to counteract it may delay the process, but cannot change it.

Automation is on its way. How rapidly it is adopted depends upon how profitable it proves. Many objects—the small table radio for example-are already being manufactured and assembled completely automatically. Airplanes and missiles are being guided to their destination by an "automatic pilot." Soon it will be possible for a person to start his car, set the dials, lean back and read the newspaper or watch television while an "automatic chauffeur" drives him to the office.

Since automation must be economical if it is to be adopted, its greatest benefit may be considered to be the virtual elimination of expensive and unpredictable human labour in the performance of routine jobs. These economic advantages of automation were stated quite precisely and accurately by Frank K. Shallenberger, President of the Shalco Engineering Corporation of Palo Alto, California, and Professor of Industrial Management at Stanford University:

Automation has given us devices which can see better, hear better, and measure better than human operators. They think and move infinitely faster than humans. They never get tired, they willingly work around the clock, they do not make mistakes, they do not talk back, they are obedient, consistent, and fully predictable. They will not go out on strike, they do not ask annually for higher wages, and they have few personal problems.

The country's defence needs have provided another major impetus toward automation. The nations of the Communist bloc outnumber the Free World in population. To offset their numerical advantage, the free nations of the world must maintain a higher man-hour production rate or risk being overtaken in the Cold War struggle. Our government recognizes this fact, and the country's tax structure and allowable depreciation encourage capital outlay for tools and automated equipment.

Besides the many potential advantages of automation, certain deterrents and problem areas must also be recognized. Because automation means change, management must make the initial difficult decision as to why, where, and how much to automate. New equipment is expensive, and cost is a major consideration. Retooling inevitably means a change in the product design, and this raises questions of consumer acceptance, an intensified sales campaign, etc. Production problems may arise, because maximum efficiency requires that automated equipment operate continuously. In a seasonal industry, continuous production may result in a large inventory with concomitant storage and cost problems. The impact of the new machinery on the labour force must also be considered, for management neither desires nor can afford to ride roughshod over its employees. The workers must be prepared, so that they accept the change, and trained, so that they can operate and maintain the equipment. Although these are primarily problem areas for business management, they are also challenges to the industrial psychologist. To make reasonably intelligent decisions, management must have information on the anticipated effects of automation. More and more, the behavioral scientist is being relied on to provide the necessary data.

There is a need for market sampling to provide information on how new products, will be received. There is a need for improved selection of personnel to fill the newly created technical jobs. There is a need for improved techniques of labour-management communication. There is a need for improved training methods to develop the new skills required by automation. There is a need for improved techniques of retraining in order to equip the semiskilled worker to handle the more technically demanding jobs in the automated plant.

The behavioral scientist must be prepared to meet these needs. Automation thus is providing new impetus for basic research in the social sciences and is expanding the industrial opportunities for the applied scientist. Fortunately, the computer—the same general purpose computer that led to the current industrial revolution and all these new problems-is providing the tool to enable the social scientist to carry on the new research.

No discussion of automation is complete without some reference to the problem of technological unemployment. The phrase "technological unemployment" has a strong emotional connotation, which often distorts objective investigation. Indisputably, automation will displace some people from some jobs. Some people will therefore be unemployed, but this does not mean that there need be any mass technological unemployment. The harness maker became unemployed when the horse and buggy was replaced by the horseless carriage, yet the over-all effect of the automobile was increased employment.

History has shown that in the long run change, invention, and automation result in a higher standard of living and increased employment. "In the long run," however, the individual worker may suffer unless he receives help. Helping the displaced worker is the continual responsibility of government, industry, and organized labour. These agencies can provide the will and the means to help. The behavioral scientist must provide knowledge about retraining, counseling, and other techniques designed to ease any suffering resulting from the new technology.Finally, one benefit that could result from automation is the shortening of the work week and increased leisure.

But leisure is valuable only if it is used constructively. Misused, it can be injurious, and there is evidence that some people are misusing the shorter work week. Increased leisure has been blamed for the increase in crime in recent years. Boredom is said to be responsible for the rise in the number of people requiring psychiatric treatment. Evidently there is need for a special programme of education designed to teach people to make constructive use of their leisure time and to divert energy to healthful channels of activity.

But what is meant by "constructive use of leisure" and "healthful channels of activity"? How is one to decide whether it is healthier to play baseball or watch the game on television? Can the behavioral scientist, the sociologist, psychologist, and educator develop programs to help?These are some of the challenges of automation, which eventually must be met if automation is to be a true tool of progress.

HUMAN THINKING

The term "thinking" will be used in this section to include *problem solving, logical reasoning, learning, creative thinking,* and *autistic thinking*. In the following paragraphs, each term is defined in relation to computing, and the limitations of a computer in accomplishing each are indicated. The definitions appear to make sharp distinctions, but it is clear that the various kinds of thinking phase into one another. Note, too, that the term "thinking" implies both the process of obtaining results and the results themselves.

Definitions. *Problem solving* is a method employed in goal-seeking behaviour. It involves the definition of the problem and the formulation and evaluation of possible solutions. A solution may be achieved by trial-and-error activity or insight.*Logical reasoning* is a scientific method of thinking that follows certain rules and involves the manipulation of symbols. There are two major types of logical reasoning:

- Induction, which is the process of inferring a general principle from a number of particular instances
- Deduction, which is the process of reasoning from general laws to particular cases

Learning is a complex process that leads to a change in behaviour as a result of practice or other experience. Learning per se cannot be measured directly but can only be inferred from a change in performance.

COMPARISON OF HUMAN THINKING WITH COMPUTER FUNCTIONS

In comparing the human activity known as thinking with computer functions, it is important to distinguish between

- The results obtained by
  The human
  The computer
- The process by which the result is obtained by
  The human
  The computer

As the succeeding paragraphs will demonstrate, it is not particularly difficult to programme a computer to obtain the same results that a human would achieve in certain problem areas. Certainly, if the concept of thinking is limited to an emphasis upon results, the computer can "think," i.e., arrive at the correct solution. Computers have been programed to perform such tasks as solving problems in arithmetic and logic, playing chess, etc. Relatively little, however, has been done to simulate the *process* of human thinking by means of a computer. An outstanding exception to this generalization is the research work of Newell and Simon designed specifically to simulate the human thought process. This research is particularly important because it clearly demonstrates the possibility of programing a general purpose computer to solve problems by using the same techniques, i.e., heuristics, that people use.

With these introductory remarks as a basis for judgment, let us examine various areas in which thinking can be compared with computer functions.

Problem Solving

The solution of mathematical problems is one example of problem-solving behaviour. How much is 2 + 2? This is a problem, and if a young child can answer it, we say that he is exhibiting intelligent behaviour. The computer can solve this and similar problems of far greater difficulty. Basically, for either man or machine, solving a problem means selecting an appropriate response from a set of initially possible solutions. The information necessary for making the selection may have been previously available as a result of learning or programing, or it may be generated during the process by means of trial-and-error activities.

Problem-solving behaviour of another type is exhibited by a child trying to fit together the pieces of a jigsaw puzzle or by a rat learning to run a maze. These are examples of trial-and-error behaviour, and the method can be used to solve problems. There are computers (more properly, robots) in existence that can run mazes. The classic example is Ashby's Homeostat, which exhibits goal-seeking behaviour; a more recent example is Shannon's maze-running rat. This "rat" exhibits trial-anderror behaviour as it goes through the maze the first time. It then "remembers" all the turns and runs perfectly the second time. Rats do not learn as quickly or as well. In this case the machine can achieve far better results than can the living organism, but the methods are different.

The ability of a computer in problem solving is not limited to the algorithmic methods useful for deriving the correct solution to an arithmetic (or purely mathematical) problem. The work of Simon and Newell in developing a General Problem Solver programme emphasizes the heuristic methods applicable to solution of logical problems. Such problems are typified by games like chess in which algorithmic methods prove impractical. That is, to reduce and analyse all possible moves contingent upon any combination of previous moves, and the possible result of each move would result in an intolerably long game. The alternate method used by humans appears to derive from analysis of a sequence of "internal plays," offering probabilities of greatest benefit or gain and execution of the play thus judged best under the given conditions. Programs modeling this probabilistic approach to problem solving are being developed.

Logical Reasoning

Possibly the quintessence of human logical reasoning is found in mathematics, and the good mathematician is considered to possess great ability in this direction. Computers have been programed to prove theorems in Euclidean plane geometry in a manner "of a clever high school student." Computers have also been programed to play games such as tic-tac-toe, checkers, and even chess. The rules of these games involve logic and logical reasoning ability. MacCallum and Smith describe a computer capable of solving the following typical problem in logic: It is known that salesmen always tell the truth and engineers always tell lies. G and E are salesmen. G states that D is an engineer. A declares that B affirms that C asserts that D says that E insists that F denies that G is a salesman. If S is an engineer, how many engineers are there? The logic machine can solve this problem, can you?

Learning

The most basic type of learning is conditioning. Pavlov

conditioned his dog to salivate at the sound of a bell, thus demonstrating a change in behaviour as a result of learning. Skinner used a somewhat different technique for conditioning animals. It was called *instrumental conditioning,* because the organism's response was instrumental to achieving the desired goal and the resulting gratification. A hungry rat was put in a box containing a lever and a food receptacle. At first, the rat exhibited random behaviour. Eventually he pressed down on the bar and received a food pellet. Each time the animal made the correct response he received a reward or reinforcement. If the rat pressed the bar several times and received no reward, the response was extinguished. In this way, Skinner was able to demonstrate that the rat could learn and could forget. A. G. Oettinger, of the Cambridge University Mathematical Laboratory, programed the EDSAC computer to adjust its output in response to a conditioning-like stimulus.

The following chart compares Skinner's and Oettinger's conditioning experiments. Skinner's rat had to learn the relation between the conditioned response (bar pressure) and the reinforcement (food). He relied on the Law of Effect to establish an associative bond between the correct action and the reward. Oettinger wanted to teach the computer to print the number 3 every time it received the stimulus signal. He, too, relied on the Law of Effect. At the beginning of the experiment, the computer printed numbers, at random. Every time a 3 appeared, however, the experimenter would input a strong positive signal as a reinforcement. Every time a number other than 3 appeared, he would input a negative signal to express disapproval or negative reinforcement. The strength of the reinforcing signal varied directly with the magnitude of the difference between the given and the desired response. In a short period of time, the computer "learned" to respond to the stimulus by printing a 3.

Since computers do not ordinarily act in accordance with the Law of Effect, Oettinger had to programme EDSAC to behave accordingly. His programme is relatively simple. The nine possible responses are held within computer memory. They can be denoted by a_0 to a_7 and X. When the machine is stimulated, it selects a number a_r and adds to it a number representing the strength of the stimulus. If the result exceeds a given minimum value, a_r is printed. In other cases, the output is an X. The figure corresponding to ar will then be increased or decreased in proportion to the strength of the approving or disapproving signal input by the operator. In this way, the desired number 3 is reached and stabilized. The computer has also been programed to "forget" if it receives no reinforcement. This is an example of the computer being used to simulate the methods employed by humans for learning.

	Skinner	Oettinger
Emitted behavior	The organism engages in food-ceking behavior when hungry.	In response to a stimulus, the computer will print a symbol 0 through 7 or an X. The symbol "X" means that the computer could not de-cide which numerical sym-bol to print.
Reinforcement	Food	Stimulus signal of varying intensities.
Conditioned response	Rat learns to press bar in order to receive food.	Computer learns to respond by printing the number every time it receives the stimulus signal.

Like Pavlov's dog and Skinner's rat, the computer can be programed to respond to conditioning and modify its, behavioral output.

Creative Thinking

For the purposes of this discussion, creative thinking was defined as the ability to organize information into novel combinations. This description implies the use of inspiration or insight as part of the creative process. Inspiration, by its very nature, cannot be planned for or programed; hence the computer cannot make inspirational guesses nor reach conclusions by insight. However, if we limit ourselves to an examination of the end result of creative thinking—namely, a novel arrangement of material or information—we find that the computer is arranging and rearranging information constantly.

So far as these combinations can be formed either on a random basis or by following a logical procedure, the computer can produce novel arrangements. But in so far as creative thinking must include inspiration or some superrational element, it cannot be accomplished by a computer. One can ask whether a construct such as inspiration must be hypothesized in order to explain creative thinking. Again, the work of Newell, Shaw, and Simon demonstrates that creative and original work can be understood by the application of the same laws of logical reasoning as are applied to all other effective problem-solving behaviour. Indeed, they go further and state that the process of creative thinking *can* be simulated on a computer.

Autistic Thinking

Like creative thinking, autistic thinking need not follow any rules or logic. Perhaps this is why some people believe that there is only a thin line separating the genius from the insane. Although computer processing must be based on definite and prescribed procedures and is not usually an end in itself, there is no inherent reason why the computer cannot be made to simulate the results of the autistic thought process and possibly even the process itself.

THE NATURE OF MECHANICAL THOUGHT

A. M. Turing raised the question "Can a machine think?" and then reformulated the problem in terms of an "imitation game." This game is played by three people, a man (A), a woman (B), and an interrogator. All three are in separate rooms, and they communicate by teleprinter. The object of the game is for the interrogator to determine which of the other two players is the man and which is the woman. He does this by asking questions of the participants and evaluating their answers. He might ask, "Are you a man?" of both participants, but then he would probably get the answer, "Yes," from both, for under the rules of the game the woman must try to get the interrogator to make a wrong identification. Now what would happen if a machine such as a computer took the part of the woman? Turing suggests that if the interrogator could not distinguish between the man and the machine on the basis of the answers he receives, then for all practical purposes—as manifested in this game—the machine can think.

In the previous discussion comparing human thinking and computer functions, a distinction was made between the process of thinking and the result obtained by following that process. The varieties of human thinking, such as problem solving, logical reasoning, learning, creativity, and autism, were specified and the behaviour of computers in such activities described. It was demonstrated that computers have been programed to obtain solutions to problems and achieve results which were comparable to the results achieved by thinking humans. The discussion also mentioned research which simulated the process of thinking by computer programs. One can therefore make this statement: to the extent that the researcher could specify behaviour in a complete and logical fashion, the computer could be programed to accomplish similar tasks. To the degree that thinking involves no logical process, as may be the case in creativity and autism, the computer cannot think.

Shannon in describing his chess playing machine makes a similar distinction. He states, "The Gordian question, more easily raised than answered, is: Does a chess playing machine of this type 'think'? The answer depends entirely on how we define thinking. Since there is no general agreement as to the precise connotation of this word, the question has no definite answer. From a behavioristic point of view, the machine acts as though it were thinking. It has always been considered that skillful chess play requires the reasoning faculty. If we regard thinking as a property of external actions rather than the internal method, the machine is surely thinking."

Even this distinction may be tangential, however, for its assumes that the question, "Do computers think?" is meaningful. This is not necessarily so, for the question does not provide an operational definition of the term "thinking." If we define thinking operationally as problem solving activity, logical reasoning, learning, etc., then the question can be answered, "Yes, computers do think because they can solve problems and perform other logically described tasks." This operational definition emphasizes the results of thinking. Alternatively, if we define thinking as a certain process or procedure used to solve problems, even then evidence could be found to support the proposition that a computer could be programed to simulate the thought process. Finally, we can take a third point of view and define thinking as an activity capable of being performed only by living organisms, and therefore, not by Computers. Re-turning then to the original question, "Do computers think?" it is clear that a positive answer presupposes a materialistic and pragmatic view of the universe with emphasis on results, whereas a negative response must be based upon a form of philosophic dualism.

Although this excursion into philosophy sheds additional light on the question, it provides no final answer. Both question and answer involve a basic semantic confusion concerning the levels of abstraction with which we are dealing. This is partially a confusion between the process and the end product, but it is also the confusion between the representation of an object and the object itself. One can represent a material object by a symbol, but the symbol must not be confused with the object itself. "Dog" stands for dog, but it is not a real dog. Similarly, symbols can represent thoughts, but the symbol is not the thought, and thoughts are not symbols. This is perhaps elementary, but it helps explain the confusion about thinking machines. The author contends that computers do not think, nor do they solve mathematical problems whatever the type of programme employed.

The computer can only perform prescribed physical operations that the human operator correlates with thinking and with mathematics. Machines can manipulate symbols but not thoughts; thus the computer output is devoid of all intellectual content. This output, however, can be made meaningful and useful when it is interpreted by the human operator. The computer performs mechanical and electronic operations. It is the human interpreter that thinks.

HISTORY AND DEVELOPMENT OF COMPUTERS

The tried, true, and trite statement, "There is nothing new under the sun," is also applicable to computers. These very modern and ingenious machines have an ancient history. Computers, in the broadest sense, are tools developed to help man calculate, standardize, and understand the events that occur in the world around him. Thus the history of computers is in part the history of man's progress in understanding his environment.

A history of that progress is beyond the scope of this text. Rather, the book presents the facts surrounding the origin and use of certain computing devices whose principles are necessary to, and incorporated in, contemporary machines. The researcher in the behavioral sciences might find a rich harvest in an investigation of the background leading to the introduction of each such device; the brief summaries in this section should be considered in the framework of an unspecified but existing social and scientific need.

Contemporary computers and their forerunners can be classified in terms of various characteristics: analog or digital, mechanical or electronic,

binary or decimal, serial or parallel, general purpose or special purpose, etc. In this chapter, we examine analog devices, which calculate by using analogies, and digital devices, which count and operate on discrete digits. Of each type, we shall consider first the mechanical precedents of the electronic model. Finally, we shall discuss some of the early automatic devices and the characteristics of present-day machines.

ANALOG COMPUTERS

To compute "by analogy" requires representation of the elements of the computation by physical variables. A direct relationship is set up between a variable occurring in the problem one is seeking to solve and a physical quantity in the computation device. Numbers are represented by the magnitude of physical quantities, such as:

- The distance between two points on a stick
- The angular displacement, velocity, or acceleration of a rotating shaft
- The electrical current in a conductor

From ancient surveying and map making, to mechanical devices including the slide rule and the flyball governor, to electronic differential analyzers, subsequent paragraphs will indicate the elaboration of the techniques for computing by analogy.

ANCIENT ANALOGIES

Probably the very earliest form of counting or numerical manipulation was of the analog type. Primitive man scratched a line on the floor of his cave in order to represent the fact that he had killed one animal. In this case there is a one-to-one relationship between the symbol and the event. Although this is still a long way from calculating by analogy, it is a start. Perhaps many hundreds of years later, yet early in history, man measured his land and made maps. The British Museum exhibits a series of clay tablets, "circular in shape, and dating back to 2300 or 2100 B.C.,which contain surveys of lands." The resemblance, or analogy, between the map and the land permits computation—interpolation and measurement—without direct use of the original computation element: the land.

GREEK COMPUTER

An analog computer, more than 2000 years old, was discovered around the turn of the twentieth century by a group of divers working off the Isle of Antikythera, near the Greek mainland. In a ship that had apparently been wrecked during the first century B. C., they found a gadget with a complicated set of dials, gears, wheels, and inscribed plates. Reconstruction proved this to be an analog computer of the solar system, designed to function as a mathematical model and used to calculate the motions of the stars and planets. Further study indicated that the mechanism was an arithmetical counterpart of the more familiar geometric models of the solar system which were known to Plato and Archimedes and which can be seen today in a planetarium.

A two-dimensional map provides an analogy only to a particular static condition. Mechanically variable models, such as this early analogy to the solar system, go beyond this static representation and accommodate calculations in which dynamic conditions or effects are important.

SLIDE RULE

The map, whether twodimensional or mechanically variable, offers the opportunity to calculate only in terms of the original systems to which the model is analogous. The slide rule is an analog device at an abstract level. Familiar to most of us, the slide rule is a true analog computer in which numbers, or more precisely their logarithms, are represented by proportional distances along a piece of wood or other rigid material. Logarithms were invented by John Napier in 1614. A few years later, in 1621, William Oughtred put two logarithmic scales together and by holding one against the other was able to multiply and divide numbers directly. In the slide rule, the product of two numbers is the sum of their scalar distance. Each position along the scale represents a real number, and every number within the range of values is represented by a position on the scale. Since there is, in theory, an infinite number of points between any two scale values, the device is a continuous function computer.

FLYBALL

In addition to calculating, the output of an analog device is frequently used as a control mechanism. This principle was first demonstrated by the steam engine governor, invented by James Watt in 1788. Although the flyball governor went out of use with the invention of the reciprocal steam engine, it embodies an important application of the feedback principle which is the basis for mechanical and electrical self-regulation.

Let us examine how this simple and ingenious device

works. Information concerning the engine speed is conveyed to the governor in the form of the rate of rotation of a shaft. This governor shaft is linked to the output shaft of the steam engine by a gear train. The arm at the top of the shaft is linked, in turn, to the valve that controls the input of steam to the engine. When the engine is started, the shaft turns, the governor spins, and the flyball weights are impelled outward by centrifugal force. If the engine should go too fast, the outward swing of the flyballs would tend to close the input valve and slow the engine down. On the other hand, if the engine were not going fast enough, the flyballs would swing inward, i.e., toward the shaft, and this would tend to open the input valve and thus speed up the engine. After a few fluctuations, a constant speed is maintained.

PLANIMETER

As mathematics became more complex, machines were developed to solve problems of mathematical integration. If you are familiar with the calculus, you may recall that the area under a curve is determined by the formula: Depending upon the complexity of the curve, this calculation may take a considerable amount of time and effort.

The planimeter is an instrument that directly measures the area bounded by an irregular curve. It was invented by J. H. Hermann, a Bavarian engineer, in 1814, and was extensively used in solving engineering problems. Jacob Amster improved upon Hermann's basic design, and in 1854 constructed the polar planimeter. Both instruments are in use today. Paralleling the relationship between a two-dimensional map and a solar system model, planimeters demonstrate the increase in degree of mechanical sophistication necessary to solve problems of greater mathematical complexity.

HARMONIC ANALYZERS AND SYNTHESIZERS

In the early part of the nineteenth century, Fourier, a French mathematician, theorized that any complex curve could be duplicated by properly combining curves of each of the simple harmonic constituents. Since each simple harmonic curve can be expressed mathematically, any complex curve could therefore be expressed and, hence, operated upon mathematically.

Harmonic analyzers and synthesizers came into being to facilitate the use of Fourier series in analyzing waveforms. The analyzer is primarily a measuring device designed to isolate the individual harmonic components (of, for example, a musical sound) and to reveal the amplitude of each. The synthesizer performs the opposite function: it accept information on the amplitude (or analogous relationship) of each of the components and produces the complex function. Mathematical analysis and synthesis permits controlled study of the changes in the function resulting from changes in any or each of the components.

Lord Kelvin faced this type of problem when he tried to predict, i.e., compute, the behaviour of tides at different ports. The harmonic components are known, for they are the gravitational effects that the sun, moon, and planets exert on the seas at a given point in time. These can be measured and the data expressed in a Fourier series. The series can then be solved for the composite effect, which in this case is the height of the tides. To aid him in these calculations, Lord Kelvin designed an analog device in which trigonometric functions, such as sines and cosines of angles, are generated by means of pulleys and cranks of adjustable lengths. When operating, the centre of each pulley describes a circular motion that is the equivalent of the sum of two simple harmonic or sinusoidal motions—one vertical and the other horizontal. The height of the tides is then calculated by adding together a number of these harmonic functions.

MECHANICAL DIFFERENTIAL ANALYZER

Mechanical instruments have been designed to solve trigonometric functions (the harmonic analyzer); integral equations (the planimeter); and differential equations (the differential analyzer). Differential equations are mathematical statements concerning rates of change rather than absolute values of quantities. The fundamental problem in the differential calculus is to measure the manner in which a function changes in value, as, for example, when computing the velocity of a falling body at any given instant. The first mechanical device for solving problems in the differential calculus was built by Vannevar Bush and his associates at M.I.T. in 1931. The basic component of this machine is the simple wheel and disc integrator plus various mechanical representations of angles and lengths. During World War II, a large mechanical differential analyzer was built and used to help solve ballistic problems.

Although effective in solving such problems, analog mechanical devices with their multitude of pulleys, gears, shafts, etc., are bulky and require both expensive precision tooling and considerable time to set up the individual problems. In order to change from one problem to another, a great deal of work with screw driver and wrenches is needed as the mechanical parts are changed from one set of values to another. This difficulty was eventually solved in a later model of the analyzer that incorporated some electrical components.

ELECTRONIC DIFFERENTIAL ANALYZER

The important distinguishing feature of the electronic differential analyzer was the elimination of the mechanical gadgetry and thus reduction of needed setup time and manufacturing difficulties. Unlike the early Greek computer, which was a direct analogy of the solar system, a differential analyzer is not a direct analogy to anything. The distinction between direct and indirect analogy characterizes the difference between special purpose and general purpose machines. The general purpose machine is designed to solve mathematical equations, including problems involving differentiation and integration.

The computer is used to solve problems connected with the design of weapon systems. In effect, it becomes an electronic analog model of a missile or craft which can then be launched or flown thousands of times under simulated flight conditions, each time providing the engineers with valuable data.

SPECIAL PURPOSE MACHINES

In contrast to the general purpose analog computer that can operate on the mathematical expressions is the special purpose analog computer that is part of a regulatory system. This device is not designed to generate the solution to an equation in the form of a numerical quantity needed by the human. Rather, it computes its data primarily to generate a signal needed to control some other part of the system.

Included in this classification are the many specially designed devices to control temperature, pressure, density, and other parameters in the chemi- cal and similar continuous process industries.

Also included are the various speed controls (governors), directional controls (autopilots), positional controls (servomechanisms), and others. These special purpose computers are applied to the solution of many diverse problems, such as aircraft design, water flow for river and harbor control, highway traffic control, fire control mechanisms, etc. The design and utilization of these devices are highly specialized fields of study, and this book can do no more than mention their existence.

DIGITAL COMPUTERS

Just as we identified the analog device as a continuous function computer, so we may call the digital device a *discrete* computer. Whereas the analog machine measured a continuous quantity, such as the distance between two points on a bar, the digital computer can only recognize and operate upon discrete numbers.

In order to trace the history of digital computing devices back to its earliest origins, we should have to start with primitive and prehistoric man who counted with the help of his fingers or digits. Indeed, it is possible to conceive of all digital devices as extensions of the basic concept of counting on one's fingers, but it is, as we shall see, a very great extension.

Subsequent paragraphs describe the contribution made by the most significant of these devices. Comptometers and mechanical calculators are not detailed, because they established no really new principles and so contributed little to the development of automatic digital computers.

ABACUS

The abacus, in its many forms, is an ancient, versatile mathematical tool in use many hundreds of years before Christ. The earliest abacus was simply a board covered with dust. Lines marked in the dust were used to represent quantities in a manner similar to lines on a slate. Later on, the dust was replaced by wax, but the purpose was the same.

At some point in history, the abacus became more formalized. A new model appeared that consisted of a tablet marked with lines. Loose counters or discs of metal, bone, glass, and other materials were placed on these lines to indicate number. Finally, these counters were fastened together on rods within a rectangular frame. Each rod represented a numerical position (units, tens, hundreds, etc.), and the value of the digit was determined by the position of the beads on the rods.

Though not a calculating device, Jacquard's loom contributed to the principles of representing information by the arrangement of holes in a card. This punched card method of data representation was used by both Babbage and Hollerith and is still in use.

The abacus and the Japanese equivalent, called the *soroban,* are still very much in use in the Orient. During and after World War II, many Americans had an opportunity to see and appreciate the remarkable speed and facility with which skilled operators manipulated the beads.

NAPIER'S BONES

John Napier was the Scottish mathematician who invented logarithms early in the seventeenth century. He also developed a set of numbering rods called "Napier's Bones" which facilitated multiplication. Widely used in the seventeenth century, the device is now forgotten, or remembered only as a forerunner of the slide rule. The value of the device as an aid in multiplication can be seen. Each "bone" has inscribed on it the multiplication table for the reference digit which appears on top of the rod. These two digit products are arranged so that the tens digit is above the diagonal while the units place is written below. Thus examining the no. 6 bone and reading down we find that 2 X 6 = 12, 3 X 6 = 18, 4 X 6 = 24, etc.

If we were to multiply 68,452 by 4 we would "throw the bones" as shown. The product is opposite the number 4 on the multiplier strip on the left. For the units place, we record the number in the lower right box under the 2 which, in this case, is the number 8. Next, we add diagonally in pairs: 0 + 0 = 0, 2 + 6 = 8, 1 + 2 = 3, 3 + 4 = 7, and finally 2.

The answer is: 4 X 68,452 = 273,808. Should the multiplier contain more than one digit, each product would have to be recorded separately and then added together as in normal multiplication.

Napier's Bones, although not a machine in the true sense of the word, was an ingenious device making the multiplication process more mechanical and thereby decreasing drudgery and the chance for human error.

ADDING MACHINE

The first true calculating machine that could add a series of numbers once the digits were set and the crank turned was invented by Pascal in 1642. Capable of doing only addition and subtraction, the machine consisted of a series of wheels on each of which were engraved the numerals 0 through 9. These wheels were mounted in a box along an axis. By using a stylus, the wheels could be advanced one-tenth to nine-tenths of a complete turn. The revolutionary aspect of this invention was the carrying device. When the wheel was advanced from 1 through 9 and on to 0, the carrying device advanced the next digit wheel to the left through one-tenth of a revolution; thus mechanizing the concept that 9 + 1 = 10.

Pascal's device was the first practical adding machine—practical in that it was used by Pascal's father and other merchants to add up their accounts. The basic design was sound, but its development was interrupted because of an apparent lack of need for calculating devices at the time.

MULTIPLICATION MACHINE

Since multiplication is really repeated addition, Pascal's machine could be made to do multiplication. Although possible, it would involve a slow process. Leibnitz, a contemporary of Pascal, developed a method of performing the repeated addition rapidly by use of a stepped wheel. This cylindrical wheel had on its outer surface nine teeth of increasing length numbered from 1 to 9. The concepts and the stepped wheel embodied in the early model are still used in present-day mechanical calculating machines.

Leibnitz conceived the idea of a multiplying machine in 1671, and the first operating model was actually constructed in 1694. This original calculating machine has been preserved in the Royal Library at Hanover where, at one time, Leibnitz was a librarian. Although the conception and the design were excellent, the machine's performance was not perfect, because skilled craftsmen of the period could not attain the high degree of precision needed for its construction.

PUNCHED

The development of punched-card machines for use in statistical calculations is credited to Dr. Herman Hollerith, a statistician employed by the United States government to tabulate the 1890 census data. In 1801, however, Joseph Marie Jacquard demonstrated the use of a punched-card system for controlling the alternation of colors of the yarn and thus of the fabric produced by weaving machines. In modern terminology, we would say that Jacquard used a punched-card programme to produce a variety of patterned fabrics. These Jacquard looms are still in use today. The writer saw such a loom in operation in a silk weaving factory in Kyoto, Japan, in 1955. He was told that the pattern woven in this fashion was more complex and elaborate than one that could be woven on the more modern machines.

The magnitude of the job Hollerith had undertaken for the Census Bureau demanded a new and more efficient approach to data collection and organization. The 1880 census, using the standard manual tabulating methods to survey a population of approximately fifty million people, took seven and one-half years to complete! At that rate, the 1890 census could not have been analyzed before a new census made it obsolete. Obviously something had to be done, and Hollerith did it. He divided a standard 3- by 5-inch card into ¼-inch squares, making a total of 240 separate areas. Each one of these squares was assigned a distinct meaning. For example, a group of 20 squares were used to designate age, from 0 to 100 years in 5-year intervals. A hole punched in a particular square would indicate that the individual was between the ages of 30 and 35 years.

The punched card is inserted in the frame located at the operator's right on the console. When the handle is depressed, the points come through the punched holes in the card and come in contact with mercury cups, making electrical contact, and causing the movement of the index of a specific dial. At the close of each day, the totals reached on these counting dials had to be transcribed to record sheets by hand.

Since the machine had only 40 dials, each card had to be tabulated more than once. To facilitate the making of these multiple sorts, a box divided into compartments was placed at the side of the operator. This sorting box had 26 compartments, each closed by a lid held against the tension of a spring by means of a catch which turned the armature of a magnet. When a card was placed in the frame and the handle depressed, one of the electrical connections—referring to age, race, or any other desired characteristic—caused the lid on a designated compartment of the box to open for the reception of the card just tabulated. Thus the cards were sorted for transmission to succeeding machines. The use of these electrical tabulating machines greatly speeded up the work of the Census Bureau and their success ushered in the era of punched-card accounting methods.

DIFFERENCE AND ANALYTIC ENGINES

The calculating devices previously discussed in this section were limited in versatility and scope of operation. Babbage's Difference Engine, conceived in 1812, was the true forerunner of the modern computer. This machine was designed to calculate and print mathematical tables, such as tables of squares. The calculations were performed by the method of differences, a standard method in numerical analysis illustrated below.

$f(x) = x^2$

Computing the Constant Differeence

x	1	2	3	4	5
x^2	1	4	9	16	25
d_1	3	5	7	9	
d_2	2	2	2		

x = Any number in a consecutive series

x^2 = The square of that number

d_1 = The first order difference, obtained by subtracting adjacent numbers in the preceding row, i. e., 4 – 1 = 3, 9 – 4 = 5, etc.

d_2 = the second order difference, obtained in the same way, i. e.,c 5 – 3 = 2, 7 – 5 = 2, etc.

By way of example, we will work with the function $f(x) = x^2$ and determine the value of x^2 for every value of x, or generate a table of squares. In using the method of differences, we must first determine the value of the constant difference. Note that in the above example, the d_2 is a constant value. Having found the constant difference, we may proceed to generate a table of squares. This can be done by reversing the previous process and adding the known difference to the table headings in the following manner.

Computing Table of Squares

d^2	d^1	x^2	
2	1	1	2+1+1=4
2	3	4	2+3+4=9
2	5	9	2+5+9=16
2	7	16	2+7+16=25
2	9	25	etc.

The method of constant differences—computing the square.

Babbage's Difference Engine could perform these

successive additions and compute large tables of polynomial functions. Also, the machine was able to print out the results, thus eliminating errors of transcription. The concept of having a machine do both the calculating and the printing of the results was a great advance in the use of automation.

The British government underwrote the cost of Babbage's Difference Engine, and he began work on it in 1823. The actual manufacture of the machine was a complex engineering problem, because every part had to be made by hand. Moreover, the project was plagued by manufacturing difficulties, personality conflicts between Babbage and his chief engineer, and financial problems. The task was officially abandoned in 1842, although work stopped as early as 1833. The British government had by this time spent £17,000 or approximately $75,000, on the Difference Engine and had only received a model of a portion of the machine.

Babbage, however, was not discouraged. At the time he stopped working on the Difference Engine, he began designing a more advanced machine, which he called the "Analytic Engine." Although the newer machine included many parts of the Difference Engine, it was to be more automatic and controlled by punched cards similar to those used by Jacquard. Unfortunately, this machine, too, was never built, but from the notes still available it is clear that Babbage was the first designer of automatic computers. Like many men of genius, he was ahead of his time; the world had to wait a hundred years before Babbage's concepts of automatic computation were realized.

EARLY AUTOMATIC UNIVERSAL COMPUTERS

With the death of Babbage in 1871, the development of computers halted. Some modifications and improvements were made in the existing machines, but there were no radically new departures. All this changed in the twentieth century. This is the century of speed and material bigness, the age of coal, steel, oil, of railroads and automobiles, of big business and bigger wars. The rapid expansion in size and complexity of business and government organizations created a need for fast and accurate computing devices. Clearly, this was the time to renew the vision of Babbage.

MARK

It was in 1937 that Howard H. Aiken of Harvard University set to work on an automatic calculating machine. Whether he was aware of the work of Babbage is unknown and beside the point. He was clearly aware of punched cards and their use in calculating machines. He solicited the support of the International Business Machines Corporation and, in collaboration with them, built the Automatic Sequence Controlled Calculator, or Mark 1.

The Mark 1 is an electromechanical, not an electronic, computer. It consists of counter wheels whose rotation is controlled by electrical relays. (Basic components of an electronic computer are vacuum tubes or transistors.) The Mark 1 receives operating instructions by means of punched paper tape. Additions or subtractions can be performed in approximately three-tenths of a second; while multiplication takes four seconds, and division about ten. Although this machine contains more than three-quarters of a million parts and 500 miles of wire, it is only about one-tenth the size of the Analytic Engine as conceived by Babbage. For all its many mechanical parts, Mark 1 is a well-built and dependable machine, operational since 1944 and still in use.

ENIAC

ENIAC stands for Electronic Numerical Integrator and Calculator, popularly called the "electronic brain." It was designed by J. P. Eckert and J. W. Mauchly at the Moore School of Engineering of the University of Pennsylvania and was completed in 1946. A general purpose computer, it was designed to solve differential equations of the type used in calculating the trajectories of bombs and shells.

The ENIAC is the first of the electronic computers. The Mark 1, as explained previously, consists of relays, but the ENIAC has no moving parts. It uses electronic techniques exclusively to set and manipulate numbers. As a result, addition and subtraction can be performed at an extremely rapid rate. The internal circuitry was such as to require different electrical connections every time a new problem was introduced. Consequently, while the actual computations could be performed very rapidly, the preparations or setup time was long, and this tended to reduce the flexibility of the computer. ENIAC is a large machine, occupying a room 20 by 40 feet and containing 18,000 vacuum tubes. A successful machine—in that it accomplished its purpose of computing ballistic tables —the ENIAC established design principles which influenced later computer development.

EDVAC

The Electronic Discrete Variable Automatic Calculator was proposed in June, 1945. John von Neumann, on behalf of a group associated with the Moore School of Electrical Engineering, issued a report containing specific proposals for a new type of computer, new as compared with the recently completed ENIAC which was already obsolete.EDVAC contained three major innovations:

- The machine was to use the binary number system, and the conversion from decimal to binary language was to be accomplished by the internal circuitry of the machine.
- Ultrasonic delay lines were used to increase memory storage capacity.
- The programme of operating instructions was to be internally stored in the enlarged memory.

EDSAC

The Electronic Delay Storage Automatic Calculator, EDSAC, is a British machine built at the Cambridge University Mathematical Laboratory under the direction of Dr. M. V. Wilkes. Work was begun in 1947 and the machine went operational in May, 1949. Like EDVAC, EDSAC is a serial automatic computer using the binary system of arithmetic and an ultrasonic memory storage. Whereas the earlier machines had to specify the location of each instruction, EDSAC introduced the use of the accumulator register and programme counter. All arithmetic operations were performed in the accumulator; i.e., numbers were added to the sum already in the accumulator, or subtracted from the accumulator. The use of the accumulator register simplified computer logic and enabled the instructions to be read into the control unit automatically in consecutive order, thus increasing operating speed.

Although EDSAC is being discussed in a chapter on history, the history is by no means ancient nor is EDSAC an obsolete machine. The word format, punched paper tape input, programing by use of subroutines, etc., all make this an up-to-date computer still in use at Cambridge.

WHIRLWIND I

Computer technology took a major step forward with the development of Whirlwind I. This machine was designed and built at M.I.T.; it contained a number of important innovations, including magnetic core storage and marginal checking.

The use of small ferrite cores for storing binary digits was originally proposed by J. W. Forrester in order to achieve high operating speeds and fast memory access. The first core matrix was fitted to the Whirlwind I computer in August, 1953. It had a capacity for 1,024 words, each word consisting of 16 binary digits. Random access to any number would require only 1 microsecond, a tremendous increase in speed. Whirlwind also innovated a system of marginal checking* intended to increase the reliability of the computer by testing it under conditions more extreme than those tolerated during normal operations. In this way, weaknesses are discovered before they cause failure under operating conditions. These faults or weaknesses can then be corrected during the time normally set aside for scheduled maintenance.

The integration of high-speed components, circuit organization, and programing techniques demonstrated by Whirlwind proved to be the forerunner to the computer used in the SAGE (Semi-Automatic Ground Environment) system. This is a real-time data processing system sponsored by the

United States Air Force to automate the air defence of the North American continent, and it involves the processing of large quantities of radar and other types of data. SAGE is probably the largest network of computers in the world today. The experience gained in planning and manning such a system has had an influence beyond air defence and has been an impetus for the further development and use of computers throughout our economy.

CHARACTERISTICS OF PRESENT DAY COMPUTERS

The preceding paragraphs outlined the history of calculating machines, emphasizing innovations that advanced the state of the art. This historical review provides us with a vantage point for extrapolating into the future and predicting the characteristics of the next generation of computers.

Charles Bourne and Dan Ford at the Stanford Research Institute collected data concerning operating characteristics of approximately 200 computers presently in use. They plotted the rates of change of various machine characteristics using a horizontal calendar scale for years from 1942 to 1965. Their investigation covered the number of computers becoming operational, speed of operation, memory size, and other characteristics.

Very obviously there has been a tremendous increase in the number of computer models. In 1950, only some 20 different types had been developed; ten years later, nearly 300 types were in use. Most likely this rate of increase will continue for some time into the future.

Total memory size shows a considerable degree of variability, but this range has remained relatively stable during the last ten years and will probably continue so with a fairly constant average value. Memory access time has not improved as rapidly as operating speeds. Components presently under development, however, may produce a breakthrough that would significantly increase the speed of access.

Many different types of memory devices are in use today, but drum and core memory appear to be the definite favorites;

and this trend will probably continue through 1965. During this period, magnetic film memory, now under development, should become commercially available.

The trend, started by EDSAC, for single-address instructions in scientific computers will probably continue, and the number of multiple address machines will become proportionally less. Index registers, a relatively new technique first used in 1951, have proved to be of great value. A large percentage of computers have one or more such registers now, and this percentage will undoubtedly increase.

From the examination of these and many other computer characteristics, the authors conclude:

The collected data seem to suggest that the majority of the computers developed between now and 1965 will show very little change in performance from that which was obtained during the last five years. However, a few research machines will definitely advance the technology, possibly as much as one order of magnitude for some of the characteristics, such as multiply times, memory sizes, and memory access times.

Chapter 2

Computer Functions and Applications

The preceding pages presupposed some acquaintance with computers; hence various aspects of these machines were discussed in general terms. This chapter specifies more precisely what computers can do and how they are used. It presupposes no prior knowledge.

COMPUTER FUNCTIONS

As the name implies, a computer can perform all the standard *arithmetic operations*. It can add, subtract, multiply, divide, extract square roots, etc. As their great advantage over earlier calculating devices, these modern machines have tremendous speed, coupled with ability to do these operations one after the other without waiting for human intervention and piecemeal instructions. In performing a continuous series of operations, it is often necessary to *look up tables of data*, such as sines and cosines, and the computer can do this when necessary. The computer can also *store data* in tables or files for future use. Files are rarely static and must be updated periodically. For example, companies keep alphabetic files of their employees, but new employees join the company and old ones leave. The computer can *collate data* and keep the files up to date.

Although manually operated calculators compute accurately, mistakes can be made in transcribing the results. This error is eliminated by today's computers which also automatically print results and reports.

Standard office machines can perform the functions described, but the computer does them faster. Further, one function can be done only by the electronic computer and not by the desk calculator. The computer can be programed to make *logical decisions*. The decisions are very rudimentary. By comparing two sets of numbers, the computer can decide which number is larger. In the hands of a good programer, this seemingly small capability enables the machine to do tremendous work.

For example, if the computer were used in inventory control and instructed to keep one dozen of a given item in stock, it could (by subtracting the latest order from the inventory) determine the number of items remaining. Programed to compare this number with 12 (the prescribed minimum shelf stock), the computer could decide whether it is necessary to reorder the item and signal this fact to the operator. The computer's capability for making this type of logical decision is one of its most valuable assets in industrial and scientific applications.

COMPUTER APPLICATIONS

Computers have many applications and diversified uses. These can be classified into the following areas:

- Mathematical and statistical computation
- Scientific and engineering computation
- Business data processing
- Military applications
- Process control

MATHEMATICAL AND STATISTICAL COMPUTATION

The impetus for modern high-speed computers came from the large amounts of statistical computation required by the 1890 census. The Census Bureau remains one of the country's largest users of highspeed computers. Other large users of computers are the military agencies. During World War I I computers were used to solve highly complex series of simultaneous equations. They helped determine the trajectories of bombs and shells by determining mass, velocity, wind direction, and other variables. But mathematical and statistical computations are not the province of government alone. Computers are being used to reduce computational drudgery wherever it is found. In the social science laboratory, this drudgery is often encountered in factor analytic studies. With the help of computers, months of hard calculations can be reduced to minutes. This ratio is typical of the economy of using computers.

SCIENTIFIC AND ENGINEERING COMPUTATION

In the scientific and engineering fields, computers are employed in calculating aircraft performance characteristics. An experimental aircraft is flown first on a computer. That is to say, the behaviour of the aircraft is determined for various flight parameters such as speed, gravitational forces, maneuverability, etc. The test results influence the final design of the aircraft. Similarly, mathematical models of other equipment and situations can be programed for testing and evaluation.

A major obstacle in scientific research results from communication and language barriers. Computers can help remove such barriers, for they can now be used to translate material from one language to another.

The techniques of machine translation are so highly developed that one company is making plans to market computer-produced language translations.

Computers are also used in the study of flood control, weather forecasting, predictions of business cycles, and the analysis of many different kinds of economic data.

BUSINESS DATA PROCESSING

Small businesses, large corporations, and governmental agencies are automating their accounting and inventory systems and thus increasing over-all efficiency. Insurance companies use computers to calculate dividends, premiums, and actuarial tables. Public utilities compute their customers' charges with the help of computers. The government processes individual income tax forms and Social Security records via the computer.

MILITARY APPLICATIONS

The military establishments of our country are entrusted with the vital task of safeguarding our nation. Maintaining an adequate degree of preparedness involves the collection and processing of quantities of data. The Army, Navy, and Air Force all use computers as part of their weapons system. The Air Defence Command, for example, operates a radar network which is constantly scanning the skies and watching for an enemy attack. Should an attack come, there will be very little time in which to take the necessary defensive measures. Time is a most critical variable, for seconds may spell the difference between survival and destruction. High-speed computers are employed to minimize the time interval between the radar recognition of an aircraft and its identification as friendly or hostile. The computers are also used to guide manned interceptors and missiles to their targets. This is the SAGE—Semi-Automatic Ground Environment—system.

Methods are being studied for using a computerized system, similar to SAGE, to control all air traffic—civilian and military—in order to reduce the danger of mid-air collisions.

PROCESS CONTROL

Process control involves a somewhat different use of computers. Oil refineries have been making extensive use of computers as control devices for some time. Without them, it would be impossible to refine enough crude oil to run our gasoline-driven economy. Computers control the input of raw materials, monitor temperature, pressure, rate of flow, etc., and perform various quality checks. In this way, it is possible to maintain production of a sufficiently high quantity and quality to meet the customer's need. Without computers, this would be impossible regardless of the amount of manpower used.

Chemical plants are operated similarly, and automobile manufacturers have automated the manufacture of automobile engines from the raw castings to the final inspection. The automated manufacturing process proceeds smoothly and with a minimum of human intervention.

COMPUTER UTILIZATION

As is obvious, computers are being used extensively in government, industry, and research installations. These expensive items of equipment range in price from less than $50,000 to more than $2,000,000. What advantages does one expect to gain from the utilization of computers? There are a number of such advantages for both the scientist in the university and the manager in a business corporation. For example, when Sir Cecil Burt, Thurstone, and others expounded the virtues of factor analysis, they found few eager follower. The computational drudgery was so great that few were anxious to use the method. The factor analysis of a correlation matrix of 35 tests (35 × 35) would take months of painstaking work even with the aid of a desk calculator. Now, all the computations, including the factor extractions and mathematical rotations, can be accomplished in ten or fifteen minutes of computer time.Computers have a number of advantages:

- *Economy*: Although computers are expensive to buy and costly to rent, they can effect operating economies in manpower costs while doing tremendous amounts of routine calculations, such as payroll, inventory control, statistical calculations, etc. The recently designed, solid-state computers are relatively compact pieces of equipment. If installed to replace punched-card accounting procedures, such a computer takes less floor space and requires fewer operating personnel. Since its files are on magnetic tape, many old records and duplicate files can be eliminated. The utilization of computer equipment will usually result in saving valuable floor space and eliminating many file cabinets. Records thus become more, rather than less, accessible.
- *Accuracy*: In addition to, and perhaps more important than, monetary savings is the improved accuracy

resulting from proper programing and utilization of computers. In a large clerical operation, a significant portion of the errors results, not from incorrect original data, but from mistakes in transcribing, typing, and filing. The computer can help eliminate these errors. Further, computer programs can be written with self-checking routines that provide even greater accuracy.

- *Speed*: Along with economy and accuracy, rapid computation is an additional obvious advantage which can be achieved in a computerized operation.

The advantages listed are in themselves sufficient to justify the use of computers in research and industry. Still other advantages are to be gained. For the research worker, the computer provides new capabilities for studying systems previously considered too complex for investigation. Such systems can now be simulated on the computer. For industrial management, the computer can provide additional and more up-to-date information concerning the operations of the company. Computers can also be used to provide for better scheduling and maintenance procedures. An outstanding example of computerized scheduling and control is the Navy PERT (Programme Evaluation Research Task) system used in scheduling the production of the Polaris missile. PERT provided Admiral Raborn with charts and time estimates, enabling him to anticipate and avoid delays and difficulties. The improved management control made possible by PERT was one of the significant factors in making the Polaris missile operational years ahead of schedule. The computer can be used to provide similar control systems for management in other governmental agencies and in private enterprise.

Utilizing computers offers opportunities, but also raises problems. Programing is one such problem. Before the computer can be put to work, a detailed list of instructions must be written in a language the machine can understand. This is the computer programme, and writing it is a timeconsuming and tedious task. Fortunately, relief is on the horizon. Computer manufacturers and users have developed, and are continuing to develop, simplified programing techniques and compiler systems. Programs involving basic mathematical routines and procedures can be written once and shared by all users. These shared programs and compilers are steps toward reducing the time and cost of programing.

A second major problem area in the use of computers is the lack of trained personnel. Extensive utilization of electronic computers is being restricted by the lack of people who can programme and operate these machines. In this problem area, no relief is in sight. The shortage will become more rather than less severe as computers become more readily available, because programers and operators are not being trained at an adequate rate. Organizations that are planning to install an electronic data processing system should also plan to train their own personnel. However, the lack of programers is not the most serious problem. One can learn the fundamentals of programing a computer in three months or less, but it is much more difficult to learn how to make optimum use of the machine—to conceive of problems worthy of computer application. Scientists, researchers, and management personnel must be trained to reorient their thinking in terms of electronic data processing equipment and away from the desk calculator. At best, such a training programme will take years, but unless these people are trained to make optimal use of the equipment, the electronic computer could become an inefficient and expensive gadget.

Programing and the need for computer-oriented executives and scientists are problem areas that must be anticipated and planned for, when installing an electronic data processing system. Since the key to a successful operation is adequate planning, this discussion is couched in terms of problems of computer utilization, rather than their advantages and disadvantages.

The behavioral scientist who is considering using computers in his research work can reap many of the same advantages and must confront many of the problems that corporate management faces. Like management, the researcher becomes capable of reducing large masses of data economically, speedily, and accurately. He also faces similar problems—how to plan suitable research and how to programme the computer. He can reduce the problems involved in programing by writing in FORTRAN or a similar system, and for most machines he will find available a number of previously written "canned" programs. In planning his research, however, the scientist encounters difficulties arising as a result of using the computer and which were not present when he was reducing data by hand. Charles Wrigley, writing in *The American Psychologist,* indicated a number of ways in which the computer influences research design. On the positive side, the researcher can deal with large amounts of data and apply relatively complex statistical techniques for reducing this data. In contrast, he must control a tendency to collect a large sample rather than a carefully selected one. A population sample of 1000 presents no more of a problem to the computer than an N of 100. A rigorously chosen sample of 100, however, provides more meaningful data than a biased sample of 1000. Large numbers cannot substitute for good experimental design. The researcher must also avoid the tendency to tailor his experimental methodology to conform to existing data reduction programs rather than to select the statistical procedures most suitable to the data and the problem.

Forewarned is forearmed; once alerted, the scientist can avoid these difficulties and use the computer as a powerful new tool in his arsenal of research devices.

DATA PROCESSING SYSTEM

A *computer* is a machine that is able to calculate and perform sequences of arithmetical and logical operations in accordance with preprogramed instructions, thus eliminating the need for human intervention at each step. A *data processing system* consists of a combination of units, including the arithmetic processing unit (which is the computer proper) plus input, output, and storage devices. Data are brought into the system by means of the *input unit.* The devices that make up this unit must be able to sense information, as coded on some medium, and transfer it to the storage unit. Information enters the system as holes in punched cards or paper tape, as magnetized spots on magnetic tape, as letters and numbers printed on paper in magnetic ink, or directly from the keyboard of an electric typewriter connected to the computer.

The *storage unit* is the computer's memory facility. Storage devices must be prepared to receive information from the input unit and to file it according to a prearranged indexing scheme. The items stored in the computer may be the instructions needed to solve a problem or the data these instructions will manipulate. The size or capacity of the memory and the speed with which its contents can be located and transferred to the central processing unit are important variables which determine the adaptability of the total system for particular commercial or scientific uses.

The *control unit* directs and coordinates the timing and operation of the entire processing system as it performs various arithmetic and logical operations and transfers the data into, and out of, storage. Although control circuits are usually dispersed throughout the system, the diagram shows the function as centralized in the control unit. By means of the control console and its many switches and signal lights, the operator starts and stops the computer and maintains cognizance of the step-bystep progress in the solution of a problem.

The *arithmetic processing unit* is the operational heart of the data processing system. This unit adds, subtracts, multiplies, and divides. It also performs logical operations, such as determining whether or not a number is zero, whether one number is larger than another, or whether a quantity is positive or negative. These determinations may seem trivial but—as will be seen—properly programed, a computer can do a great deal with these few decision capabilities.

Finally, after a problem has been solved and the answer computed, the output unit provides the means for getting the result out of the computer and into a form readable by humans. Output devices are similar to the input units and include equipment that handles punched cards, paper and magnetic tape, and printed information.

INPUT AND OUTPUT DEVICES

The units that function as input devices can often do double duty as output equipment, as their basic structures are the same. In one instance, the device is used to read unprocessed data into storage; in the other, it records the results of the computation. In both cases, the information is recorded in code on cards, tape, or other media, which the unit interprets. The methods of coding information are presented in later chapters. This chapter is primarily concerned with developing some familiarity with the equipment and its operating characteristics.

PUNCHED CARDS

The punched card is the most common input medium, probably because it is an excellent and versatile means of storing information. Installations using punched-card equipment can continue to use it even after converting to a more rapid electronic method of processing data. Both numerical and alphabetical information can be coded for card punching. Names, descriptive labels, and other items of either a numerical or non-numerical nature can be reproduced on the card from the punched holes. The card itself contains 80 or 90 columns in which information is stored. The information can be read into the computer at rates of 100 or more cards per minute depending upon the type of card reader. Considering the speed at which a computer can operate, however, this rate is not fast enough. Few computers rely on a direct card input; most convert the information from cards to paper or magnetic tape, for these can be processed at higher speeds.

The punched-card input unit consists of equipment for punching, verifying, and collating the cards. The Remington Rand Photoelectric.

PUNCHED PAPER TAPE

Long before computers came into existence, punched paper tape was used in connection with teletype equipment. It was adopted for use with the early electronic computers and remains a popular input medium. Tapes are available in various widths and can have five, six, seven, or eight channels. Ordinarily, one character occupies a row across the width of the tape. The normal speed of reading varies from 150 to 500 characters per second.

Paper tape is a faster input medium than the punched-card system. It has a further advantage: the coding can be done as a by-product of regular typing. Using a Flexowriter, or an attachment to an electric typewriter, a typist can produce a coded tape while she is preparing her standard typewritten copy. Prepared in this fashion, punched paper tape is a very efficient input device, for it eliminates the duplication of effort involved in preparing the coded data separately.

Verifying the accuracy of the tape is facilitated by preparing the tape and printed copy simultaneously, for an error in one means an error in the other, and proofreading the printed page is relatively simple.

Punched paper tape offers a third advantage: the machines needed to punch and read paper tape are cheaper than those required to handle cards or magnetic tape.

MAGNETIC TAPE

Like the punched cards and punched paper tape equipment, a magnetic tape unit can function as both an input and output device. Magnetic tapes are also used for bulk storage of data that is to be filed for future use.

The magnetic tape looks very much like the tape used in home recording devices. It consists of a plastic ribbon with magnetic surfacing. A magnetic read-write head reads or records the information. The data are recorded as magnetic spots on the tape in a prearranged seven-channel code. Computer magnetic tape differs from audio tape in that for audio recording, the signal varies with the degree of magnetization, whereas in the most popular scheme for computer application, the direction of magnetization carries the intelligence. The data are recorded in binary code; one direction of magnetization represents binary 1, and the opposite direction represents binary 0. This method of recording allows for a high signal-to-noise ratio and excellent reliability. Alternate techniques of recording, offering other advantages (such as amount of information per unit length) are also in use.

The data are recorded in blocks of information, each approximately one inch long and separated by about one-quarter inch of blank tape. This arrangement aids in locating the desired data. Commonly, counters on the tape drive equipment keep track of the blocks and activate the read heads when the specified information is located. Again, different equipment utilizes alternate identification methods.

The prime advantage of magnetic tape input is the speed with which information can be read into the computer. High-speed, high-density tapes have an effective "read rate" of more than 50,000 characters per second. A single foot of such tape, read into a computer in a fraction of a second, bears as much information as fifty punched cards (which require half a minute or more to be read into the computer). Not only is it possible to store large quantities of information on tape, but it is easy to manipulate this material and to update it. Unlike cards and paper tape, magnetic tape is reusable. Its major disadvantage is the relatively long time needed to locate a given item of information. This is basically a mechanical problem arising from the fact that one item may be on the front end of the tape whereas the next required item may be at the tail end. It takes time to move a few hundred feet of tape. Nevertheless, the great storage capacity of magnetic tape makes it an efficient medium when used to input data for high-speed computer processing.

MAGNETIC INK

One of the recent developments in data input systems was designed by the Stanford Research Institute for machine processing of letters and numerals printed in a special magnetic ink. The system, designed primarily for banks, has enabled them to process paper checks mechanically and with less clerical help. This innovation heralded a great advance in data processing technology, for it involved a compatible system understandable to both men and machines. In other systems, special coding for machine processing must be employed.

Still other equipment has been developed capable of reading symbols written in ordinary ink. Eventually, it will be possible to supply the computer with both the data and the instructions for solving a problem, in ordinary printed English. These machines will be able to recognize,

understand, and follow natural language instructions to obtain the desired solution. Some day, too, it may be possible to input data to the computer verbally. Results of recent research on machine recognition of sound are encouraging, and great progress is being made in this area.

DIRECT KEYBOARD INPUT

When a relatively small amount of input and output material is required, an electric typewriter can be connected directly to the computer. Obviously, this is a very slow method of providing data, but by using the techniques of buffering and time sharing, it need not delay computer processing. The typewriter keyboard contains many numbers and symbols: a feature not possessed by other input devices. As an output device, the electric typewriter enables the computer to supply the results in printed language for immediate interpretation and utilization.

PRINTERS

The internal operation of the computer takes place in millionths of seconds. The time-consuming aspect of the work is transferring data into, and out of, the machine. Solving a problem may take a few thousandths of a second, but obtaining a readable answer may introduce a wait of several seconds. Printing speeds are critical. They vary from 10 characters per second on the typewriter to 2000 or more per second on high-speed printers.

The typewriter is a slow printer because time is consumed in raising the key to the paper and returning it to its original position. These inertial effects are minimized in high-speed printing by using a print wheel, print chain, or matrix printer. In both the print wheel and chain, the type revolves rapidly. When a letter is properly positioned, a small hammer strikes the paper against the type. A maximum speed of up to 500 lines per minute may be obtained using this system.

Faster speeds—about 1000 lines per minute—are possible using the wire matrix printer. In this device each character in the printing line is formed by pressing the ends of selected wires (in rectangular, 5 by 7 matrices) against the paper. This procedure does not result in solid type, but the printing is legible.

STORAGE DEVICES

Storage is classified as external and internal, and the internal or main storage is further specified as static or dynamic.

EXTERNAL STORAGE

External storage may be compared to a file cabinet of data not in active use. Characteristically, external storage devices have high capacity (i.e., they store great quantities of material) and a slow access rate; hence, it takes a comparatively long time to find the information desired. Further, data contained in external storage must first be transferred to internal storage before they can be operated upon by the computer. In this sense, external storage devices are used by the input unit; in a similar manner, they may be used by the output unit for storing-data after the computer operations have been completed. Examples of external storage devices are punched cards, punched paper tape, and magnetic tape. Since the external storage devices were described previously as input-output units, the discussion will not be repeated.

Internal storage must be directly accessible to the arithmetic processing and control units of the data processing system. Access time is rapid, but capacity is somewhat limited. In *static storage*, the information is held in it fixed location in space and is always instantaneously available. Electrostatic and magnetic core memories are static. Information stored in *dynamic memories* circulates and therefore changes position and storage location with time. As a result, the stored information is not always available for instant recall. The data must be properly positioned before they can be read. Examples of dynamic memory storage devices are the Stromberg-Carlson, A Division of General Dynamics.) 1 Power supplies 9 Split prism (cutaway) 2 Paper roll take-up spindle 10 Developer section Paper cutter (accessory) 11 Cleaning chamber 4 Fuser 12 Charge grid 5 Tube control circuits 13 Xerographic drum 6 Push-button controls 14 Transfer grid 7 Metal shield 15 Paper roll 8 Charactron shaped beam tube (7-inch diameter) (cutaway) magnetic drum, disc, and acoustic delay lines. The term "memory" may be somewhat confusing and anthropomorphic. It is used interchangeably with "storage" and refers to that unit in the data processing system which holds information for later use. The information may be instructions data, reference tables, or the results of intermediate and final calculations.

All this information must necessarily be stored in code form on some medium.

All memory units have the following characteristics, and they can be rated on these dimensions:

Capacity

The term refers to the number of words of data that can be stored in the memory devices. Capacity may vary from a few hundred to a few hundred thousand digits.

Complexity of the machine logic

The ease with which the computer can move information in, and out of, storage is generally a function of the complexity of the logic (or organization) of the machine. This complexity is reflected in the variety of instructions the machine can recognize and execute. At a minimum, all computers must have a "read-out-of-memory" and a "read-out-of-memory" instruction. This may be a series of instructions rather than a single command word. In addition, some machines have indexing features and provide a means for setting up temporary storage tables that can be read out as a block of data rather than one item at a time. These features serve to increase the effective speed of operation.

Speed of access

Access time is that time required to locate a particular memory address and transfer data either into, or out of, the specified location. Access speed is measured in milliseconds (thousandths of a second) or in microseconds (millionths of a second).

Cost

The dollar value of the memory unit is a function of the construction, i.e., core, drum, disc, etc. and is directly related to the capacity, of the unit and access speed.

Volatility

Memory in which data remain intact despite power failure or equipment shutdown is called *non-volatile*. In contrast, items stored in volatile memory are lost when the power is shut off. Electrostatic storage tubes and delay line memories are examples of volatile memory; magnetic recording is non-volatile.

Before specifying the differences in storage equipment, it is useful to consider the function of the storage unit in general. A computer must have the capability of receiving information, holding it until ready, using the information (data, reference tables, or instructions) to solve the problem, and then storing the computed results before printing out the solution. When large quantities of information are to be stored, each item must be labeled and indexed so that it can be located when needed. Computer storage systems use a very simple method of indexing. The storage space is divided into a series of "bin," called *words*, in a manner analogous to the rows and columns of individual mail boxes found in most post offices. Each "bin" is given an address, and information is referred to by the address in which it is located. For example, computer instructions are written in the form: "Take the information in address no. 306 and add it to the data in address no. 307, then store the result in address no. 101." This basic reference scheme of providing each piece of data with an address holds true for all types of storage equipment.

MAGNETIC CORE STORAGE

Magnetic core memory is a static and non-volatile storage system offering random access to any item in its relatively large capacity.

The core is a tiny (less than one-tenth of an inch in diameter) ring of ferrous material. It can be magnetized in less than a millionth of a second by a few millionths of a watt, and it retains its magnetism indefinitely. A wire is passed through the hollow centre of the core; when an electrical current flows through the wire, the core becomes magnetized in one direction.

These two directions of the magnetic polarity can be called "plus" and "minus," or "1" and "0." This binary or two-state system of coding is used as a basis for storing all information in the computer.

The cores are strung together like beads in a frame. These frames (or planes) vary in size, with the more popular sizes containing approximately 4000 cores. These planes are then stacked one on top of the other; a given core address being the aggregate of cores on all planes at a particular column/ row position. Each core is located at the intersection of a vertical and horizontal wire. Such an intersection can be identified (as the coordinates in a plane).

In order to magnetize a particular core in the desired direction (i.e., to record the desired 1 or 0), it is necessary to send one-half the needed current through the horizontal wire and one-half through the vertical wire. As can be seen from the diagram, this procedure produces full current at one and only one core. The process of recording coded information by magnetically orienting selected cores is called "reading into memory." Once the information has been stored, some means for reading it out of memory must be provided. To read out, the directions in which a specific core has been previously magnetized are determined by use of a third wire, called the "sense wire." It connects each of the cores on a plane.

By activating it set of cross wires, current is directed to a specified core and orients its magnetic field. In reading out, however, our goal is not to orient that core but to determine its orientation. If the core was previously magnetized in the direction representing a zero value, the reading out process effects no change in the magnetic orientation. Hence, the detector circuit senses no change—or a zero. But had the core been magnetized in the 1 state, application of readout current produces a change in orientation, which induces a current in the sense wire. Such a current is detected as a 1.

Because it involves applying a current, reading information out of core destroys the data, or more accurately, the reading out process alters orientation of cores storing 1's. It is therefore necessary to regenerate the data. This is accomplished by an inhibiting pulse, which may be sent through the sense wire or through a fourth wire following the readout pulse and which restores the status of the core orientation. In summary, each core has a number of wires passing through its centre, and these provide the capability for writing and reading for information into, and out of, core storage. The system is efficient, reliable, has very fast access time, but is comparatively expensive and used in the more costly data processing systems.

MAGNETIC DRUM STORAGE

The most frequently employed internal computer storage device is the magnetic drum. The drum is a rapidly rotating cylinder whose ferrite-coated surface can be readily magnetized in minute discrete areas. The drums vary in diameter and in length. The number of recording channels and capacity depend on the drum size. For example, the magnetic drum in the UNIVAC Real-Time Computer

System is a very large piece of equipment. It has 128 recording bands across the length of the drum and a total capacity of 3,800,000 alphanumeric characters. A more common size of magnetic drum is the storage unit of the

UNIVAC SS 80 Data Processing System. A line drawing of this piece of equipment. There are 25 recording bands on the magnetic drum, each containing 200 word locations for a total of 5000 words. Twenty, of these storage bands are called "normal-access bands" and are provided with one read-write head per band. The remaining five bands are called "fast-access bands," because they are equipped with four read-write heads per band, spaced 50 words apart, and have an information access time four times as fast as that of the normal-access band. Also recorded on the drum are permanently magnetized control tracks, which enable the computer to locate and interpret any given address.

Electrical current is sent through the writing coil. The direction of the current flow determines the resulting polarity of the magnetic cell, which in turn is used to represent the binary digits 1 and 0. For reading data, the magnetic state of the cell is detected by the reading coil, in which the magnetic orientation induces a correspondingly polarized current. In the magnetic drum system, reading is not destructive, because the condition of the cell does not change when it passes under the magnetic head.

Besides its somewhat limited storage capacity, the rotating magnetic drum system has another important disadvantage: namely, the recording and sensing of information can take place only when the specified location is passing under the read-write head. This means that access is not instantaneous but, in fact, varies with the distance that the specified cell must travel to reach the head. To increase the access speed, some drum systems use more than one head per track.

MAGNETIC DISC STORAGE

Magnetic tapes have large storage capacities but slow access to specified data. Magnetic drums offer faster access time, but a much smaller storage capacity. Magnetic discs combine the best features of these other two systems.

The magnetic disc is approximately two feet in diameter and resembles an oversized phonograph record. It is made of thin metal and is coated on both sides with a ferrous oxide material similar to that used on the magnetic drum. Each side of the disc contains 100 concentric tracks in which the data can be stored. Fifty discs are mounted on a rotating vertical shaft. The magnetic read-write heads are mounted on an access arm that can be moved, under the control of the computer, to any track on any disc.

The magnetic disc storage system can hold large amounts of data and provides for relatively fast access on a modified random basis. This method of storage is particularly desirable for business accounting systems, which need relatively inexpensive, large capacity, random-access storage devices. The operating speed need not be extremely fast. Magnetic disc memory meets these specifications. The access arm, with its read-write heads, takes approximately a tenth of a second to move from one track to another. This is many times longer than the access time of core memory, which is measured in microseconds.

ELECTROSTATIC MEMORY

In electrostatic memory systems, information is stored on the surface of cathode ray tubes. These tubes are similar to the type used in television sets, but are generally approximately three inches in diameter. Such a tube can store a total of 256 bits. Total memory may be increased by using an array of tubes.

As in all computer memory systems, information is stored in binary code form. In the magnetic memory systems, the critical variable was the direction of magnetization, positive of negative; 1 or 0. In electrostatic memory, the presence or absence of an electrical charge on a specified portion of the surface is interpreted as 1 or 0, respectively.

The face of the cathode-ray tube is divided into a 16 by 16 matrix, which provides 256 small squares or storage positions. To record information on the tube face, an electron beam is directed to a particular square, and an electrical charge is placed on a portion of the phosphorous coating. The presence of this charge is interpreted as binary number 1. To read information out of memory, the electron beam is again directed to the selected location. If a 1 has been stored there, however, the area is already charged, and additional electrons have no effect. The lack of an output charge indicates that a 1 had been stored in that location. On the other hand, if a 0 has been stored in the selected location, the electron beam charges the area, causing an electrical pulse at the output circuitry. As in core storage, the reading out process destroys the data, which then must be regenerated.

In addition to the destructive readout, a number of other problems are inherent in electrostatic storage devices. One such problem centers in the fact that the areas in which the electrical charge must be placed are quite small, and the angle of deflection of the electronic beam is very critical. Should the electron beam be directed to one spot on the surface of the tube for any length of time, it "digs a hole" in the phosphorous coating, damaging it. Finally, differences in adjacently placed electrical charges tend to neutralize one another, producing a state of equilibrium.

This means that information stored as differences in electrical potential must be constantly regenerated to prevent loss. In summary, electrostatic storage is very sensitive—being subject to many operating difficulties-and expensive. Consequently, this type of memory system is not usually used in today's computers.

ACOUSTICAL DELAY LINE

Data can be stored as a series of electrically initiated, mechanical pulses traveling at low speed through a conducting medium. This device is called a "delay line."

Mercury-filled tubes with crystals on either end are commonly used as the storage medium. When an electric impulse is applied to the input crystal, it is converted to mechanical energy, transferred along the mercury column as an ultrasonic wave. At the other end, the output crystals reconvert the wave to a corresponding series of electrical pulses. An interval of time elapses from the moment the impulse enters the storage medium until it leaves. In a 30-inch tube of mercury, this interval is approximately 250 microseconds. This interval constitutes the "delay" that gives the storage device its name. At any given instant, a number of pulses are in transit in the mercury tube. Approximately 180 alphanumerical characters may be pulsing in the 30-inch tube at one instant, and this is the storage capacity of the unit. The storage is dynamic, for the data are constantly recirculating. As a pulse emerges from the output crystals, it may be used, and, unless modified, it flows back into the input end, recirculating as long as the equipment is powered. When needed, specific data can be located by maintaining an identification with respect to regularly spaced standard pulses (called a "clock") and transferring the information to the control unit.

Mercury ultrasonic delay line storage is volatile and relatively expensive. Although the mercury tube was successfully used in EDVAC and UNIVAC I, it is being superseded, in today's computers, by faster and more compact devices.

The ideal computer storage system should have a large capacity in a small equipment volume, fast random access, and be inexpensive both in initial production and in operation. This ideal has not yet been reached; therefore, many different systems, some of which have been described, are in use. The storage device is selected for a given data processing system on the basis of the particular feature the designer chooses to emphasize. Each system has its strengths and weaknesses.

ARITHMETIC PROCESSING UNIT

The arithmetic unit processes data in accordance with programed instructions and can add, subtract, multiply, and divide. Besides these basic operations, computers can interpret many other instructions—such as "Clear and add," "Shift right," "Branch on zero," etc. The instructions are built into the circuitry of the arithmetic unit. A variety of instructions simplifies the computer operations and provides for greater operational flexibility and speed. In performing its functions, the arithmetic unit must be furnished with information as to what operation of perform, the location of the data to use, and a place to store the results. Commonly, the same series of instructions incorporates the location of the next instruction. Thus, the computer can operate without interruption until instructed to "Halt."

In addition to arithmetical operations such as can be performed by any desk calculator, the arithmetic unit of the electronic computer is able to carry out logical operations. Logical decision making is utilized in the "Branch" instruction. Normally (i.e., without branching), the computer performs a series of operations in a prescribed sequential manner. The process starts with the computer examining instruction no. 1, and the work continues sequentially through instructions no. 2, no. 3, no. 4, etc.

The computer performs a logical decision when instructed to deviate from the sequence in accordance with the results of a prescribed test. Such an instruction is called a "conditional branching instruction" and may be considered similar to a branch or fork in the road. A traveller, reaching a fork in the road, reads the signposts. Using the information thus obtained and considering his known objective, he decides which road to follow. Computer logic is similar. For example, in calculating an arithmetic mean, we may want the computer to add an indefinite series of numbers (*N* cases). The computer, like a human operator, detects when the series is ended, for then all cases have been tallied. The next, or (*N* + 1) case, will be equal to zero.

In a manner analogous to looking for signposts, the computer is instructed to examine the contents of each new register before adding the data to the subtotal of the series and to branch on contents equal to zero. The "Branch zero" instruction provides that, if the register contains all zeros, the computer should—instead of continuing with the normal sequence of instructions—branch, or skip, to register X and follow the instruction located there.

In this manner, the computer decides, on the basis of the information it possesses and without human intervention, when to stop adding and to divide by *N* in order to obtain the arithmetic mean. This decision-making capability is part of the logic built into the arithmetic processing unit, and it helps account for the computer's tremendous versatility.

CONTROL UNIT

Although the arithmetic processing unit may be the heart of the computer system, the control unit is the brain inasmuch as it directs the operation. It selects and interprets the instructions to be performed; it moves information from one part of the computer to another as needed; it coordinates the performance of all the computer elements and insures that the system functions as an integrated unit. Specifically, the control unit must monitor the timing of every operation, and it must interpret the coded instructions. The console provides a method by which the operator communicates with the computer, and the computer with the operator.

TIMING

Electronic digital computers perform arithmetical operations in microseconds, i.e., millionths of a second. Accurate timing is critical to effective computer operation. Correct information must be in the correct location for the results to be meaningful. Required timing is accomplished by a device variously called a "clock" or "pulse generator." The basic functional unit of computer time is the time needed to process

one digit of information. If this interval is fixed at one-millionth of a second, the computer is said to operate at a 1-megacycle rate, and the clock may be a fixed frequency pulse generator, such as a crystal-controlled oscillator. This mechanism is often found in computers with magnetic core storage.

When magnetic drum storage is used, the computer clock is synchronized to the rotation of the drum, to insure that the timing will not be out of phase should the speed of the drum rotation vary slightly.

Other timing devices may also be used, but the basic principle of controlling the time sequence of the computer operation remains inviolate.

DECODING

Before information can be processed by the computer, it must be put into a numerical code (only numerically coded information can be stored in the computer). It is the function of the control unit to interpret the coded instructions and signal the other parts of the computer to take the required actions. An instruction word * may be divided into two parts: the operation code, and the data address that specifies the storage location of the data, or operand.

The instruction word 52 0364 may be interpreted to mean, "Add (code 52) the contents of storage location 0364 to number in the accumulator." As the control unit decodes this instruction word, it sets up the proper circuits to perform the addition operation as specified.

THE CONTROL CONSOLE

Every computer is equipped with a control console, and the operator and machine communicate with each other by means of the console equipment. By appropriate switch action, the operator starts and stops the computer. Other switch actions enable the operator to control the input and output units, to read the contents of a storage register, to examine the contents of the arithmetic unit, to transfer information from one location to another, and to actuate manually any operation of which the computer is capable.

Through the console, small amounts of data can be entered directly into storage. Communication is a two-way channel, and the computer communicates with the operator by means of flashing lights, bells, and other signals that are part of the console.

This is especially important when a malfunction occurs, for computers can be programed to recognize errors and to signal the condition to the operator. The console lights indicate the reason why the machine stopped—a programme error or a mechanical failure—and enable the operator to trace the cause of the difficulty.

Many computer consoles have a special maintenance panel with switches and meters designed to help the engineering personnel service and maintain the equipment. Under test conditions, the computer can indicate the unit that is not operating properly.

Since these components are often assembled on boars readily plugged into frames, any malfunctioning part can be quickly replaced.

The computer is an integrated system of input and output devices, an internal storage unit, a central processing unit, and a control section that directs and coordinates the operation of all the parts. Together these components make up the electronic data processing system.

Chapter 3

Data Representation

The functional components of computers, states that before data can be processed, they must first be coded into a language which the computer is capable of manipulating. This need for translation is not a new concept: the citizens of one country must translate their thoughts if they wish to be understood by the natives of another country. In the United Nations, for example, speeches are translated into five official languages, an even this does not guarantee universal understanding. Equally, for communication with a computer, still another language, and symbols other than the spoken or printed word, must be used in order to convey meaning. Concepts can be represented in many different symbol systems, for a concept is distinct from the symbol used to represent it.

The cahpter contains a discussion of the concepts and symbols of *machine language*; i.e., the language that the computer can manipulate. Just as one does not necessarily learn a foreign language before traveling abroad, however, one need not learn the machine language in order to understand and use the computer. The material presented in this chapter is important for those who wish to understand the inner working of the computer, but it is not a necessary prerequisite for the reader who is solely interested in learning to use the computer as a tool for solving various research problems.

The decimal, binary, and octal numbering systems, and some variations thereof, are explained, and the method for converting one system to another illustrated. The principles of binary arithmetic are described, as is a basic computer circuit for binary addition. Also included are the standard codes for representing data on cards, paper, and magnetic tape. Together, this material provides the reader with a knowledge of the essential element of machines language. But users of electronic data processing systems need not code in machine language. As a matter of fact, most users programme the computer in a problem-oriented language. The essentials of programing are discussed in Chapter 7, and those readers who do not find the mathematics and logic of computers interesting may turn immediately to that chapter.

NUMBER SYSTEM

Number are symbols. The numerical concept *eighteen* may be written as the decimal number 18—as it commonly is throughout the Western world—but it can also be written as the Roman numerals XVIII, the Hebrew character Even this is an oversimplification, for numbers have different meanings.

Numbers may be used to *denote quantity*— as in "2 apples" or "4 pencils." Numbers may also be used *as addresses in an ordered series*, and when used in this fashion the numbers need not connote quantity. The house at address 84 is not necessarily bigger than the house at address 82. The house number enables us to distinguish a given address from all others and to locate it. Finally, numbers may be used solely *for identification*, with no implication of quantity or serial location. This is true in the case of telephone number, Social Security numbers, Army serial numbers, etc. This introductory discussion emphasizes that symbols can be used to carry information, that the same information can be conveyed by different symbols, and that the same symbol can convey different information, depending upon how it is used. The meaning of the symbol is determined by convention. In communication with computers we use some familiar symbols, but we determine their meaning by new a convention. First, let us examine the common convention of numbering called "the decimal system."

DECIMAL

The decimal numbering system probably had its origin

in the accident of nature that provided man with ten fingers or digits. The common numbering system is composed of ten symbols: 0, 1, 2, 3, 4, 5, 6, 7, 8, and 9. With this system, we can count up to 9 using one symbol at a time. In order to count past 9, it is necessary to combine two symbols. By using two symbols together, the person counting can represent up to 99 objects. To count further, three symbols must be used, and so forth. Mathematically, the decimal system is described as being based on powers of 10. For example, the number 8463 can be writtern: 8463= ? (in powers of 10) (8x103) +(4x102) + (6x101) + (3X100)

8 × 1000 =	8000
4 × 100 =	400
6 × 10 =	60
3 × 1 =	3
	8463

In the foregoing example, only whole numbers were used. It is also possible to write fractions and mixed numbers in the decimal system and in the powers-of-10 convention. For example 92]! = 92.633, which can be written:

(9 × 101) + (2 + 100) + (6 × 10-1) + (3 × 10-2) + 3 × 10-3)

9×	10	=	90
2×	1	=	2
6×	0.1	=	0.6
3×	0.01	=	0.03
3×	0.001	=	0.003
			92.633

It is obvious that any numerical quantity can be expressed in this manner. but it is obvious only because we are so accustomed to dealing with decimal numbers.

The number 6 is tallied when that bulb, and no other, is lit. The computer will operate with such a system, but it requires an extremely complicated circuitry in order to add or otherwise manipulate these numbers. There are simple ways of doing things.

BINARY

Had nature provided man with eight or two prehensile

digits, we might have developed different numbering system. The electronic computer is not necessarily restricted to the use of a particular numbering system. As the example of the electric light bulb array shows, the computer can operate on a decimal numbering system. To simplify computer circuitry, we take advantage of an obvious characteristic of the electric light bulb: that it is either on or off—that it can exist in one of only two states. Not entirely by coincidence, this leads us to a consideration of a numbering system, called the "binary system," which has only two symbols: 1 and 0. The sparsity of symbols necessitates large combinations of digits, or "bits" as then, are called, to express quantity. For example, the binary, expression for the number 18 would be 10 010, or five binary bits as compared to two decimal digits.

When counting in the binary system, we start as in the decimal system and assign the symbol 0 to zero and 1 to one. Having now used up all the permissible symbols, the first symbol, namely 0, appears again in this position, while the next position to the left advances one symbol. Thus binary 10 (read one-zero and not ten) is equivalent to decimal 2. The first twenty binary and decimal numbers. Just as the decimal system is based on powers of 10, so the binary system is based on powers of 2, and any binary number may be written as a sum of powers of 2. An abbreviation list of the powers of 2. Note that fractions can be expressed as negative powers of 2.

Analyzing binary, 010 010.101 into powers of 2, we get:

$0 \times 2^5 = 0$

$1 \times 2^4 = 16$

$0 \times 2^3 = 0$

$0 \times 2^2 = 0$

$1 \times 2^1 = 2$

$0 \times 2^0 = 0$

$1 \times 2^{-1} = 0.5$

$0 \times 2^{-2} = 0.0$

$1 \times 2^{-3} = 0.125$

18.625

In order to convert a binary number into its decimal equivalent, it is only necessary to write it as the sum of its powers of 2, as was done in the example above. Thus, one calculates that binary 010010.101 is equal

Binary	Decimal
0	0
1	1
10	2
11	3
100	4
101	5
110	6
111	7
1000	8
1001	9
1010	10
1011	11
1100	12
1101	13
1110	14
1111	15
10000	16
10001	17
10010	18
10011	19
10100	20

Binary and decimal numbers.

2^{-n}

2^n	*n*	*Fraction*	*Decimal*
1	0		
2	1	1/2	0.5
4	2	1/4	0.25
8	3	1/8	0.125
16	4	1/16	0.062 500
32	5	1/32	0.031 250
64	6	1/64	0.015 625
128	7	1/128	0.007 813
256	8	1/256	0.003 906
512	9	1/512	0.001 953

1024	10	1/024	0.000 977
2048	11	1/2048	0.000 488
4096	12	1/4096	0.000 244

Positive and negative powers of two to decimal 18.625. Conversely, a decimal number may be converted into its binary equivalent by successively subtracting the powers of 2. This is readily accomplished by repeated division of the decimal number by 2. The remainder of this step of the process becomes the binary digit. An example will make this clear.EXAMPLE: Convert the decimal number 106 into its binary equivalent.

	Remainders	
2/106		
2/53	0	
2/26	1	
2/13	0	=1 101 010
2/6	1	
2/3	0	
2/1	1	
0	1	

Note that in reading the answere, we read from the bottom up, in the direction of the arrow.In summary, the following points concerning the binary numbering systems are to be stressed:

- 0 and 1 are the only two symbols used.
- It is a base 2 numbering system as compared to the decimal system, which is derived from a base 10.
- Any number or quantity may be expressed in the binary system, although to do so generally requires a longer sequence of symbols than is the case in decimal numbers.
- It is possible to convert from decimal numbers to binary and from binary to decimal. The two systems are equivalent, and the same numerical concept can be expressed in both symbol systems.

OCTAL

Whatever its advantage for use by a computer, the binary

numbering system, with its large combination of digits, is awkward for human use. Errors are likely to be made in the transcription and transmission of a long series of 1's and 0's. Fortunately, the octal system provides a method for reducing the number of binary bits to one-third while still maintaining all the advantages of that system.

A close inspection of the table reveals that there is an obvious relationship between the octal and the binary numbers such that one system can be

Decimal	Binary	Octal
0	000	0
1	001	1
2	010	2
3	011	3
4	100	4
5	101	5
6	110	6
7	111	7
8	001 000	10
9	001 001	11
10	001 010	12
11	001 011	13
12	001 100	14
13	001 101	15
14	001 110	16
15	001 111	17
16	010 000	20

Decimal, binary, octal conversion table.

converted to the other by inspection. For the numerals 0 through 7, the octal is identical with the decimal system, and both have the same binary equivalent. Since the octal numbers are derived from powers of 8, only eight symbols are utilized; the numerals 8 and 9 do not appear in this system.

Octal numbers go consecutively from 7 to 10 and from 17 to 20. It should also be noted that each octal digit has its three-bit binary equivalent and this equivalence holds true regardless of the number of octal digits, so that octal 5 = binary

101, and octal 15 = binary 001 101, and octal 55 = binary 101 101.

To convert octal to binary, or binary to octal, one must simply express the octal number as a combination of three binary bits.

Example: Convert octal 367 to binary.

3 = 011 6 = 110 7 = 111

367 = 011 110 111

Example: Convert binary 100 101 001 to octal.

100 = 4 101 = 5 001 = 1

100 101 001 = 451

It is also possible to convert an octal number into a decimal equivalent by writing it as the sum of its powers of 8.

Example: Convert octal 3075.2 to its decimal form.

3×8^3	$= 3 \times 512$	=	1536
0×8^2	$= 0 \times 64$	=	0
7×8^1	$= 7 \times 8$	=	56
5×8^0	$= 5 \times 1$	=	5
2×8^{-1}	$= 2 \times 0.125$	=	0.250
			1597.250

8^n	*n*	8^{-n}
1	0	1.0
8	1	0.125
64	2	0.015 625
512	3	0.001 953
4,096	4	0.000 244
32,768	5	0.000 031

Positive and negative powers of eight.

BINARY-CODED DECIMAL

Computers operate most efficiently using a binary code. The electronic circuitry is simpler, and the calculation can proceed at a faster rate if the computer is designed to operate with binary rather than decimal number. Input data are typically in decimal format, however; and so are the output data. For the human operator, conversion from decimal to binary is tedious, time-consuming, and subject to error. The computer would require additional circuitry to do its own converting, and this would tend to increase the size, complexity, and cost of the equipment. The solution to this dilemma was the development and utilization of a compromise and combinatory code called the "binary-coded decimal" (BCD). In this BCD system, the decimal number is converted to binary on a digit-by-digit basis using 4-bit binary equivalents for each decimal digit.

Thus 379 would be expressed as 0011 0111 1001. In pure binary, 379 would be 101 111 011. Both pure binary and binary-coded decimal are based on a two-symbol system, but the conventions that give meaning to these symbols are different and should not be confused. To the human operator, the main advantage of the binary-coded decimal system is that conversion from one system to another can be made by inspection. Computer conversion is handled on a digit-by-digit basis and requires very simple circuitry. Yet this code provides the computer with the capability for performing calculations in binary arithmetic, with its attendant advantages of simplicity and speed.

BIQUINARY

Several forms of biquinary codes are in use. The name applies to a code in which a single bit represents the quantity 5, and three or more other bits represent quantities 0 through 4. In the classic system, the biquinary code requires seven positions to represent a decimal digit. Two of these positions, the binary component, have an assigned value of 0 or 5. The other five, or quinary, positions have values of 0, 1, 2, 3, and 4. The abacus is a familiar use of one variation on this biquinary code.

	Decimal value	0	1	2	3	4	5	6	7	8	9
	0	1	1	1	1	1	0	0	0	0	0
Binary	5	0	0	0	0	0	1	1	1	1	1
	0	1	0	0	0	0	1	0	0	0	0
	1	0	1	0	0	0	0	1	0	0	0
Quinary	2	0	0	1	0	0	0	0	1	0	0
	3	0	0	0	1	0	0	0	0	1	0
	4	0	0	0	0	1	0	0	0	0	1

Biquinary code: For example, the number 7 requires a binary code 5, plus a quinary code 2. The coding of alphabetic data requires two biquinary words. The 90-column punched card of the Remington Rand UNIVAC division uses a modified biquinary code.

BINARY ARITHMETIC

We all know how to perform the basic decimal arithmetic operations, but how does one calculate in binary? Actually, it is very simple, for we use only 1's and 0's.

ADDITION

The basic operations for binary addition:

ADDITION TABLE

0 + 0 = 0

0 + 1 = 1

1 + 0 = 1

1 + 1 = 0 and carry 1

1 + 1 +1 = 1 and carry 1

As one would expect in any system of addition, 0 + 0 = 0, and 0 + 1 = 1. In binary, because there are only two symbols, when we add 1 + 1 we do not get 2 (for this does not exist). Rather, 1 + 1 = 0, and it is necessary to carry 1, i.e., add 1 to the next column on the left.

Should that column contain a 1 + 1, and we add 1, we are in effect adding 1 + 1 + 1 which equals 1, with 1 to carry. An example will make this clear.

Example: Add the following binary numbers.

Binary		Decimal equivalent
100 110		38
001 111		15
110 101	=	53

SUBTRACTION

Subtraction is equally simple, and the rules are the same as those used in decimal subtraction.

Binary Subtraction Table

0 - 0 = 0
1 - 0 = 1
1 - 1 = 0
0 - 1 = 1 and borrow 1

Example: Subtract the following binary numbers.

Binary		Decimal equivalent
101 011		43
010 110		22
010 101	=	21

MULTIPLICATION

Binary multiplication is similar to decimal multiplication as the table and example illustrate.

Binary Multiplication Table

0 X 0 = 0
0 X 1 = 0
1 X 0 = 0
1 X 1 = 0

Example: Multiply the following binary numbers.

Binary		Decimal equivalent
100 110		36
101		5
100 110		
0 000 00		
10 011 0		
10 111 110	=	180

DIVISION

Division is reduced to a process of successively subtracting the divisor from the dividednd. If the result of the subtraction yilds a positive remainder, a 1 is written in the quotient. If the remainder is negative; i.e., if the divisor is too large and cannot be subtracted, then a 0 is placed in the qoutient.

Binary Division Table

0 ÷ 1 = 0
1 ÷ 1 = 1

Example: Divide the following binary numbers.

Binary	Decimal Equivalent
1 000 001 ÷ 1 101	65 ÷ 13 = 5
101	
1 101/1 000 001	
110 1	
001 101	
1 101	
0	

BOOLEAN NOTATIONS AND COMPUTER CIRCUITRY

Section has shown how the basic arithmetic operations of addition, subtraction, multiplication, and division can be accomplished in the binary system. It has also been stated that the basic reason for using binary numbers is to simplify the electronic circuitry of the computer. It is therefore appropriate to examine a computer circuit and to determine how the process of addition is actually accomplished in the computer. But first it is necessary to learn a few symbols of logical diagraming. These symbols provide a type of shorthand notation for expressing the function of a circuit without having to draw the complete circuit diagram. The specific symbolic notation most often applied to digital computer systems is called "Boolean algebra." It was devised by George Boole, an English mathematician, in 1849 and is really a system of symbolic logic. Its application to computers is a recent development and is based upon the fact that Boolean algebra deals with functions that are either true or not true; i.e., it deals with binary conditions and therefore conveniently describes the logical circuitry of digital computer.

Without going into excessive detail, it can be briefly stated that in this application of Boolean algebra, alphabetic characters are used to represent the electrical impulses, and other symbols represent the interrelationship of the signals. For example, *A* and *B* are designated as signals. The absence of these signals can then be indicated by A + and B +, variously read as "*A* bar" or "not *A*."

If the presence of either of two input signals yields an output signal, a condition exists which can be expressed by the following Boolean notation: *A* Â" *B* = C. This is read as "*A* or *B* equals *C*." On the other hand, if both *A* and *B* must be present in order to produce an output signal then *A* Ã" *B* = *C* is the Boolean description of that condition. It is read "*A* and *B* equals *C*." In diagraming the logical operation of digital computer circuits, a few special symbols based upon the Boolean equations have been devised. The OR circuit will produce an output signal if there is an input on either *A* or *B*. In order for a signal to appear at the output of an AND gate, input signals must be present at both *A* and *B*. If the AND gate is combined with an INHIBITING INPUT signal device, then an output will be produced if and only if there is an input signal on *A* and no input for *B*, or vice versa.

These three types of units can be combined to form a logical diagram of a *half adder* circuit, a basic computer circuit for performing binary addition. When a signal is applied to either input *A* or input *B*, an output signal is produced at the sum output line.

A Ã" B = S

In binary addition, this represents 0 + 1 = 1 or 1 + 0 = 1. A signal applied to both inputs *A* and *B* would be the same as adding 1 + 1, and the answer should be 0 and carry one; that is, no signal should appear at the "sum" output, but one should appear at the "carry" output. Following the various possible inputs in the diagram of the half adder, it will be seen that if there are inputs at both *A* and *B*, then there will be but one output to "carry."

In Boolean algebra terminology, this can be expressed as follows:

- The expression above is read as *A* or *B*, but not both *A* and *B*, equals *A* and not *B*, or not *A* and *B*, which equals *S*, or sum. A + B = C meas that if there is an input at both *A* and *B*, there will only be an output at C, or carry.

The half adder is one of the circuits used in the arithmetic unit of the digital computer. ther circuits provide the capability of performing other calculations.. For our purposes, it is enough to know that both people and computers can calculate in binary arithmetic.

CODING INFORMATION

It has been shown that numerical concepts can be represented in a binary as well as in a decimal convention and that the computer can manipulate and perform arithmetic operation with binary numbers. Obviously, information must first be read into the computer, and this is accomplished by means of the various input devices. These data recording media can now be re-exmined in order fo study the methods used for coding information.

80-OLUMN PUNCHED CARD

The 80-column cárd with rectangular holes is one of the most popular devices for recording data. The card contains 80 vertical columns and twelve rows. The twelve positions in each column, i.e., the rows, contain the decimal digits 0 through 9 (with 9 being in the row nearest to the bottom edge of the card). The uppermost two rows, sometimes callled *X* (row 11) and *Y* (row 12), are the zone positions. In actual practice, the 0 row may serve the dual role of both a numeric value and a zone position.

From this brief description and illustration, it is clear that the numerals 0 through 9 can be represented, in this code, by a single punch in the proper row. To represent alphabetic data i.e., the letters of the alphabet and other nonumerical symbols—two punches in a single vertical coumn are necessary. The letters *A* through *I* are code by punching the twelfth zone and the numerical location 1 through 9 respectively.

For the letters *j* through *r*, the eleventh row and again the numerical positions 1 through 9 are used. To code S through Z, zone *0* and positions 2 through 9 are used. Special characters, such as +, -, %, *., etc., can be coded by using unique combinations of two or three punches, such as zone 12, 11, and number 1. In this manner, all numerical, alphabetic, and special characters can be represented by the 80-column punches card code. The holes are punched by a special card punch machine and interpreted by a card reader. In planning the coding of information onto a card, certain columns are reserved for specific information. Thus, columns 1 through 4 may be used for an identification code number. Age may be put in columns 5 and 6, sex in 7, etc. In the illustration, columns 75-80 were reserved for the date. Should more than 80 columns be necessary, the record can be continued by using additional cards. Continuity would be established by means of identification and sequence numbers.

Storing data by means of holes punched in cards has many advantages. It is simple and accurate, for the punches can be verified. The coded data can be printed directly onto the card as the holes are punched, facilitating identification. The cards can also be sorted into many sequences or arrangements on the basis of the data: thus it is possible to sort alphabetically by name, numerically by age, by test score, etc. By use of the card accounting machines, arithmetic operations can be performed and reports printed, all derived from the little holes in the cards. For electronic data processing, however, direct card input is too slow, and the cards are used most often as an external supplementary storage device.

90-Columns Punched Card. This card is arranged into two identical banks of 45 columns each. Each bank has six rows numbered as follows: 0, 12, 34, 56, 78 9. A hole punched into the row labeled 1 $_2$ may represent, or so it would appear, either the odd or the even digit. To make the differentiation positive, the following convention is used: a single punched hole serves to represent the 0 and all odd digits. Two punches are used to represent the even digits: one punch in the row as marked, and the other punch in 9.

To represent the number 5, one punch in the 56 row is all that is necessary, but to represent the even digit 6, two punches are required; one in row 56 and the other in row 9. Alphabetical data is equally easy to code, although, as can be seen from the illustration, three punches are often required to represent a single letter.

All the advantages, previously described, of the 80-column card are equally true of the 90-column card. The choice is dictated by the manufacturer's preference and equipment.

PUNCHED PAPER TAPE

One of the few disadvantages mentioned in connection with punched cards concerns the fixed size of the card. Each card can contain only a limited amount of information, and it is sometimes necessary to use more than one card to record all the pertinent data. Punched paper tape is a continuous recording medium not subject to the limitations of fixed record size. The only restriction concerns the size of the reel on which the tape is to be stored. Paper tape offers other important advantages: the record is less bulky and easier to store; it can be read at a fast rate; and by using a Flexowriter or similar device, punched paper tape may be coded at the same time the copy is being typewritten.

Data are recorded as a special arrangement of punched holes along the length of the tape. Portions of coded five- and eight-channel tape. Other types use six and seven channels. Although the specific codes may vary, the system is essentially the same. Using five channels, a maximum of 32 combinations of holes (i.e., $2^5 = 32$) is possible. But if one of these combinations is used to indicate a shift comparable to the shift from lower to upper case in a typewriter—the number of possible code positions can be nearly doubled. Note the different combinations of holes for letters and figures. This code also ha, the additional advantage of providing a method for indicating the space between words, carriage return, line feed, and a large selection of special characters. The five-channel code is also used for sending teletype messages, which makes this form of data input particularly valuable in an integrated data processing system where information may have to be sent from the branch office in one city to the main office in another via teletype.

MAGNETIC TAPE

The information coded on cards and paper tape is visible

to the human eye as holes in the recording media. In magnetic tape recording, we lose this knowledge, for information is recorded by magnetizing selected areas on coated plastic tape. Once recorded, this information is retained permanently, if desired. Should the information no longer be useful, however, it can be erased and new data recorded on the same tape. This reuse capability results in considerable savings.

Another advantage of magnetic tape recording is the speed at which data can be recorded and read. At the present time, magnetic tape provides a data system that can be directly and efficiently tied to the high-speed computer as an input or output device.

Magnetic tapes are available in different widths. One of the more popular sizes is ½ inch wide and has seven recording channels. From 100 to 500 characters can be recorded on 1 inch of tape, depending upon the recording density. This means that the information punched onto one 80or 90-column card could be stored in considerably less than 1 inch of tape. A full reel of tape contains 2400 feet and can be read at the rate of more than 100 inches per second. These figures provide some indication of the storage capacity and speed with which information can be made available to the computer for processing.

Magnetic tape codes are no more complex than the codes previously discussed. A seven-bit alphameric code. The *A* and *B* zones of the tape code correspond approximately to the *X* and *Y* zones on the 80-column punched card and are used for recording nonnumerical data. Numbers are recorded in a four-bit binarycoded decimal system.

Special symbols are used to identify the end of a word and the end of the message. A valuable feature of this form of tape recording is the incorporation of a check or parity bit. In the code illustrated, "even parity" is used; i.e., the number of magnetized bits in any vertical column must add up to an even number. If in the course of processing the tape, the parity check does not prove out and a column contains an odd number of bits, the computer alerts the operator to the fact that an error has occurred. This check helps insure against the loss of data as a result of mechanical difficulties in the input-output units, and it provide accurate information quickly accessible for computer processing.

The different coding techniques described in the preceding sections enable one to represent alphabetical and numerical information in a form amenable to automatic data processing.

Chapter 4

Programing Fundamentals and Machine Language

Chapter 5 and 6 described the physical structure of a computer and the methods of coding data for machine use. They also presented some basic principles of the decimal numbering system and introduced other numbering systems—binary, octal, binary-coded decimal, and biquinary—as being more useful in automatic data processing. Besides having the coded data available, however, the computer needs a programme of operating instructions. This chapter will the discuss the programer, concepts of programing, and coding techniques.

THE PROGRAMER

The profession of programing has existed for less than two decades. Those presently in this relatively new field have varying educational backgrounds. Mathematics and engineering predominate, and with reason, for a knowledge f mathematics and a familiarity with digital computer hardware is desirable for optimal utilization of the computer's capabilities. In addition, the programer must understand the content of the problem to be solved.

In the past, most computers were used to solve mathematical and engineering problems. Today, computers have much wider applicability, and more people are learning to programme and use these machines. This is especially true of the research scientist who has special problems to solve. In order to plan his work effectively, he must have some knowledge of programing, although he does not have to become an expert coder. Fortunately, the modest programing goals of the scientist user can be met with relative ease.

Programing can be divided into four phases: analysis, programme design, coding, and testing. A brief discussion of each of these will help clarify the functions of the programer.

ANALYSIS

In seeking to solve any problem, the first step usually consists of making a precise formulation of the question. This is a most difficult step, and an adequate solution requires a thorough knowledge of the content area, a knowledge of the modern mathematical techniques applicable to the specific type of problem, and enough familiarity with computers to recognize how this equipment can be most economically applied to the solution of the problem. Let us assume, for example, that as behavioral scientist we are given the task of investigating creativity by simulating the process on a computer. This is the problem as it would be presented by a researcher. How would we go about solving it? As a first step, the problem must be formulated more precisely and the area of investigation delimited.

Operational definitions of such terms as creativity" and "simulation" must be worked out. The hypotheses must be clearly stated, along with the experimental design and the statistical techniques that would be used to reduce the data to be collected.

The analysis of a problem for computer programing requires knowledge far beyond specific programing skills. The "system analyst," as he is often called, must be an expert in his field as well as in computer techniques.

Business organizations frequently call in consultants—operations research personnel—to help in the programme analysis phase of the work. In scientific research, this phase remains the responsibility of the principal investigator and cannot be delegated. Since one cannot be an expert in all fields, however, the problem formulation phase of the programme preparation is usually carried on by a team including trained mathematical programers. Their function is formulating the problem in mathematical terms and designing a mathematical model capable of solution.

PROGRAMME DESIGN

Once the programer has an operational statement of the problem, he proceeds to reanalyze the formulation in terms of the sequence of computer operations to be performed. The solution of a problem by means of a computerized data processing system is comparable to a factory production line. The input, or raw material, is the data to be processed; the Output is the finished product or solution. The data processing system, which is science's production line and factory, transmutes the raw materials into the finished product. The programer determines the operations that are to be performed on the input in order to achieve the desired output.

Part of the task is making efficient use of time and equipment. Hence, the programer is concerned with simplifying the coding, reducing execution time, and minimizing the number of storage register required. In order to help obtain an overview of the entire problem and, as an aid in visualizing the steps involved in the solution of the problem, the programer commonly designs a programme flow chart. This chart is a visual presentation of the movement of data through the Computer. It labels each stage of the process and the operations that are to be performed. It also indicates the task assigned to each computer component at every stage of the operation.

Thus the flow chart helps the programer to sys-tematize his thinking and optimize the use of his equipment. The preparation of a flow chart is a salient feature in programme design. In large organizations where there is a division of work, the person classified as a programer is responsible only for flow chart preparation. The formulator does the analysis; the programer prepares the flow charts; the coder writes out the machine instructions.

Flow charts must be detailed and comprehensive, but the level of detail is determined by the purpose for which the chart is drawn, and this varies. A management level, or systems analysis, flow chart graphically summarizes the major routines of the system and provides a comprehensive picture of the data-processing stages. This type of flow chart provides an over-all systems view of the problem; however, it is not detailed enough for coding. The detailed flow chart, its the name implies, contains a complete analysis of all the steps, in their proper sequence, which are to be followed in order to achieve the desired solution. In this detailed flow chart, the physical form of records (punched cards, paper or magnetic tape, etc.) is shown by special symbols, and there are additional chart symbols for the hardware (drum memory, processor, printer, etc.) and the processing operations. This chapter and succeeding chapters on computer applications use flow charts designed for systems analysis and not detailed coding.

The others like it have been in circulation for some years. It is part of the folklore of the programing profession, and is of unknown origin. Although somewhat facetious, it does illustrate a number of important aspects of flow charting. Looking first at the upper right-hand corner, we see a flow chart that is highly oversimplified and provides insufficient information. Getting up in the morning is a fairly complex process, and it is precily this process that we wish to chart and specify. Therefore, a single box labeled "get up" is inadequate for our purpose. Looking now at the main chart, we see depicted some of the procedures and behaviour involved in getting up. The behaviour is not linear, for it involves certain repetitions or loops, as in the case of groaning and shaking wife. There are also certain decisions to be made. These decision points are recorded as questions in oval-shaped enclosures. Note, too, that this system-oriented flow chart does not indicate the precise means by which the computer would be programed to make the decision.

FLOW CHARTING A PROGRAMME FOR DECISION MAKING

A flow chart indicating the type of logical problem solving and decision making which can be performed by a computer.

Let us once again pick up the adventures of our friend who woke up in the morning, kissed his wife good-bye, and walked to the car with keys in hand. He has three keys on the key ring: a house key, a garage key, and a car key. The keys are easily distinguishable by size. The car key is the smallest. The man—a man who think for himself—knows which key fits into his automobile ignition. Our problem is programing the computer to select from among the three keys the one that fits the car. We know that the three keys are of different sizes, and the car key is the smallest of the three, so that logically the solution hinges upon comparing the three keys and selecting the smallest.

This seems simple enough, but the question remains of *how* we shall do this. How can the computer "look at," sense, or measure, each of the three keys, and then compare the measurement, decide which is the smallest, and select that one? One possibility is to put into the computer the size characteristics of the car key, use this as a standard, and compare all given keys to this standard. The key that matches would be the one selected. Another possibility is to compare two of the three keys and eliminate the larger, compare the remaining two, again eliminating the larger, and thus the smallest, or car key, left. There are undoubtedly other possibilities, but for our purposes, these suffice.At this point, we ask our mathematisian programer to help decide which method for solving the key selection problem would be the most efficient. The criteria for efficiency in this case are simplified coding reduce execution time, and minimized storage facilities. The mathematisian makes a mathematical model for each possibility and select the simples. In this case, the second choice is, by far, the best solution.Our mathematisian is not through, however; he must write a set of equations for the solution. Let's see what these look like.Let A, B, and C= the three keys

- A < B, A < C 4" A is the smallest
- A < B, C < A 4" C is the smallest
- B < A, C < B 4" C is the smallest
- B < A, B < C 4" B is the smallest

The systems analysis of the problem ends with the writing of the mathematical model of the problem and its solution. The programme designer now draws the flow chrat, and the coder writes the programme that will enable the computer to solve the problem.

CODING

An mathematical part of the programing process consists of translating the mathematical formulation of a problem into machine language. Coding is exacting and detailed, but it is not difficult. To understand coding, one needs to be aware that the computer, in contrast to the human being, cannot think for itself. In order to function at all, the computer must be given instruction for every operation. Writing these instructions is the coder's job.

Computer instructions are written as a combination of letters and numbers in accordance with a predetermined code. This code differs for the different computer system, although the basic concept remains the same. The coder be well versed in the logic of the computer system, the purpose, the use of each code symbol. He must follow the machine logic precisely and systematically.

TESTING

Once the programme has been coded, it must be tested to insure that it operates properly and arrives at the correct solution to the problem. Programme testing, or "debugging" as it is usually called, involves trying the programme in a properly operating computer and observing the results at various stages in the computation. Occasionally the programme will not "cycle"; i.e., an incorrect instruction will cause the computer to stop prematurely. The error must be located and corrected. In other instances, the programme may, go into a continuous loop, repeating the same few instructions over and over, and not process all the required data. As can be imagined, many types of coding errors result in improper cycling of the programme of instructions. All of these errors must be located and corrected.

After determining that the programme does cycle, it must be tested to insure that the results of computer processing are accurate. One might process a problem having a known solution by the, as yet, untested programme. If the end results agree, it can be assumed that the programme is accurate. To be sure, this assumption will not necessarily hold true in all cases. It is possible for a programme to function properly with one set of data and not with another, for there may be an aspect of the programme that was not exercised by the trial data. These intermittent errors are very difficult to locate. The situation is analogous to the problem faced by an automobile owner who takes his car to a garage because he hears a "knock." When the mechanic drives the car, the "knock" is not there. To locate this type of difficulty, more rigorous systematic testing than simply comparing results is necessary. A new programme is checked by using programed test routines, which print out the contents of selected registers as each instruction in the programme is completed, and by other similar techniques.

The four phases of system analysis, programme design, coding, and testing together constitute the programing process from the start to the finished product.

COMPUTER WORDS

Both the programme of instructions and the data to be processed are stored in the internal memory of the computer. The basic unit of information is the computer word, which is a series of binary digits stored in a register. Each register has its own address.

Commonly, the size of the computer word, i.e., the number of bits, is constant for a given computer, but different machines may have larger or smaller words. Computer words are of two kinds: instruction words and data words. In memory, these are indistinguishable from each other. If an instruction word is entered into the arithmetic unit, it will be treated as a data word. When the instruction word enters into the control unit, however, it is interpreted as an instruction and executed. Having instructions and data in the same format adds to the versatility of the computer, for instruction words can be processed and modified in the same manner as data words. This is another way of saying that the computer can be programed to modify its own instructions—an extremely interesting concept and one that has many ramifications.

INSTRUCTION WORD FORMAT

Computer instructions can be classified, on the basis of function, into three general categories: transfer of data, arithmetic operations, and branching or conditional instructions. At the start of the computing process, the data and the instructions for solving the problem have been coded on to external storage media, such as punched cards, paper, or magnetic tape.

Transfer instructions direct the transfer of information from these storage devices to the internal memorn system on which the computer can operate. This category of instruction also transfers data out of internal storage to output tapes or printer. Other uses involve the transfer of information from the main memory area to the arithmetic registers, between registers, and back to memory.

Instructions for *arithmetic operations* direct the computer to add, subtract, multiply, and divide. Normally, computation moves sequentially from one instruction to the next on the programme list. *Conditional instructions* provide a means for interrupting sequential processing and allowing the programme to skip to a designated place in the list of instructions. Conditional instructions compare the contents of two registers, and the branching is contingent upon the of this comparison. For example, instructions may be written to compare A and B, and if A is larger, continue the normal sequence; but if:A is smaller, branch to a predetermined instruction, which would then start a new sequence.

Computer instructions consist of two parts: the operation and the address. The operation portion specifies the action the computer is to perform; the address specifies the location in memory of the operand—i.e., the data word on which the operation is to be performed.

Instructions of the type described may be written in the following form:

One-address Word Format

OP a

The rectangular box represents the word as stored in a register. "OP" stands for operation, and "*a*" for address. This schema is called a "one- address" word format, or one-address logic, and their instructions are interpreted as, for example, add (the operation) the contents of register "*a*" (the address) to the accumulator. It is implicit in the logic of this system that the results of the operation will be retained in the accumulator until transferred. The *accumulator* is a working storage register located in the arithmetic unit. Having performed the specified operation, the control units locates the following instruction in the next address location; that is, if the first instruction was in memory "*m*," then the next one would be in location (*m* + 1). To accomplish this sequencing of instructions, the machine stores the address of the instruction being executed and, by means of a sequence counter, adds a "1" to that address in order to obtain the address of the next instruction.

The basic components of the computer are the input and output units, the storage unit, the control unit, and the arithmetic unit. Let us examine the basic computer operating cycle in terms of the function of each of these components.

The input *and output units*are peripheral equipment used to bring data into the main storage or to transfer or print out information from storage.

The *storage unit* is the repository of all information, both instructions and data.

The *control unit* contains an instruction register. Most machines also contain one or more sequence or index registers.

The *arithmetic unit* contains one or more accumulator registers.

The computation cycle is regulated by the control unit and is divided into a "fetch" phase and an "execute" phase operating as follows:

Fetch: The fetch phase is under the guidance of the

sequence register; the address of the next instructions is located; the information (namely, the operation to be performed and the address of the operand) is transferred into the instruction register; and the operand is fetched.

Execute: The execute phase is under the direc5ion of the instruction register which sees to it that the instructions are carried out and the sequence register updated.

If one wanted to add X to Y using one-address logic, the sequence of instructions would be:

Fetch: Transfer the instruction to the instruction register.

Execute: Clear the accumulator and add the number *X* to it. Add 1 to the sequence register.

Fetch: Transfer the next instruction to the instruction register.

Execute: Add Y to the accumulator.

The sum of $X + Y$ is now stored in the accumulator. If we were interested in this sum, our next instruction would be to transfer the contents of the accumulator to a specified register located in the main memory storage. Then, if we wished, we could have the contents of that register printed out.

Keep these points clearly in mind: the control unit contains the instruction to be executed and the sequencing needed to locate the next instruction. The computational work is done by the accumulator register of the arithmetic unit; this work includes the arithmetic processing and also the various logical tests and branching instructions.

The IBM 709, Burroughs 220, and Packard-Bell PB 250 are examples of computers that use a one-address word format. Instruction word formats differ in other machines. The more common systems and their interpretations listed below. In the examples, the operation part of the word (OP) will, for purposes of simplicity, be considered as an add instruction.

One-and-one-half-address Word Format

OP a_1 a_2

In the one-address format, the instructions are stored and processed in sequences; in the one-and-one-half-address format (since instruction words are not stored sequentially), the location of the next instruction word must be specified. IBM 650 and UNIVAC Solid State 80 and 90 computers use the one-and-one-half-address logic.

Two-address Word Format†

OP a_1 a_2

Even though the word format is the same for both the one-and-one-halfand the two-address words, the computer logic that interprets the instructions is different. The IBM 395 and the RCA 301 use the twoaddress instruction word.

Three-address Word Format

OP a_1 a_2 a_3

Three-address logic is used by Honeywell 80 and National Cash Register 304.

Four-address Word Format†

OP a_1 a_2 a_3 a_4

The National Cash Register 390 Data Processing System uses the four-address word format.

The very diversity of instruction word format in use by different manufacturers indicates that no system has a clear advantage over any other. The one-address machine operates at a relatively fast rate, but requires a number of instructions to perform a particular function, such as adding two numbers together. A three-address machine could perform this same addition in one instruction, but the over-all execution time might be slower. At any rate, for most machines, the computer logic is fixed, and it is the responsibility of the programmer to know his computer and to make optimal use of its capabilities.

DATA WORD FORMAT

In contrast to the relative complexity of the instruction word, the data word format is simplicity itself. The sign and the magnitude constitute the only information necessary to represent numerical data. The data word can be represented schematically:

Sign Magnitude

So, with reference to the instruction, "Add the contents of a1 to the accumulator," a data or number, in the form indicated above, would be the contents stored in address a_1.

Depending upon the computer, the data word format can become somewhat more complex by using variable length configurations, floating point numbers, overflow bits, and similar items. Each computer has its own special idiosyncrasies, which the programmer must learn and use in coding the machine.

PROGRAMING LANGUAGE

Machine computation is carried on by means of a set of programing instructions that precisely define every step in the computational process. As was pointed out, the programme must be written in a code called the "machine language." Each of various computers has its own unique machine language, and a programme written for one type of computer does not operate in another machine. All this adds to the complexity of prograining. To help alleviate this difficulty, a number of more abstract symbolic programing languages have been developed, enabling the user to communicate with many types of computers. Programs are written in the symbolic language and then translated automatically, by the computer itself, into the specific machine language to process the data.

Machine language consists of the specific codes and formats directly interpretable by a given computer. In most cases, the representation of alphabetical or numerical data in machine language is simply the binary expression for each letter or number. Nevertheless, enough variation exists in the word format of the different computers to make the machine language relatively unique. In dealing with instructional codes, there is even greater variability. The very strangeness and preciseness of machine languages tend to decrease computational flexibility and cause clerical errors in programing.

Problem-oriented language are designed to be more meaningful to the human writing the programme than to the machine processing the codes. For example, the instruction "add" in machine language might be written as binary 23 (010 111), but in problem-oriented language it would be written as ADD. Obviously, the latter symbol is easier for a person to understand and remember, The task of programing any given machine is simplified by this procedure and made relatively independent of the computer hardware. Before executing the programme, the symbolic instructions must be translated into machine code. The translation is accomplished by a large set of machine-language instructions, which convert the problem-oriented language symbols into machine language. Writing this translator programme is a very difficult and time-consuming process requiring skilled programers, but once available, it can be used with ease. FORTRAN, coined from "*formula trans*lation," is such a problemoriented language developed for the IBM 700 series computers. An example of its use will be given in a subsequent section of this chapter.

At present, each problem-oriented language requires a translator to convert it into a suitable machine language. In addition, since not all computers can use the same problem-oriented language, various manu- facturers develop their own versions of these symbolic languages. The entire procedure is very inefficient, because it requires many translators and monopolizes the talents of skilled programers (who are in short supply) to develop these automatic translation programs. One possible solution to this dilemma lies in the creation of a common computeroriented language. This would be a synthetic language into which all problem-oriented languages would be translated, and from which all machine languages would be translated.

The present procedures can be diagramed as follows:

- It has been suggested that a more generally applicable, and therefore more efficient system, would have the following form:

A programme written in problem-oriented language would be processed, by means of a "generator" programme, into the universal computer-oriented language. Since a number of problem-oriented languages exist, different generator programs would be required to convert them into the universal 'language, which would be the same for all computers. When a given computer was selected for use, the universal computer-oriented language would be processed through a translator programme into the proper machine language. The universal type of language has its main advantage, potential ability to make every computer programme, originally written in a problem-oriented language, usable in all computers.

The concept is excellent, and although many difficulties must be overcome before it becomes a reality, the initial research is already under way. At the System Development Corporation, a special research project called UNCOL is investigating the programing feasibility of a *un*iversal *c*omputer-*o*riented *l*anguage. Other organizations are also working toward the standardization of computer languages. One of the most significant of these efforts was the proposal made by the ACM (Association for Computing Machinery) and the GAMM (German-Swiss Applied Mathematical Society) for an international standard algorithmic language (ALGOL) for use in scientific numerical work. In a similar vein, a conference on data system language, sponsored by the U.S. Department of Defence, helped prepare the specifications for COBOL—*c*ommon *b*usiness *o*riented *l*anguage for business data processing.

For the average computer user, especially the scientist who is less interested in programming techniques than in the computer applications, these developments in symbolic programing languages help take the drudgery out of programing and make the computer a more useful and usable tool.

AN ILLUSTRATIVE FORTRAN PROGRAMME

To illustrate the ease and simplicity with which a modern, complex, high-speed, electronic digital computer can be programed, a FORTRAN programme for the IBM 709 is analyzed in detail. The programme chosen as illustration involves the calculation of an arithmetic mean, variance, and standard deviation for a set of data.

Although these calculations are simple enough to be

performed on a desk calculator, they can become tedious and timeconsuming. At any rate, the example is a useful one to illustrate FORTRAN programing. FORTRAN is a problem-oriented language designed for use with the IBM 704 and 709 data processing systems. It enables the programer to write instructions in a relatively simple language, which resembles ordinary usage. This FORTRAN language is then automatically translated into an efficient 709 machine language by use of a special programme called a compiler. The programer need not know, and does not use, the machine language.

As was pointed out earlier in this chapter, programing consists of four phases: analysis, programme design, coding, anti testing, Let us examine these phases in terms of the example.

Analysis

Analysis consists of the precise formulation of the problem and a design of a mathematical model to be used in its solution. The problem under consideration is the calculation of an arithmetic mean and standard deviation. The formulas for these calculations are already well known and no special analysis work is needed. The formulas selected are those designed for use with the original, ungrouped data.

Arithmetic Mean:

Standard Deviation:

Variance:

" = the sum of

X = the individual measurements

N = the number of cases

$"X^2$ = each measurement squared and then summed

$("X)^2$ = all measurements summed and the total squared

Programme Design

Programme design involves the analysis of the mathematical formulas in terms of the computer operations to be performed. The flow chart represents the movement of the data through the computer. The flow chart as drawn is more elaborate than necessary for FORTRAN cooling. The chart shows each stage of the data processing as a discrete step. The FORTRAN language, how-ever, is powerful enough to combine a number of these steps, and the actual coding is simpler than the flow chart indicates. For example, the chart shows the reading into the computer of one item of data, i.e., one test score, at a time. In practice, six or ten scores are punched on one card and read into memory simultaneously and then processed in the same way. Nevertheless, for clarity each logically separate procedure is illustrated.

In examining the chart, we see that the first item of business after "start" is to read into memory the number of cases in the sample. Then three accumulator registers are set to zero. One (K) keeps a record of the number of data cards processed: a second accumulates the sum of X by adding the score value (X) to the "X accumulator; and the squared X value (X^2) is summed in the third register. When these steps have been completed, a test is made to determine whether the value of N equals the number of cards processed (K). If the two numbers, are not equal, the computer control loops back to read in another data card and the process is repeated. When $N = K$. all the cases have been processed, and so the next step calls for the computation of the arithmetic mean (M). Then the value in the register containing "X is squared ("X)^2, and the value in the other accumulator ("X^2) is multiplied by N. All the figures needed to compute the variance and the standard deviation are now available, and so these statistics are computed. M,ó^2, and ó are printed and the machine stopped.

Coding

To write the coding for this problem in machine language would pose a fair-sized problem. The programer would have to assign each item of data in the sam-ple to a particular storage location in memory and then transfer the information from memory to the accumulator for processing. A long series of instructions would be required. With the FORTRAN problem-oriented language, all this is unnecessary. One simply states the problem in accordance with the formal rules of FORTRAN, and the compiler programme translates the statement into machine language.

FORTRAN Statement

	1	2 5	6	7		76	80
1	C				Jøhn Jønes Programer		
2	C				Prøgram Tø Calculate The Mean,		
3	C		1		Variance, And Standard Deviatiøn		
4				Førtran			
5					Dimensiøn Data (1000)		
6		900			Førmat (I 5)		
7		901			Førmat (5f: 10.2)		
8		902			Førmat (3f: 20.2)		
9					Read Input Tape 5, 900, N		
10					Read Input Tape 5,901 [Data (I), I = I, N]		
11					Sumx = 0.0		
12					Sumxx = 0.0		
13					Fln = N		
14					Dø 10 I -- I,N		
15					Sumx = Sumx + Data (I)		
16		010			Sumxx = Sumxx + Data (I) ** 2		
17					Av = Sumx/Fln		
18					Var = (Fln * Sumxx -- Sumx ** 2)/ Fln ** 2		
19					Std = Sqrtf (Var)		
20					Write Øutput Tape 6, 902, Av, Var, Std		
21					Call Exit		
22					End		

FORTRAN statement of programme to compute arithmetic mean, standard deviation, and variance.

Analysis of the FORTRAN Statement

All the alphabetical characters written in FORTRAN language must be in capital letters. The letters "I," "O," and "Z" are handwritten as, and

The asterisk followed by FORTRAN signifies a message to the FORTRAN compiler indicating the start of the compilation. This form of notation is a FORTRAN convention standard throughout most of the country. A "C" punched in column 1 identifies the card as a comments card, which is not to be processed by the FORTRAN compiler, but is to be listed as part of the programme printout.

Line 1: Gives the name of the progamer and other identifying data, if any.

Line 2: Contains the title of the programme.

Line 3: The 1 in column 6 indicates that the statements on this card is a continuation of the previous card. Up to nine conitnua-tion cards are allowed.

Line 4: is the word FØRTRAN, indicating that the translation is to be accomplished by the FORTRAN compiler.

Line 5: DIMENSIØN DATA (1000): reserves 1000 memory loca- tions for input data.

Line 6: 900 FØRMAT (15): means that the data are in the *I*nteger mode, literal notation, and occupy the first *5* columns on the punched card. This FORMAT is used to read in sample size; see 9.

Line 7: 901 FØRMAT (5 F 10.2): means that there are 5 data items in the *F*loating mode, literal notation: each vari-able occupying a *10*-column field; and there are 2 digits following the decimal point.

Line 8: 902 FØRMAT (3 F 20.2): means that there are 3 data items in the *F*loating point mode, literal notation: each vari- able occupying a *20*-column field; and there are 2 digits following the decimal point.

Line 9: READ INPUT TAPE 5, 900, N: names the Input Tape unit No. *5*; the *900* refers to the statement numbers at the associated FORMAT; *N* is the variable denoting the sample size.

Line 10: READ INPUT TAPE 5, 9021 [DATA (I), I = 1, N]: names the tape unit no.*5*; 901 refers to the statement number of the associated FORMAT; and the rest of the statement indicates that a list of variables is read into the array labeled *DATA;*

I = *1* sets Index register *I* to *1*, and the index register is incremented until it reaches limit *N*, which is the sample size. This instruction reads all input data into the memory locations reserved by the statement on Line 5

Line 11: SUMX = 0.0: is an arithmetic statement; *SUMX*, the ex-pression to the left of the equal sign, is a variable meaning the sum of the X's. The equal sign means compute the value of the expression to the right of the equal sign and assign this value to the variable on the left of the equal sign. The expression to the right of the equal sign, 0.0, is a con-stant chosen so as to convey a meaningful mathematical computation. This expression sets the value of *SUMX* equal to zero at the start of the computations.

Line 12: SUMXX = 0.0: is an arithmetic statement and is inter-preted in a manner similar to that of the preceding state- ment. *SUMXX* is the sum of the squared *X* values.

SMXX is set to zero at the start of the computations.

Line 13: FLN: = N: is an arithmetic statement that converts N, orig-inally written in the Integer mode, into the Floating pointmode for use in Floating point arithmetic.

Line 14: DØ 10 I = 1, N is a *DO* statement which is an instruction for a loop or sequence of statement to be executed one or more times. It means *DO* all the following statements up to, and including, statement 10; set *I* (the *I*ndex register) = *1*, then repeat the process, incrementing the index by 1 each time the loop is repeated, until *I* = *N* which would mean that all of the data in the sample had been processed. When *I* = *N*, the loop is broken, and the next instruction is the one following statement 10 which, in this case, would be on line 17.

Line 15: SUMX = SUMX + DATA (I): is an arithmetic statement and part of the DO loop. It is an instruction to read an item of *DATA* in the Integer mode and to add this value to *SUMX* which had been set to zero at the start of the problem. In the next iteration of the loop, a new value will be added to *SUMX*, and so on.

Line 16: SUMXX = SUMXX + DATA (I) **2: is referred to in the programme (Line 14) as statement number 10. It is an arithmetic statement and is part of the *DO* loop. *DATA (I)* **2 is an instruction to read an item of *DATA*, written in the Integer mode, and square it. The symbol ** indi-cates an exponential expression and the 2 specifies the power. The entire expression is an instruction to read the data, square the value, add it to *SUMXX* (which had been started at zero). Then iterate and read the next value, etc.

Line 17: AV = SUMX/FLN: is an arithmetic statement in FOR-TRAN for computing an arithmetic mean. *AV* is the *AV*erage or mean which is obtained by dividing the sum of the *X*'s by the sample size. *M* = X/N.

Line 18: VAR = (FLN * SUM XX - SUM X **2)/FLN **2: is an arithmetic statement containing the FORTRAN instruc- tions for computing the *V AR*iance or, ó^2.

Line 19: STD = SQRTF (VAR): is an arithmetic statement which says that the *ST*andard *D*eviation is to be obtained by taking the *SQ*uare *Root*, using Floating point mode, of the v ARiance:

Line 20: WRITE ØUTPUT TAPE 6, 902, AV, VAR, STD: is an output statement and provides for the transmittal of in-formation from computer memory to an output tape and from here to the printed page. In this case, *T APE* Unit 6 is specified as the output tape. The variables to be written on this tape are the *AV*erage, *V AR*iance, and *ST*andard Deviation, and the spacing is to be as specified in FORMAT 902.

Line 22: CALL EXIT: is a termination statement used at the com-puter centre for the subroutine that terminates the execu- tion phrase of the programme and transfers control back to the executive programme. In this way, the next FORTRAN pro- gram can be processed without loss of computer time.

Line 23: *END:* is the statement used to conclude all instructions in this programme. The statement notifies the executive routine to initiate the compilation phase of this programme.

FLOATING POINT ARITHMETIC

One of the troublesome details in numerical computation concerns the handling of the decimal point. In ordinary hand multiplication, the decimal point in the product is located so that it is to the left of the sum of the decimal places in both the multiplier and the multiplicand. This is illustrated in the following example:

741.9527 × 62.834 ______________ 46619.8559518

In multiplying numbers either by hand or in a digital computer, it is possible to set the number of decimal places in advance and decide to treat all numbers as having, for example, three decimal places. This system has certain disadvantages, however, as the following example illustrates.

0.034 X 0.025 ________ 0.000850

Since we are limited to three digits to the right of the decimal point, we lose all the non-zero digits.

To avoid this type of difficulty, most computers engaged in scientific computational work use floating point arithmetic. Although the term may be strange, the procedure is familiar.

Basically, the numbers are so arranged that the decimal point precedes the first digit; they are then multiplied by a power of 10 in order to locate the decimal point in its proper place: 0.7419527 X 10^3.

In computers designed with special circuits for floating

point operation, the floating point numbers are aligned so that the exponents are equal before addition and subtraction.

In multiplication, the exponents are added; in division, the exponent of the divisor is subtracted from the exponent of the dividend. All this is done automatically, requiring no special programing instructions, and is therefore fast and efficient.

Chapter 5

The Computing Centre

The scientific utility of an electronic computer is great, but so also is the expense. In the fifteen years since ENIAC was built, scientists and administrators have had to become accustomed to computers which may cost hundreds of thousands or even millions of dollars, and where the rate that has to be charged to the user in any self-supporting installation may amount to hundreds of dollars per hour. The needs of the early behavioral scientists were much more modest. In the laboratory experiments in psychology in the nineteenth century, equipment often consisted only of a pencil, a stopwatch and some paper. Subjects were usually volunteers and unpaid; if outside subjects were unavailable, psychologists could always experiment on each other. At that time, the scientist who was sufficiently dedicated could meet his expenses from his own pocket. The philosophy of self-support extended into the twentieth century. In the nineteen-thirties and the nineteen-forties, punched-card machines began to be rented by universities. The researcher would then pay hourly charges for the privilege of using the machines. If he had research funds of any sort, the costs were probably charged to that source. Failing that, he paid the bills himself.

This method of financing was obviously inadequate for electronic computers. Even the most dedicated of scientists could not hope to purchase his needed time on a computer from his personal income. Some system had to be devised whereby some central organization provided a machine free of charge to those scientists who were unsupported by research grants. Hence, there have been two problems in making computers available to scientists. The first is the obvious technical one of providing machines which possess the requisite speed, reliability, and storage. The second has been the administrative one of developing organizational and financial arrangements so that the machines are effectively used by researchers. At the university level, the answer has proved to be the Computing Centre operated on the Robin Hood principle of charging those who have research funds, but of supplying the machine free of charge to those who do not. This chapter will be concerned with some of the administrative and technical problems involved in building up these centers.

The part played by instrumentation in the history of science will be considered in Section. The next three sections will be devoted to the three M's of the University Computing Centre: machines, men, and methods. Machine selection and financing will be discussed in Section, and the training of computer specialists in Section. Methods are the next ingredient; existing ones have to be revised, and new ones created. This topic forms the subject of Section.

Examples are often drawn from the experience of the University of Illinois. This is partly because of my own familiarity with that experience, but primarily because Illinois was the first university to own its computer on an unrestricted basis and therefore was able to give scholars in all fields easy access to a computer. As a result, the first computer analyses in many areas of science were carried out at the University of Illinois. An electronic computer has been available there since 1951. Hence, there is by now ten years of experience in the problems of transition to computers. The lessons of the decade may serve as a guide in our charting of progress for the next ten-year span.

INSTRUMENTATION IN THE HISTORY OF SCIENCE

The Platonic tradition bequeathed to us by the Greeks has stressed the role of ideation and theory in the history of science. It is not surprising, therefore, to find historians of science emphasizing the epochal new theories, for instance, the Copernician view of the solar system, the Newtonian laws of motion, the Darwinian evolutionary theory. These are presented as the great landmarks in the development of science, the dramatic moments which every schoolboy is expected to know about.

Each of these theoretical reconstructions, however, has been preceded by a long period of accumulation of factual knowledge. Darwin's field studies of island floras and faunas made during his voyage on the *Beagle* preceded by twenty years his promulgation of the theory of evolution; Kepler's and Newton's insights depended upon the planetary observations of Tycho Brahe, made years before; and the stimulus to Copernicus' heliocentric astronomy was the increasing body of astronomical information which led to frequent amendment of the original Ptolemaic system of epicycles and deferents.

The rate of scientific fact finding, in turn, has been influenced by the discovery and improvement of scientific instruments. A history of science is needed which focuses not upon the theoretical reconstructions but upon the instrumental inventions and their scientific outcomes. Following the invention of glass, there is the birth of modern chemistry; the telescope is the forerunner of modern astronomy; the microscope, of cellular physiology and of microbiology. In each case, the order of scientific development has been (a) the invention of the new instrument and its perfection, (b) the meticulous accumulation of scientific observations—e.g., by the early observatories, by the seventeenth-century microscopist—and then, perhaps a century or more later, (c) the theoretical reconstruction. The twentieth century has added its own important share to the instruments designed to supplement man's unaided power of observation and analysis, e.g., the betatron, the radio telescope, the electron microscope. Judging from past scientific history, these instruments will provide a vast accession in our store of factual knowledge, and from this knowledge will arise the theories of the future.

The electronic computer bids to rank as one of the great twentieth-century inventions. It stands as man's latest and so far his most successful effort to supplement his powers of calculation. Viewed from the wider perspective of history, its rate of expansion has been remarkable. In 1946, there was only ENIAC; five years later, when psychologists first caught up with electronic computers, they were to be counted by tens; ten years later, by hundreds; and now, only fifteen years later, by thousands. They are being used in all areas of science, physical and social. Calculations impracticable only twenty years ago are now routine.

Initially designed to aid in computation, computers are taking over an increasing range of clerical duties. It is probably not exaggerating to speak of this as a second industrial revolution, when the menial chores of the clerk will be lightened, as were those of the laborer in the Industrial Revolution of a century or more ago; and the hope is increasing that these machines created by man will even be able to supplement his powers of problem solving and decision making. If generality of application is taken as the criterion for evaluating the importance of any scientific invention, then the computer promises to be one of the most important inventions of all time.

This book is concerned with only one part of this history-making change. It is restricted to one segment of the scientific effort, namely, that of the behavioral sciences, and to only a ten-year time span, so that we are still actively engaged in finding answers for some of the initial technical problems. It is, in effect, a case study of what happens when social scientists try to adapt to the challenge of a new scientific instrument which promises to offer almost unlimited powers of calculation, relative to the tools of a decade ago.

Let me remind those who are sceptical, and who consider that this may overstate the influence of a scientific instrument, of the experiences of Galileo. Upon hearing of the invention of the telescope by the Dutch lensmakers, he set to work to construct his own. His task completed, he trained his homemade telescope upon the heavens and was rewarded with an unparalleled burst of discoveries. He saw the shadows of the rising and the setting sun cast by the mountains of the moon upon its plains; he observed the phases of Venus and saw four satellites of Jupiter; sunspots and the rings of Saturn became visible; and turning from the planets to the stars, he found multitudes of them not visible to the naked eye, so that only a small part of the assemblage had previously been known. In awe, he wrote, "I am quite beside myself with wonder, and infinitely grateful to God that it has pleased Him to permit me to discover such great marvels."

There is a danger, of course, in random fact finding. Perhaps the most amusing reminder of this danger is to be found in the words of Gulliver when he visited the scientists of the Grand Academy of Lagado:

The first professor I saw was in a very large room, with forty pupils about him. After salutation, observing me to look earnestly upon a frame, which took up the greatest part of both the length and breadth of the room, he said perhaps I might wonder to see him employed in a project for improving speculative knowledge by practical and mechanical operations. But the world would soon be sensible of its usefulness, and he flattered himself that a more noble exalted thought never sprang in any other man's head. Every one knew how laborious the usual method is of attaining to arts and sciences; whereas by his contrivance the most ignorant person at a reasonable charge, and with a little bodily labour, may write books in philosophy, poetry, politics, law, mathematics, and theology, without the least assistance from genius or study. He then led me to the frame, about the sides whereof all his pupils stood in ranks. It was twenty foot square, placed in the middle of the room. The superficies was composed of several pieces of wood, about the bigness of a die, but some larger than others. They were all linked together by slender wires. These bits of wood were covered on every square with paper pasted on them, and on these papers were written all the words of their language, in their several moods, tenses, and declensions, but without any order.

The professor then desired me to observe, for he was going to set his engine at work. The pupils at his command took each of them hold of an iron handle, whereof there were forty fixed round the edges of the frame, and giving them a sudden turn, the whole disposition of the words was entirely changed. He then commanded six and thirty of the lads to read the several lines softly as they appeared upon the frame; and where they found three or four words together that might make part of a sentence, they dictated to the remaining four boys who were scribes. This work was repeated three or four times, and at every turn the engine was so contrived that the words shifted into new places, as the square bits of wood moved upside down.

Six hours a day the young students were employed in this labour, and the professor showed me several volumes in a large folio already collected, of broken sentences, which he intended to piece together, and out of these rich materials to give the world a complete body of all arts and sciences; which however might be still improved, and much expedited, if the public would raise a fund for making and employing five hundred such frames in Lagado, and oblige the managers to contribute in common their several collections.

He assured me, that this invention had employed all his thoughts from his youth, that he had emptied the vocabulary into his frame, and made the strictest computation of the general proportion there is in books between the number of particles, nouns, and verbs, and other parts of speech.

How useful a computer would have been to this good professor! Any scientific instrument can be, and sometimes will be misused. Perhaps that does not matter too much in the full course of scientific history. The futilities are winnowed out like chaff. To try to strike some balance between Galileo and Lagado, let us turn to Richardson's treatise on weather forecasting written in 1922. The meteorologist is attempting to make the best estimates of future weather that he can from the known weather of the present and the past. With observations from all over the world, if he needs them, and from the upper atmosphere as well as from the ground, the voluminousness of his records can be oppressive.

In the midst of a book that is mostly technical and mathematical, Richardson devoted two pages to a fantasy. He pictured the weather forecasters of the future working in teams in a huge circular room resembling London's Albert Hall. Each team was analyzing one segment of the data. The weather director was in the centre of the assemblage. Like the conductor of some immense orchestra, he would shine a green light of approval upon those teams which were up to schedule, but a red light of disapproval upon those who had fallen behind in the race to finish the calculations so that the forecast could be available ahead of the weather being predicted. Less than fort years later, the fantasy is actuality, but instead of teams of clerks and their conductor, meteorologist have had recourse to a computer and its programers.

MACHINE ACQUISITION AND CONTROL

Obviously, the first stage in computer adaptation is getting a machine. Because of their low cost, desk calculators spread rapidly through university laboratories; it was feasible for each administrative unit to acquire its own machines. An electronic computer presents a much more formidable problem. University administrators were faced with a dilemma. Financially, they felt they could not afford a computer, but scientifically, that they could not afford to be without one. It is a tribute to their resourcefulness that within ten years almost all research-oriented universities have accepted the computer as a legitimate piece of scientific equipment and have found the means to acquire one. The financial support given by the National Science Foundation, the generous discount policies of the commercial firms, and the "build-your-own-machine" movement have each played their part.

ACHIEVING COMPUTER ACCEPTANCE

In order to win acceptance of the computer as part of the research support facilities of the university, four early misconceptions had to be cleared away:

- Early estimates of potential computer usage were much too conservative. It was thought at first that a single university could not support a high-speed computer with sufficient workload, so that a few machines located on a regional basis across the country would be better. For example, Hartree, a pioneer computer designer at Cambridge University, believed that four or five computers would suffice for all British needs in scientific computing. I must confess to the same misjudgment. When I started using ILLIAC in 1951, I was so impressed by its high speed—since it operated at what then seemed to me the fantastic speed of 1400 multiplications per second—that I failed to foresee that within less than five years this machine would prove to be too limited for the university's needs and that a supplemental machine would have to be obtained to handle the overload.

- Some administrators wanted to charge the heavy hourly machine rates directly to the scientist, so that the computer might be selfsupporting. On the cheaper punched-card machines, this policy had worked moderately well. Fast computers, however, might cost $100 or more per hour, so that under this policy only those adequately provided with research funds would have gained access. Computers would have been priced beyond the means of the independent researcher or the graduate student. The University of Illinois seems to have been the first to promulgate the enlightened policy of charging those supplied with research funds, but providing the machine free of charge to those without. This procedure seems to have become standard by now.
- Many administrators, including some computer directors, thought machine time to be so valuable that it should be used only for tasks which could not be carried out with any other calculating aid. For example, one administrator questioned the desirability of using a computer to calculate a series of fifty matrix inversions of order six. His grounds were that the scientist could work each one with the

aid of a desk calculator in an hour or two. In psychology, this policy would have meant use of a computer for principal axes factor analysis and for analytic rotation, but not for calculation of correlations or preparation of contingency tables; the latter tasks seemed to be regarded as insufficiently respectable. This philosophy of computer scarcity deified the machine, overlooking the primary purpose of a computer, i.e., saving men's time and supplying them with much needed research assistance not previously available. Perhaps the extreme of this philosophy is represented by the university which imposed a nominal charge, as computer rates go (about $10 hourly for the use of a fairly fast computer), not to add appreciably to revenue, but mainly to dissuade any frivolous or wasteful use of the machine. Admittedly, any heavily loaded machine must be carefully scheduled to avoid waste and inefficiency, but this was a machine still only partly loaded. Such a charge deters the scientist from experimenting. He tends to keep to his old ways when, as we shall see later in this chapter, a main problem in using computers is finding better methods of analysis. At the worst, he may not use the computer at all but may prefer to stay with the desk calculator, thereby saving his money and wasting only his own time. Once again, the Illinois administration set a most valuable precedent by the liberality of its provision of machine time.

- Some physical scientists were of the opinion that computers should be reserved primarily for mathematicians, physicists, and engineers, who might be expected to have the appropriate level of mathematical sophistication and rigor. Behavioral scientists were regarded (often correctly) as mathematically rather naive. The volume of the behavioral scientist's input was often surprising, and that of his output even more so. However, the voluminous input so often found should be regarded as a challenge rather than as an occasion for merriment by computer engineers. The computers of the nineteen-forties and of the early nineteen-fifties, designed both by and for physical scientists, were ill balanced, with input and output facilities much inferior to the main arithmetical unit.

COMPUTER OBSOLESCENCE

In dealing with issues involving machine acquisition, it is necessary to comment on the question of computer obsolescence. This problem may be worded thus: Since rapid technical advances continue in machine speed, storage capacity, machine reliability, and input and output systems, is it better to acquire a machine immediately, despite the obsolescence risk, or to wait for the brave new models of the future?

There are two stages in obsolescence. The first occurs when some scientific analyses, not practicable upon current machines, become feasible upon newer machines of greater capacity and speed. Rather than disrupt the over-all research effort by changing a computer so as to cope with these problems, it may often be preferable to give the scientist concerned funds with which to buy time at some other computing centre. The second stage-occurs if and when the cost per calculating unit has become sufficiently lower on some newer machine to justify the effort of changing facilities, with its associated chores of reprograming. Provided that the university has started with as modern and as powerful a machine as is available at the time of acquisition, this second stage is reached only after quite a long time. The University of Illinois started with what was then one of the best machines in the world. In terms of the standards of the nineteensixties, its storage capacity is limited (1024 immediate-access locations, 12,800 memory drum locations). Those who need large storage space will need to look elsewhere until ILLIAC II, currently under construction, is ready. This means that the first stage of obsolescence has been reached. But it is doubtful whether the

Illinois machine is yet at the second stage. After ten years of service, ILLIAC remains a comparatively economical machine.

Two features of computer economics are relevant here. It has been an American tradition to change last year's model for a new one. Should the same be done with computers? In my judgment, the answer is emphatically "No." Changing a computer is much more disruptive than trading in an automobile because of the labour of preparing the standard programs for a computer and of getting researchers familiar with them. It is not always realized that the programs may cost as much as or even more than the machine itself. Frequent computer changes mean that the same programs are written over and over again, and for a large part of the time the installation is not effectively used.

Another aspect of computer transition should be stressed. It is a false economy to take out the old machine at the same time as bringing in the new. Until a programme library is established for the new machine, it will be of limited usefulness. The old machine retains its value so long as there are programs available for it which have not yet been written for the new one. This labour of reprograming will probably be substantially reduced, or possibly eliminated, as newer machines are built which have programme compatibility with the older machines they are intended to replace, and as more programs are written in languages, such as FORTRAN, applicable to various machines. But in the past decade, the evidence seems clear that institutions, such as Illinois, which have stayed with one machine have fared better, with respect to building up a substantial library of programs, training graduate students in machine use, and widespread scientific application of the computer, than have the installations which changed computers frequently.

The second factor in computer economics is that the more powerful and more expensive machines are cheaper per unit of calculation than the less costly but less speedy ones. Increases in machine speeds have more than offset the increased expense, provided there is the workload to keep the giant busy.

These two factors mean, in my estimation, that a university spends its money most wisely if it concentrates upon one centralized installation, equipping it with the most modern and powerful machine available at the time of acquisition. Many universities have had separate punchedcard facilities for business and for research use, but it is likely that this tradition will have to be abandoned. A machine of the sixties is so fast that with proper scheduling a wide variety of work can be handled. The cost of a modern computer is so formidable that it would be a financial luxury to have two of these giants on a campus until such time as the first becomes overloaded. There remains the possibility of getting two smaller machines, one for business use and one for research, instead of the one large one. One disadvantage of this course of action has already been pointed out: namely, that the two machines jointly cannot handle the same workload that the one centralized installation can. A second disadvantage is that, if both have smaller capacity, some campus analyses then cannot be handled on either machine.

An administrative consequence is that determined efforts must be made to avoid factionalism among the various units of the university affected by computer developments. Because computers represent a new area for universities with few established precedents, factionalism seems to be found rather frequently. At present the punched-card equipment is often under different control from the electronic computer, and the two organizations may view themselves in a competitive rather than in a complementary role. Separate schools, such as the School of Business or the School of Engineering, may hope to acquire their own machines. The Director of the Computing Centre should be given sufficient authority to insure that a consistent university-wide computational policy is followed. His position requires that he should be responsive to the special needs of the various groups for whom computers are important. Computers have been shown relevant to so many areas of scholarship that there are inevitably going to be many differences of opinion and need.

Two trends have been evident during the last ten years:

- A great increase in the volume of work emanating from any campus as the computer becomes better known and a versatile programme library is established,
- A great increase in the volume of work which can be handled by one computer. Presumably these two curves will sooner or later change to plateaus, but this still seems to be a long way off. So far, the two increases seem roughly to have balanced each other, as the experience of the University of Illinois appears to show. One general purpose machine, ILLIAC, sufficed for the computational needs of the early fifties; ILLIAC II will probably suffice for the early sixties. Present indications are that each of the twenty or thirty major universities with extensive research programs and large numbers of doctoral students (Big Ten, Ivy League, etc.) will be able to use at least one machine of present maximal power (such as the Bendix G-20, the Control Data Corporation 1604, or the IBM 7090). Smaller universities which do not have sufficient work to keep one of these machines occupied—even when allowing for a dramatic upsurge in demand once a computer is installed—face a difficult problem of machine selection. Computer economics indicate the financial advantages of the regional machine. Yet there remains a great research convenience in having a computer close at hand upon one's own campus. The best answer may prove to be a compromise, with a medium-speed machine handling most analyses on the campus, and a transfer of those problems requiring greater speed or storage capacity to one of the major universities.

If the upward curve of machine speeds should exceed the upward curve of usage, this argument for a regional machine might hold even for the larger universities. When machines of the power of LARC and STRETCH become generally available, we may find that a single university, even the largest, cannot keep the computer fully occupied. The pattern for the future may then become that of each university maintaining its own machine for the tasks less demanding of speed and storage, and a regional group of universities supporting one of the larger computer installations. This would be equivalent to the present library system by which each Middle Western university maintains its own library, but transfers some less used titles to the Midwestern Library Centre rather than retaining them locally. The position is complicated by the fact that for numerical operations which only take a few minutes, a speed gain by a factor of ten does not make much difference. What does it matter whether a large set of correlations takes fifty seconds or five? That is why I think we are more likely to go to a mixed system than to the complete regionalism originally prophesied by Hartree. The convenience of getting most of one's calculations on one's own campus is simply too great to be sacrificed.

However, prophecies in any area of rapid technological advance are always risky. An effective system of satellite machines might be organized over an entire state or an even larger region, where inputs are flashed to a central machine in some convenient location and the outputs are flashed back to the campus of origin.

If the curve of usage heads upward faster than the curve of speed, then the answer is easier. If and when any university can maintain one of the most powerful current machines and this too becomes overloaded, then the university can add to its computer installation with the aim either of diversifying or of decentralizing its facilities.

COMPUTER CONSTRUCTION, RENTAL OR PURCHASE?

Any computing centre has to decide whether it is better advised to rent a commercial machine, or to buy one, or to build its own machine. Early centers had no choice. Until the Remington Rand UNIVAC was marketed in 1952, high-speed commercial computers were not available. Each computer before that had to be custom-built. Even after that, universities usually acquired a computer more cheaply by building their own than by getting a commercial machine. The universities that have built copies of ILLIAC have found themselves equipped with fast computers and extensive programme libraries for comparatively low cost.

As computers have become progressively larger and more complex, the disadvantages of individual effort and the advantages of commercial production have become increasingly apparent. The task of successfully building a computer becomes more and more formidable, and the economics of mass manufacture are more evident. For most universities, the effective choice is therefore between buying or renting a commercial machine.

Rentals are high in comparison with purchase prices. A machine may be purchased for no more than three or four years' rental. The reason for this rapid depreciation is, of course, the obsolescence issue. With a rented machine, a change can be made whenever an improved new model becomes available, while a purchased computer has to be held for a longer period. A secondary advantage of rental is that computer maintenance is then generally supplied free of charge, whereas with purchase either a maintenance contract is needed at comparatively high price, or, alternatively, the university's engineering school has to have or to add qualified computer technicians to its own staff.

The viewpoint expressed in this section has been that a university should aim at getting a very good computer and holding it for probably at least ten years. During the early part of the period, it will have an outstanding installation relative to other centers, and even in the latter part, any university with a machine such as a G-20, a 1604 or a 7090 is certainly not going to be saddled with what can in any sense be called an inferior machine, no matter what the technical progress may have been during the period. A machine that makes many thousands of multiplications and divisions per second remains in an absolute sense a very impressive acquisition. Over the ten-year span, purchase will have proved markedly cheaper than rental. The money so saved could with advantage be devoted to strengthening the consultancy and programing services of the centre, the topic to be discussed in the next section. More important perhaps than the financial saving will be the programme stability so achieved. At least until full programme compatibility is achieved, any university which rents a machine with the express aim of changing its computer each two or three years is going to spend a disproportionate amount of its effort upon the writing and rewriting of programs.

PROGRAMING AND PERSONNEL

Now that many universities have good machines, the main emphasis must turn to their effective use. This includes recruiting and training good programers, reporting programs in a foolproof way, providing courses for both graduate and undergraduate students in numerical methods appropriate for computers, and supplying consultant services to insure that machines are used efficiently. Most universities have already recognized this need to some extent by offering programing courses and by making computer staff available for consultation with would-be users. It is my opinion, however, that we have not done enough in this direction.

THE PROGRAMME LIBRARY

The key to effective use of a computer is a good programme library. The problem is deciding where the responsibility for building it should lie. Salesmen sometimes suggest that there is no longer any problem; their company is said to be able to supply all programs that are needed. Likewise, organizations such as SHARE—the Society to Help Avoid Repetitive Effort—have been launched to place programing efforts on a cooperative basis. Yet the national practice seems still to be greatly inferior to the national aspirations.

Universities have had IBM 650's for many years now; yet the social scientists who use these machines find that their programing needs are still formidable. Either they cannot secure copies of the programs which have been written elsewhere, or the reports are not intelligible, or the other university's machine is not compatible with their own. The commercial firms seem to me to be to some extent culpable in this sorry state of affairs, since they have the financial resources needed to set the matter right, and it would also appear to be entirely in their own self-interest to do so. I doubt whether any one of them has so far spent even a tiny fraction of 1 per cent of its budget upon this coordinating effort. If they will not take the lead, then perhaps some national foundation may be willing to do so. Two journals in our area (*Behavioral Science* and *Educational and Psychological Measurement*) now include computer sections, including brief reports upon newly prepared programs. This is a helpful development, but it does not go far enough.

Sooner or later there will come the recognition that a computer programme is just as important a part of our scientific effort as a research report and requires as careful dissemination and preservation. Indeed, it will probably be regarded as more important than the average run-of-the-mill article, because it is used by so many more persons. When that time arrives, what is written here will be out of date. Some central organization might meanwhile fruitfully undertake the same sort of responsibility for computer programs that the American Documentation Institute has accepted for the care and distribution of unpublished research material. A charge should be made for each programme sent out. The system would still be much cheaper for the recipient than the present one where he may in the end have to write his own programme. The organization might also try to insure that programme reports follow a uniform format whenever possible and that the directions are intelligible. Authorship and date should also be indicated. Not only is this fair to the author, but an doubtful points can then be checked with him. In the past, there have probably been many cases where recipients have not used programs which they have been sent because of obscurities in the operating instructions.

At present, however, the issue remains as to the policy a university should adopt to insure an adequate programme library. The University of Illinois has followed the practice of arranging for the computer staff to write a few staple routines, but for the most part expecting the user to write his own. This policy has had its merits. Not only have a number of social scientists learned to write programs, but also their library remains probably the most extensive one available at present in the social sciences. This is remarkable when it is remembered that Illinois has had to rely upon its own efforts and upon those of the three other universities with compatible machines, namely, Iowa State University, Michigan State University, and the University of Sydney. Yet I doubt whether the Illinois policy provides the long-term answer.This collection of programs is somewhat one-sided, reflecting too much the research interests of those who participated in its preparation; e.g., factor analysis and pattern analysis are well represented, but analysis of variance and covariance is not.

Furthermore, computer programs serve the interest of so many researchers that I am uncertain about the wisdom of expecting every man to become his own programer, any more than we expect him to become his own librarian. In many calculations and clerical tasks, use of a computer can save much time when a programme is available, but the task can be carried out more quickly by hand than by writing a special programme. The calculation of correlations is one example; the clerical operation of transposing matrix rows and columns is another. Yet programs for these, once written, will be very widely used. Likewise, it is doubtful whether the research director, who can be assumed to be a man of high productivity, should take time away from his researches to teach himself the specialized skill of programing. It seems better for this skill to be delegated to a specialist. Discussion will therefore turn to the training and employment of computer personnel.

PERSONNEL

In my opinion, each larger department of psychology should include a computer specialist. Perhaps he could also serve other departments with similar computational needs, e.g., sociology, anthropology, communications, political science, if they do not have sufficient work for a programer of their own. Colleges of agriculture, of business, and of education seem to me to use computers enough to train and employ their own specialists. Duties of a computer consultant should include:

- Writing basic programs;
- Training and assisting other members of the department in their programme writing;
- Maintaining the programme library, i.e., insuring adequate reporting of local programs and obtaining copies of programs written elsewhere;
- Helping machine users in the mechanics of card and tape production;
- Acting as a statistical and mathematical consultant for those who need such help (many poor theses in psychology are attributable to mathematical and statistical inadequacies; the computational adviser invariably finds himself giving statistical advice as well);
- Training a few especially selected graduate students to handle other computational consultancies similar to the one which he holds. The appointee should have academic rank, because the best men will not usually be willing to accept non-academic positions. This rank should be held jointly in the psychology department and at the computing centre. If possible, he should be supported by graduate assistants who can help with the consultancy and programing, and can themselves be trained as computer specialists. This would help overcome the present growing shortage of qualified men in the field.

Administrators may ask whether we can afford such appointments. We cannot afford to be without them. The computer has become so well accepted that universities, with the willing support of the National Science Foundation, are prepared to spend as much as a million dollars on a machine; and the giants of the future, such as LARC and STRETCH, may cost many times as much again. Having made this immense investment, universities will then have to be prepared to supply a staff of data processing specialists to insure effective use of the machine. Some might urge that this assignment should be left entirely to the central computer staff. However, there are two reasons why the task should be kept at the departmental level. First, the amount of consultancy across the university is too great. Even within one department, the work can be burdensome. At Michigan State University, there is a list of 88 articles, theses, and convention papers in psychology which include computer results, and the list may not be complete. This holds for a period of less than four years since MISTIC (the Michigan State computer) became available. Secondly, the usual computer mathematician or engineer is not well qualified to advise a behavioral scientist upon his computations. He cannot be expected to know psychological theories and objectives or standard psychological methods. Obviously, the best consultant is one who has an intimate knowledge of the area of research.

European visitors have commented that American universities do not encourage men to give their maximal effort to consultancy. The reason, no doubt, is the emphasis placed in the United States upon personal publications in deciding upon promotions. The person who can adequately fill a computer consultancy such as has been outlined must be highly qualified, and as a rule such men will be available only if we insure that they have as good opportunities for advancement as do their competitors.

Should personal publication be expected from these men before they are promoted? My inclination is to think it should. The best consultant is probably one who has first-hand experience in research; his own efforts help him appreciate the problems of others. So long as personal produc-tion is expected from him, it is only fair that anyone appointed as computer consultant be guaranteed a proportion of uninterrupted time for his own research.

The alternative is for administrators to be willing to judge and promote computer consultants in terms of their catalytic effect upon others' research production. Two or three of the best computer men I have known have been singularly unselfish persons who seem able to get just as interested in the research of others as in their own.

Perhaps a place should be reserved in our larger universities for persons of this temperament, just as it seems generally agreed that there is an important place for those whose gifts lie in the field of university administration rather than individual research. Perhaps, so as to maintain good academic form in the matter, it might be arranged for them to appear as highly productive by:

- Including computer programs among their publications—this would be just, since as much creative thinking is likely to go into a programme as into a research manuscript—
- Listing them as co-authors in all research publications in which they have played an advisory role; they will then appear to be unusually productive researchers.

Computer programing and the organization of computer analyses have gone beyond the reach of careful clerks with high school education. There seems to be a growing demand for persons who are simultaneously competent researchers, experienced in the use of multivariate methods, and skilled as computer users and programers. To try to meet this demand, behavioral science departments should introduce courses in the numerical methods appropriate for computers both for graduate and undergraduate students and should recruit and train good programers. Most universities have already recognized this need to some extent by offering programing courses and by making the computer staff available for consultation with would-be users. These efforts have usually been made by the computing centre. It is my opinion that their work should be supplemented by the behavioral science department themselves. All graduate students nowadays should know of the existence and potentialities of computers; many should be given an opportunity of using a computer for the analysis of their own data; some of the more enthusiastic should be encouraged to try their hand at the writing of programs; and occasional ones with the requisite ability, temperament, and mathematical knowledge should be trained specifically as computer specialists to act in the roles already discussed.

INNOVATION IN NUMERICAL METHODS

The good programer in the behavioral sciences also has to be a numerical innovator, expert in his knowledge of the use that is going to be made of his work, and willing to break away from customary statistical practices. Old techniques have been revised to make them convenient for computers, and completely new methods are being created that would not be feasible were it not for the existence of computers. Factor analysis provides a striking example because of the historical role played in it by subjective judgment. Ten years ago each factorist had to rely upon his own experience and wisdom in deciding upon the number of factors to extract, where to locate axes on his graphs, how to estimate communalities, and so on, so that two persons who started from the same data could never be guaranteed to reach the same answer. By contrast, factor analysis now can be applied with all judgment eliminated.

Computers have provided the spur to these technical changes, and these revisions had to be made before effective programs could be prepared. The steps of such an objective system will merely be itemized here. The principal axes method gives a unique initial factoring; Guttman's communalities provide exact rank-reducing values for those concerned only with the common variance; the Kiel-Wrigley criterion provides a logical basis for the decision upon the number of factors to be rotated; analytic methods have been developed both for orthogonal and for oblique rotation; and matrix algebra methods are now available for the matching of factors. The important point in this context is that, associated with the programing effort, there has had to be a series of technical and logical reappraisals of factor analysis. Factor analysis may seem to be an exceptional case, because it has traditionally been more judgmental and imprecise than any of our other main procedures. To show that these technical revisions apply to even the most standard of methods, I should like to illustrate by the staple of psychological statistics, the correlation coefficient.

CALCULATING THE CORRELATION COEFFICIENT (A CASE STUDY)

As an undergraduate, I was taught to plot the bivariate frequency distribution of x and y on graph paper. Numbers were kept to single digits so far as possible by use of class intervals and assumed means. A slide rule was available for the final multiplications and divisions, and a table of squares for extraction of the square root. Special work sheets were available to systematize the order of operations. This procedure could be successfully taught to any reasonably intelligent clerk with a high school education and a patient temperament. Two hours might be needed for a correlation when the sample was large.

Squares and products could be calculated directly from the scores without introducing class intervals and assumed means to simplify the figuring. Various dodges were available for calculating and checking sums of squares and products, such as the now well-known one of entering x on one side of the keyboard and y on the other, and then squaring, thereby getting x^2, y^2 and $2xy$ in different parts of the upper register. Once again, the operation could be successfully taught to any reasonably intelligent and careful person. Thirty minutes might be needed for a correlation.

My next transition was to punched-card machines. An entirely different method was used for calculation of squares and products; known in the United States as *progressive digiting* and in Britain as *summary multiplication*, it apparently was originally devised by a Danish actuary, Tetens, in 1785. The procedure enables the square of x and the product of x with a number of other variables to be obtained simultaneously. The procedure reduces multiplication to a series of additions. The operator using this method requires more than a rote understanding if he is to be efficient. He must be familiar with plugboards and maintain good organization. By working with duplicate sets of cards, he can arrange for tabulations to proceed on one set, while the sorter is getting the cards ready for the tabulation to follow. A couple of hundred correlations may now be calculated and checked in a period of eight or ten hours. That means perhaps twenty completed correlations per hour.

Twery's method for calculating correlations, devised in 1952, seems to be the best for an electronic computer. All scores for one person are input, and then every square and product is formed for that person, each being stored in a different location. It is as if a large number of desk calculators were placed around a hall, with a separate one used for accumulation of each square and each product, and then a clerk went from one to the other, recording one square or product on each. This unconventional order of work has two advantages. First, data in the behavioral sciences are usually arranged with all scores for one person together; punching of card or tape is therefore easier. Secondly, scores for any individual are no longer needed, once squares and products have been formed from them. The method accordingly permits a practically unlimited number of persons in the sample, even when storage capacity of the computer is quite limited. With this procedure, a set of 700 correlations can be calculated in ILLIAC for a sample of 500 persons in about twenty minutes, i.e., 35 correlations per minute, with most of the time required for input, so that with more modern machines with faster input systems, there is a further appreciable reduction in the time.

This example has been introduced to illustrate the extensive changes often needed even in the most standard computations in order to take advantage of the special characteristics of a computer. There may well be a negative rather than a positive transfer from knowledge of the traditional desk calculator and punched-card methods.

Patterns and Types

Whereas the correlation coefficient ranks among the older of the techniques of psychological statistics. McQuitty's ([4]) method of agreement analysis is among the newer. This procedure handles problems which remained unanswered before the computer period. Specifically, it is designed

- To provide a method of classification for dichotomous and categorical data based directly upon the responses and the point frequencies, with no reference to correlation; (b) to group persons into types at the same time it is assembling items into patterns;
- To identify configurations of items (referred to here as *syndromes*) in which non-linear relations as well as linear relations between the elements can be identified.

The traditional multivariate methods have adopted a linear and compensatory model. Variables have been assumed to be additive, both in predicting some outcome (as in multiple regression) and in determining a man's standing upon a factor (as when calculating factor measurements). Any deficit on any one variable can always be offset by a surplus upon another. Computational convenience seems to have been the main reason for this linearity assumption. Non-linearities are quite often found in meteorology and other physical sciences, and no convincing logical reasoning or empirical evidence has ever been provided to show that they will not be found in psychology. Indeed, this possibility can hardly be put to the test so long as we do not have satisfactory non-linear methods.

Variables can be conceived as either disjunctive or conjunctive rather than compensatory in their effects. To insure a certain favorable outcome, either *a* or *b* may suffice. Since elementary school work is not very hard, either reasonable ability *or* a modicum of hard work may enable a child to perform well. This is the disjunctive situation.

Alternatively, both a and b may be needed if the favorable outcome is to occur. A Ph.D. is probably unobtainable unless the candidate has reasonably high ability and is willing to work hard. This is the conjunctive situation. On this view, genius might be hypothesized to be a total con- figuration of aptitudes and traits, each playing an essential part in the man's realizing his fullest achievement. With any key element lacking, the configuration would no longer be appropriate, and performance might then be relatively undistinguished. Political history indicates that neither a female nor a Negro may at present be elected to the American presidency, no matter how talented the person may be in other respects. There is no overcoming the single biological disability. The logic is conjunctive rather than compensatory. (Political configurations change. There was a time when a Catholic was also automatically excluded from Presidential consideration.) Davison discovered that frustration tolerance of nursery school children was sharply lowered whenever (a) they were blocked by some situation which they were unable to master, *and* (b) they were very persistent in trying to reach their goal. Frustration was very much less whenever inability and persistence were not conjoined, i.e., when they failed but were not very highly motivated to accomplishment, or when their prolonged effort led eventually to the desired outcome.

The practical difficulty is the considerable number of patterns to be found in any empirical analysis. If the sample of items is large, one often cannot find two identical patterns, e.g., no two senators in the United States 83rd Congress voted in exactly the same way. The great step forward, introduced by McQuitty in agreement analysis, has been to shift the focus to the acceptance of partial patterns, so that persons are classified in terms of their predominant patterns of responses. Operationally, this means extracting the largest person-item submatrices characterized by perfect agreement that can be found in the data. Each submatrix consists of a subset of persons and a subset of items. The group of persons may be defined to form a *type*. The items upon which they agree are defined to be the *pattern*. The technique is one of multiple classification. Any person can appear in more than one type, and any item can appear in more than one pattern. There are several different ways in which these submatrices can be isolated. This description applies to the system recently worked out and programed by Hemingway.

His first step is formation of the agreement matrix. The computer, having been supplied with the responses for *n* persons, calculates the number of items on which each person agrees with each other. There are accordingly $n(n-1)/2$ agreement scores. Items may be either dichotomous or multichotomous. The data matrix remains in the computer, since it will be referred to again and again.

The machine next finds the two persons with highest agreement, and they are grouped together. (Special rules which will not be given here deal with ties.) The computer prepares a scoring key itemizing the responses on which the two persons agree. The logic is that items on which they disagree cannot be essential to the pattern. All other persons are then scored with respect to the scoring key, which contains the items provisionally accepted as belonging to the pattern.

The person who has the highest score on this key is obviously the one who has most in common with the two persons already provisionally grouped into a type, so that he is added to the group. The scoring key is once more revised, now including only those responses on which all three persons agree. Remaining persons are scored in terms of this further revision, and the person with highest score joins the type in his turn. Thus, as the number of persons in the type increases, the number of items in the pattern declines. The process of building the type and more precisely defining the pattern continues until the maximal product of accounted-for responses is reached, i.e., when the product of the persons provisionally in the type and items provisionally in the pattern is at a maximum. The maximal product of persons times items is found empirically. The computer continues adding to the provisional type as long as any remaining persons have any items in common with those in the type, and then selects the stage in the chain when the persons times items product is largest. These product functions seem characteristically to reach a mode, and thereafter decline rather rapidly, as losses of items outweigh gains of persons. The computer then prints the $j \times k$ submatrix and deletes the $j \times k$ responses from the data matrix.

Other submatrices are calculated in the same way as the first. A new agreement score matrix is formed for the unused item responses. The pair of persons with highest agreement form the nucleus of a second type. There is the same process of revising the scoring key after the addition of each person, and next adding to the type the person with highest score on the key. At any stage of building up the submatrix, the key, by its method of construction, consists of responses on which there is perfect agreement among subgroup members.

Here is a procedure with the simplest of arithmetic, consisting only on counting and of finding the highest agreement score. Yet agreement analysis is feasible for any large set of persons and items only on a computer. Indeed, even for a computer the operation is a lengthy one. MISTIC probably ranks as a high-speed computer, even in these times of faster machines, with its speed of about 10,000 additions per second. However, about 15 minutes may be needed to extract one submatrix from a group of 100 persons and as many items. An agreement analysis for the

United States 83d Senate, based upon the voting records of the senators, disclosed as many as forty type-patterns; about ten hours were needed for its computation. The machine indicates the number of responses included in each submatrix at the time of printing it out, so that at any stage it is easy to determine how much of the data matrix has been used and deleted. If the machine is needed for other work, the residual data matrix can be punched on cards, and the operation can start again later.

Any item may appear in more than one submatrix; so may any person. In analysis of voting records, this multiple classification enables one to recognize the varying affiliations and alliances. For example, a senator may vote with the civil rights advocates on one group of votes, with the economy bloc on another, and with agricultural interests on a third. Likewise any one roll call vote can appear in more than one pattern, i.e., it has different meaning and significance for various Senate groups.

Thus, briefly, we may see the interplay between the computer, the programer, and the methodologist. For effective computer use, methods often have to be drastically revised. There is also a greater incentive to create completely new procedures, in the knowledge that the computer can readily complete the calculations, even if a human would be loath to do so. Results provided by the computer enable new techniques to be evaluated much more quickly, providing a spur to the methodologist to revise and to reformulate. Computers are demanding radical changes in our numerical methods.

COMPUTERS AND THE SCIENTIFIC EFFORT

My prediction is that the electronic computer will prove to be the most versatile and influential scientific instrument so far invented and that it will play a larger role in the scientific histories of the future than even such obvious challengers as the microscope and the telescope. There are two reasons for this judgment:

- The large number of sciences that are benefiting from computers,
- The very varied numerical, clerical, and logical activities which form part of the computer workload. To the scientist with limited time and energy, the computer means extra research assistance. Unlike its human counterparts, this assistant is indefatigable. incredibly fast, and remarkably accurate; but it shares, with the humans it is superseding, the need to be given extremely precise instructions. It is moronic in the literalness with which it does what it is told to do. In this chapter, our concern has so far been with the problems of transition. We are still learning how to handle the facilities available to us. This section deals with the long-term influence of computers upon scientific method and experimental design in the social sciences, once our problems of machines, of men, and of methods have been resolved.

FUNCTIONS OF THE UNIVERSITY COMPUTING CENTRE

The modern American university has become so complex

that it threatens to divide into a set of small empires, made up of its various departments and institutes, each encircled by high walls and too preoccupied with its own problems and affairs to have any time left for effective scholarly communication with its neighbors. In this fissioning, the computer centre stands out as one centripetal force and the university library as another.

If I were the architect designing a functional twentieth-century campus, I should place these two institutions at the two main vantage points, with all roads leading to them. These are the two central organizations to remind us of the unity of scholarship and science.

Nearly every computing centre has been preoccupied so far with hardware problems. The dream of acquiring a computer has been realized at most universities. Now, faced with the nightmare of an overloaded facility, committees are writing their memoranda to urge the case (and it is generally a good case) for computers of higher capacity and power. The pattern of hardware change therefore continues. If one inquires about the computer position at

University X, a rather stock reply is: "At present we have only Machine Y, but Machine Z is on order." Viewed at the microcosmic local level, computer policy sometimes seems bedevilled by politics.

The over-all view, however, shows an amazingly rapid international acceptance of computers. There may be controversies about the machine to be acquired (there will be many complaints that the current macnine is not good enough) and as to how it should be controlled (criticisms are often heard that the current administration is insufficiently helpful and does not fully realise the scientific and economic importance of getting analyses completed as rapidly as possible), but there seems to be virtually complete acceptance that any university with pretensions to scientific respectability must have some reasonably fast computer. I do not have the facts, but my guess is that telescopes and microscopes never spread around the scientific world at this rate; I doubt if even Caxton's momentous discovery of printing did.

The duties of university computing centers must gradually be widened to include the dissemination of knowledge about computer numerical techniques, language translation, computer simulation models, Monte Carlo methods, and all the other new procedures emerging as a result of computer development.

Alternatively, this work will have to be initiated in other departments of the university. Before the introduction of computers, numerical analysis was a somewhat unpopular subject. It was unattractive, for example, to study solutions of equations which were either too involved for any practical use or which required an unreasonable amount of time and effort in their application. Likewise, matrix algebra, after its golden nineteenth-century days, had settled down into a rut. The field has now come alive again and is bustling with activity. There is, however, a formidable problem in getting this information into an intelligible form for the computer user. Clearly, behavioral scientists must be better trained in calculus, matrix algebra, and mathematical statistics than in the past.

Quite a large proportion of graduate students in the behavioral sciences, and perhaps even the undergraduates, should be expected to take mathematics as a minor. Computing activities will help by showing students the utility of mathematics and providing an incentive for its study; the interdisciplinary coteries which form around computing centers are often mathematically very stimulating. While improvement of mathematical standards should proceed as fast as possible, a generation or two may be required for behavioral scientists to reach the standards currently found in the physical sciences.

In the interim, mathematical and statistical information must be presented in simpler form. Special textbooks are needed for those with limited mathematical training, even if this means an expansive and verbal style that is irksome for professional mathematicians. The need for improved consultancy services at the university has been discussed earlier. Because of these augmented functions, the time may not be very far distant when the computing centre will have to be allocated as large a proportion of any university's budget as the library currently gets.

THE INTERPLAY OF THEORY, METHOD, EXPERIMENT, AND INSTRUMENTATION IN THE HISTORY OF SCIENCE

We can now return to the problem of the role of instrumentation in the history of science. There is an elaborate interweaving of theorization, of fact finding, of method construction, and of instrument development. No one technique can be assigned a logical or a chronological primacy over the others. The response to one problem in science is generally the stimulus for another. Any advance in methodology leads to more fruitful fact finding; better experimental evidence means theorization is more likely to be relevant; and so on.

Instrumentation plays its part in determining the form, not only of the methods and the experimental results, but even of the theories. The differences between the American and the British view of factor analysis may have been the product of their different computational facilities. For historical and cultural reasons, psychological research has not been as generously financed in Britain as in the United States. There has been less research assistance and fewer punched-card machines and electronic computers. Factor analyses have generally been conducted with smaller test batteries, so that fewer factors have been extracted. It is not surprising, therefore, that Vernon's description of human ability is more parsimonious in its admission of factors than Thurstone's. British reluctance to accept the desirability of rotation may be attributable to the same circumstance.

As long as one operates with only three or four factors, the main groups of tests can be discerned readily enough by inspection of the centroid sign pattern, so that there is no need for rotation. Once twelve or sixteen factors have been extracted, however, the sign pattern becomes so complicated that a rotated solution with many near-zero loadings becomes essential if the test clusters are to be clearly distinguished.This interplay between method, experiment, and theory can be illustrated from the British history of the study of individual differences.Here are some landmarks:

Darwin: We have already seen how years of painstaking observation preceded his theory. His sequence is: observation theory.

Galton: Stimulated by the Darwinian theory to examine the evidence upon human inheritance, he devised the correlation coefficient to measure resemblances in persons with varying amounts of common inheritance; then he made a multitude of observations. His sequence is: theory method observation.

Karl Pearson: His professional career was devoted to elaborating upon the idea of correlation and other statistical techniques relevant for biological research. He stayed with method throughout. Instrumental consideration influenced his results. Tables in his articles appear to eight decimal places because that was the capacity of his hand-activated Brunsviga.

Spearman: He started with his concept of general intelligence, then devised a method intended to establish its existence, and then collected the data on which to test his theory. His sequence is: theory method observation.

Burt: He seems to have been of a more empirical temperament, concerned initially with certain educational problems. His observations led him to considerations of refinement of psychological measurements. His sequence is: observation method.

There is no general order. What happens seems to depend upon the temperament of the man, upon his times, and upon what his predecessors have done.

Our interest in computers has sprung from the time-consuming nature of our multivariate methods. The initial sequence has been: method instrumentation. I have tried to show how the computer transition is not a rote process of programing the extant methods. The need now is for revision of methods to meet the computer requirements. The sequence has become: instrumentation method. My prediction is that computers will also bring us a great accession in empirical knowledge (remember Galileo and his telescope). Behavioral science theories hardly ever seem to fit the facts well; the facts are generally too complex. Any spate of fact finding will inevitably reveal discrepancies in our theories, and there will then be a heroic attempt to restate them so as to overcome their defects. The later computer sequence will therefore be: instrumentation fact finding theory.

Biological history is informative about the effects of new instrumentation and the time span over which this operates. The compound microscope was invented at about the beginning of the seventeenth century. By the middle of the century, decisive advances began to be made in technique. Red blood corpuscles were seen; then bacteria; then spermatozoa; and then muscle striations. Thus blood chemistry, bacteriology, embryology, and histology had their origins. With accumulation of vast amounts of data, there was an impetus to classification which culminated in Linnaeus' *Systema Naturue* in the middle of the eighteenth century. In the nineteenth century, with the empirical foundations of biology so much better established, there came a period of great theories and generalizations. Thus two hundred years or more lapsed from the invention of the microscope to its theoretical harvest. The intervening period had been devoted to perfection of the microscope as a research instrument, to observation and to classification, which provided the seeds for the theoretical accomplishments to follow. The computer impact on science may be expected to take a similar course, but with more compressed time span because of the greater proportion of human time and energy being given to scientific research.

THE SCIENTIFIC PARADIGM IN THE BEHAVIORAL SCIENCES :

The scientific task in the behavioral sciences is isolation of functional relations. Much has been written about the stimulus-response sequence. This has been oversimplified. Except for reflexes, there is not usually a one-one correspondence between stimulus and response. Behaviour in any situa-tion depends in part upon the set of stimuli impinging on the organism and in part upon the organism, i.e., its present state, its inheritance, its prior learning, and its expectancies. Any single segment of behaviour is generally the resultant of a large number of determinants pertaining both to the stimulus configuration and to the organism itself. Stimuli and organismic variables will be called the *antecedents,* and the sequence of behavioral responses will be called the *subsequents*. The functional relations needed are those which link a set of antecedents and a set of subsequents. These neutral terms have been selected to avoid imputation of causality and its metaphysical problems.

The functional relations will generally be both multivariate and probabilistic. The reason for their multivariateness is obvious; many determinants affect the outcome. They are probabilistic because not all determinants can usually be accounted for. Meteorology provides an analog from the physical sciences. The outcome, which is the weather, is the product of many atmospheric and geophysical factors, so that its predictions are probabilistic.

Probably no one will have disagreed to this point. The controversies about method occur mostly at the tactical level of how best to attain to these multivariate functions. There are those who support the univariate procedure by which only one antecedent is varied, with all others held constant. This procedure has been favored not only by experimental psychologist but throughout the natural sciences, and it is probably unequaled for its precision and ease of interpretation.

With these methods, various aspects of the stimulus-and-organism configuration can be considered jointly. The complexity of the experimental situation is disentangled by the multivariate statistics. Until recently, these methods have had the common characteristic of being extremely laborious computationally. Despite this, multiple regression and factor analysis came into regular use before the arrival of computer. Because behavioral scientists were already familiar with these techniques, they have been first to be programed. Canonical analysis involves finding the best linear functions between a set of antecedents and a set of subsequents, an objective which is essentially similar to the formal scientific one of finding the functions which link stimulus and organismic variables with the behavioral responses. Combining as it does some elements of multiple regression and

some of factor analysis, canonical analysis was extremely laborious, and hence was hardly ever used in our desk calculator period. Because it is not well known, it remains little used even though we have the computers to handle it. The multiple discriminant function, designed to achieve the best classification into known groups (surely similar in form to the objective of the clinical psychologists), is another method that was developed before computers, but even now remains practically unused. There are the new multivariate techniques, such as MCQuitty's agreement analysis and Lingoes' multiple scalogram analysis, which have been devised since the advent of computers, and whose calculations have been organized in such a way as to make full use of computer capabilities. The era of invention of new multivariate techniques is evidently not yet over. We are likely to see many more during the next half century.

Experimental designs may be classified in yet another way. The variables can be controlled and manipulated, or they can be observed in some systematic way in real-life observations in the field. We are accustomed to think of laboratory experiments as having some sort of intrinsic merit not possessed by material gleaned in the field. Astronomy, however, serves to remind us that high rigor can be attained even when the scientist must rely upon observation. Until the ascent of Sputnik in 1957, there had been no manipulated experiment in astronomy.

Thus there is a two-by-two classification: univariate-controlled, univariate-observational, multivariate-controlled, multivariate-observational. We are dealing here with oblique rather than orthogonal factors. Not all designs are equally likely. Instead, controlled laboratory studies are more likely to be univariate, and field studies to be multivariate. The distinction should not, however, be made too sharply. The *k*-way analysis of variance has been used increasingly in the laboratory. By suitable balancing of the numbers of subjects receiving the various experimental treatments, the effects of each factor can be examined independently from the others. The economy of a procedure in which several variables are experimented upon simultaneously is one advantage of the design. Another is the feasibility of examining the interactions (non-linearities) between the variables, in which the outcome is influenced by the simultaneous level on two variables. The laboratory psychologist is evidently willing to adopt multivariate techniques whenever he can get the controls and the precision he wants.

The strengths of the multivariate field experiment lie in its realism. Behaviour is observed in *situ*. Applications of psychology will incline toward multivariate designs, because in making predictions and recommendations, we shall always want to utilize our information as fully as we can.

It is not helpful to have behavioral scientists feuding about which is the right method to follow. The complexity of behaviour is sufficiently great to warrant trying all roads which may add to our knowledge. The extremes are clear. The univariate laboratory experiment excels in precision; the multivariate field investigation is strong on realism. Both are admirable goals, and each investigator has to use his own judgment as to the best balance between the two. His decision will no doubt be influenced by his temperament and his training as well as by his objective appraisal of the situation.

There is one fundamental difference between the methods. So far as the history of modern science goes, the univariate method is comparatively old, extending back to Galileo or before. The multivariate method is much newer, with its main development occurring within about the last hundred years (although I believe the resolution of forces into components goes back several centuries before that). The multivariate logic seems to have owed its formal inception to John Stuart Mill's" canon of concomitant variation. Galton's discovery of correlation came forty years later, at a time when there was an intensive search in progress for a reliable method of measuring association; Bio*metrika*, the statistical journal, dates from the beginning of the twentieth century; and the multivariate statistical procedures considered in this book have emerged since then. This is not a long period in terms of the history of science. The preoccupation with methods which has characterized a number of multivariate researchers is explicable in terms of the infancy of their field.

Computers are significant because they have opened the way to easy use of multivariate statistics. We can now readily take a multivariate approach to the search for functional relations. The tactical routes open to us have been widened. It is entirely premature to say what proportion of future behavioral science research will be multivariate and what proportion will be univariate.

Multivariate analysis is still too new, and both its logic and its techniques are insufficiently elaborated. That there will be some significant place for multivariate analysis and for the computer as its instrument does not have to be argued.

Chapter 6

Data Processing in Psychological Research

HISTORICAL ANTECEDENTS AND METHODOLOGICAL PROBLEMS

Psychologists were among the first behavioral scientists to recognize and utilize the high-speed digital computer in data processing. The modern computer was developed by mathematicians and engineers primarily for application in their own fields (and in the physical sciences). At most universities, responsibility for the operation of computers is usually assigned to mathematicians or engineers, yet the records of such centers show that psychologists rank high in actual use of computer time.

Furthermore, this high level of use occurs even though, in the early days at least, psychologists found that using the computer demanded that they first spend hundreds or even thousands of hours in writing new programs for the particular types of data analysis they wished to carry out. There seem to have been two reasons for this development:

But the readiness of psychologists to adopt the computer as a tool and their widespread use of computers point to a prior question: Why have psychologists historically been so active in the development of statistical methods, in the use of aids to computation, and in concern with experimental design? The answer to this question appears to lie in the unique problems faced by psychologists and in the nature of their subject matter. Whether the psychologist is primarily interested in theory or in application, certain special problems make his task both difficult and complex.

These problems confront all social scientists, but psychologists are peculiarly sensitive to them, perhaps because they are more concerned with their status vis-à-vis their colleagues in the physical sciences. Four of the most critical of these problems are:

- Sampling of subjects,
- Experimental controls,
- Selection of variables,
- The measurement of variables.

SAMPLING OF SUBJECTS

The psychologist is concerned with behaviour, but he cannot study behaviour in the abstract; he must study a behaving organism, whether it be a rat, a cat, a monkey, or a human subject. But even after he has selected the species, he still must choose a sample. From the standpoint of simplicity, it would be pleasant to have a ready supply of "standard subjects" of each species, much as the chemist can reach for chemically pure reagents.

As every one knows, however, no two living organisms are identical, not even litter mates or identical twins. Instead, individual differences are the rule and are especially pronounced among higher organisms. Every psychologist, then, is forced to restrict his study to a sample of subjects selected from the larger population of possible subjects and to be concerned with the adequacy of that sample for any particular investigation.

For experimental psychologists interested primarily in psychological processes, this means using a sample sufficiently large to yield stable estimates of population parameters and adequate tests of hypotheses. For many other psychologists, the primary focus of interest is individual differences among subjects, their origin, their interrelationships, and their relationships to life criteria. In either case, the research psychologist is likely to be confronted with a considerable amount of statistical analysis. Computers permit him to process his data far more efficiently and accurately than was heretofore possible.

PROBLEMS OF EXPERIMENTAL CONTROLS

An investigator interested in studying the factors involved in the linear acceleration of an object, for example, needs to know certain facts, e.g., the mass of the object, the force applied and its point of application, the inertial properties of the object and of the medium through which it must pass, and many others besides. Next, he must vary each of the relevant variables, systematically, one at a time, in order to generate some laws about linear acceleration as a function of these variables. Having measured, controlled, and observed, he can then analyse and formulate. A fairly simple set of mathematical expressions in the form of general and special laws would result from these procedures. Finally, he must test his formulations, i.e., replicate the experiments.

In essence, the foregoing exemplifies the experimental model of the physical sciences. Control of all but a single variable is the essence of experimentation in the physical sciences and the ideal in psychology as well. For a variety of reasons, some of which are indicated below, such experimental control often is not possible or not acceptable in experimentation with human subjects. Thus, the psychologist finds it necessary to permit several or even many variables to covary as in nature and can no more manipulate them than can the astronomer. In such instances, the univariate model must be replaced or supplemented by the multivariate; probability and the use of statistics then must supplant the isolation and manipulation of variables. The physical scientist comes closest to this problem in the fields of meteorology, astronomy, and quantum physics. But even though he cannot control, isolate, or accurately measure the relevant variables in these areas, the physical scientist's knowledge of them far surpasses the equivalent knowledge of the behavioral scientist.

There are still other differences: Human objects differ from other objects in a number of respects, not the least of which is in our attitudes toward them. Social and moral restraints, the evidence from the Nuremburg trials notwithstanding, deter the scientist from inflicting pain or discomfort upon another person, however noble the cause or intent. ([9]) Further differences from physical objects relate to the variability, complexity, and highly reactive nature of human organisms. A psychological probe into the inner emotions of another may result in a blank stare or a poke in the nose. (How unlike the well-behaved physical object!) Here no simple laws are possible and certainly none with the esthetic elegance of a mathematical equation.

Opportunities for direct manipulation of variables are limited, not only because of ethical reasons or emotional involvement but also because such control either introduces artificiality or destroys the variables we wish most to assess. We always stand the chance of losing what we seek, almost in direct proportion to our efforts to reach it. The probabilistic model, rather than univariate experimentation, is thus the most obvious and natural choice of the psychologist for many problem areas. With this choice goes a necessary tolerance for ambiguity and indeterminancy, a need for passive rather than active control, for sampling, and for satisfaction with approximation rather than certitude.

When samples are used instead of populations, where parameters require estimation, where natural experiments replace laboratory control, when likelihoods need evaluation, in short, when we operate within the confines of the multivariate probability model, a computer becomes a potentially powerful ally. It can free the social scientist of a great deal of drudgery in the organization of data; it can allow him to use what were, B. C. (before computers), forbidding statistical techniques. With some ingenuity on his part, computers offer the opportunity for testing models and simulating behaviour. This last area, as yet not fully explored, is extremely exciting and challenging for the behaviour scientist concerned with thinking, emotional, and motivational processes. It is likely that clinical psychologists of the future may find it necessary to utilize computers for situations requiring more than a crude diagnostic evaluation. Currently, it seems unlikely that computers will be used in psychotherapy, but with the development of language translation programs, it is not inconceivable that a future computer could serve as a valuable aid in therapy.

PLETHORA OF PSYCHOLOGICAL VARIABLES

The nomenclature of variables in psychology is almost as bewildering as their number. Thus, we have molecular variables and molar ones, those which are environmental and organismic, quantitative and qualitative, observable and inferred, complex and simple, stimulus and response, independent and dependent, etc. It would be interesting to speculate on the reasons for this meta-language. Does it reflect the complexity and range of variables required for understanding human behaviour—as opposed to those needed for physical objects, our incomplete comprehension of what is relevant, or our frustration? Possibly all three. In any event, the number of variables is indeed large, many are difficult or impossible to isolate, some defy analysis, and quite a few are vague and lack operational significance. A Linnaeus is needed to identify a psychological hierarchy of behaviorrelevant variables. Short of finding this genius, we can employ the limited capabilities of a computer to help us discover the underlying dimensionality of this universe. Having done this, we will be in a much better position to measure the variables and to design experiments to test their effects.

PROBLEMS OF MEASUREMENT IN PSYCHOLOGY

Last, but certainly not least, are the multitude of problems connected with measurement of psychological variables, once they have been selected. How does one go about measuring a complex variable: for example, anxiety? But first, what is meant by this term? The psychological literature is replete with definitions, operational and otherwise, of this central concept. Almost as much has been written on this "variable" as on love, and with about as much understanding. Psychologists not only do not agree upon the "meaning" of this term, but they set about measuring it in different ways. As a consequence, several studies have shown little or no relation between alternative measures and symptoms of anxiety. This is clearly an unsatisfactory state of affairs for research, even though the use of this term and others like it often suffices for action in a clinical setting or in the everyday world.

Perhaps one of the chief difficulties in this area exists because we carry many of our language habits over into the research setting, even though it is chimerical to suppose that the complexities of psychological reality will correspond to the forms of language. An obvious, but unpalatable, solution of this dilemma is giving up our theoretical pretensions and matching our research language with the complexity and often highly specific nature of life. Another, and related, solution is the painful and long-drawn-out process of empirical investigation. Integral to this enterprise is reliable and meaningful quantification.

For variables that are either too complex or difficult to isolate from the observation matrix, as well as for those discontinuous in nature, some numerical value can be assigned. The important thing, however, is not the number as such, but the intra-individual and inter-individual reliability with which it is given.

Although some information is lost by having too few categories, even dichotomous data can yield valuable insights. A number of techniques are available to the clinician for quantifying even the most recalcitrant variable, e.g., scaling methods, Q-sorts, check lists, etc. That old standby, rating scales, although subject to a number of distorting influences, can also be used to good advantage. Despite our best efforts, there will be variables which we feel are important but which elude quantification.

If we can accurately specify what the variable's presence means for any given bit of behaviour and what its absence indicates, and if we can do this reliably, then it can be quantified. On the other hand, if we cannot do these things, we are either working with an epiphenomenon or are confused in our thinking. In any event, a computer does not as yet have the logical powers of a human. It is restricted in its manipulations to machine representations (often binary) of the data we input. The output, or results, can be no better or worse than our conceptualizations.

Before turning to illustrative examples of the extremely profitable and often necessary use of digital computers by psychologists for data processing, it is important to note what the modern computer cannot do and what it can.

The computer cannot design an experiment, select the variables to be studied, select the measuring instruments, or collect the data. It cannot specify which among alternative methods of statistical analysis are to be applied. It cannot even read data until they are coded and punched in a specified language and format.

It cannot do anything with the data it reads until supplied with a set of specific sequential instructions called a "programme."

But with the appropriate programme stored in its memory, the computer can read large amounts of data rapidly, carry out elaborate sequences of computations at high speeds, with almost complete accuracy, and then print out the results in an easy-to-read format specified in the programme. Taken together, these operations are termed "data processing."

Because of both the cost and the capacity of modern computers, psychologists are rarely the sole users of any computer. Usually they process their data through a general purpose computing centre, so highly automatized that not even the immediate operator of the computer is aware of the specific type of problem the computer is working on at any given moment.

As noted above, psychologists who pioneered in the application of computers had to write entirely new programs for the special types of data analyses in which they were interested. Preparing and debugging such programs typically required far more time than the particular statistical analysis for which they were written.

Once written, however, a programme could be used over and over again. More important, the programme could be made available to fellow psychologists at other universities, with access to the same type of computer; thus it became possible to develop libraries of shared programs.

In spite of the variety of computer types and the rapidity of technological change in the computer field, most computer centers are now supplied with a library containing tested programs for carrying out the most frequently used techniques of statistical analysis. Thus the tremendous advantages of the modern computer in routine data processing are immediately available to the research psychologist who need only

- Prepare his data in the proper format,
- Specify to the computer operator the particular programme (or programs) to be used in processing his data,
- Specify certain parameters which must be inserted before a generic programme can begin computing on a specific problem. A few hours (or even minutes) later, depending on the demand for computer time, he picks up his printed results of a data analysis, which only a few years ago would have required several man-weeks or even months of hand computation, and in many cases would have been completely unattainable at any cost.

The foregoing picture of the psychologist's almost effortless use of the computer in data processing is admittedly somewhat rosier than that which exists in many localities. Unfortunately, many psychologists work in institutions without a computer.

Those with access to a computer may discover that only a limited number of needed programs are available for the particular make and model locally available; hence they are forced to learn to write programs. And with the rapid technological changes, one finds that just about the time an adequate library of programs is established, a decision has been made to acquire a new computer.

Even though the new model may have a much larger memory and compute many times faster than the old one, the user now must write or otherwise acquire an entirely new library of programs; consequently, it may be months before he can take full advantage of the potentiality of the new computer. Finally, like all man-made machines, computers both new and old are subject to operational breakdown. Although breakdowns rarely result in inaccurate computation, they can result in annoying delays, especially after one has become accustomed to high-speed data processing.

For these, as well as other reasons, it is hardly surprising that the most extensive and most effective use of computer occurs in institutional settings, where one or more staff members specialize in the application of computers to the particular sorts of problems and analyses of interest to behavioral scientists.

To be maximally effective, such a specialist must be thoroughly familiar with both the terminology and techniques employed by behavioral scientists on the one hand, and with the programing and operation of the local computer on the other.

Although he need not (and perhaps should not) serve as a consultant in research design or in decisions regarding statistical analyses of data, he must be at least sufficiently well grounded in both mathematics and statistical techniques to establish and maintain an up-to-date library of programs, to write new programs as needed, to recommend the most appropriate and efficient programs for carrying out analyses as specified by the research scientist, and generally to assist the would-be user to make maximal use of the computer. In a few university settings, specialists of this sort hold joint appointments on the staff of the computer centre and the staff of an instructional department.

Several of the larger psychological research institutes have found it necessary to appoint one or more such full-time specialists to facilitate computer use by other research personnel.

The great potentialities of the computer in data processing seems to have been first realized by psychologists at the University of Illinois. Its School of Engineering had built the ILLIAC for university use at the same time it built the ORDVAC for use by the Ordnance Department of the United

States Army. Thanks to the cooperative attitude of the engineers in charge of this installation, to the vision and diligent programing efforts of Charles F. Wrigley, J. Neuhaus, K. Dickman, and others, and because of the computational needs of R. B. Cattell, Charles Osgood, L. L. McQuitty, and others of the department of psychology, a most effective data processing facility was developed by 1955. For the first time, psychologists were able to complain, not about finding time to analyse their data, but about having so many analyzed results available that they could not find time to prepare them for publication.

The influence of this pioneering development at the University of Illinois was far more than local. Because of the size and speed of the ILLIAC, local scientists could not utilize its full capacity in the early years, and the University of Illinois generously made the computer and its programs available to scientists from other universities.

Thus, many psychologists first learned of the real potentialities and the actual necessity of computers in present-day research. Today, all major universities have some type of computer installation available for data processing; for present-day psychological research, it is as essential as is a good library for historical research.

The remainder of this chapter presents illustrative examples of data analysis of special interest to psychologists. No effort has been made to assess systematically the impact of computers on published research; rather the authors have attempted to select a variety of problems and techniques in order to emphasize for research psychologists the range of application and ability of computers.

PSYCHOLOGICAL DATA PROCESSING

FACTOR ANALYTIC STUDIES

Even a cursory survey of the literature indicates that the most extensive application of computers in psychology has been in factor analytic studies. There are at least two reasons: (1) the versatility of the technique, and hence its utility in a wide variety of research designs, and (2) the extremely large number of computations required for factor analysis and analytic rotational solutions.

In fact, before the development of computers and of appropriate programs for factor extraction and analytic rotation, psychologists were unable to undertake any but relatively small problems, i.e., those involving relatively few variables. Now, because of these developments, it is entirely feasible for an investigator to complete, within a matter of minutes, a factor analysis that formerly would have required two or three manyears of laborious computation. In fact, several such analyses may be carried on as a part of a doctoral dissertation.

The most ardent proponent of factor analytic techniques in psychology is Cattell, who was also one of the first to employ computers extensively in his research. Cattell was also the first to clarify and label the distinction between three types of factor analysis—all of potential interest to the psychologist. The essential differences between the R and P techniques are:

- In the number of persons or cases studied, and
- In the number of occasions on which observations are made. Both the R and P techniques represent an effort to identify basic or underlying sources of covariation among a larger number of observed variables. In R technique, the correlation between variables is based on the covariation of individual differences of the several variables across many individuals. The resulting factor (or underlying variable) is thus said to be a common factor across persons. In P technique, the correlation is based on the covariation of correlated changes in variables *for the same person* on many successive occasions. The resulting factor is thus common to the variables, but it may be unique to the individual. Q technique, on the other hand, is designed to identify subgroups of persons who have such similar scores on a sample of variables as to justify treating them as a common type of person.

Data matrix	R	P	Q
Each row is an:	Entity (person or subject)	Occasion	Attribute (variable or test)
Each column is an:	Attribute (variable or test)	Attribute (variable or test)	Entity, person or subject
Scattergram plotted column *vs.* column	Variable against variable. Each en-try refers to the paired scores of one person on two variables.	Variable against variable. Each en- try refers to the scores on two variables made by the same person on that occasion.	Person against person. Each entry refers to the scores of two persons on the same variable.
Correlation matrix	*r* between variables	*r* between variables	*r* between persons
Resulting factors:	Underlying dimensions common on two or more variables.	Underlying dimensions common to two or more variables	Underlying types common to two or more persons.
Factor loadings is correla- tion of:	A variable and underlying di- mension on which persons vary.	A variable and an underlying di-mension on which the individual varies from time to time.	A person and an underlying type representing a subgroup of persons.
Typical *N* of:	Persons	Many (100-100)	One
Attributes	Several (10-50)	Several (10-50)	Many (100 f possible)
Occasions	One	Many (100 if possible)	One

Essential characteristics of R, P, and Q factor analyses. with computers. R technique has been most widely utilized in the development of personality assessment devices of interest to clinical psychologists and in studies concerned with the empirical identification of theoretical constructs. Examples of the use of the R technique in the development of psychological tests include the well-known tests of Primary Mental Ability (Thurstone), the 16PF Personality Test (Cattell), and the Guilford-Zimmerman Temperament Test. In addition, Cattell has made extensive use of factor techniques in developing his O-A Battery, objective personality tests, and in seeking to find matchings among the personality factors found in different domains of personality test variables: self-ratings, ratings by others, objective tests.

A number of investigators have utilized R-factor analysis in an effort to identify the dimensions underlying observed behaviour of neurotic and psychotic patients, regardless of their psychiatric diagnosis. The first one developed by Wittenborn reduces 52 symptom-ratings to 9 cluster scores established by factor analyses. Later Lorr, Jenkins, and Holsopple developed the Multidimensional Scale for Rating Psychiatric Patients. Some 40 rating scales provide 11 "factor" scores. A still later form devised by Lorr, Rubinstein, and Jenkins for use with psychotic outpatients provides scores on ten personality and symptom variables. Each of these instruments has proved extremely useful in providing relatively objective scores in a series of relatively uncorrelated dimensions.

Of considerable interest and utility to psychologists has been the extensive series of R-factor analytic studies of Osgood and his students concerned with the development of the connotative dimensions of meaning and utilizing the technique known as the "Semantic Differential." This technique first requires the subjects to rate objects, concepts, or people on a series of adjectival bipolar scales; the resulting ratings are inter correlated, and then the matrix is factored. Small, in a doctoral dissertation, followed these procedures to study age and sex differences in semantic stimuli of fourth, eighth, and twelfth grade boys and girls. Shortly thereafter, Smith applied the same technique to identify the dimensions of the self-concept of neuropsychiatric patients; he was able to identify clearly five such dimensions and replicate them on a second sample of patients. In a doctoral dissertation under the senior author's direction, Lin is following the same general procedures in studying age and sex differences in the self-concept of fourth, eighth, and twelfth grade boys and girls.

The second most widely used of the three factor analytic techniques by psychologists is Q technique in which some index of association (r, tau, coefficient of profile similarity, etc.) is computed between all possible pairs of individuals in a group, and the resulting matrix of coefficients is analyzed in an attempt to find natural clusters (families or types) of persons. The first such application seems to have been the study by Moore, Stafford, and Hsu in 1947 (long before the availability of computers) aimed at identifying pre-psychotic syndromes in a population of college students.

More recently, Guertin utilized what he termed "inverted factor analysis" to identify types of schizophrenic patients, but failed to find any evidence of a general factor of schizophrenia. Borko also used an inverse or obverse factor analysis to determine clusters or types of patients based on MMPI responses. And still more recently, by means of a cluster analysis of a group of poor readers, Smith and Carrigan identified five types of reading cases, each of which they regarded as requiring different kinds of remedial treatment.P-factor analytic technique is most similar to the type of intuitive analysis represented by the intensive case study so much preferred by clinical pyschologists. In fact, it is a method for doing systematically what the clinician attempts to do intuitively, i.e., to identify the essential (or basic or genotypic) variable(s) influencing the day-to-day fluctuations in the behaviour of a single patient. The reader may therefore be surprised to learn that P technique has been but rarely used by clinical psychologists. Why is this so? There are at least three possible reasons:

- Like all types of statistical analysis, P technique

requires that the observational data be quantified, i.e., expressed as numbers, and unfortunately, many clinical psychologists object to any form of quantification of their observations of patients, arguing that it is impossible to express in symbols or numbers the complexities of the phenomenon which they observe. Actually, this is not a well-justified concern, since the investigator is free to use as many variables (symptoms, traits, mechanisms) as he wishes and may rate each on as many categories as he chooses.

- Unfortunately, a great many clinicians are antagonistic to any proposal to apply statistical techniques of any kind to the single case. Because of this orientation, they often fail to acquire any real competence with the methods of multivariate statistics and hence could not utilize P-factor analysis even if they wanted to. If their training has included some familiarization with the technique, they are apt to argue that since the assumptions underlying it are not met (e.g., linear relationships among variables), the technique is not applicable to real clinical problems, where interactions and curvilinear relationships supposedly abound.
- The most rational reason for the paucity of P-factor studies is the admittedly serious problem involved in securing meaningful data on enough variables on enough successive occasions for a single case to provide reliable correlations and a stable factor structure. It requires considerable testing time on each occasion to obtain scores on each of several variables. More important, since the goal is determining the covariation in the day-to-day fluctuations of states of the subject, it is essential that the measures obtained not be influenced by virtue of repeated measurements. Unfortunately, this requirement is not easily met in psychological measurement, because of practice effects, memory,

boredom, etc. Ideally, one would use tests for which there were 100 equivalent forms, but unfortunately, none exist.

It is not surprising, therefore, to find that the most extensive use of Pfactor analysis has been in the analysis of physiological and psychophysiological variables, for which the measures are presumably relatively uninfluenced by repetitive testing. Thus Williams, in a single subject tested on 100 occasions, identified a cyclical factor, or state, characterized by low cholinesterase in serum, high pulse pressure, high pH of saliva, low pH of urine. Another factor was characterized by high per cent lymphocytes, low per cent neutrophils, high blood glucose, and small difference flicker fusion thresholds. A third factor, perhaps the best substantiated of all factors defined by the P techniques, is one characterized by large PGR deflections, high initial skin resistance, low glucose concentration, marked upward drift in skin resistance during relaxation, short dark adaptation, high daily urine volume, and other variables.

But P-technique studies of the single case need not be limited to physiological variables. Cattell and Luborsky have shown that ingenuity on the part of the investigator permits the inclusion of often repeated measures of needs, moods, and attitudes in P-technique studies. Furthermore, Cattell and Cross present rather convincing evidence that certain personality factors originally identified by the R technique with many subjects also appear in a single case analyzed by the P technique.

An interesting application of R technique of factor analysis to the single case occurs in a study recently completed by Rosenthal, who explored its possibility as a technique for discovering the implicit personality theory utilized by a judge in his assessment of others. In this study, Rosenthal asked each of several subjects (judges) to rate a number of others (targets) on some 40 variables, utilizing each target's autobiography as a basis for the ratings. For each judge, correlations were computed be-tween all pairs of rated variables, the *N* being the number of targets rated. Thus, it was possible to carry out an R-technique factor analysis for each judge. Rosenthal found marked differences in the resulting factor structures, e.g., differences in the number of factors required to account for 95 per cent of the variance, in the relative amount of variance accounted for by the most salient factor, and also in the loading of specific variables. Equally important from the standpoint of methodology, he found that, with 50 or more targets, intrajudge factor similarity (i.e., replicability) was considerably greater than interjudge factor similarity.

MULTIPLE REGRESSION

Perhaps some of the best examples of the use of the regression model for prediction can be found in the studies by Horst and his associates at the University of Washington. This source has issued a series of publications which are truly impressive in the thoroughness of their documentation. Particularly noteworthy is the excellent reporting of many IBM 650 computer programs needed for such analyses. A cursory glance through these articles and the programme write-ups will clearly demonstrate the close interdependency of research and computers. A major part of the work done at this centre relates to predicting college success differentially for a number of different course areas. The analog for the clinician might be the differential prediction of therapeutic success as a function of type of therapy, therapist-patient similarity, initial status of the patient, diagnosis, etc. Quite typically, because of the problems involed, the clinician attacks this type of research in a piecemeal fashion. Nothing comparable to the number of cases (Horst reports using as many as 15,000) and variables (up to 46) has been attempted in the clinical area. Let us here illustrate the procedures involved in one kind of predictive study and how the computer is integral to the analysis.

As Talbott has pointed out, batteries composed of intellective measures have reached a certain point of predictive efficiency relative to the complex criterion of college success. The search for additional variables tapping aptitude and achievement does not offer much promise of raising the level of prediction. Not altogether unfamiliar to the personality psychologist has been the suggestion that personality and interest variables might result in a significant improvement in predicting college grades. Talbott rightly anticipates, however, a prior problem, i.e., that of the predictive value of normative versus ipsative measures. Common sense, mathematics, and empirical findings suggest contradictory answers to this problem. Talbott addressed himself to this issue by comparing the relative predictive efficiency of an ipsative and a normative personality measure for college grades. The responses of 171 University of Washington college students to Edwards Personal Preference Schedule (the ipsative measure) and Wright's Rating Scale form of this same test (the normative measure) served as the basis for predicting college grade point averages in nine different course areas plus the all-University grade point average. His principal finding was that the two measures did not yield significantly different predictions, although it was expected that the normative measure would be superior.

The following steps in the analysis of these data nicely demonstrate the advantages of having a computer as helpmate. First, there is the timeconsuming and often boring matter of scoring the test protocols. It is much cheaper, quicker, and quite probably more reliable to let a machine do this for us. Second, each variable from both forms of the test (15 on each) must be correlated with every other and with the 10 criterion measures, representing some 750 correlations. Third, the two 15-order matrices must be inverted in order to obtain the regression weights and the multiple correlations.

Fourth, vectors of criterion correlations must be estimated by multiplying the inverse obtained by vectors based upon subsamples of Ss in the nine course areas. Finally, some test of significance must be devised and calculated for the differences between the predictions of the two forms of the test for the ten criteria. Although each of these steps has been separately programed, efficiency would dictate an integrated programme, * starting with the new data and ending with the various tests of significance. On a high-speed computer, a job of this magnitude would probably not exceed 30 minutes in time. This saving would mean that the researcher could easily investigate many different hypotheses in the space of a week or a month.

In those cases where one has many criteria or a complex multidimensional criterion and a number of predictors, the regression model is wedded to the factor model to yield what has been called "canonical analysis" by Hotelling. The next example illustrates a complex analysis employing a principalaxis factor analysis and a least-squares multiple regression analysis in yet another manner.

FACTOR SPACE D2 ANALYSIS

The method of multivariate analysis to be described is particularly appropriate in those cases where there is reason to believe that the treatment effects we are evaluating may be a function of a small number of underlying factors. Overall and Gorham report on the use of such a method for clinical experimental data. Briefly, the particular project reported by these investigators was a double-blind study of 12 weeks' duration using drugs administered to 80 newly admitted schizophrenic patients, randomly assigned to six different drug groups. Three psychiatric evaluations were made using Lorr's Multidimensional Scale for Rating Psychiatric Patients, i.e., before treatment, 4 weeks after initial administration, and after 12 weeks. Since it could not be assumed that the 11 "factor" or scale scores used on this test represented independent dimensions for this particular sample of patients, *factor space* D^2 *analysis* offered a potentially powerful tool for evaluating significant treatment differences, which might not otherwise become apparent from a univariate analysis. For any sizable sample of cases and number of groups and/or variables, such an analysis would be prohibitive with a desk calculator.

The kinds of calculations, rather than a detailed procedure, will be outlined here. As reported by Overall and Gorham, the essential steps involved in this type of analysis are:

- The calculation of the correlation matrix, based upon the within groups sums of squares and cross products, corrected to the treatment means and summed over groups;

- A principal-axis solution of the correlation matrix to yield a few orthogonal variates accounting for the maximum of variance;
- The rotation of the reference axes to meaningful structure;
- Estimation of factor scores by regression analysis;
- The testing of differences among the various group means on the underlying dimensions, which is provided by Mahalanobis-D^2 statistic.

Two factors resulted from the seven Lorr scales analyzed, four having been omitted from the study because of previous findings. The first factor was interpreted as representing improvement in ward behaviour; the second related to improved mental processes. Factor scores were differentially related to drug treatment. With the increased accessibility of computers, this method of analysis with many more variables may well prevail in the clinical literature.

PATTERN ANALYTIC METHODS

Two general classes of techniques will receive attention here:

- Those methods which relate to ordered data, e.g., testing, classifying, and comparing profiles or patterns of standings on linear continua;
- Those which relate to *unordered data*, e.g., discovering that set of elements or items which has a predictive validity not possessed by its constituent parts. The first class of methods has come to be known as "profile analysis"; the second has unhappily assumed the generic term of "pattern analysis," or one of its cognates, e.g., "configural analysis." We shall use the latter term for the second class of procedures

Profile Analysis

As Gengerelli and Butler state the issue, "The problem of profile analysis is essentially a matter of specifying by means of a single real number the mutual quantitative discrepancies existing among a set of measures or scores *x1, x2, x3*... earned by a given individual." The authors then proceed to generate unique, unambiguous numbers to describe any profile of scores. This is accomplished by obtaining rank differences among the set of variables and adding a fractional portion to each coefficient from a table of prime numbers. The latter maneuver insures that to each profile there corresponds one number and to each number there is but one profile. By these procedures, profiles can be ordered in a discrete replicable series, thus permitting the use of a statistic to describe the average profile of a group of Ss. One is then able to determine whether any particular group of Ss can be discriminated from any other. It is also possible to classify any particular profile as being more like another (group or individual) profile than unlike it. Gengerelli and Butler report that, in their experience, where the difference between the mean profile scores of two groups was significant at better than the.01 level, misclassification of profiles did not exceed 30 per cent.

Although it is not known whether this method has been programed for a computer, it is a very simple programme to write. Here is one case where the clinician can easily gather thousands of protocols, set up norms, test differences, and then proceed to classify test protocols individually in the clinical setting. The authors cite a study of five nosological groups:

- Paranoid schizophrenics,
- Manic depressives,
- Alcoholics with psychosis,
- Alcoholics without psychosis,
- College students, who were tested on the MMPI. Each group was found to have an average profile which significantly differed from the *null* or flat profile at better than the.001 level. When significance tests were applied to the differences among groups, only one group was found to be discriminable from the others, i.e., the college group. Having established essentially two classes of profiles, i.e., disturbed and normal, classification was then at- tempted. The

percentage misclassified was 16.7 for the disturbed patients and 20.0 for the college group. The addition of the *elevation* variable did not improve the differentiations; i.e., there were still two classes of profiles. This method treats *shape* and *elevation* separately and hence leaves open the question of a possible interaction between the two as contributing to discriminations.

Other methods have been suggested for profile analysis, e.g., an analysis of variance technique by Block, Levine, and McNemar and the use of intraclass correlation by Haggard. The latter technique offers a very interesting application as illustrated by the author, i.e., determining the reliability over time of a set of profiles taken from one individual. One of Haggard's findings was that the profiles of different persons were more similar than that of the same person (five MMPI testings of a psychiatric patient, admitted many times), over a period of 3 1/2 years. If this were not so, one would begin to question seriously either our treatment methods or the test employed. Haggard suggests many other applications which would interest both the clinician and the personality psychologist.

A somewhat different use of the profile matching technique was used by Kelly and Fiske in an analysis of the relative accuracy of qualitative (judgmental) and quantitative (objective) matching of personality descriptions of subjects assessed first as beginning graduate students in clinical psychology and assessed several years later on the basis of professional performance. In brief, it was found that the purely statistical matching of all possible pairs of rated personality profiles resulted in 74 per cent of the cases being correctly matched, as compared with 70 per cent correct matches by judges using two verbal descriptions of the same subjects. This example is included less because of the resulting findings than to indicate the range of applicability of computers to research of interest to clinical psychologists. The *tau* statistic used is perhaps the most appropriate statistic for comparing the shapes of profiles, but its hand computation is laborious if more than a few variables are included in profiles to be matched.

Another example of the utility of a computer in computing *tau* is a study by Hoffman who was interested in comparing the problem-solving abilities of small homogeneous and heterogeneous groups. All members of a pool of potential subjects in this experiment were administered the Guilford-Zimmerman Temperament Survey, which yields scores on 10 variables. Hoffman used a computer to obtain the *tau* of each subject with every other subject in a large subject pool and then assigned his Ss to experimental groups on the basis of their similarity or dissimilarity.

All the foregoing methods presuppose the existence of some group or groups from which the analysis proceeds. The techniques to be discussed below are designed to *find* these groups empirically. Thus, logically and experimentally, the procedures of configural analysis should precede those of profile analysis. The order of presentation was reversed because of the greater familiarity of profile analysis as contrasted with configural analysis.

Configural Analysis. Basic to the methods to be discussed is what is known as the Meehl Paradox; i.e., two or more test items can severally have a zero correlation with a criterion and yet jointly be perfectly correlated with it. This possibility arises from the statistical definition of independence, i.e., two or more items are independent if, and only if, each variable has a zero relationship with every other item when taken separately and with every combination of variables. McQuitty has clearly outlined the issues involved and has offered many different methods for analyzing data configurally. In this chapter, we shall content ourselves with illustrating but two configural techniques: *agreement analysis* and *similarity analysis*. *Agreement analysis* is a method excellently suited for solving those problems which are of utmost significance to the clinician, i.e., patterns of behaviour. Implicit in the pattern or configural approach is the assumption that other than linear relationships may exist among variables. Based on Zubin's agreement score, McQuitty has devised a general method for classifying or clustering persons or items in terms of patterns. An agreement score based on two or more persons is simply the number of items responded to in the *same* way. Thus, e.g., if at least 2 Ss gave "true" responses to 10 items of an inventory and "false" responses to 4, the agreement score would be 14 for those persons.In one of its simplest versions, agreement analysis involves the following five steps:

- Calculate agreement scores for all pairs of persons; this basic symmetric matrix represents the common components of agreement existing among the *N* individuals.
- Select the highest entry in the matrix as a basis for combination.
- Reduce or condense the agreement matrix by one row and column and use the common answers of the preceding combination to score all individuals not in the pattern.
- Substitute this array of agreement scores for the one deleted and note who is included in the new combination; e.g., if *A* and *B* were combined, the column and row designations could be represented as *AB*.
- Reiterate steps b to d, successively combining individuals, groups, or individuals and groups, until all Ss have been classified or until all patterns merge into one.

The foregoing procedures result in a hierarchical organization of the data not unlike that of a Linnaean system. Although it is not too difficult to perform an agreement analysis, addition being the most complex of the mathematics involved, any sizable sample of Ss and items would soon tire the most ambitious researcher. The scoring, re-scoring, and counting are well adapted to computer operations. Despite the method's adaptability to clinical and personality problems, not much research has been done in this area. McQuitty has shown in one study on psychological well-being that mental hospital patients differ from other persons primarily in terms of their response patterns. Further work with this method is needed.In contrast to the version of agreement analysis presented above, the method of *similarity analysis* differs in three main respects:

- It has a generality beyond qualitative or ordinal data.
- Indices of association form the basis for determining all higherorder relationships (one does not refer back to the actual responses for combining).
- A classification assumption is involved based on similarity rather than identity of response patterns.

The basic matrix from which an analysis proceeds can contain frequency counts (e.g., agreement scores), correlations, or other indices of association or concomitance. The method can be used on continuous or discrete variables, where the relationships are either linear or curvilinear. Thus, as a clustering method, similarity analysis is more general than agreement analysis. To the degree, however, that its assumptions are in error when combining individuals, items, or variables, then agreement analysis would seem to be the more powerful method. Let us see how the method works by giving an illustration.

Wrigley has presented a study on the divisional structure of the American Psychological Association, which had been previously analyzed by both factor and cluster methods. The first step, after having obtained indices of membership for the 17 APA divisions, was to reduce the order of the matrix by 1. This was done by combining the two divisions of Personality-Social and SPSSI, representing the largest coefficient in the matrix. One row and column is then deleted from the matrix and an *average* is calculated for the newly combined division and substituted for one of those deleted. The procedure is then identical with the foregoing version of agreement analysis for further combinations. Each time a reduction is made, average indices are calculated, based upon the number of elements in the pattern. This method resulted in a number of groupings, which were then compared with the results of two factor analyses and a cluster analysis.

After having made these comparisons, Wrigley proceeded to list the advantages of similarity analysis in comparison with factor analysis. Briefly, he concluded that similarity analysis:

- Allows one to select the number of groups after analysis;
- Is quicker;
- Is more objective;
- Has an immediate appeal to the uninitiated. Factor analysis, on the other hand, uses more information, allows for multiple classification (another version of similarity analysis also provides for this), and probably yields more stable results.

To conclude this section on pattern analytic methods, it seems obvious that clinical psychologists now have the opportunity for extensively testing their beliefs about the pervasiveness and importance of patterns. The methods just described represent only a small proportion of those available for research use.

We now turn to an illustration of a technique from scaling theory, whose development was materially aided by a computer.

MULTIPLE SCALOGRAM ANALYSIS

Multiple scalogram analysis (MSA) represents a generalization of Guttman's scaling method. As such, its aims are:

- To provide an empirical and statistical basis for scaling items,
- To produce as many unidimensional scales as is consistent with the underlying dimensionality of the matrix. The kinds of items which are particularly appropriate to scale analysis are cumulative in nature: when either endorsement or passing of an item implies the en-dorsement or passing of another item which is more popular or less difficult. Thus, for example, the following three items are cumulative in respect to the underlying ability of arithmetic knowledge: (1) 3 + 2 = 5; (2) a + b = b + a; and (3) x2 - 9 = (x + 3) (x - 3). That is, a person passing the third item would in all likelihood pass the other two, and a person failing the first would fail the two more

difficult ones. Each item is assumed to represent increasing amounts of arithmetic knowledge.Based on Ss' responses to such items as the above, we can order the people in respect to their possession of the trait being measured. To the extent that a univocal ordering of Ss and items can be obtained, the items are said to be "scalable" or to form a unidimensional scale. Such scales have these important formal properties:

— Scale scores permit a reconstruction of the Ss' answers to all items;
— Maximum predictability with relatively few items is attained for *any* external criterion;
— Error of measurement is minimized for both scale scores and responses to individual items.The following five formal criteria were employed for linking items and for testing the scale hypothesis:
  (a) Positive manifold. All adjacent items in a Guttman-Lingoes scale are required to be positively related. If the items are negatively related, one of them is reflected, i.e., 1's are changed to 0's and 0's to 1 1's, where 1 represents an endorsement or passing of the item and 0 its converse.
  (b) Mononicity of item marginals. The proportion of 1's is not allowed to increase when items have been ordered from easy to difficult or from popular to unpopular. If a positively related item (or one that has been made positive by reflection) fails to meet this criterion, that item is not considered a candidate for the scale.
  (c) Minimum distances between adjacent items of a scale. The measure of distance is the symmetric set difference, i.e., items are as similar as possible in their 11 and 00 correspondences.

(d) Minimum errors. The number of 01's, when items have been ordered from easy to difficult, should be the smallest value obtainable for the smallest distance. If one minimizes the following function of distance and error, the third and fourth criteria can be collapsed, i.e., the square of the distance plus the number of errors.

(e) Statistical significance. The fourfold table resulting from any two adjacent items must be significant at or beyond the.01 level as evaluated by either the x2 or Fischer's exact test. This last criterion provides a test for rejecting the scale hypothesis, sets a lower bound on the coefficient of reproducibility, and requires differential reproducibilities for items with extreme marginals and for varying sample sizes.

The first item of any scale is chosen on the basis of that item marginal that is largest when all items whose marginals are less than *N*/2 have been reflected. Scales are terminated either when there is no positively related item with the preceding item of a scale when the marginals are required to be monotonic decreasing or, if there is such an item, when the relationship is not significant, according to the fifth criterion above.

Without going any further into the theory of scale analysis, suffice it to say that many different kinds of items have been found to scale, from fear symptoms to the voting behaviour of United States senators.

Lingoes has presented an excellent example of a configuration or pattern possessing validity not possessed by its constituent parts. In an analysis of a personality inventory (MMPI), it was found that although scale scores on selected variables could not discriminate patients from nonpatients (identical means and variances), a measure based on the concept of deviation from perfect scaling did so significantly (P d".003).

Without going into great detail, the MSA procedure is based on what might be called "chain theory." The essential premise of this theory is that variables may concatenate in many different ways other than the linear for which we have adequate measures. A more general measure of relationship has been used based on probability considerations. What this entails for the MSA technique is a calculation of exact probabilities for multivariate distributions. In the dichotomous case, this means that Fisher's exact test must be applied between each and every item (a substantial enterprise even with tables of log factorials).

Two items are considered to be relevant to the same domain if, and only if, they yield a significantly small probability value. As each successive link in the chain is developed, an order emerges among the elements of the chain which can be described sometimes as a Guttman unidimensional scale, sometimes as a factor, as a cluster, or as of some other form. Thus, it can be seen that no restrictions are imposed on the data, be they linearly related or otherwise, qualitative or quantitative, etc.

Computers are essential to the use of this technique with even moderately large matrices. An analysis of 100 items and 100 Ss took only three minutes on an IBM 704, but would take at least a month to do by hand.

We conclude this chapter by presenting an illustration of an integrated set of computer programs (an example of an executive routine) for multivariate analysis.

AN EXECUTIVE SYSTEM PROGRAMME

Tryon has conceptualized the various methods of multidimensional analysis as representing different arbitrary decisions at successive stages of a general programme of analysis. Any particular method of analysis, according to Tryon, is a variant of the general programme, which has been programed for the IBM 704 computer. For example, Thurstone's *centroid factor analysis* is defined by the following decisions in regions A to G, representing V-analysis (i.e., variable analysis): A2, B3, Cn, C4, E4 or E5, F2, and G2. All of these decisions are controlled by a parameter card which is read in ahead of the data cards. Such an integrated programme allows a researcher to make many different comparisons on the same data. The several programs are so organized that new subroutines may be added to the executive routine (a programme to select and monitor other programs). Tremendous latitude is available with such a flexible routine. There are more than 2,000 possible patterns of major decisions within V-analysis alone. Let it be noted that some kinds of analyses (in general those to the right of the schema) are highly abstracted variations, whereas those that deal with directly observed, finite, less constructed kinds of variation appear to the left.

Here is represented a graphic illustration of a three-dimensional subspace, where highly correlated clusters of variables are encircled by dashed lines. Such a printed output can be easily prepared for publication, thus saving a great deal of expense and time in preparing special charts.

In the preceding pages, we have outlined the most pressing methodological problems and some of the more extensive uses of computers by psychologists. We have also paid some attention to techniques which, although less used, are nonetheless adaptable to computers. Many methods and designs have not been mentioned, e.g., that of complex analysis of variance, discriminant function analysis in classification, and non-parametric statistics like chi-square, to name but a few. Nevertheless, such procedures as these have been programed.

A concluding word of caution seems appropriate. When trying to decide whether to use a computer (granting availability of both machines and programs), this is a good general rule: If the cost in time and/or money of clerical and computational assistance is greater than the cost involved in preparing data for machine analysis, then a computer is, of course, recommended; if the cost is equal, a computer is still preferable because of its greater reliability. Even at commercial rates of $300 to $500 an hour for large machines, substantial savings over desk calculations are possible because of the tremendous speed of analysis.

Some types of analyses are best handled by low-speed computers and/or ancilliary equipment, such as card-sorters, collators, etc. The value of such devices is not to be minimized.

Nevertheless, as Wrigley has pointed out on several occasions, the increased availability of computers and the problems associated with programme libraries often tempt some potential user to use statistical models which are either inappropriate or are little understood.

Others may be tempted to correlate anything and everything just because the capacity of the programme permits it. The computer is no substitute for good and long cerebration by its human user. This he can do best, despite the story of the computer, which when asked, "Is there a God?" allegedly printed out the reply, "There is now!"

Chapter 7

Factor Analysis

QUESTIONS THAT CAN BE INVESTIGATED BY FACTOR ANALYSIS

Factor analysis starts with a matrix of the correlations among a set of *n* variables and seeks to investigate questions about it, such as the following:

- Can the observed relationships be represented or reproduced, with little error or loss of information, from a set of *r* reference variables smaller in number than the *n* variables with which the analysis was begun?
- Can the *r* (*n*) reference variables be interpreted to represent basic dimensions in the field of investigation of which the observed variables are linear weighted composites?
- Are these basic variables completely independent in the population (represented on orthogonal reference axes), or related (represented on oblique reference axes)?

In order to investigate the first question, the test variables can be repre-sented by vectors of length proportional to their common variability and separated by an angle so that the correlation between two variables, $r_{ij} = Vs_i\, V_j \cos ö_{ij}$. A reference system of coordinate axes is then introduced into the test space and each test vector is expressed in terms of the *r* coordinate axes of the reference system. Estimating the length of the vectors representing variables, which has the effect of reducing the test space to the common factor space, and determining the dimensionality of the reference space are problems that must be dealt with in factoring the reduced correlation matrix. Various methods and computer programs, such as the centroid method, the principal axes method, and the multiple-group method, have been devised to deal with the factoring problems.

The second question involves the determination of a set of coordinate axes that is most useful and meaningful for the reference purposes of the investigator. Are there locations of the reference axes, determined by the structure of the interrelationships of the variables in *r*-space or by theory, or both, that are most useful for meaningful interpretation and reference? This is the problem of rotation, or translation of axes about the origin. A number of solutions, such as the two-factor, bifactor, and simple structure models, and a number of analytical methods, such as the varimax, quartimax, and oblimax programs, have been developed to deal with rotational problems.

With reference to the third question, it should be pointed out that the quartimax and varimax analytical rotation programs insert an orthogonal reference frame. The oblimax, biquartimin, and several other rotation programs insert an oblique frame of reference axes, the degree of obliquity being determined by the structure of the data being analyzed.

The investigator must select an orthogonal or oblique rotational solution. The mathematics of orthogonal solutions are simpler, and in many cases the structure is so nearly orthogonal that little is gained by introducing the complications of oblique factors. Also the theoretical framework used by some investigators requires orthogonal reference factors, regardless of the obliquity of the data.

In some areas of investigation there is considerable obliquity in the data. Where this is the case, a better simple structure fit can be obtained with oblique axes. A part of the information obtained from the analysis is the degree of obliquity or correlation among factors for a given set of data.

In addition to the questions and problems posed above, a number of other problems may be considered in connection with factor analysis. The general problem of matching factors from different studies will be considered in Section and use of marker reference variables in Section. The generation of factor scores will be considered in Section, and some influences of computers on research in factor.

INTERCORRELATIONS

As applied in the behavioral sciences, the method of factor analysis generally starts with an intercorrelation matrix. From a mathematical point of view, the matrix to be factored need not be composed of correlation coefficients, but the examples in this chapter will be concerned with the factorization of a matrix composed of Pearson product-moment correlation coefficients.

Strictly speaking, the technique of obtaining correlations need not be treated in a chapter on factor analysis. The procedure is generally familiar, however, and it affords an excellent opportunity to mention some basic differences between solving problems on a hand calculator as opposed to solving them by means of an electronic computer. When one seeks to obtain a matrix of correlations by hand methods, one normally considers two variables at a time. The sums, sums of squares, and cross products for the two variables are laboriously collected, and eventually the correlation coefficients are computed. Then the process is repeated for two more variables and continued until all possible coefficients have been obtained. Because of time-consuming input-output considerations, as well as programme logic, the technique just described would be a very inefficient way to utilize the capacity of an electronic computer.

A flow chart of a simple correlation routine which might be written for an electronic computer. Within the boxes, k refers to the number of variables which are to be intercorrelated. In box 2, the term "record" refers to some type of input, such as punched cards, magnetic tape, paper tape, etc. The same consideration applies to box 15 regarding output. Notice that all summary information is collected before any of the correlation coefficients are computed. It may be inferred from the entry in box 6 that the sum of squares for a variable is regarded as being a special case of a cross product (i.e., the cross product of the variable with itself). Developing the programme logic in this manner makes it unnecessary to write a separate loop for the sums of squares. Similarly, reference to box 14 indicates that the programme would produce the correlation of each variable with itself along with all of the other correlations. A typical complete programme would contain provisions for optional output of the summary data before box 9 and the variances after box 10.

Observe that $(k)\ (k + 1)/2$ storage locations are necessary to contain the cross products. As the covariances are formed, however, the cross products are no longer needed. Similarly, as the correlationbetween two variables is formed, the covariance of the two variables is no longer needed and the correlation can be stored in the location which previously contained the covariance. Thus, the internal structure of memory can be visualized as a matrix which is replaced by succeeding ones at various stages in the process. This allows a maximum amount of memory to be used for computational storage purposes and a minimum number of memory locations to be devoted to storage of the end products. It is difficult to overemphasize the value of being able to visualize machine analysis problems in terms of matrices.

METHODS OF FACTORING

The basic equation for factoring the reduced correlation matrix,† R, on orthogonal axes is

$$R = F\,F'$$

where F represents the orthogonal factor matrix. The methods of factoring presented in this section all yield arbitrary orthogonal axes which must be rotated to orthogonal or oblique reference positions for meaningful factor interpretation. Before electronic computers, factor extraction done by pencil and paper arithmetic, or with the aid of a desk calculator, was a laborious process. Large-scale correlation matrices may be factored with relative ease on the modern electronic computer.

As previously mentioned, a number of analytical techniques are available for extracting factors from a matrix of intercorrelations. Examples are given in this chapter for two of the methods. The illustrative data are obtained from Fruchter. ([4]) All the sample analyses presented in this chapter were obtained by means of an IBM Type 650 Magnetic Drum Data Processing Machine, but the procedures may be generalized to other in-ternally programed digital computers.

It is important to realise that computers are symbol manipulators. As such there is theoretically almost no limit to the magnitude of a problem which can be solved utilizing the computer. Practical limitations exist in abundance, however. Consider a correlation matrix consisting of fifty variables; 2500 storage locations would be required to store the entire square matrix. Theoretically, even if the machine contained only 2000 storage locations, the matrix could still be factored by cycling the data through the machine one column at a time. Operationally, such a solution rarely is used, particularly when the machine is input-output limited. In this particular case, a compromise can be effected by entering only the triangular matrix; this procedure reduces the storage problem but increases the complexity of the programing.

Computers vary with regard to speed, capacity, accuracy, etc. It is important, therefore, to realise that in the discussion which follows, the comments are true, in general, for all general purpose stored programme computers, but the task of implementing the procedures on a particular machine varies in complexity, depending upon the characteristics of the machine and the skill of the programer.

One of the decisions to be made in programing for factor analysis is whether to enter into the computer a square matrix of correlations or only the triangular matrix. A 5 × 5 square correlation matrix (a). If all elements in the square matrix are stored in memory, the numbers within the cells represent a possible memory location for each element. (b) contains the same amount of information, because of the redundant nature of correlation matrices since *rij* = *rji*, but utilizes ten fewer memory locations. (a) have consecutive memory locations when considered by row, and are displaced consistently by five when examined by column. (b) that the ele- ments for column 3 are located in addresses 3, 7, 10, 11, and 12, which at first glance does not appear consistent. The mapping function for the displacement of consecutive elements in a triangular matrix is not difficult to calculate, but it does require additional programing. Additional programing usually requires more processing time, and the additional instructions themselves require memory locations. It is possible in a small problem for the additional programing to require more memory space than is saved; at the same time the processing time may be increased. In this example, only ten memory locations are saved, but in a 40-variable problem 780 locations would be saved. Frequently, it is difficult to achieve an optimum solution to a problem such as this. The solution depends upon what is expected from the programme in the way of generality, on the characteristics of the machine for which the programme is to be coded, and on the skill of the programer.

On a very large machine, it is relatively simple to enter raw data into the computer and receive rotated factor loadings as the final output, with optional provisions for intermediate output, such as correlations and centroid loadings. For smaller machines, and particularly for those without magnetic tape attachments, it is not feasible to link the steps together in a continuous process. The boxes with the "corner cuts" represent decks of punched cards containing the indicated information. The rectangular boxes represent the computer with the indicated programme loaded in the memory. Frequently, the output format for one programme will not match the input requirements of the next programme in a process, even when the programs have been coded for the same machine. Suppose, for example, that the output in box 3 represents a triangular matrix but the programme in box 4 requires a square matrix.

A number of solutions to this dilemma are possible. Probably the best procedure is revising the programme at box 2 to produce the output in the proper format for box 4, or revising the programme at box 4 to accept the format of box 3. There is a natural reluctance, however, to tamper with programs which have been checked out and are known to work well. Commonly, not enough storage remains in either programme to make the necessary changes; and wading through pages of machine language coding (frequently necessary in programme revision) can become tedious. Also on drum machines, where optimization is an important consideration, changing a number of instructions may increase processing time considerably.

Alternately, the data can be rearranged by a key punch operator. More important than the time taken is the possibility of keypunching errors. If the programme at box 4 has a symmetry checking routine for the matrix and there are errors, it may take longer to debug the data than it took to debug the programme.

A compromise procedure is writing a computer programme that will accept cards of one format and rearrange the data for output in a different format. Routines of this nature are simple to write and they run very quickly. In this type of operation, however, the computer is being used as a glorified reproducer. In some situations, therefore, the expense or the ethics of employing valuable machine time for a task which does not properly utilize the full capacities of the computer should enter into the decision of whether to adopt this method of making the output of one programme compatible with the input of a succeeding programme.

Centroid Method

Where frequency of use is the criterion, the centroid method of factor analysis has been more popular than other methods. As high-speed computing facilities become more available and the problem of computational laboriousness becomes less important, the centroid method is likely to lose some of its appeal. Excellent theoretical and illustrative material pertaining to the centroid technique is available in several references. The 11-variable example used for illustration is small and the advantages of solution on a computer are not as great as for larger problems. It was chosen because its size allowed using the same example many times for different procedures without obscuring major points, as might occur with larger tables. For additional details of the solution, see Fruchter. The values in the table were obtained using a programme written for a *basic* 650; i.e., none of the instructions in the programme utilizes the floating point device, index registers, core storage, or magnetic tape. These values may be compared with those Fruchter obtained by desk calculator, if desired.

Table of Centroid Factors*

	Factor					
Variable	**I**	**II**	**III**	**IV**	**V**	**h2**
1. Dial and table reading	7001	-2901	-0816	-1098	1512	6159
2. Spatial orientation I	5008	-2478	3771	-1532	-0927	4866
3. Reading comprehension	5749	1149	-2912	-1560	-1107	4652
4. Instrument comprehension	5731	1697	1079	-0645	1643	4001
5. Mechanical principles	5026	5141	0790	1625	-0199	5500
6. Speed of identification	4726	-1602	3931	-1251	-1509	4421
7. Numerical operations I	5008	-5090	-3278	1486	1592	6649
8. Numerical operations II	5661	-4588	-3521	2161	0217	7022
9. Mechanical information	2962	5213	0646	2155	-1275	4265
10. Practical judgment	4832	2526	-2192	-1498	-1859	4024
11. Complex coordination	4991	1039	2257	-0693	2199	3640
$\sum\sum a^2/\sum r_{ii}$	.568	.812	.952	.999	1.040	

In general, the number of decisions which must be made by the operator at the console of a computer during a programme run is inversely related to the economic efficiency of the programme. Even though economic efficiency is not a major concern of the scientist, shortage of available machine time, or of money to pay for it may force him to accept procedures he might not consider best if he had an indefinite amount of time and facilities available. Often, therefore, decision functions which are the judgments of an informed operator are programed. In factor analysis, two of the major decisions which must be made concern the communality estimates and the point at which to cease extracting factors. In the programme just mentioned, zeros are originally entered as the values in the principal diagonal of the correlation matrix, and the programme is instructed to select and insert the highest correlation in the column in the principal diagonal of the correlation matrix, as the original communality estimate.

In the programme used for computing the example, the criterion for the cessation of factoring is obtained as follows: The original communality estimates are summed. After each factor is extracted, the loadings are squared and summed. This value is added to all previous sums of squares of factor loadings, and the total sum is divided by the sum of the original communality estimates. When this ratio becomes larger than 1.00, the programme ceases. If it should be decided that more centroid factors are needed after this criterion is reached, they can be obtained by resetting some of the control kncbs on the console and starting the computer again. The ratio is reported below each column of the centroid factor matrix.

Since the value for the criterion is merely an estimate, this procedure is not the only one used in determining the dimensionality of the reduced correlation matrix. Basically, the number of meaningful, interpretable factors must be determined. This is done best during the rotation process.

Principal Axes Method

The principal axes method of factor analysis has long been regarded as superior to the centroid method from a mathematical point of view. Because of the computational difficulties involved, very few matrices of any size were factored by the principal axes method until computers became available. The chief advantage of the method is the fact that each factor extracted makes a maximum contribution to the remaining communality. The principal axes solution is obtained by computing the eigenvalues for the original correlation matrix. Associated with each eigenvalue is an eigenvector. The eigenvalues are also referred to as "characteristic roots," or "latent roots," of the matrix. The loadings in the table were determined by taking the square root of the eigenvalue for a particular factor and multiplying it by the associated elements of the eigenvector.

Table of Principal Axis Factors*

		Factor				
Variable	I	II	III	IV	V	h^2
1. Dial and table reading	7301	-2076	0313	-0201	-0947	5864
2. Spatial orientation I	5096	-0387	4432	0676	0672	4667
3. Reading comprehension	5722	0887	-2441	1945	-0488	4350
4. Instrument comprehension	5544	2298	0627	-0782	-1158	3836
5. Mechanical principles	4417	5283	-1300	-1047	0354	5033
6. Speed of identification	4681	0500	4524	1050	1631	4639
7. Numerical operations I	5658	-5548	-1686	-1283	0299	6737
8. Numerical operations II	6219	-4700	-2371	-0556	1322	6844
9. Mechanical information	2239	5796	-1864	-1464	1946	4801
10. Practical judgment	4592	2493	-2391	2813	-0380	4107
11. Complex coordination	4828	2021	1992	-1653	-1863	3756
$\sum a^2$	3.0427	1.3545	.6987	.2183	.1495	

*All entries to four decimal places.

The programme used to obtain the solution was written

by Wright and is based on Hotelling's iterative procedure. One of the important characteristics of the programme is the fact that as each latent root and vector is found, the rank of the matrix is reduced, enabling subsequent roots to be determined with less computation.

Table of Eigenvalues and Eigenvectors*

	Eigenvectors				
Varirable	I	II	III	IV	V
1. Dial and table reading	4186	-1784	0375	-0430	-2450
2. Spatial orientation I	2921	-0333	5302	1447	1739
3. Reading comprehension	3280	0762	-2920	4162	-1261
4. Instrument comprehension	3178	1974	0750	-1673	-2994
5. Mechanical principles	2532	4539	-1556	-2240	0916
6. Speed of identification	2683	0430	5411	2248	4218
7. Numerical operations I	3244	-4766	-2017	-2746	0773
8. Numerical operation II	3565	-4038	-2836	-1191	3418
9. Mechanical information	1284	4980	-2229	-3132	5032
10. Practical judgment	2632	2142	-2860	6019	-0983
11. Complex coordination	2767	1736	2383	-3536	-4816
Eigenvalues	3.0433	1.3548	.6990	.2185	.1496

*All entries to four decimal places.

ROTATION

Rotation of the frame of reference axes to a meaningful interpretable position is one of the valuable aspects of factor analysis as it is applied in the behavioral sciences. Although theoretical criteria (such as simple structure) for the location of the reference frame have been proposed, the determination of simple structure for a given set of variables has required a combination of skill and objectivity when done by graphical methods. Computers have not only reduced the laboriousness of the task but have made it feasible to apply objective analytical criteria, such as maximizing the variance of the squared factor loadings, to the determination of a unique set of reference axes for a given set of data.

The methods of factoring presented in the previous section yield arbitrary factor matrices. Each of the obtained factor matrices is merely one of the theoretically infinite number of orthogonal factor matrices from which the reduced correlation matrix can be reproduced by the basic formula R = F F2 + ñ, where ñ represents the residual partial correlation matrix after removal of the portion of the correlations accounted for by the r common factors. The residual correlation may be due to errors of measurement (unreliability), computational errors such as rounding, or common factors if all of the common factors have not been removed.

For the rotational problem, it is desired to rotate or transform the arbitrary factor matrix into one more suitable for reference or interpretation.

Several models have been proposed for specifying the location of the reference axes; the most widely used of these is Thurstone's simple structure concept. The rotated factor matrix may be on orthogonal reference axes, in which case it is represented by $F_{1;}$ and the matrix which transforms it from its arbitrary to its rotated position is designated by A. If the arbitrary orthogonal factor matrix is designated by F_{0}, the orthogonal rotated matrix may be designated by

$$F_1 = F_0 \ddot{E}$$

The quartimax and varimax methods discussed later in this section are analytical methods which yield rotated solutions on orthogonal axes.

If orthogonal reference axes are not specified, the reference structure determined from the data may consist of oblique axes. The matrix of factor loadings on oblique simple reference axes is represented by the letter V, so that

$V = F_0 \ddot{E}$

The reduced correlation matrix is

$R = V (\ddot{E}2\, \ddot{E})^{-1} V'$

and $\ddot{E}2\ \ddot{E} = C$ is the matrix of cosines of the angular separations among the oblique reference vectors or, in other words, the matrix of correlations among the oblique factors. The C matrix may be factored, rotated, and interpreted, if the factor structure at the second and higher orders is desired.

ANALYTICAL ORTHOGONAL ROTATION

Although attempts have been made over the years to reduce rotation procedures to analytical methods, little progress was made until computers became available. Several objective, analytic methods are now in use that transform an obtained arbitrary factor matrix to one useful for reference or interpretation. Various claims have been made for the different methods, but each aims at achieving a final solution which meets some or all of the criteria for Thurstone's simple structure concept.

Basically, they depend on minimizing the sum of the cross products of squared factor loadings. Even though the behavioral scientist may not always be convinced that an obtained solution is best, in the sense that it is the most simple, at least he can report the analytical criterion he has used to reach the rotational solution. Either the analytical solution as obtained from the computer will be acceptable to the investigator or it will approach an acceptable solution. In the latter case, further rotations of the axes can be done by graphical methods.

Either an orthogonal or oblique frame of reference axes is specified by an investigator. If he wishes to use uncorrelated reference factors, an orthogonal method should be used. In orthogonal rotation, the reference axes maintain right-angle separations. If the investigator is willing to accept factors that are correlated, he should choose an oblique method which does not specify the angular separation of the axes.

The degree of obliquity of the reference axes is determined from the data. Currently, two of the most popular techniques for orthogonal analytical rotation are the quartimax method and the varimax method. Examples of both are given in this section.

THE QUARTIMAX METHOD

Only limited information will be given concerning the analytical formulas. Those interested in programing specific routines require more detailed information than it would be feasible to include in this chapter. These details are available elsewhere.

With regard to the quartimax method and, in general, for all the analytic rotational procedures, it is desired to obtain a matrix, generally called a "transformation matrix," which, when used to post-multiply the originally obtained factor matrix, yields a rotated factor matrix that meets the requirements for simple structure and meaningful interpretation. The programs that have been developed so far to obtain this transformation matrix are based on iterative procedures in which a given function is maximized or minimized. For the quartimax method, the function maximized is the sum of the fourth powers of factor loadings; hence the name "quartimax."

The centroid factor matrix was rotated analytically by the quartimax method. The rotated loadings. The solution is called a "straight" or "nonnormalized" quartimax solution.

When the original centroid loadings are used as the basic factor structure from which to begin the analytic procedure, the process is such that tests or variables that have high communalities influence the rotation more than variables with lower communalities.

If the vectors representing the variables are extended to unit length before the analytic process is begun and then brought back to their original length after the process, the disproportionate weighting is eliminated.

The table contains the loadings for the same example when rotated by the normalized quartimax method. In normalized quartimax, the vectors are extended to give equal weight to all variables in determining the rotational solution

Table of Non-normalized Quartimax Rotated Factor Solution*

	Factor					
Variable	**I**	**II**	**III**	**IV**	**V**	**h2**
1. Dial and table reading	6608	1572	3240	1052	1959	6159
2. Spatial orientation I	2574	0854	6425	0077	0101	4866
3. Reading comprehension	4003	3848	0693	3891	0247	4652
4. Instrument comprehension	2476	4474	2732	0333	2506	4001
5. Mechanical principles	0390	7344	0902	-0086	0296	5500
6. Speed of identification	1799	1458	6216	0123	-0426	4421
7. Numerical operations I	8107	-0676	0201	-0424	0288	6649
8. Numerical operations II	8296	0330	0219	-0113	-1104	7022
9. Mechanical information	-1003	6361	-0077	-0245	-1056	4265
10. Practical judgment	2214	4423	0613	3913	-0289	4024
11. Complex coordination	1898	3530	3393	0591	3910	3640
	N	M	P	V	S	

N = Numerical
M = Mechanical
P = Perceptual
V = Verbal
S = Spatial orientation

Transformation Matrix*

	I	II	III	IV	V
I	6602	5941	4330	-1281	0846
II	-5549	7585	-2684	-1548	1432
III	-4464	0300	7666	4583	0434
IV	1890	2611	-3327	7658	-4458
V	1449	-0499	-2047	4036	8784

*Entries to four decimal places.

indicates that they are structurally very similar; i.e., variables which have high loadings on certain factors in one solution tend to have high loadings on the same factors in the other solution. The magnitude of the loadings do differ somewhat. The values in the two figures can be compared with a solution obtained by a graphical method, if desired.

Table of Normalized Quartimax Rotated Factor Solution

	Factor					
Variable	**I**	**II**	**III**	**IV**	**V**	**h2**
1.Dial and table reading	6129	1692	4024	1182	1890	6159
2. Spatial orientation I	1829	0756	6686	0188	-0081	4860
3. Reading comprehension	3717	4023	1170	3884	0231	4652
4. Instrument comprehension	1988	4461	3165	0343	2454	4001
5. Mechanical principles	0044	7320	1128	-0211	0311	5500
6. Speed of identification	1064	1346	6392	0202	-0604	4421
7.Numerical operations I	8058	-0442	1087	-0286	0325	6649
8. Numerical operations II	8217	0583	1103	-0006	-1063	7022
9. Mechanical information	-1187	6327	-0058	-0397	-1021	4265
10. Practical judgment	1935	4548	0891	3862	-0309	4024
11. Complex coordination	1382	3461	3761	-0557	2837	3640
N = Numerical M = Mechanical P = Perceptual V = Verbal S = Spatial orientation *Entries to four decimal places.	N	M	P	V	S	

Giving an extensive interpretation to the factors would serve little purpose here, but they are identified for reference. Factor I is labeled a numerical (N) factor, since its two highest loadings are for the two Numerical Operations scores. Because of the nature of the tests having high loadings on the factors, Factor II is labeled mechanical (M); Factor III, perceptual (P) Factor IV, verbal (V); and Factor V, spatial orientation (S).

The quartimax solutions can be obtained very quickly on a computer, but they have limitations for some purposes. Since the quartimax procedure attempts to simplify the rows (variables) of the matrix, a tendency exists for a general factor to appear if the unrotated matrix had a strong general factor. The normalized solution in changes the pattern only slightly. It does not have a great deal of meaning for a variable that purports to measure reading comprehension to have a higher loading on a numerical factor than on a verbal factor. In Fruchter's graphic solution, for example, the loadings on Reading Comprehension on (N) and (V) were.29 and.54 respectively, which makes more psychological sense. For some theories and sets of data, however, where a general factor is indicated, the quartimax solution may be the most appropriate.

THE VARIMAX METHOD

The appearance of the general factor, which the quartimax method produces under some circumstances, is less common in rotated solutions obtained by the varimax method, because the varimax method simplifies the columns (factors) of the factor matrix as well as the rows (variables). The varimax method gives a rotational solution which is usually closer to the simple structure criterion of multiple factor analysis than does the quartimax method. Also, for some conditions, the loadings are less variant over a series of analyses, allowing for more valid generalization of the results.

Procedurally, the varimax solution is very similar to the quartimax method. That is, an iterative procedure that maximizes a function is employed to determine a transformation matrix which, when used to post-multiply the original factor matrix, results in the rotated matrix. The function maximized in the varimax method is the variance of the squared loadings of the factor columns.

Table of Non-normalized Varimax Rotated Factor Solution*

	Factor					
Variable	**I**	**II**	**III**	**IV**	**V**	**h2**
1.Dial and table reading	6073	0880	3529	1970	2756	6159
2. Spatial orientation I	2058	0487	6573	0481	0865	4866
3. Reading comprehension	3488	2823	1022	4965	0824	4652
4. Instrument comprehension	1963	3816	2811	1545	3361	4001
5. Mechanical principles	0127	7051	1151	1534	1261	5500
6. Speed of identification	1318	1140	6381	0579	0345	4421
7. Numerical operations I	8060	- 0643	0694	0152	0782	6649
8. Numerical operations II	8282	0435	0877	0662	-0474	7022
9. Mechanical information	-1062	6350	0172	1023	-0350	4265
10. Practical judgment	1738	3453	0889	4944	0235	4024
11. Complex coordination	1416	3020	3372	0399	3707	3640
	N	M	P	V	S	

N = Numerical
M = Mechanical
P = Perceptual
V = Verbal
S = Spatial orientation

*Entries to four decimal places.

The straight varimax and normalized varimax solutions, respectively, for the example. Observe that the general factor is absent in both solutions. The normalized varimax solution reflects a relationship of Reading Comprehension to (N) and (V), which is more logically meaningful. The magnitudes of the two loadings are almost identical with those obtained by the graphical method, and the entire solution is very similar to the graphical solution.

Table of Normalized Varimax Rotated Factor Solution*

	Factor					
Variable	I	II	III	IV	V	h2
1.Dial and table reading	5474	0029	3588	2732	3358	6159
2. Spatial orientation I	1591	0151	6576	0756	1513	4866
3. Reading comprehension	2834	2037	1112	5596	1332	4652
4. Instrument comprehension	1510	3036	2633	2156	4115	4001
5. Mechanical principles	-0060	6598	1071	2268	2274	5500
6. Speed of identification	0894	0884	6391	0835	1037	4421
7. Numerical operations I	7879	- 1051	1027	0997	1123	6649
8. Numerical operations II	8110	0122	1323	1634	0046	7022
9. Mechanical information	-1057	6235	0165	1550	0468	4265
10. Practical judgment	1149	2804	0942	5441	0744	4024
11. Complex coordination	1039	2328	3139	0880	4389	3640
	N	M	P	V	S	
N = Numerical M = Mechanical P = Perceptual V = Verbal S = Spatial orientation *Entries to four decimal places.						

The different methods may be selected merely by specifying the one desired on a parameter card preceding the data into the computer. This parameter card also contains the tolerance value, which indicates to the computer to cease computing when the increase in the function to be maximized is less than the indicated amount. Obviously, different tolerance values produce slightly different results.

In some studies, the investigator has an hypothesis concerning the factors on which each test will have its major loadings. A computer programme has been developed by Saunders to find the best-fitting orthogonal factors for a given hypothesis.

ANALYTICAL OBLIQUE METHODS

N oblique rotation, the angles between the reference axes are determined by the structure of the data. One might, therefore, infer that orthogonal rotation can be considered as a special case of an oblique solution. Once again, the attempt is made to maximize or minimize some function iteratively. The possibility exists that the solution which yields the maximum or minimum is an orthogonal one. In actual practice, such a result is rare, but it is theoretically possible. The oblique method is a more general method for this reason.

Currently, the oblimax method—of which this section gives an example-is the most widely used of the analytic oblique methods. Another analytic oblique method (for which an example is not shown) is the quartimin method. The quartimin criterion requires that the sum of cross products of squared factor loadings be minimized. Still another method, covarimin, requires that the covariances of the squared elements be a minimum. The quartimin criterion tends to yield axes that are too close; the covarimin yields axes that are too separated. Biquartimin is an oblique solution which averages the tendencies of quartimin and covarimin by requiring that the sum of the two functions be a minimum.

The function to be maximized by the oblimax method is the ratio formed by the quotient of the sum of the fourth powers of all values in the matrix to the square of the sum of all the squared values in the matrix. The values in the table may be compared with those obtained by an oblique graphical method.(4) If.30 is taken as an arbitrary minimum value for presence on the factor, the structures of the two solutions are identical, with the exception that Variable 1 appears in the graphical solution with a loading of.32, but not in the analytical solution.

It is interesting to note again the behaviour of Variable 3, Reading Comprehension, on (N) and (V). The loadings are.01 and.40 in the oblimax solution. The transformation matrix and the C matrix of the cosines of the angular separations between the oblique axes.

FACTOR MATCHING

A recurring problem in factor analysis concerns the generalization of results over studies and the matching of factors from different studies. Several methods have been developed for this purpose, and the one proposed by Ahmavaara will be illustrated here. A matrix is to be obtained with the elements representing the relationships between the factors across samples. The matrix (T) is computed by T = (F2 1F1) -1 F2 1F2

where F1 = the rotated factor matrix from one study F2 = the rotated factor matrix from another study.

Notice how simple the computational logic of the problem becomes when conceived in terms of matrix operations. Follow the flow chart. Except for input-output functions, every step is a matrix operation.

It is possible, therefore, to programme a problem of this nature with standard coded matrix operations procedures. Normal precautions concerning numerical analysis may not be ignored, however. For example, some matrix inversion routines produce rounding errors of unacceptable magnitude as the order of the matrix increases. A good subroutine description contains relevant information about its restrictions and capacities; within those limits, it can be used by the coder without detailed knowledge of the internal mechanics of the subroutine.

Table of Oblimax Rotated Factor Solution*

Variable	I	II	III	IV	V
1. Dial and table reading	0895	-1164	0504	1466	-1974
2. Spatial orientation I	-0112	-0307	4422	0046	-0269
3. Reading comprehension	3999	-0203	-0249	0149	0001
4. Instrument comprehension	0246	0664	-0196	-0568	-2956
5. Mechanical principles	0135	4032	-0162	0311	-1189
6. Speed of identification	-0006	0341	4623	-0036	0190
7. Numerical operations I	-0436	-0334	-0531	4611	-0336
8. Numerical operations II	0004	0869	0319	5422	0964
9. Mechanical information	0064	4435	0194	0540	0235
10. Practical judgment	4073	0435	0125	-0518	0474
11. Complex coordination	-0762	0339	0138	-0841	-3415
	V	M	P	N	S
N = Numerical M = Mechanical P = Perceptual V = Verbal S = Spatial orientation					

To demonstrate the factor matching technique, the factors obtained from the varimax rotation of the centroid solution and the varimax rotation of the principal axis solution were compared. The relationships between the factors from the two methods. The near-unity diagonal elements indicate the high similarity of the corresponding factors and the off-diagonal near-zero values reveal the essential dissimilarity of the other factors. The method may be used to match factors from batteries having all or some of the same test variables. The variables common to the two batteries are used to compare the factors.

ESTIMATION OF FACTOR LOADINGS

In some situations an estimate is desired of the loadings of variables not included in the original factor analysis. These loadings can be estimated by a regression procedure, if the correlations of the new variables with the variables in the factored battery are available.

The variables whose loadings are to be estimated may be new tests which were not available at the time of the original analysis, or they may be criterion measures which matured after the factor analysis was done. For some experimental studies, it is desirable to separate the variables into two categories: independent, or predictor, variables; and dependent, or criterion, variables. The independent variables may serve as a reference

Table of Factor Matching For Normalized Varimax Rotation of Centroid and Principal Axis Method*

Varimax factors derived from centroid factors							
		I	II	III	IV	V	
	I	9986	0137	0090	-0464	0133	N
Varimax factors derived	II	-0384	9986	0164	-0304	-0029	M
	III	-0099	0056	9998	0083	-0138	P
from principal	IV	2117	-0690	-0206	9742	0286	V
axis factors	V	-0158	-0310	-0039	0045	9993	S
		N	M	P	V	S	
N = Numerical M = Mechanical P = Perceptual V = Verbal S = Spatial orientation *Entries to four decimal places.							

Battery for several sets of criterion variables. Only the independent reference battery is factor analyzed. The loadings of the dependent variables on the reference factors are then estimated by the regression technique.

Table of Normalized Varimax Rotated Factor Solution Based On Principal Axis Factors

	Factor					
Variable	I	II	III	IV	V	h2
1.Dial and table reading	5653	0585	3451	2240	3067	5864
2. Spatial orientation I	1745	0142	6338	0665	1727	4667
3. Reading comprehension	4495	1202	1098	4430	1005	4350
4. Instrument comprehension	1790	3210	2784	1930	3657	3836
5. Mechanical principles	0209	6254	1204	2141	2263	5033
6. Speed of identification	0954	0860	6599	0708	0824	4639
7. Numerical operations I	7992	-1079	1128	0444	0922	6737
8. Numerical operations II	8047	0082	1344	1364	0011	6844
9. Mechanical information	-0923	6799	0106	0887	0347	4801
10. Practical judgment	1456	3026	0886	5329	0779	4107
11. Complex coordination	1112	2376	3113	0637	4536	3756
	N	M	P	V	S	
N = Numerical M = Mechanical P = Perceptual V = Verbal S = Spatial orientation *Entries to four decimal places.						

This procedure has the advantage that the structure of the reference factors is unaffected by the criterion variables; only the common factors in the reference space are used to make comparisons between the factor content of different sets of dependent variables. Variables with well-established factor content may be used as "marker" variables in the reference space.

By way of illustration, the validity correlations between the 11 tests used in the example, and pass-fail training criteria for three air crew positions. To estimate the loadings of these 3 criterion variables on the 5 factors derived from the analysis of the 11 tests, the formula provided by Mosier is Vtp = 2 tj2 jm (Fmj2 jm)-1

where Vtp represents the matrix of factor loadings of the new variables on the rotated factors.

R2 Tj represents the transpose of the matrix of intercorrelations of the new tests (t) with the tests (j) in the original analysis.

Fmj represents the matrix of factor loadings of analyzed tests on rotated factors.

The estimated loadings were obtained with a programme developed by King. It may be observed that the pilot training criterion has its highest loadings on the spatial orientation and mechanical factors; the bombardier criterion has no appreciable variance on any of the factors; and the navigator criterion has its highest loadings on the verbal and numerical factors.

FACTOR SCORES

After the factors in a battery of test variables, or other measures, have been defined, it is frequently desired to represent the scores of individuals on the factors for further work, such as multiple regression.

Before the advent of the computer, relatively little use was made of this procedure because of the amount of computational labour involved.

Variable 1 (Dial and Table Reading), Variable 7 (Numerical Operations I), and Variable 8 (Numerical Operations II) have loadings of appreciable magnitude on the factor we have labeled "numerical.

Table of Validity Correlations of Eleven Tests For Three Pass-fail Training Criteria

Variable	Criteria	Pilot	Bombardier	Navigator
1. Dial and table reading		28	18	55
2. Spatial orientation I	20	13	33	
3. Reading comprehension	17	13	38	
4. Instrument comprehension	32	23	28	
5. Mechanical principles	37	10	25	
6. Speed of identification	18	06	18	
7. Numerical operations I	-01	12	38	
8. Numerical operations II	03	12	41	
9. Mechanical information	28	00	08	
10. Practical judgment	13	14	35	
11. Complex coordination	39	13	27	
*Entries to two decimal places.				

Table of Estimated Loadings of Three Criterion Variables on Five Rotated Factors*

x			*Factor*			
Criterion	I	II	III	IV	V	h^2
Pilot	-0128	3656	1740	-0087	5260	4409
Bombardier	0872	-0164	0511	1589	2879	1186
Navigator	3951	0696	2178	4070	2580	4406
	N	M	P	V	S	
N = Numerical M = Mechanical P = Perceptual V = Verbal S = Spatial orientation *Entries to four decimal places.						

" In certain situations, it would be advantageous to have

an estimate of an individual's numerical ability represented by one score rather than three. When such a score is developed from the factor matrix, it is called a "factor score." From the entire battery of II tests, 5 factor scores can be developed for each individual by the appropriate weighting of his scores on the original variables.

In computing a factor score, the goal is finding a weighted combination of the tests which best predict a factor.

The general formula is:

Xf = the factor score âi = the weighting coefficient for the ith variable Xi = the raw score for an individual on the ith variable p = the number of tests which load on the factor

The weighting coefficients are obtained by multiple correlation. The matrix to be assembled is the correlation matrix composed of the *p* variables, with the factor loadings serving as validities.

The regression weights obtained are used as the weighting coefficients in the formula. The determination of *p* is arbitrary. One possible procedure is to include all of the variables for each factor score. In practice, variables which load highest on a factor are used. Obviously, separate weighting coefficients must be derived for each factor score.

The use of factor scores as independent variables in multiple prediction work overcomes, to some extent, one of the liabilities of using electronic computers. Computers can generate nonsense at the same wondrous pace that they can generate sense.

Where the labour of computation is no longer a paramount barrier in research, it may be tempting to add a few variables to a research battery to see what happens. Such a procedure may seem justified in factor analysis because of the experimental character of many tests.

The content of a test is not established just because the originator of the test gave it a label. The sheer amount of data available for interpretation, however, can be quite discouraging in many cases. Reducing the number of variables by means of factor scores appears to be one useful method of reducing the number of predictor variables in multiple correlation or other analyses without losing the contributions of the individual tests.

EFFECT OF COMPUTERS ON FACTOR METHODS

The availability of the computational capacity of modern electronic computers has made it possible to apply desirable procedures which would be prohibitive without such powerful computational machines.

A programme library for factor analysis studies should contain, as a minimum, routines for intercorrelation of large numbers of variables, matrix multiplication, and the inversion of real, symmetric, positive semidefinite matrices. A principal axes factor extraction programme, and analytic rotation programs for orthogonal and oblique solutions are also desirable.

With the aid of a computer, it is possible to investigate many problems of theoretical interest that it would not be feasible to investigate without such aid. Some of these problems are the effect of reiterating the factoring with communality estimates derived from the previous factoring, to determine whether the communality estimates will stabilize studying the effect of eliminating some of the variables in a battery on the factor structure, and trying out rotational solutions with varying numbers of factors to help determine the best estimate of the dimensionality of the correlation matrix.

There are a number of procedures which have desirable mathematical or statistical properties, but whose computational labour would be prohibitive without the use of a large-scale computer. These include Lawley's maximum-likelihood method of factor analysis in which a running chisquare test for the number of factors is provided, and Rao's canonical factor analysis, which also yields a test of significance. With the widespread availability of large-scale computers that can be expected in the future, much investigation of factor analysis methods will be possible, and great improvements in the objectivity and usefulness of the methods will occur.

Chapter 8

Automated Teaching

THE "TEACHING MACHINE" AS AN EDUCATIONAL TECHNIQUE

"Automated teaching" is an educational technique having the following characteristics:

- A series of instructional materials, or "items," is presented to the student. An item may contain a statement of information, a question, or both.
- The student attempts to answer each question contained in the instructional items, usually by some overt action, e.g., choosing a correct alternative or writing one or more missing words in a sentence.
- The student is generally given knowledge of results immediately after he responds to each question; i.e., he is given information from which he can determine whether his answer was right or wrong.

The device by which automated teaching is conducted or controlled is called a "teaching machine." Teaching machines range in complexity from textbooks with special page format and instructions, to elaborate electromechanical devices costing thousands of dollars. The functional components of a teaching machine.

Teaching machines bring to education a means by which teachers may be relieved of certain routine, repetitive instructional tasks and thus be given time to perform the more creative activities for which the human is uniquely qualified. In this way, the teacher can, for the most part, avoid the role of drillmaster or record keeper and concern himself more with the motivational, social, and inspirational aspects of the instructional process.

Automated teaching offers further advantages as an effective educational technique in its own right. First, the overt responses required of students by most machines, for example, help to insure active participation and thus help to maintain interest on the part of the student. Secondly, the teaching machine allows each student to proceed systematically and independently through the instructional materials. He is required to answer questions on one topic or concept before he can advance into new concepts. This differs greatly from many conventional classrooms in which a teacher lectures at a rate that is too fast for some students, and too slow for others. Thirdly, teaching machines provide immediate reinforcement for desired response behaviour, whereas in many conventional classrooms, students receive reinforcement only through test papers returned days or weeks after the administration of the test.

Teaching machines are also useful as research tools for investigating basic variables in human learning. They make possible precise control and replication of experimental conditions. Spurious effects caused by the personality of the experimenters and similar uncontrolled factors can be held to a minimum.

Adaptability in Teaching Machines

Although the design of the machine is important, no teaching machine can provide effective instruction without a well-prepared, well-tested set of items. The machine may present the instructional materials either in a fixed, predetermined sequence, or in a sequence that varies with the student's specific responses to each item.

A teaching machine that presents materials in a predetermined sequence can be extremely simple in design. With minor embellishments, it can also keep error records and help prevent student cheating. Such a machine, however, cannot be responsive to individual student differences; i.e., it cannot give each student a particular sequence of materials and type of reinforcement suited to his individual needs, as these needs are progressively revealed by the adequacy of his responses. For this reason, the further development of teaching machines appears to lie in the direction of making them flexible and adaptive to the student's responses.

To show concretely what is involved in developing such flexibility and to illustrate the means by which it can be achieved, we shall later describe a particular experimental teaching machine that has been developed by the System Development Corporation's (SDC) Automated Teaching Project. This machine uses a small general purpose digital computer, the Bendix G-15, and its control unit. The computer is programed to adapt its teaching behaviour to the needs of the student. During an instructional session, it can determine what sequence of items to present and what feedback messages to provide the student, so as to make learning relatively efficient.

Incorporation of a computer in the teaching machine provides a second type of flexibility, one of great importance when the machine is used as a research tool. The machine's operation can readily be altered between instructional sessions. This is done by changing the computer programme, a change more readily effected than would be an equipment modification.

Many changes can be made in the operation of the machine by minor changes of a few numbers in the programme. Such alterations permit different teaching procedures and machine characteristics to be investigated. The teaching machine used at SDC is sufficiently adaptable to allow a wide range of automated teaching research. Investigators can manipulate many types of experimental variables without major restrictions arising from machine limitations. Thus the computer-based teaching machine is, in effect, not just one machine but many different machines.

Computer-controlled Teaching Machines

A brief account of some explorations of the uses of computers to control teaching machines will illustrate the technique and its application. The feasibility of using a computer as a teaching machine was probably first established by a research group of the International Business Machines Corporation. Rath, Anderson, and Brainerd at IBM demonstrated the use of an IBM 650 to teach binary arithmetic. The lesson taught the student to count in the binary system, then to add, subtract, multiply, divide, and finally to convert from decimal numbers to binary and from binary to decimal. In this application, the machine typed out the questions for the student, who then responded by pressing the appropriate keys of a typewriter. The answer was scored by the computer, one key stroke at a time. The instant an error occurred, the computer stopped the student, typed out "wrong," and presented another problem. If the student was making few errors, he was asked whether or not he wanted to skip some items. When the student typed his choice, the computer complied either by presenting additional items or by skipping. When the programme advanced to a new problem in response to an error, the new problem chosen was a function of the number of errors made in that section of the lesson. Thus the new problem could be equally or less difficult. The average student completed the lesson in binary arithmetic in approximately one hour. Upon completion, the student was tested by the machine on each of the six topics taught. The test was individualized and contained more items relating to those topics on which the student had made the most training errors.

Alan Perlis at the Carnegie Institute of Technology has written a special programme of feedback messages designed to provide computer programers with knowledge of where they made errors in their programs. During the testing phase, when an error is encountered, an appropriate message is printed out supplying the student programer with information designed to help him avoid that type of error on future occasions. Although this is not strictly a teaching machine application, it does have some educational value and represents an interesting method of teaching computer programing.

Bolt, Beranak and Newman, Incorporated,* of Cambridge, Massachusetts is using a computer called the Programed Data Processor, manufactured by the Digital Equipment Corporation, as a teaching machine for vocabulary, spelling and foreign language instruction. The computer presents a word from a set *A* of words of language X. The student then tries to type a corresponding word in language Y. If the student's response is correct, the computer confirms its correctness, posts a score, offers a compliment, eliminates the presented item from *A*, and presents a new item from *A*.

If the student's response is incorrect, the computer says so, moves the item to a "missed" set *B* and offers him the choice of trying again or seeing the correct answer. When the student has replied correctly, or has seen the answer, the computer posts a score, makes a suitable remark, and presents a new item from *A* or a missed item from *B*. Another programme for automatic instruction in sound recognition was developed to investigate techniques for improving the methods of teaching people to differentiate between similar sounds. The programme presents tones for the student to identify which differ in frequency, amplitude, duty cycle, repetition cycle, and length of total signal. It grades the student's answers as right or wrong, providing immediate playback of right and wrong answers for comparison and continually modifying itself to keep pace with the student, stressing sounds which trouble him and discarding those he seems to know well.

At the Coordinated Science Laboratory,† an engineering department at the University of Illinois, a teaching machine system has been developed which is named PLATO (Programed Logic for Automatic Teaching Operations). The system uses the ILLIAC computer as a control unit, a slide reservoir, a storage tube which will permit material given by the student or by the computer to be displayed along with the slides, the screen of a closed-circuit television system, and the student's control panel. PLATO will adjust to individual ability of the student; it will allow the exceptional student to progress at high speed, while a less capable one proceeds at a slower rate.

An educational application of computers, somewhat related to teaching machines, uses simulation procedures. ([3]) An IBM 650 has been used by the American Management Association for training top management personnel, through simulation procedures. Trainees make judgments concerning production, sales, advertising, etc., in connection with competitive business situations. These decisions are entered into the computer, which then processes the information, interrogates the trainee further, and supplies him with knowledge of results indicating probable consequences of his actions. In this way, the student learns to estimate the probability of various consequences that are contingent on his decisions. At SDC, a computer is used in training exercises to simulate an air defence environment which includes hostile attacks by "enemy" missiles and aircraft. During the training exercise, Air Force personnel man their normal positions in an air defence centre. They see and respond to the simulated air defence problem and take whatever actions are necessary to cope with the simulated situation. Each crewman in the system receives information which reflects the consequences of his own actions, as well as the actions of other members of the system. In addition, computer programs provide both individual and subsystem scores on a number of problem-solving situations in the simulated exercise.

THE AUTOMATED TEACHING PROJECT OF THE SYSTEM DEVELOPMENT CORPORATION

By way of a concrete example, we shall describe the Automated Teaching Project sponsored by SDC.14.2.1 Description of the Experimental Teaching Machine. The experimental teaching machine at SDC consists of three major units: (a) a Bendix G-15 computer; (b) a random access slide projector; and (c) an electric typewriter.

- Bendix G-15 computer. The Bendix G-15 is a relatively small, general purpose computer. It has a photoelectric unit with which it can read information from punched paper tapes. A bell mounted in the computer frame can be rung under computer control, thus permitting programed auditory signals. This computer serves as the central control unit for the teaching machine. It determines, at all times during a training session, the materials that are to be presented to the student. The computer analyzes student responses to the instructional items and compares these responses with stored data.

- Random access slide projector. This projector, developed by the engineering staff at SDC, is used to display instructional materials to the student. It holds up to six hundred 35mm slides, arranged in 15 magazines of 40 slides each. Each slide contains one item. The projector receives instructions from the G-15, selecting and projecting slides in the sequence indicated by the computer. The use of an external random access slide projector contrasts with the methods of Anderson and Rath, and of Perlis, who used internal computer storage for problem materials.
- Electric typewriter. This typewriter, which is linked to the computer, serves two important functions. First, the student uses the keyboard to insert his answers to the instructional materials, normally in multiple-choice form. Second, the computer programme takes control of the typewriter to print messages telling the student how successful he has been in answering the questions.
- One additional piece of equipment is used in the automated teaching project, although it is not actually part of the experimental teaching machine. It consists of a direct punched card input to the G-15 computer. Information about the instructional items can be manually punched on IBM cards; these cards can then be read into the computer, where the information can be transcribed directly onto punched paper tape.
- 14.2.2 Operation of the Machine. In its application as the control unit for a teaching machine, the computer has two somewhat unusual characteristics. First, in

automated teaching the student can be regarded as "on line" with the computer. That is, the computer and the student interact during the entire lesson; for much of the time the computer is simply waiting for the student to take some switch action, i.e., answer a question. This contrasts with the more common computer usage in which a large mass of data is fed to the computer and is then processed at a rapid rate until the required solution is reached. In a low duty cycle application such as automated teaching, costly equipment can be justified only by time-sharing the central computer among other users.

- A second unusual characteristic of the computer's performance in automated instruction involves the small amount of arithmetic calculation. Most of the computer's work in a teaching machine involves storing data, transferring data, and making "logical decisions" based on these data. Only rarely does it perform the mathematical operations usually regarded as the primary role of computers.
- A lesson begins with the student seated in front of the typewriter. The slide projector displays a question or a multiple-choice item for the student to answer. The student reads the item and, if an answer is required, insert his choice of answer by pressing the typewriter key corresponding to the number of his choice, e.g., 1, 2, 3, 4, or 5.

  The student may change his answer by inserting another choice before requesting an evaluation of his answer. When the student presses the "Enter" key on the typewriter keyboard, the machine evaluates the last answer inserted. Once the "Enter" key is activated, the answer cannot be changed. The typewriter, then under computer control, informs the student whether his choice was correct. The "Enter" key is pressed again and a new slide is presented. This cycle is repeated for each item until the end of the lesson.

- Instructional slides are selected by the computer on the basis of four aspects of the student's behaviour:
  - Errors in answering questions;
  - Speed of the student's responses;
  - The student's evaluation of his own
- performance; and (4) pre-inserted information about the student, for example, aptitude, personality, and achievement indices. When a student is in trouble, the computer recognizes this fact and supplies extra remedial material. When the student is doing well, some materials are omitted.
- The procedures appear to be simple and logical, yet a vast amount of effort must precede the presentation if the lesson is to be effective. To provide the reader with a realistic example of the preparation involved in using a computer as a research tool in an auto-instructional experiment, the steps required for preparing a short lesson are described in some detail.
- 14.2.4 Preparation of the Lesson. The first step is the preparation of instructional material. The items to be presented must be written, tested, revised, and prepared in the form of slides. Branching procedures have to be designed, and the information about the items and the branching decisions must be specified on special manuscript forms. The manuscripted material must then be coded onto punched paper tapes for interpretation by the computer programme. The entire process is checked, using the slides, the paper tapes, the typewriter, and the internally stored computer programme. Only after these tasks are completed is the lesson ready for presentation. Preparation of a two-hour lesson may take several months.
- *STEP 1:* Instructional items. In developing a set of items one must decide what is to be taught by the machine and then prepare a set of questions covering the material.
- This provides a skeleton of the teaching sequence.

> The gaps are then filled in with new items that provide information prerequisite to answering the original questions. Cues or prompts are added to help the student give the correct answer. The material is pretested. Gross oversights, including items which can be answered correctly without reading explanatory information, items with ambiguities, and other faults are detected and removed in the next revision.

The preparation of instructional items is the very heart of effective machine teaching. In fact, many workers in the auto-instructional field view the machine as nothing more than the "binding of the book." This is an extreme view, for the computer may or may not make full use of the materials. If students are permitted to skip items which they do not need in order to learn the material, considerable time can be saved, allowing the student to go on to more advanced topics. If students have difficulty in certain areas, they can be given extra remedial work on those topics Code Number Message

- (No message—go immediately to next slide.)
- "Very good"
- "You are correct; the answer is _____"
- (No printed message—a bell is sounded instead.)
- "The correct answer is _____"
- "Wrong!"
- "No! No! Try again"

If the student is making no errors, responding rapidly, and confident about his progress, then items will be skipped, and he will be permitted to cover the material more rapidly.

Some of the multiple-choice items contain distractors—a common type of misunderstanding. If one of these distractors is chosen, the student is immediately branched to remedial items designed to clarify that particular point.

At the end of each topic, or at the end of the lesson, the student may be given the option to repeat items for review. If the student has performed very poorly he may have no choice but to accept the review items. Branching decisions are made by the computer during the lesson, but the criteria for each branch are prespecified by the educator preparing the materials.. In this flow chart, there are 12 items and 5 decision points. Each circle beneath an item represents a possible answer to the question. The first circle to the left would be the computer response to choice No. 1; the second to choice No. 2, etc. The numbers in these circles designate feedback codes.

ITEM MANUSCRIPTING

After the items have been written and the flow chart completed, all the information contained therein must be converted to a form that can be interpreted by the computer. The first stage of this conversion consists of coding or "manuscripting."

For each item, the following descriptive information is required: an item number uniquely assigned to each item, the number of the correct multiple-choice answer (option), transfers, feedback messages, and concept counters. These last three terms, perhaps, require a little more explanation. A "transfer" is used if it is desired to branch the student on the basis of his answer to a single multiple-choice item. The number of the item to which he will be transferred is entered in the column corresponding to the choice of option on which the transfer will be executed.

After the student responds to an item he will receive information, or "feedback," regarding the correctness of his answer.

This feedback message may be printed out on the typewriter or presented as part of the next slide.

If the messages are to be typed out, they must be prestored in the computer and an identification number assigned to each. The coded identification numbers on the item manuscript form insure that the proper feedback will occur after the appropriate response to a given item.

The student's errors on any set of items covering a particular topic or concept may be tallied by using "concept counters."

A counter is a register located in the internal storage of the computer where a record may be accumulated. The number of a particular counter is entered opposite each item of the set, and a count is kept of student errors.

COMMAND MANUSCRIPTING

Commands are special computer instructions, which may also be used to implement the branching decisions. The commands are manuscripted along with the items and refer to the items by number. As an example of the use of commands consider the first decision which appears after the fourth item in the flow chart. The decision is to branch to one of four new items, depending upon how many errors are made on Items 1-4. If no errors are made, branch to Item 12; if two errors, branch to Item 8; if three or four errors, branch to Item 6. Item 5 asks the student whether he wants to review or would rather go on to the next topic. Item 2 will be indicated as a transfer on option 2 so that the student will be returned to Item 2 if he chooses to repeat a few items before continuing to the next topic. If he does not want a review, he will be transferred to the next topic.

PREPARATION OF PUNCHED PAPER TAPE

After the item and branching information has been manuscripted, it is punched onto cards. By using a special tape preparation computer programme, the information on the cards is converted to punched tape. The computer programme records the information on a five-channel paper tape in the form of punched holes. This tape is called the "item tape." The punched holes on the item tape represent two classes of information: item data and commands for branching.

Note that the item tape is entirely separate from another tape containing the computer programme, which selects the slides to be presented to the student. This second tape is called the "slide selection programme" and is stored inside the computer on the magnetic drum. The slide selection programme requires certain input data in order to perform its function of selecting slides for presentation. These input data are contained on the item tape. Several blocks of data from the item tape are read into the computer at a time. After the slide selection programme has used these data, it may call for more data from the item tape. This process continues at a rate depending on the speed with which the student responds to the items.

LESSON CHECKOUT

After the tapes have been prepared, they must be checked for errors. The internally stored slide selection programme is read into the computer. After the slide selection programme has been entered, the tape containing information on the items and on the branching is mounted on the computer and the lesson is started. As the internally stored slide selection programme interprets the answers received via the typewriter, it reads the item tape. Using the information contained on the item tape and the information from the typewriter responses, the slide selection programme records and evaluates the inserted responses.

The programme also prints feedback messages and selects appropriate slides for subsequent presentation, dependent on the branching decisions which have been executed. Every possible branch must be tried and found to occur under the conditions originally specified in the flow chart. The information on the slides must also be consistent with the flow chart. A student must not be reinforced for answering items incorrectly. Neither should the student be incorrectly branched to wrong items at inappropriate times. Once the programs are checked, the lesson may be presented whenever desired without further preparation; the programme tapes have merely to be read into the computer. The instructions on the tape will cause the machine to perform the teaching operations in proper sequence.

THE COMPUTER-CONTROLLED TEACHING MACHINE AS A RESEARCH TOOL

Computer-controlled automated instruction does not stand divorced from existing knowledge about education and the learning process; rather, it is a new tool through which this knowledge can be applied and extended. Traditional research variables, such as the mode of presentation of materials, whole versus part learning, student aptitude and personality characteristics, etc., are still relevant. However, since one of the main advantages of using a computer as a control element for a teaching machine is its capacity to modify the sequence of instructional items during the tutoring session, the problem of determining the nature of a good sequence of items has been a central issue for research by workers in this field.

Different research workers have contrasting points of view about the nature of an optimal sequence of instructional items (often called a "programme". Various opinions prevail on questions such as, "What is an optimal sequence of items on a topic?" and "To what extent should items be tailored to individual students?" T

he computer-based teaching machine developed at SDC represents one tool by which such problems may be explored. One question currently being studied at SDC is, "What decision criteria should be used in determining when to branch a student to less difficult remedial items?" For example, in theory it may be desirable to minimize errors for optimal learning on a programme, but at the same time it may be necessary to use errors as a criterion for branching. Studies may consequently be directed toward the evaluation of methods of reducing the number of items needed to determine branching (i.e., the number of test items). This approach assumes a distinction between test items and teaching items. The function of the test item is to yield a maximally valid and reliable measure of individual differences, whereas the teaching item attempts to reduce individual differences with respect to the content of the item.

One possible method of reducing the number of test items required is the sequential test, by which the selection of each test item to be presented to a student depends upon his previous responses to other test items. Instead of keeping a test score on each individual by the number of correct answers to a long series of test items, the score is determined by the path traversed by the student through a branching tree of test items. Hence, a given student will never see more than a few of the test items. The resulting measure may provide validity and reliability equivalent to measures obtained by having each student traverse, in order, each test item in a long series.

Other examples of studies that may have relevance to the branching criterion problem involve a comparison of post-test scores and training time for alternative branching criteria. For example, a criterion based largely on type of error may be superior to one based on error rate. Branching in one experimental programme may be entirely contingent upon the selections of particular multiple-choice options on single items which transfer the student immediately to remedial items. In another programme, using the same teaching items, the student will be branched to alternative remedial items contingent upon how many error were committed on a series of test items.

Still further comparisons may be made using a combination of criteria for branching. A flow chart containing branching decisions based on the response latency, the type of error, the student's self-evaluation, and the number of errors accumulated over several items. During the course of the lesson, weights may be assigned to non-error criteria, such as response latency and self-evaluation, depending upon how accurately these criteria reflect the student's performance.

Other questions relating to branching concern the interaction effects between individual difference variables, content variables, and the effectiveness of different branching criteria. For example, from some rationale one may deduce that highly motivated over-achievers would benefit more from response latency branching criteria than from error rate criteria on conceptual material, but the two methods may be predicted to be effective in the reverse order on rote material. Such a study might lead to a procedure whereby the branching criteria are weighted differentially on the basis of measured student characteristics, and the appropriate technique is selected by inserting the weighted scores into the computer as part of the initial conditions. In an alternate procedure, the decision might be made during the teaching sequence to branch to a different weighting system determined by the results of the ongoing testing.

An important consideration in any study is the development of a criterion, or set of dependent variables, which is sufficiently sensitive to variations among independent variables to detect their effect in small-scale pilot explorations using relatively few subjects and items. One approach to this problem is establishing different levels of criteria for evaluating the effect of different decision schemes. For example, one level of criteria may use the stimulus characteristics of the branching structure as rational or facevalidity evidence of its effectiveness. A programme which contained all branching decision points in the same location would be clearly suspect, since certain decisions are contingent on the outcomes of previous decisions in the programme. A second criterion level may use response data on the training items. Ideally, an optimal branching structure should minimize errors on training items as well as total number of training items presented. At yet a third level, a post-training objective or performance test may be used as a criterion. The nature of this criterion may vary with respect to its similarity to the training task. Ultimately, we are primarily interested in the student's ability to transfer this learning to new situations.

The results of research studies, such as those described above, not only provide information on the effectiveness of decision criteria for branching, but also furnish data for the revision and improvement of the instructional items that were used in the experiment. With each revision, the items become more useful in promoting student learning. Items are organized into topics, each topic being covered at several difficulty levels. If a student is doing exceptionally well at one level of a topic, he may be branched to more advanced material. If he is not doing well, he will be branched down to a lower level of difficulty.

FUTURE DEVELOPMENTS

With the completion of the computer-based teaching machine, a number of studies were undertaken to determine its operational feasibility and the teaching effectiveness of the adaptive "branching" mode of instruction. Preliminary findings from current experiments indicate that computer-based teaching machines are indeed feasible and that such machines can function very effectively by adapting the materials to the individual student. The programme described in the previous section represents only one of many possible designs which can be programed for the teaching machine.

At present, SDC is developing an expanded educational facility, using a more powerful digital computer, the Philco 2000. With this computer, large numbers of students can simultaneously receive individualized automated instruction. The computer will have in storage detailed information about the instructional material and about each of the students being taught. It will receive input information from each student, perform logical decisions concerning the next item or feedback message to be shown to the student, and send necessary output messages to the display devices.

Because of its high speed, it will be able to process the information for each student so rapidly and so frequently that no student need wait any appreciable time for the computer to respond to his insertions. At any given time, different students might be working on a different portion of the lesson, or even on different subject areas. Ten or fifteen students might be receiving instruction in algebra, for example, while other are learning English composition. Thus it will be possible, when using the Philco 2000, to obtain experimental data on many students concurrently, rather than working with one at a time as is the case with the present machine.

The new facility, designated CLASS (Computer-based Laboratory for Automated School Systems), will provide an individualized item display panel and a response device for each of many students. Simple displays will also be provided for teachers, so that the teacher can monitor individual student or group progress and can intervene when a particular student is having unusual difficulty.

Separate rooms will be provided in CLASS for school administration and counseling functions normally associated with the operation of an educational system. The computer will receive and process many types of data, such as registration, class attendance, test, and previous educational background. These data will be made available in digested forms as requested by teachers, administrators, and counselors.

The CLASS facility will permit investigation not only of the individual learning process, but of an entire integrated educational system. Interactions among students, and between students and teachers, might be studied. Conventional methods of instruction would be used in addition to automated teaching. The effectiveness of different combinations of techniques, including textbooks, instruction by human teachers, film and television presentations, as well as teaching machines, would be evaluated. Hopefully, the results of these studies will provide information on the direction that should be taken by future educational systems.

One area in which future progress might be expected is in the generation of a set of items on some basis other than a completely prespecified branching structure. The earlier description showed that the instructional sequence was specified by the items and branching decisions as described in the flow chart. The exact sequence of items in any branch of the sequence is completely specified before the lesson begins. An alternative to this procedure is programing certain general rules to be used by the computer in selecting slides. To illustrate the operation of such a programme, a design similar to the following might be used.

The programme will contain a large store of items with a description of each. Instead of the lesson planner's having to go through all of the items in order to select the members of each remedial branch, the computer will be programed to select items according to certain constraints or legality rules. For example, one rule might specify the order in which different types of items should be selected; first the lead-in, or orientation items; then items stating the principle; next practice examples, review items; and finally, test items. Another rule may specify the proportions of each type of item to be used for each topic; 5 per cent lead-in, 10 per cent review, 15 per cent examples, 5 per cent test items, etc. Each item would have to be classified by topic, type of item, difficulty level, and its prerequisite topics.

Items might also be classified as belonging to a remedial series or a basic series, depending on whether they are prespecified by the experimenter or selected by the computer. A *basic series* is any sequence of prespecified items constituting a central stream of interlocking items which are presented in sequence to the student. In contrast, the items in the remedial detour are selected from a library of items by the computer in accordance with certain rules. If several items in the remedial library are parallel, i.e., if they have the same coded characteristics, the computer might select an item at random by resorting to a random number generator.

Using a computer to assist in preparation of sequences of instructional items is particularly important when items are written for extensive educational application. A single two-hour lesson may incorporate several hundred items. A four-year high school programme will require thousands of items. The task of organizing such extensive sequences becomes enormous, and computer assistance would constitute a major breakthrough in the area of automated teaching.

In cases where the number of items is small and the rules required for selection are simple, the computer can already generate practice or drill exercises for the student. For instance, in a multiplication lesson where the student is required to practice multiplying single-digit numbers, the machine can randomly compose exercises by assigning digits to be multiplied. Rather soon, the computer should be capable of selecting, from a large pool of items, a series that will uniquely meet the needs of any given student.

Another area in which future progress might be expected is the programing of a "learning" feature in the machine itself. One of the remarkable characteristics of the master teacher is ability to modify his teaching with experience and thus progressively increase his skill in helping others to learn. One might assume that this process of improvement stems from trying different teaching approaches, retaining those which work well, and abandoning the methods which are not effective. The teaching machine of the future may also contain this property. The computer would have stored information on aptitude, personality, and previous achievement of each student. It would then select the teaching method which had been found to work best with this type of student.

Performance on test items in the programme would provide a standard against which different methods would be compared. Methods that are highly correlated with performance on the test questions would be assigned weights fo. their teaching effectiveness. In subsequent teaching sessions, methods with the highest weights would be tried first. If none of the machine methods were helpful, the experimenter would have to add new approaches to the programme. But it is also possible that the computer may derive new methods from the existing available techniques. The emerging methods, obtained by combining the existing methods with the highest weights, would then be added to the list of available methods and assigned weights on the basis of their effectiveness. As the teaching machine gained in experience, those unique combinations of methods which were found to be most effective would gain priority in the hierarchy of techniques and less effective procedures would drop out.

Finally, in future auto-instructional systems, a student may be given much more freedom in the kinds of information he can insert and receive from the teaching machine. He may be allowed to answer questions posed by the machine, or even ask questions of his own, using conventional English. The enormous storage capabilities of computers may be used to allow the student to call up reference materials needed in the solution of problems. In general, efforts are being made to eliminate arbitrary restraints imposed by machine design and to allow the student a wide variety of modes of expression, as well as alternative methods of solution to different problems. Of course, the scope of applications of computers to education will grow. Computers are already being used in processing test scores, in registration and scheduling, attendance and grade reporting, etc.

Computers are also used for predicting school population, for estimating future school costs, salary bill projections, capital outlay for school plant, and other management forecasting and optimization problems. In the future, it is not unreasonable to expect such applications to be integrated with the instructional function and processed in a central, general purpose, high-speed digital computer. School administrators, teachers, counselors, supervisors, and curriculum specialists will have instant access to information heretofore available only at great cost to assist them in making educational decisions for an entire school district, whether at the local, county, state, or national level. Certainly, the computer will play a paramount role in the school of the future.

CANONICAL ANALYSIS

Our attempts to chart the wilderness of behaviour have resulted in an increasingly entangled geography of terms and boundaries. The surveyor's task is twofold: identifying clusters of related events to be included in the domain of a concept, and then developing refined procedures for analyzing the relationships among these complex, multivariate events. Concepts of aptitude, ability, or function have become collective terms representing many related, and often quite highly specific behaviors. In prediction problems, for example, we no longer are concerned with a simple single predictor—single criterion relationship. Rather, the increasing use of multiple regression analysis has suggested that many advantages are to be gained from the utilization of a battery of variables as predictors of our criterion.

In another case, we find it expedient to determine the relationships between a number of variables through correlational methods; subsequently, we reduce the correlations to their principal factors. We hope, of course, to be able to identify unifying principles and at the same time discard nonrelated phenomena. Note, however, that while we are happily conducting multivariate analyses on one side of the statement, predictor "! criterion, we are just as happily assuming the other side to be N univariate for our analysis.

This seems to be so whichever side of the statement we are examining. Obviously, our logic is faulty. Certainly, the milieu of data collecting and impatient theory building has perpetuated this fallacy, but the position taken in practice by many a behavioral scientist that method is secondary to theory building is hardly defensible. The numerous conflicting factor analytic studies of a single phenomenon clearly reflect the extent of this problem. A way out of this dilemma has been available for many years, but it has been largely ignored.

A a method for determining what he designated "the most predictable criterion." His procedure makes it possible to determine the maximum correlation between a set of predictor variables and a set of (rather than a single) criterion variables. In other words, weights are found for the various parts of the criterion which, like the weights found for the predictors, will cause the combined sum of the criterion variables to correlate maximally with the combined sum of the predictor variables. These weights generally will be different for each battery. Although it is convenient to speak of "predictor" and "criterion" batteries, it should be obvious that with this procedure the distinction between them breaks down; we simply have two batteries that must be weighted in order to determine the maximum correlation between them. Hotelling termed this method "canonical analysis."

The advantages of this procedure are several. Primarily, the burden of forming a composite criterion is reduced. The reseacher is no longer required either to pick and choose among criteria, in order to select that one which *seems* best to reflect the behaviour being studied, or to assign arbitrary weights to the criterion variables. Secondarily, the sets of variables being studied do not have to conform to the predictor—criterion model. Indeed, the relationship between *any* two sets of variables may be studied by canonical analysis. Certain problems are attendant upon this application, however, and these will be discussed later.

HISTORY OF CANONICAL ANALYSIS

Canonical analysis has had a rather short history.

Hotelling's original articles in 1935-36 created something less than a stir when they orig-inally appeared. Not until 1947, when the *British Journal of Psychology* added a Statistical Section devoted to the application of mathematical models to psychological problems, was canonical analysis brought to the attention of the psychological public. At that time three articles appeared simultaneously. Of these, only one attempted to illustrate the method as a working model for psychologists.

An examination of these articles shows one of the major difficulties of canonical analysis. The computations involved in even a simple problem, such as that presented by Thompson, are complex and quite timeconsuming, even when carried out by a mathematically sophisticated researcher. Further, the computational model requires several approximations by interpolation; this is seldom an accurate process. The advent of the high-speed electronic computer has all but eliminated the tedious and laborious mathematical computations required for canonical analysis. Complex computations have become routine; the related time element has become almost negligible, and computational errors all but vanish. With this advance in computation, the mechanical aspects of canonical analysis can be made routine and practical. It is to the presentation of such a routine that we now turn.

The procedure to be illustrated here was worked out on MISTIC, a high-speed automatic digital computer, and is based on the method presented by Thompson. For a discussion of the mathematical rationale of canonical analysis, the reader is referred to Hotelling.

The complete model for canonical analysis begins with the determination of the intercorrclations of the variables within each of two batteries, and the cross correlations between them. The first solution, utilizing one battery as "Predictor" and the other battery as "criterion," then yields a matrix of correlations between the battery of predictors and the *composite* criterion as well as a matrix of regression weights for the battery of predictors. The second solution yields the reverse: the matrix of correlations between the battery of criteria and the composite predictor, and a matrix of regression weights for the criteria. These weights then may be substituted in regression equations for purposes of prediction. On the other hand, if the original variables represent independent tests or measures, customary tests for the significance of a correlation coefficient may be employed.The computation of the two sets of regression weights from raw data is relatively straightforward, involving only four standard programs on the average high-speed computer. Only one step will require special programing; this step could easily be accomplished by desk calculator if experienced programers are not available, even if analyses of several different sets of data are contemplated. The programs necessary for the complete canonical analysis are, in order of use:

- Computation of the Pearson product-moment coefficient of correlation (*r*), or its equivalent
- Computation of the inverse of a matrix. Postmultiplication of a matrix by another matrix †
- Computation of ë: ‡ the matrix of latent roots (i.e., eigenvalues) and computation of U: the matrix of latent vectors (i.e., eigenvectors, or, more commonly factors loadings). This may be accom-

$C_{ij} = A_{i1} B_{j1} + A_{i2} B_{j2} + \cdots + A_{in} B_{jn}$

Note that the number of columns of the first matrix must be equal to the number of rows of the second matrix.

Example:

$C_{11} = A_{11} B_{11} + A_{12} B21$ $C_{12} = A_{11} B_{12} + A_{12} B_{22}$ $C_{21} = A_{21} B_{11} + A_{22} B_{21}$ $C_{22} = A_{21} B_{12} + A_{22} B_{22}$

plished by a programme which solves a determinantal equation of the form:

$|A - \lambda B| U = 0$

With the foregoing programs available, a high-speed computer * should permit the analysis of 10 predictors with 10 criteria in less than 30 hours. Only about three hours will be spent in actual computer running time; the remainder is consumed in casting the data into the proper format for computer input and checking the accuracy of the format (i.e., card or tape verification).

In the following presentation of the canonical analysis

method, the outline of the steps in matrix manipulation will be paralleled by an arithmetic example. This example utilizes the set of hypothetical correlations employed by Thompson in his reformulation of Hotelling's original method.

Consider the matrix:

In this matrix, the letter symbols † represent the following quantities:

A = the matrix of intercorrelations of the "predictors"

B = the matrix of intercorrelations of the "criteria"

C = the matrix of cross correlations between "predictors" and "criteria"

C2 = the matrix C with rows and columns interchanged (i.e., the transpose of C)

Our procedure for extracting the maximum correlation between the batteries, and the regression weights of *each* battery on the other, is an extension of Thompson's(9) formulation. As he points out, in matrix terms, the maximum correlation between the batteries is found from the following equation:

Where b = the weights of the criterion that will maximize R^2, or the multiple coefficient of correlation between battery and criterion.

Solving for R^2 (i.e., ë) and b, and given the matrix:

As can be seen, our solution has yielded two sets of regression weights, one absolute and one normalized, for both batteries, as well as the set of squared multiple coefficients of correlation. The latter are, of course,

If one begins the analysis of predictors on criteria with |B – Y+03BBA|V = 0 as in Step 4, the V matrix so determined must be rearranged in decreasing order of magnitude of ë, i.e., column 2, column 1. Note that column 3 vanishes, since ë3 = 0. identical for both parts of the solution. These computations may be summarized as follows:

- $R^2 = \lambda$ from and
- P, the absolute regression weights of the predictors, = (A^{-1}) (C2 U) $(U2\ BU)^{-½}$ and Q, the absolute regression weights of the criteria, = (B^{-1}) (CV) $(V2\ AV)^{-½}$

- Ba, the normalized regression weights of the predictors, = (A^{-1}) (C2 U) $(U2\ BU)^{-1/2}$ and b^b, the normalized regression weights of the criteria, = (B^{-1}) (CV) $(V2\ AV)^{-1/2}$
- V, the matrix of vectors of predictors on criteria (analogous to U), is given by the normalization of $A^{-1}C2\ U$
- A check on computational accuracy is given by [(C2 U) $(U2\ BU)^{-1/2}]2$ [P] = ë = [(CV) $(V2\ AV)^{-1/2}]2$ [Q]

It should be pointed out that we have computed V without solving the second determinantal equation. Instead, by using a link through U in the determination of V, a major saving in computer running time has been provided. For example, in the analysis of a matrix of 17 predictors and 4 criteria, *one* solution of the determinantal equation required 4¾ hours of actual computer operation before convergence was reached and the latent roots and vectors determined. The transformation of U, replacing the second solution, required only 22 minutes on a desk calculator. It may be stated that as a general rule, when the size of the matrix increases, the time to reach convergence increases disproportionately.

The multiple correlation found by this method may be interpreted as is any *R*. The advantage peculiar to canonical analysis lies in the fact that the second set of variables has been weighted in terms of the amount of variance contributed by each single variable. This seems far superior either to arbitrary weighting by summation or to computing separate multiple cor-relation coefficients for each of the criterion variables. For example, imagine a situation where one is attempting to predict university achievement.

The criterion usually employed is "grade-point average," representing the mean of grades earned in several areas of endeavor. Simple summation assumes that each area contributes equally to the total variances; in view of varying content, varying instructors, varying levels of difficulty, varying examinations and measures, etc., this assumption seems hardly reasonable. On the other hand, the computation of a set of multiple correlations between one's battery of predictors and the score for each separate criterion area may yield scanty information about the *over-all* adequacy of one's predictors. The canonical analysis *R*, combining all criteria with all predictors, should provide a much stronger index of association.The weights for predictors and criteria offer a couple of possibilities for further experimentation. For instance, they may be plugged into a standard prediction formula; the predicted scores thus obtained may then be compared with actual scores from a flesh sample. Again, weights found by canonical analysis might be used in hypothesis testing. For example, the two batteries may represent sets of variables one is attempting to interrelate, such as indicators on psychodiagnostic tests and nosological categories in psychopathology.

In such a situation, it would seem that the canonical analysis solution offers a far more rigorous criterion of association than does chi-square or than do statistical treatments involving a univariate model.At this point, we should note that we do not yet know which method of multivariate analysis is most appropriate for a particular kind of data. The considerations for using canonical analysis can be identified only after further experience with the method. At the present time, selection of the appropriate multivariate method for a given problem can be determined only through empirical evaluation, though with sufficient experience we should eventually be able to establish adequate methodological criteria. For the present, we ought to utilize the results of several alternative procedures in a comparative fashion before we attempt to draw conclusions from the results of a canonical analysis method. In this connection, several alternative approaches for evaluating the relations between two sets of variables:

- The full canonical analysis model;
- Reduction of the "criteria" to their independent dimensions by rotated factor analysis and the independent prediction of each "factor";
- Combining the variables into one all-inclusive factor analysis, finding the independent predictor-with-

criterion dimensions, and correlating these with the independent dimensions of predictors and the independent dimensions of criteria;

- Making separate rotated factor analyses of "predictors" and "criteria," determining these factor scores.

It would perhaps be wise for the experimenter to test at least several of these models on his own particular type of data before committing himself to a single approach.

Perhaps one additional issue should be mentioned. Although it appears obvious that one chooses variables that "seem" to belong together for manipulation—whether the choice is by hunch or hypothesis—the temptation of a data-engulfing computer is hard to resist. A shotgun approach certainly yields data: however, one is often hard pressed to interpret the results obtained. As an alternative to this indefensible procedure, I might suggest we meet temptation with rigorous self-discipline, since we can hardly defend our *model* if we cannot interpret the results it provides.

One last aspect of the canonical analysis model is worth noting. Horst has recently developed a model extending solution from the relations between two sets of variables to the relations between several sets of variables. This logical extension should also offer exciting possibilities for further study. For illustrating this technique, Hillmer,a student of Horst's, developed the common factor structure of a set of personality items administered under three different conditions. He established several common factors, at the same time minimizing noncorresponding factor correlations. It would seem to be a promising technique, especially in the area of reliability of test.

Like factor analysis, canonical analysis and the other multivariate techniques are on the frontier of psychological research. As with any method of experimentation, the researcher needs to expend fully as much energy exploring his model as he expends exploring his psychological domain. The search must be not only for methods of multivariate analysis that are mathematically defensible (which is an issue for psychological statistics generally), but also for methods that are readily interpretable psychologically.

STUDIES OF PERCEPTION

Benjamin W. White is a staff member in the Psychology Group of Lincoln Laboratory, Massachusetts Institute of Technology, where, since 1955, he has been working on problems of human pattern recognition. His interest in perception began at an undergraduate seminar with Hans Wallach at Swarthmore College. Individual differences in measures of perceptual functioning formed a topic of his doctoral dissertation in psychology at the University of Michigan. While at Lincoln, he has concentrated on studying the use of the high-speed genera *l purpose digital computer for generating precisely specified and complex visual and auditory stimuli.*

Rapid technological advances during the years following World War II have led to development of devices of unprecedented capability for handling visual and auditory material. There now exist sensitive microphones, film, and tape which can rapidly record sights and sounds with fidelity, and projectors, amplifiers, and speakers which can present this recorded information to our eyes and ears with such realism that it is sometimes difficult to distinguish the live from the canned. Such a technology allows the psychologist engaged in research on perception to exercise a degree of control over his stimulus material that would have been impossible 20 years ago—when the favored device for creating visual displays was a pen and India ink.

Much of the impetus behind these developments has stemmed from a need to provide human operators with reliable information to guide a vehicle or device traveling through space in real time toward a destination that might also be traveling through space in a path by no means perfectly predictable. In such a situation, the human engineer has the problem of presenting the necessary information so that the human operator can guide the vehicle to its destination with greatest accuracy.

It is easy to specify completely the information necessary to carry out such a guidance task. It is by no means easy to discover how this information can be so presented that the operator can make best use of it.

An operator has to know the present position, speed, and course of the vehicle he is guiding, and of the target, in order to solve the problem. But, displaying this information to him in the form of a compact table of numbers may not enable him to act upon it either promptly or accurately. Previous research in perception has remarkably little to offer toward the solution of such problems; hence, the psychologists faced with these display problems have had to rely on their own, often hastily conceived, research studies.

Problems relating to the display of information to human operators have cast a rather different light on the ancient and muddled question of veridicality in perception. Commonly, our ability to interact with and to manipulate our environment was assumed to be limited by the accuracy with which the perceptual world reflected the "real" world. Human engineering studies of displays have indicated that the accuracy of a display is only one of the factors involved in display effectiveness. In certain tracking tasks, large amounts of error are tolerable as long as data are presented in a proper form.

This need to present incoming information to the operator in a form he can readily assimilate has led to the introduction of special purpose computers linking the raw incoming data to the display system. Such devices may provide a number of links between the operator and the computer to enable the operator to insert or delete parts of the display, to alter its scale, and to interrogate the computer for additional information.

As a result of these developments, those of us concerned with research in perception can take advantage of a technique of great flexibility for the generation and control of visual and auditory displays. Further, we now recognize that some of the most important and far-reaching problems in perception concern the kind of information processing that we perform on the waveforms and images impinging on our ears and eyes, in order to make rapid and accurate adjustments to events around us.

USING THE COMPUTER TO GENERATE VISUAL DISPLAYS

STUDIES USING COMPUTER-GENERATED VISUAL DISPLAYS

Comparatively few studies using computer-generated displays have as yet appeared in the psychological literature. One can account for this by the small number of computers equipped with a video output and the small number of psychologists engaged in perceptual research. Green presented one of the first accounts of this use of the computer in 1957. His presentation summarizes the programing involved in generating such displays and illustrates some of the displays generated. Several of these illustrations show patterns of vertical or horizontal bars composed of dots in a matrix, alternate bars having differing probabilities of a dot's occurring in this region. These patterns illustrate the use of a random number generator for such work. In generating the film strips for this study, the random number generator was used to determine whether a dot should be painted in each matrix position, to determine whether, on a given frame, the orientation of the bars should be vertical or horizontal, and to determine the number of bars.

This work on the detection of bar patterns might also be described as a study in contour detection as a function of the distribution of elements in adjacent regions of the visual field. As such, it is similar to a different study of stereoscopic depth done by Julesz. The displays in this study were dot matrices, in some respects similar to those used by Green*et al.* Instead of producing these displays on line, Julesz used the computer to produce a magnetic tape containing a list of brightness values so arranged that they could be read into a television transducer to produce the dot matrices on the cathode ray tube (CRT), where they were photographed. This method circumvents some of the annoying problems of generating displays on line with a computer. On the other hand, Julesz' technique makes it more difficult to change certain display characteristics. Complete control of the CRT display by digital tape would be convenient. Such a system for display generation would make more efficient use of computer time with no sacrifice in flexibility. The demand for such equipment has not yet been sufficient to make its commercial production feasible.

With these displays, Julesz has not only produced a novel and intriguing stereoscopic depth effect, but has given careful consideration to the kind of model which can account for the conditions under which this effect does and does not occur. The elimination of alternative explanations necessitated generating displays with particular characteristics such that one model would predict the occurrence of the effect and the alternative model would not. Without the computer, it would have been difficult to create some of these displays in order to sort out alternative hypotheses.

An exploration of the stimulus factors affecting the kinetic depth effect, has been undertaken by Green and by Braunstein. These studies both used movies made with the computer. The displays consisted of sets of points or lines which were changed between each frame in such a way as to represent the rigid rotation of a three-dimensional constellation in space. A subject was asked to view a short movie of 250 frames showing the movements of such a constellation of points or lines and then to rate the coherence of the elements in the display. Parameters, such as the number of points or lines in the display, speed of rotation, axis of rotation, degree of linear perspective, and symmetry of element placement, were all varied to ascertain their effect on perceived coherence.

An unpublished study by the author involved the recognition of static, computer-generated displays of alphanumeric characters, the elements of which had undergone a number of two-dimensional random walks. Subjects were shown these displays in scrambled order and asked to identify the character in each. The proportion of correct identifications declined regularly with the number of walks the points in a given figure had undergone, and the rate of this decline was markedly affected by the size of the step which a point could take on any given walk.

EQUIPMENT

Comparatively few high-speed, general purpose digital computers are equipped with a cathode ray tube output to enable the programer to generate pictures directly. However, the IBM 709 does have

such an output device as optional equipment, and the following description of the technique of generating visual patterns will be in terms of this equipment. This machine has two cathode ray tubes as outputs, a 5-inch tube with fast decay phosphor, and a 21-inch tube with a slower phosphor. The latter is used only for monitoring; the former has mounted over it a 35mm camera whose shutter is normally open and whose film can be indexed by a pulse under programme control. Three instructions are provided: one to select the unit and prepare it for data transmission, one to display a dot at one of two intensities and at some position within a raster 3.36 inches square, and a third to advance the film one frame in the camera. Dots may be written in this raster at maximum speeds in excess of 7100 dots per second. The square raster has 1024 positions on each (*X* and *Y*) axis.Suppose, using this equipment, we wished to make a simple movie of a dot moving across the centre of the frame at constant speed starting at the leftmost position and moving to the rightmost position. The display programme would look something like this:

- Put the integer 512 in "*Y*"
- Put the integer 0 in "*X*"
- Put a 1 in "Inc"
- Display a point at *X*, *Y*
- Add "Inc" to X
- Advance film one frame
- Is *X* now greater than 1024?
  No: go to 4
  Yes: go to next instruction
- Stop

Should this movement be too rapid, the programme could be altered to take two or more frames at each dot position. Should the programer wish to introduce some acceleration, a constant could be added to "Inc" after each frame. Exchanging *X* and *Y* will produce vertical motion; adding "Inc" both to *X* and *Y* will produce diagonal motion. What would be the effect of exchanging instructions 6 and 7?

REPRESENTING VISUAL PATTERNS IN THE COMPUTER

In the moving dot programme above, on any given frame the pattern was represented in the computer by a pair of numbers, the *X*, *Y* coordinates. When writing display programs in some languages, such as FORTRAN, this is the only, straightforward way of representing a pattern. Should the pattern be large and intricate, such representation will involve two long lists for the *X* and *Y* coordinate values so that there is very little storage left over for the programme designed to manipulate this pattern. Even with 32,000 available registers, this extravagant use of storage for representing a pattern may limit the programer severely if he wishes to perform any but the most simple transformations. Another method for representing patterns in memory.

Here we see the letter T in a matrix consisting of five columns and seven rows. Each cell in this matrix has been given a number. The sequence of numbers from 1 to 35 traces an orderly path through the matrix. As we trace this path, let us write in a line a 0 for each empty cell we encounter, and a 1 for each filled cell which contains part of the T. This string of 35 O's and 1's is shown below the matrix. Such a string of binary digits can be directly represented in a single computer register (of sufficient length). In some sense, we have now represented the pattern T in one register. In our previous method, we would have required 22 registers, 11 for the *X* coordinate values and 11 more for the corresponding *Y* values. Actually, we could have done somewhat better than this by putting the paired *X* and *Y* values into one register, since only 10 bits are required to specify an integer between 0 and 1023.

Even so, the method of storing the string of 1's and O's in a single register saves a great deal of space.

Some of this advantage must be sacrificed when the time comes actually to display this T pattern. If the *X, Y* coordinates are stored as paired numbers in 11 successive registers, we simply write a programme to display 11 points whose coordinate values are to be found in these 11 registers. When the T is stored in a single register in the form of a string of 1's and O's, however, we must write a subroutine which will enable the computer to convert this representation into an appropriate series of *X, Y* coordinate values. To do this, we need to furnish several things: a starting position for cell no. 1 of the 35-cell matrix, a dot separation value, and the information about the nature of the path through the matrix. With this, the subroutine can then simply consider each of the 35 bits in turn, painting a dot in the appropriate position if the bit is a 1, or skipping that locus if the bit is a 0. This method of pattern representation was used for the alphanumeric characters.

Patterns need not be reduced to a sequence of 1's and O's. If the display equipment has the capability, and if the photographic equipment can deal with more depth of contrast, the number of brightness levels may be increased considerably above 2; in which case the pattern is stored as a sequence of numbers between 0 and the maximum dot intensity desired. In making the display, these numbers can be used either to control dot intensity on the cathode ray tube or to programme the number of times a dot in a given position in the pattern will be painted on the scope. With each additional paint, up to some maximum, the photographed brightness in the region will increase.

INPUT TECHNIQUES

No matter how the pattern is represented in the computer the problem remains of how to put it there. If the display is regular and simple, such as a dot matrix, one can write a programme to generate a matrix of a given size, grain, and location, and get around the problem of reading in the original pattern. Patterns composed of random sets of points may be similarly generated by the programme. Aside from these special cases, however, one must face the problem of reducing some picture to a form which can be read into computer memory.

If the pattern is reduced to a list of *X*, *Y* coordinates, these may be put on cards or on magnetic tape for read-in. This can be a laborious process and one in which clerical errors are extremely difficult to correct. Manually reducing a pattern to a string of 1's and O's is equally tedious. This whole problem could be by-passed with special equipment, such as a photoelectric device which could scan the pattern to be stored in the computer. Such a photoelectric device could scan the image and emit a pulse whenever the brightness of the area under scrutiny exceeded some threshold value. This pulse could either be used to activate some off-line device for preparing a tape or cards, or it could be used with a suitable input programme and direct data entry provisions to store the train of pulses on line in successive registers as strings of O's and 's.

Alternately, the CRT could be programed to display a raster of dots. If the pattern to be entered in memory were a transparency, this could be placed over the scope face. Over this, a suitable optical system and photomultiplier tube could be used to transmit the train of pulses to the computer in a form suitable for storage.

PATTERN TRANSFORMATIONS

The whole point of going to all this trouble to get a pattern into a computer is to be able to operate on it in some way that will take advantage of the computer's unique capabilities: its speed and its enormous logical and computational facility. To put a pattern in storage only to display it unchanged would probably be the most expensive way of degrading an image yet devised. In what ways might a psychologist doing research in visual perception want to change the patterns which he had gone to such trouble to insert into computer memory?

To illustrate some of the more obvious transformations

which the computer can perform on visual patterns, it will simplify the exposition to assume that the patterns are stored as lists of *X*, *Y* coordinates with integral values between 0 and 1023—in other words as lists of numbers. As far as the computer is concerned, these may be treated like any other numbers: they may be compared to ascertain whether two numbers are identical or not, they may be added, subtracted, multiplied, or divided. Rigid transformations of a two-dimensional figure are thus very simply computed. Hozizontal or vertical movements are accomplished simply by adding a constant to all the coordinate values on the *X* and/or the *Y* axis, as was done in the sample programme above. A programme to generate one of Michotte's *lancement* displays would be simple to write and would require very little storage, since the figures and the movement patterns are so simple.

Size transformations and rotations about the *X*, *Y*, or *Z* axes are computed with ease, especially if subroutines are available for the trigonometric functions. More interesting, perhaps, are elastic transformations which can be performed with ease on the computer, but which would be difficult to realise by any other means. The variety of these is limited only by the programer's ingenuity. Blurring of the pattern can be introduced by computing the brightness value of each point in the pattern on the basis of a local average of that point and its neighbors. Such averaging could be repeated several times until the pattern was unrecognizable. Shearing or stretching portions of the pattern are two more prosaic examples of nonrigid transformations which the computer can perform and which may be difficult to do by other means.

Among the useful capabilities of the computer is that of being able to generate a series of pseudo random numbers. Subroutines for this purpose exist which are surprisingly simple and rapid. With a random number generator in the display programme, it is easy to introduce noise into the pattern, or to have the points in the pattern undergo a two-dimensional random walk. A random number generator provides an extremely flexible method of producing textures in a wide variety of specifications.

AUDITORY PATTERNS GENERATED BY THE COMPUTER

STUDIES EMPLOYING COMPUTER-GENERATED AUDITORY DISPLAYS

Computer-generated melodies, recorded on magnetic tape, have been used in one experiment on the recognition of distorted melodies. The first 24 notes of 10 familiar melodies were stored in the computer as paired numbers representing pitch and the duration of each note. No information was stored about amplitude. One of the bits in the accumulator was brought out to an amplifier and speaker which provided input to the tape recorder. Actually, the distortions in the melodic patterns were computed not in the machine, but by hand, and fed to the machine, a labour which the author could have avoided had he been a more expert programer. The distortions introduced were not of the usual kind encountered in auditory research, but involved transformations such as doubling or halving the size of the musical intervals between each successive note in the melody, eliminating all pitch or all duration information.

A research programme recently begun on auditory discrimination training dramatically illustrates the potentialities of the digital computer for psychological research. Using a small (4000 words of core storage), highspeed machine equipped with a digital-to-analog converter and special output equipment and two electric typewriters for on-line input and output, a two-subject psychophysical experiment can be run entirely under programme control. The subjects are presented with a sound which can have any of five values on five dimensions: frequency, amplitude, repetition rate, duty cycle, and duration. The subject's task is to identify the sound. This he may do by typing a series of numbers on the typewriter. The computer then informs him whether his response was correct, and if wrong, in what respects it differed from the correct response. Having done this, the computer then selects the next stimulus on the basis of the subject's pattern of past responses. Two subjects may be run at once. The computer also keeps necessary records and computes summary statistics. The stimuli here are simple waveforms, but this is by no means a necessary limitation.

In its present form, the computer generates the patterns by producing a digitized signal corresponding to the desired sound and then playing these time-quantized data through a digital-to-analog converter. Here the computer is being used to generate the stimuli, compute the sequence of their presentation, feed back information to the subject, and analyse results. Seemingly a tour de force, this novel application of a computer only foreshadows widespread use in psychological research, as the increasing availability of high-speed general purpose machines makes more practical their acquisition by laboratories and universities.

Perhaps the most common use of the computer as an auditory display generator has been in connection with the efforts to devise ways of transmitting speech using narrow bandwidth channels. This work is best summarized in the two-volume proceedings of a conference on this topic, which was held in 1959 at the Air Force Cambridge Research Centre. When a system has been devised for introducing the speech signal into a digital computer, has the signal been rendered unintelligible in the process? To ascertain this, the data are put out through a digital-to-analog converter to form a new auditory signal, which is presented to subjects whose accuracy in identifying the spoken words is evaluated.

TERMINAL EQUIPMENT

As with visual patterns, special terminal equipment is needed in order to get sounds into and out of a computer. Simple patterns, such as a sine wave of a certain frequency and amplitude, can be generated by the computer from a stored programme. An approximation to white noise might be produced in a similar manner.

To put a complex waveform such as human speech into the computer requires a different approach and special input equipment. A typical system designed to introduce a sample of speech into a digital computer is described by Forgie and

Forgie. A microphone picks up the speech and feeds it to a bank of 35 bandpass filters. Filter outputs are sampled at a rate of 180 times a second, the amplitude of each filter at each sampling period being converted to binary digital form and fed directly to the computer. Such a system can be used on line with a live speaker or in connection with a tape-recorded speech sample.

When the set of patterns to be generated is small and fixed, patterns may be stored on some device like a magnetic drum. The computer acts as a kind of switching device to select a given sequence of these messages. Generating patterns from a larger set and placing various parameters of these patterns under computer control require equipment which is the reverse of the input equipment described above. A series of binary numbers corresponding to relative amplitudes of various frequencies is read out and changed in a digital-to-analog converter to a corresponding series of voltages. These may, in turn, be fed to a device such as a vocoder to generate the waveform.

A simple way to produce noise from a computer is to connect one of the flip-flops in the accumulator to an amplifier and speaker. With such an arrangement, one can programme this bit in the accumulator to change its state at a given rate for a given duration and in this way act as a squarewave generator. The pitch of the tone emitted from the speaker is determined by the rate at which the bit in the accumulator is changing its state. Some computers have such an arrangement as standard equipment to enable the operator to detect "loops" when a programme is running. If the pitch of the tone is high, he knows that the loop is a small one; if it is low, he knows that the loop involves a number of instructions in the programme. Such information is frequently useful in debugging a new programme. This arrangement can easily be programed to play melodies.

AUDITORY PATTERN REPRESENTATION IN THE COMPUTER

From the foregoing description of the techniques for

getting auditory patterns into and out of a computer, it is evident that the ways in which such patterns are represented in computer memory are parallel to those which were discussed for visual patterns. To generate melodies using the amplifier and speaker directly coupled to one bit in the accumulator, it is necessary merely to write a programme which will put in memory a list of pitch and duration values for each note in the melody, a representation formally identical to the *X, Y* coordinate list method of representing a two-dimensional visual pattern.

The representation of speech which has been put in memory with the bandpass filter bank arrangement described above is formally identical with the matrix representation of a visual pattern when only one bit of amplitude information is desired.

OPERATING ON STORED AUDITORY PATTER

Just as visual patterns, once in the computer, can be subjected to a wide variety of transformations employing all the arithmetic and logical circuitry at the programer's disposal, so may auditory patterns be manipulated once they have been represented in computer memory. Actually, very little such manipulation of auditory patterns has been performed on computers—partly because many efficient special purpose analog devices exist for transforming such patterns. By using appropriate filters, amplifiers, choppers, and by changing tape speed at playback time, one can easily transform auditory patterns in many ways which are of interest to researchers in this area.

These methods impose some distortion such as noise or periodic interruption on the pattern (which is uncorrelated with the pattern); or, such as bandpass filtering (which is correlated with the microstructure of the pattern and not with its macrostructure). For such operations, special purpose analog devices work admirably, but when auditory patterns must be manipulated at a more macroscopic level, a digital computer is useful.

Those, for example, who are manipulating speech at the

level of the phoneme, are finding the high-speed general purpose digital computer a powerful tool.

COMPUTER DISPLAYS FOR OTHER SENSE MODALITIES

As yet, the literature does not contain studies employing computergenerated displays designed for senses other than vision or audition. However, several research efforts are directed toward the use of the tactile modality as an information channel.

Geldard's laboratory at the University of Virginia has for some years been doing basic psychophysical work in this area, and Geldard has described experiments successful in transmitting English text by means of vibrators attached. The particular equipment used in Geldard's research transmitted text at such slow speeds that a computer was not required for generating and sequencing the signals. Were someone to modify this system to enable people to receive English text at speeds comparable to those achieved in ordinary visual scanning of printed text, or in auditory reception of spoken English, the speeds involved might make the use of the computer more attractive for such work.

Related to this area of reading machines for tactual input are the efforts to automate the production of Braille books. A programme has been written for one of the large digital computers to enable it to turn clear English text punched on cards into grade 2 Braille, also punched on cards, which can be used with automatic equipment to set the plates for producing Braille books.

Since grade 2 Braille involves a number of special characters and many contractions and abbreviations, the translation from clear English text is more complicated than a one-to-one mapping.

Also under development are automatic devices to present the Braille code to the fingers of the human reader. These developments, together with the growing research interest in devices to aid those with sensory or motor deficits in navigation and communication, may well stimulate interest in the use of the computer for generating displays other than auditory or visual.

AUTOMATIC PATTERN RECOGNITION

Thus far we have outlined the use of the computer to generate patterns for perceptual research. Instead of programing the computer to generate stimuli for people to respond to, we may wish to study how the computer will respond to a pattern under various conditions. There are pressing demands for automatic pattern and character recognizers. An automatic handwriting recognizer would be of immense value to the Post Office Department. A machine to read handwritten numbers could expedite the processing of checks in clearing houses. Military agencies are interested in the development of automatic devices to aid in photo interpretation. There is a long-standing need for a device that can "read" a printed page and emit a train of signals which the blind can interpret.

The astonishing thing is that such pattern recognition is performed so readily by human beings. Postmen every day correctly sort mail addressed in handwriting which no machine now in existence could decipher. The need for automatic recognition devices has given rise to a considerable research and development effort, much of which is not relevant to this chapter, since it is concerned with engineering devices which will read a particular set of characters, rather than with the investigation of human pattern recognition.

TEMPLATE MATCHING

Devices for character recognition now in commercial use depend upon a particular type font and a particular format in the document to be read. Every effort is made to eliminate sources of variation in the characters. In striking contrast, the human being is distinguished by his ability to recognize accurately characters of astonishing variety under conditions of severe pattern degradation.

As long as the variety of inputs which can be correctly classified is comparatively small, pattern recognition devices can be built which depend upon a matching of the input patterns with templates stored in memory. The template yielding the best match determines the response. Most of the automatic devices mentioned above operate on such a system. This system encounters difficulties when the class of permissible inputs is enlarged, a point clearly made in Selfridge and Neisser's discussion. A theory of human pattern recognition based upon a process of template matching would have grave difficulty in coping with the realities of human recognition behaviour.

NEURAL NETS

There is an alternative view of pattern recognition which has formed the basis for psychological models, which some workers have attempted to simulate on digital computers. Estes' earlier learning model conveys some flavour of this approach. He hypothesizes that on successive learning trials some subset of stimulus elements is consistently associated with reinforcement. At the outset of learning, all the stimulus elements impinging on the organism are associated with the first success. After the second success, some of these stimulus elements will no longer be the same, while others will. The connections between the latter and the correct responses will be twice reinforced; the connections between stimulus elements unique to the first or second trial will have been reinforced but once. Thus, after a number of trials, a subset of stimulus elements emerges which has received more reinforcement than others. Thus is an S-R connection formed.

This fiction of a subset of stimulus elements common to all trials may be convenient in the context of the usual learning experiment where every effort is made to keep the physical environment of the organism constant from trial to trial; but it is hard to invoke it in the context of the recognition experiment where two patterns with no stimulus elements in common may be readily and correctly placed in the same category. Nevertheless the idea has been extended to a two-stage process in some attempts to simulate neural networks on a digital computer. Here the computer is programed to simulate a network of randomly connected nonlinear elements which are assigned parameters borrowed from neurophysiology: thresholds and refractory periods. The network is divided into four groups of elements: two fixed input groups and two output groups. An output is defined at any instant by the difference in the number of elements fired in the two subgroups during the instant. One input consists of firing all the elements in the first input group and none in the second. The alternative input is the reverse. An element that receives excitation above its threshold fires, and transmits excitation to all elements to which it is connected- the effectiveness of this excitation, known as its "weight," being a property of that particular connection.

The object of the programme was to ascertain whether, by manipulating these weights following each input presentation, the network could be organized so that a given input would be reliably associated with one of the two outputs. Clark and Farley found that such a network can be organized in this manner to classify the inputs in the desired manner with a probability significantly above chance. More interesting is their finding that such a network can do this even when the inputs are noisy; i.e., when they are not disjoint subsets of the input ensemble. That so disorderly a system could yield such orderly discriminations was suggested some years ago by Hebb in his discussion of the cell assembly and its role in recognition. Further work with computer simulation of a randomly organized network has been done by Rosenblatt. Roberts has investigated the effects of various methods of reinforcing the network, discovering that the kind of reinforcement scheme employed makes a significant difference in the rapidity with which the network can be taught to make a given discrimination. In these random network pattern recognizers, learning is much more rapid if the characters are first centered on the "retina" and made the same size.

The random network experiments have been among the first attempts to use the computer to, simulate a psychological process. The model employed has been essentially neurological, in that the characteristics of the "elements" comprising the networks have borne an obvious relationship to neurophysiological concepts. The interesting properties of such networks and their possible relation to neural networks were frst suggested by McCulloch and Pitts.

PARALLEL PROCESSING

Pointing out that the random net has severe limitations as a system which can be taught to make a number of discriminations under noisy conditions, Selfridge and Neisser propose a fundamentally different model for pattern recognition. The model has been realized in the form of a digital computer programme designed to recognize "sloppy hand-printed characters." This programme depends upon a number of tests being made of the pattern to be recognized. Is there a cross bar in the pattern? Is there an upward concavity? Is there a vertical line? During the training phase of the programme, these tests are performed on a number of examples of each character in the set. After each example is presented, the correct "answer" is fed back to the computer so that eventually the machine builds up a number of probabilities linking the outcome of each test with each character.

On the test trials, a pattern is again presented, the many tests are performed, and a "vote" is taken to determine, given the outcomes of these tests, which character has the highest probability of being associated with this set of outcomes. This strategy employed in a programme to recognize "sloppy, hand-printed characters," made about 10 per cent fewer correct identifications than human readers made with the same material. Selfridge thinks that such a programme can cope with much wider variability in the inputs than the random net approach without enlarging the size of the machine unduly. He points out that the training procedure could do more than alter the probabilities linking test outcomes with responses. Conceivably, the machine could be programed to abandon certain tests which failed to yield differential predictions and to alter the way in which probabilities are combined to make the final decision.

Notice that this model of recognition does not assume that there is some invariant in all instances of a pattern. The assumption is that there are features more or less characteristic of a given pattern, any of which may be present in a given instance.

A strategy of pattern recognition basically similar to the letter recognition programme described above has been programed by Forgie and Forgie for the recognition of spoken English by a digital computer. With special equipment for direct input of speech to the computer, the programme examines the amplitude of the whole sound envelope sampled at the rate of 180 times per second. When the amplitude is above a fixed threshold, all subsequent samples are classified as belonging to one of the ten possible sounds being studied. These decisions are continued until the amplitude falls below the threshold, at which point a "vote" is taken of the decision for all samples and a final decision determined. The decision for each slice of speech is based upon a rough localization of the first two formants. The outcome of this processing determines which of a series of confusionelimination operations will be performed before reaching a final decision for the sample. This programme, which combines parallel and sequential processing, correctly classified 93 per cent of the utterances of 11 male and female speakers saying 10 English vowels.

When computers are equipped to deal directly with human outputs like the written and the spoken word, social scientists from many disciplines are going to find new and significant applications for them. There is already considerable interest in the use of a computer as a teaching machine. Were the computer capable of understanding the student's speech, its pedagogic possibilities would be significantly broadened. Social psychologists and sociologists, interested in studying communication practices of small groups or organizations, would have at their disposal a device which could greatly facilitate the tedious job of initial data reduction. Experimenters interested in psychophysics, discrimination learning, pattern recognition, rote learning, concept formation, or, in fact, any domain in which the subject is required to make a series of responses over a period of time, will find that the computer can be programed to make the next presentation, display, or trial, dependent in any desired degree upon the outcomes of previous trials. In short, automatic pattern recognition programs will make possible a much more intimate linking of man and computer than has been possible up to now.

EXISTING PATTERN RECOGNITION PROGRAMS AS PSYCHOLOGICAL THEORIES

The relevance of this work for the psychology of perception is not easy to assess. Neurophysiologists today are less and less satisfied with the model of the neuron as something which fires or does not fire when its threshold is exceeded and hence are dubious about the value of continued computer simulation of neural nets based upon such a simplified model. There is no doubt about the finding that such nets can be trained to make discriminations of noisy inputs, provided the number of outputs is modest, but there is some uncertainty about the way in which such demonstrations can advance our understanding of human pattern recognition.

Similarly, Selfridge's parallel processing programme is in some sense a model, though not a neurological model, of human pattern recognition. Selfridge rules out the random network as a reasonable model for pattern recognition, because the size of the network required to perform the discriminations we know the human has to make, and make reliably, is unreasonably large by current estimates. He regards the parallel processing strategy as more consistent with our present knowledge of human performance in this domain. It has indeed been shown to work with noisy human products like hand-sent Morse code and hand-printed letters, but much more needs to be done before such programs can be viewed as testable theories of human pattern recognition.

The fact remains, however, that a cleverly programed computer can learn to recognize patterns under conditions which are far from trivial. It is impossible to be involved in the construction of such a computer programme without being forced to consider many facets of human pattern recognition and perception from a very different viewpoint. None of these computer recognition programs, for example, has tackled the problem of segmentation. In every case, it is assumed that there is but one letter, one vowel, one pattern in the computer to be recognized. No attempt is made to isolate the spoken vowel in a stream of connected speech nor, to isolate a single letter in cursive script. The Morse code programme described by Selfridge is almost the only recognition programme which deals with such segmentation problems, and it is significant that a large part of the processing done in this programme is devoted to segmentation—isolating the sequence of dots and dashes to be recognized. Work is being done on this problem in spoken English, but the problem is far from solved. These difficulties focused renewed attention on the whole problem of unit formation in perception—a problem which has received little or no attention from psychologists since the heyday of the Gestalt school.

It is only natural that there should be a rush to prove that the powerful new high-speed general purpose digital computers can perform many tasks previously thought to be uniquely human. Can computers think? Can they be original? Can they solve problems? Can they recognize patterns? Non-trivial affirmative answers have now been given to all these questions. Programs to do all these things have been written, and they work, so the existence proofs are in. Now it is time to go on to other things.

Since the computer has been shown to be capable of pattern recognition, it becomes a possible tool to use for testing psychological models of this process. As yet almost no studies have had this orientation. The study of the detection of bar patterns in statistically defined dot matrices is one of the first perceptual studies using the computer as a stimulus generator which examines the empirical data from the standpoint of a particular theoretical model—statistical detection theory. This model influenced the choice of independent variables, certain aspects of the analysis, and served as a focus for the interpretation of the results, which in some instances were at variance with the model.

Julesz' work with stereoscopic depth is another instance of a fruitful use of a computer in a series of studies designed to test a first approximation to a model for stereoscopic depth perception. The model predicts certain conditions under which the effect will and will not occur. These are put into the computer as parameters and displays generated to these specifications in order to see whether observers report the effect under these conditions.

AREAS FOR FUTURE APPLICATION OF COMPUTER TECHNIQUES TO PERCEPTUAL RESEARCH

The computer has thus far been used in the field of perception *either* as a recognizer or as a generator of patterns. There is no reason it can't do *both* and, in so doing, act as a powerful tester of hypotheses about human pattern recognition. The computer could, for example, generate a series of patterns which varied along some parameter known to make recognition increasingly difficult for human beings. These same displays could be fed back to the computer programed as a pattern recognizer to study the degree its recognition performance matched that of human observers. To the extent that it did, the programme on that machine could be said to be an adequate theory of human pattern recognition.

This approach looks promising, but a word of caution is perhaps in order. Those who have labored to introduce multidimensional arrays like pictures and complex time-varying waveforms into a digital computer for processing are uneasy about the awkwardness of the procedure.

They contend that the speed and reliability with which people handle the same information indicate that the representation of patterns in human memory must be significantly different from the techniques used thus far in storing pictures in digital computers. Because of the stepped-up programme of research in outer space, rapid advances in the technology of optical image processing are being made. Such devices may ultimately be more appropriate tools than digital computers for perceptual research. Lettvin's recordings from the optic nerve of the frog suggest that before the information arrives at the cortex considerable image processing may be done by a multiply-connected system which could be simulated by a network of resistors and diode. Initial processing of visual images might best be done by such an analog device before attempting to read them into a digital computer for further processing. The current enthusiasm for digital computers should not blind us to the possibilities of analog devices in this area. Certainly the neurophysiological data available on end organ and central nervous system behaviour make it obvious that there is room for both models.

The computer could be of immediate use in generating stimulus materials for certain perceptual studies. The extremely important research being done by Gibson and his colleagues at Cornell on the perception of slanted surfaces requires the use of stimulus materials which are complex and difficult to manufacture so that the statistical properties of the textures are known. The generation of such material on a computer with a video output would be rapid and would give the experimenter the chance to get a number of independent samples of a given texture, as well as a number of different textures whose parameters could be stated exactly. Gradients of texture within one display are easily programed.

Attneave and his associates have published a number of studies using nonsense two-dimensional forms constructed according to certain welldefined rules so that all forms so generated can properly be said to be members of this family of figures. A recent study employed such a technique to generate a set of stimuli for a discrimination experiment. The cells of a 300 X 300 matrix were filled or not filled according to a rather elaborate set of rules. Out of this matrix, the shapes used in the experiment were cut. Such a procedure must have required hundreds of manhours. The same displays could have been generated with a computer programme in a matter of seconds, with considerably less opportunity for error. The very fact that the rules for generating such figures are so explicit makes their computer generation simple to programme.

The most far-reaching development is foreshadowed by the recently initiated research of Swets· Here the computer is serving a number of functions which an experimenter cannot usually encompass with such precision. It has stored within it a set of rules for generating a finite set of stimulus patterns, a set of rules for determining which member of the set will be presented next, a method of matching the subject's response with the stimulus and displaying the discrepancy between the two, and provision for giving the subject control over a number of stimulus parameters. With audio and video outputs, and on-line communication with the computer by the electric typewriter, this system comes about as close to being the all-purpose automatic experimenter as one could hope.

Interestingly, some will see this arrangement as a machine for studying human learning, thinking, or problem solving, whereas others viewing the same elephant will be inclined to see it as the perfect machine for studying perception. Both are correct, of course, and those who are doing this work are well aware that they are studying discrimination learning. With rare exceptions such as Lashley and Harlow, workers in the field of learning have been content to leave the stimulus alone or to vary it in only one dimension; and workers in perception have been cavalier about the response. Use of the computer in psychological experiments may offer a unique opportunity to the many disciplines of experimental psychology to recognize and correct former limitations.

Chapter 9

Computer Simulation of Cognitive Processes

The study of cognitive processes—the higher mental processes involved in activities generally referred to as "thinking" and "problem solving"—has attracted considerable attention in recent years. A major reason for this attention has been the development of a method for studying human cognitive processes by simulating these processes on a large, high-speed digital computer. The behaviour of the computer is determined by a programme; hence the major effort in this method centers around writing a programme that will cause the computer to perform a task the same way that people do. The statements of such a programme form a theory or model of human behaviour in the task situation. The implications of the model are determined by running the programme on the computer and observing the resulting behaviour.

Although the method of studying human cognitive processes by computer simulation is only a few years old, a number of important results have already been achieved. The first major contribution was made by Newell,

Shaw, and Simon who programed a computer to simulate the behaviour of subjects solving problems in symbolic logic. Solution of a logic problem requires that a given logic expression be converted into a desired formulation by the application of certain rules to the given expression. The problem-solving programme is an explicit model of problem-solving behaviour in this task. The programme proceeds to solve these problems by finding differences between the two expressions and selecting rules which, when applied to the given expression, will lead to a reduction of those differences. The application of a single rule to the given expression usually yields an expression intermediate between the original expression and the one desired. This intermediate expression is then compared to the desired expression, the differences detected, and once again the appropriate rule is applied. This procedure is repeated until the desired expression is obtained. The behaviour of this programme is quite similar in procedure to human problem-solving behaviour.

A second contribution to our understanding of cognitive processes has resulted from the computer model of verbal learning behaviour developed by Feigenbaum. This programme is designed to simulate the behaviour of humans learning lists of nonsense syllables. The programme learns these syllables by constructing a series of tests based on the differences between the syllables. These tests form a discrimination mechanism for a list of syllables. The performance of this programme in learning lists of nonsense syllables reveals marked similarities to the activity of human subjects engaged in the same task. Our understanding of cognitive processes will be further increased by the computer models that have been or are being developed to simulate human behaviour in portfolio selection, concept formation, and music composition. The purpose of this report is to introduce the method of studying cognitive processes by computer simulation. The method will be presented by describing the author's work on computer simulation of behaviour in the binary choice experiment. This form of presentation has the advantage of discussing techniques and problems in specific contexts rather than in the abstract. The reader is cautioned, however, that the material presented here is descriptive rather than prescriptive.

SIMULATION OF BINARY CHOICE EHAVIOUR–AN EXAMPLE OF SIMULATION OF COGNITIVE PROCESSES

THE BINARY CHOICE EXPERIMENT

In the binary choice experiment, the subject is asked to

predict which of two events, E1 or E2, will occur on each of a series of trials. After the subject makes each prediction, he is told which event actually occurred. The order of the events is determined by a random process, but the subject is not given this information. The subject is instructed to make as many correct predictions as he can.

A STATISTICAL LEARNING THEORY EXPLANATION OF BINARY CHOICE BEHAVIOUR

One model of behaviour in this experiment has been offered by the statistical learning theorist.([2], [9]) In its simplest form, this model says that the probability that the subject will predict that event E1 will occur on trial *t* is increased if event E1 occurred on trial *t* - 1. Conversely, the probability that the subject will predict that event E1 will occur on trial *t* is decreased if event E2 occurred on trial *t* - 1. The more often one event occurs, the greater the probability that the subject will predict that event.

The simple statistical learning model is consistent with some characteristics of the behaviour observed in the binary choice experiment, notably that subjects usually predict each event about as often as it occurs. But the simple statistical learning model is not consistent with other characteristics of behaviour observed in the experiment. For example, after several successive occurrences of one event, subjects tend to predict the occurrence of the other event.

This behaviour is quite frequently observed in nonexperimental situations and is referred to as "gambler's fallacy" or "negative recency." This behaviour is, of course, not consistent with a model that predicts that successive occurrences of one event increase the probability that the subject will predict that event.

Evidence has also been presented that the statistical learning model does not adequately predict the subject's responses when the subject is predicting an event series that contains conditional probability relationships; e.g., the probability that E1 will follow E1 is not the same as the probability that E1 will follow E2.

A COMPUTER MODEL OF BINARY CHOICE BEHAVIOUR

The difficulties of the simple statistical learning model and the comments of investigators of binary choice behaviour would seem to indicate that binary choice behaviour is much more complex than the statistical learning model would indicate. The subject's response is not determined simply by the frequency and recency with which an event has occurred, as the statistical learning model implies. Post-experimental interviews and analysis of trial-by-trial responses suggest that subjects entertain hypotheses about patterns in the event series. The subject is apparently not a passive mechanism being conditioned to make responses with a certain probability. He is more adequately depicted as an active information-processing mechanism that views the binary choice task as the problem of finding the structure of the event series. Such a complex information-processing model can be stated in the form of a computer programme, and the model can be studied by running the programme on the computer.

Before the computer model can be written, information must be obtained about the cognitive processes involved in binary choice behaviour. The data available from previous experimentation did not provide sufficient information, and a new set of experiments was run in which the subject was asked to "think aloud" while making his choices.

"THINKING ALOUD."

The "thinking aloud" procedure is not new. Woodworth says it was advocated by Claparéde in 1917. Heidbreder used the "thinking aloud" procedure in her work on concept formation, and Duncker also made very effective use of the same procedure in his work on problem solving. The procedure has been used in several computer simulation studies of thought processes in addition to the study of binary choice behaviour.

The "thinking aloud" procedure consists simply of asking the subject to verbalize while performing a task. The statements of the subject and the experimenter are recorded.

This record is called a "protocol." The "thinking aloud" procedure is not to be confused with introspection. The distinction made by Duncker is worth repeating:

This instruction, *"Think aloud,"* is not identical with the instruction to introspect which has been common in experiments on thought-processes. While the introspecter makes himself as thinking the object of his attention, the subject who is thinking aloud remains immediately directed to the problem, so to speak, allowing his activity to become verbal. When someone, while thinking, says to himself, "One ought to see if this isn't...," or, "It would be nice if one could show that...," one would hardly call this introspection; yet in such remarks something is revealed [p. 2].

The following excerpts from the protocol of subject DH predicting a series of "+" symbols and "✓'" symbols in a 200-trial binary choice experiment give some indication of the information obtained with this technique:

The ninth one will be a ✓ I think that you just gave me the + to throw me off, and you'll continue the progression.

The fourteenth one will be a ✓ You're beginning a new progression with + 's.

The sixteenth one will be a ✓'.... to throw me off now.

Ninety-nine is a ✓'. You've begun a progression of three +'s and three ✓''s. You've already had the three +'s. Ninety-eight (sic) will be a ✓'.

One-twenty-nine will be a ✓'. You've begun a progression of two +'s and two ✓''s.

One-thirty-two will be a +. You're alternating the signs now.

The "thinking aloud" protocols not only furnished additional information on the cognitive processes of the subject, but also transformed the goal of the research. The goal became the explanation of the behaviour indicated by the protocol. The strategy followed in the study of binary choice behaviour was construction for each subject of a model that would make the same predictions as the subject for the same reasons that the subject gave. In the next section, the development of a model for one of the subjects, DH, will be retraced, and in the following section the model for DH will be described.*

ANALYSIS OF THE PROTOCOL

The protocol obtained with the "thinking aloud" technique was the raw data for the construction of the computer programme. Cursory examination of the protocol provided some understanding of the processes the subject used in the formulation of his responses. The protocol of DH in the binary choice experiment seemed to corroborate the conjecture about hypothesis behaviour in the experiment, i.e., that the subject entertained hypotheses about patterns in the event series. But a casual examination of the protocol did not provide detailed information about which hypotheses the subject entertained and under what conditions these hypotheses were evoked and selected.

This detailed information was obtained from a careful analysis of the protocol. The first step in this analysis was to code the subject's statements on the basis of their apparent meaning. For example, DH's comment, "You're following with a ✓' and two +'s," was coded as the patternhypothesis ✓' + +. The comment, "You've begun a progression of two +'s and two ✓''s," was coded as the pattern-hypothesis + + ✓' ✓'. The second step was to investigate the seemingly plausible conjecture that a relationship existed between the subject's hypotheses and the sequences of events and predictions preceding the statement of those hypotheses. Some regularities were uncovered. For example, after several ✓''s occurred, DH would say that a progression of ✓''s was beginning. After the event sequence + ✓' + ✓', the subject would say that the signs were beginning to alternate. The analysis also revealed that DH usually changed hypotheses after incorrect predictions and retained hypotheses after correct predictions. The hypotheses were also consistent with the subject's symbol predictions.

THE MODEL FOR DH

On the basis of the information obtained from the analysis of the protocol, together with some conjectures where this analysis could not supply the necessary information, a rough outline of a model of DH's behaviour in the binary choice experiment was obtained:

A hypothesis is generated about the structure of the event series on the basis of the preceding events. This hypothesis is used to obtain a prediction of the next event. The prediction performs the role of a test of the hypothesis. If the prediction is correct, the hypothesis is retained unless a decision is made that the pattern of events will be interrupted ("negative recency"). If the prediction is incorrect, either the event is explained as an interruption of the pattern ("you just gave me the + to throw me off") or a new hypothesis is generated.

The completion of the model was a lengthy task involving the iterative procedure of proposing a detailed model, testing the model against the data, modifying the model, testing again, and so on. During this procedure, almost every part of the model originally proposed was modified or replaced. In addition, modifications of the model led to new interpretations of the data, and these interpretations led to further modifications of the model.

The completion of the model for DH's behaviour in the binary choice experiment began with attempts to specify the mechanism for pattern selection. Several mechanisms were considered, only to be rejected. Similarly, several negative recency mechanisms were tried. The representations of certain basic elements of the model, e.g., the patterns and hypotheses, were also the subject of experimentation. After much experimentation, the model for DH described below was completed.

The basic element of this model is the hypothesis. Every hypothesis has a pattern component, e.g., progression of –"s, simple alternation (+ –'), double alternation, etc. Some hypotheses have a second component which is a negative or "guess-opposite" component. If the guess-opposite component is not present, the prediction of the hypothesis is the prediction of the pattern component; e.g., the prediction of the hypothesis which has a pattern component "progression of –"s" and no guess-opposite component is a –'. If the guess-opposite component is present, the prediction of the hypothesis is the "opposite" of the prediction of the pattern component; e.g., the prediction of the hypothesis which has a pattern component "progression of –''s" and a guess-opposite component is a +.

The model itself is divided into two phases. Phase 1 is concerned with the processing for the pattern component of the model. The output of this phase may also be interpreted as the subject's explanation of the preceding event (the explanation hypothesis). Phase 2 is concerned with the processing of the guess-opposite component of the model. The output of this phase becomes the subject's hypothesis for predicting the event of the next trial (the prediction hypothesis).

The model sharply distinguishes between patterns that predict an event correctly and those that do not. Indeed, this simple idea of retaining hypotheses that predict correctly and changing, or at least considering the possibility of changing, hypotheses that predict incorrectly is a basic premise of the model. The distinction is made between the ability of the hypothesis to predict an event and the ability of the pattern to predict the event. If the hypothesis contains a guess-opposite component and it predicts an event *correctly*, the pattern will not be able to predict correctly and will be considered for change. If the hypothesis is negative and it predicts incorrectly, the pattern will be able to predict correctly and will not be considered for change.

The pattern-change mechanism, composed of the evocation mechanism and the selection mechanism, is really a device for choosing a pattern from the basic list of nine patterns that the subject uses. The choice is made in two stages. In the evocation stage, a subset of the patterns is nominated. In the selection stage, a single pattern is selected.

The model says the experimenter tried to "throw me off" on trial t when a pattern failed to predict the event of trial t, but the pattern-change mechanism does not select another pattern. Otherwise, the explanationhypothesis contains only a pattern.

This phase of the model first tests whether the prediction hypothesis for trial t contained a guess-opposite component. If the guess-opposite component is present, it is processed in much the same fashion that the pattern is processed in the pattern-selection phase. If the negative hypothesis predicted correctly, the guess-opposite component is saved. If the negative hypothesis did not predict correctly, the guess-opposite component is considered for retention in a fashion analogous to the throw-me-off consideration in the pattern phase.

If the guess-opposite component was not present in the prediction hypothesis for trial *t*, the model considers whether or not the guess-opposite component should be introduced. This consideration is made in the following way: The model determines the number (N_1) of events including and preceding trial *t* in which the explanation hypothesis for trial *t* could have predicted correctly. Then the number (N_2) of contiguous events that could have been predicted by the last occurrence of the explanationhypothesis is determined. If $N_2 > N_1$, the guess-opposite component is not introduced; and the prediction hypothesis for trial *t*+1 is the explanation-hypothesis for trial *t*. If $N_2 = N_1$, the prediction hypothesis for rial $t + 1$ is guess-opposite the explanation hypothesis for trial *t*. If $N_2 < N_1$, the model concludes that the previous occurrence of the explanation hypothesis as represented by N_2 is not really pertinent. The model then searches for an occurrence of the explanation hypothesis preceding the occurrence represented by N_2 and repeats the process. If no occurrence is found, the guess-opposite component is not introduced, and the prediction hypothesis for trial *t*+1 is the explanation hypothesis for trial *t*.

THE STUDY AND TESTING OF THE COMPUTER MODEL

After the model was specified in a form such as that of the flow charts the coded computer programme was written. The first attempts at coding revealed logical contradictions and inadequate specifications in earlier flow chart formulations.

After these inaccuracies and the coding errors that inevitably occur in programs were corrected, the programme was ready for study and testing. The study and testing involved a comparison of the human behaviour and the programme behaviour as determined by running the programme on the computer.

Even in the case of computer simulation of specific individuals, the comparison of the program's behaviour with the subject's behaviour does not involve a word-for-word comparison. The model of DH's behaviour in the binary choice experiment certainly was not designed to produce a wordfor-word facsimile of DH's protocol. The computer programme was designed to match a coded representation of the protocol, such as was discussed above.

The model's protocol can be compared with the subject's protocol which served as a basis for the derivation of the model. This comparison is, of course, not a rigorous test, but it does give some idea of the adequacy of the model. Even though the model was derived from the subject's protocol, the model's protocol and the subject's protocol are not identical. Thus, some procedure is required for determining the relative adequacy of the model.

SIMPLE DIFFERENCE COUNT

The most obvious method of testing the adequacy of the computer programme to simulate behaviour is to count the differences between the coded form of the subject's protocol and the machine's protocol. In the binary choice case, this comparison will give the number of differences in hypotheses and symbol predictions between the subject's behaviour and the machine's attempt to simulate this behaviour. Unfortunately, this simple error count can be misleading. Human behaviour and models of this behaviour generally contain a large number of interdependencies. The model's decision at any given point in time *t* depends quite heavily on its prior decisions, and if one of these prior decisions is different from the subject's decision, the model is quite likely to make a decision different from that of the subject at *t*. The ability of the model of DH's behaviour to select the same hypothesis as the subject does at trial *t* depends on the ability of the model to select the same hypothesis that the subject did at trial *t* - 1. If the model's hypothesis at trial *t* - 1 was different from the subject's, the model's hypothesis at trial *t* is most likely to be different, too. Because of the interdependencies in the behaviour and the model, two differences would result. The second difference, however, may have resulted from the first and not from any in- adequacy in the model. Thus the difference count would be exaggerated. By similar reasoning, the difference count might be reduced. *

TURING'S TEST

One solution to the problems involved in comparing the behaviour of complex models and the behaviour of the subjects that the models are simulating is to use a version of the "blindfold" test. We are all familiar with the advertisements that challenge the reader to distinguish between oleomargarine and the "high-priced spread." This same type of test might be used to see whether an expert could distinguish between the subject's protocol and the machine's protocol. A pragmatic solution to the debate over whether machines could think. Turing proposed that an interrogator question a machine and a person on a variety of topics via a teletype. If the interrogator could not distinguish the machine's responses from the human's, Turing was willing to conclude that machines could think. Such a test has been applied in at least one case. McGovern has programed a computer to answer questions about the weather.

These questions were also asked of nine people. McGovern then listed the questions and the answers given by the computer programme and the humans. Another group of 10 people was asked to pick out the program's response to each question out of the 10 responses listed for each of the 25 questions. These 10 people made 42 correct choices out of 250 opportunities, which is not better than would be expected if these judges were choosing randomly. Newell and Simon have proposed that a version of Turing's test, such as the one used by McGovern, might be used to determine the adequacy of computer simulations of human cognitive processes. Thus, judges might be handed the protocol obtained by computer simulation and coded versions of nine human protocols and be asked to pick out the machine's protocol.

Turing's test lacks the rigor that the computer simulation of cognitive processes promises to restore to the study of cognitive processes. It is certainly true that the use of judges is a respectable test, and statistical techniques are available for determining the ability of judges to discriminate beyond mere guessing. The use of Turing's test, however, implies that no good operational criteria exist for comparing human protocols and machine protocols.

Furthermore, the ability of the computer simulation of cognitive processes to achieve its goal—the creation of a model that will produce a reasonable facsimile of the subject's behaviour—is probably not very well tested by Turing's test. Turing's test is adequate for telling the researcher whether or not he has achieved a programme that will produce behaviour that is indistinguishable from human behaviour. But Turing's test is not adequate for matching the protocol of the machine's behaviour and the subject's behaviour; since even though these protocols may be quite different, judges cannot determine which is the machine's protocol. In statistical terminology, Turing's test is not very powerful for testing simulation models. The probability of an error of the second kind, i.e., accepting the model when it is in fact wrong, is quite high.

CONDITIONAL PREDICTION

Another method for obviating the difficulties that arise in the simple difference-counting method of comparing the machine's protocol and the subject's protocol involves an attempt to eliminate the interdependencies that vitiate the difference-counting method. Every time the programme makes a decision different from that of the subject, the programme can be set back on the track, i.e., the subject's decisions imposed on the model, so that the differences between the subject's behaviour and the program's behaviour at any point in time will not be caused by the differences that occurred earlier. Thus the decisions of the model at any point in time are conditional on the preceding decisions of the model's being the same as those of the subject.

This system of conditional prediction was applied to the binary choice model of DH that has been presented above. The programme of DH's behaviour was subdivided into segments, each of which was capable of making a decision that could be compared to a decision of the subject, e.g., pattern evocation, pattern selection, pattern prediction, etc. After each segment was executed, the decision of the segment was compared to that of the subject by a test; e.g., "Did the pattern-evocation mechanism evoke the subject's pattern?" If a difference between the program's decision and the subject's decision was detected by any of these tests, the program's decision was replaced by the subject's decision. The programme itself was not modified. Thus, if the pattern-evocation mechanism failed to evoke the subject's pattern, the subject's pattern was added to the list of evoked patterns. This corrected list of evoked patterns was then used as the input to the pattern-selection mechanism. Thus, the inputs to the pattern- selection mechanism and each of the other programme segments were correct or at least contained the information required by the segments to make a correct decision.

The results of using the programme of DH to predict in this conditional fashion are given a restatement of the flow chart with the addition of the tests and control statements required for conditional prediction.

If he did not, an error was tallied (three trials) and control was transferred back to the simulation programme beginning with the pattern-evocation mechanism. The conditional prediction system performed similar functions after the programme made any decision that could be checked against the protocol. Thus the input to each segment of the programme was eliminated as a source of error.

This type of conditional prediction offers several advantages as a device for comparing machine protocols and subject protocols. The first advantage—the elimination of the interdependencies in the model as a cause of spurious differences between the model's behaviour and the subject's behaviour—has already been mentioned. A second advantage derives from the ability to test each segment of the model separately. For example, the number of times the pattern-evocation mechanism fails to evoke the subject's pattern and the number of times the pattern-selection mechanism fails to select the subject's pattern are determined independently of each other.

This separation allows easy identification of those segments of the model that make large numbers of errors. A third advantage derives from the greater number of tests given each component of the model by the use of the conditional prediction technique. If the pattern-evocation mechanism fails to evoke the subject's pattern, the subsequent operation of the pattern-selection mechanism cannot be considered a valid test for reasons that have been previously discussed. If the mistake of the pattern-evocation mechanism is corrected before the pattern-selection mechanism is used, however, the pattern-selection routine will be given a valid test.

The problem of comparing the program's behaviour and the subject's behaviour can be summarized as follows: The errors made by a model in predicting the subject's behaviour result from either erroneous inputs to the model or incorrect specification of the model. The difficulty with the simple difference count is that it confuses these two sources of error. Turing's test is not sharp enough to determine specific inadequacies of the model. The major virtue of the conditional prediction technique is its separation of the two types of errors; thus, it permits identification of the components of the model that are inadequately specified.

TESTING MODELS OF GENERALIZED INDIVIDUALS

In the cases where the computer programme represents a generalized individual rather than a specific individual, the simple difference-count comparison of behaviour is certainly not appropriate. The conditional prediction technique is of less value than in the case of simulation of specific individuals.

Turing's test suffers from the same inadequacies in this case as in the case of specific individuals.

Perhaps the traditional statistical comparisons are the most useful tests in this situation. For example, the serial position curve generated by a verbal learning programme simulating behaviour in a nonsense syllable learning experiment can be compared to the curve obtained from human behaviour in the same experiment. Other summary statistics of the program's behaviour can also be compared with those of the subjects' behaviour.

Chapter 10

Computer Synthesis of Human Language Behaviour

Robert F. Simmons was born May 14, 1925, in Massachusetts. He received his Ph.D. in industrial psychology from the University of Southern California in 1954. He worked for three years at Psychological Services, Inc., in Los Angeles, primarily in research on flying safety with USAF pilots and aircraft. The subsequent two years were spent at Douglas Aircraft developing computerized methods for predicting man-hour costs of building newly designed airplanes. For the past five years, he has been employed at The RAND Corporation and System Development

Synthex is the name of a research project at the System Development Corporation. The project has as goals the development of research methodologies and vehicles for the eventual creation of a computerized system which will synthesize human cognitive functions, particularly in the area of human language behaviour.

This chapter attempts to summarize the results of a wide body of research pertinent to the development of such a language synthesizer. It also outlines the major problems and methods of research involved in the construction of machine systems that will ultimately be successful in synthesizing language behaviour.

LANGUAGE AND COGNITION

The processes used by humans in their thinking, learning, and perceptual behaviors are a matter of neverfailing interest to the psychologist. "How does a man know?" has remained a central question in psychology from the time of the Greek similacra, through the associationists, introspectionists, behaviorists, even to this mid-twentieth century age of computer technology.

The questions "What does a man know?" and "How does a man learn?" have more frequently been studied by means of language in verbal types of testing instruments and in learning experiments with language materials than by any other methods. In rebelling against introspectionism, the early behaviorists threw out the subjective verbal report only to have it reintroduced as a class of behaviour as much deserving of study as any other; and many of today's studies of thinking, of human perception, and of learning are equally interpretable as studies of the human use of language. Obviously not all of psychology can be encompassed by studying man's use of language, but to the extent that man uses his language to symbolize, to communicate, perhaps to remember, even to perceive much of his world, the study of human language behaviour is the study of human cognition.

LANGUAGE AND ACTION

One great portion of the study of man not obviously related to his use of language is the whole area of motor skills, muscular behaviour toward a particular end. But the release of a sequence of complex laryngeal behaviour in phonation or the careful control of the myriad tiny responses required in writing or typing are examples of perhaps the most complex of all human motor skills. Most other motor skills can also be mediated by the use of language. Thus, to a significant extent, the study of language even includes the study of how particular words and sentences can be related to motor behaviour.

It soon becomes apparent in the study of language behaviour that if a psychologist could understand all aspects of man's use of language, he probably would in the process have developed a complete functional blueprint of the relations holding in the vast area between the stimulus input and the response. This functional understanding would be independent of the particular symbology or coding used by any given sense modality.

Such is the thesis of this study of language behaviour. In the discovery of the functional relations necessary for transforming a language input to a language output for any given purpose, it is believed that, in symbolic form, the functions necessary for the transformation of any other behavioral input to output are being studied also. For example, if in hearing and answering a question, a subject must encode a sequence of sounds, correlate certain aspects of this string with stored information, evaluate the result, then recode it into an appropriate motor output, is it not reasonable to conclude that these procedures are typical of the functions used in reacting to a visually perceived situation?

SYNTHESIS AND SIMULATION

In synthesizing a complex molecule, the chemist builds it by combining elements or simpler molecules. If he is copying an existing material, the ideal result is a molecule alike in every particular to the one copied. If, as often is the case, he is attempting to construct a molecule that he calculates can exist, his success is measured by comparing his results with his computations (or even by the discovery of unexpected by-products).

Computer studies of human behaviour fall untidily into both classes: the copying or simulation of human processes and the creation of other procedures not necessarily used by man to achieve a comparable output. Usually the term "simulation" loosely embraces both approaches (as well as a much broader area of mathematical modeling, war-gaming, etc.). This section draws a distinction believed to be important in furthering the progress of computer research on cognitive behaviour. *Simulation* is used for work that explicitly attempts to copy or model the processes used by humans in their cognitive behaviour. *Synthesis* is used for research aimed at the construction of systems which, given the same inputs as a human, produce outputs comparable in kind and amount. The synthetic system, in contrast to the simulated one, may use any convenient means to go from input to output and is not necessarily limited to modeling what is known or observable in human behaviour. The method of synthesis has this advantage: the researcher is not limited by prevailing notions as to his procedures for attaining a behaviour comparable to that of a human.

As in the Newell-Simon simulation approach, it is argued here that a computer programme, which accepts a human type of inputs and generates a product comparable to that of a human, using gross stages that are apparently similar to those of humans, will in itself be a testable theory of that human behaviour. But since the resulting programs are based on a computer whose internal switching logic may be vastly different from that of the brain, a language synthesizer may turn out to be a functional analog of human language behaviour only in the sense that a wheeled vehicle performs the function of locomotion. If this type of functional relationship is found, the synthesized system may have furnished a testable hypothesis about human behaviour, but one later found to be invalid. Considering the success of the wheel and the airplane wing from a practical viewpoint, perhaps more is to be gained in the long run if computer-synthesized behaviors eventuate in ersatz rather than truly simulated human behaviors.

PRACTICAL USEFULNESS FOR LANGUAGE MACHINES

One other sense of the word synthesis is important in the discussion of language-processing machines. Philosophers have long used the word to communicate the idea of combining separate elements of thought or sensation into a whole, of simple into complex conceptions. Such an idea is basic to any conceivable purpose to which a language machine might be oriented. The essence of any use of language appears to be the selection and recombination of ideas or objects symbolized now by one set of words and later by another. In practical application, a language-processing system faces the exceedingly difficult task of extracting and recombining concepts or meanings from widely varying sources, and synthesizing these into a reasonably concise response to a question or command.

The social value of language synthesizers lies in the potential creation of "thinking" systems of much greater memory capability than that of a single person. An ultimate language processor could be expected to store vast quantities of information, which might have been extracted from whole libraries of human endeavor. Depending on the degree to which these machines have a logic for creative synthesis of widely separated facts, they could routinely apply interdisciplinary discoveries from the entire breadth of science and scholarship to the answering of a question or the solving of a problem.

More immediately, many large bureaucracies are faced by ever-increasing communications problems in which the volume of written communications simply exceeds the capacity of the human executives. Scientific reports, market reports, progress reports, business summaries, etc., all flood the control arm of any large corporation. Even the daily business activities of cataloging, inventory control, and purchasing are to a large extent simple examples of language-processing tasks in which a vocabulary of numbers and a syntax of permitted combinations evolve into a new natural language of our age.

Recently Kellogg outlined a fact retrieval machine which showed clearly how a language synthesizer could serve a factory executive by accepting written or graphic material and maintaining a capability of showing the entire picture, big or small, of the current operation, in response to questions in a special simplified language. Such machines obviously become of increasing importance as the complexity of an already vastly complicated economy continues to grow.

But perhaps the most important aspect of the eventual importance of language-processing machines lies in the capability of language to serve as a model, precise or rough as required, of any given set of experiences or actions. Just as the digital computer is a general purpose machine that can be connected between any input-output devices, so will the language synthesizer probably become a much more easily programed mediator between a human society and the work it wishes to accomplish at any given time. Already the current generation of compilers translates from problem-oriented languages close to natural English into the bits and operations of the computer. In some tomorrow, perhaps not so distant, the logic of the compiler-translator and the research in language processing will be merged into a computer with the wired-in capability of computing with natural language.

RESEARCH TRENDS

In the fifteen years that have seen computers become widely available, there has been a corresponding growth in attempts to use them to simulate or synthesize various aspects of human behaviour. One is tempted to believe that almost every programer or computer engineer immediately senses a rough analogy between logic switching and thinking; the least sophisticated have been known to rush into print with remarkably inadequate descriptions of "mechanical brains" or "thinking machines." The literature, however, bears witness to an ever-growing number of computer-associated researchers who have paused long enough to formulate hypotheses about a particular behaviour and who have then programed a computer in the attempt to duplicate that behaviour and test their hypotheses.

SIMULATION OF COGNITIVE PROCESSES

A recent survey of attempts to simulate human cognitive processes on computers found more than four hundred published articles. As many as half of these were theoretical formulations, verbal or mathematical; but almost as many described an already constructed system which in some manner appeared to duplicate complex human processes. It is both interesting and significant that more than half of these documents were written since 1958. Although many of the techniques and findings developed by these researchers in synthesis of cognitive processes are pertinent to the study of language behaviour, lack of space must limit discussion of their findings to a few general statements. Gelernter, Newell, Shaw, and Simon, and Wang have all been concerned from varying points of view with the development of programme systems which can use heuristic methods or specially designed algorithms to prove geometric or logical theorems.

Newell and Simon have generalized from their work to the development of GPS (General Problem Solver) which shows considerable promise as an approach to computerized problem solving. Also as an outgrowth of this work, Shaw and Simon have built several versions of IPL (Information Processing Language) a list-structured programing system. This programme serves to allow a general purpose computer to simulate a computer whose wiring makes easy many of the operations required in studying human cognitive behaviors.

The Rosenblatt Perceptron and a large family of more practical pattern-recognition devices have demonstrated means by which computersynthesized learning can be accomplished, particularly in a perceptual context. In regard to learning of the conditioned response type, a whole genus of machines exists. Interestingly enough, the earliest models of these predate computers and are to be found in the psychological journals of the 1930's.

Since the main theme of this section is recent computer research in the area of language behaviour, we must reluctantly ignore the highly instructive work in the development of chess, checker, bridge, and other gameplaying systems and the whole area of the development of hardware to translate from printed or spoken patterns of language into bit patterns of use to the computer. For surveys of this work, see Fatehchand and for a definitive summary in the field of artificial intelligence.

The remainder of this section will focus on current work in mechanical translation, information retrieval, recent linguistic and psychological research pertinent to language, and on a discussion of a few prototypes of general purpose language-processing machines.

MECHANICAL TRANSLATION AND INFORMATION RETRIEVAL

These two topics, each of which has its own fairly large literature, can be considered together as simply differing emphases in research on the computer processing of natural language. Researchers in each area are usually acquainted with work in the other and, in fact, often contribute to both. Together, the two fields include the bulk of present research in natural language processing and are a rich mine of hypotheses, programing techniques, and methods of approach to the synthesis of human language behaviour.

The problems of mechanical translation have recently been described in detail by Oettinger and by Reifler. In the information retrieval area, BarHillel has made a highly critical review of progress toward a theoretical understanding, with particular emphasis on the pitfalls into which he believes most researchers have already stumbled. For a general survey of current research in computer processing of language information, the National Science Foundation, *Current Research and Development in Scientific Documentation,* periodically lists the work in progress in this and other countries.

The mechanical translation work began with the oversimplified hypothesis that, given a large enough bilingual dictionary, a computer could successfully substitute words from one language for words from the other and that the result would be a translation useful for some purposes. In fact, the early result turned out to be largely gibberish. It is still possible, however, to argue that, if the dictionary were so arranged that any word, phrase, or sentence in the one language had an appropriate correspondent in the other, mechanical translation would indeed be easy. But the completion of such a dictionary is an impossible task (because languages are open sets of words and sentences in which theoretically a new item may always be added to the existing set).

Even the approximation of such a dictionary would be a task so vast as to be unfeasible. Moreover, every human translator knows that a vocabulary of words and a set of syntactical rules are a much more efficient approach to translation; but although every competent speaker of the language is proficient in the use of its grammatical or syntactic rules, not even the linguists or the grammarians have completely stated them.

The inadequate knowledge of these syntactic rules may be considered as the current major obstacle to successful machine translation of languages. As this barrier of syntactic ignorance yields to the attack of linguists and other researchers, an equally inadequate knowledge of the rules for forming semantic categories will probably become apparent. To date, it is generally believed that a thorough syntactic analysis will resolve problems of translating from a word with multiple meanings in one language to one of the many words which sometimes carry similar meanings in the target language. At least, today, the problem of selecting from multiple meanings is less bothersome than that of translating word sequences from one language to another.

The importance of mechanical translation to the synthesis of language behaviour is threefold. One, the work itself is the first major example of computers processing language data in a way previously possible only to humans. Second, the work has generated a renewed interest in the detailed development of means for syntactically analyzing language and has been a major motivating force in the recent linguistic developments to be reviewed below. Finally, the language translation work has developed specialized research methods by which one may attack and eventually solve language problems with the aid of computers.

In the area of information retrieval, in contrast to mechanical translation, it appears that the major logical difficulty for computers is one of semantic or meaning analysis. Here the primary problem is to accept a request for a fact or a document, to search mechanized files for the terms stated in the request, and to deliver all, and only, those documents which the requestor considers pertinent. Unfortunately, many pitfalls lie between the requestor's desire and the retrieval system's response. Most of these difficulties are in the use of language.

For example, the requestor may be searching for literature on machines or systems that simulate human cognitive processes. Assume that the mechanized library contains all such documents that have been written.

Very obviously, the words, "simulated cognitive processes," have been used only infrequently in the titles (or for that matter, in the contents). Titles such as *"A Machine that Learns,"* or *"Teaching the Computer to Play Chess,"* or *"A Theorem Proving System,"* will be far more frequent representatives of the genre desired. If a machine is programed to find synonyms, it will not only miss what the ingenious author has devised as a unique and attention-commanding title, but it will also begin to gather many kinds of irrelevant documents. And of course, to top off the difficulties, what the requestor really wanted might have been a group of mathematical articles on conditional probability machines. At any rate, discovering what the request is actually aimed at is a critical problem.

Further developments of automated indexing are currently being investigated. Doyle is studying the usefulness of indexing associative paths between words as discovered by computer analysis of their bivariate frequency in a set of documents. Maron is studying means of weighting index words according to empirical probabilities of their being used to call forth a particular document. Methods for evaluating the effectiveness of various indexing procedures have been studied and applied on small samples of literature by Cleverdon and by Swanson. However, the comparative evaluation of various IR methods is still a matter for future resolution. This chapter, however, is less concerned with the practical utility of various computerized IR approaches than with their implications for the synthesis of language behaviour. These implications appear significant.

Automated indexing techniques hint at a direction of research that may allow computer processing of quantities of text toward the development of a fairly inclusive set of the semantic categories found in natural language. Automatic abstracting techniques, which score each sentence in proportion to the number of a particular set of content words it contains, may be significant in the development of methods for evaluation. Of text as the computer selects an answer to a natural language question.

The particular emphasis of this section on automatic indexing and abstracting in IR research should not be interpreted to mean that these problems are at the heart of the IR problem. Nor should the preoccupation with semantic categories be understood to imply that IR does not have syntactic problems as well. To the contrary, the important work of Perry and Kent at Western Reserve owes much of its success to their use of a limited syntactic analysis carried in "role indicators," which distinguish such terms as "ballistic missile" from the similar appearing but considerably different "missile ballistics." Probably, as appear the opposite of the situation in mechanical translation, the most important current problem in IR is semantic categorization and organization. As this problem approaches solution, one may expect the syntactic organization of language to assume ever-increasing importance.

LINGUISTIC AND PSYCHOLOGICAL RESEARCH.

In the field of linguistics, some important developments have occurred in the past few years. Most important of these appears the truly significant work of Zellig Harris and his students at the University of Pennsylvania. Harris and Chomsky have developed a means of syntactic analysis which on the one hand promises eventually to become a system and a mathematical model for the generation of many or all grammatical English sentence forms. On the other hand, the approach is being developed at Pennsylvania as a method of analyzing sentences in text into constituent grammatical structures and into "subsentences" and transformations. Harris's project is computer-oriented and he has so far succeeded in programing the UNIVAC to make a syntactic analysis "... adequate for the writing that appears in scientific articles...... " Harris' work can be expected to yield methods useful to any language synthesizing system both for analysis of input text and for the generation of output in grammatical English sentences.

At Indiana University, Householder and Lyons are working on a systematic syntactic and semantic analysis of English with the aid of an electronic computer. They, too, report some success in the automation of methods of syntactic analysis, particularly in the area of computer determination of the syntactic function of words in the text. Other linguists, like Garvin and Oettinger, are working with the specific problem of mechanical translation and making significant progress toward computerized treatment of the structure of languages.

Osgood, studying linguistic behaviour from a psychological point of view, has developed a measuring instrument called the "semantic differential." By factor analyzing subjects' scaled evaluation of words, he measures the placement of each test word in a semantic space whose dimensions are the evaluation factors so extracted. Osgood's work has given rise to a significant number of psychological studies of various aspects of language usage by means of the semantic differential. A fairly remarkable consistency in factors underlying the evaluation of words has been found. Seemingly, factors named "Evaluation," "Potency," and "Activity" underlie most subject's ratings. To the synthesis of language behaviour, the semantic differential suggests similar procedures as a possible means for finding other types of semantic categories.

Bruner, Goodnow, and Austin in their already classic *Study of Thinking* suggest other important semantic categories. They are willing to argue that all cognitive activity depends on the formation of categories of events and the subsequent treatment of such categories. They distinguish carefully between concept formation, or the development of categories, and concept attainment, or the achievement of distinguishing features which separate categories from each other. Although the work of these psychologists is not directed precisely at the human use of language, it does show that one can hardly study human cognitive activity without learning more about the human's use of language in the process. The concept categories of Bruner serve equally well as concept or meaning categories for the use of language. And interestingly enough, one subclass of meaning categories includes those that deal with the structure of syntactic meanings or uses of words. Techniques of Bruner and of Osgood, useful in studying cognitive activity from their own particular emphasis, transfer easily to means profitable for the development of a language synthesizer.

Thus, from current linguistic research it becomes apparent that means for computer processing of syntax are almost developed to a practical state. Means for the formation and processing of semantic categories are suggested by some of the current studies in IR and in the psychology of thinking, but many key concepts are yet lacking for the computer synthesis of language behaviour.

PSEUDO-COGNITIVE LANGUAGE SYSTEMS

In the last two years, at least three programs have been started toward the development of general purpose language processing systems. Lindsay, using one of the RAND Information Processing Language systems, has developed a computer programme which analyzes English syntax and constructs a semantic model that makes explicit the implicit meanings of some words. His programme is concerned with sentences about family relationships, such as father, mother, brother, etc. His syntactic analyzer, however, is designed to work with a very large class of sentences composed of Basic English words. His process, essentially, is to make a detailed syntactic analysis of sentences in such a manner as to clarify nouns, subjects, objects, and the particular grammatical relations existing among them. The semantic section of the programme has routines which can work with the words, "mother, father, brother, sister, and offspring," using the results of the syntactic analysis to relate them to names that have been mentioned in the text. The programme then "annexes" these names to appropriate branches of a hierarchical family tree. By the nature of the family tree structure, it is possible to infer that if John is the brother of Mary, and Mary, the daughter of Meg, Meg is the mother of Mary, Meg is the mother of John, etc.

The generality of Lindsay's reading machine can be seen to derive from the use of syntactic analysis as a means for developing semantic maps or models. Because these models represent in their structure a broad frame of relationships between the objects (or words) modeled, it becomes possible to deduce from the model more information than is actually given in any sentence that the system reads.

Another system based on a hierarchical classification of data is that of Green and Selfridge which is now being programed to answer questions expressed in English about baseball scores. Their programs break into four parts; syntactic analysis, content analysis, data finding, and data processing of the answer. Their approach puts a heavy emphasis on the analysis of the question into a set of terms that call forth an appropriate sequence of routines which can extract pertinent data from the wellorganized computer storage. A third language processing system still in early stages of development is the author's Synthex system. The Synthex approach will attempt to develop a completely general data organization for the material read in a way such that the machine's store of information can grow as a function of the commands and questions given it and of the quantity of reading it does. Methods aimed toward these hopeful goals and an example of the author's approach are to be found in the following sections.

The three systems outlined here and a few others, either less general or in earlier stages of progress, begin to show how the research findings from mechanical translation, information retrieval, linguistics, and psychological research can be integrated into general purpose language synthesizers. In passing, it is probably significant to note that both Green and Lindsay are psychologists and that Lindsay develops at considerable length the relationship of his work to the study of human cognitive processes with rather cogent suggestions for additional research on human subjects.

PROBLEMS IN COMPUTER LANGUAGE SYNTHESIS

In this section, problems associated with computer

synthesis of the human ability to read, remember, organize information, and write statements in response to questions are examined in detail. For convenience, these problems are categorized into the three broad areas of syntactic analysis, logical analysis, and semantic analysis. Unfortunately, the problems are not so clearly distinct as the categories would imply, and it will often become apparent that there are complex interrelationships among each of the three areas. As means generally available for computer processing of language data are discussed, the distinction made earlier between computer synthesis and computer simulation of human behaviour will be clarified. Methods found to be convenient and apparently necessary for computer solution of language problems will not always be those used or required by humans.

SYNTACTIC ANALYSIS

Why need a language be analyzed syntactically? People seem to read, write, and talk very adequately without necessarily being able to diagram a sentence or even to recognize parts of speech. In fact, the whole business of grammatical analysis is often to be summarized in an adult by some negative feelings toward a particular grammar teacher who insisted that a number of apparently arbitrary lines and subdivisions be superimposed on a sentence obviously much more meaningful without them.

In computer uses of language, the extent and type of syntactic analysis appears to be a function of the task. In information retrieval work of some types, the only use of syntax to be observed is the sequence of topic words in a request. If this sequence is preserved in the search, the use of syntax remains implicit. In mechanical translation where two languages differ significantly in grammatical structure, the syntactic relations in one must be translated to grammatical relationships in the other. The syntax of one language is related to that of another by analyzing both in terms of the sequence rules for combining categories that may be common to both, such as nouns, verbs, prepositions, subjects, objects, tenses, etc. For a reading and question-answering machine, syntactic analysis of questions is required at the very least to translate them into information retrieval commands. If the system is to do even such simple things as to find the noun to which a pronoun refers or determine major topics of a sentence, a fairly complete syntactic analysis is essential.

Syntactic analysis may be looked upon as the derivation of a structural interlingua between sentence organization and storage organization, or between question structure and the structure of information in memory, or between grammatical sequences in two languages. So from this viewpoint, unless the input-output language sequences are built into the storage and programme organization, any language processing machine must undertake such syntactic analysis as is required to make a common linguistic structure for input, storage, and output.

SYNTACTIC ANALYSIS–WORD CLASS

Underlying any grammatical analysis of sentences or larger units is the requirement that each word in the sentence be categorized into such word classes as noun, verb, pronoun, etc., or into some comparable categorization, such as Fries' (11) form-classes and function words. The practical value of word class is minimizing the number of grammatical rules needed for analyzing sentences. By dealing with all words that have certain grammatical functions in common as a single category, e.g., "nouns," it is often possible to ignore their differences in structure and meaning. This economy is particularly worthwhile in customary analyses of sentences where eight or nine word classes are generally found sufficient for most grammatical op- erations. Depending on the depth of analysis, however, some researchers in mechanical translation find it desirable to distinguish twenty or thirty different parts of speech. The new word classes account for certain, not too frequent, anomalies that grammarians have typically been willing to list as exceptions to their rules of analysis.

Computer assignment of word class to each word in a sentence is most frequently accomplished by dictionary look-up procedures. The dictionary used includes not only equivalent verbal meanings of each word, but also its part of speech, its possible inflections, and a host of other grammatical codes as well. Since a very large number of words in any natural language may be used as more than one part of speech, determining word class from a dictionary is not simply a matter of table look-up. Depending on position and sequence, or on tense and number, a very complex logic is required to make an adequate syntactic classification of the particular use of a word. Sometimes, too, the word cannot be classified until the context phrase or sentence has been partially analyzed at a higher level.

A second possible approach to identifying parts of speech without using a complete dictionary has some evidence in its favour. Some preliminary experiments by the author have given support to the hypothesis that human subjects can recognize parts of speech from grammatical context without the aid of cues from the word to be identified. The procedure in these experiments was that of blanking out the content words in a sample of text while leaving unchanged such grammar-loaded forms as prepositions, conjunctions, articles, and certain bound morphemes. For example, "These _____s also _____the _____to _____ _____ly along." * The subject is required to identify the part of speech of each word that has been blanked out. Scores from a sample of five subjects on a fairly simple 500-word text ranged from 90 per cent to 99 per cent correct classifications. In addition, no error was common to all subjects. Finally, the subjects reported that the bound morphemes (such as _____ly or _____al) were often misleading and usually helpful only as secondary cues to confirm a hypothesis based on word sequences.

The direction of this evidence is toward the idea that if human subjects can indeed identify parts of speech with a high degree of accuracy without knowing the actual word involved, then it should be possible to determine the cues of sequence and sentence structure that they use and formulate them into a computer programme to accomplish the same task. Such a programme would work with a small dictionary of function words and sequence rules and allow the language processer to accept words it had never before encountered, without failing in its task of syntactic analysis.16.3.1.2 Syntactic Analysis—Sentences. After the parts of speech or word classes have been recognized, it is possible and customary to break the sentence into such larger functional units as clauses, phrases, subjects, predicates, objects, and complements. Or for a particular purpose, the sentence may be transformed into a hierarchical tree structure of dependencies or of constituents. In general, the analysis at this functional level reveals what units of the sentence include what other subunits. Thus, in "The old man sat down," the subject is not *man*, but *old man*, and the predicate includes both the verb and its adverb. In most types of analy sis found useful with computers, the tree structure would list *old* beneath *man*, and *down* beneath *sat*, to show these relations.A general way of looking at English sentences is to conceive of them as sequences made up as follows:

Sentence:

Nominative (or noun phrase)

Modifiers

Complements

Verbal (or verb phrase)

Modifiers

Complements

The *nominative* is a word or phrase acting as a noun. It may include other words, phrases, or clauses, which limit or add breadth to its meaning, in the form of modifiers or complements. The nominative may be the subject of a sentence, or the complement or the object of a verb, or the complement or modifier of another nominative. In a similar manner, verbs may be complemented or modified by other words or phrases. The modifiers and complements may each be made up of nominative-verbal units, etc., so that, theoretically at least, a sentence need never end. The task of syntactic analysis is separating out and making clear these and other types of relationships which hold among the words in a sentence. A number of procedures for the analysis of sentences have been developed into fairly practical form by researchers in the language processing area. Among these, the *predictive analysis* methods of Ida Rhodes which have been further developed by Oettinger and the Harvard Mechanical Translation Group, Zellig Harris'*kernel analysis* approach and David Hays' *dependency analysis* all appear to be the quite general type of tech- nique which can prove adaptable to many language processing uses. Each of these approaches exists in more or less usable form as a computer programme system, and of course, none is so well developed as to handle anything approaching all possible structures of English.

LOGICAL PROBLEMS

Logical aspects of language thoroughly permeate both the syntactic and semantic areas. On the syntactic level, Reichenbach devoted a long chapter of his *Symbolic Logic* to the analysis of conversational language. He suggested that traditional grammatical analysis simply ignored many of the logical relations inhering in the structure of sentences. He proposed the beginnings of a grammar based on the calculus of functions. In such a grammar, a sentence like "The sky is blue," would be analyzed Blue (sky), where the parentheses indicate the simple following relationship: sky belongs to a category of blue objects. Another example is more to the point. "John gave the book to Jack"; is converted to Gave (John, book, Jack) to indicate the complex directional relationship of *John, book,* and *Jack* as determined by gave. Reichenbach believed that his approach could be generalized to give a grammar far more useful than those available from the usual formulas of grammarians.

Clearly, with a grammar in terms of logical functions, the propositional calculus would become more easily applicable to the determination of truth values of statements. The calculus of propositions can be considered in this light as a syntax of argument which studies the connective relationships between statements and furnishes principles for recognizing and testing the of validity of deductions. The word classes used by such a logical grammar would be quite different from the usual parts of speech. For example, the brother of, the father of, or the employer of, might all belong to different structural categories because they each predicate different relationships between subject and object. Such terms as *and, or, not,* the blanks between sentences, and a host of other connectives would occupy special categories in the grammar. And perhaps most important of all, the line between syntactic and semantic categories would obviously become a meaningless division.

This last point calls attention to two facts of importance in natural language and their grammars. Usually syntax is taken to include the rules for the categorization of parts of speech and the rules for the sequencing of parts of speech in sentences. But there appears to be a continuation of categorization and sequencing rules throughout the area of language usually considered as semantic.

The rules are apparently implicit in natural languages for the formation of such semantic categories as synonymity, oppositeness, family relationship, and hierarchical relationship. Equally implicit are the rules by which semantic categories are combined into meaningful statements. So the first fact appears to be that in natural languages the difference between rules of grammar and rules of meaningful usage is simply that the former syntax has been made more explicit than the latter.

This principle explains the second fact mentioned earlier in this section that the indicators of logical conjunction and logical deduction are to be found both in the "grammar" and the "semantics" of a natural language.

As a consequence, from the customary linguistic viewpoint, the logician, for all his care in distinguishing function and content of words, seems to be dealing with a hodgepodge mixture of syntax and semantics. And from the logician's view, the natural languages are imprecise and undisciplined.

Thus, looking at language from Reichenbach's vantage point leads to a better understanding of the problems of syntax and semantics. A most important problem in semantics is the determination of the categories of meaningfulness and the rules for arranging meaning categories into meaningful statements. A second important problem is the discovery and inventory of the cues of language that serve as logical connectives and as signs of equivalence, subordination and superordination between words. Defining the language problem in these terms helps to guide the research effort through a largely unmapped semantic territory.

SEMANTIC PROBLEMS

Semantic problems may be classified as either problems of word meanings or problems of the meanings of questions and sentences.

Word Meaning

To deal at all with semantics, it is necessary first, to find a referent or an operational definition of the term "meaning." For working with computers, the word has a number of convenient referents. In mechanical translation, the meaning of a Russian word is one of the English entries in a bilingual dictionary. In a question-answering system, the meaning of a word would be the subroutine it calls forth for a particular type of answering operation. In a general language-processing system, the meaning of a word might be a set of coordinates relating it to a hierarchical structure or meaning space. Generally, at least for computer operations, the meaning of a word is taken as a definition of what the computer does with it or because of it.

Words may have many meanings even when treated in the simplified sense described above. For example, in mechanical translation, there may be several entries in the dictionary. Which one is to be chosen?

In the question-answering machine, the word *which* in a question may call forth a routine to find, evaluate, and rearrange data, whereas in a statement, *which* calls forth a subordinating conjunction routine to operate on the oncoming clause. How is a computer to select the appropriate meaning or action?

The answer tends to define *context*. The meaning of a word depends on its context, and dictionaries frequently give examples of the context in which a particular meaning applies. For the computer, a set of rules is required; e.g., "if the word is a Russian verb, select the second English equivalent, if a noun, select the third," or "if *which* is in a statement followed by a question mark, take routine 74; otherwise, routine 22."

In this manner, context will mean to the computer that it must determine to what categories a word belongs in order that it may select a particular meaning or action. Thus, the function and need for extended syntactic and semantic categories conjoined with appropriate action routines becomes apparent in any language synthesizer. And some of the most important of all problems in constructing such a system centre on defining increasingly precise categories for operations on words.

The Meaning of Questions and Sentences

If the meaning of a word can be understood as the selection of a particular routine for storage or for action, what of the meaning of sentences and questions? Once again it must depend on the purpose of the machine. To a computer translator, the only meaning of a string of Russian words is to transform it into an English string according to its programme. To such a computer, the meaning of a Russian string of words is the activation of an *appropriate sequence* of analysis and transformation routines.

In the general purpose language synthesizer, a sentence may call forth several different sequences, depending on whether the machine is in a reading, writing, or question-answering mode. But the idea of meaning as an *appropriate sequence* of operations applies in every case, and the statement or question must be so analyzed as to reveal appropriate syntactic and semantic cues for the selection of operations to be performed.

With this view of meaning, a language synthesizer can be considered a system in which a string of input words is a set of events that map onto a meaning space whose coordinates might be the various modes of operation and whose metric might be in terms of categories which could call forth particular subroutines to operate on the input. Regardless of the model through which the system may be conceptualized, however, the significant problem remains of designing and programing a sufficient set of routines to do the various particular tasks which in their totality form the Gestalt of language behaviour synthesis.

METHODOLOGY FOR SOLVING LANGUAGE PROBLEMS ON THE COMPUTER

A problem can generally be measured as easy or difficult not so much in terms of the number of operations required, but by completeness of the description available for those operations. Thus the building of an automobile or ten thousand of them is a complex but well-understood task which can be accomplished by unskilled labour following detailed instructions. On the other hand, the design of an automobile is a very difficult task insomuch as it requires a set of procedures which are not completely defined or completely describable. Both research in general and the designing of a language synthesizer obviously fall in the category of work whose operations are poorly defined.

Yet the basic principles of scientific method apply as much to computer research as to any other type and go far toward simplifying the task of the language researcher. In the language of systems science, the principles of scientific method form a feedback loop of hypothesis formation, hypothesis testing, hypothesis revision, retesting, and successive revision until deviations of reality from the hypothesized reality fall within tolerable limits. In the area of computer research on languages, workers have developed their own special variations of scientific method to make feasible the exceedingly difficult tasks in which they are engaged. These methods are more often used than formally discussed by researchers in the field,* but they are nonetheless basic to the successful accomplishment of their work.

THE METHOD OF SIMULATION

Underlying all the research on simulated or synthesized

cognitive functions is the existence theorem of an organism which can accomplish the task in question.

If an animal can solve a problem by a series of observable or semiobservable operations, why not also a machine? In conjunction with some understanding of how the neural control of organic behaviour may be reduced to the action of switching circuits, and the extent to which a general purpose digital computer can simulate any finite switching network, the simple, often poorly defined existence theorem rapidly comes to generate research hypotheses testable by building a computer programme.

The Newell and Simon protocol approach shows most clearly how this method works. Given a complex human behaviour, such as problem solving, describe the behaviour as precisely as possible by giving human subjects samples of the type of problem to be solved by the computer. Observe their behaviour and obtain from them protocols describing in as much detail as possible the steps the subjects went through in coming to a solution.

Reduce these descriptions to a sequence of binary decisions and the data which determined the direction of each, and the behaviour is then described in terms amenable to computer programing. In the attempt to write the programme, it often becomes apparent that the behaviour has not been described adequately, so it then is necessary to observe more closely and to describe more thoroughly any neglected aspects of the behaviour.

The simulation method, in an informal sense, appears basic to the writing of any computer programme. What does a programer do except find an approach that he as a human can use to solve a particular problem and then translate it into a machine programme?

The technique must be completely described if a programme is to be written, and it is validated by a programme that accomplishes the task.

The advantage of formulating the simulation approach via protocols as a formal method, and thus the significant contribution of Newell and Simon, lies in the researcher's being directed to a set of operations which eventually converge to a solution of his problem.

THE METHOD OF ITERATION

Mechanical translation researchers have developed their own version of scientific method in application to their language problems. Although just as dependent on the procedures of humans, their method is not explicitly or necessarily the simulation of human behaviour (except in the sense that any programme records the programer's solution to a problem). This methodology can be seen clearly in the mechanical translation programme of Hays (Chapter 17). The general approach could begin with a specialized Russian-English dictionary on magnetic tapes, a simple set of rules for assigning English prepositions to substitute for Russian case endings, and a programme which examined each word in succession, looked it up in the dictionary, and printed the dictionary output on the translation tape. The output of such a translation system would be a hash of English in the sequence of Russian, and with all English equivalents listed for each Russian word.

By setting up a parallel system in which a human translator translates the same text, a criterion is obtained against which the machine output can be compared. Where the machine output falls short, the human editor attempts to write a rule to improve the system. This rule is then programed as an additional condition for words that fall in its category. Over a long enough period of time and a large enough sample of text, eventually a set of programs will be obtained that can translate the kind of text that the editor-computer system has experienced.

This iterative approach can set up a man-machine system that routinely improves itself as a function of experience. Although the computer does not learn, the editor continually modifies the programme to minimize its errors. The computer serves as a high-speed hypothesis tester which continually tests the programs against an ever-increasing sample of situations. With the computer-editor learning system, it is usually desirable also to have special analysis routines which can make statistical summaries of all the translations of a particular word, or all the uses of a given rule or procedure, in such a manner as to simplify the editor's task of discovering under what circumstances the programme failed and so to lead him in profitable directions toward correcting it.

METHODOLOGY FOR LANGUAGE BEHAVIOUR SYNTHESIS

The protocol method of simulation and the iterative method of the language translator reduce to similar forms emphasizing slightly different aspects of a basic computer-researcher methodology. The simulation method emphasizes the formalization of means for developing hypotheses; the iterative approach is more concerned with the testing and improving of hypotheses. Together or singly, each method defines a research task in such a manner as to minimize wasted effort and almost to insure success if enough time and effort are expended. This section will attempt to demonstrate how the methods in combination apply to the problems of language behaviour synthesis.

At the syntactic level of word class analysis, the approach presents human subjects with the problem of determining parts of speech for content words that have been blanked out of a sample of text. * Protocols with particular emphasis on the cues for word class recognition are then collected. These cues are translated into a programme system which reads a sample of text until it comes to a content word, then transfers to a table of routines associated with the preceding and following function words. On the basis of these routines or rules, the system tentatively assigns a part of speech, and reads until it reaches the next content word, at which it repeats its basic procedure. At the end of a sentence, the system tests for consistency (presence of noun and verb, absence of illegal construction, etc.).

If inconsistencies are found, it applies alternate permissible rules until the sentence is consistent or until it runs out of rules. At the end of a run through a set of text, the program's diagnostic routines would compare the results with the editor-supplied criterion which showed the correct word-class assignments and would summarize and print out the errors made and the rules used in each case. The human editor is then in a position to analyse the errors and revise the programme system.

A similar approach is obviously applicable to the more complex aspects of syntactic analysis. Fortunately, in the area of analysis of sentences, the language researcher can begin with a fairly well-tested computer logic and thus, by building on the shoulders of the considerable work already accomplished, shorten the number of iterations necessary to achieve a system that meets his requirements.

The methods apply equally well in the semantic areas, particularly in a question-answering system. The semantic problem, as discussed previously, is largely one of developing and organizing myriads of subroutines at both word, phrase, and sentence levels; inference routines (for example: "The king's name is George" = "KingGeorge," or "The eel is a fish" = "*eel* is a subcategory under *fish*"); routines for translating questions into retrieval requests; routines for scoring and evaluating data produced in response to a request; routines for making words into meaningful sequences; routines for casting sequences of words into grammatical statements; and hosts of special rules for varying basic systems in accordance with the categories to which the words belong.

But complex as the resulting system will undoubtedly be, it can be constructed programme by programme with the aid of an error feedback loop and editors to infuse the system with additional intelligence.

A question-answering system can begin with a very simple logic and a small set of rules. As the system of editor and programme gains experience, the rules become increasingly adequate and the failures less frequent. The output of the programme, compared against the editor's criterion of what the answers should be, continually focuses effort on those portions of the system which are inadequate. By such means, eventually a large enough sample of question types can be answered adequately by the machine so that it gradually achieves the status of a useful language processer.

A SIMPLE QUESTION ANSWERING MACHINE

As an illustration of how the methods described in the preceding section work, a simple question-answering machine that the reader can build with a card file is described below. Simple as the system is, it nevertheless shows how a computer can be simulated in a card file in the early stages of developing the logic of what may eventually become a very complex programme system.

By limiting the operations possible in the system to computations, comparisons, and transfers, the card file allows a researcher to develop the logic for programs needed to answer questions submitted in ordinary English.

First, a sample of English text is selected; for example, a one-page article about electric fishes. Each content word in the text is assigned a sequence number. The lowest sequence number is the first content word in the first article "read" to the machine; the highest sequence number is the last content word that has so far been "read" to the system.

The card file is then constructed so that a card exists for each different content word that the system has experienced. On each card is a record (or index) of all the different sequence numbers in which the word occurred in the sequenced text. Additional cards are placed in the file for question-making words, such as *how, what, why, which,* etc. Under each such word is a list of rules for recognizing an answer to a question that it signifies.

Also on the card file in conjunction with each word is a growing list of cross references to other words in the file. These cross references are developed empirically as a result of discovering that if the question had used a different word, it could have found an answer.

To use the system the researcher (henceforth, the editor) takes a question that he (or preferably, someone else) has written, and converts it by simple syntactic rules into the form of a declarative statement that ends with the question words. For an example, "How powerful is the shock of an electric eel?" is transformed to, "The shock of an electric eel is how powerful."

Shock	Electric	Eel	Powerful	How (Adj.)
4	4	20	63	-----is-----enough to
13	11	26	163	
11	19	34		-----so-----as to
56	22	42		
64	33	55		-----as-----as
80	41	112		
117	49	169		-----is the most-----
132	67	174		
164	94			-----is the least-----
167	104			
170	111			-----is more-----than
184	113			
188	131			-----is less-----than
	151			
	168			

The content words and the question word are then extracted as the key words for an information request. The index records for *shock. electric, eel,* and *powerful* are reproduced. This table also shows the rules that have so far been developed for distinguishing the answer to a "How (adj.)" question from other statements containing the key words.

Shock	Electric	Eel	Powerful
51	41	42	63
56	49	55	
64	67		
80			
164	151	169	163
167	168	174	
170			

Intersection of content words in the question.

Thus shows two ranges of text in which all four words of the question intersect. These are then extracted from the text in such a manner as to complete the paragraph at the beginning and the end and to find a referent for every pronoun. The human reader easily sees that the first of the two statements contains an answer. This answer is: "The shock of an electric eel is strong enough to stun a horse. It is the most powerful shock found among the electric fishes."

By finding those paragraphs which contained an intersection of all the question terms, the simulated computer provided two statements which might contain answers to the question.

Unfortunately, the logic for determining which statement, if either, contains an answer is very complex. Notice that what the first statement actually contains is, "The shock they give is said to be strong enough to stun a horse. It is the most powerful shock found among the electric fishes"; *they* refers back to, "electric batteries give the shock said to be strong enough to stun a horse, etc." In the second statement, *this fish* refers back to the electric catfish which gives a powerful shock. Thus there is no simple statement that tells how powerful the shock of an electric eel is, and the rules under "How (adj.)" do not apply.

Any simple rule for selecting the statement in which shock of the electric eel is the subject predicating *powerful* immediately fails by rejecting both statements. A rule is needed that will allow the system to synthesize the information that:

- The shocking organs found along both sides of the eel give shocks;
- The shocking organs give shocks strong enough to stun a horse;
- *Strong enough* is a measure of *how powerful.*

The preposition *of* in *shocking organs of the eel* allows the editor to formulate a rule that "if a subject term is in an 'of' relationship to a term in the question, the latter term may be substituted for the former." The editor also cross-references *strong* and *powerful.*

As a result of applying the newly formulated rules and of having substituted antecedents for pronouns, the first statement is computed to read, "... the *shock* (*electric* batteries or *shocking* organs = they = *eel*) give is said to be *strong enough to* stun a horse [It = the *shock* (*electric* batteries or *shocking* organs = *eel*) give] *is the most powerful shock* found among the *electric* fishes...." The first statement now contains two sentences in which not only do all four terms intersect, but in which the predicates include *enough to* and *is the most,* both of which have previously been determined as conditions for answering a "How (adj.)" question. The system can now select the first statement, or the particular sentences in it, as answering the question. A validation test of the editor-devised rules occurs every succeeding time one of the rules is used for answering a question.

Thus by failing a question, the system focused on a worthwhile problem for the editor's attention and forced him to write a rule of inference for use by the programme. As the set of rules grows, some validated by additional questions, some found wanting and eventually rejected, the computer-in-a-box accumulates the design for a true computerized questionanswering system.

Eventually a point is reached at which the original sequence-organized memory system may become too cumbersome, but by that time the difficulties which define cumbersome will probably also have indicated the direction for improvements.

Some readers may have wondered whether there may not be simpler methods for selecting the statement which contains the answer to the question.

For example, an application of Luhn's logic for weighting content words comes quickly to mind. Although a simple count shows that the content words of the question are more frequently represented in the second statement (which does not contain an answer) than in the first (which does), it appears that an iterative method could equally well be applied to the development of statistical criteria for distinguishing the two.

Sooner or later, however, a statistical weighting approach not based on the syntax and semantic rules of language would almost certainly reach a limit far short of the precision of word meaning and grammatical cues for signaling the answers to questions.

Even more important, the research goal in this work is a system that synthesizes human language behaviour.

To achieve an eventual synthesis at a level at all comparable to the level of humans, it will unquestionably be necessary to use as many as possible of the cues to meaning that language provides. Thus, even at the beginning, it is important that a language synthesizer take the most general approach possible.

Index

Encyclopaedia of

COMPUTERS APPLICATIONS IN MANAGEMENT

Encyclopaedia of
COMPUTERS APPLICATIONS IN MANAGEMENT

Volume 2

Sumit Sethi

ANMOL PUBLICATIONS PVT. LTD.
NEW DELHI - 110 002 (INDIA)

ANMOL PUBLICATIONS PVT. LTD.
H.O.: 4374/4B, Ansari Road, Daryaganj,
New Delhi-110 002 (India)
Ph.: 23278000, 23261597
B.O.: No. 1015, Ist Main Road, BSK IIIrd Stage
IIIrd Phase, IIIrd Block,
Bangalore - 560 085 (India)
Visit us at: www.anmolpublications.com

Encyclopaedia of Computers Applications in Management

First Edition, 2009
ISBN 978-81-261-3912-5 (Set)

PRINTED IN INDIA

Printed at Mehra Offset Press, Delhi.

Contents

Preface

This Encyclopaedia is designed to provide a comprehensive introduction to the design and analysis of computer algorithms and data structures. In terms of the computer science and Computer Application, this encyclopaedia to be primarily focused on the Junior-Senior level Algorithms course.

This Encycloparedia owes its existence to the collaboration made possible by the Internet and the free software movement. Its author — a college professor, have yet to meet face to face, but we have been able to work closely together and have been aided by many wonderful folks who have donated their time and energy to helping make this encyclopaedia better.

Author

Chapter 1

Computer Fundamentals

This unit aims at introducing you to today's most commonly used electronic device – the computer. The study of this unit will highlight the characteristics and evolution of computers. It will also help you to understand the basic terminology associated with computers.

OBJECTIVES

After studying this unit, you should be able to

- Understand the basic characteristics of computers,
- Understand how the computers evolved,
- Understand the components that make up a computer,
- Differentiate between hardware and software,
- Differentiate between system and application software,
- Understand the difference between bits and bytes,
- Classify devices as input and output devices,
- Differentiate between ROM and RAM, and
- Appreciate the use of various secondary storage devices.

WHY COMPUTER?

The word 'Computer' literally means to 'Compute' or to 'Calculate'. Stated simply, it is an electronic device which processes information based on the instructions provided, to generate the desired output. It, therefore, requires two types of input – raw data, and the set of instructions to process or act upon the data.

This can schematically be shown in Figure.

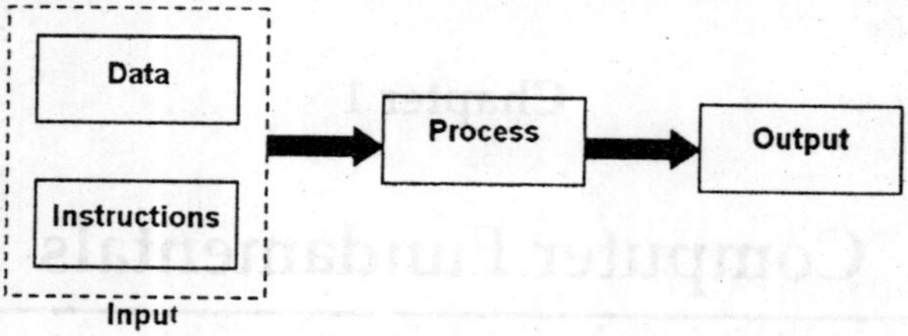

Fig. Processing Information

Data can be of any type – text, numeric, alpha-numeric, image, picture, sound etc. The instructions that act upon this data are also called the programme or software in computer terminology.

CHARACTERISTICS OF COMPUTERS

The characteristics of computers that have made them so powerful and universally useful are speed, accuracy, diligence, versatility and storage capacity.

Speed

Computers work at an incredible speed. The speed with which it performs is way beyond human capabilities. As a comparison, it can do in one minute what a human being would probably take a lifetime!

When we refer to the speed of computers, we now talk in terms of milliseconds (hundredth of a second), microseconds (millionth of a second), nanoseconds (billionth of a second), and even picoseconds (trillionth of a second). A powerful computer is capable of performing about 3-4 million simple instructions per second.

Accuracy

In addition to being fast, computers are also accurate. Errors that may occur can almost always be attributed to human error (inaccurate data, poorly designed system or faulty instructions/programmes written by the programmer) rather than technological weaknesses. In fact, a special term GIGO (Garbage In Garbage Out) has been coined to represent a scenario where faulty results are got due to inaccurate instructions or faulty data.

Diligence

Unlike human beings, computers are highly consistent. They do not suffer from human traits of boredom and tiredness resulting in lack of concentration. Computers, therefore, score high over human beings in performing voluminous and repetitive jobs.

Versatility

Computers are versatile machines and are capable of performing any task as long as it can be broken down into a series of logical steps. This means that their capability is, once again, limited only by human intelligence. As is evident, in today's fast developing technology-world, it is almost inconceivable to find an area where computers are not being used. The presence of computers can be seen in every sphere – Railway/Air reservation, Banks, Hotels, Weather forecasting and many more.

Storage Capacity

Today's computers can store volumes of data. Unlike human memory where unimportant information is relegated to the back of the mind and forgotten as time progresses, a piece of information once recorded (or stored) in the computer, can never be forgotten and can be retrieved almost instantaneously! Information can, therefore, be retained as long as desired (using secondary storage – a type of detachable memory).

Identify the characteristics of a computer that have contributed towards making it such a popular device.

EVOLUTION OF COMPUTERS

The history of computers can be traced back to almost 2000 years ago, with the advent of abacus, a wooden rack holding two horizontal wires with beads strung on them. Numbers are represented using the position of beads on the rack. Fast and simple calculations can be carried out by appropriately placing the beads.

In 1620, an English mathematician by the name *William Oughtred* invented the slide rule – a calculating device based on the principle of logarithms. It consisted of two graduated scales devised in such a manner that suitable alignment of one scale against the other, made it possible to perform additions, compute products etc. just by inspection.

Blaise Pascal, a French mathematician, is usually credited for building the first digital computer in 1642. He invented the mechanical calculating machine. Numbers were entered in this machine by dialing a series of numbered wheels. Another series of toothed wheels transferred the movements to a dial, which showed the results.

In 1671, *Gottfried von Leibnitz,* a German mathematician, invented a calculating machine which was able to add and perform multiplications. He invented a special stepped gear mechanism for introducing the addend digits, which is still being used.

The prototypes made by *Pascal* and *Leibnitz* were not used in many places. It was only about a century later that *Thomas of Colmar* created the first successful mechanical calculator which could add, subtract, multiply, and divide. A lot of improved desktop calculators by various inventors followed, such that by 1890 a range of improvements like accumulation of partial results, storage of past results, and printing of results were not uncommon.

THE FIRST COMPUTER

Charles Babbage, a professor of mathematics at Cambridge University, England, realised that many long calculations usually consisted of a series of actions that were constantly repeated and hence could possibly be automated. By 1822, he designed an automatic calculating machine that he called the 'Difference Engine'. It was intended to be steam powered and fully automatic (including printing of result tables), commanded by a fixed instruction programme. In short, he developed a prototype of a computer which was 100 years ahead of time and is, therefore, considered as the father of modern day computers.

A step towards automated computing was the development of punched cards which were first successfully used by *Herman Hollerith,* who worked in the US Census Bureau in 1890. He along with *James Powers* developed devices that could read information that had been punched into cards, without any human help. This resulted in reduced reading errors, increased workflow and availability of unlimited memory (punched cards could be used as easily accessible memory of unlimited size).

These advantages were seen by various commercial companies and soon led to the development of improved punch-card using computers by companies like International Business Machines (IBM) and Remington.

SOME WELL KNOWN EARLY COMPUTERS

Mark I

After World War II there was a need felt for advanced calculations. By that time, many reliable mechanical desk calculators had been developed. *Howard A. Aiken* of Harvard University, while working on his doctorate in physics, in the year 1937, designed a machine that could automatically perform a sequence of arithmetic operations. He completed this in 1944 and named it Mark I. This machine performed a multiplication and division at an average of about four and eleven seconds respectively. The results were printed at a rate of one result per five seconds.

ENIAC

The World War II also produced a large need for computer capacity especially for the military. New weapons were made for which trajectory tables and other essential data were needed. In 1942, Professors

John P. Eckert and *John W. Mauchly* at the Moore School of Engineering of the University of Pennsylvania, USA, decoded to build a high speed computer to do the job. This was called the Electronic Numeric Integrator and Calculator (ENIAC).

It used 18,000 vacuum tubes, about 1,800 square feet of floor space, and consumed about 180,000 watts of electrical power. It had punched cards I/O and its programmes were wired on boards.

ENIAC is accepted as the first successful high-speed electronic digital computer and was used from 1946 to 1955.

EDVAC

Fascinated by the success of ENIAC, *John Von Neumann*, a mathematician, undertook an abstract study of computation in 1945. In this he aimed to show that a computer should be able to execute any kind of computation by means of a proper programmed control. His ideas, referred to as 'stored programme technique', became essential for future generations of high-speed digital computers and were universally accepted. The basic idea behind the stored programme concept was that data as well as instructions can be stored in the computer's memory to enable automatic flow of operations.

Between 1947 and 1950, the More School personnel and the Ballistics Research Laboratory of the US army built a computer named Electronic Discrete Variable Automatic Computer (EDVAC), which was based on Von Neumann's concept of stored programme.

UNIVAC

The Universal Automatic Computer (UNIVAC), developed in 1951, was the first digital computer to be produced and was installed in the Census Bureau.

The first-generation stored-programme computers needed a lot of maintenance, reached 70per cent to 80per cent reliability of operations and were used for almost 10 years. EDVAC and UNIVAC fell into this group of computers and were the first commercially available computers.

Computer Generations

Generation' in computer terminology is a 'step' ahead in technology. As you go through the history of evolution of s, you will find that the earliest computers were big onsumed a lot of power and heated up quickly, due h it had to be shut down, frequently to be cooled. They very expensive in terms of development and enance.

s technology improved, computers became compact, r and more powerful. From a user's perspective, they become user friendly and more affordable. This has largely contributed towards the popularity that computers have gained these days.

The term 'generation' was earlier used only to distinguish between varying hardware technologies but was later extended to include both hardware and software. A comparison of generations is made below.

First Generation Computers (1940 to 1956)

The first generation of computers was characterized by vacuum tubes in the circuitry and magnetic drums for memory.

These computers were enormous in size, used great deal of electricity and were expensive to operate. They also had limited storage capacity.

First generation computers relied on machine language (binary-coded programme) to perform operations and could solve only one problem at a time. Punched cards and paper tapes were used to input data and instructions, and output was displayed on printouts.

Early computers like ENIAC, EDVAC and UNIVAC can all be classified as first generation computers.

Second Generation Computers (1956 to 1963)

In the early 1950s, the discoveries of Transistor and Magnetic core memory changed the image of computers – from unreliable to highly reliable machines with increased capability, and higher storage capacity.

The transistor was far superior to the vacuum tube, allowing computers to become smaller in size, cheaper, reliable and more energy efficient. Though transistor still generated a great deal of heat, it was a substantial improvement ove vacuum tube.

Second generation of computers was also characterized b allowing programmers to specify instructions in symbolic (or assembly) language rather than cryptic binary machine language. High level programming languages like COmmon Business Oriented Language (COBOL) and FORmula TRANslation (FORTRAN) were also being developed at this time. Due to the increase in the cost of expanding programming, these machines were expensive to purchase and operate. Such computers were, therefore, mostly found in large computer centres or government/private laboratories with many programmers and support professionals.

Third Generation Computers (1964 to 1971)

The development of Integrated Circuit by *Jack Kilby*, an engineer with Texas Instruments, in 1958, was the hallmark of the third generation of computers. Punched cards and printouts gave way to devices like keyboards and monitors making it easier for the user to interact with the computer. Computer manufacturers could provide a range of accessories like the cathode ray tube display devices, page printers, consoles etc.

Existence of an operating system allowed the device to run various applications at one time with the central programme monitoring the memory.

For the first time, computers were being widely used in business for areas like:

- Accounting
- Payroll
- Billing
- Tracking Inventory, etc.

Third generation computers were substantially smaller and cheaper than their predecessors.

Fourth Generation Computers (1971 to present) The trend in 1970s was to move from single-purpose but powerful computers towards cheaper computer systems that could support a large range of applications.

A new revolution in computer hardware came about which could shrink the computer logic circuitry and its components using the Large Scale Integration (LSI) technology. Hundreds of components could now fit onto a single chip!

Fig. IC Chips

Fig. Intel Pentium Microprocessor Chip

In the 1980s, Very Large Scale Integration (VLSI) squeezed hundreds of thousands of components onto a single chip. This shrinking trend continued and led to the introduction of personal computers (PCs) – programmable machines that are small enough and inexpensive so that these can be purchased and used by individuals. Companies like Apple Computers and IBM introduced very successful PCs.

The IC technology was not only used to construct the processor, but also for the construction of memory. The first memory chip was constructed in 1970 and could hold 256 bits.

Fifth Generation Computers (the Road Ahead)

The fifth generation of computers characterized by artificial intelligence is in the process of development. The goal here is to develop devices that are capable of learning and responding to natural language input. This generation of computers is using new technologies in very large scale integration, along with new programming languages and will be capable of amazing feats, in the area of artificial intelligence, such as voice recognition. What unique features classify computers into different generations?

COMPONENTS OF A COMPUTER

The computer system essentially comprises three important parts – input device, central processing unit (CPU) and the output device. The CPU itself is made of three components namely, the arithmetic logic unit (ALU), memory unit, and the control unit. In addition to these, auxiliary storage/secondary storage devices are used to store data and instructions on a long-term basis.

Input Unit

Data and instructions must be entered into the computer system for processing, and results obtained from computations must be displayed or recorded for the user. The input device serves the purpose of receiving data and instructions in a form that can be understood by the computer.

Central Processing Unit

Data and instructions (programmes) are stored in the computer's memory after which all the major calculations and computations are carried out within the CPU. The CPU is also responsible for controlling the operations of various units of the computer system.

Arithmetic Logic Unit (ALU)

All calculations and comparisons, based on the instructions provided, are carried out within the ALU. It performs arithmetic functions like addition, subtraction, multiplication, division and also logical operations like greater than, less than and equal to.

Main Memory

The main memory holds data and instructions after input, till they are needed. It also holds the processed results that are awaiting output.

Control

The function of the control unit is to execute the instructions of a programme, one by one, in the desired sequence. It interprets each instruction and then prompts its execution by one of the units like input, output, ALU, storage.

For example, a comparison of two numbers (a logical operation) to be performed by the ALU may require loading the two numbers into the main memory which is a function performed by the control unit. It will then pass on the execution of the 'compare' function to the ALU.

Output Unit

The processed data, stored in the memory of the computer is sent to the output unit, which then converts it into a form that can be understood by the user. The output is usually produced in one of the two ways – on the display device, or on paper (hard copy).

Secondary Storage

Also termed as 'auxiliary' or 'backup' storage, it is typically used as a supplement to main storage. It is much cheaper than the main storage and stores large amount of data and instructions permanently. Hardware devices like magnetic tapes and disks fall under this category.

HARDWARE VS SOFTWARE

The electrical, electronic, mechanical and magnetic components that make up the computer system are together termed as 'hardware'. These include components that are responsible for user input, display and mathematical processing. The CPU, disk drives, internal chips and wiring, modem, peripheral devices like the monitor, keyboard, mouse, printer, speakers etc. are together termed as computer hardware. Computer hardware cannot perform any manipulation or calculation without being instructed as to what to do and how to do it. Programmes (or instructions) are required to tell the computer what to do. The generic term for computer programmes is 'software'. Software comes in two main types – system software and application programmes.

SYSTEM VS APPLICATIONS SOFTWARE

System software consists of programmes that control the operations of the computer system itself. It consists of a group of programmes that control the operations of a computer equipment including functions like managing memory, managing peripherals, loading, storing, and is an interface between the application programmes and the computer. MS DOS (Microsoft's Disk Operating System), UNIX are examples of system software. Software that can perform a specific task for the user, such as word processing, accounting, budgeting or payroll, fall under the category of application software. Such programmes run on top of an operating system (like Windows, UNIX, Linux, Macintosh) and are used to carry out specific functions. Word processors, spreadsheets, database management systems are all examples of general purpose application programmes.

BITS AND BYTES

All information in the computer is handled using electrical components like the integrated circuits, semiconductors, all of which can recognize only two states – presence or absence of an electrical signal. Two symbols used to represent these two states are 0 and 1, and are known as BITS (an abbreviation for BInary DigiTS). 0 represents the absence of a signal, 1 represents the presence of a signal. A BIT is, therefore, the smallest unit of data in a computer and can either store a or 1.

Since a single bit can store only one of the two values, there can possibly be only four unique combinations:

00 01 10 11

Bits are, therefore, combined together into larger units in order to hold greater range of values. BYTES are typically a sequence of eight bits put together to create a single computer alphabetical or numerical character. More often referred to in larger multiples, bytes may appear as Kilobytes (1,024 bytes), Megabytes (1,048,576 bytes), Giga Bytes (1,073,741,824), TeraBytes (approx. 1,099,511,000,000 bytes), or PetaBytes (approx. 1,125,899,900, 000,000 bytes).

Bytes are used to quantify the amount of data digitally stored (on disks, tapes) or transmitted (over the internet), and are also used to measure the memory and document size.

State TRUE or FALSE

– All code or data is stored and processed in computers using two symbols – 0 and 1

– A 'Byte' is a group of four bits and is often used to store characters.

INPUT AND OUTPUT DEVICES

The computer will be of no use unless it is able to communicate with the outside world. Input/Output devices are required for users to communicate with the computer. In simple terms, input devices bring information INTO the computer and output devices bring information OUT of a computer system. These input/output devices are also known as peripherals since they surround the CPU and memory of a computer system.

Some commonly used Input/Output devices are listed in table below.

Input Devices	Output Devices
	Keyboard
	Mouse
	Joystick
	Scanner
	Light Pen
	Touch Screen Monitor
	LCD
	Printer
	Plotter

INPUT DEVICES

Keyboard

It is a text base input device that allows the user to input alphabets, numbers and other characters. It consists of a set of keys mounted on a board.

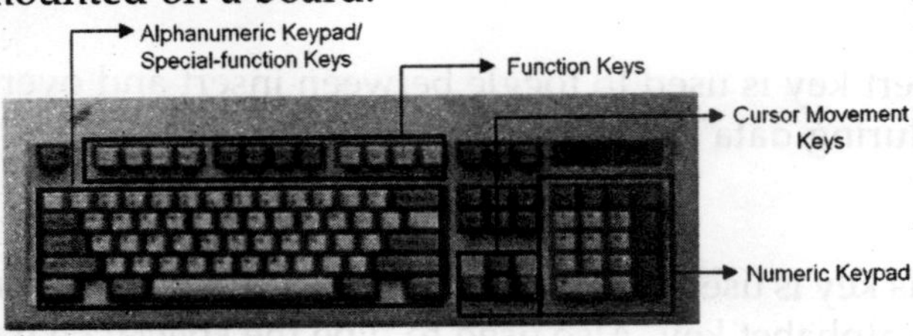

mounted on a board.

Fig. Qwerty Keyboard Layout

Alphanumeric Keypad

It consists of keys for English alphabets, 0 to 9 numbers, and special characters like + - / * () etc.

Function Keys

There are twelve function keys labeled F1, F2, F3, ..., F12. The functions assigned to these keys differ from one software package to another. These keys are also user programmable keys.

Special-function Keys

These keys have special functions assigned to them and can be used only for those specific purposes. Functions of some of the important keys are defined below.

Enter

It is similar to the 'return' key of the typewriter and is used to execute a command or programme.

Spacebar

It is used to enter a space at the current cursor location.

Backspace

This key is used to move the cursor one position to the left and also delete the character in that position.

Delete

It is used to delete the character at the cursor position.

Insert

Insert key is used to toggle between insert and overwrite mode during data entry.

Shift

This key is used to type capital letters when pressed along with an alphabet key. Also used to type the special characters located on the upper-side of a key that has two characters defined on the same key.

Caps Lock

Cap Lock is used to toggle between the capital lock feature. When 'on', it locks the alphanumeric keypad for capital letters input only.

Tab

Tab is used to move the cursor to the next tab position defined in the document. Also, it is used to insert indentation into a document.

Ctrl

Control key is used in conjunction with other keys to provide additional functionality on the keyboard.

Alt

Also like the control key, Alt key is always used in combination with other keys to perform specific tasks.

Esc

This key is usually used to negate a command. Also used to cancel or abort executing programmes.

Numeric Keypad

Numeric keypad is located on the right side of the keyboard and consists of keys having numbers (0 to 9) and mathematical operators (+ - * /) defined on them. This keypad is provided to support quick entry for numeric data.

Cursor Movement Keys

These are arrow keys and are used to move the cursor in the direction indicated by the arrow (up, down, left, right).

MOUSE

The mouse is a small device used to point to a particular place on the screen and select in order to perform one or more actions.

It can be used to select menu commands, size windows, start programmes etc.

The most conventional kind of mouse has two buttons on top: the left one being used most frequently.

Fig. Mouse

Mouse Actions

Left Click: Used to select an item.

Double Click: Used to start a programme or open a file.

Right Click: Usually used to display a set of commands.

Drag and Drop: It allows you to select and move an item from one location to another. To achieve this place the cursor over an item on the screen, click the left mouse button and while holding the button down move the cursor to where you want to place the item, and then release it.

Joystick

The joystick is a vertical stick which moves the graphic cursor in a direction the stick is moved. It typically has a button on top that is used to select the option pointed by the cursor. Joystick is used as an input device primarily used with video games, training simulators and controlling robots.

Scanner

Scanner is an input device used for direct data entry from the source document into the computer system. It converts the document image into digital form so that it can be fed into the computer. Capturing information like this reduces the possibility of errors typically experienced during large data entry.

Fig. A Flat-bed Scanner

Hand-held scanners are commonly seen in big stores to scan codes and price information for each of the items.

Light Pen

It is a pen shaped device used to select objects on a display screen. It is quite like the mouse (in its functionality) but uses a light pen to move the pointer and select any object on the screen by pointing to the object.

Users of Computer Aided Design (CAD) applications commonly use the light pens to directly draw on screen.

Touch Screen

It allows the user to operate/make selections by simply touching the display screen. Common examples of touch screen include information kiosks, and bank ATMs.

OUTPUT DEVICES

Monitor

Fig. Monitor

Monitor is an output device that resembles the television screen and uses a Cathode Ray Tube (CRT) to display information. The monitor is associated with a keyboard for manual input of characters and displays the information as it is keyed in. It also displays the programme or application output. Like the television, monitors are also available in different sizes.

Liquid Crystal Display (LCD)

LCD was introduced in the 1970s and is now applied to display terminals also. Its advantages like low energy consumption, smaller and lighter have paved its way for usage in portable computers (laptops).

Printer

Printers are used to produce paper (commonly known as hardcopy) output. Based on the technology used, they can be classified as Impact or Non-impact printers. Impact printers use the typewriting printing mechanism wherein a hammer strikes the paper through a ribbon in order to produce output.

Dot-matrix and Character printers fall under this category. Non-impact printers do not touch the paper while printing. They use chemical, heat or electrical signals to etch the symbols on paper.

Inkjet, Deskjet, Laser, Thermal printers fall under this category of printers.

When we talk about printers we refer to two basic qualities associated with printers: resolution, and speed. Print resolution is measured in terms of number of dots per inch (dpi). Print speed is measured in terms of number of characters printed in a unit of time and is represented as characters-per-second (cps), lines-per-minute (lpm), or pages-per-minute (ppm).

Plotter

Plotters are used to print graphical output on paper. It interprets computer commands and makes line drawings on paper using multicoloured automated pens. It is capable of producing graphs, drawings, charts, maps etc.

Fig. A Flatbed Plotter

Computer Aided Engineering (CAE) applications like CAD (Computer Aided Design) and CAM (Computer Aided Manufacturing) are typical usage areas for plotters.

RAM/ROM

Computer's memory can be classified into two types – RAM and ROM.

RAM or Random Access Memory is the central storage unit in a computer system. It is the place in a computer where the operating system, application programmes and the data in current use are kept temporarily so that they can be accessed by the computer's processor. The more RAM a computer has, the more data a computer can manipulate.

Random access memory, also called the Read/Write memory, is the temporary memory of a computer. It is said to be 'volatile' since its contents are accessible only as long as the computer is on. The contents of RAM are cleared once the computer is turned off.

ROM or Read Only Memory is a special type of memory which can only be read and contents of which are not lost even when the computer is switched off. It typically contains manufacturer's instructions. Among other things, ROM also stores an initial programme called the 'bootstrap loader' whose function is to start the computer software operating, once the power is turned on.

Read-only memories can be manufacturer-programmed or user-programmed. While manufacturer-programmed

ROMs have data burnt into the circuitry, user-programmed ROMs can have the user load and then store read-only programmes. PROM or Programmable ROM is the name given to such ROMs.

Information once stored on the ROM or PROM chip cannot be altered. However, another type of memory called EPROM (Erasable PROM) allows a user to erase the information stored on the chip and reprogram it with new information. EEPROM (Electrically EPROM) and UVEPROM are two types of EPROMs.

SECONDARY STORAGE DEVICES

RAM is volatile memory having a limited storage capacity. Secondary/auxiliary storage is storage other than the RAM. These include devices that are peripheral and are connected and controlled by the computer to enable permanent storage of programmes and data.

Magnetic medium was found to be fairly inexpensive and long lasting medium and, therefore, became the preferred choice for auxiliary storage. Floppy disks and hard disks fall under this category. The newer forms of storage devices are optical storage devices like CDs, DVDs, Pen drive, Zip drive etc.

Floppy Disk

These are small removable disks that are plastic coated with magnetic recording material. Floppy disks are typically 3.5² in size (diameter) and can hold 1.44 MB of data. This portable storage device is a rewritable media and can be reused a number of times.

Floppy disks are commonly used to move files between different computers. The main disadvantage of floppy disks is that they can be damaged easily and, therefore, are not very reliable.

Hard Disk

Hard disks are made up of rigid material and are usually a stack of metal disks sealed in a box. The hard disk and the hard disk drive exist together as a unit and are a permanent part of the computer where data and programmes are saved. These disks have storage capacities ranging from 1GB to 80 GB and more. Hard disks are also rewritable and are more reliable when compared with floppies.

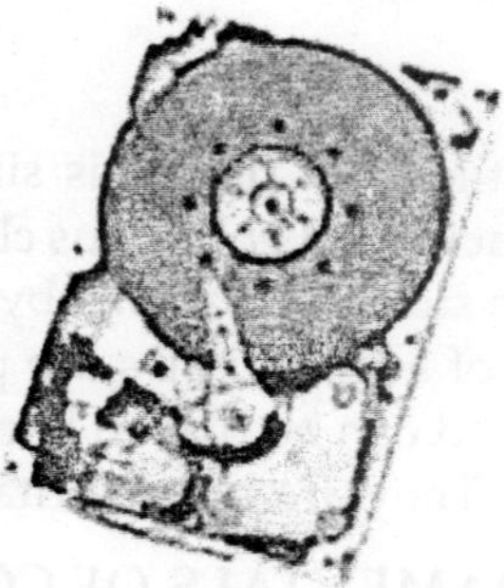

Fig. A Floppy Disk

Fig. A Winchester Disk

Depending on the way they are packaged, hard disks can be classified as Disk packs or Winchester disks. Disk packs are removable, in the sense that they can be removed and kept offline when not in use. They must be mounted on the disk drive before use. Winchester disks on the other hand, consist of disk platters sealed in a contamination-free container and form a permanent component of the computer.

CD

Cmpact Disk (CD) is portable disk having data storage capacity between 650-700 MB. It can hold large amount of information such as music, full-motion videos, and text etc. It contains digital information that can be read, but cannot be rewritten. Separate drives exist for reading and writing CDs.

Since it is a very reliable storage media, it is very often used as a medium for distributing large amount of information to large number of users. In fact today most of the software is distributed through CDs.

DVD

Digital Versatile Disk (DVD) is similar to a CD but has larger storage capacity and enormous clarity. Depending upon the disk type it can store several Gigabytes of data (as opposed to around 650MB of a CD). DVDs are primarily used to store music or movies and can be played back on your television or the computer too. They are not rewritable media.

FUNDAMENTALS OF COMPUTER

Richard Hamming, a former researcher at Bell Labs, once observed that a change of an order of magnitude in quantity causes a change in quality.

A racing car that can go 1000 km/hour in the Nevada desert is a fundamentally different machine than a normal car that goes 100 km/hour on a highway. Similarly, a 100-story skyscraper is not just a scaled up 10-story apartment building. So, too, with computers.

Type	Price	Example Application
Disposable computer	1	Greeting cards
Embedded computer	10	Watches, toys, appliances
Palmtop computer	100	Home video games, PDA
Personal computer	1K	Desktop or laptop computer
Server or workstation	10K	Network server, professional use
Workstation clusters	100K	Departmental mini-supercomputers
Mainframe computer	1M	Batch data processing in a bank
Supercomputer	10M	Weather prediction

DISPOSABLE COMPUTER

Single chips, perhaps glued to the inside of greeting cards, play tunes such as "Happy Birthday" or "Here Comes the Bride".

SMART CARDS

A smart card is a credit-card sized plastic card with an embedded computer chip. The chip can either be a microprocessor with internal memory or a memory chip with non-programmable logic. The chip connection is either via direct physical contact or remotely via a contactless electromagnetic interface.

ACTIVE BADGES

The Active Badge system provides a means of locating individuals within a building by determining the location of their Active Badge. This small device worn by personnel transmits a unique infra-red signal every 10 seconds.

EMBEDDED COMPUTERS

Computers embedded inside telephones, microwave ovens, cameras, CD players, toys, dolls, and a thousand other devices. Within a few years, almost everything electrical will have a computer in it.

The number of embedded computers will be measured in the billons, dwarfing all other computers combined by orders of magnitude. These computers hold a processor, less than a megabyte of memory, and I/O capability.

PALMTOP COMPUTERS

Computers the size of a credit card, cell-phone, or calculator. Portable digital assistants, limited graphical display. These systems typically contain a few megabytes of memory, a small display, and a touch sensitive input area or limited keyboard.

PERSONAL COMPUTERS

Personal computers, including both desktop and notebook devices, that are most associated with the word computer.

Personal computers come with many megabytes of memory, hard disks in the gigabytes, DVD or CD drives, keyboard, pointing devices, full-size display, multimedia, and communication devices.

SERVER OR WORKSTATION

High-performance computers, often with multiple processors, with gigabytes of memory, terabytes of disk space, and high-speed networking capability.

The Sun Ultra™ 80 workstation brings multiprocessing power, industry-standard PCI I/O, and dual-UPA graphics capability to the desktop. This next-generation workstation uses the processing power of UltraSPARC™ -II processors, PGX32™ and Sun Elite3D and Expert3D graphics technology, UltraSCSI disks, and the innovative high-performance peripheral component interconnect (PCI) I/O bus. With the tower system enclosure, Sun Ultra 80 workstation provides all the modular and expandable features that users have grown to expect from Sun Workstation™ systems. Sun's commitment to high-performance computing means the Ultra 80 workstation delivers increasing levels of performance and preserves 100 percent binary compatibility with application software.

WORKSTATION CLUSTERS

Standard workstations connected by advanced networks, and running special software that allow all the machines to work together on a single problem or application.

Included here are "farms" of network servers, graphics rendering machines, and enterprise-support systems.

Clusters scale easily from a handful of machines to thousands of them.

Avalon

Avalon is a 140 processor Alpha Beowulf cluster constructed entirely from commodity personal computer technology. It is a co-operative venture of the Los Alamos National Laboratory Centre for Nonlinear Studies and Theoretical Division.

MAINFRAMES

Room-size computers with massive storage systems, extensive I/O capability, and capable of handing enormous numbers of transactions.

These are the direct descendants of the corporate computing facilities first acquired decades ago. While extremely expensive, they are often kept running because of the enormous investment in software, data, operating procedures, and personnel that they represent.

Mainframes are notorious as the source of the Year 2000 problems caused by COBOL or FORTRAN programmes written in the 1960s and 1970s by programmers who never envisioned their software lasting three or four decades.

UNISYS ES7000 SERVER

A CMP-based ES7000 contains numerous "cells" to form

a powerful, reliable, agile, and cost-effective Intel® mainframe. These cells can be configured flexibly to create a server with:

- as many as 32 CPUs
- 4 crossbar intra-connects
- 256MB of third-level cache
- 64GB of memory
- 96 PCI adapters

with partitions running up to eight operating systems

Supercomputers

Supercomputers have extremely fast CPUs, disks and networks. Typically they are highly parallel machines, similar to workstation clusters, but with faster components and specialized processors.

Supercomputers are used to solve computationally intensive problems in science and engineering, such as modeling climate systems, modeling fluid-flow systems such as aircraft structures, synthesizing new molecules for medical or genetic studies, and simulating large economics systems.

Ohio Supercomputer Centre

The CRAY SV1 computer system at the Ohio Supercomputer Centre (OSC) is a powerful parallel vector processor (PVP) super-computer that features 16 (500 MHz) vector processors and 32 Gbytes of physical RAM for large memory jobs. Serial jobs, auto-tasked and parallel jobs are scheduled on the 16 single streaming processors (SSP). Four of the SV1 SSP processors can be combined into one multi-streaming processor (MSP). Multi-streaming is a feature that automatically divides loop iterations among the four CPUs. You may get speedup factors of up to four on loops to which this technique can be applied.

Chapter 2

Central Processing Unit and Operating System

A CPU and memory aren't much use without a keyboard and screen, and a disk drive, i.e. a useful computer is actually a computer system.

Figure shows the organisation of a simple computer system with one CPU, memory and three input-output (I/O) devices - *peripherals*: a disk and a keyboard & screen. As always, the components are connected by a system bus - this is the same as the bus mentioned above; communication with peripherals can be done in a manner similar to memory reading/writing.

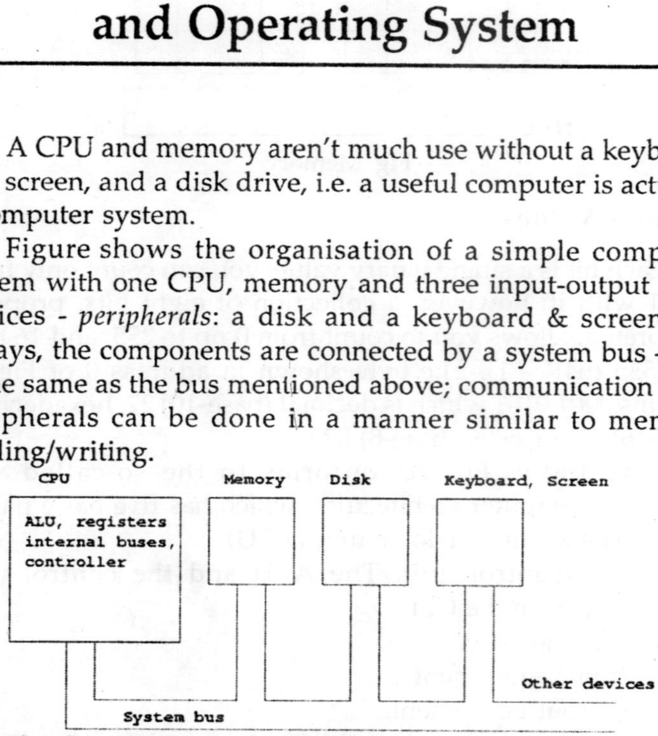

Fig. Organisation of a Simple Computer System

Figure shows main memory; it is essentially a sequential collection of cells, each of which, typically, can store eight binary digits - bits - BInary digiTs. Each bit is like a *sub-cell* that can be '0' or '1'. Bits have much in common with light-bulbs - they are either on - value 1, or off - value 0.

We commonly term a collection of eight bits a byte.

Each cell has an address.

Addresses run from 0 to N-1, where N is the size of the memory; on a typical PC these days, N is 64 Mega(bytes) - Mega = million, well actually 1048576 = 2^{20}.

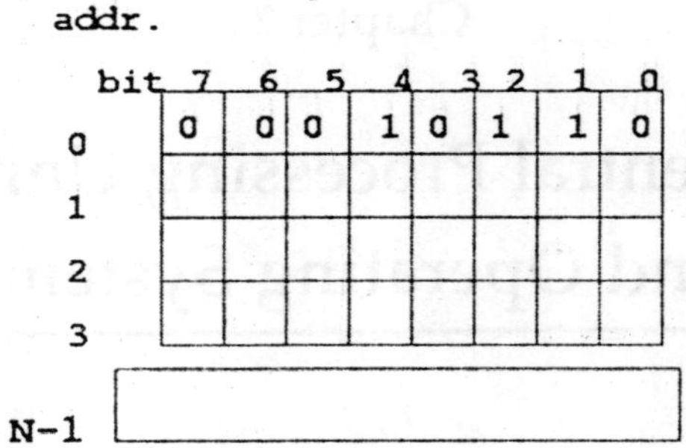

Fig. Memory

Numeric Values

Each bit is a single binary value: you can count only from 0 to 1 with it; however, a collection of eight bits, properly interpreted, allows you to count from 0 up to 255; and 16 bits, 0...65535 (64K - 1). The byte shown in address 0 of Figure contains 0001 0101 which is decimal (base-10) 22, hexadecimal (base-16) 15, or octal (base-8) 025..

Essentially, Figure conforms to the so-called von Neumann computer architecture, which has five basic parts:

1. The arithmetic-logic unit (ALU).
2. The control unit. The ALU and the control unit comprise the CPU.
3. The memory.
4. Input equipment.
5. Output equipment.

As we have already said, memory may contain, in addition to data, programme instructions - coded as numbers. One major breakthrough of the von Neumann architecture was that data - the things that are processed - and instructions - that describe the processing to be done - are both numbers, and both reside in the same memory.

However, *inside the machine,* there is nothing to distinguish data from instructions, nor, for that matter, data from addresses - except in how they are used.

A memory location, therefore, can store:

- True numerical values.
- Numerical values which are eventually translated to other meanings, e.g. ASCII text character codes.
- Addresses (of other locations, cells) - pointers, indirection.
- Programme instructions.

CENTRAL PROCESSING UNIT

INTRODUCTION

As indicated, the CPU consists of an Arithmetic-Logic-Unit (ALU) - the calculator, and a controller - to do the fetching and executing of the programme instructions; in addition, we need a few local memory registers - for storage of temporary data, and buses to transfer data and addresses throughout the CPU.

ARITHMETIC LOGIC UNIT - ALU

The ALU is the calculator part. The ALU takes the contents of ALU input buses A and B and combines them in some way (add, subtract, logical OR, etc.) and passes the result onto a C data bus. Let us assume that this is a 16-bit machine, i.e. the buses and ALU take 16-bit numbers - they are 16-bits wide.

A simple ALU is shown in Figure . It has a number of functions which are selected by function selection control lines F; the control lines are equivalent to selecting the operation on a calculator, e.g. add, subtract. Two condition flags are output: N, set to 1 if last operation caused a negative result; Z, last operation, if a zero result; result flags are important for constructing conditional instructions (if, else).

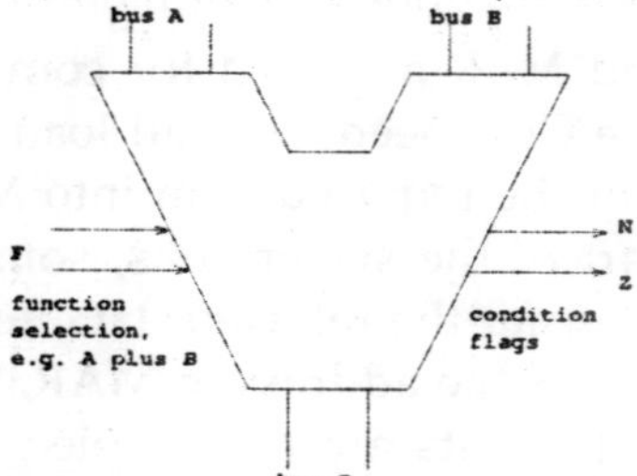

Fig. Arithmetic and Logic Unit (ALU)

SIMPLIFIED CPU

Figure gives a view of a simplified CPU - but not so simplified that we cannot describe how an actual programme might operate in it; with few additions figure would actually work. The major thing we have left out is control.

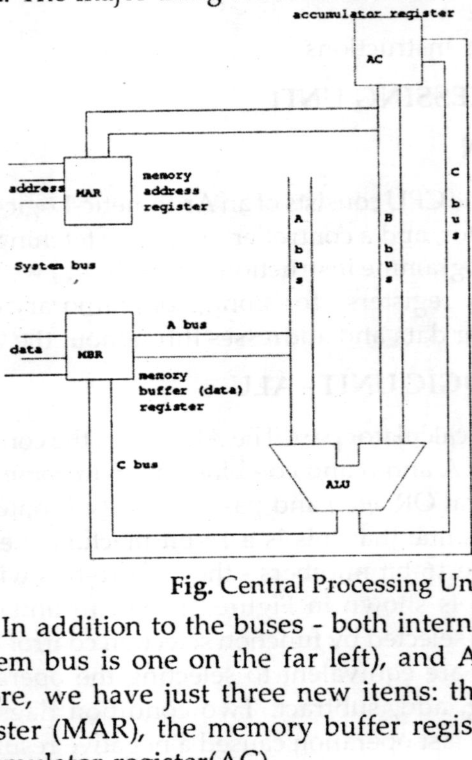

Fig. Central Processing Unit

In addition to the buses - both internal and system - the system bus is one on the far left), and ALU, all mentioned before, we have just three new items: the memory address register (MAR), the memory buffer register (MBR), and the accumulator register(AC).

Conceptually, registers are no different from main memory cells.

The MAR and MBR are used for communicating with memory: when the CPU needs to read load from memory, it puts the address of the required item into MAR, asserts *read* on the control part of the system bus, some time later, the system bus will transfer the relevant data item into the MBR; for write store, it puts the address in MAR, the data in MBR, and asserts *write*, the data are then copied into the relevant memory location.

The AC is used as a general holding register for operand (input) data and results.

All will become clear if we return to the example programme statement:

z = x + y;

As in the introduction, assume that z corresponds to location 2, x to 0, and y to 1. The programme, as it would appear in machine instructions, is:

P1.

Load contents of location 0 (x, 22) into AC.

P2.

Add contents of 1 (y, 33) to AC, with result going to AC.

P3.

Store contents of AC in location 2 (z).

VIRTUAL MACHINES, ABSTRACTION, LEVELS OF CONCERN

Here, and in other modules, you will frequently encounter the term *abstraction,* most often in the context of an antidote to *complexity*. It crops up under a variety of guises: separation of concerns, structured levels, modular this and that, information hiding, modelling.

A dictionary definition of abstraction (the verb) is: the process of considering (extracting) certain essential properties of objects while omitting other properties that are not relevant (usually inessential details); the act of abstraction or abstracting produces an abstraction (noun) which collectively refers to the set of chosen properties.

From our point of view abstraction does have two important facets which are related but different, namely, extraction (of the essential from the inessential) and idealisation (i.e. the irrelevant details are deviations from the ideal). Often, somewhat loosely, an abstraction may be called a model. In the following paragraphs I give examples of abstraction applied to computing and more mundane fields.

Systems Engineering

Systems engineering, in general, is one of the great

breakthroughs of the 20th century. Without it, only very clever people, who could carry the plans for the total system (cathedral, television, satellite...) in their heads, could be effective engineers. With systems engineering a bit of clever decomposition can yield a problem that is solvable by teams of mere mortals.

The key concept here is probably that of a *black-box* abstraction; a black-box is completely characterised by: (a) what it expects as inputs; (b) what it produces as outputs; and (c) the relationship between inputs and outputs.

MULTILEVEL VIEW OF COMPUTING MACHINES ......

It is impossible and undesirable for engineers or programmers to carry in their minds the hundreds of thousands of transistors, resistors, connections..., and software that make up a computer system. Thus it is necessary to decompose (break-up) the system, into chunks or sub-systems. But we have to be methodical about this: if you break a 2,000,000 component computer into 200,000 sub- systems, you are not much further ahead - where next?

A computer can be viewed as a hierarchy of levels as shown below. At any one time you make up your mind what level concerns you.

Level 6 Application Level

Here the computer is viewed as a machine which performs a specific function, e.g. a spreadsheet, a word-processor; the user at this level shouldn't have to be concerned with any details of computer science or engineering, just as the average car driver need not be concerned with the internal details of car engines.

Level 5 High-level Language Level

Here the computer is viewed as a (virtual) machine which obeys the instructions or understands the statements of a high-level language such as C, C++, Java, COBOL, etc. A compiler or interpreter converts these instructions into lower level machine or assembly code.

Level 4 Assembly Language Level

At this level, we view the computer as being run by a programme (a sequence) of so called assembly level instructions.

Here we see instructions that explicitly move data around between registers, accumulators, programme counters, ports and memory addresses; and instructions that transform or combine their contents (e.g. ADDD, SUBD, LODD). To be effective at this level, the programmer must have a model of the machine - its *architecture*, or, more specifically, its *instruction set architecture (ISA)* that properly expresses: (a) the interconnection of registers to indicate allowable data movements, and (b) the repertoire of transformations and combinations that can be performed in the arithmetic-and-logic unit and elsewhere.

Assembly language is just a symbolic form of the language understood by level 2 below (which are coded as numbers). Assembly language is translated into machine language using an *assembler*.

Level 3 Operating System Machine Level

At this level, we have operating system software in charge of running the assembly language. In some contexts, this level is absent.

Level 2 Machine Language Level

Here are the same sort of instructions that we described for the previous level: major difference, they are now coded as numbers, rather than alphanumeric symbols (e.g. 2501 instead of (say) ADDD x). Two points: (a) they are ready for execution in the processor - the Level 1 machine 'understands' them; and, (b) human programmers have great difficulty in understanding them!

Level 1 Microprogram Level

This level is concerned with the (underlying) engine that implements individual Level 2 instructions by appropriately directing the the components and their interconnections at that level. In some (mostly earlier, but also some modern RISC machines) machines this level does not exist and machine instructions are implemented directly by digital logic.

Level 0 Digital Logic Level

Here we are at the level of gates and memory cells. The language is made up of 1s and 0s or, at best, binary numbers.

There are certainly levels below level 0 - transistors, p-n junctions, molecules, atoms,...!), but the six above should be enough for us. In fact, we shall be mainly concerned with level 2 and above, though, just for completeness, we will show how some basic components may be built from digital logic *gates*At each level, the programmer or engineer or physicist must pay attention to different sorts of object or quantity. At level 5 (high-level language,), the programmer deals with the data types provided by the language.

At level 4 you are forced to deal with physical storage locations, registers and the like. And so on, until at level 0 you are concerned with bits (1s and 0s).

The major point is that, the higher the level of abstraction, the more powerful the machine becomes. For example, you want to type a letter on a word-processor. At level 6 you just do it. At level 5 you first have to write a word-processor programme - allocate a few years or so for that! At level 4 you have to write a compiler so that you can write the word-processor - there isn't much point in trying to write a word-processor in assembler, it'll take so long and be so error prone that the project will never end. And so on. Down to level 0, where you first have to make a computer from thousands of chips, then write the microcode,..., then write the compiler, the write the word-processor,..., then type the letter.

The difference between working at level 4 (say) and level 2 is like discovering that you can take 100 metre strides, instead of the 1.5 meters of ordinary mortals.

OPERATING SYSTEMS
OPERATING SYSTEMS I

A batch system is one in which jobs are bundled together

with the instructions necessary to allow them to be processed without intervention.

Often jobs of a similar nature can be bundled together to further increase economy

The basic physical layout of the memory of a batch job computer is shown below:

Monitor (permanently resident)

User Space

(compilers, programmes, data, etc.)

The monitor is system software that is responsible for interpreting and carrying out the instructions in the batch jobs. When the monitor started a job, it handed over control of the entire computer to the job, which then controlled the computer until it finished.

A sample of several batch jobs might look like:

```
JOB user_spec      ; identify the user for accounting purposes
FORTRAN            ; load the FORTRAN compiler
ource programme cards
LOAD               ; load the compiled programme
RUN                ; run the programme
Data cards
EOJ                ; end of job
JOB user_spec      ; identify a new user
LOAD application
RUN
data
EOJ
```

Often magnetic tapes and drums were used to store intermediate data and compiled programmes.

- Advantages of batch systems
  - Move much of the work of the operator to the computer
  - Increased performance since it was possible for job to start as soon as the previous job finished
- Disadvantages
  - Turn-around time can be large from user standpoint
  - More difficult to debug programme

- Due to lack of protection scheme, one batch job can affect pending jobs (read too many cards, etc)
- A job could corrupt the monitor, thus affecting pending jobs
- A job could enter an infinite loop

As mentioned above, one of the major shortcomings of early batch systems was that there was no protection scheme to prevent one job from adversely affecting other jobs.

The solution to this was a simple protection scheme, where certain memory (e.g. where the monitor resides) were made off-limits to user programmes. This prevented user programmes from corrupting the monitor.

To keep user programmes from reading too many (or not enough) cards, the hardware was changed to allow the computer to operate in one of two modes: one for the monitor and one for the user programmes. IO could only be performed in monitor mode, so that IO requests from the user programmes were passed to the monitor. In this way, the monitor could keep a job from reading past it's on $EOJ card.

To prevent an infinite loop, a timer was added to the system and the $JOB card was modified so that a maximum execution time for the job was passed to the monitor. The computer would interrupt the job and return control to the monitor when this time was exceeded.

SPOOLING BATCH SYSTEMS

One difficulty with simple batch systems is that the computer still needs to read the the deck of cards before it can begin to execute the job. This means that the CPU is idle (or nearly so) during these relatively slow operations.

Since it is faster to read from a magnetic tape than from a deck of cards, it became common for computer centres to have one or more less powerful computers in addition to there main computer. The smaller computers were used to read a decks of cards onto a tape, so that the tape would contain many batch jobs. This tape was then loaded on the main computer and the jobs on the tape were executed. The output from the jobs would be written to another tape which would then be removed and loaded on a less powerful computer to produce any hardcopy or other desired output.

It was a logical extension of the timer idea described above to have a timer that would only let jobs execute for a short time before interrupting them so that the monitor could start an IO operation. Since the IO operation could proceed while the CPU was crunching on a user programme, little degradation in performance was noticed.

Since the computer can now perform IO in parallel with computation, it became possible to have the computer read a deck of cards to a tape, drum or disk and to write out to a tape printer while it was computing. This process is called spooling: Simultaneous Peripheral Operation OnLine.

Spooling batch systems were the first and are the simplest of the multiprogramming systems.

One advantage of spooling batch systems was that the output from jobs was available as soon as the job completed, rather than only after all jobs in the current cycle were finished.

MULTIPROGRAMMING SYSTEMS

As machines with more and more memory became available, it was possible to extend the idea of multiprogramming (or multiprocessing) as used in spooling batch systems to create systems that would load several jobs into memory at once and cycle through them in some order, working on each one for a specified period of time.

Monitor
(more like a operating system)
User programme 1
User programme 2
User programme 3
User programme 4

At this point the monitor is growing to the point where it begins to resemble a modern operating system. It is responsible for:

- Starting user jobs
- Spooling operations
- IO for user jobs

- Switching between user jobs
- Ensuring proper protection while doing the above

As a simple, yet common example, consider a machine that can run two jobs at once. Further, suppose that one job is IO intensive and that the other is CPU intensive. One way for the monitor to allocate CPU time between these jobs would be to divide time equally between them. However, the CPU would be idle much of the time the IO bound process was executing.

A good solution in this case is to allow the CPU bound process (the background job) to execute until the IO bound process (the foreground job) needs some CPU time, at which point the monitor permits it to run. Presumably it will soon need to do some IO and the monitor can return the CPU to the background job.

TIMESHARING SYSTEMS

Back in the days of the "bare" computers without any operating system to speak of, the programmer had complete access to the machine. As hardware and software was developed to create monitors, simple and spooling batch systems and finally multiprogrammed systems, the separation between the user and the computer became more and more pronounced.

Users, and programmers in particular, longed to be able to "get to the machine" without having to go through the batch process. In the 1970s and especially in the 1980s this became possible two different ways.

The first involved timesharing or timeslicing. The idea of multiprogramming was extended to allow for multiple terminals to be connected to the computer, with each in-use terminal being associated with one or more jobs on the computer. The operating system is responsible for switching between the jobs, now often called processes, in such a way that favoured user interaction. If the context-switches occurred quickly enough, the user had the impression that he or she had direct access to the computer.

Interactive processes are given a higher priority so that

when IO is requested (e.g. a key is pressed), the associated process is quickly given control of the CPU so that it can process it. This is usually done through the use of an interrupt that causes the computer to realise that an IO event has occurred.

It should be mentioned that there are several different types of time sharing systems. One type is represented by computers like our VAX/VMS computers and UNIX workstations. In these computers entire processes are in memory (albeit virtual memory) and the computer switches between executing code in each of them. In other types of systems, such as airline reservation systems, a single application may actually do much of the timesharing between terminals. This way there does not need to be a different running programme associated with each terminal.

PERSONAL COMPUTERS

The second way that programmers and users got back at the machine was the advent of personal computers around 1980. Finally computers became small enough and inexpensive enough that an individual could own one, and hence have complete access to it.

REAL-TIME, MULTIPROCESSOR, AND DISTRIBUTED/NETWORKED SYSTEMS

A real-time computer is one that execute programmes that are guaranteed to have an upper bound on tasks that they carry out. Usually it is desired that the upper bound be very small. Examples included guided missile systems and medical monitoring equipment.

The operating system on real-time computers is severely constrained by the timing requirements.

Dedicated computers are special purpose computers that are used to perform only one or more tasks. Often these are real-time computers and include applications such as the guided missile mentioned above and the computer in modern cars that controls the fuel injection system.

A multiprocessor computer is one with more than one

CPU. The category of multiprocessor computers can be divided into the following sub-categories:

- Shared memory multiprocessors have multiple CPUs, all with access to the same memory. Communication between the the processors is easy to implement, but care must be taken so that memory accesses are synchronized.
- Distributed memory multiprocessors also have multiple CPUs, but each CPU has it's own associated memory. Here, memory access synchronization is not a problem, but communication between the processors is often slow and complicated.

Related to Multiprocessors are the Following:

- Networked systems consist of multiple computers that are networked together, usually with a common operating system and shared resources. Users, however, are aware of the different computers that make up the system.
- Distributed systems also consist of multiple computers but differ from networked systems in that the multiple computers are transparent to the user. Often there are redundant resources and a sharing of the workload among the different computers, but this is all transparent to the user.

UNIX OPERATING SYSTEM OVERVIEW

UNIX was developed at Bell Labs in the early 1970s. The first version was written by Ken Thompson in assembler for the PDP- 7 minicomputer. This was soon followed by a version for the PDP-ll, written in a new language called C that was devised and implemented by Dennis Ritchie. In 1974, Ritchie and Thompson published a landmark paper about UNIX (Ritchie and Thompson, 1974). For the work described in this paper they were later given the prestigious ACM Turing Award (Ritchie, 1984; Thompson, 1984). The publication of this paper stimulated many universities to ask Bell Labs for a copy of UNIX. Since Bell Labs' parent company, AT&T, was a regulated monopoly at the time and was not permitted to be in the computer business, it had no objection to licensing UNIX to universities for a modest fee.

In one of those coincidences that often shape history, the PDP-11 was the computer of choice at nearly all university computer science departments, and the operating systems that came with the PDP-l1 were widely regarded as being dreadful by professors and students alike. UNIX quickly filled the void, not in the least because it was supplied with the complete source code, so people could, and did, tinker with it endlessly.

One of the many universities that acquired UNIX early on was the University of California at Berkeley. Because the complete source code was available, Berkeley was able to modify the system substantially. Foremost among the changes was a port to the V AX minicomputer and the addition of paged virtual memory, the extension of file names from 14 characters to 255 characters, and the inclusion of the TCP/IP networking protocol, which is now used on the Internet (largely due to the fact that it was in Berkeley UNIX).

While Berkeley was making all these changes, AT&T itself continued to develop UNIX, leading to System III in 1982 and then System V in 1984. By the late 1980s, two different, and quite incompatible, versions of UNIX were in widespread use: Berkeley UNIX and System V. This split in the UNIX world, together with the fact that there were no standards for binary programme formats, greatly inhibited the commercial success of UNIX because it was impossible for software vendors to write and package UNIX programmes with the expectation that they would run on any UNIX system (as was routinely done with MS-DOS). After much bickering, a standard called POSIX (Portable Operating System-IX) was created by the IEEE Standards Board. POSIX is also known by its IEEE Standards number, PlO03. It later became an International Standard.

The POSIX standard is divided into many parts, each covering a different area of UNIX. The first part, PlO03.l, defines the system calls; the second part, PlO03.2, defines the basic utility programmes, and so on. The PlO03.l standard defines about 60 system calls that all conformant systems must support. These are the basic calls for reading and writing files, creating new processes, and so on. Nearly all UNIX systems now support the PlO03.l system calls. However many UNIX systems also support extra system calls, especially those defined by System V and/or those in Berkeley UNIX. Typically these add up to perhaps 100 system calls to the POSIX set. The operating system for the UltraSPARC II is based on System V and is called Solaris. It also supports many of the Berkeley system calls.

A rough breakdown of the Solaris system calls by category is given in Fig. 629. The file and directory management system calls are largest and the most important categories. Most of these come from PIO03.l. A relatively large fraction of the others are derived from System V.

Category	**Some examples**
File management	Open, read, write, close, and lock files
Directory management	Create and delete directories; move files around
Process management	Spawn, terminate, trace, and signal processes
Memory management	Share memory among processes; protect pages
Getting/setting parameters	Get user, group, process ID; set priority
Dates and times	Set file access times; use interval timer; profile execution
Networking	Establish/accept connection; send/ receive message
Miscellaneous	Enable accounting; manipulate disk quotas; reboot the system

One area that is largely due to Berkeley UNIX rather than System V is networking. Berkeley invented the concept of a socket, which is the endpoint of a network connection. The four-pin wall plugs to which telephones can be connected served as the model for this concept. It is possible for a UNIX process to create a socket, attach to it, and establish a connection to a socket on a distant machine. Over this connection it can then exchange data in both directions, typically using the TCP/IP protocol. Since networking technology has been in UNIX for decades and is very stable and mature, a substantial fraction of the servers on the Internet run UNIX.

Since there are many implementations of UNIX, it is difficult to say much about the structure of the operating system since everyone is somewhat different from all the others. However, in general, Fig. 6-30 applies to most of them. At the bottom, there is a layer of device drivers that shield the file system from the bare hardware. Originally, each device driver was written as an independent entity, separate from all the others. This arrangement led to a lot of duplicated effort, since many drivers must deal with flow control, error handling, priorities, separating data from control, and so on. This observation led Dennis Ritchie to develop a framework called streams for writing drivers in a modular way. With a stream, it is possible to establish a two-way connection from a user process to a hardware device and to insert one or more modules along the path. The user process pushes data into the stream, which then is processed or transformed by each module until it gets to the hardware. The inverse processing occurs for incoming data.

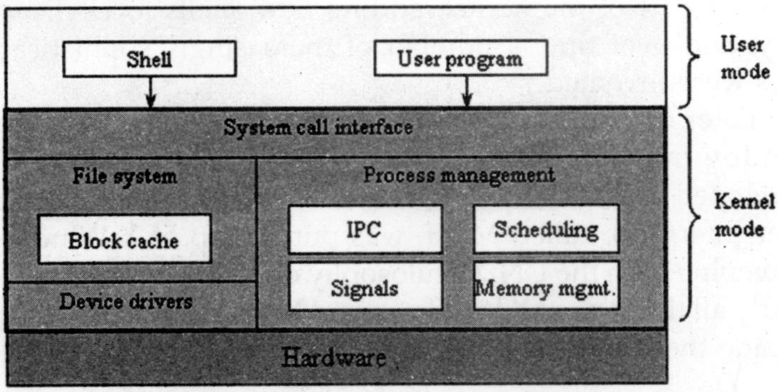

Fig. The Structure of a Typical UNIX System.

On top of the device drivers comes the file system. It manages file names, directories, disk block allocation, protection, and much more. Part of the file system is a block cache, for holding the blocks most recently read in from disk, in case they are needed again soon. A variety of file systems have been used over the years, including the Berkeley fast file system.

The other part of the UNIX kernel is the process management portion. Among its various other functions, it handles IPC (InterProcess Communication), which allows processes to communicate with one another and synchronize to avoid race conditions. A variety of mechanisms are provided. The process management code also handles process scheduling, which is based on priorities. Signals, which are a form of (asynchronous) software interrupt, are also managed here. Finally, memory management is done here as well. Most UNIX systems support demandpaged virtual memory, sometimes with a few extra features, such as the ability of multiple processes to share common regions of address space.

From its inception, UNIX has tried to be a small system, in order to enhance reliability and performance. The first versions of UNIX were entirely text-based, using terminals that could display 24 or 25 lines of 80 ASCII characters. The user interface was handled by a user-level programme called the shell, which offered a command line interface. Since the shell was not part of the kernel, adding new shells to UNIX was easy, and over time a number of increasingly sophisticated ones were invented.

Later on, when graphics terminals came into existence, a windowing system for UNIX, called X Windows, was developed at M.I.T. Still later, a full-fledged GUI (Graphical User Interface), called Motif, was put on top of X Windows. In keeping with the UNIX philosophy of having a small kernel, nearly all the code of X Windows and Motif runs in user mode, outside the kernel.

WINDOWS NT OPERATING SYSTEM OVERVIEW

When the original IBM PC was launched in 1981, it came equipped with a 16-bit real-mode, single-user, command-line oriented operating system called MS-DOS 1.0. This operating system consisted of 8 KB of memory resident code. Two years later, a much more powerful 24-KB system, MS-DOS 2.0, appeared. It contained a command line processor (shell), with a number of features borrowed from UNIX. When IBM released the 286-based PC/AT in 1984, it came equipped with MS-DOS 3.0, by now 36 KB. Over the years, MS-DOS continued to acquire new features, but it was still a command-line oriented system.

Inspired by the success of the Apple Macintosh, Microsoft decided to give MS-DOS a graphical user interface that it called Windows. The first three versions of Windows, culminating in Windows 3.x, were not true operating systems, but graphical user interfaces on top of MS-DOS, which was still in control of the machine. All programmes ran in the same address space and a bug in anyone of them could bring the whole system to a grinding halt.

The release of Windows 95 in 1995 still did not eliminate MS-DOS, although it introduced a new version, 7.0. Together, Windows 95 and MS-DOS 7.0 contained most of the features of a full-blown operating system, including virtual memory, process management, and multiprogramming. However, Windows 95 was not a full 32-bit programme. It contained large chunks of old 16-bit code (as well as some 32-bit code) and still used the MS-DOS file system, with nearly all its limitations. The only major change to the file system was the addition of long file names in place of the 8 + 3 character file names allowed in MS-DOS.

Even with the release of Windows 98 in 1998, MS-DOS was still there (now called version 7.1) and running 16-bit code. Although a bit more functionality migrated from the MS-DOS part to the Windows part, and a disk layout suitable for larger disks was now standard, under the hood, Windows 98 was not very different from Windows 95. The main difference was the user interface, which integrated the desktop, the Internet, and television more closely. It was precisely this integration that attracted the attention of the U.S. Dept. of Justice, which then sued Microsoft claiming that it was an illegal monopoly.

While all these developments were going on, Microsoft was also busy with a completely new 32-bit operating system being written from the ground up. This new system was called

Windows New Technology, or Windows NT. It was initially hyped as the replacement for all other operating systems for Intel-based PCs, but it was somewhat slow to catch on and was later redirected to the upper end of the market, where it found a niche. It is gradually becoming more popular at the low end as well.

NT is sold in two versions: server and workstation. These two versions are nearly identical and are generated from the same source code. The server version is intended for machines that run as LAN-based file and print servers and has more elaborate management features than the workstation version, which is intended for desktop computing for a single user. The server version has a variant (enterprise) intended for large sites. The various versions are tuned differently, each one optimized for its expected environment. Other than these minor differences, all the versions are essentially the same. In fact, nearly all the executable files are identical for all versions. NT itself discovers which version it is by looking at a variable in an internal data structure (the registry). Users are forbidden by the license from changing this variable and thus converting the (inexpensive) workstation version into the (much more expensive) server or enterprise versions. We will not make any further distinction between these versions.

MS-DOS and all previous versions of Windows were single-user systems. NT, however, supports multiprogramming, so several users can work on the same machine at the same time. For example, a network server may have multiple users logged in simultaneously over a network, each accessing its own files in a protected way.

NT is a true 32-bit multiprogramming operating system. It supports multiple user processes, each of which has a full 32-bit demand-paged virtual address space. In addition, the system itself is written as 32-bit code everywhere.

One of NT's original improvements over Windows 95 was its modular structure. It consisted of a moderately small kernel that ran in kernel mode, plus a number of server processes that ran in user mode. User processes interacted with the server processes using the client-server model: a client sent a request message to a server, and the server did the work and returned the result to the client via a second message. This modular structure made it easier to port it to several computers besides the Intel line, including the DEC Alpha, IBM PowerPC, and SGI MIPS. However, for performance reasons, starting with NT 4.0, pretty much all of the system was put back into the kernel.

One could go on for a long time both about how NT is structured internally and what its system call interface is like. Since our primary interest here is the virtual machine presented by various operating systems (i.e., the system calls), we will give a brief summary of the system structure and then move on to the system call interface.

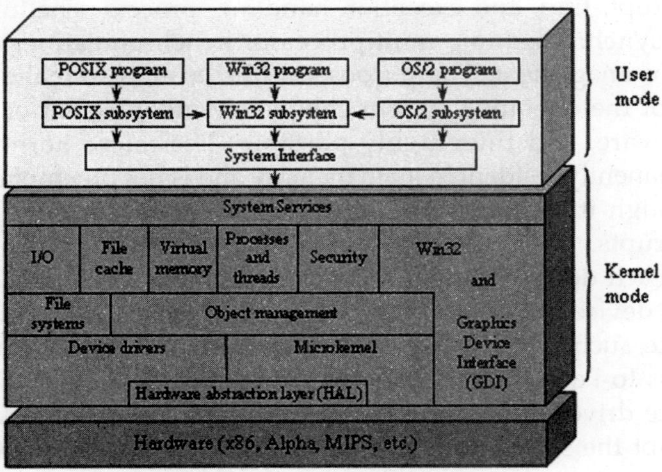

Fig. The structure of Windows NT.

The structure of NT is illustrated in Fig. 6-31. It consists of a number of modules that are structured in layers and work together to implement the operating system. Each module has some particular function and a well-defined interface to the other modules. Nearly all the modules are written in C, although part of the graphics device interface is written in C++ and a tiny bit of the lowest layers are written in assembly language.

At the bottom is a thin layer called the hardware

abstraction layer. Its job is to present the rest of the operating system with abstract hardware devices, devoid of the warts and idiosyncracies with which real hardware is so richly endowed. Among the devices modeled are off-chip caches, timers, I/O buses, interrupt controllers, and DMA controllers. By exposing these to the rest of the operating system in idealized form, it becomes easier to port NT to other hardware platforms, since most of the modifications required are concentrated in one place. User mode

Above the hardware abstraction layer is a layer containing the microkernel. and the device =drivers. The microkernel and all the device drivers have direct access to the hardware when needed, as they contain hardware-dependent code.

The microkernel supports the primitive kernel objects, interrupt, trap, and exception handling, process scheduling and synchronization, multiprocessor synchronization, and time management. The purpose of this layer is to make the rest of the operating system completely independent of the hardware, and thus highly portable. The micro kernel is permanently resident in main memory and is not preemptable, although it can temporarily give up control to service I/O interrupts.

Each device driver can control one or more I/O devices, but a device driver can also do things not related to a specific device, such as encrypting a data stream or even just providing access to kernel data structures. Since users can install new device drivers, they have the power to affect the kernel and corrupt the system. For this reason, drivers must be written with great care.

Above the microkernel and device drivers is the upper portion of the operating system, called the executive. The executive is architecture independent and can be ported to new machines with relatively little effort. It consists of three layers.

The lowest layer contains the file systems and the object manager. The file systems support the use of files and directories. The object manager handles objects known to the kernel. These include processes, threads (lightweight processes within an address space), files, directories, semaphores, I/O devices, timers, and many others. It also manages a namespace in which newly created objects can be placed so they can be referred to later.

The next layer consists of six major parts, as shown in Fig. 6-31. The I/O manager provides a framework for managing I/O devices and provides generic I/O services. It uses the services of the file system, which in turn uses the device drivers, as well as the services of the object manager.

The cache manager keeps the most recently used disk blocks in memory to speed up access to them in the (likely) event that they are needed again. Its job is to figure out which blocks are probably going to be needed again and which ones are not. It is possible to configure NT with multiple file systems, in which case the cache manager works for all of them, so each one does not have to do its own cache management. When a block is needed, the cache manager is asked to supply it. If it does not have the block, the cache manager calls upon the appropriate file system to get it. Since files can be mapped into processes' address spaces, the cache manager must interact with the virtual memory manager to provide the necessary consistency.

The virtual memory manager implements NT's demand-paged virtual memory architecture. It manages the mapping of virtual pages onto physical page frames. It thereby enforces the protection rules that restrict each process to only access those pages belonging to its address space and not to other processes' address spaces (except under special circumstances). It also handles certain system calls that relate to virtual memory.

The process and thread manager handles processes and threads, including their creation and destruction. It is concerned about the mechanisms used to manage them, rather than policies about how they are used.

The security manager enforces NT's elaborate security mechanism, which meets the U.S. Dept. of Defence's Orange Book C2 requirements. The Orange Book specifies a large number of rules that a conforming system must meet, starting with authenticated login through how access control is handled to the fact that virtual pages must be zeroed out before being reused.

The graphics device interface handles image management for the monitor and printers. It provides system calls to allow user programmes to write on the monitor or printers in a device-independent way.

It also contains the window manager and hardware device drivers. In versions of NT prior to NT 4.0, it was in user space but the performance was disappointing, so Microsoft moved it into the kernel to speed it up. The Win32 module also handles most of the system calls. It, too, was originally in user space but was also moved to the kernel to improve performance.

On the top of the executive is a thin layer called system services. Its function is to provide an interface to the executive. It accepts the true NT system calls and calls other parts of the executive to have them executed.

Outside the kernel are the user programmes and the environmental subsystems. The environmental subsystems are provided because user programmes are not encouraged to make system calls directly (although they are technically capable of it).

Instead, each environmental subsystem exports a (different) set of function calls that user programmes can use. Win32 (for NT or Windows 95/98 programmes), POSIX (for UNIX programmes that have been ported), and OS/2 (for OS/ 2 programmes that have been ported).

Windows applications use the Win32 functions and communicate with the Win32 subsystem to make system calls. The Win32 subsystem accepts the Win32 function calls and uses the system interface library module to make the necessary true NT system calls to carry them out.

There is also a POSIX subsystem, which provides minimal support for UNIX applications. It supports only the P1003.1 functionality and little else.

It is a closed subsystem, meaning that its applications cannot use the facilities of the Win32 subsystem, which greatly restricts what they can do. In practice, porting any real UNIX programme to NT using this subsystem is nearly impossible.

It was included only because parts of the U.S. government require operating systems for government computers to be PlOO3.1 compliant.

This subsystem is not selfcontained so it uses the Win32 subsystem for some of its work, but without exporting the full Win32 interface to its user programmes.

The OS/2 subsystem is similarly limited in functionality and may be dropped in some future release. It also uses the Win32 subsystem. There is also an MS-DOS environmental subsystem (not shown in the figure).

Having looked briefly at the structure of NT, let us now turn to our main subject, the services offered by NT. This interface is the programmer's main connection to the system. Unfortunately, Microsoft has never made the complete list of NT system calls public, and it also changes them from release to release. Under such conditions, writing programmes that make system calls directly is nearly impossible.

What Microsoft has done is define a set of calls called the Win32 API (Application Programming Interface) that are publicly known. These are library procedures that either make system calls to get the work done, or, in some case, do the work right in the user-space library procedure or in the Win32 sub system.

The Win32 API calls do not change with new releases, to promote stability. However, there are also NT API calls that may change between releases of NT. Although the Win32 API calls are not all NT system calls, it is better to focus on these here rather than the true NT system calls because the Win32 API calls are well documented and more stable over time.

The Win32 API philosophy is completely different from the UNIX philosophy.

In the latter, the system calls are all publicly known and form a minimal interface: removing even one of them would reduce the functionality of the operating system. The Win32 philosophy is to provide a very comprehensive interface, often with three or four ways of doing the same thing, and including many functions that clearly should not be (and are not) system calls, such as an API call to copy an entire file.

Many Win32 API calls create kernel objects of one kind or another, including files, processes, threads, pipes, etc. Every call creating a kernel object returns a result called a handle to the caller.

This handle can be subsequently used to perform operations on the object. Handles are specific to the process that created the object referred to by the handle. They cannot be passed directly to another process and used there (just as UNIX file descriptors cannot be passed to other processes and used there).

However, under certain circumstances, it is possible to duplicate a handle and pass it to other processes in a protected way, allowing them controlled access to objects belonging to other processes. Every object also has a security descriptor associated with it, telling in detail who may and may not perform what kinds of operations on the object.

NT is sometimes said to be object-oriented because the only way to manipulate kernel objects is by invoking methods (API functions) on their handles. On the other hand, it lacks some of the most basic properties of object-oriented systems such as inheritance and polymorphism.

number of exceptions. For example, Windows 95/98 do not have any security, so those API calls that relate to security just return error codes on Windows 95/98. Also, NT file names use the Unicode character set, which is not available on Windows 95/98.

There are also differences in parameters to some API function calls.

On NT, for example, all the screen coordinates given in the graphics functions are true 32-bit numbers; on Windows 95/98, only the low-order 16 bits are used (for backward compatibility with Windows 3.1). The existence of the Win32 API on several different operating systems makes it easier to port programmes between them but also points out more clearly that it is somewhat decoupled from the actual system calls.

Some of the differences between Windows 95/98 and NT are summarized in Figure.

Item	Windows 95/98	NT 5.0
Win32 API?	Yes	Yes
Full 32-bit system?	No	Yes
Security?	No	Yes
Protected file mappings?	No	Yes
Private address space for each MS-DOS programme?	No	Yes
Plug and play?	Yes	Yes
Unicode?	No	Yes
Runs on Alpha	Intel 80x86	80x86,
Multiprocessor support?	No	Yes
Re-entrant code inside aS?	No	Yes
Some critical as data writable by user?	Yes	No

OPERATING SYSTEMS II

INTRODUCTION

- The CPU is essentially a glorified calculator;
  - That main-memory is a large collection of 'pigeon-holes' each of which can hold one number; each number can represent:
  - An actual numeric quantity;
  - A text character coded as a number;
  - etc..
  - An instruction to be executed by the CPU;
- That a disk or other magnetic memory is a place to store:
  - Pieces of memory that need to be stored after the computer is switched off - non-volatile storage;
  - Later we will see that a disk can also be used to hold pieces of (main) memory that have got too big for the physically available memory size, i.e. virtual memory on disk.

Software

Without software, the system in Figure just sits there

quietly, doing nothing!. It must be programmed with appropriate software.

Roughly speaking, software can be divided into two categories:

System Software

Operating system and utilities;

Application Software

e.g. wordprocessing, spreadsheets,..., including user-developed software.

The divide, between system and application, can be somewhat blurred. In general, the more general purpose and *ordinary* the function performed - like copying or deleting files, or compiling or assembling programmes - the closer to system software; the more special purpose - like a database management system - the closer to application category.

Originally, the system software was likely to be developed by the computer *hardware* manufacturer; however, since the 1980s, the PC revolution has turned this on its head. This chapter is concerned primarily with the operating system - which is definitely system software.

WHAT DOES AN OPERATING SYSTEM DO?

The system software, particularly the operating system, mediates between the user (and the application software) and the hardware. Thus, though in reality (hardware) a disk may be lots of circles with bits (1 or 0) arranged along their circumference, that is very difficult for a programmer or user to handle. For example, instead of clicking on FILE/SAVE, you would have to concoct some machine code to do: 'save the first 128 bytes on circle 22, head 2, sector 4 and save the second 128 bytes on...', all the time checking, and updating your list of occupied sectors. The operating system handles the whole filing system for you. You just give the file name and it does the rest.

From the point of view of a user at the keyboard, the

operating system makes the computer act 'intelligent' and alive. From the programmer point of view, it provides several services. The user of the service can be an application programme - via invocation of a service function, e.g. System.output.println(); - or a human user - via the operating systems human-interface,

With Windows NT and Linux, we are moving away from single-user operating systems to multi-tasking - where, for example, the user can set the computer to compiling a large file, while he/she starts to edit another file.

Microsoft Windows-95/98 offers some multi-tasking features. Windows NT is truly multi-tasking.

Since the late 1960s, operating systems on large computers have been multi-user; they allow a large number of users to use a single computer at one time, with each having the sensation of being the sole user of the machine. In the multi-user case, in addition to normal operating system duties, the operating system must:

- Allocate the CPU on a fair basis, and so that users, or a singles user's separate programmes, do not notice much delay;
- Keep each programme, or bits of them, in memory at once - a difficult juggling trick;
- Keep each programme from interfering with another program's memory, whether maliciously or by error;
- Manage a private area of disk for each user/ programme;
- Perform accounting tasks (perhaps) - so that users can be charged for the use of each service.

VIRTUAL MACHINE LEVELS AND THE OPERATING SYSTEM

The multilevel view of a computer. At each level there is a different virtual machine which obeys its own language.Figure recalls this view.

Except for levels 0 and 1 each level is, in fact, virtual, in the sense that it is created by a computer programme or interpreter.

The operating system also provides a higher-level abstraction for parts of the underlying hardware, e.g. a hierarchical file directory structure as an abstraction for a complex system of spinning disks, controllers etc.

It would be a good idea, at this stage, for you to get these different levels clear in your head. You should also convince yourself of the value of working at the highest level possible - employing the highest level of abstraction possible. If you need more convincing, consider reworking your last Java assignment in assembly language! Employing a higher level of abstraction is like a walker being able to take 10, 20 or maybe 500 steps at a time - for no extra effort; or, like travelling across the Atlantic by air, rather than swimming or rowing a boat.

HISTORICAL DEVELOPMENT OF OPERATING SYSTEMS

Computers were treated as electronic instruments and could only be programmed using binary codes (machine code). The methods of inserting the codes varied: switches, paper tape, punched cards or, at the beginning, *patched* in with wires which connected High or Low voltages to indicate '1' or '0'.

OPEN SHOP

By this time (say 1959) there were compliers - like FORTRAN. Users would run their own programmes - much like users of personal computers do nowadays. Users booked the machine for (say) 1/2 hour at a time. Programmes were prepared off-line - onto punched cards - computers were too expensive for such menial tasks.

It was up to the new user to load whatever programme was required onto the machine - from cards; executable and source code were both on cards.

You may be able to imagine the following scenario if you think of an organisation with a single small, slow microcomputer, with one floppy drive, no hard disk and no resident operating system.

- At the appointed hour, you would charm/threaten/ cajole the previous user out of the computer room.

- First, the FORTRAN compiler had to be loaded - a huge deck of cards - via the card reader; note: before this there was no software in the computer, except for a small card reader programme. Such a programme was sometimes called a 'bootstrap' or card-loader - these were the great-great-grand-daddy of todays operating systems; a typical card-loader occupied, maybe, 50 to 100 bytes of memory.
- Then your new source was read in, and compiled.
- If there were compiler errors, you noted them and left the computer room. The next user took over - or the computer lay idle until the next half-hour slot began. You would then book another 1/2 hour (maybe the next free was 2 days away - or, you could come in in the middle of the night), try to locate the error, and retype the offending card(s); NB. there was no editing facility in the computer.
- If there were no compilation errors, the machine would punch the object code onto cards.
- The next stage was to link and load the object code with the library of system subroutines - also object code. To do this, the linker programme, followed by library, followed by users object code, had to be read in via the card reader.
- If no linker errors - they were plentiful - you ended up with a programme in the computers memory, ready to execute.
- Now, you could either run the programme - by putting the start address into the PC register, via switches, or punch out the executable programme - the equivalent of a '.exe' file.
- If the programme ran correctly (and, you didn't run out of time) you left to celebrate. Otherwise, you noted the error - very difficult, if the programme just crashed. Big installations had line printers, which allowed printing of a full dump of the memory - in Hex or Octal - at the time of crashing. If you had no line printer, you noted the contents of a few memory

locations using the console switches and lights - you could dial any memory location using switches and examine the contents on a light panel (one switch for every address bit and one light for every data bit). Or; in desperation, you could try to 'patch' the machine code to try to get it to do something.

Clearly, much time was wasted:

- Loading programmes;
- Idle time, if a user did not take an allocated time slot;
- Users scratching their heads wondering what was wrong with a programme;
- etc....- but, note, no computer games!

All this on a machine that costed a few million pounds.

Side-bar:

In 1960, an average programmer salary was about £1500, a computer cost around £1,500,000: ratio person annual salary to computer capital cost, 1 to 1000. Today, salary £30,000, powerful PC, £1000: ratio 30 to 1. Thus, compared to 1960, computers are ,times the cost; or programmers 30,000 times more expensive!

OPERATOR SHOP

The next stage was to hire an operator. The operator performed all interaction with the computer. Users submitted 'jobs' on cards, and received the results back on line printer paper.

The operator was more skilled and quicker at operating the computer.

Also, similar jobs could be batched, e.g. all the FORTRAN compilations - allowing the FORTRAN compiler programme to be loaded only once, followed by all the linking, etc.

Furthermore, the operator could assert priority:

- To a user who was prepared to pay more;
- To a small job, or one which used an already loaded programme;
- ,Also, the operator could halt jobs that ran too long.

These are all feature that can be seen in modern operating systems.

OFF-LINE INPUT-OUTPUT AND RESIDENT MONITOR

Reading cards was not much of a job for a X million pound computer!

Better to create - on a cheaper *satellite* machine - a magnetic tape, that contained many jobs, and get the expensive machine to work its way through the tape. Maybe there were two tape decks - one to replace the card input, one to replace the card output. Also the system software (compiler, linker/loader) could be kept on a tape.

Most significant, however, from an operating systems point of view, was the addition of a small resident monitor programme which remained in memory all the time and which ran each job in turn. This was the great-grandfather of today's OSs. The term operating system crept in because of the similarity of the resident monitor's role to that of a human operator.

The previous instructions to the operator (in English) now had to be coded for the resident monitor. These instructions had to be punched on cards — a typical convention was to precede resident monitor commands with an asterisk, '*', to distinguish them from source programme statements, or data; i.e. the resident monitor had a rudimentary command language interpreter.

A typical resident monitor was IBM's FORTRAN Monitor System - FMS — that ran on the IBM 709.

SPOOLING SYSTEMS AND SCHEDULERS

Early resident monitor systems used polled input-output, to read from and write to their magnetic tapes; thus, when they needed input, or needed to output, the CPU gave up all other activity and attended to the tape. Polled i-o is very inefficient inefficient; most of the time is wasted waiting for 'status-ready' and things like that. Therefore, the next elaboration was to add software to the resident monitor to allow it, simultaneously, to read from tape, do CPU processing, and, perhaps, write to an output tape or printer.

For slower devices like tapes, interrupt driven device drivers, were sufficient. Eventually, disks were added to the main machine. The off-line tape preparation machines would be dispensed with, since the card jobs could be read-in on the main machine (using interrupts) and placed on disk to await execution. In addition, running jobs could write to disk files (faster), with the disk files being printed fairly independently.

A primitive scheduler was added to the resident monitor:

- When a job was read-in from cards (or tape), its name and characteristics were placed in a queue;
- The scheduler was run at the end of each job, to select the next job from the queue and set it running.

Operators tasks are now limited to:

- Mounting tapes - for large data files, too big for cards - only very privileged users were allowed to keep data on the disk;
- Restarting the resident monitor when it crashed, or a user programme crashed it;
- Loading cards;
- Unloading printer paper.

This mode of running was called spooling: simultaneous peripheral operations on line - spool.

The operation is somewhat evocative of a spool of thread:

- Jobs wound on to the outside;
- Scheduler winds them off from the inside;
- Ditto with the output: CPU winds output data on; interrupt driven printer programme winds them off — onto line-printer paper.

Spooling systems are the grand-daddies of modern OSs.

MULTIPROGRAMMING

Nevertheless, spooling doesn't totally remove I/O waiting. Consider a programme which is doing a stock update, and the stock files is on mag. tape: very often the CPU has to issue a *read-from-tape* and can do nothing until the data arrives.

The job is then said to be input-output bound - no amount of interrupt handling can help in this case.

Multiprogramming comes to the rescue.

If the memory is big enough - or the jobs small enough:

- You can place a number of them in memory at once;
- When one becomes I/O bound, transfer to another (*).
- However, using only the simple rule: CPU bound jobs are favoured. The problem with this rule is that a big number crunching programme with no I/O could hog the CPU for ever.

Thus, the scheduler becomes a good deal more complicated. CPU time is one of the main resources that jobs are in competition for - implementing policies for sharing such resources is a big part of an operating system's task.

Multiprogramming also introduces competition for memory space. Also, the resident monitor and other programmes must be protected from malicious or faulty programmes that try to write to parts of memory not owned by them. What we have just described is called batch multiprogramming: each user job may be considered to batch together a set of steps - e.g. compile-pass1...-pass2...link...run. Each step is independent - provided its results are stored safely on disk. Thus, the resident monitor can schedule each (sub)task independently. The term process is used to mean an executing programme that performs a subtask; more about processes later. At this stage the resident monitor has become a true operating system, albeit still batch.

In addition to queuing and running processes, the OS provides services to the process via service calls. Programmes and processes can no longer access input-output devices directly - they must - in the terminology of multi-level machines - execute an OS machine level instruction that does that for them.

Of course, two processes may require the same resource at the same time, e.g. tape, printer; CPU time and memory are also resources that are in heavy demand. The business of granting resources in a fair way is not a trivial one.

INTERACTIVE MULTIPROGRAMMING AND TIME-SHARING

The batch multiprogramming described above was fine

for the computers - but not for people - if programmers can be considered people, which, in organisations, is rare! In developing a programme you could spot an error five seconds after getting your batch job back from the machine, and have to wait a day to get another try. Programmers needed quicker response.

Interactive multiprogramming or time-sharing was the solution.

Instead of interacting, indirectly, via cards and printout, each user has an on-line interactive terminal. They also have access to the disk - perhaps their own directory - to store programmes and data between sessions.

The whole basis of time-sharing is that there may be 5, 10 or 100 users connected to a single computer - with one CPU - with each of them getting the impression that she/he is the sole occupant.

Of course, if all these users are running heavily CPU intensive programmes (number crunching), the impression of having a machine to yourself quickly subsides. However, that will rarely be the case; at any instant, out of 20 connected users, 7 might be editing (requires little or no CPU time), 10 might be thinking about what to do next, and only 3 doing anything that really exercises the CPU — e.g. compiling or running programmes.

Incidentally, operating systems have ways of discouraging heavy CPU and memory users from peak interactive times. For these users, a form of batch service is offered. The user submits a job to a batch queue much the same way as before - except the job is specified

- Interactively
- In a disk file, and
- The inputs and outputs also use disk files.

The batch queue is treated differently from the queue associated with the interactive users - it is probably only given a chance at night, or when the interactive use gets very slack.

Massachusetts Institute of Technology (MIT) were the first to demonstrate a time-sharing system - about 1960; that was CTSS. It ran on a converted IBM 7094. But, on machines whose hardware was meant to run one programme/user at a time, time-sharing was not easy — see later.

Multics

The next step was MIT, Bell Labs. and General Electric co-operating in producing MULTICS (MULTiplexed Information and Computing Service). MULTICS was way ahead of its time. For the companies involved, maybe too far ahead, for it was costly to produce, and was not commercially successful.

But, MULTICS was enormously influential on the technical development of operating systems. MULTICS begat UNIX. Scratch the surface of most modern operating systems and you will find some MULTICS or UNIX influence.

Minicomputers

Up to 1961 computers were a bit like electricity generating plants — they took up whole buildings or, at least, floors or rooms. They cost $millions.

In 1961 Digital Equipment Corporation (DEC) introduced the PDP-1. The PDP-1 had 4K of 18-bit words. It cost a mere $ 120,000. For some jobs it was nearly as fast as an IBM 7094 - the 7094 cost $2 million). Personal computing was on the horizon.

A whole family of PDPs, so-called mini-computers were developed, leading to the PDP-8 - the first true personal, or, at least, laboratory computer - and the PDP-11.

UNIX

After Bell Labs. dropped out of the MULTICS project, Ken Thompson, one of the MULTICS team at Bell Labs., wrote a single user version of MULTICS for a PDP-7. It was written in assembly language. It was called UNIX - as a pun on Multics.

Note that the PDP-7 had 4K memory.

Yet this early UNIX featured:

- A file system;
- A process control mechanism;
- File utilities;

- A command interpreter.

Next step: UNIX was ported onto a PDP-11/20 and later a PDP-11/45.

But, besides its power and elegance, the next step was to ensure UNIX's fame and fortune. Dennis Ritchie joined the team and developed the C programming language. Around 1972, a new version of UNIX was written, almost entirely in C. Now UNIX could be ported onto any machine that had a C compiler.

HISTORY OF OPERATING SYSTEMS-GENERATIONS, SUMMARY

This section summarises OS history in the form of generations.

1ST GENERATION (1945-1955): VACUUM TUBES AND PLUGBOARDS

- Plugboards;
- Vacuum Tubes;
- Machine language;
- The computer is the eighth wonder of the world!

2ND GENERATION 1955-1965): TRANSISTORS AND BATCH SYSTEMS

- Transistors: greater reliability, smaller, less power, faster than vacuum tubes - all the factors you want in a computer;
- PDP-1 from DEC - interactive computing;
- PDP-1 from DEC - cheap(ish) computing;
- PDP-8 from DEC - personal computing;
- jgc in short pants;-)

3RD GENERATION (1965-1980): ICS, MULTIPROGRAMMING AND TIMESHARING

- People becoming more important than the computer;
- OS written in a high-level language.

4TH GENERATION (1980-1991): PCS AND DISTRIBUTED COMPUTING

- Ordinary people using computers;

- Computers become a consumer item;
- Need for *user-friendly* operating systems and software - people are no longer prepared to go to college for three years just to learn how to use a computer;
- Networks of PCs replace mainframes.

THE FUTURE (1993-)

- World-wide-web;
- Left as exercise for student.

PREVIEW OF THE WORK OF A TIME-SHARING OPERATING SYSTEM

If each task required nothing but CPU time then multiprogramming would have little advantage over running tasks consecutively. Figure shows two tasks labelled A and B, each of which requires different resources (VDU, disk and CPU) in the order in which they are shown.

If task A were allowed to run to completion before task B was started, valuable processing time would be wasted. We show below how the tasks may be scheduled to make more efficient use of resources, each step takes one unit of time, and they are done entirely sequentially, then the total time is 10 steps.

Contrast Figure - timeshared -, which takes just 6 steps. It is worth noting that if the CPU is to be available to one task while another is accessing a disk or using a printer, then these devices must be capable of autonomous operation, i.e. they must either be able to transfer data by DMA without the active intervention of the CPU or must be able to receive a chunk of data at high speed from the CPU and process it at their leisure.

The next chapter will look at some of the details of how a time-sharing operating system schedules many tasks, and allocates resources to them in a fair or otherwise optimal manner.

This comes down to:

- CPU allocation;
- I/O resource allocation, i.e. disks, printers, tapes;
- Memory resource allocation, i.e. virtual memory.

OPERATING SYSTEMS

The operation - in the sense of 'driving' them - of computers evolved through users operating them, to operators, and finally through various sophistications of operating system software to timesharing operating systems.

First, we give a demonstration of the effect of multiprogramming.

Assume that the jobs/processes/programmes are in memory to start with, that they do some computation (taking 10 millisec) which results in the requirement to read a particular record from a disk file (taking 10 millisec), finally they do some more computation (again 10 millisec). Viewed as executions of single programmes this may not appear too useful - where do the results go to - but, in fact, the jobs are quite typical of what would be encountered by a timesharing during the execution lifetime of three processes

Figure shows how the jobs would have to run on a single user system like MS-DOS. The computer is *I/O blocked* during each disk input - regardless of whether the input is by polled I/O, interrupts, or DMA.

Figure shows the effect of multiprogramming; when one process become I/O bound, the CPU can do processing for another. Thus, a 90 millisec of computer usage can be reduced to 60; add more jobs and you get a greater increase in efficiency. NB. in this case, you are concerned with the method of I/O transfer - ideally the CPU asks for the data, and receives an interrupt when they are placed in memory.

The work that a modern timesharing operating system performs is a good deal more complex than that of, for example, a simple resident monitor - or even a single user OS like MS-DOS. Nevertheless, like all complex systems, the analysis of operating systems responds to breaking them into subsystems/components.

The following functions are required:

- Dispatching or scheduling. Switching the processor from one process to another; allowing jobs to enter queue.
- Interrupt handling.

- Resource allocation. Allocation of the computer's resources to processes: memory, I/O devices, CPU time.
- Resource protection. Ensuring that no process can access any resource which has not been allocated to it.
- Provision of (virtual) I/O and other services.
- Provision of a file system - to processes, and to human users.
- Analysing and decoding user commands - and requests from programmes, and converting these into procedure and programme names.

We shall now briefly look at a selection of topics that pertain to these requirements.

PROCESSES

General

The concept of a process is central - first used by MULTICS. Sometimes referred to as a task. Definition can be difficult: 'a programme in execution' may be the best.

During its life, a process goes through a series of discrete states:

- Running - if it currently has the CPU resource;
- Ready - if it could use the CPU if the CPU were available;
- Blocked - if it is waiting for some event to happen before it can proceed.

When a job is admitted to the system, a corresponding process is created and placed at the back of the queue and it is marked ready; alternatively, there may be separate queues. It gradually moves to the top of the ready list - see scheduling/ dispatching below; when the CPU becomes available the process makes a state transition from ready to running. Strictly speaking this is dispatching.

To prevent any one process, say process A, monopolising the system - i.e. to provide time-sharing it must be possible possible to stop the process after it has consumed its allocated amount of CPU time. This is done via an interrupting clock (hardware) which allows a specified time quantum - a time-slot to pass; if process A is still using the CPU the clock generates an interrupt, causing the system to regain control. Process A now makes the state transition back to ready, i.e. A is put back in the ready queue.

The next process, process B, say, on the ready queue is now put into the running state; and so on....

If a running process initiates an I/O operation before its time-slot expires then the process is forced to release the CPU; it enters the blocked state and releases the CPU.

If a process is in the blocked state and the event for which it is waiting completes, then the process makes the transition from blocked to ready.

PROCESS CONTROL BLOCK (PCB)

Because of this 'switching on and off' of processes is is necessary to have housekeeping information associated with each process. A process control block PCB which is a record containing important current information about the process, for example: current state of the process, unique identification of the process, the process's priority, open files and I/O devices, use of main memory and backing store, other resources held, a register save area.

THE KERNEL

All of the operations involving processes are controlled by a portion of the OS called its nucleus, core or kernel. The kernel represents only a small portion of the code of the entire OS but it is intensively used and so remains in primary storage while other portions may be transferred in and out of secondary storage as required.

One very important function of the kernel is interrupt processing. In large multi-user systems, the kernel is subjected to a constant barrage of interrupts. Clearly, rapid response is essential: to keep resources well utilised, and to provide acceptable response times for interactive users.

In addition, while dealing with an interrupt, the kernel disables other interrupts. Thus, to prevent interrupts being disabled for long periods of time, the kernel is designed to do the minimum amount of processing possible on each interrupt and to pass the remaining processing to an appropriate system process.

The kernel of a sophisticated OS may contain code to perform:

- Interrupt handling;
- Process creation and destruction;
- Process state switching and dispatching;
- Inter process communication;
- Manipulation of PCB;
- Support of I/O activities;
- Support of memory allocation and deallocation;
- Support of the file system;
- Support of system accounting functions.

Supporting hardware and microcode is often provided - even for portable operating systems like UNIX.

The kernel has privileges that allow it to do things that normal processes cannot do, e.g. access I/O devices. Privilege is usually conferred by the processor state, i.e. privilege level is stored in hardware, so a process has a different processor state from the kernel. In the original Intel 8086/88 and 80286, there was limited support for processor states; however, in the 80386 and after, full time-sharing was supported.

SCHEDULING

The goal of scheduling (the method by which processor time is managed) is to provide good service to all the processes that are currently competing for resources, including the CPU.

Three type of scheduling may be identified: long term scheduling, medium term scheduling, and short term scheduling. We will be concerned only with short-term scheduling - also called dispatching, which decides how to share the computer among all the processes that currently want to compute. Such decisions may be made frequently - tens of times per second.

There are several competing goals that scheduling policies aim to fulfill - one is *good throughput*. For short term scheduling, this minimizes the number of process switches. Another goal is good (quick) service.

Scheduling Objectives

Some of the - often conflicting - objectives of a good scheduling algorithm/policy are:

1. Be fair - all processes should be treated equitably;
2. Maximize throughput and service, i.e. as many processes as possible per unit time;
3. Maximize the number of interactive users receiving acceptable response times;
4. Be predictable - a given job should run in about the same amount of time regardless of the load on the system;
5. Balance resource use - processes using underutilized resources should be favoured;
6. Achieve a balance between response and utilization;
7. Avoid indefinite postponement - as a process waits for a resource its priority should grow (aging);
8. Enforce priorities;
9. Give preference to processes holding key resources;
10. Give better service to processes exhibiting desirable behaviour e.g. low paging rates,
11. Degrade gracefully under heavy loads.

Thus, scheduling may appear to be a complex problem.

SCHEDULING POLICIES, ALGORITHMS

First Come, First Served (FCFS)

Under FCFS, the short term scheduler runs each process until it either terminates or leaves because of I/O or resource requests. Processes arriving wait in the order that they arrive.

FCFS is non-preemptive, so a process is never blocked once it has started to run until it leaves the domain of the short term scheduler.

FCFS is usually unsatisfactory because of the way that it favours long (greedy) processes - like the person in the bank queue in front of you with the weeks takings from a shop!

Round Robin (RR)

The intention is to provide good response ratios for short as well as long processes. This policy services (allocates CPU to) a process for a single time slot (length = q), where q = between 1/60 and 1 second; if the process is not finished it is interrupted at the end of the slot and placed at the rear of the ready queue and will wait for its turn again. New arrivals enter the ready queue at the rear.

RR can be tuned by adjusting q. If q is so high that it exceeds the service requirements for all processes, RR becomes the same as FCFS. As q tends to 0, process switching happens more frequently and eventually occupies all available time. Thus q should be set small enough so that RR is fair but high enough so that the amount of time spent switching processes is reasonable.

RR is preemptive, i.e. it will stop a process, if the process has not completed before the end of its time-slot.

SHORTEST PROCESS NEXT (SPN)

SPN (like FCFS) is non-preemptive. It tries to improve response for short processes over FCFS. But, it requires explicit information about the service time requirements for each process. The process with the shortest time requirement is chosen.

Unfortunately, long processes wait a long time or suffer starvation. Short processes are treated very favourably.

CONCLUSION

- Preemption is worth the extra switching cost. Since context must switch at every interrupt from the running process back to the kernel, it does not usually cost much extra for the kernel to make a decision and allow a different process to run.
- The time-slot should be large enough so that preemption cost does not become excessive, e.g.. if a process switch costs 100 microseconds, the quantum should be about 100 times as long.
- Some policies are more expensive than others to

implement. FCFS only requires a queue for the ready list.

- Many OSs use a hybrid policy, with RR for short processes and some other method for long.
- Space management affects scheduling. Processes that need a substantial amount of memory are often given larger time-slots so that they can get more work done while they are occupying main store.

MEMORY MANAGEMENT

Data that is currently accessed most frequently should be in the highest level of storage hierarchy. Each offers about an order of magnitude faster access than its lower neighbour.

The relationship between each layer and the one below it can be considered as similar to that between cache and main memory - cache. If we need to cache an item from a higher level then access is significantly slower. We call such a situation a cache miss. In contrast a cache hit is when we find the data we need in a cache and need not turn to the associated slower memory.

PHYSICAL AND VIRTUAL STORE

The OS must arrange main memory so that processes remain ignorant of each other and still share main memory. A guiding principle is that the more frequently data are accessed, the faster the access should be. If swapping in and out of main storage becomes the dominant activity, then we refer to this situation as thrashing. Physical store is the hardware memory on the machine, usually starting at physical address 0. Certain locations may be reserved for special purposes; the kernel may reside in in the low addresses. The rest of physical store may be partitioned into pieces for the processes in the ready list.

Each process has its own virtual memory - the memory perceived by the process. As far as the process is concerned all address references refer to virtual space. Each process' virtual memory is limited only by the machine address size.Virtual memory can also be very useful even in a single user system - if the computer has a larger address space than physical memory, and if programmes need a large amount of memory; compare overlaying - in which the programmer takes responsibility for segmenting the programme into memory sized chunks.

CHOICE OF PAGE SIZE

The choice of page size determined at the design stage is a trade- off between various considerations:

- Overhead space - least with large pages, since page tables have fewer entries.
- Internal waste - smallest with small pages.
- Cold start faults - lower with large pages. These are the faults needed to bring the programme into main store the first time. With larger pages there are fewer total pages, hence fewer cold start faults.
- Page fault rate - generally lower with small pages, assuming that a fixed amount of main store is available.
- Efficiency of transfer between main memory and disk store - best with large pages, since they take about the same amount of time to transfer as small pages.

Larger pages are usually better, unless they become so large that too few processes in the ready list can have pages in main store at the same time. Common page sizes are from 512 bytes to 4K bytes but can be as large as 8K.

PAGE REPLACEMENT POLICIES

The storage manager must decide to keep some pages in main store and other pages in secondary store - unless virtual space requirements are less than the available physical space.

These decisions may be made at any time but when a page fault occurs a decision must be made; the process that suffered the page fault cannot continue until the appropriate page is swapped in.

A page replacement policy (PRP)/algorithm is used to decide which page frame to vacate ie. swap out its page.

Some commonly quoted strategies are:

Note: pages being heavily used should be preserved. One

goal is to minimize the number of page faults. Swapping can reach a level at which all processes present need to swap so no progress can be made. If this persists, the OS is spending all its time transferring pages in and out of main store - known as thrashing.

FIRST IN, FIRST OUT (FIFO)

Also called longest resident.

When a page frame is needed, the page that has been in main store for the longest time is chosen. This policy tends to save recently used pages which have a higher probability of being used again soon. However a frequently used page still gets swapped out when it gets to be old enough, even though it will have to be brought in immediately.

LEAST RECENTLY USED (LRU)

This method is based on the assumption that the page reference pattern in the recent past is a mirror of the pattern in the near future. Pages that have been accessed recently are likely to continue to be accessed and ought to be kept in main store. It is expensive to implement exactly since in order to find the page least recently used, either a list of pages must be maintained in use order or each page must be marked with the time it was last accessed.

Chapter 3

Computer Arithmatic and Devices

FRACTIONS AND FLOATING POINT

Often, the quantities we want to represent and compute are not integers. Furthermore, the intermediate results in a computation may not be integer.

To represent non integers, the following are required:

- Representation of the digits of the number - on both sides of the 'point';
- Representation of the position of the 'point'.

In a fixed point representation, the point is assumed to be in some fixed position - and, since it is fixed, the position need not be stored. In a floating point representation, the position of the point can be varied according to the size of the number. Floating point is by far the most common and useful on general purpose computers.

FIXED POINT

To represent fractional numbers, we simply extend the positional system, introduced in section 2.3.1, to include digits corresponding to negative powers. We do this by introducing a *point* '.'; the integer number is as before, and is shown to the left of the point; the fraction part is shown to the right of the point. Therefore, generalising what was given in section 2.3.1, a number which includes a *q*bit fractional part - for a total of *p+q* bits - is written:

$$d_{p-1} d_{p-2} \ldots d_2 d_1 d_0 . d_{-1} d_{-2} \ldots d_{-q+1} d_{-q}$$

and its value is:

$$value = d_{r-1} \times b^{p-1} + d_{m-2} \times b_{p-2} + ... d_2 \times b_2 + d_1 \times b + d_o + d_{-1} \times b_{-1} + d_{-2} \times b_{-2} + ... + d_{-q+1} \times b_{-q+1} + d_{-q} \times b_{-q}$$

$$\begin{aligned} 123.45_{10} &= 1 \times 10^2 + 2 \times 10^1 + 3 \times 10^0 + 4 \times 10^{-1} + 5 \times 10^{-2} \\ &= 1 \times 100 + 2 \times 10 + 3 \times 1 + 4 \times 0.1 + 5 \times 0.01 \\ &= 100 + 20 + 3 + 0.4 + 0.05 \\ &= 123.45 \end{aligned}$$

In binary,

$$\begin{aligned} 0.1 &= 1 \times 2^{-1} = 1 \times 0.5 = 0.5 \\ 0.01 &= 1 \times 2^{-2} = 1 \times 0.25 = 0.25 \\ 0.001 &= 1 \times 2^{-3} = 1 \times 0.125 = 0.125 \end{aligned}$$

Example. Convert 11.101_2 to decimal.

$$\begin{aligned} 11.101 &= 1 \times 2^1 + 1 \times 2^0 + 1 \times 2^{-1} + 0 \times 2^{-2} + 1 \times 2^{-3} \\ &= 2 + 1 + 0.5 + 0 + 0.125 \\ &= 3.625 \end{aligned}$$

The the magnitude of the number depends on the fixed position of the point. The problem arises that sometimes we want most of the digits after the 'point', i.e. small numbers, sometimes we want most of them before the 'point', i.e. large numbers. A single fixed-point representation cannot do both.

Other methods that have been proposed for storage of fractions:

- Store the number as a logarithm - actually, logarithms are peripherally involved in floating point representation;
- Store the number as a pair (*a*,*b*) representing a rational number.

But, floating point is the widely adopted solution.

FLOATING POINT

A floating point number is composed of two parts:

1. The digits of the number, the fraction; the fraction is often called the mantissa, but, strictly, this is an abuse of the term.
2. The position of the point - the exponent.

The floating point representation is similar to the 'scientific', or 'exponential' representation of very large and very small numbers on some calculators and in books; e.g. 123.56 = 0.12345 E + 03, i.e. 0.12345×10^3. In this scientific representation, you can think of the exponent as representing the 'point' position.

In fact, the exponent is the integer part of the logarithm to which the base must be raised in order to place the point in the right position.

Examples of decimal floating-point with five digit fraction and three digit exponent are shown in Table.

Table: Examples of floating-point

Fraction	Exponent	Floating-point	Fixed-point
12345	003	0.12345×10^3	123.45
12345	002	0.12345×10^2	12.345
12345	001	0.12345×10^1	1.2345
12345	000	0.12345×10^0	0.12345
12345	-001	0.12345×10^{-1}	0.012345

BINARY FLOATING POIN

We will explain binary floating point using a total of 8 bits (1 for sign, 3 for exponent, 4 for fraction); most practical systems use 32 bits, but the following explains the principles without the confusion of many bits. The bits are arranged as follows,

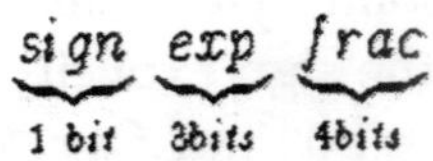

The fraction (mantissa) is just a straight fraction, i.e. the (virtual) point is at the left hand side of the four bits. The exponent is stored as a signed number, using excess 4 (biased by 4) representation, i.e. biased by 4 - recall Table. Thus, the bit patterns in the exponent represent values as shown in Table .

Table: 3-bit, excess 4

bits	111	110	101	100	011	010	001	000
value	3	2	1	0	-1	-2	-3	*

Of course, you don't have to look up Table, simply subtract 4 from the stored number.

The value, v, of the stored floating point number.

$$v = f \times r^e$$

where f is the fraction, r is the radix (base) of the exponent and e is the exponent.

Or, to make the excess in the exponent more explicit, $v = f \times r^{e-q}$

where q is the excess.

Normalisation

Unless otherwise stated, f is bounded as follows:

$.1000 \leq f \leq .1111\, f \times r^{e-q}$

i.e. the top bit of the fraction is always set.

The most common practical floating point number system (IEEE Standard 754, single precision) uses 8 bits for exponent, 23 for fraction - including 1 for sign; a total of 32 bits. There is a double precision format at 64 bits and extended precision at 80 bits.

Hidden Bit

Notice that, in a normalised number, eqn 2.4, the top bit is always set; thus, we don't really have to store it - this is a trick that the IEEE standard uses to 'steal' an additional bit for the fraction; actually, they work it so that the top bit is assumed to be just to the left of the 'point'. We will adopt this trick for our floating-point-byte system. Where we show the hidden bit, and make the sign explicit,

$$v = (-1)^3 \times 1.f \times r^{e-q}$$

Denormalised Numbers

In special circumstances, IEEE 754 allows numbers to be stored with a denormalised fraction; for such cases they use exponent 000 which flags the special case. The major advantage is that we can store a 'pure' zero.

Henceforth, we will call this small floating point number system flob - floating-point byte.

Example: Stored representation is 01101011, what is the value?

Sign 0→+ Stored exponent = 110 = 6_{10}, actual exponent =

+2. Fraction = 1011, i.e. with hidden bit, 1.1011. Therefore,

Example: Stored representation is 10111100, what is the value?

Sign 0→– Stored exponent = 011 = 3_{10}, actual exponent = –1. Fraction = 1100, i.e. with hidden bit, 1.1100. Therefore,

$$\begin{aligned} v &= -1.1100 \times 2^{-1} \\ &= -.11100 \times 2^{0} \\ &= -.11100 \\ &= -(0.5 + 0.25 + 0.125) \\ &= -0.875 \end{aligned}$$

None: In the following we will assume that the only allowed denormalised number is 0; i.e. 0000000→0; there is no other allowable case where stored exponent can be 000.

ROUNDING AND TRUNCATION

As mentioned in the introduction, section 2.2.4, the real numbers form a continuum. However, instead of infinity of them, exactly 225can be represented in flob. In flob there are three legal regions on the real line, and four illegal.

```
-infinity -15.5      -0.125        0          0.125     15.5 +inf
-----------+----------+-----------+----------+----------+-------

            ............                      ............

-----------+----------+-----------+----------+----------+-------

  illegal   | legal    | illegal   | illegal  | legal    | illegal
  (1)          (2)        (3)        (4)  (5)      (6)         (7)


  Negative    Negatives  Neg.       Zero Pos.   Positives  Pos.
  Overflow               Underflow      Underflow          Overflow
```

Fig. The Seven Regions of The Real Number Line.

The dots (...) in Figure are meant to show that, even within the legal regions, we do not have a continuum, but a discrete set of numbers. So, in reality, there are many other *illegal* regions:

For actual numbers, we must compromise and represent

them with a close legal number; this entails *rounding* or *truncation*. Rounding is probably the best - it takes the closest; e.g. in a one digit representation, 0.34→0.3, 0.36→0.4; therefore, the maximum error = 0.05, i.e. half the step between legal numbers (0.1).

Truncation

Truncation chops off the insignificant digits, e.g. 0.34→0.3; in this case, the maximum error is 0.09.

ADDITION AND SUBTRACTION IN FLOATING POINT

Here, we merely show the principle; and, to avoid some detail we use a decimal format.

Example: $2\times10^6+13\times10^3$. Ans. $2.031\times10^6=2013\times10^3=2013000$.

The general method for addition and subtraction, (*A*+/-*B*) is:

1. Line up points by making exponents equal:
   a. Identify the operand with the smaller exponent, say A - *expA*;
   b. Do. Successively shift A's fraction right while increasing its exponent;
   c. until *expA* = *expB*.
2. Add (or subtract) the fractions.
3. Normalise the result.

Example: $0.28\times10^1+0.12\times10^0$.

0.280×10^1

$+ 0.012\times10^1$

$= 0.292\times10^1$

Example. $0.28\times10^2-0.24\times10^2$.

0.280×10^2

$- 0.240\times10^2$

$= 0.040\times10^2$

$= 0.400\times10^1$ after normalisation

MULTIPLICATION AND DIVSTRANGELY, THESE ARE EASIER THAN ADD AND SUBTRACT

MULTIPLICATION

- Multiply the fractions;

- Add the exponents;
- Normalise the result.

DIVISION

- Divide the fractions;
- Subtract the exponents;
- Normalise the result.

$$x = f_x \times r^{ex}$$

$$y = f_y \times xr^{ey}$$

$$x \times y = (f_x \times f_y) \times r^{(e_x + e_y)}$$

$$\frac{x}{y} = \frac{f_x}{f_y} \times r^{(e1-e2)}$$

Example: $0.120 \times 10^1 \times 0.253 \times 10^2 = 1.2 \times 25.3$ ·

$0.120 \times 10^1 \times 0.253 \times 10^2 = 0.030360 \times 10^3$,

$= 0.030 \times 10^3$

$= 0.300 \times 10^2$

FIXED VERSUS FLOATING POINT

Speed

Where there is no dedicated floating-point hardware, fixed - point arithmetic can be performed faster and easier, see below;

Ease of Implementation

Fixed point may be easier to implement easier; in the past, many computers-have only integer arithmetic units, and so must use software to do floating point.

Up to the Intel 80386 series - great-great-grand-daddy of the

Pentium III - you had to have a special purpose floating-point co-processor (the 80387) for Intel XX86 microprocessors; modern digital-signal-processors (DSPs) may not have any floating-point;

Ease of Programming

Generally, floating point saves the programmer any worry about over/under-flow;

Range

Fixed point limits the range of the numbers being represented. Floating point gives greater range - at the cost of resolution; see below for definitions of range and resolution.

ACCURACY

Strictly speaking, accuracy is not a feature of the number system. Accuracy is determined by the error inherent in the production of the number, for example, the error in reading a metre. Thus, 12.34 ± 0.01; this indicates that the actual number could be anywhere between 12.33 and 12.35. It might be possible to include better *resolution* e.g. express it as 12.34567, but, due to the *accuracy* limitation, the 567would be meaningless.

REAL NUMBERS AND FLOATING-POINT FORMATS.

This section describes how real numbers are represented in floating-point format in the Intel Architecture FPU. It also introduces terms such as normalized numbers, denormalized numbers, biased exponents, signed zeros, and NaNs. Readers who are already familiar with floating-point processing techniques and the IEEE standards may wish to skip this section.

REAL NUMBER SYSTEM

The real-number system comprises the continuum of real numbers from minus infinity (-·) to plus infinity (+·).

Binary Real Number System

Because the size and number of registers that any computer can have is limited, only a subset of the real-number continuum can be used in real-number calculations. As shown at the bottom of Figure, the subset of real numbers that a particular FPU supports represents an approximation of the real number system. The range and precision of this real-number subset is determined by the format that the FPU uses to represent real numbers.

FLOATING-POINT FORMAT

To increase the speed and efficiency of real-number computations, computers or FPUs typically represent real numbers in a binary floating-point format. In this format, a real number has three parts: a sign, a significand, and an exponent.

The binary floating-point format that the Intel Architecture FPU uses. This format conforms to the IEEE standard.

The sign is a binary value that indicates whether the number is positive (0) or negative (1). The significand has two parts: a 1-bit binary integer (also referred to as the J-bit) and a binary fraction. The J-bit is often not represented, but instead is an implied value. The exponent is a binary integer that represents the base-2 power that the significand is raised to.

Binary Floating-Point Format

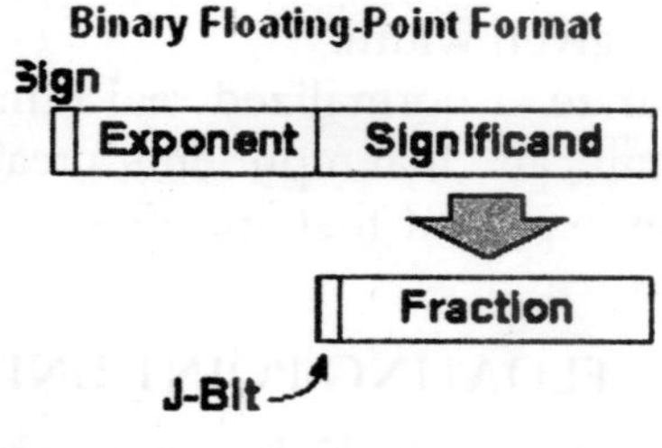

The real number 178.125 (in ordinary decimal format) is stored in floating-point format. The table lists a progression of real number notations that leads to the single-real, 32-bit floating-point format (which is one of the floating-point formats that the FPU supports). In this format, the significand is normalized and the exponent is biased For the single-real format, the biasing constant is +127.

Normalized Numbers: In most cases, the FPU represents real numbers in normalized form. This means that except for zero, the significand is always made up of an integer of 1 and the following fraction:

- 1.fff...ff

For values less than 1, leading zeros are eliminated. (For each leading zero eliminated, the exponent is decremented by one.)

Real Number Notation

Notation		Value	
Ordinary Decimal		178.125	
Scientific Decimal		$1.78125E_{10}2$	
Scientific Binary		$1.0110010001E_{2}111$	
Scientific Binary (Biased Exponent)		$1.0110010001E_{2}10000110$	
Single-Real Format Normalized	Sign	Biased Exponent	Significand
	0	10000110	011001000 10000000000000 1. (Implied)

Representing numbers in normalized form maximizes the number of significant digits that can be accommodated in a significand of a given width.

To summarize, a normalized real number consists of a normalized significand that represents a real number between 1 and 2 and an exponent that specifies the number's binary point.

FLOATING-POINT UNIT

The Intel Architecture Floating-Point Unit (FPU) provides high-performance floating-point processing capabilities. It supports the real, integer, and BCD-integer data types and the floating-point processing algorithms and exception handling architecture defined in the IEEE 754 and 854 Standards for Floating-Point Arithmetic.

The FPU executes instructions from the processor's normal instruction stream and greatly improves the efficiency of Intel Architecture processors in handling the types of high-precision floating-point processing operations commonly found in scientific, engineering, and business applications.

COMPATIBILITY AND EASE OF USE OF THE INTEL ARCHITECTURE FPU

The architecture of the Intel Architecture FPU has evolved in parallel with the architecture of early Intel Architecture processors. The first Intel Math Coprocessors (the Intel 8087, Intel 287, and Intel 387) were companion processors to the Intel 8086/8088, Intel 286, and Intel386 processors, respectively, and were designed to improve and extend the numeric processing capability of the Intel Architecture.

The Intel486 DX processor for the first time integrated the CPU and the FPU architectures on one chip. The Pentium processor's FPU offered the same architecture as the Intel486 DX processor's FPU, but with improved performance. The Pentium Pro processor's FPU further extended the floating-point processing capability of Intel Architecture family of processors and added several new instructions to improve processing throughput.

Throughout this evolution, compatibility among the various generations of FPUs and math coprocessors has been maintained. For example, the Pentium Pro processor's FPU is fully compatible with the Pentium and Intel486 DX processors's FPUs.

Each generation of the Intel Architecture FPUs have been explicitly designed to deliver stable, accurate results when programmed using straightforward "pencil and paper" algorithms, bringing the functionality and power of accurate numeric computation into the hands of the general user. The IEEE 754 standard specifically addresses this issue, recognizing the fundamental importance of making numeric computations both easy and safe to use.

For example, some processors can overflow when two single-precision floating-point numbers are multiplied together and then divided by a third, even if the final result is a perfectly valid 32-bit number. The Intel Architecture FPUs deliver the correctly rounded result.

Other typical examples of undesirable machine behaviour in straightforward calculations occur when computing financial rate of return, which involves the expression (1 + i)n or when solving for roots of a quadratic equation:

$$\frac{-b \pm \sqrt{b^2 - 4ac}}{2a}$$

If *a* does not equal 0, the formula is numerically unstable when the roots are nearly coincident or when their magnitudes are wildly different. The formula is also vulnerable to spurious over/underflows when the coefficients *a*, *b*, and *c* are all very big or all very tiny. When single-precision (4-byte) floating-point coefficients are given as data and the formula is evaluated in the FPU's normal way, keeping all intermediate results in its stack, the FPU produces impeccable single-precision roots. This happens because, by default and with no effort on the programmer's part, the FPU evaluates all those sub-expressions with so much extra precision and range as to overwhelm almost any threat to numerical integrity.

If double-precision data and results were at issue, a better formula would have to be used, and once again the FPU's default evaluation of that formula would provide substantially enhanced numerical integrity over mere double-precision evaluation.

On most machines, straightforward algorithms wili not deliver consistently correct results (and will not indicate when they are incorrect). To obtain correct results on traditional machines under all conditions usually requires sophisticated numerical techniques that go beyond typical programming practice.

General application programmers using straightforward algorithms will produce much more reliable programmes using the Intel architectures. This simple fact greatly reduces the software investment required to develop safe, accurate computation-based products.

Beyond traditional numeric support for scientific applications, the Intel architectures have built-in facilities for commercial computing. They can process decimal numbers of up to 18 digits without round-off errors, performing exact arithmetic on integers as large as 264 (or 1018). Exact arithmetic is vital in accounting applications where rounding errors may introduce monetary losses that cannot be reconciled.

The Intel FPU's contain a number of optional numerical facilities that can be invoked by sophisticated users. These advanced features include directed rounding, gradual underflow, and programmed exception-handling facilities.

These automatic exception-handling facilities permit a high degree of flexibility in numeric processing software, without burdening the programmer. While performing numeric calculations, the processor automatically detects exception conditions that can potentially damage a calculation (for example, $X \div 0$ or

$\sqrt{X}$

when $X < 0$). By default, on-chip exception logic handles these exceptions so that a reasonable result is produced and execution may proceed without programme interruption. Alternatively, the processor can invoke a software exception handler to provide special results whenever various types of exceptions are detected.

BIASED EXPONENT

The FPU represents exponents in a biased form. This means that a constant is added to the actual exponent so that the biased exponent is always a positive number. The value of the biasing constant depends on the number of bits available for representing exponents in the floating-point format being used. The biasing constant is chosen so that the smallest normalized number can be reciprocated without overflow.

Real Number and Non-number Encodings

A variety of real numbers and special values can be encoded in the FPU's floating-point format. These numbers and values are generally divided into the following classes:

- Signed zeros.
- Denormalized finite numbers.
- Normalized finite numbers.
- Signed infinities.

- NaNs.
- Indefinite numbers.

(The term NaN stands for "Not a Number.")

The encodings for these numbers and non-numbers fit into the real number continuum. The encodings shown here are for the IEEE single-precision (32-bit) format, where the term "S" indicates the sign bit, "E" the biased exponent, and "F" the fraction. (The exponent values are given in decimal.)

The FPU can operate on and/or return any of these values, depending on the type of computation being performed. The following sections describe these number and non-number classes.

SIGNED ZEROS

Zero can be represented as a +0 or a -0 depending on the sign bit. Both encodings are equal in value. The sign of a zero result depends on the operation being performed and the rounding mode being used.

Signed zeros have been provided to aid in implementing interval arithmetic. The sign of a zero may indicate the direction from which underflow occurred, or it may indicate the sign of an · that has been reciprocated.

NORMALIZED AND DENORMALIZED FINITE NUMBERS

Non-zero, finite numbers are divided into two classes: normalized and denormalized. The normalized finite numbers comprise all the non-zero finite values that can be encoded in a normalized real number format between zero and ·. In the single-real format this group of numbers includes all the numbers with biased exponents ranging from 1 to 254_{10} (unbiased, the exponent range is from -126_{10} to $+127_{10}$).

When real numbers become very close to zero, the normalized-number format can no longer be used to represent the numbers.

This is because the range of the exponent is not large enough to compensate for shifting the binary point to the right to eliminate leading zeros.

When the biased exponent is zero, smaller numbers can only be represented by making the integer bit (and perhaps other leading bits) of the significand zero.

The numbers in this range are called denormalized (or tiny) numbers.

The use of leading zeros with denormalized numbers allows smaller numbers to be represented. However, this denormalization causes a loss of precision (the number of significant bits in the fraction is reduced by the leading zeros).

Real Numbers and NaNs

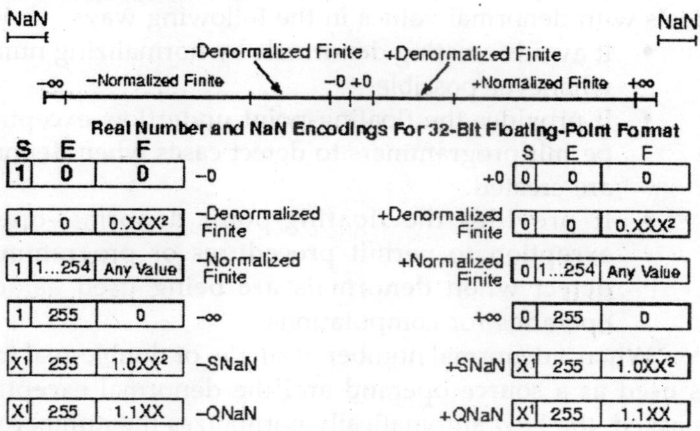

NOTES:
1. Sign bit ignored.
2. Fractions must be non-zero.

When performing normalized floating-point computations, an FPU normally operates on normalized numbers and produces normalized numbers as results. Denormalized numbers represent an underflow condition.

A denormalized number is computed through a technique called gradual underflow.

Here the single-real format is being used, so the minimum exponent (unbiased) is -126_{10}. The true result in this example requires an exponent of -129_{10} in order to have a normalized number. Since -129_{10} is beyond the allowable exponent range, the result is denormalized by inserting leading zeros until the minimum exponent of -126_{10} is reached.

Denormalization Process

Operation	Sign	Exponent*	Significand
True Result	0	-129	1.01011100000...00
Denormalize	0	-128	0.10101110000...00
Denormalize	0	-127	0.01010111000...00
Denormalize	0	-126	0.00101011100...00
Denormal Result	0	-126	0.00101011100...00

NOTE: Expressed as an unbiased, decimal number.

In the extreme case, all the significant bits are shifted out to the right by leading zeros, creating a zero result. The FPU deals with denormal values in the following ways:

- It avoids creating denormals by normalizing numbers whenever possible.
- It provides the floating-point underflow exception to permit programmers to detect cases when denormals are created.
- It provides the floating-point denormal-operand exception to permit procedures or programmes to detect when denormals are being used as source operands for computations.

When a denormal number in single- or double-real format is used as a source operand and the denormal exception is masked, the FPU automatically normalizes the number when it is converted to extended-real format.

Signed Infinities

The two infinities, +· and -·, represent the maximum positive and negative real numbers, respectively, that can be represented in the floating-point format. Infinity is always represented by a zero significand (fraction and integer bit) and the maximum biased exponent allowed in the specified format (for example, 255_{10} for the single-real format).

The signs of infinities are observed, and comparisons are possible. Infinities are always interpreted in the affine sense; that less than any finite number and +· is greater than any finite number. Arithmetic on infinities is always exact. Exceptions are generated only when the use of an infinity as a source operand constitutes an invalid operation.

Whereas denormalized numbers represent an underflow condition, the two infinity numbers represent the result of an overflow condition. Here, the normalized result of a computation has a biased exponent greater than the largest allowable exponent for the selected result format.

NaNs

Since NaNs are non-numbers, they are not part of the real number line. In Figure, the encoding space for NaNs in the FPU floating-point formats is shown above the ends of the real number line. This space includes any value with the maximum allowable biased exponent and a non-zero fraction. (The sign bit is ignored for NaNs.)

The IEEE standard defines two classes of NaN: quiet NaNs (QNaNs) and signaling NaNs (SNaNs). A QNaN is a NaN with the most significant fraction bit set; an SNaN is a NaN with the most significant fraction bit clear. QNaNs are allowed to propagate through most arithmetic operations without signaling an exception. SNaNs generally signal an invalid-operation exception whenever they appear as operands in arithmetic operations. Exceptions are discussed in "Floating-Point Exception Handling".

See "Operating on NaNs", for detailed information on how the FPU handles NaNs.

Indefinite

For each FPU data type, one unique encoding is reserved for representing the special value indefinite. For example, when operating on real values, the real indefinite value is a QNaN.The FPU produces indefinite values as responses to masked floating-point exceptions.

FPU ARCHITECTURE

From an abstract, architectural view, the FPU is a coprocessor that operates in parallel with the processor's integer unit. The FPU gets its instructions from the same instruction decoder and sequencer as the integer unit and shares the system bus with the integer unit. Other than these connections, the integer unit and FPU operate independently and in parallel. (The actual microarchitecture of an Intel Architecture processor varies among the various families of processors. For example, the Pentium Pro processor has two integer units and two FPUs; whereas, the Pentium processor has two integer units and one FPU, and the Intel486 processor has one integer unit and one FPU.)

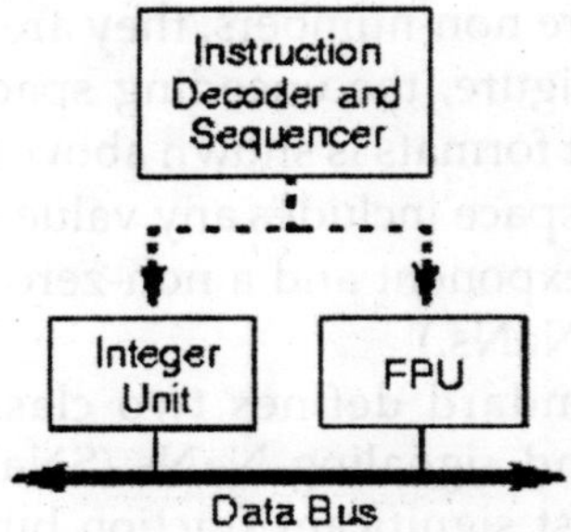

Fig. Relationship Between the Integer Unit and the FPU

The instruction execution environment of the FPU consists of 8 data registers (called the FPU data registers) and the following special-purpose registers:

- The status register.
- The control register.
- The tag word register.
- Instruction pointer register.
- Last operand (data pointer) register.
- Opcode register.

These registers are described in the following sections.

The FPU Data Registers

The FPU data registers consist of eight 80-bit registers. Values are stored in these registers in the extended-real format. When real, integer, or packed BCD integer values (in any of the formats shown in Figure are loaded from memory into any of the FPU data registers, the values are automatically converted into extended-real format (if they are not already in that format). When computation results are subsequently transferred back into memory from any of the FPU registers, the results can be left in the extended-real format or converted back into one of the other FPU formats (real, integer, or packed BCD integers).

The FPU instructions treat the eight FPU data registers as a register stack.All addressing of the data registers is relative to the register on the top of the stack. The register number of the current top-of-stack register is stored in the TOP (stack TOP) field in the FPU status word. Load operations decrement TOP by one and load a value into the new top-of-stack register, and store operations store the value from the current TOP register in memory and then increment TOP by one. (For the FPU, a load operation is equivalent to a push and a store operation is equivalent to a pop.)

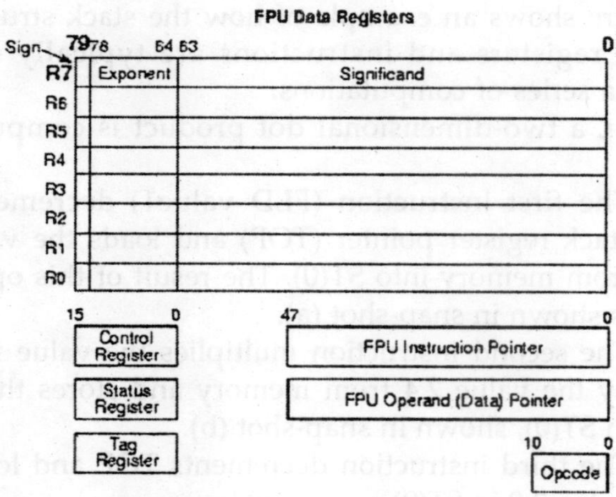

Fig. FPU Execution Environment

If a load operation is performed when TOP is at 0, register wraparound occurs and the new value of TOP is set to 7. The floating-point stack-overflow exception indicates when wraparound might cause an unsaved value to be overwritten.

Many floating-point instructions have several addressing modes that permit the programmer to implicitly operate on the top of the stack, or to explicitly operate on specific registers relative to the TOP. Assemblers supports these register addressing modes, using the expression ST(0), or simply ST, to represent the current stack top and ST(i) to specify the *i*th register from TOP in the stack ($0 \leq i \leq 7$). For example, if TOP contains 011B (register 3 is the top of the stack), the following instruction would add the contents of two registers in the stack.

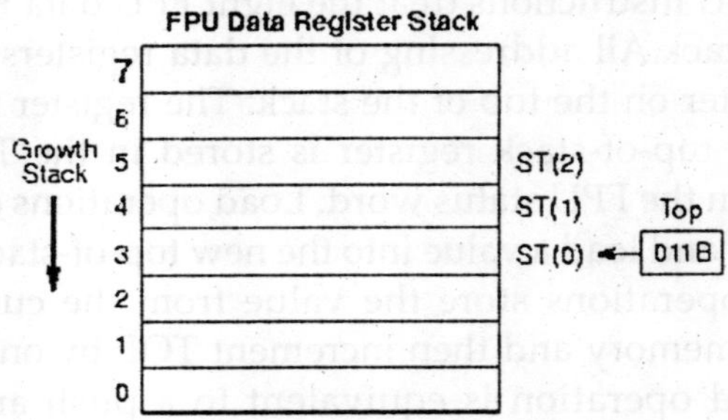

Fig. FPU Data Register Stack

Figure shows an example of how the stack structure of the FPU registers and instructions are typically used to perform a series of computations.

Here, a two-dimensional dot product is computed, as follows:

1. The first instruction (FLD value1) decrements the stack register pointer (TOP) and loads the value 5.6 from memory into ST(0). The result of this operation is shown in snap-shot (a).
2. The second instruction multiplies the value in ST(0) by the value 2.4 from memory and stores the result in ST(0), shown in snap-shot (b).
3. The third instruction decrements TOP and loads the value 3.8 in ST(0).
4. The fourth instruction multiplies the value in ST(0) by the value 10.3 from memory and stores the result in ST(0), shown in snap-shot (c).
5. The fifth instruction adds the value and the value in ST(1) and stores the result in ST(0), shown in snap-shot (d).

The style of programming demonstrated in this example is supported by the floating-point instruction set. In cases where the stack structure causes computation bottlenecks, the FXCH (exchange FPU register contents) instruction can be used to streamline a computation.

Parameter Passing With the FPU Register Stack

Like the general-purpose registers in the processor's integer unit, the contents of the FPU data registers are unaffected by procedure calls, or in other words, the values are maintained across procedure boundaries. A calling procedure can thus use the FPU data registers (as well as the procedure stack) for passing parameter between procedures. The called procedure can reference parameters passed through the register stack using the current stack register pointer (TOP) and the ST(0) and ST(i) nomenclature. It is also common practice for a called procedure to leave a return value or result in register ST(0) when returning execution to the calling procedure or programme.

Example FPU Dot Product Computation

Computation

Dot Product = (5.6 x 2.4) + (3.8 x 10.3)

Code:

```
FLD   value1 ; (a) value1=5.6
FMUL  value2 ; (b) value2=2.4
FLD   value3 ;     value3=3.8
FMUL  value4 ; (c) value4=10.3
FADD  ST(1)  ; (d)
```

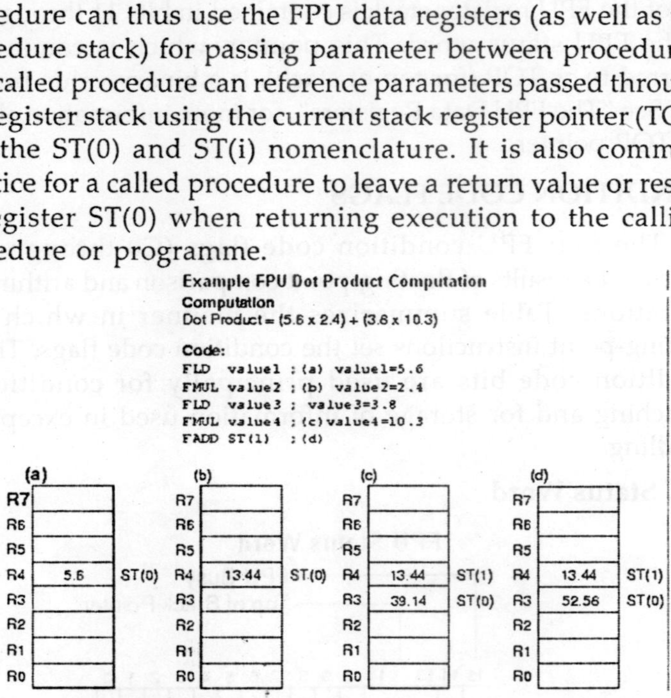

Figure. FPU Dot Product Computation

FPU STATUS REGISTER

The 16-bit FPU status register indicates the current state of the FPU. The flags in the FPU status register include the FPU busy flag, top-of-stack (TOP) pointer, condition code flags, error summary status flag, stack fault flag, and exception flags. The FPU sets the flags in this register to show the results of operations.

The contents of the FPU status register (referred to as the FPU status word) can be stored in memory using the FSTSW/ FNSTSW, FSTENV/FNSTENV, and FSAVE/FNSAVE instructions. It can also be stored in the AX register of the integer unit, using the FSTSW/FNSTSW instructions.

TOP OF STACK (TOP) POINTER

A pointer to the FPU data register that is currently at the top of the FPU register stack is contained in bits 11 through 13 of the FPU status word. This pointer, which is commonly referred to as TOP (for top-of-stack), is a binary value from 0 to 7. See "The FPU Data Registers", for more information about the TOP pointer.

CONDITION CODE FLAGS

The four FPU condition code flags (C0 through C3) indicate the results of floating-point comparison and arithmetic operations. Table summarizes the manner in which the floating-point instructions set the condition code flags. These condition code bits are used principally for conditional branching and for storage of information used in exception handling

FPU Status Word

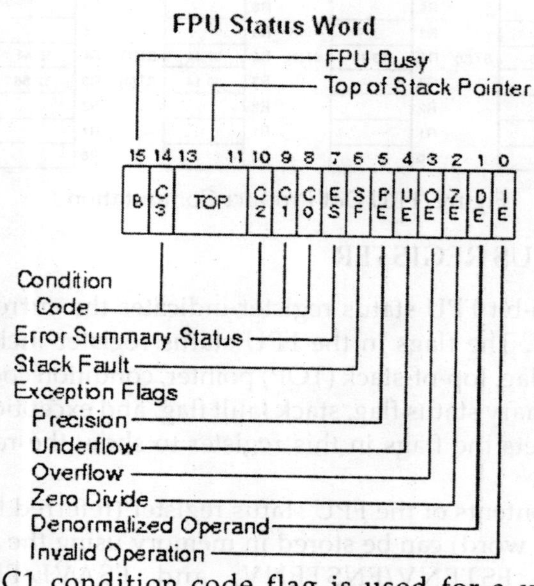

The C1 condition code flag is used for a variety of

functions. When both the IE and SF flags in the FPU status word are set, indicating a stack overflow or underflow exception (#IS), the C1 flag distinguishes between overflow (C1=1) and underflow (C1=0). When the PE flag in the status word is set, indicating an inexact (rounded) result, the C1 flag is set to 1 if the last rounding by the instruction was upward. The FXAM instruction sets C1 to the sign of the value being examined.

The FPTAN, FSIN, FCOS, and FSINCOS instructions set the C2 flag to 1 to indicate that the source operand is beyond the allowable range of $\pm 2^{63}$.

Where the state of the condition code flags are listed as undefined in Table 31-3, do not rely on any specific value in these flags.

FPU Condition Code Interpretation

FPU Condition Code Interpretation				
Instruction	**C0**	**C3**	**C2**	**C1**
FCOM, FCOMP, FCOMPP, FICOM, FICOMP, FTST, FUCOM, FUCOMP, FUCOMPP	Result of Comparison		Operands are not Comparable	0 or #IS
FCOMI, FCOMIP, FUCOMI, FUCOMIP	Undefined. (These instructions set the status flags in the EFLAGS register.)			#IS
FXAM	Operand class			Sign
FPREM, FPREM1	Q2	Q1	0=reduction complete 1=reduction incomplete	Q0 or #IS
F2XM1, FADD, FADDP, FBSTP, FCMOVcc, FIADD, FDIV, FDIVP, FDIVR, FDIVRP, FIDIV, FIDIVR, FIMUL, FIST, FISTP, FISUB, FISUBR,FMUL, FMULP, FPATAN, FRNDINT, FSCALE, FST, FSTP, FSUB, FSUBP, FSUBR, FSUBRP,FSQRT, FYL2X FYL2XP1	Undefined			Roundup or #IS
FCOS, FSIN, FSINCOS, FPTAN	Undefined		1=source operand out of range.	Roundup or #IS (Undefined if C2=1)
FABS, FBLD, FCHS, FDECSTP, FILD, FINCSTP, FLD, Load Constants, FSTP (ext. real), FXCH, FXTRACT	Undefined			0 or #IS
FLDENV, FRSTOR	Each bit loaded from memory			
FFREE, FLDCW, FCLEX/FNCLEX, FNOP, FSTCW/FNSTCW, FSTENV/FNSTENV, FSTSW/FNSTSW,	Undefined			
FINIT/FNINIT, FSAVE/FNSAVE	0	0	0	0

Exception Flags

The six exception flags (bits 0 through 5) of the status word indicate that one or more floating-point exceptions has been detected since the bits were last cleared. The individual exception flags (IE, DE, ZE, OE, UE, and PE) are described in detail in "Floating-Point Exception Handling". Each of the exception flags can be masked by an exception mask bit in the FPU control word.The exception summary status (ES) flag (bit 7) is set when any of the unmasked exception flags are set. When the ES flag is set, the FPU exception handler is invoked, using one of the techniques described in "Software Exception Handling". (Note that if an exception flag is masked, the FPU will still set the flag if its associated exception occurs, but it will not set the ES flag.)

The exception flags are "sticky" bits, meaning that once set, they remain set until explicitly cleared. They can be cleared by executing the FCLEX/FNCLEX (clear exceptions) instructions, by reinitializing the FPU with the FINIT/FNINIT or FSAVE/FNSAVE instructions, or by overwriting the flags with an FRSTOR or FLDENV instruction.

The B-bit (bit 15) is included for 8087 compatibility only. It reflects the contents of the ES flag.

STACK FAULT FLAG

The stack fault flag (bit 6 of the FPU status word) indicates that stack overflow or stack underflow has occurred. The FPU explicitly sets the SF flag when it detects a stack overflow or underflow condition, but it does not explicitly clear the flag when it detects an invalid-arithmetic-operand condition. When this flag is set, the condition code flag C1 indicates the nature of the fault: overflow (C1 = 1) and underflow (C1 = 0). The SF flag is a "sticky" flag, meaning that after it is set, the processor does not clear it until it is explicitly instructed to do so (for example, by an FINIT/FNINIT, FCLEX/FNCLEX, or FSAVE/FNSAVE instruction).

BRANCHING AND CONDITIONAL MOVES ON FPU CONDITION CODES

The Intel Architecture FPU (beginning with the Pentium Pro processor) supports two mechanisms for branching and performing conditional moves according to comparisons of two floating-point values. These mechanism are referred to here as the "old mechanism" and the "new mechanism."

The old mechanism is available in FPU's prior to the Pentium Pro processor and in the Pentium Pro processor. This mechanism uses the floating-point compare instructions (FCOM, FCOMP, FCOMPP, FTST, FUCOMPP, FICOM, and FICOMP) to compare two floating-point values and set the condition code flags (C0 through C3) according to the results. The contents of the condition code flags are then copied into the status flags of the EFLAGS register using a two step process:

1. The FSTSW AX instruction moves the FPU status word into the AX register.

2. The SAHF instruction copies the upper 8 bits of the AX register, which includes the condition code flags, into the lower 8 bits of the EFLAGS register.

When the condition code flags have been loaded into the EFLAGS register, conditional jumps or conditional moves can be performed based on the new settings of the status flags in the EFLAGS register.

Moving the FPU Condition Codes to the EFLAGS Register

Moving the FPU Condition Codes to the EFLAGS Register

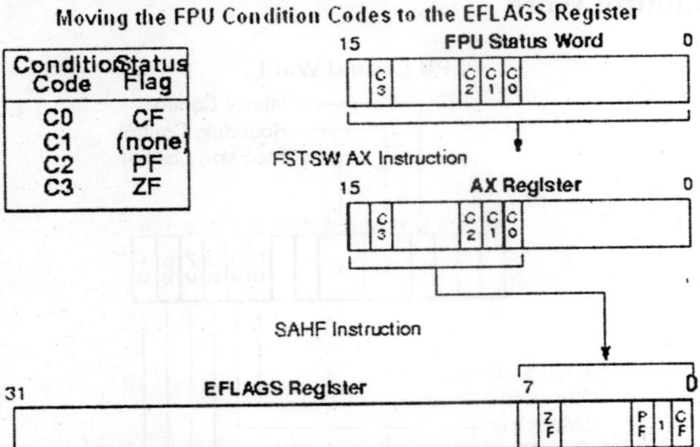

The new mechanism is available only in the Pentium Pro processor. Using this mechanism, the new floating-point compare and set EFLAGS instructions (FCOMI, FCOMIP, FUCOMI, and FUCOMIP) compare two floating-point values and set the ZF, PF, and CF flags in the EFLAGS register directly. A single instruction thus replaces the three instructions required by the old mechanism. Note also that the FCMOV*cc* instructions (also new in the Pentium Pro processor) allow conditional moves of floating-point values (values in the FPU data registers) based on the setting of the status flags (ZF, PF, and CF) in the EFLAGS register. These instructions eliminate the need for an IF statement to perform conditional moves of floating-point values.

FPU CONTROL WORD

The 16-bit FPU control word controls the precision of the FPU and rounding method used. It also contains the exception-flag mask bits. The control word is cached in the FPU control register. The contents of this register can be loaded with the FLDCW instruction and stored in memory with the FSTCW/FNSTCW instructions.

When the FPU is initialized with either an FINIT/FNINIT or FSAVE/FNSAVE instruction, the FPU control word is set to 037FH, which masks all floating-point exceptions, sets rounding to nearest, and sets the FPU precision to 64 bits.

FPU Control Word

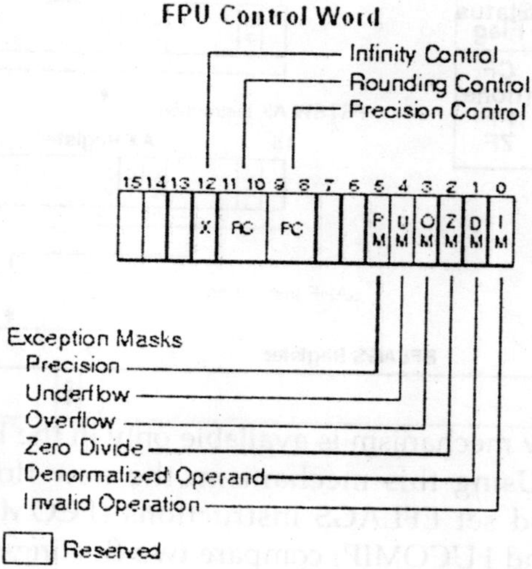

Exception-Flag Masks

The exception-flag mask bits (bits 0 through 5 of the FPU control word) mask the 6 exception flags in the FPU status word (also bits 0 through 5). When one of these mask bits is set, its corresponding floating-point exception is blocked from being generated.

Precision Control Field

The precision-control (PC) field (bits 8 and 9 of the FPU control word) determines the precision (64, 53, or 24 bits) of floating-point calculations made by the FPU.The default precision is extended precision, which uses the full 64-bit significand available with the extended-real format of the FPU data registers.

This setting is best suited for most applications, because it allows applications to take full advantage of the precision of the extended-real format.

Precision Control Field (PC)

Precision	PC Field
Single Precision (24-Bits*)	00B
Reserved	01B
Double Precision (53-Bits*)	10B
Extended Precision (64-Bits)	11B

*Includes the implied integer bit.

The double precision and single precision settings, reduce the size of the significand to 53 bits and 24 bits, respectively. These settings are provided to support the IEEE standard and to allow exact replication of calculations which were done using the lower precision data types. Using these settings nullifies the advantages of the extended-real format's 64-bit significand length. When reduced precision is specified, the rounding of the significand value clears the unused bits on the right to zeros.

The precision-control bits only affect the results of the following floating-point instructions: FADD, FADDP, FSUB, FSUBP, FSUBR, FSUBRP, FMUL, FMULP, FDIV, FDIVP, FDIVR, FDIVRP, and FSQRT.

ROUNDING CONTROL FIELD

The rounding-control (RC) field of the FPU control register (bits 10 and 11) controls how the results of floating-point instructions are rounded.

Four rounding modes are supported: round to nearest, round up, round down, and round toward zero. Round to nearest is the default rounding mode and is suitable for most applications. It provides the most accurate and statistically unbiased estimate of the true result.

Fig. Rounding Control Field (RC)

Rounding Mode	**RC Field Setting**	**Description**
Round to nearest (even)	00B	Rounded result is the closest to the infinitely precise result. If two values are equally close, the result is the
even		value (that is, the one with the least significant bit of zero).
Round down (toward -·)	01B	Rounded result is close to but no greater than the infinitely precise result.
Round up (toward +·)	10B	Rounded result is close to but no less than the infinitely precise result.
Round toward zero (Truncate)	11B	Rounded result is close to but no greater in absolute value than the infinitely precise result.

The round up and round down modes are termed directed rounding and can be used to implement interval arithmetic. Interval arithmetic is used to determine upper and lower bounds for the true result of a multistep computation, when the intermediate results of the computation are subject to rounding.

The round toward zero mode (sometimes called the "chop" mode) is commonly used when performing integer arithmetic with the FPU.

Whenever possible, the FPU produces an infinitely precise

result in the destination format (single, double, or extended real).

However, it is often the case that the infinitely precise result of an arithmetic or store operation cannot be encoded exactly in the format of the destination operand.

For example, the following value (*a*) has a 24-bit fraction. The least-significant bit of this fraction (the underlined bit) cannot be encoded exactly in the single-real format (which has only a 23-bit fraction):

(*a*) 1.0001 0000 1000 0011 1001 0111E_2 101

To round this result (*a*), the FPU first selects two representable fractions *b* and *c* that most closely bracket *a* in value ($b < a < c$).

(*b*) 1.0001 0000 1000 0011 1001 011E_2 101

(*c*) 1.0001 0000 1000 0011 1001 100E_2 101

The FPU then sets the result to *b* or to *c* according to the rounding mode selected in the RC field. Rounding introduces an error in a result that is less than one unit in the last place to which the result is rounded.

The rounded result is called the inexact result. When the FPU produces an inexact result, the floating-point precision (inexact) flag (PE) is set in the FPU status word.

When the overflow exception is masked and the infinitely precise result is between the largest positive finite value allowed in a particular format and +·, the FPU rounds the result as shown in Table 31-6.

Table. Rounding of Positive Numbers With Masked Overflow

Rounding Mode	Result
Rounding to nearest (even)	+·
Rounding toward zero (Truncate)	Maximum, positive finite value
Rounding up (toward +·)	+·
Rounding down) (toward -·)	Maximum, positive finite value

When the overflow exception is masked and the infinitely precise result is between the largest negative finite value allowed in a particular format and -·, the FPU rounds the result.

Table: Rounding of Negative Numbers With Masked Overflow

Rounding Mode	Result
Rounding to nearest (even)	-·
Rounding toward zero (Truncate) value	Maximum, negative finite
Rounding up (toward +·) value	Maximum, negative finite
Rounding down) (toward -·)	-·

The rounding modes have no effect on comparison operations, operations that produce exact results, or operations that produce NaN results.

Infinity Control Flag

The infinity control flag (bit 12 of the FPU control word) is provided for compatibility with the Intel 287 Math Coprocessor; it is not meaningful for the Pentium Pro processor FPU or for the Pentium processor FPU, the Intel486 processor FPU, or Intel 387 processor NPX. See "Signed Infinities", for information on how the Intel Architecture FPUs handle infinity values.

FPU Tag Word

The 16-bit tag word indicates the contents of each the 8 registers in the FPU data-register stack (one 2-bit tag per register). The tag codes indicate whether a register contains a valid number, zero, or a special floating-point number (NaN, infinity, denormal, or unsupported format), or whether it is empty. The FPU tag word is cached in the FPU in the FPU tag word register. When the FPU is initialized with either an FINIT/FNINIT or FSAVE/FNSAVE instruction, the FPU tag word is set to FFFFH, which marks all the FPU data registers as empty.

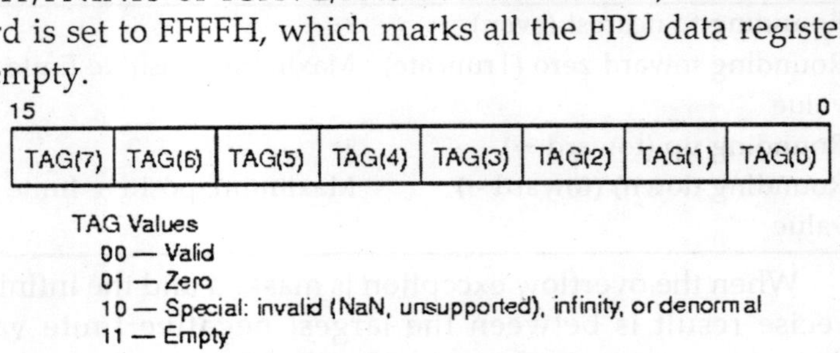

Figure. FPU Tag Word

Each tag in the FPU tag word corresponds to a physical register (numbers 0 through 7). The current top-of-stack (TOP) pointer stored in the FPU status word can be used to associate tags with registers relative to ST(0).

The FPU uses the tag values to detect stack overflow and underflow conditions. Stack overflow occurs when the TOP pointer is decremented (due to a register load or push operation) to point to a non-empty register. Stack underflow occurs when the TOP pointer is incremented (due to a save or pop operation) to point to an empty register or when an empty register is also referenced as a source operand. A non-empty register is defined as a register containing a zero (01), a valid value (00), or an special (10) value.

Application programmes and exception handlers can use this tag information to check the contents of an FPU data register without performing complex decoding of the actual data in the register. To read the tag register, it must be stored in memory using either the FSTENV/FNSTENV or FSAVE/FNSAVE instructions. Software cannot directly load or modify the tags in the tag register. The FLDENV and FRSTOR instructions load an image of the tag register into the FPU; however, the FPU uses those tag values only to determine if the data registers are empty (11B) or non-empty (00B, 01B, or 10B). If the tag register image indicates that a data register is empty, the tag in the tag register for that data register is marked empty (11B); if the tag register image indicates that the data register is non-empty, the FPU reads the actual value in the data register and sets the tag for the register accordingly. This action prevents a programme from setting the values in the tag register to incorrectly represent the actual contents of non-empty data registers.

The FPU Instruction and Operand (Data) Pointers

The FPU stores pointers to the instruction and operand (data) for the last non-control instruction executed in two 48-bit registers: the FPU instruction pointer and FPU operand (data) pointer registers. (This information is saved to provide state information for exception handlers.)

The contents of the FPU instruction and operand pointer registers remain unchanged when any of the control instructions (FINIT/FNINIT, FCLEX/FNCLEX, FLDCW, FSTCW/FNSTCW, FSTSW/FNSTSW, FSTENV/FNSTENV, FLDENV, FSAVE/FNSAVE, FRSTOR, and WAIT/FWAIT) are executed. The contents of the FPU operand register are undefined if the prior non-control instruction did not have a memory operand.

The pointers stored in the FPU instruction and operand pointer registers consist of an offset (stored in bits 0 through 31) and a segment selector (stored in bits 32 through 47).

These registers can be accessed by the FSTENV/FNSTENV, FLDENV, FINIT/FNINIT, FSAVE/FNSAVE and FRSTOR instructions. The FINIT/FNINIT and FSAVE/FNSAVE instructions clear these registers.

For all the Intel Architecture FPUs and NPXs except the 8087, the FPU instruction pointer points to any prefixes that preceded the instruction. For the 8087, the FPU instruction pointer points only to the actual opcode.

LAST INSTRUCTION OPCODE

The FPU stores the opcode of the last non-control instruction executed in an 11-bit FPU opcode register. (This information provides state information for exception handlers.) Only the first and second opcode bytes (after all prefixes) are stored in the FPU opcode register. The encoding of these two bytes. Since the upper 5 bits of the first opcode byte are the same for all floating-point opcodes (11011B), only the lower 3 bits of this byte are stored in the opcode register.

SAVING THE FPU'S STATE

The FSTENV/FNSTENV and FSAVE/FNSAVE instructions store FPU state information in memory for use by exception handlers and other system and application software. The FSTENV/FNSTENV instruction saves the contents of the status, control, tag, FPU instruction pointer, FPU operand pointer, and opcode registers. The FSAVE/

FNSAVE instruction stores that information plus the contents of the FPU data registers. Note that the FSAVE/FNSAVE instruction also initializes the FPU to default values (just as the FINIT/FNINIT instruction does) after it has saved the original state of the FPU.

Contents of FPU Opcode Registers

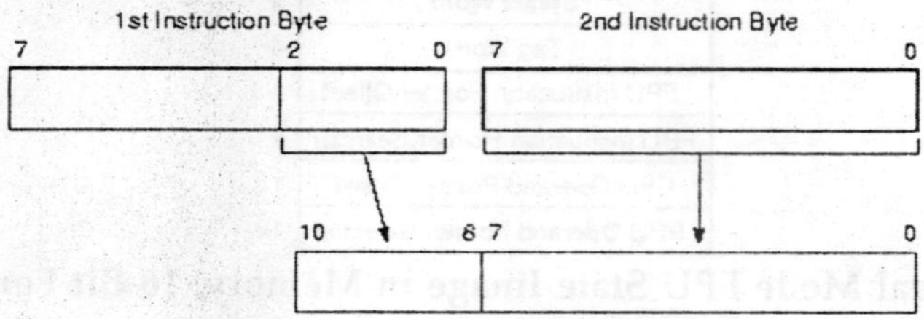

FPU Opcode Register

Protected Mode FPU State Image in Memory, 32-Bit Format

32-Bit Protected Mode Format

31 ... 16	15 ... 0	
	Control Word	0
	Status Word	4
	Tag Word	8
FPU Instruction Pointer Offset		12
0000 Opcode 10...00	FPU Instruction Pointer Selector	16
FPU Operand Pointer Offset		20
	FPU Operand Pointer Selector	24

☐ Reserved

Real Mode FPU State Image in Memory, 32-Bit Format

32-Bit Real-Address Mode Format

31 ... 16	15 ... 0	
	Control Word	0
	Status Word	4
	Tag Word	8
	FPU Instruction Pointer 15...00	12
0000 FPU Instruction Pointer 31...16	0 Opcode 10...00	16
Reserved	FPU Operand Pointer 15...00	20
0000 FPU Operand Pointer 31...16	000000000000	24

☐ Reserved

Protected Mode FPU State Image in Memory, 16-Bit Format

Protected Mode FPU State Image in Memory, 16-Bit Format

16-Bit Protected Mode Format

15 — 0	Offset
Control Word	0
Status Word	2
Tag Word	4
FPU Instruction Pointer Offset	6
FPU Instruction Pointer Selector	8
FPU Operand Pointer Offset	10
FPU Operand Pointer Selector	12

Real Mode FPU State Image in Memory, 16-Bit Format

Real Mode FPU State Image in Memory, 16-Bit Format

16-Bit Real-Address Mode and Virtual-8086 Mode Format

15		0	Offset
Control Word			0
Status Word			2
Tag Word			4
FPU Instruction Pointer 15...00			6
IP 19..16	0	Opcode 10...00	8
FPU Operand Pointer 15...00			10
OP 19..16	0	0 0 0 0 0 0 0 0 0 0 0 0	12

The FLDENV and FRSTOR instructions allow FPU state information to be loaded from memory into the FPU. Here, the FLDENV instruction loads only the status, control, tag, FPU instruction pointer, FPU operand pointer, and opcode registers, and the FRSTOR instruction loads all the FPU registers, including the FPU stack registers.

FLOATING-POINT DATA TYPES AND FORMATS ....

The Intel Architecture FPU recognizes and operates on seven data types, divided into three groups: reals, integers, and packed BCD integers.

Figure shows the data formats for each of the FPU data types. Table gives the length, precision, and approximate normalized range that can be represented of each FPU data type.

Denormal values are also supported in each of the real types, as required by IEEE Std. 854.

With the exception of the 80-bit extended-real format, all of these data types exist in memory only. When they are loaded into FPU data registers, they are converted into extended-real format and operated on in that format.

Floating-Point Unit Data Type Formats

Floating-Point Unit Data Type Formats

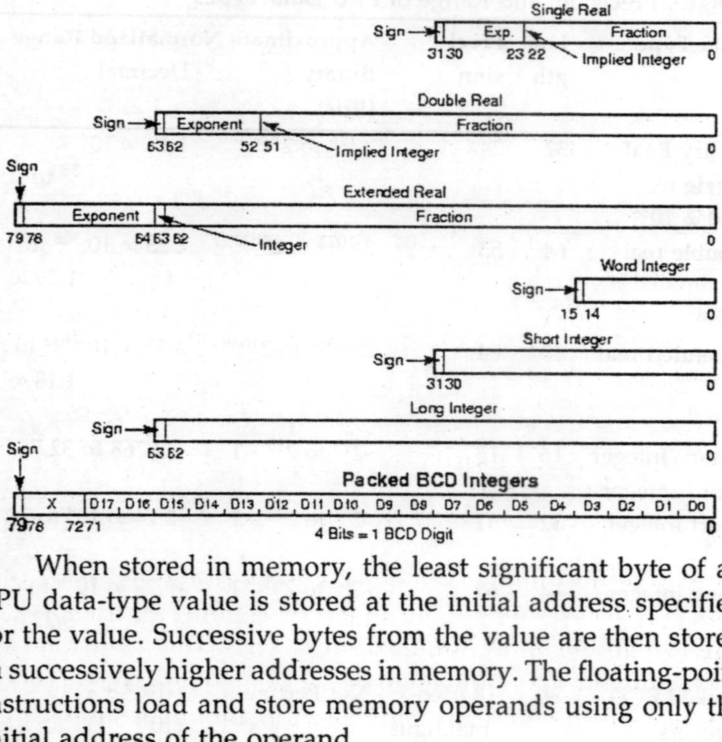

When stored in memory, the least significant byte of an FPU data-type value is stored at the initial address specified for the value. Successive bytes from the value are then stored in successively higher addresses in memory. The floating-point instructions load and store memory operands using only the initial address of the operand.

REAL NUMBERS

The FPU's three real data types (single-real, double-real, and extended-real) correspond directly to the single-precision, double-precision, and double-extended-precision formats in the IEEE standard. The extended-precision format is the format used by the data registers in the FPU.

For the single-real and double-real formats, only the fraction part of the significand is encoded. The integer is assumed to be 1 for all numbers except 0 and denormalized finite numbers. For the extended-real format, the integer is contained in bit 63, and the most-significant fraction bit is bit 62. Here, the integer is explicitly set to 1 for normalized numbers, infinities, and NaNs, and to 0 for zero and denormalized numbers.

Length, Precision, and Range of FPU Data Types

Data Type	Length	Precision	Approximate Normalized Range: Binary (Bits)	Approximate Normalized Range: Decimal
Binary Real Single real	32	24	2^{-126} to 2^{127}	1.18 ∞ 10^{38} to 3.40 ∞ 10^{38}
Double real	64	53	2^{-1022} to 2^{1023}	2.23 ∞ 10^{-308} to 1.79 ∞ 10^{308}
Extended real	80	64	2^{-16382} to 2^{16383}	3.37 ∞ 10^{-4932} to 1.18 ∞ 10^{4932}
Binary Integer Word integer	16	15	-2^{15} to 2^{15} - 1	-32,768 to 32,767
Short integer	32	31	-2^{31} to 2^{31} - 1	-2.14 ∞ 10^{9} to 2.14 ∞ 10^{9}
Long integer	64	63	-2^{63} to 2^{63} - 1	-9.22 ∞ 10^{18} to 9.22 ∞ 10^{18}
Packed BCD Integers	80	18 (decimaldigits)	Not Pertinent	(-10^{18} + 1) to (10^{18} - 1)

The exponent of each real data type is encoded in biased format. The biasing constant is 127 for the single-real format, 1023 for the double-real format, and 16,383 for the extended-real format.

The encodings for all the classes of real numbers (that is, zero, denormalized-finite, normalized-finite, and ·) and NaNs for each of the three real data-types. It also gives the format for the real indefinite value. When storing real values in memory, single-real values are stored in 4 consecutive bytes in memory; double-real values are stored in 8 consecutive bytes; and extended-real values are stored in 10 consecutive bytes.

Table: Real Number and NaN Encodings

Class		Sign	Biased Exponent	Significand Integer[1]	Fraction
	+	0	11..11	1	00..00
	+Normals	0	11..10	1	11..11
		.	.	.	.
		0	00..01	1	00..00
Positive	+Denormals	0	00..00	0	11.11
		.	.	.	.
		0	00..00	0	00..01
	+Zero	0	00..00	0	00..00
	-Zero	1	00..00	0	00..00
	-Denormals	1	00..00	0	00..01
		.	.	.	.
		1	00..00	0	11..11
Negative	-Normals	1	00..01	1	00..00
		.	.	.	.
		1	11..10	1	11..11
	-	1	11..11	1	00..00
	SNaN	X	11..11	1	0X..XX[2]
NaNs	QNaN	X	11..11	1	1X..XX
	Real Indefinite (QNaN)	1	11..11	1	10..00
			←8 Bits →		←23 Bits →
	Single-Real:		←11 Bits →		←52 Bits →
	Double-Real:		←15 Bits →		←63 Bits →
	Extended-Real				

As a general rule, values should be stored in memory in double-real format. This format provides sufficient range and precision to return correct results with a minimum of programmer attention. The single-real format is appropriate for applications that are constrained by memory; however, it provides less precision and a greater chance of overflow. The single-real format is also useful for debugging algorithms, because rounding problems will manifest themselves more quickly in this format. The extended-real format is normally reserved for holding intermediate results in the FPU registers and constants. Its extra length is designed to shield final results from the effects of rounding and overflow/underflow in intermediate calculations. However, when an application requires the maximum range and precision of the FPU (for data storage, computations, and results), values can be stored in memory in extended-real format. The real indefinite value is a QNaN encoding that is stored by several floating-point instructions in response to a masked floating-point invalid-operation exception. Integer bit is implied and not stored for single-real and double-real formats. The fraction for SNaN encodings must be non-zero.

BINARY INTEGERS

The FPU's three binary integer data types (word, short, and long) have identical formats, except for length. Table 31-8 gives the precision and range of these data types and Figure gives the formats. Table gives the encodings of the three binary integer types.

Fig. Binary Integer Encodings

Class	Sign	Magnitude		
Positive	Largest	0	11..11	
		⋮	⋮	
	Smallest	0	00..01	
Zero	0	00..00		
Negative	Smallest	1	11..11	
		⋮	⋮	
	Largest	1	00..00	
Integer Indefinite	1	00..00		
		Word Integer:	15 bits	
		Short Integer:	31 Bits	63 Bits
		Long Integer:		

The most significant bit of each format is the sign bit (0 for positive and 1 for negative). Negative values are represented in standard two's complement notation. The quantity zero is represented with all bits (including the sign bit) set to zero. Note that the FPU's word-integer data type is identical to the word-integer data type used by the processor's integer unit and the short-integer format is identical to the integer unit's doubleword-integer data type.

Word-integer values are stored in 2 consecutive bytes in memory; short-integer values are stored in 4 consecutive bytes; and long-integer values are stored in 8 consecutive bytes. When loaded into the FPU's data registers, all the binary integers are exactly representable in the extended-real format.

The binary integer encoding 100..00B represents either of two things, depending on the circumstances of its use:

- The largest negative number supported by the format (-2^{15}, -2^{31}, or -2^{63}).
- The integer indefinite value.

If this encoding is used as a source operand (as in an integer load or integer arithmetic instruction), the FPU interprets it as the largest negative number representable in the format being used. If the FPU detects an invalid operation when storing an integer value in memory with an FIST/FISTP instruction and the invalid-operation exception is masked, the FPU stores the integer indefinite encoding in the destination operand as a masked response to the exception. In situations where the origin of a value with this encoding may be ambiguous, the invalid-operation exception flag can be examined to see if the value was produced as a response to an exception.

If the integer indefinite is stored in memory and is later loaded back into an FPU data register, it is interpreted as the largest negative number supported by the format.

DECIMAL INTEGERS

Decimal integers are stored in a 10-byte, packed BCD format. Table 31-8 gives the precision and range of this data type and Figure shows the format. In this format, the first 9 bytes hold 18 BCD digits, 2 digits per byte The least-significant digit is contained in the lower half-byte of byte 0 and the most-significant digit is contained in the upper half-byte of byte 9.

The most significant bit of byte 10 contains the sign bit (0 = positive and 1 = negative). (Bits 0 through 6 of byte 10 are don't care bits.) Negative decimal integers are not stored in two's complement form; they are distinguished from positive decimal integers only by the sign bit.

Table 31-11 gives the possible encodings of value in the decimal integer data type.

The decimal integer format exists in memory only. When a decimal integer is loaded in a data register in the FPU, it is automatically converted to the extended-real format. All decimal integers are exactly representable in extended-real format.

The packed decimal indefinite encoding is stored by the FBSTP instruction in response to a masked floating-point invalid-operation exception. Attempting to load this value with the FBLD instruction produces an undefined result.

UNSUPPORTED EXTENDED-REAL ENCODINGS ....

The extended-real format permits many encodings that do not fall into any of the categories shown in Table 31-9. Table 31-12 shows these unsupported encodings. Some of these encodings were supported by the Intel 287 math coprocessor; however, most of them are not supported by the Intel 387 math coprocessor, or the internal FPUs in the Intel486, Pentium, or Pentium Pro processors. These encodings are no longer supported due to changes made in the final version of IEEE Std. 754 that eliminated these encodings.

The categories of encodings formerly known as pseudo-NaNs, pseudo-infinities, and un-normal numbers are not supported. The Intel 387 math coprocessor and the internal FPUs in the Intel486, Pentium, and Pentium Pro processors generate the invalid-operation exception when they are encountered as operands.

The encodings formerly known as pseudo-denormal numbers are not generated by the Intel 387 math coprocessor and the internal FPUs in the Intel486, Pentium, and Pentium Pro processors; however, they are used correctly when encountered as operands. The exponent is treated as if it were 00..01B and the mantissa is unchanged. The denormal exception is generated.

Fig. Packed Decimal Integer Encodings

Class		Sign	Biased Exponent	Significand	
				Integer	Fraction
Positive Pseudo-NaNs	Quiet	0	11..11	0	11..11
		.	.		.
		0	11..11		10..00
	Signaling	0	11..11	0	01..11
		.	.		.
		0	11..11		00..01
Positive Reals	Pseudo-infinity	0	11..11	0	00..00
	Unnormals	0	11..10	0	11..11
		.	.		.
		0	00..01		00..00
	Pseudo-denormals	0	00..00	1	11..11
		.	.		.
		0	00..00		00..00
Negative Reals	Pseudo-denormals	1	00..00	1	11..11
		.	.		.
		1	00..00		00..00
	Unnormals	1	11..10	0	11..01
		.	.		.
		1	00..01		00..00
	Pseudo-infinity	1	11..11	0	00..00
Negative Pseudo-NaNs	Signaling	1	11..11	0	01..11
		.	.		.
		1	11..11		00..01
	Quiet	1	11..11	0	11..11
		.	.		.
		1	11..11		10..00
			←15 bits →		←63 bits →

NOTE: * UUUU means bit values are undefined and may contain any value.

FPU INSTRUCTION SET

The floating-point instructions that the Intel Architecture FPU supports can be grouped into six functional categories:

- Data transfer instructions
- Basic arithmetic instructions
- Comparison instructions
- Transcendental instructions
- Load constant instructions
- FPU control instructions

The following section briefly describes the instructions in each category. Detailed descriptions of the floating-point instructions are given in "Instruction Page Key".

Unsupported Extended-Real Encodinlgs

Class		Sign	Biased Exponent	Significand	
				Integer	Fraction
	Quiet	0	11..11	0	11..11
		.	.		.
		0	11..11		10..00
Positive Pseudo-NaNs	Signaling	0	11..11	0	01..11
		.	.		.
		0	11..11		00..01
	Pseudo-infinity	0	11..11	0	00..00
	Unnormals	0	11..10	0	11..11
		.	.		.
Positive Reals		0	00..01		00..00
	Pseudo-denormals	0	00..00	1	11..11
		.	.		.
		0	00..00		00..00
	Pseudo-denormals	1	00..00	1	11..11
		.	.		.
		1	00..00		00..00
	Unnormals	1	11..10	0	11..01
Negative Reals		.	.		.
		1	00..01		00..00
	Pseudo-infinity	1	11..11	0	00..00
Negative Pseudo-NaNs	Signaling	1	11..11	0	01..11
		.	.		.
		1	11..11		00..01
	Quiet	1	11..11	0	11..11
		.	.		.
		1	11..11		10..00
			←15 bits→		←63 bits→

Escape (ESC) Instructions

All of the instructions in the FPU instruction set fall into a class of instructions known as escape (ESC) instructions. All of these instructions have a common opcode format, which is slightly different from the format used by the integer and operating-system instructions.

FPU Instruction Operands

Most floating-point instructions require one or two operands, which are located on the FPU data-register stack or in memory. (None of the floating-point instructions accept immediate operands.)

When an operand is located in a data register, it is referenced relative to the ST(0) register (the register at the top of the register stack), rather than by a physical register number. Often the ST(0) register is an implied operand.

Operands in memory can be referenced using the same operand addressing methods available for the integer and system instructions.

Data Transfer Instructions

The data transfer instructions perform the following operations:

- Load real, integer, or packed BCD operands from memory into the ST(0) register.
- Store the value in the ST(0) register in memory in real, integer, or packed BCD format.
- Move values between registers in the FPU register stack.

Data Transfer Instructions

Real		Integer		Packed Decimal	
FLD	Load Real	FILD	Load Integer	FBLD	Load Packed Decimal
FST	Store Real	FIST	Store Integer		
FSTP	Store Real and Pop	FISTP	Store Integer and Pop	FBSTP	Store Packed Decimal and Pop
FXCH	Exchange Register Contents				
FCMOV*cc*	Conditional Move				

Operands are normally stored in the FPU data registers in extended-real format (see "Precision Control Field"). The FLD (load real) instruction pushes a real operand from memory onto the top of the FPU data-register stack. If the operand is in single- or double-real format, it is automatically converted to extended-real format. This instruction can also be used to push the value in a selected FPU data register onto the top of the register stack.

The FILD (load integer) instruction converts an integer operand in memory into extended-real format and pushes the value onto the top of the register stack. The FBLD (load packed decimal) instruction performs the same load operation for a packed BCD operand in memory. The FST (store real) and FIST (store integer) instructions store the value in register ST(0) in memory in the destination format (real or integer, respectively). Again, the format conversion is carried out automatically.

The FSTP (store real and pop), FISTP (store integer and pop), and FBSTP (store packed decimal and pop) instructions store the value in the ST(0) registers into memory in the destination format (real, integer, or packed BCD), then performs a pop operation on the register stack. A pop operation causes the ST(0) register to be marked empty and the stack pointer (TOP) in the FPU control work to be incremented by 1. The FSTP instruction can also be used to copy the value in the ST(0) register to another FPU register [ST(i)].

The FXCH (exchange register contents) instruction exchanges the value in a selected register in the stack [ST(i)] with the value in ST(0).

The FCMOV*cc* (conditional move) instructions move the value in a selected register in the stack [ST(i)] to register ST(0). These instructions move the value only if the conditions specified with a condition code (*cc*) are satisfied. The conditions being tested with the FCMOV*cc* instructions are represented by the status flags in the EFLAGS register. The condition code mnemonics are appended to the letters "FCMOV" to form the mnemonic for a FCMOV*cc* instruction.

Table: Floating-Point Conditional Move Instructions

Instruction Mnemonic		**Status Flag States**
Condition Description		
FCMOVB	CF=1	Below
FCMOVNB	CF=0	Not below
FCMOVE	ZF=1	Equal
FCMOVNE	ZF=0	Not equal
FCMOVBE	(CF or ZF)=1	Below or equal
FCMOVNBE	(CF or ZF)=0	Not below nor equal
FCMOVU	PF=1	Unordered
FCMOVNU	PF=0	Not unordered

Like the CMOV*cc* instructions, the FCMOV*cc* instructions are useful for optimizing small IF constructions.

They also help eliminate branching overhead for IF operations and the possibility of branch mispredictions by the processor.

Load Constant Instructions. The following instructions push commonly used constants onto the top [ST(0)] of the FPU register stack:

FLDZ	**Load +0.0**
FLD1	Load +1.0
FLDPI	Load
FLDL2T	Load $\log_2 10$
FLDL2E	Load $\log_2 e$
FLDLG2	Load $\log_{10} 2$
FLDLN2	Load $\log_e 2$

The constant values have full extended-real precision (64 bits) and are accurate to approximately 19 decimal digits. They are stored internally in a format more precise than extended real. When loading the constant, the FPU rounds the more precise internal constant according to the RC (rounding control) field of the FPU control word. See "Pi", for information on the constant.

BASIC ARITHMETIC INSTRUCTIONS

The following floating-point instructions perform basic arithmetic operations on real numbers. Where applicable, these instructions match IEEE Standard 754:

FADD/FADDP	**Add real**
FIADD	Add integer to real
FSUB/FSUBP	Subtract real
FISUB	Subtract integer from real
FSUBR/FSUBRP	Reverse subtract real
FISUBR	Reverse subtract real from integer
FMUL/FMULP	Multiply real
FIMUL	Multiply integer by real
FDIV/FDIVP	Divide real

FADD/FADDP	Add real
FIDIV	Divide real by integer
FDIVR/FDIVRP	Reverse divide
FIDIVR	Reverse divide integer by real
FABS	Absolute value
FCHS	Change sign
FSQRT	Square root
FPREM	Partial remainder
FPREM1	IEEE partial remainder
FRNDINT	Round to integral value
FXTRACT	Extract exponent and significand

The add, subtract, multiply and divide instructions operate on the following types of operands:

- Two FPU register values.
- A register value and a real or integer value in memory.

Operands in memory can be in single-real, double-real, short-integer, or word-integer format. They are converted to extended-real format automatically.

Reverse versions of the subtract and divide instructions are provided to foster efficient coding. For example, the FSUB instruction subtracts the value in a specified FPU register [ST(i)] from the value in register ST(0); whereas, the FSUBR instruction subtracts the value in ST(0) from the value in ST(i). The results of both operations are stored in register ST(0). These instructions eliminate the need to exchange values between register ST(0) and another FPU register to perform a subtraction or division.

The pop versions of the add, subtract, multiply and divide instructions pop the FPU register stack following the arithmetic operation. The FPREM instruction computes the remainder from the division of two operands in the manner used by the Intel 8087 and Intel 287 math coprocessors; the FPREM1 instructions computes the remainder is the manner specified in the IEEE specification.

The FSQRT instruction computes the square root of the source operand.

The FRNDINT instructions rounds a real value to its nearest integer value, according to the current rounding mode specified in the RC field of the FPU control word. This instruction performs a function similar to the FIST/FISTP instructions, except that the result is saved in a real format.

The FABS, FCHS, and FXTRACT instructions perform convenient arithmetic operations. The FABS instruction produces the absolute value of the source operand. The FCHS instruction changes the sign of the source operand. The FXTRACT instruction separates the source operand into its exponent and fraction and stores each value in a register in real format.

Comparison of real values differ from comparison of integers because real values have four (rather than three) mutually exclusive relationships: less than, equal, greater than, and unordered.

The unordered relationship is true when at least one of the two values being compared is a NaN or in an undefined format.

This additional relationship is required because, by definition, NaNs are not numbers, so they cannot have less than, equal, or greater than relationships with other real values.

The FCOM, FCOMP, and FCOMPP instructions compare the value in register ST(0) with a real source operand and set the condition code flags (C0, C2, and C3) in the FPU status word according to the results. If an unordered condition is detected (one or both of the values is a NaN or in an undefined format), a floating-point invalid-operation exception is generated.

The pop versions of the instruction pop the FPU register stack once or twice after the comparison operation is complete.

The FUCOM, FUCOMP, and FUCOMPP instructions operate the same as the FCOM, FCOMP, and FCOMPP instructions. The only difference is that with the FUCOM, FUCOMP, and FUCOMPP instructions, if an unordered condition is detected because one or both of the operands is a QNaN, the floating-point invalid-operation exception is not generated.

Table: Setting of FPU Condition Code Flags for Real Number Comparisons

Condition	**C3**	**C2**	**C0**
ST(0) > Source Operand	0	0	0
ST(0) < Source Operand	0	0	1
ST(0) = Source Operand	1	0	0
Unordered	1	1	1

The FICOM and FICOMP instructions also operate the same as the FCOM and FCOMP instructions, except that the source operand is an integer value in memory. The integer value is automatically converted into an extended real value prior to making the comparison.

The FICOMP instruction pops the FPU register stack following the comparison operation.

The FTST instruction performs the same operation as the FCOM instruction, except that the value in register ST(0) is always compared with the value 0.0.

The FCOMI and FCOMIP instructions are new in the Intel Pentium Pro processor. They perform the same comparison as the FCOM and FCOMP instructions, except that they set the status flags (ZF, PF, and CF) in the EFLAGS register to indicate the results of the comparison instead of the FPU condition code flags. The FCOMI and FCOMIP instructions allow condition branch instructions (J*cc*) to be executed directly from the results of their comparison.

Table: Setting of EFLAGS Status Flags for Real Number Comparisons

Comparison Results	**ZF**	**PF**	**CF**
ST0 > ST(*i*)	0	0	0
ST0 < ST(*i*)	0	0	1
ST0 = ST(*i*)	1	0	0
Unordered	1	1	1

The FUCOMI and FUCOMIP instructions operate the same as the FCOMI and FCOMIP instructions, except that they do not generate a floating-point invalid-operation exception if the unordered condition is the result of one or both of the operands being a QNaN.

The FCOMIP and FUCOMIP instructions pop the FPU register stack following the comparison operation. It also sets the C1 flag to indicate the sign of the value.

Branching on the FPU Condition Codes

The processor does not offer any control-flow instructions that branch on the setting of the condition code flags (C0, C2, and C3) in the FPU status word. To branch on the state of these flags, the FPU status word must first be moved to the AX register in the integer unit.

The FSTSW AX (store status word) instruction can be used for this purpose. When these flags are in the AX register, the TEST instruction can be used to control conditional branching as follows:

1. Check for an unordered result. Use the TEST instruction to compare the contents of the AX register with the constant 0400H. This operation will clear the ZF flag in the EFLAGS register if the condition code flags indicate an unordered result; otherwise, the ZF flag will be set.
   The JNZ instruction can then be used to transfer control (if necessary) to a procedure for handling unordered operands.

Table: TEST Instruction Constants for Conditional Branching

Order	Constant	Branch
ST(0) > Source Operand	4500H	JZ
ST(0) < Source Operand	0100H	JNZ
ST(0) = Source Operand	4000H	JNZ
Unordered	0400H	JNZ

2. Check ordered comparison result. The TEST instruction to test for a less than, equal to, or greater than result, then use the corresponding conditional branch instruction to transfer programme control to the appropriate procedure or section of code.

If a programme or procedure has been thoroughly tested nd it incorporates periodic checks for QNaN results, then it not necessary to check for the unordered result every time comparison is made.

See "Branching and Conditional Moves on FPU Condition Codes", for another technique for branching on FPU condition codes.

Some non-comparison FPU instructions update the condition code flags in the FPU status word. To ensure that the status word is not altered inadvertently, store it immediately following a comparison operation.

TRIGONOMETRIC INSTRUCTIONS

The following instructions perform four common trigonometric functions:

FSIN	Sine
FCOS	Cosine
FSINCOS	Sine and cosine
FPTAN	Tangent
FPATAN	Arctangent

These instructions operate on the top one or two registers of the FPU register stack and they return their results to the stack. The source operands must be given in radians.

The FSINCOS instruction returns both the sine and the cosine of a source operand value. It operates faster than executing the FSIN and FCOS instructions in succession.

The FPATAN instruction computes the arctangent of ST(1) divided by ST(0). It is useful for converting rectangular coordinates to polar coordinates.

Pi

When the argument (source operand) of a trigonometric function is within the range of the function, the argument is automatically reduced by the appropriate multiple of 2π through the same reduction mechanism used by the FPREM and FPREM1 instructions. The internal value of that the Intel Architecture FPU uses for argument reduction and other computations is as follows:

$\pi == 0.f * 2^2$

where:

f = C90FDAA2 2168C234 C

(The spaces in the fraction above indicate 32-bit boundaries.)

This internal π value has a 66-bit mantissa, which is 2 bits more than is allowed in the significand of an extended-real value. (Since 66 bits is not an even number of hexadecimal digits, two additional zeros have been added to the value so that it can be represented in hexadecimal format.

The least-significant hexadecimal digit (C) is thus 1100B, where the two least-significant bits represent bits 67 and 68 of the mantissa.)

This value of π has been chosen to guarantee no loss of significance in a source operand, provided the operand is within the specified range for the instruction.

If the results of computations that explicitly use π are to be used in the FSIN, FCOS, FSINCOS, or FPTAN instructions, the full 66-bit fraction of π should be used. This insures that the results are consistent with the argument-reduction algorithms that these instructions use. Using a rounded version of π can cause inaccuracies in result values, which if propagated through several calculations, might result in meaningless results.

A common method of representing the full 66-bit fraction of π is to separate the value into two numbers (high π and low π) that when added together give the value for π shown earlier in this section with the full 66-bit fraction:

π = high π + low π

For example, the following two values (given in scientific notation with the fraction in hexadecimal and the exponent in decimal) represent the 33 most-significant and the 33 least-significant bits of the fraction:

high π (unnormalized) = $0.C90FDAA20 \times 2^{+2}$

low π (unnormalized) = $0.42D184698 \times 2^{-31}$

These values encoded in standard IEEE double-real format are as follows:

high π = 400921FB 54400000

low π = 3DE0B461 1A600000

(Note that in the IEEE double-real format, the exponents are biased (by 1023) and the fractions are normalized.)

Similar versions of π can also be written in extended-real format.

When using this two-part π value in an algorithm, parallel computations should be performed on each part, with the results kept separate. When all the computations are complete, the two results can be added together to form the final result.

The complications of maintaining a consistent value of π for argument reduction can be avoided, either by applying the trigonometric functions only to arguments within the range of the automatic reduction mechanism, or by performing all argument reductions (down to a magnitude less than π/4) explicitly in software.

LOGARITHMIC, EXPONENTIAL, AND SCALE

The following instructions provide two different logarithmic functions, an exponential function, and a scale function.

FYL2X	Compute log ($y*\log_2 x$)
FYL2XP1	Compute log epsilon ($y * \log_2(x + 1)$)
F2XM1	Compute exponential ($2^x - 1$)
FSCALE	Scale

The FYL2X and FYL2XP1 instructions perform two different base 2 logarithmic operations. The FYL2X instruction computes the log of ($y * \log_2 x$). This operation permits the calculation of the log of any base using the following equation:

$\log_b x = (1/\log_2 b) * \log_2 x$

The FYL2XP1 instruction computes the log epsilon of ($y * \log_2 (x + 1)$). This operation provides optimum accuracy for values of epsilon (ε) that are close to 0.

The F2XM1 instruction computes the exponential ($2^x - 1$). This instruction only operates on source values in the range -1.0 to +1.0.

The FSCALE instruction multiplies the source operand by a power of 2.

TRANSCENDENTAL INSTRUCTION ACCURACY

The algorithms that the Pentium and Pentium Pro

processors use for the transcendental instructions (FSIN, FCOS, FSINCOS, FPTAN, FPATAN, F2XM1, FYL2X, and FYL2XP1) allow a higher level of accuracy than was possible in earlier Intel Architecture math coprocessors and FPUs. The accuracy of these instructions is measured in terms of units in the last place (ulp). For a given argument x, let $f(x)$ and $F(x)$ be the correct and computed (approximate) function values, respectively. The error in ulps is defined to be:

$$\text{error} = \left| \frac{f(x) - F(x)}{2^{k-63}} \right|$$

where k is an integer such that

$$| \leq 2^{-k}(f(x) < 2|$$

With the Pentium and Pentium Pro processors, the worst case error on transcendental functions is less than 1 ulp when rounding to the nearest-even and less than 1.5 ulps when rounding in other modes. The functions are guaranteed to be monotonic, with respect to the input operands, throughout the domain supported by the instruction.

With the Intel486 processor and Intel 387 math coprocessor, the worst-case, transcendental-function error is typically 3 or 3.5 ulps, but is sometimes as large as 4.5 ulps.

FPU CONTROL INSTRUCTIONS

The following instructions control the state and modes of operation of the FPU. They also allow the status of the FPU to be examined:

FINIT/FNINIT Initialize FPU
FLDCW Load FPU control word
FSTCW/FNSTCW Store FPU control word
FSTSW/FNSTSW Store FPU status word
FCLEX/FNCLEX Clear FPU exception flags
FLDENV Load FPU environment
FSTENV/FNSTENV Store FPU environment
FRSTOR Restore FPU state
FSAVE/FNSAVE Save FPU state
FINCSTP Increment FPU register stack pointer
FDECSTP Decrement FPU register stack pointer

FFREE Free FPU register

FNOP No operation

WAIT/FWAIT Check for and handle pending unmasked FPU exceptions

The FINIT/FNINIT instructions initialize the FPU and its internal registers to default values.

The FLDCW instructions loads the FPU control word register with a value from memory. The FSTCW/FNSTCW and FSTSW/FNSTSW instructions store the FPU control and status words, respectively, in memory (or for an FSTSW/FNSTSW instruction in a general-purpose register).

The FSTENV/FNSTENV and FSAVE/FNSAVE instructions save the FPU environment and state, respectively, in memory. The FPU environment includes all the FPU's control and status registers; the FPU state includes the FPU environment and the data registers in the FPU register stack. (The FSAVE/FNSAVE instruction also initializes the FPU to default values, like the FINIT/FNINIT instruction, after it saves the original state of the FPU.)

The FLDENV and FRSTOR instructions load the FPU environment and state, respectively, from memory into the FPU. These instructions are commonly used when switching tasks or contexts.

The WAIT/FWAIT instructions are synchronization instructions. (They are actually mnemonics for the same opcode.) These instructions check the FPU status word for pending unmasked FPU exceptions. If any pending unmasked FPU exceptions are found, they are handled before the processor resumes execution of the instructions (integer, floating-point, or system instruction) in the instruction stream. The WAIT/FWAIT instructions are provided to allow synchronization of instruction execution between the FPU and the processor's integer unit. See "Floating-Point Exception Synchronization" for more information on the use of the WAIT/FWAIT instructions.

WAITING VS. NON-WAITING INSTRUCTIONS

All of the floating-point instructions except a few special

control instructions perform a wait operation (similar to the WAIT/FWAIT instructions), to check for and handle pending unmasked FPU exceptions, before they perform their primary operation (such as adding two real numbers). These instructions are called waiting instructions. Some of the FPU control instructions, such as FSTSW/FNSTSW, have both a waiting and a non-waiting versions. The waiting version (with the "F" prefix) executes a wait operation before it performs its primary operation; whereas, the non-waiting version (with the "FN" prefix) ignores pending unmasked exceptions. Non-waiting instructions allow software to save the current FPU state without first handling pending exceptions or to reset or reinitialize the FPU without regard for pending exceptions.

Note: When operating a Pentium or Intel486 processor in MS-DOS compatibility mode, it is possible (under unusual circumstances) for a non-waiting instruction to be interrupted prior to being executed to handle a pending FPU exception. The circumstances where this can happen and the resulting action of the processor are described in "No-Wait FPU Instructions Can Get FPU Interrupt in Window". When operating a Pentium Pro processor in MS-DOS compatibility mode, non-waiting instructions can not be interrupted in this way.

Unsupported FPU Instructions

The Intel 8087 instructions FENI and FDISI and the Intel 287 math coprocessor instruction FSETPM perform no function in the Intel 387 math coprocessor, or the Intel486, Pentium, or Pentium Pro processors. If these opcodes are detected in the instruction stream, the FPU performs no specific operation and no internal FPU states are affected.

Operating on NaNs

As was described in "NaNs", the FPU supports two types of NaNs: SNaNs and QNaNs. An SNaN is any NaN value with its most-significant fraction bit set to 0 and at least one other fraction bit set to 1. (If all the fraction bits are set to 0, the value is an ·.) A QNaN is any NaN value with the most-significant fraction bit set to 1. The sign bit of a NaN is not interpreted.

As a general rule, when a QNaN is used in one or more arithmetic floating-point instructions, it is allowed to propagate through a computation. An SNaN on the other hand causes a floating-point invalid-operation exception to be signaled. SNaNs are typically used to trap or invoke an exception handler. They must be inserted by software; that is, the FPU never generates an SNaN as a result.

The floating-point invalid-operation exception has a flag and a mask bit associated with it in the FPU status and control registers, respectively.

The mask bit determines how the FPU handles an SNaN value. If the floating-point invalid-operation mask bit is set, the SNaN is converted to a QNaN by setting the most-significant fraction bit of the value to 1. The result is then stored in the destination operand and the floating-point invalid-operation flag is set.

If the invalid-operation mask is clear, a floating-point invalid-operation fault is signaled and no result is stored in the destination operand.

When a real operation or exception delivers a QNaN result, the value of the result depends on the source operands.

Except for the rules given at the beginning of this section for encoding SNaNs and QNaNs, software is free to use the bits in the significand of a NaN for any purpose. Both SNaNs and QNaNs can be encoded to carry and store data, such as diagnostic information.

Rules for Generating QNaNs

Source Operands	QNaN Result
An SNaN and a QNaN.	The QNaN source operand.
Two SNaNs.	The SNaN with the larger significand converted into a QNaN.
Two QNaNs.	The QNaN with the larger significand.
An SNaN and a real value.	The SNaN converted into a QNaN.
A QNaN and a real value.	The QNaN source operand.

Neither source operand is a NaN and a floating-point invalid-operation exception is signaled.	The default QNaN *real indefinite.*

Uses for Signaling NANs

By unmasking the invalid operation exception, the programmer can use signaling NaNs to trap to the exception handler. The generality of this approach and the large number of NaN values that are available provide the sophisticated programmer with a tool that can be applied to a variety of special situations.

For example, a compiler can use signaling NaNs as references to uninitialized (real) array elements. The compiler can preinitialize each array element with a signaling NaN whose significand contained the index (relative position) of the element.

Then, if an application programme attempts to access an element that it had not initialized, it can use the NaN placed there by the compiler. If the invalid operation exception is unmasked, an interrupt will occur, and the exception handler will be invoked. The exception handler can determine which element has been accessed, since the operand address field of the exception pointers will point to the NaN, and the NaN will contain the index number of the array element.

Uses for Quiet NANs

Quiet NaNs are often used to speed up debugging. In its early testing phase, a programme often contains multiple errors. An exception handler can be written to save diagnostic information in memory whenever it was invoked. After storing the diagnostic data, it can supply a quiet NaN as the result of the erroneous instruction, and that NaN can point to its associated diagnostic area in memory.

The programme will then continue, creating a different NaN for each error. When the programme ends, the NaN results can be used to access the diagnostic data saved at the time the errors occurred. Many errors can thus be diagnosed and corrected in one test run.

In embedded applications which use computed results in further computations, an undetected QNaN can invalidate all subsequent results. Such applications should therefore periodically check for QNaNs and provide a recovery mechanism to be used if a QNaN result is detected.

FLOATING-POINT EXCEPTION HANDLING

The FPU detects six classes of exception conditions while executing floating-point instructions:

- Invalid operation
  - Stack overflow or underflow
  - Invalid arithmetic operation
- Divide-by-zero
- Denormalized operand
- Numeric overflow
- Numeric underflow
- Inexact result (precision)

The nomenclature of "#" symbol followed by one or two letters is used in this manual to indicate exception conditions. It is merely a short-hand form and is not related to assembler mnemonics. Each of the six exception classes has a corresponding flag bit in the FPU status word and a mask bit in the FPU control word. In addition, the exception summary (ES) flag in the status word indicates when any of the exceptions has been detected, and the stack fault (SF) flag (also in the status word) distinguishes between the two types of invalid-operation exceptions.

When the FPU detects a floating-point exception, it sets the appropriate flags in the FPU status word, then takes one of two possible courses of action:

- Handles the exception automatically, producing a predefined (and often times usable result), while allowing programme execution to continue undisturbed.
- Invokes a software exception handler to handle the exception.

The following sections describe how the FPU handles exceptions (either automatically or by calling a software exception handler), how the FPU detects the various floating-point exceptions, and the automatic (masked) response to the floating-point exceptions.

ARITHMETIC VS. NON-ARITHMETIC INSTRUCTIONS

When dealing with floating-point exceptions, it is useful to distinguish between arithmetic instructions and non-arithmetic instructions. Non-arithmetic instructions have no operands or do not make substantial changes to their operands. Arithmetic instructions do make significant changes to their operands; in particular, they make changes that could result in a floating-point exception being signaled. Table 31-19 lists the non-arithmetic and arithmetic instructions. It should be noted that some non-arithmetic instructions can signal a floating-point stack (fault) exception, but this exception is not the result of an operation on an operand.

Automatic Exception Handling

If the FPU detects an exception condition for a masked exception (an exception with its mask bit set), it sets the exception flag for the exception and delivers a predefined (default) response and continues executing instructions. The masked (default) responses to exceptions have been chosen to deliver a reasonable result for each exception condition and are generally satisfactory for most floating-point applications. By masking or unmasking specific floating-point exceptions in the FPU control word, programmers can delegate responsibility for most exceptions to the FPU and reserve the most severe exception conditions for software exception handlers. Because the exception flags are "sticky," they provide a cumulative record of the exceptions that have occurred since they were last cleared. A programmer can thus mask all exceptions, run a calculation, and then inspect the exception flags to see if any exceptions were detected during the calculation.

Table: Arithmetic and Non-arithmetic Instructions (Sheet 1 of 2)

Non-arithmetic Instructions	**Arithmetic Instructions**
FABS	F2XM1
FCHS	FADD/FADDP
FCLEX	FBLD
FDECSTP	FBSTP
FFREE	FCOM/FCOMP/FCOMPP
FINCSTP	FCOS
FINIT/FNINIT	FDIV/FDIVP/FDIVR/FDIVRP
FLD (register-to-register)	FIADD
FLD (extended format from memory)	FICOM/FICOMP
FLD constant	FIDIV/FIDIVR
FLDCW	FILD
FLDENV	FIMUL
FNOP	FIST/FISTP
FRSTOR	FISUB/FISUBR
FSAVE/FNSAVE	FLD (conversion)
FST/FSTP (register-to-register)	FMUL/FMULP
FSTP (extended format to memory)	FPATAN
FSTCW/FNSTCW	FPREM/FPREM1
FSTENV/FNSTENV	FPTAN
FSTSW/FNSTSW	FRNDINT
WAIT/FWAIT	FSCALE
FXAM	FSIN
FXCH	FSINCOS
	FSQRT
	FST/FSTP (conversion)
	FSUB/FSUBP/FSUBR/FSUBRP
	FTST
	FUCOM/FUCOMP/FUCOMPP
	FXTRACT
	FYL2X/FYL2XP1

Note that when exceptions are masked, the FPU may detect multiple exceptions in a single instruction, because it continues executing the instruction after performing its masked response. For example, the FPU can detect a denormalized operand, perform its masked response to this exception, and then detect numeric underflow.

SOFTWARE EXCEPTION HANDLING

Native Mode

The native mode for handling floating-point exceptions is selected by setting the NE flag in control register CR0 to 1. In this mode, if the FPU detects an exception condition while executing a floating-point instruction and the exception is unmasked (the mask bit for the exception is cleared), the FPU sets the flag for the exception and the ES flag in the FPU status word. It then invokes the software exception handler through the floating-point-error exception (#MF, vector 16), immediately before execution of any of the following instructions in the processor's instruction stream:

- The next floating-point instruction, unless it is one of the non-waiting instructions (FNINIT, FNCLEX, FNSTSW, FNSTCW, FNSTENV, and FNSAVE).
- The next WAIT/FWAIT instruction.
- The next MMX instruction.

If the next floating-point instruction in the instruction stream is a non-waiting instruction, the FPU executes the instruction without invoking the software exception handler.

MS-DOS* Compatibility Mode

If the NE flag in control register CR0 is set to 0, the MS-DOS compatibility mode for handling floating-point exceptions is selected.

In this mode, the software exception handler for floating-point exceptions is invoked externally using the processor's FERR#, INTR, and IGNNE# pins. This method of reporting floating-point errors and invoking an exception handler is provided to support the floating-point exception handling mechanism used in PC systems that are running the MS-DOS or Windows* 95 operating system.

The MS-DOS compatibility mode is typically used as follows to invoke the floating-point exception handler:

1. If the FPU detects an unmasked floating-point exception, it sets the flag for the exception and the ES flag in the FPU status word.
2. If the IGNNE# pin is deasserted, the FPU then asserts the FERR# pin either immediately, or else delayed (deferred) until just before the execution of the next waiting floating-point instruction or MMX™ instruction. Whether the FERR# pin is asserted immediately or delayed depends on the type of processor, the instruction, and the type of exception.
3. If a preceding floating-point instruction has set the exception flag for an unmasked FPU exception, the processor freezes just before executing the next WAIT instruction, waiting floating-point instruction, or MMX instruction. Whether the FERR# pin was asserted at the preceding floating-point instruction or is just now being asserted, the freezing of the processor assures that the FPU exception handler will be invoked before the new floatingpoint (or MMX) instruction gets executed.
4. The FERR# pin is connected through external hardware to IRQ13 of a cascaded, programmable interrupt controller (PIC). When the FERR# pin is asserted, the PIC is programmed to generate an interrupt 75H.
5. The PIC asserts the INTR pin on the processor to signal the interrupt 75H.
6. The BIOS for the PC system handles the interrupt 75H by branching to the interrupt 2 (NMI) interrupt handler.
7. The interrupt 2 handler determines if the interrupt is the result of an NMI interrupt or a floating-point exception.
8. If a floating-point exception is detected, the interrupt 2 handler branches to the floating-point exception handler.

If the IGNNE# pin is asserted, the processor ignores floating-point error conditions. This pin is provided to inhibit floating-point exceptions from being generated while the floating-point exception handler is servicing a previously signaled floating-point exception.

"Guidelines for Writing FPU Exception Handlers", describes the MS-DOS compatibility mode in much greater detail.

Typical Floating-Point Exception Handler Actions

After the floating-point exception handler is invoked, the processor handles the exception in the same manner that it handles non-FPU exceptions. (The floating-point exception handler is normally part of the operating system or executive software.) A typical action of the exception handler is to store FPU state information in memory (with the FSTENV/ FNSTENV or FSAVE/FNSAVE instructions) so that it can evaluate the exception and formulate an appropriate response (see "Saving the FPU's State"). Other typical exception handler actions include:

- Examining stored FPU state information (control, status, and tag words, and FPU instruction and operand pointers) to determine the nature of the error.
- Correcting the condition that caused the error.
- Clearing the exception bits in the status word.
- Returning to the interrupted programme and resuming normal execution.

If the faulting floating-point instruction is followed by one or more non-floating-point instructions, it may not be useful to re-execute the faulting instruction. See "Floating-Point Exception Synchronization", for more information on synchronizing floating-point exceptions.

In cases where the handler needs to restart programme execution with the faulting instruction, the IRET instruction cannot be used directly. The reason for this is that because the exception is not generated until the next floating-point or WAIT/FWAIT instruction following the faulting floating-point instruction, the return instruction pointer on the stack may not point to the faulting instruction. To restart programme execution at the faulting instruction, the exception handler must obtain a pointer to the instruction from the saved FPU state information, load it into the return instruction pointer location on the stack, and then execute the IRET instruction.

In lieu of writing recovery procedures, the exception handler can do the following:

- Increment an exception counter for later display or printing.
- Print or display diagnostic information (such as, the FPU environment and registers).
- Halt further programme execution.

See "FPU Exception Handling Examples", for general examples of floating-point exception handlers and for specific examples of how to write a floating-point exception handler when using the MS-DOS compatibility mode.

FLOATING-POINT EXCEPTION CONDITIONS

Invalid Operation Exception

The floating-point invalid-operation exception occurs in response to two general types of operations:

- Stack overflow or underflow (#IS).
- Invalid arithmetic operand (#IA).

The flag for this exception (IE) is bit 0 of the FPU status word, and the mask bit (IM) is bit 0 of the FPU control word. The stack fault flag (SF) of the FPU status word indicates the type of operation caused the exception. When the SF flag is set to 1, a stack operation has resulted in stack overflow or underflow; when the flag is cleared to 0, an arithmetic instruction has encountered an invalid operand. Note that the FPU explicitly sets the SF flag when it detects a stack overflow or underflow condition, but it does not explicitly clear the flag when it detects an invalid-arithmetic-operand condition. As a result, the state of the SF flag can be 1 following an invalid-arithmetic-operation exception, if it was not cleared from the last time a stack overflow or underflow condition occurred. See "Stack Fault Flag", for more information about the SF flag.

Stack Overflow or Underflow Exception (#IS)

The FPU tag word keeps track of the contents of the registers in the FPU register stack.It then uses this information to detect two different types of stack faults:

- Stack overflow-an instruction attempts to write a value into a non-empty FPU register
- Stack underflow-an instruction attempts to read a value from an empty FPU register.

When the FPU detects stack overflow or underflow, it sets the IE flag (bit 0) and the SF flag (bit 6) in the FPU status word to 1. It then sets condition-code flag C1 (bit 9) in the FPU status word to 1 if stack overflow occurred or to 0 if stack underflow occurred.

If the invalid-operation exception is masked, the FPU then returns the real, integer, or BCD-integer indefinite value to the destination operand, depending on the instruction being executed. This value overwrites the destination register or memory location specified by the instruction.

If the invalid-operation exception is not masked, a software exception handler is invoked (see "Software Exception Handling") and the top-of-stack pointer (TOP) and source operands remain unchanged.

The term stack overflow comes from the condition where the a programme has pushed eight values onto the FPU register stack and the next value pushed on the stack causes a stack wraparound to a register that already contains a value. The term stack underflow refers to the opposite condition from stack overflow. Here, a programme has popped eight values from the FPU register stack and the next value popped from the stack causes stack wraparound to an empty register.

INVALID ARITHMETIC OPERAND EXCEPTION (#IA)

The FPU is able to detect a variety of invalid arithmetic operations that can be coded in a programme. These operations generally indicate a programming error, such as dividing · by ·. Table 31-20 lists the invalid arithmetic operations that the FPU detects. This group includes the invalid operations defined in IEEE Std. 854.

When the FPU detects an invalid arithmetic operand, it sets the IE flag (bit 0) in the FPU status word to 1. If the invalid-operation exception is masked, the FPU then returns an indefinite value to the destination operand or sets the floating-point condition codes. If the invalid-operation exception is not masked, a software exception handler is invoked and the top-of-stack pointer (TOP) and source operands remain unchanged.

DIVIDE-BY-ZERO EXCEPTION (#Z)

The FPU reports a floating-point zero-divide exception whenever an instruction attempts to divide a finite non-zero operand by 0. The flag (ZE) for this exception is bit 2 of the FPU status word, and the mask bit (ZM) is bit 2 of the FPU control word.

The FDIV, FDIVP, FDIVR, FDIVRP, FIDIV, and FIDIVR instructions and the other instructions that perform division internally (FYL2X and FXTRACT) can report the divide-by-zero exception.

When a divide-by-zero exception occurs and the exception is masked, the FPU sets the ZE flag and returns the values shown in Table 7-21. If the divide-by-zero exception is not masked, the ZE flag is set, a software exception handler is invoked, and the top-of-stack pointer (TOP) and source operands remain unchanged.

Table: Divide-By-Zero Conditions and the Masked Responses to Them

Condition	**Masked Response**
Divide or reverse divide operation with a 0 divisor.	Returns an · signed with the exclusive OR of the sign of the two operands to the destination operand.
FYL2X instruction.	Returns an · signed with the opposite sign of the non-zero operand to the destination operand.
FXTRACT instruction. is set to 0 with the	ST(1) is set to -·; ST(0) same sign as the source operand.

Denormal Operand Exception (#D)

The FPU signals the denormal-operand exception under the following conditions:

- If an arithmetic instruction attempts to operate on a denormal operand (see "Normalized and Denormalized Finite Numbers").
- If an attempt is made to load a denormal single- or double-real value into an FPU register. (If the denormal value being loaded is an extended-real value, the denormal-operand exception is not reported.)

The flag (DE) for this exception is bit 1 of the FPU status word, and the mask bit (DM) is bit 1 of the FPU control word.

When a denormal-operand exception occurs and the exception is masked, the FPU sets the DE flag, then proceeds with the instruction.

The denormal operand in single- or double-real format is automatically normalized when converted to the extended-real format. Operating on denormal numbers will produce results at least as good as, and often better than, what can be obtained when denormal numbers are flushed to zero.

In fact, subsequent operations will benefit from the additional precision of the internal extended-real format. Most programmers mask this exception so that a computation may proceed, then analyse any loss of accuracy when the final result is delivered.

When a denormal-operand exception occurs and the exception is not masked, the DE flag is set and a software exception handler is invoked.

The top-of-stack pointer (TOP) and source operands remain unchanged.

When denormal operands have reduced significance due to loss of low-order bits, it may be advisable to not operate on them.

Precluding denormal operands from computations can be accomplished by an exception handler that responds to unmasked denormal-operand exceptions.

Numeric Overflow Exception (#O)

The FPU reports a floating-point numeric overflow exception (#O) whenever the rounded result of an arithmetic instruction exceeds the largest allowable finite value that will fit into the real format of the destination operand. For example, if the destination format is extended-real (80 bits), overflow occurs when the rounded result falls outside the unbiased range of $-1.0 * 2^{16384}$ to $1.0 * 2^{16384}$ (exclusive). Numeric overflow can occur on arithmetic operations where the result is stored in an FPU data register. It can also occur on store-real operations (with the FST and FSTP instructions), where a within-range value in a data register is stored in memory in a single- or double-real format. The overflow threshold range for the single-real format is $-1.0 * 2^{128}$ to $1.0 * 2^{128}$; the range for the double-real format is $-1.0 * 2^{1024}$ to $1.0 * 2^{1024}$.

The numeric overflow exception cannot occur when overflow occurs when storing values in an integer or BCD integer format.

Instead, the invalid-arithmetic-operand exception is signaled. The flag (OE) for the numeric-overflow exception is bit 3 of the FPU status word, and the mask bit (OM) is bit 3 of the FPU control word.

When a numeric-overflow exception occurs and the exception is masked, the FPU sets the OE flag and returns one of the values shown in Table 31-22. The value returned depends on the current rounding mode of the FPU.

Table: Masked Responses to Numeric Overflow

Rounding Mode	**Sign of True Result**	**Result**
To nearest	+	+·
	-	-·
Toward -·	+	Largest finite positive number
	-	-·
Toward +·	+	+·
	-	Largest finite negative number
Toward zero	+	Largest finite positive number
	-	Largest finite negative number

The action that the FPU takes when numeric overflow occurs and the numeric-overflow exception is not masked, depends on whether the instruction is supposed to store the result in memory or on the register stack.

If the destination is a memory location, the OE flag is set and a software exception handler is invoked (see "Software Exception Handling"). The top-of-stack pointer (TOP) and source and destination operands remain unchanged.

If the destination is the register stack, the exponent of the rounded result is divided by 2^{24576} and the result is stored along with the significand in the destination operand. Condition code bit C1 in the FPU status word (called in this situation the "round-up bit") is set if the significand was rounded upward and cleared if the result was rounded toward 0. After the result is stored, the OE flag is set and a software exception handler is invoked.

The scaling bias value 24,576 is equal to $3 * 2^{13}$. Biasing the exponent by 24,576 normally translates the number as nearly as possible to the middle of the extended-real exponent range so that, if desired, it can be used in subsequent scaled operations with less risk of causing further exceptions.

When using the FSCALE instruction, massive overflow can occur, where the result is too large to be represented, even with a bias-adjusted exponent. Here, if overflow occurs again, after the result has been biased, a properly signed · is stored in the destination operand.

Numeric Underflow Exception (#U)

The FPU reports a floating-point numeric underflow exception (#U) whenever the rounded result of an arithmetic instruction is "tiny" (that is, less than the smallest possible normalized, finite value that will fit into the real format of the destination operand). For example, if the destination format is extended-real (80 bits), underflow occurs when the rounded result falls in the unbiased range of $-1.0 * 2^{-16382}$ to $1.0 * 2^{-16382}$ (exclusive). Like numeric overflow, numeric underflow can occur on arithmetic operations where the result is stored in an FPU data register. It can also occur on store-real operations (with the FST and FSTP instructions), where a within-range value in a data register is stored in memory in a single- or double-real format. The underflow threshold range for the single-real format is $-1.0 * 2^{-126}$ to $1.0 * 2^{-126}$; the range for the double-real format is $-1.0 * 2^{-1022}$ to $1.0 * 2^{-1022}$. (The numeric underflow exception cannot occur when storing values in an integer or BCD integer format.)

The flag (UE) for the numeric-underflow exception is bit 4 of the FPU status word, and the mask bit (UM) is bit 4 of the FPU control word.

When a numeric-underflow exception occurs and the exception is masked, the FPU denormalizes the result (see "Normalized and Denormalized Finite Numbers"). If the denormalized result is exact, the FPU stores the result in the destination operand, without setting the UE flag. If the denormal result is inexact, the FPU sets the UE flag, then goes on to handle the inexact-result exception condition (see "Inexact-Result (Precision) Exception (#P)"). It is important to note that if numeric-underflow is masked, a numeric-underflow exception is signaled only if the denormalized result is inexact. If the denormalized result is exact, no flags are set and no exceptions are signaled.

The action that the FPU takes when numeric underflow occurs and the numeric-underflow exception is not masked, depends on whether the instruction is supposed to store the result in memory or on the register stack.

If the destination is a memory location, the UE flag is set and a software exception handler is invoked. The top-of-stack pointer (TOP) and source and destination operands remain unchanged.

If the destination is the register stack, the exponent of the rounded result is multiplied by 2^{24576} and the product is stored along with the significand in the destination operand. Condition code bit C1 in the FPU the status register (acting here as a "round-up bit") is set if the significand was rounded upward and cleared if the result was rounded toward 0. After the result is stored, the UE flag is set and a software exception handler is invoked.

The scaling bias value 24,576 is the same as is used for the overflow exception and has the same effect, which is to translate the result as nearly as possible to the middle of the extended-real exponent range.

When using the FSCALE instruction, massive underflow can occur, where the result is too tiny to be represented, even with a bias-adjusted exponent. Here, if underflow occurs again, after the result has been biased, a properly signed 0 is stored in the destination operand.

Inexact-Result (Precision) Exception (#P)

The inexact-result exception (also called the precision exception) occurs if the result of an operation is not exactly representable in the destination format. For example, the fraction 1/3 cannot be precisely represented in binary form. This exception occurs frequently and indicates that some (normally acceptable) accuracy has been lost. The exception is supported for applications that need to perform exact arithmetic only. Because the rounded result is generally satisfactory for most applications, this exception is commonly masked. Note that the transcendental instructions [FSIN, FCOS, FSINCOS, FPTAN, FPATAN, F2XM1, FYL2X, and FYL2XP1] by nature produce inexact results.

The inexact-result exception flag (PE) is bit 5 of the FPU status word, and the mask bit (PM) is bit 5 of the FPU control word.

If the inexact-result exception is masked when an inexact-result condition occurs and a numeric overflow or underflow condition has not occurred, the FPU sets the PE flag and stores the rounded result in the destination operand. The current rounding mode determines the method used to round the result (see "Rounding Control Field"). The C1 (round-up) bit in the FPU status word indicates whether the inexact result was rounded up (C1 is set) or "not rounded up" (C1 is cleared). In the "not rounded up" case, the least-significant bits of the inexact result are truncated so that the result fits in the destination format.

If the inexact-result exception is not masked when an

inexact result occurs and numeric overflow or underflow has not occurred, the FPU performs the same operation described in the previous paragraph and, in addition, invokes a software exception handler (see "Software Exception Handling"). If an inexact result occurs in conjunction with numeric overflow or underflow, one of the following operations is carried out:

- If an inexact result occurs along with masked overflow or underflow, the OE or UE flag and the PE flag are set and the result is stored as described for the overflow or underflow exceptions (see "Numeric Overflow Exception (#O)" or "Numeric Underflow Exception (#U)"). If the inexact-result exception is unmasked, the FPU also invokes the software exception handler.
- If an inexact result occurs along with unmasked overflow or underflow and the destination operand is a register, the OE or UE flag and the PE flag are set, the result is stored as described for the overflow or underflow exceptions, and the software exception handler is invoked.
- If an inexact result occurs along with unmasked overflow or underflow and the destination operand is a memory location, the inexact-result condition is ignored.

EXCEPTION PRIORITY

The processor handles exceptions according to a predetermined precedence. When an instruction generates two or more exception conditions, the exception precedence sometimes results in the higher-priority exception being handled and the lower-priority exceptions being ignored. For example, dividing an SNaN by zero can potentially signal an invalid-arithmetic-operand exception (due to the SNaN operand) and a divide-by-zero exception. Here, if both exceptions are masked, the FPU handles the higher-priority exception only (the invalid-arithmetic-operand exception), returning a real indefinite to the destination. Alternately, a denormal-operand or inexact-result exception can accompany a numeric underflow or overflow exception, with both exceptions being handled.

The precedence for floating-point exceptions is as follows:

- Invalid-operation exception, subdivided as follows:
  - Stack underflow.
  - Stack overflow.
  - Operand of unsupported format.
  - SNaN operand.
- QNaN operand. Though this is not an exception, the handling of a QNaN operand has precedence over lower-priority exceptions. For example, a QNaN divided by zero results in a QNaN, not a zero-divide exception.
- Any other invalid-operation exception not mentioned above or a divide-by-zero exception.
- Denormal-operand exception. If masked, then instruction execution continues, and a lower-priority exception can occur as well.
- Numeric overflow and underflow exceptions in conjunction with the inexact-result exception.
- Inexact-result exception.

Invalid operation, zero divide, and denormal operand exceptions are detected before a floating-point operation begins, whereas overflow, underflow, and precision errors are not detected until a true result has been computed. When a pre-operation exception is detected, the FPU register stack and memory have not yet been updated, and appear as if the offending instructions has not been executed. When a post-operation exception is detected, the register stack and memory may be updated with a result (depending on the nature of the error).

FLOATING-POINT EXCEPTION SYNCHRONIZATION

Because the integer unit and FPU are separate execution units, it is possible for the processor to execute floating-point, integer, and system instructions concurrently. No special programming techniques are required to gain the advantages of concurrent execution. (Floating-point instructions are placed in the instruction stream along with the integer and system instructions.) However, concurrent execution can cause problems for floating-point exception handlers. This problem is related to the way the FPU signals the existence of unmasked floating-point exceptions. (Special exception synchronization is not required for masked floating-point exceptions, because the FPU always returns a masked result to the destination operand.). When a floating-point exception is unmasked and the exception condition occurs, the FPU stops further execution of the floating-point instruction and signals the exception event. On the next occurrence of a floating-point instruction or a WAIT/FWAIT instruction in the instruction stream, the processor checks the ES flag in the FPU status word for pending floating-point exceptions. It floating-point exceptions are pending, the FPU makes an implicit call (traps) to the floating-point software exception handler.

The exception handler can then execute recovery procedures for selected or all floating-point exceptions. Synchronization problems occur in the time frame between when the exception is signaled and when it is actually handled. Because of concurrent execution, integer or system instructions can be executed during this time frame. It is thus possible for the source or destination operands for a floating-point instruction that faulted to be overwritten in memory, making it impossible for the exception handler to analyse or recover from the exception.

To solve this problem, an exception synchronizing instruction (either a floating-point instruction or a WAIT/ FWAIT instruction) can be placed immediately after any floating-point instruction that might present a situation where state information pertaining to a floating-point exception might be lost or corrupted. Floating-point instructions that store data in memory are prime candidates for synchronization. For example, the following three lines of code have the potential for exception synchronization problems:

Fild Count; Floating-point instruction
INC Count; Integer instruction
FSQRT; Subsequent floating-point instruction

In this example, the INC instruction modifies the result of a floating-point instruction (FILD). If an exception is signaled during the execution of the FILD instruction, the result stored in the COUNT memory location might be overwritten before the exception handler is called. Rearranging the instructions, as follows, so that the FSQRT instruction follows the FILD instruction, synchronizes the exception handling and eliminates the possibility of the exception being handled incorrectly.

Fild Count; Floating-point instruction

FSQRT; Subsequent floating-point instruction synchronizes; any exceptions generated by the FILD instruction.

INC Count; Integer instruction

The FSQRT instruction does not require any synchronization, because the results of this instruction are stored in the FPU data registers and will remain there, undisturbed, until the next floating-point or WAIT/FWAIT instruction is executed. To absolutely insure that any exceptions emanating from the FSQRT instruction are handled (for example, prior to a procedure call), a WAIT instruction can be placed directly after the FSQRT instruction.

Note that some floating-point instructions (non-waiting instructions) do not check for pending unmasked exceptions. They include the FNINIT, FNSTENV, FNSAVE, FNSTSW, FNSTCW, and FNCLEX instructions.

When an FNINIT, FNSTENV, FNSAVE, or FNCLEX instruction is executed, all pending exceptions are essentially lost (either the FPU status register is cleared or all exceptions are masked). The FNSTSW and FNSTCW instructions do not check for pending interrupts, but they do not modify the FPU status and control registers. A subsequent "waiting" floating-point instruction can then handle any pending exceptions.

Floating-Point Exceptions Summary

Table lists the floating-point instruction mnemonics in alphabetical order. For each mnemonic, it summarizes the exceptions that the instruction may cause. "Floating-Point

Exception Conditions", for a detailed discussion of the floating-point exceptions. The following codes indicate the floating-point exceptions:

- #IS Invalid-operation exception for stack underflow or stack overflow.
- #IA Invalid-operation exception for invalid arithmetic operands and unsupported formats.
- #D Denormal-operand exception.
- #Z Divide-by-zero exception.
- #O Numeric-overflow exception.
- #U Numeric-underflow exception.
- #P Inexact-result (precision) exception.

DEVICES

BINARY TO BCD CONVERTER

- Shift the binary number left one bit.
- If 8 shifts have taken place, the BCD number is in the *Hundreds, Tens,* and *Units* column.
- If the binary value in any of the BCD columns is 5 or greater, add 3 to that value in that BCD column.
- Go to 1.

Operation	Hundreds	Tens	Units	Binary
HEX				F F
Start				1111 1111

Example: Convert hex E to BCD

Operation	Tens	Units	Binary
HEX			E
Start			1 1 1 0
Shift 1		1	1 1 0
Shift 2		1 1	1 0
Shift 3		1 1 1	0
Add 3		1 0 1 0	0
Shift 4	1	0 1 0 0	
BCD	1	4	

Example: Convert hex FF to BCD

Operation	Hundreds	Tens	Units	Binary	
HEX				F	F
Start				1 1 1 1	1 1 1 1
Shift 1			1	1 1 1 1	1 1 1
Shift 2			1 1	1 1 1 1	1 1
Shift 3			1 1 1	1 1 1 1	1
Add 3			1 0 1 0	1 1 1 1	1
Shift 4		1	0 1 0 1	1 1 1 1	
Add 3		1	1 0 0 0	1 1 1 1	
Shift 5		1 1	0 0 0 1	1 1 1	
Shift 6		1 1 0	0 0 1 1	1 1	
Add 3		1 0 0 1	0 0 1 1	1 1	
Shift 7	1	0 0 1 0	0 1 1 1	1	
Add 3	1	0 0 1 0	1 0 1 0	1	
Shift 8	1 0	0 1 0 1	0 1 0 1		
BCD	2	5	5		

Truth Table for Add-3 Module

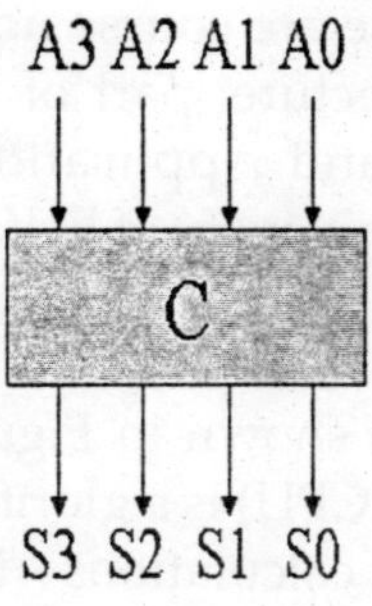

A3	A2	A1	A0	S3	S2	S1	S0
0	0	0	0	0	0	0	0
0	0	0	1	0	0	0	1
0	0	1	0	0	0	1	0
0	0	1	1	0	0	1	1
0	1	0	0	0	1	0	0
0	1	0	1	1	0	0	0
0	1	1	0	1	0	0	1
0	1	1	1	1	0	1	0
1	0	0	0	1	0	1	1
1	0	0	1	1	1	0	0
1	0	1	0	X	X	X	X
1	0	1	1	X	X	X	X
1	1	0	0	X	X	X	X
1	1	0	1	X	X	X	X
1	1	1	0	X	X	X	X
1	1	1	1	X	X	X	X

Here is a Verilog module for this truth table.

BINARY-TO-BCD CONVERTER MODULE

Here is a structural Verilog module corresponding to the logic diagram.

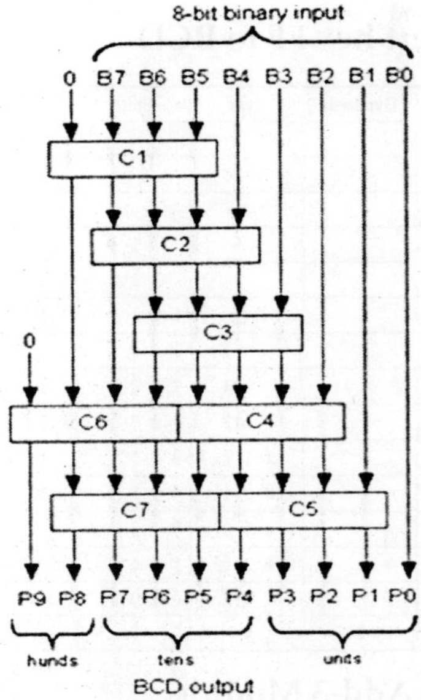

SCOPE

These notes provide an introduction to the architecture and organisation of digital computers. These are course notes for the module CSC 722 Computer Architecture, part of the course MSc/PgDip in Computer Science and Applications, School of Computer Science, The Queen's University of Belfast.

OVERVIEW

A very simple model of a computer is shown in Figure. At its simplest, the Central Processing Unit (CPU) is a glorified calculator, the memory stores the results of calculations - it is a set of labelled cells - the label is called the address, each cell contains a number - data. The bus is simply a pipeline along which data and addresses can flow.

Both data and addresses are stored as numbers, though data numbers may be *interpreted* otherwise, e.g. as text characters.

As well as containing data, the memory also contains the programme - in the form of numeric instructions. Ultimately, everything is reduced to numbers.

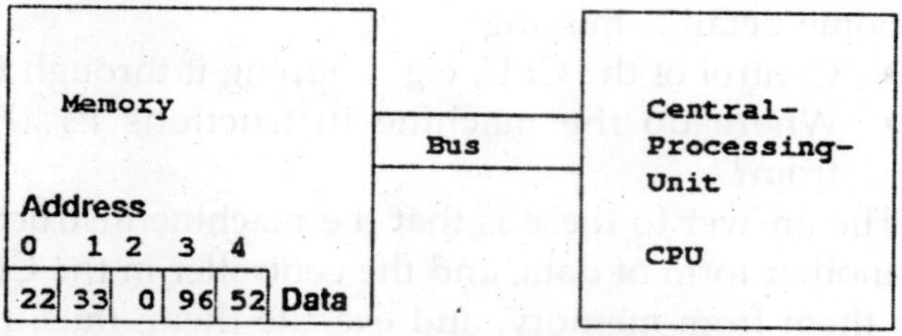

Fig. Overview of a Computer: CPU and Memory

What is a computer programme? Take, for example, the C/C++/Java instruction:

z = x + y; /* add variables x and y, result in z*/

In a programming language, each variable is associated with a memory cell: e.g. x at location 0, y at 1, z at 2; therefore in Figure the value in x is 22, in y, 33, and in z, 0. Note the difference between address (for y, it is 1) and data or value (for y it is 33).

Java - Interpreted?

The fact that Java is *interpreted*, rather than compiled, makes it a little different. Nonetheless, what we say about general computer organisation remains valid. To execute the instruction, the CPU may need to execute a number of sub-instructions (machine instructions), e.g.

P1.

Read the contents of memory cell corresponding to x.

P2.

Read the contents of memory cell corresponding to y.

P3.

Do the addition,

P4.

Write the result in the memory cell corresponding to z.

Four or *five* machine instructions per high-level language instruction is typical. Although we usually talk of just bus, there are three parts to a normal bus: the data-bus, the address-bus, and the control part. The bus operates as follows, take P2 above: first the address (1) is put on the address-bus, then control asserts read-memory, some time later the contents of address 1 (33) is put on the data-bus.

Some detail is missing:

- Control of the CPU, e.g. stepping it through P1...P4.
- Where do the machine instructions P1...P4 come from?

The answer to these is that the machine instructions are just another form of data, and the controller in the CPU must fetch them from memory, and execute them; thus, there are two sorts of data flowing along the bus - actual numeric values, and machine instructions; the controller is in a continuous cycle:

- Fetch P1.
- Execute P1.
- Fetch P2...Execute P2.
- .and keep on until it reaches a halt instruction.

This is the famous fetch-execute cycle.

In the remainder, I will fill in some more detail - going from an overview to increasing detail; the idea is that you stop when the detail gets too much.

Chapter 4

Microsoft Office

MICROSOFT WORD

This unit seeks to introduce you to MS Word. You will learn about MS Word menus and its commands, basic information required to create, save, print, open and modify documents. These documents can be letters, faxes, emails, resumes, reports, brochures, newsletters, web pages and advertisements. You will also learn to work with the standard toolbar and the formatting toolbar.

Objectives

After studying this unit, you should be able to

- Identify the MS Word screen layout and its components,
- Identify the various menus and their functions,
- Understand the standard toolbar and its options, and
- Understand the formatting toolbar and its options.

Windows and MS Office are Microsoft's two most popular programmes. One is an operating system and the other a bundle suite comprising MS Word (word processor), MS Excel (spreadsheet), MS Power Point (graphics presentation programme), MS Access (relational database), MS Outlook, MS Publisher and MS FrontPage. Together, these two flagship programmes have a worldwide vice-like grip and a near monopoly over the personal computer packaged software market. Not only are they the most preferred and widely used programmes in this segment, they have become a benchmark against which all other products are evaluated. If all this sounds like an ad-copy of Microsoft's Office, it was not meant to be.

From your (and our) point of view, this simply means that once having learnt and mastered these packages, in spite of a high rate of technological obsolescence in the computer industry, the skills acquired would never go waste. No matter where you work and what you do, MS Office and specially MS Word, MS Power Point and MS Excel would be of great use to computer users.

Microsoft Word is a full-featured word processing programme, which can be used for any work involving creating and managing text. You can use it from the simplest to the most complex of word processing applications. Using Word, you can write letters and reports, prepare bills and invoices, prepare office stationery –letter heads, envelopes, forms, etc., design brochures, pamphlets, newsletters, magazines, etc.

In short, you would find it extremely difficult to think of a word processing feature not available in Microsoft Word. For most tasks, Word offers several ways of doing the same thing.

It is left to the user to find which one is preferable to him. Since covering all the different methods for doing the same task would require a book running into thousand pages, we have taken the liberty to illustrate the methods(s) we considered most user-friendly. As you gain more proficiency in using Word you will yourself discover other methods of doing your tasks.

STARTING MS WORD

To start Word click once on the Start button, choose All Programmes and click once on Microsoft Word.

On starting Word you would see a Word main screen with the Tip of the Day (unless somebody had instructed not to do so, in the last session).

These tips are Word's way of teaching you new tricks and techniques while you work. Most of these tips are quite informative and some are even entertaining.

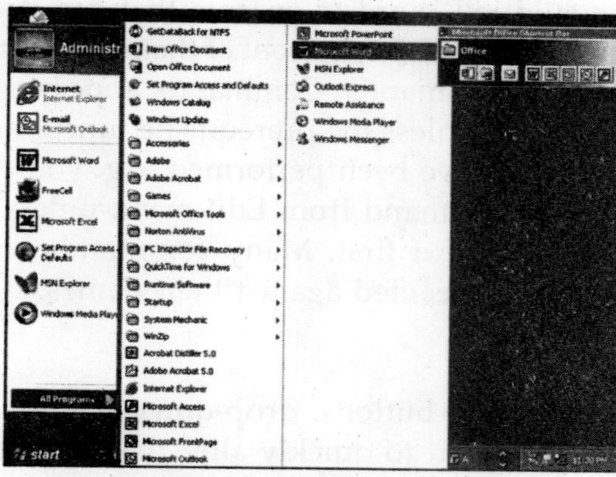

Read the tip, if you have the time and the inclination, then click once on OK button in the dialogue box to start working on the document.

MS WORD SCREEN LAYOUT

Parts of a Word Window is described below:

Title Bar

This tells you which application package is currently running and which document is currently open.

Menu Bar

This is the traditional Windows style drop-down menu. When you point to any menu title and click once with the mouse, the menu will open, displaying all the commands available under this menu title. Clicking on the desired command would tell Word to execute that command. Some commands have ellipses (...) in front of them. These commands have further sub commands. Commands appearing dimmed cannot be executed unless the prerequisite functions required by that command have been performed, e.g. you cannot use the Copy or Cut command from Edit menu unless you have selected a piece of text first. Many commands also have a keyboard shortcut specified against their names.

Standard Toolbar

Toolbars contain buttons, drop-down menus and other controls that help you to quickly alter that appearance and arrangement of documents by executing a variety of Word commands. Toolbars are very helpful and convenient in quickly executing commands without having to go through the menus. The standard toolbar contains icons for basic functions like opening files, saving files, printing files, cut, copy, paste etc.

Formatting Toolbar

This contains icons for changing the look of your text (called "formatting" in computer jargon); for example, there are icons for changing fonts, styles, font sizes, text alignment etc.

Ruler

The ruler lets you make changes in margins and indents, and helps in creating document as per required dimensions.

Scroll Tools

It helps you to travel within your document. You can go anywhere, up and down, right and left in your document mainly by two ways: Using the horizontal and vertical scroll bars with the help of the mouse; or using the keyboard to press PgUp, PgDn, Home, End and arrow keys.

Status Bar

Also called the Status Area, it is normally the last line on your screen. This gives the following information about your work:

- Current page
- Section number

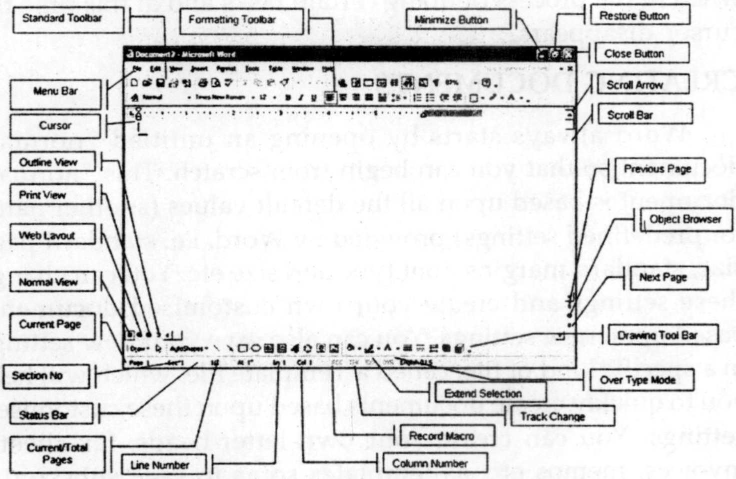

- Current/Total pages in the document
- Current cursor position (where the cursor is presently located)
- Current line number Record macro – whether macro recording is on or not
- Track Revision – whether revisions have been made or not
- Extend Selection
- Over type Mode – whether you are in Insert mode or Overwrite mode
- Help for WordPerfect users – whether on or not.

Cursor

Also called the Insertion Pointer, it denotes the place where text, graphics or any other item would be placed when you type, overwrite or insert it. This looks like a tall, skinny toothpick and keeps blinking so that you can locate it easily.

Mouse Pointer

When your mouse pointer looks like an I-beam you should

be able to move it freely about the screen. This is used for either placing the cursor at the desired place (take the mouse pointer there and click) or choosing any command either from the menu or from toolbars. The mouse pointer changes shape when in the process of doing certain tasks and at this time the cursor disappears.

CREATING DOCUMENTS

Word always starts by opening an untitled "normal" document so that you can begin from scratch. This "normal" document is based upon all the default values (another name for predefined settings) provided by Word, i.e. standard page size, standard margins, font type and size etc. You can change these settings and create your own customised documents based upon new settings. You can also save your new settings in a specific kind of file, called a Template file, which will help you to quickly create documents based upon these customised settings. You can create your own letter-heads; fax sheets, invoices, memos etc. as templates so as to save substantial work and printing costs. Since these templates are like ready-made, pre-printed forms, all you have to do is fill in the blanks, very similar to filling in paper forms manually. Templates have been covered in more detail later.

How to Type in Word

Once Word has been started, you can immediately start typing. When you press character keys on the keyboard, you can see the corresponding characters appear in the Word window. Use the spacebar when you want to separate characters and words from each other. Use the Tab key when you want to move the cursor or text from one Tab stop to another, and also when you want to create a blank longer than one space between words.

Insert and Overtype Modes

Word normally uses the insert mode. In this mode, Word does not overtype the existing text but pushes it forward. By pressing the Ins key, you can switch to overtype mode. In this mode, the new text replaces the old text after the cursor. To switch between Overtype/Insert modes, press the Insert key. In the Insert mode, when you place the cursor in the middle of two words and start typing, the new text is inserted between the two words and all the text below this line is automatically adjusted. In the overtype mode, when you place the cursor in the middle of two words and start typing, the new text overwrites the previous text.

VISUALIZING AND PLANNING FOR A NEW DOCUMENT

Just like you visualize an entire building before it is constructed (the blueprint), it is a good habit to think about the overall look and contents of the document before you actually start creating it. Word gives you onscreen clues about how your printed document would look like before it is actually printed.

If you provide some basic information such as paper size and orientation (portrait or landscape, i.e. lengthwise or widthwise printing respectively), Word would display, while you are creating the document, simple information like margins, page endings, line endings, the relative size and placement of text and graphics and so on. Therefore, it is always a good idea to start by specifying the page size, printer, margins etc. before entering text.

TYPING TEXT

Typing text in word is similar to typing it on a normal typewriter, except for three major differences (there are over a million minor differences!). Unless you want to start a new paragraph don't press the 'Enter' key. The moment you reach the end of the right margin of your page, word automatically places the cursor at the beginning of the next line. This feature is called word wrap and it does away with the irritating necessity of either having to yank a lever (like in a typewriter) at the end of each line or pressing Enter after every line. While typing, when you reach the end of a line Word automatically figures out whether the next word that you are typing can fit within the current line, if not, the next word is automatically placed in the next new line. This means that you don't have to bother about left or right margins while typing. Simply go ahead and keep on typing, word would take care of these things automatically.

Do not bother if you make mistakes while typing. Thanks to Word's editing features, you can always go back anywhere in your document and correct the mistakes, make alterations, additions or deletions. Not only this, Word's spelling programme would help you to rectify all spelling mistakes. Do not bother about how your text looks – in form of size, looks or placement. Again, Word's advanced formatting features would help you later, to really beautify your work. Normally, it is faster to type "Plain vanilla" text first, finish entry and then bother about formatting the document ("formatting" includes specifying font type, font size, font attributes like bold, italics, underline, colour, placement etc.). However, as explained earlier, page setup details should ideally be specified right in the beginning before typing the text.

SOME 'DON'TS'

- Don't use the spacebar to indent paragraphs. Instead, use the tab key for the indent control in Word's ruler (the top handle on the left hand side).
- Don't use spacebar to centre or otherwise position text. Use the left, right and centre alignment buttons from formatting bar instead.
- Don't use spacebar to create columns. Use Word's table or column command instead.
- Don't hit enter key repeatedly for starting the matter on new page. Use insert page break command instead.

MS WORD MENUS

The Menu bar located below the title bar consists of a drop down menu and the sub menu along with the keyboard shortcut commands against their names. For executing most tasks, the user has three options.

- Choose the desired command from the Menu option provided by either using the mouse or using cursor movement keys, or
- Press the appropriate shortcut keys and combination from the keyboard, or
- Click once on the relevant Icon from the displayed toolbar.

Although there is no right or wrong approach, most users find the third option the simplest and the fastest.

This section deals with the various menu options available in MS Word.

File Menu

New

Creates a new blank document based on the default template.

Open

Opens an existing document or a template.

Close

Closes the active document without exiting Ms Word and prompts you to save any unsaved changes.

Save

Saves the active document with the same file name, format and in the current location.

Save As

Saves the active document with the different file name or format and location, as desired.

Save as Web Page

Saves the current document as a Web Page in the form of an Internet file.

Search

Finds files, web pages and outlook items based on the search criteria you enter.

Versions

Saves and manages multiple versions of the document in a single file.

Web Page Preview

Shows your active document as a web page in your browser.

Page Setup

Allows you to set the margins, orientation, paper size and source, and other layout options for your document.

Print Preview

Shows you the preview of your document, exactly the way it will look on the paper.

Print

Allows you to print and define the print settings of your current document to the defined printer.

Send To

Sends the active document as an email or a fax to the desired recipient.

Properties

Displays the properties of the current document, i.e. the

creation date, the title, author, number of paragraphs, lines, words, characters, pages etc. in the file.

Exit

Closes the MS Word Software after prompting you to save any unsaved documents.

Edit Menu

Undo Last Commands

Reverses the last command.

Replace Last Commands

Restores the last command again once you undo it.

Cut

Removes a word, line or a block, as selected and places it in the special memory called the clip board, from where it can be retrieved.

Copy

Copies the cut word, line or a block and places it on the office clipboard.

Office Clipboard

Is a special place in the computer's memory from where cut or copied word, line or block can be retrieved.

Paste

Inserts the cut or copied selection at the defined point and replaces any active selection.

Paste Special

Inserts the cut or copied selection at the defined point and replaces any active selection in the specified format.

Paste as Hyperlink

Defines the inserted cut or copied selections as a link to another document.

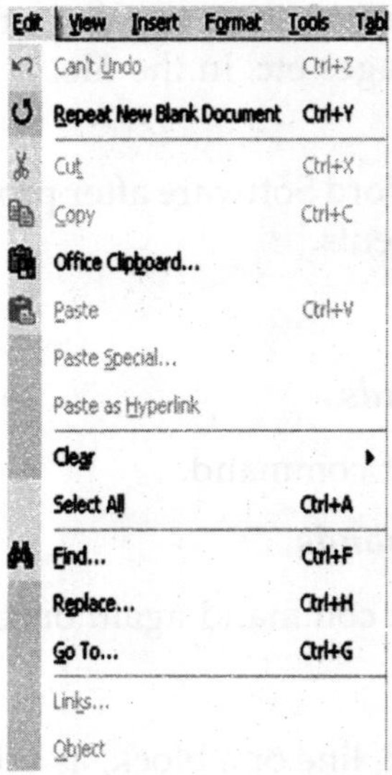

Clear

Directly removes the selected character, word, line or a block without putting it on the clipboard.

Select All

Selects all the contents of the active document including the text and graphics.

Find

Searches for a specified character, word within the active document.

Replace

Searches for and replaces a specified character or a word in the active document.

Go To

Moves the cursor to the desired page, section line, bookmark, comment etc.

Links

Displays or changes information for each link in the current document including the name and location of the source file, the item, the type and also define the updating of the link.

Objects

Activates the application in which the selected object was created so that you can modify it.

View Menu

Normal

Shows the document in the normal view. This is the default document view.

Web Layout

Shows your active document as a webpage, as it will appear in the web browser.

Print Layout

Shows your active document as it will appear on paper after printing.

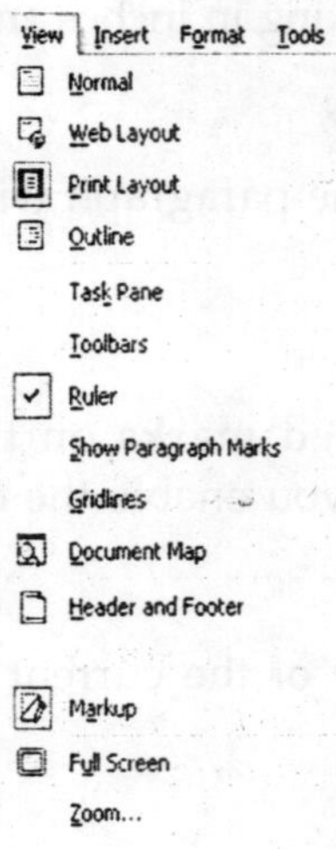

Outline

Shows your active window so that you can examine and work with the structure of your file in the classic outline form.

Task Pane

Window which pops out on the right side of the document screen and has the options to choose from the recently opened documents, new documents, WebPages or emails, the clip board menu, basic search menu, inserting clip arts, style and formatting of your document and mail merge etc.

Toolbars

Give you the option to display the required tool bar in form of buttons, menus or a combination of both, making the commands available to you at a single click. The most important Toolbar is the Menu bar, which is permanently on the top of the screen.

The rest of the tool bars like Standard toolbar, Formatting toolbar, Drawing toolbar and the Picture toolbar can be added or removed from the screen as and when desired.

Ruler

Allows you to keep a track of the margins and tabs. When this option is activated, you can see the horizontal and the vertical ruler along with the marking in inches and the tab marks.

Show Paragraph Marks

Shows the end of the paragraph with a special character which is non printable.

Gridlines

Shows the checkered marks on the work area of the current document once you enable the option.

Document Map

Shows the structure of the current document in the left hand side pane.

Header and Footer

Defines a common text, picture or both which has to appear on the top (header) and bottom (footer) of every page. These can be page numbers, dates, references, company logo etc.

Footnotes

Defines comments, or provide references that appear at the end of each page in a document.

Markup

Marks the comments, and tracks and defines all the changes done in the document.

Full Screen

Once this option is activated, the entire menu and tool bars are hidden and you can view the document on the whole screen without any rulers, startup bar and tool bars etc.

Zoom

With this option you can reduce or enlarge the view of your document. Zoom options include zoom to page widths, text width, whole page etc.

Insert Menu

Break

Inserts page break, column break, and text wrapping break or section breaks.

Page Numbers

Inserts page numbers in your document on every page that is automatically updated when you add or delete a page.

Date and Time

Inserts the current date and time which is automatically updated when you open or print the document.

Auto Text

Stores text or graphics you need to frequently use.

Field

Inserts a field at the insertion point. Use fields to insert a variety of up-to-date information.

Symbol

Inserts special characters and symbols from the installed fonts in your list.

Comment

Inserts a comment at the desired insertion point.

Reference

Inserts a reference, which can be a footnote, caption, cross-reference or an index table, at the desired insertion point.

Web Component

Inserts a component for use on the webpage, such as lines, bars for the navigation and lists views of document libraries.

Picture

Inserts pictures from clip art, word art, charts and diagrams, auto shapes from the libraries, scanners cameras or other documents.

Diagram

Inserts diagrams in the form of organization charts, cycle, radial, Venn and target diagrams.

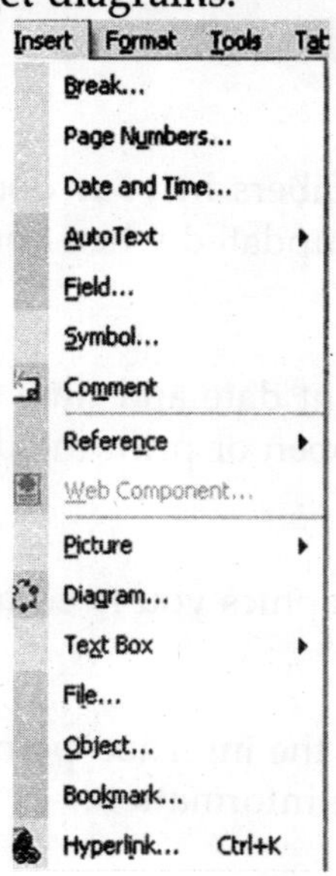

Text Box

Inserts a box where you can click and type text in a horizontal or a vertical fashion in an active window at the desired insertion point in your active document.

File

Inserts a file or a part of your file at the desired insertion point in the active document.

Object

Inserts an object such as image, media clip, presentation, table, chart, slide, picture, video, sound etc.

Bookmark

Creates a bookmark which you can use to mark selected points in your active document.

Hyperlink

Inserts a link through which you can directly connect to a location in the current document, webpage, or a file created in a different programme.

Format Menu

Font

Changes the font style, font size, font effect, text effect and character spacing for the selected text.

Paragraph

Changes the paragraph indents and spacing, line and page break and other paragraph formatting options.

Bullets and Numbering

Adds or modifies the bullets or numbers in the selected paragraphs.

Borders and Shading

Applies shading in the selected paragraph and creates borders around the selected area in different styles and colours.

Columns

Changes the number of columns along with the column width and spacing in the document or a section of the document.

Tabs

Defines the position and alignment of the tabs and determines the type of leader character for each tab stop.

Drop Cap

A drop cap is traditionally the first letter in the paragraph and it appears in the left margin or dropped from the base line of the first line in the paragraph. The drop cap formats a letter or word or the selected text with a large initial or dropped capital letter.

Text Direction

Changes the orientation of desired/selected text from horizontal to vertical in a table cell.

Change Case

Changes the sentence case; upper, lower case, toggle case etc. for the desired/selected text.

Fit Text

Changes the width for the selected text so that it fits horizontally.

Asian Layout

Changes the layout of the selected text, i.e. the phonetic guide, enclosed characters, horizontal or vertical, combined characters, or enclose two lines in one.

Backgrounds

Fills colours, effects printed watermarks from selected picture and adds it as a background to the document.

Theme

Applies a new or different design to a document, webpage, email, or data access page.

Frames

Creates a table of content by using the heading of your page and formats it on the left frame of the page.

Auto Format

Analyses the content of the active document and then automatically formats it.

Style and Formatting

Displays the style and formatting task pane, where you can re-apply formatting easily, create styles, and select all the text with the same formatting.

Reveal Formatting

Finds the text with similar formatting and then can also compare it with another selection.

Object

Formats the line, colour, fill and pattern size, position and other properties of the selected objects.

Tools Menu

Spelling and Grammar

Checks the writing style, spellings and grammar of the active document and suggests the possible corrections.

Language

Provides an option to choose a language for the selected text in the document that contains more than one language.

Word Count

Shows the exact number of characters, words, lines and paragraph in the active document.

Auto Summarize

Displays a summary of the sentences which are most relevant to the theme.

Speech

It has the inbuilt speech recognition software, which converts your speech into text. It also sets up the speech recognition software to select menus, toolbars and dialogue item boxes.

Track Changes

It marks and keeps a track of changes in your current document, by the reviewer's name.

Compare and Merge Document

You can compare your document with any other document with the option to merge the two. The changes can be displayed as markup in a new document or any of the old documents.

Protect Document

It gives you an option to protect your document or part of your online form except as specified. It also gives you the option to protect it with a password so that only privileged users can make changes to the document, mark revisions, or fill in the online form.

Online Collaboration

Starts a spontaneous online net meeting by sending an invitation to other participants, who are also online using Microsoft

Net meeting on their computers. It also has the feature of scheduling an online meeting by using names from the address book of your email programme, and displays the discussions toolbar, where you can insert a new discussion.

Letters and Mailings

It has the letter wizard feature which quickly helps you create letters.

The Mail merge wizard helps you create form, letters, mailing labels, envelops, catalogs and different types of mail merge documents that have the same or different address, and send the same body text to different users, without having to type the letter again and again.

Tools on the Web

Connects you to the Microsoft Office tools available online for further information and integrated e-services of Microsoft.

Macro

Is a series of actions, which you can record for repetitive execution. With the Macro dialog box you can edit, run or delete. You can also record a new macro in the visual basic editor.

Templates and Add-ins

Attaches a different template to the active document, with an option to load add-in programmes and update document styles.

Auto Correct Options

Sets the option to automatically correct text for any typing error as you type, and also stores and reuses frequently used text.

Customise

Gives you an option to customise the toolbar buttons, menu commands and shortcut key assignments including the icon size, font and the menu animation etc.

Options

Provides you an option to customise the Microsoft Office Program's default settings, such as the screen appearance, printing, editing, spell check, file location, typography, track changes etc.

Tables Menu

Draw Table

Gives you the option to draw customised tables in your active document. You can also have nested tables.

Insert

Allows you to insert tables, rows, columns or cells in the selected table.

Delete

Allows you to delete tables, rows, columns or cells in the selected table.

Select

Allows you to select tables, rows, columns or cells.

Merge Cells

Combines the contents of the selected adjacent cell into a single cell.

Split Cells

Splits a single cell into multiple cells, i.e. you can increase the number of rows or columns.

Split Table

Divides a table into two separate tables and inserts a paragraph mark above the row that contains the insertion point.

Table Auto Format

Automatically formats the table with a predefined format including the borders and shading of the table. It also resizes the table to fit the contents of the table cells.

Auto Fit

Gives you the option to automatically fit the contents in the table or fit the table in the window, or define the table width or distribute the rows and columns evenly.

Heading Rows Repeat

If your table spans more than one page, you can designate a particular row to be the table heading that is repeated on every subsequent page.

Convert

Gives an option to convert the selected text into a table or converts a selected table into text.

Sort

Arranges the data in the required order, i.e. ascending or descending, based upon the criteria, i.e. the column on which you want to sort.

Formula

Gives you the option to perform mathematical calculations on numbers.

Hide Gridlines

Gives you the option to show or hide the table gridlines. Gridlines are dotted lines on your table, which help to see which cell you are working in. Gridlines are not printable. In case you want to print the gridlines, you can use the borders and shadings command from the format menu.

Table Properties

Sets various options to format the table, i.e. options like table size, alignment, text wrapping etc.

Windows Menu

New Window

Opens a new window with exactly the same contents making it easier for you to view different parts of the file at the same time.

Arrange All

Displays all the open files in separate windows on the screen making it easier for you to cut-copy-paste between files.

Split

Splits the active window into panes or removes the split from an already split window.

Currently Open Files

These are the list of currently open files. It also tick marks and shows the file you are currently working within the active window.

Help Menu

Microsoft Word Help

Launches the MS Office Assistant, which provides help and tips to accomplish your tasks.

Hide the Office Assistant

Displays or hides the office assistant from the active screen.

What's This

Provides help on the topic clicked on.

Office on the Web

Connects to Microsoft's website, where you can get help and updated information on office programmes.

Active Product

Launches the activation wizard so that you can activate or update your copy of Microsoft Office.

WordPerfect Help

Helps you learn the MS Word equivalent for WordPerfect for DOS commands and key combinations.

Detect and Repair

Automatically finds and fixes all the errors in Microsoft Office.

About Microsoft Word

Displays the basic information about your computer and operating system along with the version details, copyright, legal and licensing notices, the user name, organization name and the software serial number.

STANDARD TOOLBAR

The standard toolbar contains buttons, with the help of which you can execute commands, quickly without going through the menus.

With the standard toolbar you can create, open, save and print your documents.

With the help of the standard toolbar icons, you can send your documents as e-mails; insert tables, objects, pictures, charts, diagrams in your document.

New

To create a new document based on the default template.

- Choose New from the File menu.
- Click on Blank Document in the New Document menu on the right panel.

Open

To open an existing document or a template.

- Choose Open from the File menu;
- Choose the directory where your document is saved;
- Type in your file name here;
- Click once on Open; and
- Double click on the file name.

Save

To save the active document or template.

- Choose Save command from the File menu.

Save As

To save the active file with a different filename or in a different location.

- Choose Save As command from the File menu;
- Choose the directory where you want to save the document;
- Type in the file name you want to save the file as;

- Click once on Save.

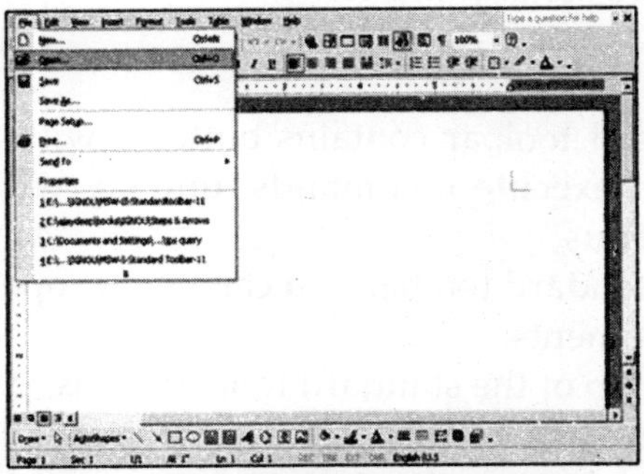

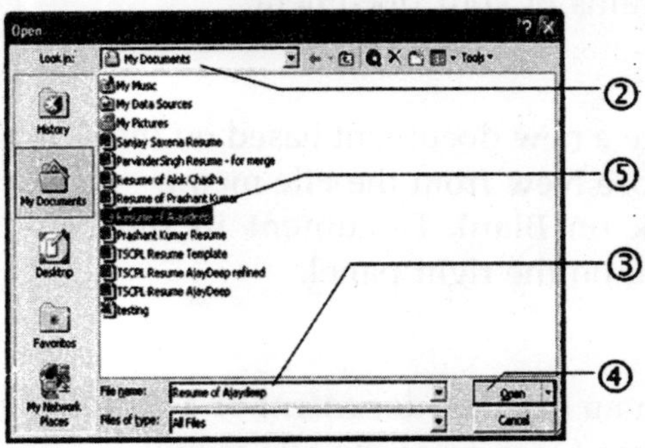

Page Setup

To modify the page setup

- Choose Page Setup from the File menu; and
- Click on OK once you have defined your page settings.

Page Setup allows you to set options like Paper margins, Paper settings, Page Layout and Document Grid. These options are provided through the following three tabbed sub-menus.

- *Margins:* You can set the margins here.
- *Paper:* You can change the paper size or source here.
- *Layout:* You can change the paper layout here.

Margins

- Click here to define the Top, Bottom, Left, Right, Gutter and Gutter Position.

- Click on the desired Orientation, i.e. Landscape or Portrait.
- Click here to set options for multiple pages.
- Click here to define the portion of the document you want to apply these settings to.
- Click here to get the default settings.

Paper

- Click here to define the paper size or define the custom size here.
- Click here to define the printer tray you want to print the first page from and the rest of the pages can be defined in the subsequent column.
- Click here to define the portion of the document you wish to apply these settings to.
- Click here to define the print options.
- Click here to get the default settings.

Layout

- Click here to define the beginning of the new section.
- Click here to define the header and footer pages.
- Click here to define the distance between the edge of the page and top of the header/footer.
- Click here to define the vertical alignment of the page.
- Click here to define the portion of the document you wish to apply these settings on.
- Click here to add or remove the line numbers from the portion of document currently selected in the apply to option.
- Click here to apply the borders around each document.
- Click here to get the default settings.

Print

To print the document or the template.

- Click on the Print option from the File menu;
- Select the Printer name here; and
- Click on OK after you have defined all the settings

- Click here to change the printing options for the selected printer.
- Click here to find the network printer based on the printer name, model etc.
- Click here to print your document in a file instead of a printer.
- Click here to define the number of copies you want to print.
- Click here to print multiple copies on a single sheet of paper.
- Click here to print multiple papers on single sheet.
- Click here to scale the paper size.
- Click here to define the printing options.
- Click here to select the page or the page range you want to print.
- Choose the document or the part of document you want to print.

Print Preview

It shows a preview of the document as it will be printed on paper.

- Click on the Print Preview option in the file menu.
  - This will show how your page will look on paper (when printed).

Spell Check

Checks the grammar of your document and also identifies any spelling mistakes within the current document.

- Click on the Spelling and Grammar option in the Tools Menu.
  - This displays a dialogue window, that displays spelling mistakes in red and grammatical errors in green. You can choose from the following options to check your document.
  - Ignore leaves the highlighted spelling mistake or grammatical error unchanged and finds the next error.

- Ignore All leaves all instances of the error unchanged throughout the document continuing with the spell/grammar check.
- Add to Directory option adds the highlighted word in the Not in the Dictionary option in the custom dictionary.
- Change accepts the current selection in the suggestion box. You can also edit the text and then click change.
- Change All changes all instances of the word not in the dictionary or capitalization box to the word in the suggestion box. You can also edit the text in the suggestion box and then click on Change All.
- Auto Correct adds the spelling error and its correction in the auto correct list so that it will automatically correct errors as you type it.
- Choose the directory language from here.
- Options defines the spelling and grammar checking details.
- Click here to undo the last change.

Cut-Paste

The **Cut** command cuts the selection and puts it on the clipboard, whereas the **Paste** command inserts the clipboard contents at the insertion point.

- Select the portion of the document you want to remove. Drag your mouse pointer on the selection and press the right mouse button. Choose the Cut option from the drop down menu.
- Place the cursor on the insertion point and press the right mouse button. Choose the Paste option.
  - You will notice the selected text has been moved from the original place to the new specified location.

Copy-Paste

The **Copy** command copies the selection and adds it on

the clipboard, whereas the Paste command inserts the clipboard contents at the insertion point.

- Select the portion of the document you want to copy. Drag your mouse pointer on the selection and press the right mouse button. Choose the Copy option.
- Place the cursor on the insertion point and press the right mouse button. Choose the Paste option.
  - You will notice the selected text has been moved from the original place to the new specified location.

Undo-Redo

Undo reverses certain commands and Redo reverses the action of undo command.

- Click on Undo or Redo buttons to perform the desired task.

Tables

Inserts tables in your active document and also customises your table according to your requirement. You can also create nested tables.

- Click on the Draw Table option from the Table menu.
- Click here to draw a table.
- Click on the Insertion point and drag your mouse.
- Once you release the mouse you will find your table. You can similarly add more rows and/or columns.
  - You will see the Tables and Borders toolbar. You can use the toolbar options to create your tables and format your table borders.

Zoom

Enlarges or reduces the display of your active document between 10 and 400 percent.

- Click here to enlarge or reduce the display of your active window, according to your requirement.
  - What the Standard toolbar is used for?
  - What is the difference between 'Save' and 'Save As'?

- What is the difference between 'Cut' and 'Copy' commands?
- What are the three most commonly used commands while printing any document?

FORMATTING TOOLBAR

The formatting toolbar contains buttons, drop-down menus and other controls, which help you to format and align your document, like changing font style, size, colour, text alignment, bulleting and numbering etc. These buttons help you quickly execute commands without having to go through menus.

Font

Highlight the text you want to format

- Click on the Font option in the Format Menu of the Standard Toolbar. A dialogue box is displayed where you can choose options to format your text.
  - Choose the Font from the scroll down arrow.
  - Choose the Font Style from the scroll down arrow.
  - Choose the Font size here, i.e. bold, italics or underline.
  - Choose the Font Colour here.
  - Click here to get the predefined default font formatting.
- Click on OK once after you have selected your formatting settings.

Bullets

To add or remove bullets from the selected paragraph or text.

- Choose the Bullets and Numbering option from the Format menu.
- Click on the Bulleted option from the pop up menu.
- Choose your desired Bullet style.
- Click once on OK.

Numbering

To add or remove bullets and/or numbering from the selected paragraph or text.

- Choose the Bullets and Numbering option from the Format menu.
- Click on the Numbered option (or Bullets in case you wish to add bullets to your text) from the pop up menu.
- Choose your desired Number style.
- Click once on OK.

Left-Right-Centre Alignment, Justify

- Select the text you want to align.
- Click on the Left Align button on the Formatting toolbar if you wish to align the text on the left side of the page.
- Click on the Right Align button on the Formatting toolbar if you wish to align the text on the right side of the page.
- Click on the Centre Align button on the Formatting toolbar if you wish to align the text in the centre of the page.
- Click on the Justify button on the Formatting toolbar if you wish to align the text with both the margins of your page.
  - You can see your text aligned to the left of your page.
  - You can see your text aligned in the centre of your page.
  - You can see your text aligned to the right of your page.
  - You can see your text aligned with both the margins of your page.

Line Spacing

It changes the space between the lines of your text.

- Select the text by highlighting it.
- Click on the Line Spacing button on the Formatting toolbar and select the desired spacing from the drop-down menu.
  - You will get your desired line spacing for the selected text.

Right Indenting

It indents the paragraph to the next Tab.

- Place the cursor at the beginning of the paragraph you want to indent.
- Click on the Increase Indent button on the Formatting toolbar.
  - You can see your paragraph has moved to the next tab.

Left Indenting

Indents the paragraph to the previous Tab.

- Place the cursor at the beginning of the paragraph you wish to indent.
- Click on the Decrease Indent button on the Formatting Toolbar.
  - You can see your paragraph has moved to the Previous tab.

Highlighter

Highlighter marks the text so that it is highlighted and stands out from the surrounding text.

- Select the text you wish to highlight.
- Click on the Highlighter button on the Formatting toolbar and select the desired colour.
- The selected text is highlighted in the selected colour.
  - For what purpose the Formatting toolbar is used?
  - What are the four possible text alignments?
  - What is the difference between bullets and numbered list?

SUMMARY

In this unit, you have studied about MS Word, the full featured, easy to use word processor. You have also studied the various menu options and commonly used toolbars – Standard and Formatting.

Menu Options

- File menu displays the commands to open a new or an

existing file, saves and closes the file, prints and defines the page settings. It also has an option to display the file properties along with a list of the four most recently used files.

- Edit menu displays the commands to edit or format your text, find or find and replace a particular word or a line. It also has an option to cut-copy-paste a part or a paragraph.
- View menu displays the commands to select the toolbars to be displayed each time you open the word window, to hide or show the task pane, gridlines, header and footer, paragraph marks etc.
- Insert menu displays the commands to insert page breaks, section breaks. It also displays the options to insert pictures, diagrams, text boxes, files, objects, bookmarks and hyperlinks.
- Format menu allows you to format your text/ paragraph by changing text fonts, adding bullets or numbering, borders and shading, tabs, columns etc.
- Tool menu displays the commands to check for spelling mistakes and grammatical errors, languages, fix broken text, compare and merge documents, track changes etc.
- Table menu displays the commands to draw, modify and format tables. It also has options to define the formulas for calculations in the tables.
- Windows menu displays the option to create a new window, splits an existing window or arranges all the open windows. It also displays the currently open files.
- Help displays the commands to launch the MS Word help, hides or shows the office assistant.

Toolbars

The Standard Toolbar

With standard tool bar, you can perform the following tasks:

- New creates a new document.
- Open opens an existing document.
- Save saves your document for future use.

- E-mail sends your document as an e-mail through MS Outlook.
- Print prints your document on paper.
- Print Preview allows you to see your document as it will look when printed.
- Spell Check checks spellings and grammar of your current document.
- Cut moves the selected part of the document onto the clipboard.
- Copy moves the selected text to another place.
- Paste copies the cut or copied text selection to the insertion point.
- Undo reverses the last command.
- Redo reverses the action of the last command.
- Tables inserts customised tables in your document.

The Formatting Toolbar

The formatting toolbar helps you perform the following tasks:

- Font style, Size and Colour change the font style, size and colour.
- Bulleting applies bullets to the selected text.
- Numbering applies numbering to your selected lines/ paragraph.
- Alignment aligns your paragraph (Left, Right, Centre, and Justify).
- Line Spacing defines the distance between your lines.
- Right Indenting indents your selected paragraph to the right.
- Left Indenting indents your selected paragraph to the left.
- Highlighter highlights the selected text in the colour selected.

Microsoft Word is a full-featured word processing programme, which can be used for any work involving creating and managing text. You can use it from the simplest to the most complex word processing applications. Using Word, you can write letters and reports, prepare bills and invoices, prepare office stationery – letter heads, envelopes, forms etc., design brochures, pamphlets, newsletters, magazines etc. In this unit, you will learn how to create, save, close, open and print a simple document. You will also learn how to create a document using MS Word templates. We shall also learn creating and modifying tables and various formatting commands like changing fonts, font size, text colour and alignment of the text.

Objectives

After studying this unit, you should be able to

- Create, save, open and print your document,
- Save your document as a web page,
- Create tables and modify them,
- Insert tables, pictures, diagrams, charts and objects in your document,
- Define your page setup and printing options,
- Align and format your document,
- Create bullets and numbered lists,
- Format your document; define the font style, font size, font colour etc., and
- Check your document for spelling mistakes and grammatical errors.

CREATING A SIMPLE DOCUMENT

Word always starts by opening an untitled "normal" document, so that you can begin from scratch. This "normal" document is based upon all the default values (another name for pre-defined settings) provided by Word, i.e. standard page size, standard margins, font type and size etc. You can change these settings and create your own customised documents based upon new settings. You can also save your new settings in a specific kind of file, called a Template file, which will help you to quickly create documents, based upon these customised settings. You can create your own letterheads; fax sheets, invoices, memos etc. as templates so as to save substantial work and printing costs. Since these templates are like ready-made, pre-printed forms, all you have to do is fill in the blanks, very similar to filling in paper forms manually. Templates have been covered in more detailed later.

TYPES OF COMPUTER INFECTION

When you go through or rather listen the news, you hear about many different forms of electronic infection. The most common are:

Viruses

Computer viruses are called viruses, because they share some of the traits of biological viruses. A computer virus passes from computer to computer, like a biological virus passes from person to person.

A virus is a small piece of software, that piggybacks on real programmes. Once it is running, it is then able to infect other programmes or documents. For example, a virus might attach itself to a programme such as a spreadsheet programme. Each time the spreadsheet programme runs, the virus runs too, and it has the chance to reproduce (by attaching to other programmes) or wreak havoc.

E-mail Viruses

An e-mail virus moves around in e-mail messages, and usually replicates itself by automatically mailing itself to dozens of people in the victim's

e-mail address book.

Worms

A worm is a small piece of software that uses computer networks and security holes to replicate itself. A copy of the worm scans the network for another machine that has a specific security hole. It copies itself to the new machine using the security hole, and then starts replicating from there, as well.

Trojan Horses

A Trojan horse is simply a computer programme. The programme claims to do one thing (it may claim to be a game) but instead does damage when you run it (it may erase the data stored in your hard disk). Trojan horses have no way to replicate automatically.

ANTI-VIRUS SOFTWARE

In order to combat the menace of viruses, specialized companies have developed special purpose software typically called *"anti-virus software"* to help the users to detect, remove, and prevent further invasion of viruses.

Some of the commonly used anti-virus packages are:

- Norton Antivirus
- McAfee Antivirus
- Escan
- Trend Micro
- AVG

Starting MS Word

To start Microsoft Word

- Click once on the Start button, choose All Programmes and click once on Microsoft Word; or
- Directly click on the Word icon from the Office Shortcut Bar on the Desktop; or
- Click on the Microsoft Word icon on the recently used programmes list above the Programmes Menu.

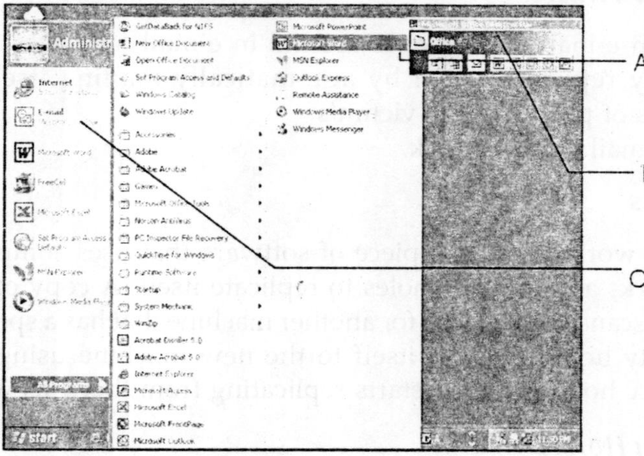

Opening a New Document

- Click on New from the File menu to create a new template;

- Click on Blank Document in the New Document option on the right panel.

Entering Text

- Click here and start typing in your text.
  - Don't worry about the formatting of the text. Keep on typing your text without pressing enter key. Once you need to start a new paragraph press the enter key.

Changing the Font Style

- Highlight the heading by clicking the left mouse button from the starting of the text you want to change the font, and drag it till the end of the text.
- Click on the Font Box of the formatting toolbar. Click once on the pull down arrow symbol and a list of the available fonts will drop down. Browse the list with the mouse and click on the desired font, i.e. Garamond in this case.
  - Once you click on the desired font, the drop down list will disappear and the desired font will be applied on the selected text.

Changing the Font Size

- Highlight the text as explained earlier; and
- Click on the Font Size Box of the formatting toolbar. Click once on the down arrow symbol and a list of the available font sizes will drop down. Browse the list with the mouse and click on the desired Font Size, i.e. 16 in this case.
  - Once you click on the desired font size, the drop down list will go and the desired font size will be applied on the selected text.

Changing the Font Colour

- Highlight the text as explained earlier; and
- Click on the Font Colour Box of the formatting toolbar. Click once on the pull down arrow symbol and a list of the available font colours will drop down.

Browse the list with the mouse and click on the desired Font Colour, i.e. blue grey in this case.

- Once you click on the desired font colour, the drop down list will go and the desired font colour will be applied on the selected text.

Changing Text Attribute

Applying the Bold Attribute

- Highlight the text as explained earlier; and
- Click once on the Bold Button of the formatting toolbar.
  - Once you click on the Bold button, you can see your text attribute to be bold.
  - Similarly, you can apply the bold attribute to the sub headings also.

Underlining the Text

- Highlight the text as explained earlier; and
- Click once on the Underline Button of the formatting toolbar.
  - Once you click on the Underline button, you can see your selected text has been underlined.

Italicizing the Text

- Highlight the text as explained earlier; and
- Click once on the Italic Button of the formatting toolbar.
  - Once you click on the Italic button, you can see that the attribute of your text has been changed to Italics.

Bullets

- Highlight the text as explained earlier;
- Click once on the Bullets and Numbering option from the format menu;
- Click on the Bullet style you wish to use from the options on the pop up screen; and
- Click on OK once.

- Once you click on the OK button you can see your text has been bulleted.

Numbering the Text

- Highlight the text as explained earlier;
- Click once on the Bullets and Numbering option from the format menu;
- Click on the Number style you wish to use from the options on the pop up screen; and
- Click on OK once.
  - Once you click on the OK button, you can see your text is numbered.

Aligning the Text

Centreing the Text

- Highlight the text as explained earlier; and
- Click on the Centre icon once on the formatting toolbar.
  - Once you click on the Centre button you can see your heading in the centre of the page.

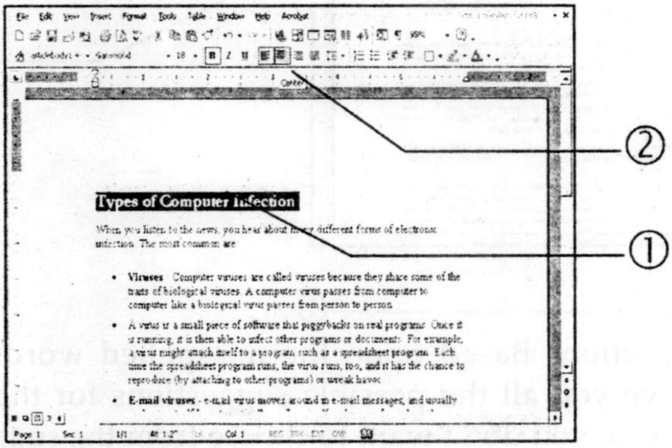

Justifying the Text

- Highlight the text as explained earlier; and
- Click on the Justify icon once on the formatting toolbar.
  - Once you click on the Justify button, you can see

that your paragraph has been justified to both the horizontal edges of the page.

Spelling and Grammar Check

- Place the cursor right in the beginning of the document to ensure that the complete document is checked for spelling and grammatical errors. (Although even if you will place the cursor anywhere in the middle, Spelling check feature will prompt you and start from the beginning);
- Choose Spelling and Grammar command from the Tools menu;
- Once you click on the Spelling and Grammar command, the spell check dialog box appears. The spell check dialog box gives you the following options. Click on the options you want to use. Click on OK once.

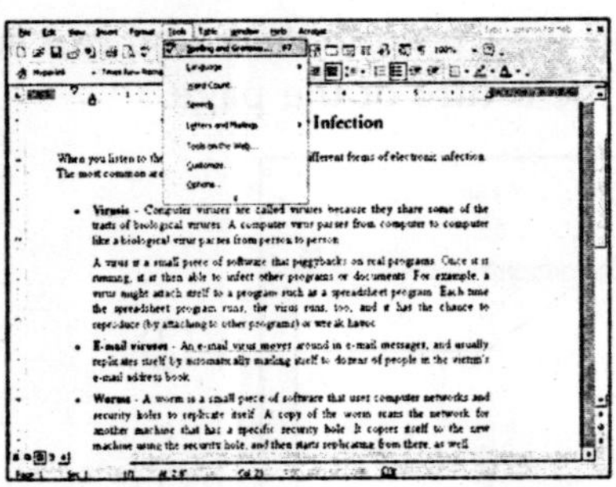

②

①

Suggestions Based upon the misspelled words, Word would give you all the possible suggestions for the correct word. In case you don't want to choose from the suggestions, you can simply type the correct word and click once on the change button.

Ignore Though this word is not found in the dictionary, leave it unchanged.

Ignore All	Ignore this word for all subsequent occurrences.
Change	Change this word with the specified

	suggestion.
Change all	Change this word for all subsequent occurrences, with the suggestion specified.
Add	Add this word to the dictionary.
Auto-Correct	Add the suggested corrections to Auto-Correct.
Options	For changing Spell Checks default settings.
Undo Last	Cancel for the previous replacement.
Cancel	Terminate Spell Check and return to the document.

Print Preview

- Choose Print Preview command from File menu.
  - This is how your document will look like on print. Click on the Print option if you don't have to make any changes and print the document or click on the Close option and make the relevant changes.

Print

- Choose Print command from the File menu;
- Choose your printer from the list;
- Click here to choose All. This would print all of the pages of the current document; and
- Click on OK button to print.

Saving the Document

- Choose Save command from the File menu;
- Type the file name by which you wish to save your file; and
- Click on the Save button.

Closing the Document

- Choose Close command from the File menu.

Opening the Document

- Choose Open command from the File menu;

- Specify the correct directory path where you have saved your file;
- Choose the file by clicking it once; and
- Click once on the Open button to open the selected file.

Exiting MS Word

Choose Exit command from File command menu to end your MS Word session.

CREATING A DOCUMENT THROUGH TEMPLATE

Every Microsoft Word document is based on a *template.* A template determines the basic attributes for a document such as default font, font size, page margins, page size, page orientation etc. The two basic types of templates are *global templates* and *document templates.* Global templates, including the *Normal template* (on which all new documents are based by default), contain settings that are available to all documents. Document templates, such as the memo or fax template (accessed by selecting the New Document dialog box from the File → New command), contain settings that are available only to documents based on these templates. For example, if you create a memo using the memo template, the memo can use the settings from both the memo template as well as the settings in any global template.

Word provides a variety of pre-defined document templates. You can also *create your own document templates* such as templates for your company's letter head, fax form, invoice etc.

We shall now work on an exercise involving *Creating an Inter Office Memo* created using MS Word's Elegant Memo template.

INTEROFFICE MEMO

Date: 12/25/2005
To: All TSCPL Members
Cc: The Managing Directors
From: ajaydeep
RE: New Year Party

All TSCPL staff members along with their family members are cordially invited to the New Years Party at 10:00 PM on 31st Dec at Maharaja Hall, The Radisson Hotel, New Delhi.

Dress Code is Smart Casuals.

AjayDeep Singh
Office/Chief Admin Officer

Selecting a Template

- Start MS Word;
- Click on the New Blank Document from the file menu;
- Click on the General Templates option from the New form Template option on the right panel;
- Choose Memo Wizard in the Memo option from the Template popup menu; and
- Click once on the OK Button.

STARTING A TEMPLATE AND SELECTING THE TEMPLATE STYLE

- Click once on the Next button to start the Memo wizard Template;
- Click once on the Elegant Style radio button to select it; and
- Click once on Next to continue.

HEADER AND THE HEADER ITEMS

- Click on the Yes Radio button and type in the text here, if you want to include a title;
- Click once on the Next button;
- Click on the header items you want to include in the memo and type in the item here; and
- Click once on the Next button.

RECIPIENT'S NAMES AND THE CLOSING ITEMS

- Type in the Recipients address here and click on the To radio button;
- Type in the Second Recipients address here and click on the Cc radio Button;

- Click on the option here to have as separate page for your distribution list;
- Click once on the Next button;
- Tick and type in the closing items you would like to include in the memo; and
- Click once on the Next button.

HEADER AND FOOTER

- Tick the header you want to include in your memo;
- Tick the footer you want to include in your memo;
- Click once on the Next button; and
- Click once on the Finish Button.

MS Word provides an easy to use Table Menu, through which you can create very sophisticated tables in a matter of minutes.

These tables once created can be easily modified to insert, delete, merge or split, existing rows and columns. Let us follow the instructions, given below, to create the invoice sample given in Exercise 4.3.

It may be kept in mind that although you can create tables of any kind using MS Word, in case these tables involve lot of figure and calculations it is better to use MS Excel rather than MS Word, since MS Excel has been specifically designed for this purpose.

CREATING ROWS AND COLUMNS

- Type in your text and place the cursor on the point where you want to insert the Table;
- Click on the Table sub menu in the Insert Option from the Table Menu;
- Type here the Number of columns desired;
- Type here the number of rows desired; and
- Click on OK once.
  - You get your desired Table box once you release the mouse button.

Inserting Rows and Columns

- Click once on the Rows above option in the Insert option of the Table.

– You will find a row inserted above your column.

- Click once on the Columns to the Left option in the Insert option of the Table Menu.
  - You will find a column inserted to the left of your table. Similarly, you can add in more rows.

Merging Cells

- Now you can type in your text in the cells. You need to merge the last row of the table so as to fit in the amount in words.
- Highlight the cell you want to merge; and
- Click on the Merge Cell Option from the Table Menu.
  - Your cells of the last rows have merged to one cell and now you can type in your text.
  - Your final table is ready to use now. You can now type and format the rest of your text as explained earlier to complete your exercise.

Now, you can type in the rest of your text and complete your exercise.

- What is a Template?
- List and define the types of templates.
- What is the difference between a normal document and a normal template?

Chapter 5

Digital Gates

LOGIC

Since at least 400 B.C. human beings have been studying what it means to think and to reason. Two closely related aims can be identified:

- To understand the process of mental reasoning.
- To develop methods to mechanise thinking and reasoning, e.g. to develop procedural methods for doing mathematical proofs, or simply to give procedures by which a thinker could come up with a rational answer to a difficult question, or, more lately, as in the study of Artificial Intelligence, to develop methods by which computers may be programmed to perform tasks that require *intelligence.*

Broadly speaking, logic is the study of the principles and patterns of reasoning, argument and proof. Again generalising, we can say that logic uses a language that is a formalisation of certain types of natural language statements.

You should be aware that there are two distinct but related forms of logic:

- Propositional logic - which is closely related to Boolean algebra. We will have cause to use elements of propositional logic in this course. And, you will come across it frequently in your other courses. Note: in programming, where you will have already come across statements like: if(x == 10 && y == 20) (test the truth of the logic statement *x is-equal-to 10* and *y is-equal-to 20.*

- Predicate calculus, which is at the basis of the Prolog programming language.

PROPOSITIONAL LOGIC

Propositional logic deals with statements (propositions) which make claims which can be either true or false. Thus, valid propositions are:

- Dublin is the capital of Ireland.
- Belfast has more than 100,000 inhabitants.
- Manchester United are Premiership Champions.
- Joe Bloggs is a first year QUB student.

The test for validity is as follows: you must be able to meaningfully append to the statement "is true" (or "is false").

Thus "Dublin is the capital of Ireland is true".

Notice, however, how "Manchester United are Premiership Champions" may need time/date qualification.

The following are invalid propositions.

- What is the capital of Ireland? (a question)
- Has Dublin a large population? (a question)
- Go now to room 1.15! (a command)
- Will you come to the Botanic Inn with me on Thursday? An invitation - variations on which may be called a "proposition" in everyday language!

Generalisation/Abstraction: Symbolic Logic

We can make symbols stand-for any proposition, e.g.

p = "Dublin is the capital of Ireland"

Hence, in propositional calculus, the 'Boolean' variable p has the truth value *true.*

q = "Belfast has more than 100, 000 inhabitants"

Compound Propositions

We can now combine elementary propositions using logic connectives to make compound or complex propositions.

Conjunction - and

Dublin is the capital of Ireland and Belfast has more than 100,000 inhabitants is true.

The combined proposition is true if-and-only-if both elements are true. In this case, let us agree that both are true, so that the statement: Arsenal are European Champions and Belfast has more than 100,000 inhabitants is false. The meaning of and can be neatly summarised with a truth-table using abstract symbols:

Table: Truth-table for Conjunction

p	*q*	*p and q*
F	*F*	*F*
F	*T*	*F*
T	*F*	*F*
T	*T*	*T*

Other symbols for conjunction are: $\wedge$ (looks like an A), and, in C/C++/Java, &&.

Disjunction - or

Note that or has two natural language meanings: exclusive-or, only one of the statements can be true at any time; inclusive-or, only either one or the other needs be to be true, or *both*; without any qualification, *or* generally means inclusive-or. The meaning of or is given by the following truth-table:

Table: Truth-table for Disjunction

p	*q*	
F	*F*	*F*
F	*T*	*T*
T	*F*	*T*
T	*T*	*T*

Other symbols for disjunction:, and, in C/C++/Java,.

Negation - not

If a proposition *p* is true, then not(*p*) is false.

The meaning of not is given by the truth-table:

Table: Truth-table for negation

p	*not q*
F	*T*
T	*F*

SET THEORY

The propositional calculus on truth values is equivalent to (*isomorphic* with) the calculus of set operations:

$$\textbf{and} \leftrightarrow \cap \text{ (intersection)}$$
$$\textbf{or} \leftrightarrow \cup \text{ (union)}$$
$$\textbf{not} \leftrightarrow \sim \text{ (complement)}$$

DIGITAL LOGIC

Digital computers are constructed from switching circuits which implement propositional calculus - Boolean algebra; indeed, the term *switching algebra* is sometimes used. 'Switch-on' might be associated with true and 'off' with false. However, equally, so long as everyone is agreed as to the convention, 'on' could be associated with false and 'off' with true.

Likewise, the physical entities representing the values could be {voltage-low, voltage-high} or {light-off, light-on}, or whatever. Very often, we use {0, 1} - the binary digits - to represent {false, true}.

The essence of Boolean algebra is that we have only two allowable values, which we can label whatever we like, usually: {false, true}, or {0, 1}, and the two *binary* operations mentioned above: *conjunction* (and), and *disjunction* (or), together with the *unary* operation *negation* (not). There are other binary operations, but they can be expressed in terms of these three.

Let us now examine these operations or functions - to emphasise that they are functions, we write them in *prefix* notation, remarking, however, that the *infix* notation conveys exactly the same meaning. In addition, we use the value set {0,1}, recalling that the set {false, true} is entirely equivalent.

Conjunction - and

and (0,0) = 0
and (0,1) = 0

and (1,0) = 0
and (1,1) = 1

Of course, this is the same thing as Table.

Because there is a slight analogy with numerical multiplication, and is sometimes denoted by the infix '.', or just concatenation of the input variables; also, and itself is often written in infix form. Thus, for Boolean variables *p*, *q*, and *r*, the following are equivalent:

$$r = \text{and } (p, q)$$
$$r = p \text{ and } q$$
$$r = p \wedge q$$
$$r = p \cdot q$$
$$r = pq$$
$$r = p \text{ and } q$$

Disjunction or

and (0,0) = 0
and (0,1) = 0
and (1,0) = 0
and (1,1) = 1

Of course, this is the same thing as Table.

Because there is a slight analogy with numerical addition, or is sometimes denoted by '+'. Thus, for Boolean variables *p*, *q*, and *r*, the following are equivalent:

$$r = \text{or } (p, q)$$
$$r = p \text{ or } q$$
$$r = p \vee q$$
$$r = p + q$$

NEGATION-NOT

not (0) = 1
not (1) = 0

This is the same thing as Table.Because there is a slight analogy with numerical negation, or is sometimes denoted by variations of - and ~. Thus, for Boolean variables p, q, the following are equivalent:

$$q = \text{not } (p)$$
$$q = \neg p$$

$$q = p^{-}$$
$$q = \sim p$$
$$q = p'$$

0, 1 are not numbers!

The analogies with arithmetic (and 'ordinary' algebra) may cause confusion for the unwary; remember that {0,1}stand for {false, true}and that it makes no sense at all to do arithmetic on them - no more sense than, for example, attempting to multiply a Java text String by.

AND, OR ARE BINARY, NOT IS UNARY AND THE ASSOCIATIVE LAW

Although it is not uncommon to see $p + q + r = p$ or q or r, you must remember that both or and and are *binary* - meaning two parameter functions. Thus, strictly,

$p + q + r = p + (q + r) = \text{or}(p, \text{or}(q, r))$,

just as in Java, if(x==2||y==3||z==4) strictly could be written if(x==2||(y==3||z==4)).

Of course, in 'ordinary' algebra, + and X-, etc. are also binary, but the *associative law,* see section 3.3.2 for these operations allows us to string a series of them together. Note: in 'ordinary' algebra, there are two minuses, a unary one (-1) and a binary one (3 - 1 = 2); always remember that if you have to write an expression evaluator programme.

EQUIVALENCES OF BOOLEAN ALGEBRA

Just as it helps to know that in ordinary algebra, $a \times x\ b \times x + a \times y + b \times y = (a + b) \times (x + y)$, or that $x + (-x) = 0$, it is useful to be aware of the more useful equivalences (or identities or laws) of Boolean algebra. Some of them are shown in Table 3.4. Some of these are intuitive, some not. For each equivalence there are duals - where and is swapped for or and *vice-versa*. For completeness, we show the table in two forms, Table 3.4, using the mathematicians $\wedge, \vee, \neg$ notation, and Table, using the engineers., + –, notation.

LOGIC GATES

Logic gates are the hardware implementation of logic

functions. Again, all Boolean functions can be implemented using a combination of and, or, and not gates. The term gate comes from the operation of the and gate, see below, which, if one of its inputs is false, blocks or gates the other input, even if it is true.

Microprocessors, and other digital logic integrated circuits (chips) are simply massive collections of interconnected gates.

Because of a particular twist of fate in the physics of transistors - of which logic gates are constructed - it turns out that real circuits tend to employ nand and nor gates a good deal in preference to and and or:

Nand

p nana *q* = not (*p* and *q*)
Nor:
p not *q* = not (*p* or *q*)
Nor:

TRANSISTOR IMPLEMENTATIONS

For completeness, we show transistor implementations of not (also called an *inverter*), nand and nor. Again for completeness, we give the following model of a transistor when it is operated in so-called *switching* mode.

Transistor as a Switch

There are three connections - collector, base, and emitter. The positive power supply (e.g. +5 volts) is applied to the collector via a resistor; the emitter (the one with the arrow) is connected to ground/earth. The input signal is applied to the base. When the input signal is high, say > 3 volts when the power is 5 volts, the transistor switches on, i.e. current is allowed to flow down to the emitter and out to ground. When the input signal is low, the transistor switches off i.e. little or no current is allowed to flow.

The net effect of the transistor in Figure switching on is that the output is connected to ground and V_{out} takes the voltage of ground - ~ 0 volts. Thus high input (V_{in}) - logic 1 - yields low output - logic 0; thus, not, inversion.

The net effect of the transistor switching off is that the output takes on the voltage ~ V_{cc} volts. Thus low input (V_{in}) - logic 0 - yields high output - logic 1; thus, not, inversion.

With this model in mind, it is easy to verify that the circuits in Figures do in fact operate as nand and nor.

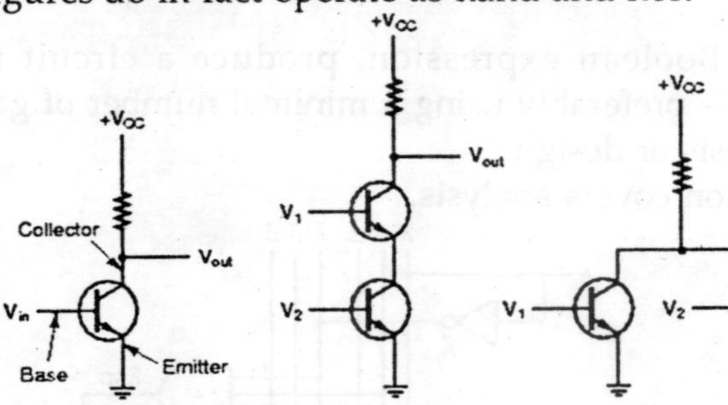

(a) (b) (c)

Fig. (a) Not (b) nand (c) nor

If you would like to see mechanical implementations of gates (levers, also water valves), see [Hillis, 1999].

Symbols for Logic Gates

Figure shows the symbols, and truth-tables, for the five basic logic gates.

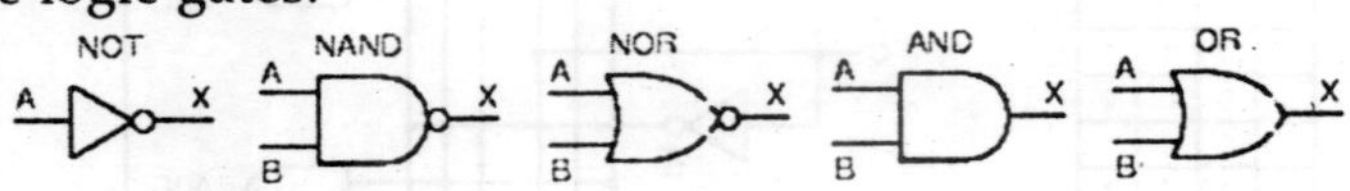

A	X
0	1
1	0

(a)

A	B	X
0	0	1
0	1	1
1	0	1
1	1	0

(b)

A	B	X
0	0	1
0	1	0
1	0	0
1	1	0

(c)

A	B	X
0	0	0
0	1	0
1	0	0
1	1	1

(d)

A	B	X
0	0	0
0	1	1
1	0	1
1	1	1

(e)

Fig. Symbols and truth-tables for (a) not (b) nand (c) nor (d) and (e) or

The circles denote negation-not, inversion. It is possible to have negation on inputs too.

LOGIC CIRCUIT ANALYSIS

There are two fairly distinct activities in working with digital logic, analysis, and synthesis.

Analysis

Given a circuit, what does it do? i.e. what Boolean function does it implement.

Synthesis

Given a Boolean expression, produce a circuit that implements it - preferably using a minimal number of gates. This is synthesis or design.

This section covers analysis.

A	B	C	M
0	0	0	0
0	0	1	0
0	1	0	0
0	1	1	1
1	0	0	0
1	0	1	1
1	1	0	1
1	1	1	1

(a)

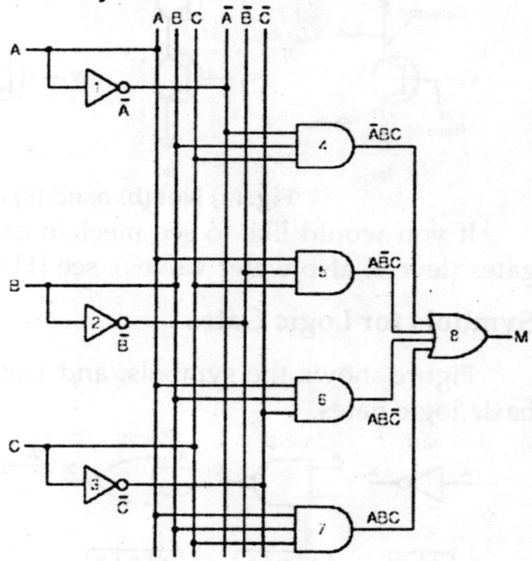

(b)

Fig. Truth-table (a) and Circuit (b) for Majority of three Circuit

It takes a majority vote over the three inputs.

Exercise. Verify the truth-table in Figure by creating an expanded truth table containing columns for. Note: starting from scratch, and not knowing the answer, this is the way you would normally do it - you cannot hope to work out column *M* in your head.

GENERATIONS OF INTEGRATED CIRCUITS

Integrated circuits started to appear in the late 1960s. A typical single chip of that age - but still available to buy today

- is shown in Figure; it contains four nand gates and has 14 pins.

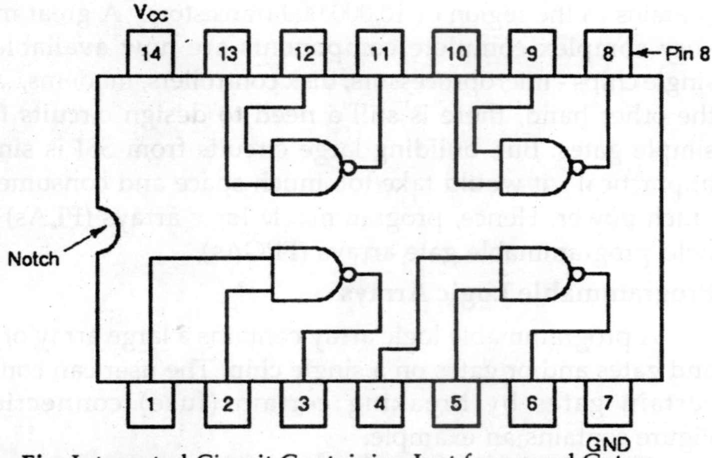

Fig. Integrated Circuit Containing Just four nand Gates

Nowadays, an integrated circuit such as Figure is said to be *small scale integrated* (SSI). Small scale integrated circuits contain up to 10 gates (up to about 100 transistors). In the late 1960s, complete computers were made from SSI; still, this was a lot better than the individual devices (transistors, resistors, etc.) of the 1950s and 60s. And, a fantastic improvement over the vacuum tubes used in the 1940s.

You will still find SSI circuits, e.g. Transistor-transistor-logic (TTL) 74xx00 quad 2-input nand used on the periphery of computer systems, and as the 'glue' which connects the more complex circuits/chips together. In SSI chips, as many gates of a given type as possible are put in the package (chip). The number of gates is limited by the number of pins, and to a lesser extent by the ability to dissipate the heat generated by the circuit. On the 74xx00 you have: power 2 pins + 4 *x* (2 *inputs* + 1 *output*) = 3 for each NAND gate = total of 14 pins. An additional consideration is the area taken up by such an SSI chip, roughly. 2.5 *Cm*× 1*Cm*. In the case of early TTL each chip would consume about 10 milliWatts of power. Later medium scale integrated (MSI) circuits began to appear - containing 10-100 gates. Later on large scale integrated (LSI) containing 100-100,000 gates. The first microprocessors (1971 - the 4 bit Intel

4004) would have been classified LSI. Now we have very large scale integrated (VLSI), and beyond. The latest Pentium III contains in the region of 10,000,000 transistors. A great many very complex complete components are now available on single chips - microprocessors, disk controllers, modems,.... On the other hand, there is still a need to design circuits from simple gates. But, building large circuits from SSI is simply impractical - it would take too much space and consume too much power. Hence, programmable logic arrays (PLAs) and field programmable gate arrays (FPGAs).

Programmable Logic Arrays

A programmable logic array contains a large array of not, and gates and or gates on a single chip. The user can connect certain gates by breaking certain (fuse) connections. Figure contains an example.

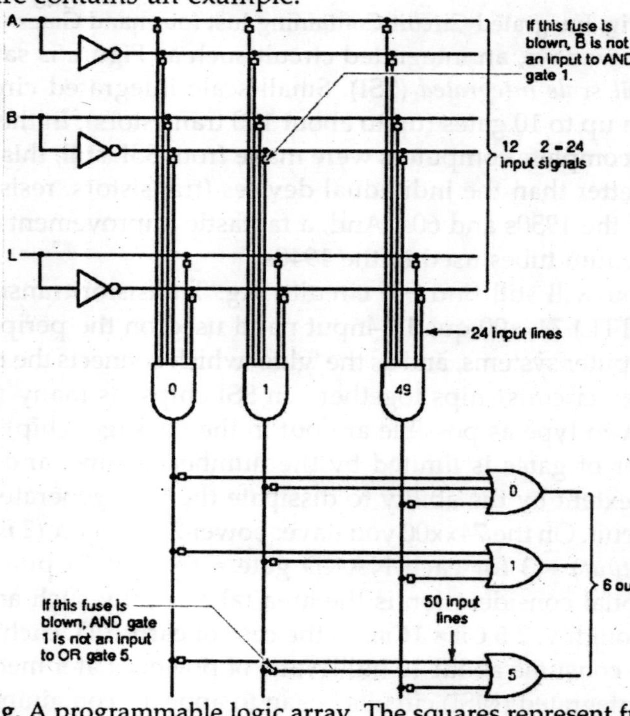

Fig. A programmable logic array. The squares represent fuses which can be blown to disable connections, and so determine which function is implemented, i.e. programmed

Chapter 6

Programming Basics

MAILING LISTS ALL OVER AGAIN

History is repeating itself. It's mailing lists all over again. Businesses have long understood that the key to winning is finding and contacting people who have their wallets out. That idea gave birth to the special interest publication whose main business proposition to advertisers is its mailing list — a targeted demographic ready to spend money on something specific.

Why else would they be reading the special interest publication? They must be looking for something to buy. Millions of businesses exist solely for the purpose of assembling and distributing these targeted lists.

Before the Internet came along, however, list impurity was a major issue.

The older a list, the more likely it was that the list's members had put away their wallets, and the less valuable the list became. But the Internet is enabling businesses with real-time lists with a purity that's nearly 100 percent. These lists immediately answer the question of who has money to spend, who is about to spend it, when they'll spend it, and who is willing to spend it online. It's the 21st century version of a customer list, a.k.a. McNealy's online directory of transactional IDs.

Assembling these directories has put the war between Java and.NET ahead of all other battles, because in the future no transaction will be completed without the presence of one of these technologies in the customer's hands.

Who do You Bet on?

While both technologies could co-exist for the foreseeable future, Sun and Microsoft appear hell bent on disintermediating the other. If either company succeeds, virtually everybody who bet on the wrong horse — businesses, IT managers, programmers, and vendors — would be sent back to the drawing board. This is a potentially devastating setback, because deciding on one technology forces you into making so many other decisions across your entire solution matrix.

For example, thousands of mobile phones and credit cards are already entering the market with Java preloaded. While Web services standards like XML and SOAP should make it possible for these Java clients to conduct a transaction with a server driven by either Java or.NET, the odds of the transaction completing successfully and securely are increased when the same technology is on both ends of the network.

Furthermore, popularity of one technology over the other could create a vicious circle. Merchants who see more potential customers using Java-enabled devices will develop for Java. If more merchants develop for Java, then more mobile phone makers will put Java into their phones. If one technology develops enough momentum over the other, the game could be over.

To keep that from happening, Sun and Microsoft are waging a war that includes smear campaigns, innuendo, personal attacks between the executives, litigation, entire technology and development platforms, and, most interestingly, a no-holds-barred effort to marry those platforms to the most transactional IDs.

The focus of this struggle has now turned to the part of Java and.NET that promises to allow customers to move seamlessly from one site to another without having to use separate user IDs and passwords. In Microsoft's world, this is called Passport. Sun's implementation is called Project Liberty. Getting users to adopt one or the other is one way to complete the aforementioned marriage. To do this as quickly as possible, and to claim bragging rights for the most number of transactional IDs, Microsoft and Sun are taking two completely different approaches.

Microsoft is busy gating virtually every service it runs with Passport. Not a week goes by where I don't find some clever trick that Microsoft uses to convert another one of its constituencies into a clan of Passport holders. A Passport is now required to access all the reseller areas on Microsoft.com. The same goes for Hotmail users.

Last week, my son got a new computer from eMachines. Using a huge rebate, Microsoft subsidized 75 percent of his Internet service costs in exchange for using MSN as his ISP. As an MSN user, he automatically becomes a Passport holder. So does his mother, thanks to Windows XP's multi-user support. Get the picture? Just yesterday, I attempted to play with Microsoft's UDDI directory. (UDDI is a white pages standard that will play an important role in the future of Web services.) I couldn't get in without a Passport. A freshly installed version of Windows XP asks you to sign up for Passport no fewer than five times. The wording of the request is very disingenuous. I showed the message to several less computer-literate people and all were misled into thinking that they wouldn't be able to access the Internet unless they signed up for a Passport.

The Power of Partners

Sun on the other hand has no existing services or products that people are registered to use. As a result, Sun has no way of doing what Microsoft has done: converting over 165 million constituents into Passport holders. However, according to McNealy, the number of transactional IDs that use Liberty will blow right past Passport once his 34 partners in the Liberty Alliance start enabling their customers. VodaFone's hundreds of millions of customers, says McNealy, will be authenticating with Liberty. If other Alliance members — Fidelity, Bank of America, American Airlines, Sprint — follow suit, the number of transactional IDs suddenly married to Java could easily dwarf the universe of Passport users. For example, American Airlines could require a smart card enabled with Sun's

JavaCard technology that authenticates the cardholder against a Liberty-based authentication server before that person is allowed to board a flight.

At the Gartner conference, Microsoft CEO Steve Ballmer said, "Liberty has zero probability of mattering." Considering the way Microsoft has its pedal to the metal in order to work. NET into as many transactional hands as possible, I'm not so sure. Sun has managed to get Java into just about every digital device out there. The company has focused on the market leaders: some form of Java is on smart cards from American Express, Visa, and MasterCard. It's still in almost all Windows-based devices (except for recently shipped XP systems and Pocket PC). The world's leading mobile phone, digital TV, set top box, and gaming system manufacturers have all included Java. When I asked Richard Green, Sun's Vice President of Java and XML Software, what he charged everyone for that, he wouldn't say. My bet is pennies. For pennies, no one had anything to lose. And Sun had everything to gain.

Considering how Java's tentacles have extended into everything everywhere, it should come as no surprise to see Microsoft working hard to catch up. To get more transactional customers, Microsoft's goal is to get the.NET equivalent of Java into as many of those devices as possible, even if it has to make them itself. Can you say "XBox?"

The gaming constituency wouldn't be a bad group to turn into Passport holders, would it? Microsoft's.NET Developer Platform group product manager, what the company calls that piece of.NET they're trying to put into all those devices out there and how Microsoft plans to get it there. Montgomery calls it the ".NET Framework." He says Microsoft will soon announce three huge partners for the mobile version that they want to put into phones to compete with J2ME, the micro-edition of Java. Earlier this week, I learned that Microsoft's code name for this is ".NET Compact" and my bet is that Microsoft will do a lot more than give it away in order to disintermediate J2ME. I have no idea who the partners are, but only a handful of phone manufacturers matter. My guess is Microsoft has found three of them willing to manufacture a new model based on Windows

CE for mobile phones (code-named Stinger). In that scenario, Stinger would come with.NET Compact built-in. Another scenario is where Microsoft ports.NET Compact to the existing OS from Symbian that's used by many existing smart phones.

ASSEMBLY LANGUAGE PROGRAMMING

PROGRAMMES IN ASSEMBLY CODE

We now want to write some programmes for the Mac-1A. For completeness, We can write in binary machine code, but, that is tedious and error prone - because of the distraction of having to translate into a numeric code. It is better to use the mnemonics. The assembly code can then be assembled to machine (executable) code; this is done using a programme called an assembler.

For the purposes of this chapter, assembly language is a language in which there is one-to-one relationship between symbolic instructions and machine instructions; we will come across pseudo-instructions that are really instructions to the assembler programme, but these will be obvious.

CONVENTIONS

In the following examples, if we need to mention actual addresses, we will start all code at 100*H* and all data at 500*H*. Note again that the largest address is *FFFH* (12 bits). Also, be careful with *FFFC* onwards (4092_{10} to 4095_{10}, which are used for memory-mapped input-output,

Often, for brevity, we will assume variables that variables a0, a1, a2... (integers) have been declared and are already in locations 500, 501, 502,.... Alternatively, we will use symbols for data. Use these assumptions in the exercises where appropriate.

SIMPLE PROGRAMME - ADD TWO INTEGERS

Programme. Add the integer in a1 to the integer in a0 and put the result in a2, i.e.

a2 = a0 + a1;

In assembly code:

```
Start: LODD a0 /get a0 into accum.
 ADDD a1 /accum. gets a0+a1
 STOD a2 /store result in a2
```

There are four fields in an assembly instruction:

Label

Optional, only necessary if you need to jump to that instruction; can also be useful as comment, e.g. above. Always followed by ':', otherwise assembler will try to interpret it as an instruction.

Instruction mnemonic.

Operand

I.e. address of thing to suffer the operation. Either:

- Symbolic name, e.g. above.
- Symbolic label, or numeric address, to jump to.
- Constant - for immediate addressing.

Comment

Comments are even more important for assembly language programmes than the are for high-level language programmes. Make your code maintainable by someone else!

DECLARING VARIABLES

For a real assembler, we would have to declare all variables. And, tell it where to start main programme at. E.g. in the example above,

```
DW a0 10H /a0 is a WORD type, initialised to 10H
DW a1 22H /these are not executable instructions
DW a2 /but pseudo-instructions
/ie. directives to the assembler to allocate
/storage and associate names with that storage
/ just like you declare variables in Pascal
ORG 100H /start prog. at 100H
```

IF-THEN

High-level language

```
if(a0 ==a1) a2 = a2 + 1;
else next instructions...
```

Assembly language

```
If: LODD a0
  SUBD a1
  JZER Then
  JUMP Next
Then: LOCO 1 /load constant 1
  ADDD a2
  STOD a2
EndThen: JUMP Next /Unnecessary
Next:...
```

IF-THEN-ELSE

High-level Language

```
if(a0==a1) a2 = a2 + 1;
else a2 = a2 + 2;
//next instructions...
```

REPETITION

High-level language

```
//sum first n integers
int sum=0;
int i=0;
while(i<=n){
sum= sum + i;
i++;
}
```

Assembly Language

```
init: LOCO 0
  STOD sum
  STOD i
loop: LODD n
  SUBD i
  JPOS loopend
loopbody:
  LODD sum /load sum into accumulator
```

```
  ADDD i /add i to it
  STOD sum / and don't forget to store the result!
incr: LOCO 1
  ADDD i
  STOD i
  JUMP loop
loopend:...
```

It is straightforward to define deterministic loops, for example,

```
for(i = 0; i<n; i++)
{sum= sum + i;}
```

in terms of do-while. Likewise do-until - the continuation test is merely carried out at the end of the loop, instead of at the beginning for do-while.

MACHINE CODE, MEMORY MAPS

Let us see how the If-then-else from the previous section would *assemble* into machine code. We use Figure to translate.

Thus, we can identify two separate sections of memory: (a) programme, (b) data.

Of course, there is nothing really separating these, and there is nothing to stop assembly programmers modifying instructions as data, nor, for that matter, runaway programmes attempting to execute data!

Actually, as shown in Figure, in a C or C++ programme, we can identify four sections of memory. Exact implementation detail may differ depending on compiler, machine architecture and operating system. In some contexts, Figure is called a memory map.

THE ASSEMBLY PROCESS

Assembly is the process of translating the symbolic assembly code into (numeric) machine code.

Example

Assemble (translate) the following assembly programme into binary machine code. Assume a0, a1... at 500, 501 etc. Start code at 100.

Two-Pass Assembler

This section describes how a two-pass assembly programme works. We said that one assembly language instruction maps to one machine instruction; thus, it would appear natural to run through the list of assembly instructions and translate them.

This works fine until we get to JZER Then; what address is Then?

You don't know until you have assembled up to Then.

Therefore, we must have a symbol table - - which is a list of (symbol, address) pairs. If a symbol has been entered in the table, then you can look up its value. Initially, the table is empty.

Also we must have an operation-code (op-code) table - similar to the symbol table, only it is fixed, and contains a table relating instruction code (LODD, STOD,...) to the 4-bit op-code part of the instruction (0001, 0010,...). In general, this should also contain the length of each instruction, or some means of calculating it. Unlike most machines, Mac-1a has a single fixed instruction length of one; most machines have instruction lengths which vary according to the instruction.

MANUAL ASSEMBLY

Here in a slightly less formal way, is a recipe for assembling manually. We do it in a table, first write down the assembly code, the make two columns, one for address, the other for instruction or data. Then translate using Figure .

Do it in two passes. Leave Jump addresses blank first time round - you don't know the Jump destination addresses until after you have coded the Jump destination.

Use Hexadecimal for the machine code. If necessary, separate the binary fields in Figure into groups of four - one for each Hex. digit, and add another column to Figure to contain the Hex. representation of the operation code (op-code).

LINKING AND LOADING

If the programme above was viable to work on their own,

it would be possible to load it into the addresses given: 100 to 107 for programme and 500 to 50b for data, set the PC to 100, and the programme would run.

Unfortunately, programmes are usually made up from more than one module, and the results of each module translation - object files - must be linked together to produce an executable programme.

Essentially, at the end of pass two, there will be symbols for which you do not have an address; these will refer to subprograms that are contained in other modules. Also, the ILC will need to contain relative addresses, not absolute addresses as above.

In linking and loading the main jobs to be done are:

- Resolve references to external objects (symbols for which you have no value after pass two), these will be given in the symbol tables of another module.

Relocate relative addresses to yield absolute addresses.

FURTHER ASSEMBLY PROGRAMMING

The instruction set (Mac-1a) introduced was severely limited - particularly in its inability to call subprograms. We now extend our coverage to the remainder of the Mac-1 instruction set, and attempt some more ambitious programmes.

Firstly, we will introduce the additional instructions - especially those based on the stack; we will explain the purpose of a stack and its use for handling subprograms.

In addition, we will describe the memory addressing modes found on most general purpose computers. Next, we will show how some more real programmes can be constructed, from simple three or four liners, to subroutines, input-output and interrupts.

Although this chapter is entirely about Mac-1, the presentation is such that the principles of general-purpose computers are emphasised. Thus, someone who follows this chapter will have little difficulty in understanding Motorola

68000, Intel 80x86 series, or virtually any conventional computer.

ADDRESSING-GENERAL

In a computer, memory locations can hold instructions or data. In addition, as we shall see the data can be interpreted either as a plain value, e.g. 100, or as an address or reference to another data item. Those of who are familiar with C/C++ will recognise pointers; and Java people will recognise references.

In general, machine instructions usually take zero, one, or two operands (e.g. in lodd a0; a0 is the single operand; lodd is the operation;

Actually Mac-1 has no multi-operand instructions. For a start, it is an accumulator machine, i.e. in instructions like addd, lodd, the second - implicit - operand is AC, the accumulator.

Operands can be data, or can refer to data - i.e. address of data, or can be labels - which translate to addresses - of instructions, e.g. for jumps. The question of addressing is concerned with how operands are interpreted. In the case of data the operand can be:

- A so-called immediate constant, e.g. LOCO 10;
- A value held in a register - no example in Mac-1;
- A value held in memory, e.g. LODD a0;
- In addition we can *qualify* the operand to say in which mode it should be interpreted:

Immediate:

When an operand is interpreted as an immediate value, e.g. LOCO 5, it is the actual value '5' that is put in the accumulator. In the case of Mac-1, the value '5' is part of the instruction: LOCO 5; 0111 0000 0000 0101;

Direct:

The specified name or number is the 'direct' address of the intended operand, e.g. LODD a0, which is the same as LODD 501 - if our usual definitions apply -, so that the contents of memory cell '501' are loaded into the accumulator. Thus, 0000 0101 0000 0001; lodd 501;

Register

The number or name of a register is given, which contains the real operand; conceptually similar to direct except that the register name/number is substituted for memory address;

Indirect

The specified name or number contains the address of the operand, i.e. the operand is the 'indirect' address of the true operand, e.g. let us invent LODI 501, so that the *contents of the contents of* memory cell '501' are loaded into the accumulator. Thus, xxxx 0101 0000 0001 lodi 501; if memory cell 501 contains '50a', and memory cell 50a contains '3'.

Indexed

Lets us assume that we have an integer array stored in an array of N (= 9, say) contiguous locations starting at location 1230 (say), and we want to successively add them into the accumulator:

```
\lodd 1230
loop: addi 1230+SI;ac<- [ac]+m[1230+si]
\inc SI
\...test for end
\jump loop
```

Of course, because Mac-1 has no index registers, I have had to invent one (SI), and an addressing mode for add: addi - add direct using SI as an index; also I had to invent an 'increment instruction. Indexing is a bit like running your finger along a table of figures. The instructions 'lodl'...'subl' introduced below are a bit like indexed - but they use a very special index register called the stack-pointer (SP).

Addressing modes look complicated, but if you are careful to analyse what a construct means - by drawing a diagram, if necessary - then there are no real pitfalls.

Also, for those who are not specialists in assembly programming, you should keep to the simple modes and only use the complex modes when they are absolutely essential.

MAC-1 INSTRUCTION SET EXTENSIONS

The Mac-1 instruction set extended to the full repertoire, we do not bother with the binary version of the instruction since we will not be assembling programmes using the additional instructions, nor writing them in machine code.

THE ADDITIONAL JUMPS

jneg x Jump on negative if ac<0: pc <- x
jnze x Jump on nonzero if ac!=0: pc <- x

These save some of the trouble encountered using just jpos and jzer; however, as we have seen, they are not essential.

THE STACK

In Mac-1, the register SP is the stack-pointer and is dedicated to maintaining the stack; the stack itself - the data *pointed-to* - is actually part of main-memory.

The stack is a memory into which values can be stored and from which they can be retrieved on a last-in-first-out (LIFO) basis. Ideally, you store with a PUSH and retrieve with a POP. It may help to think of an analogy such as a spring loaded canteen tray dispenser, or a bus conductor's coin dispenser; the main point is that you can only put on the top (PUSH), get from the top (TOP) or remove the value at the top (POP). In spite of its simplicity this device has a remarkably large impact on the computational capability of a computer. A stack gives us a *sort-of* indirect addressing and also a *sort-of* indexed addressing via a the stack pointer; but a stack does much more than that, it is the basis of the implementation of functions and procedures, and blocks in block-structured high-level languages. SP points to the top of the stack - i.e. to the memory location where the last value was pushed.

In the case of Mac-1, the stack grows from high memory towards low memory. PUSH increases the size of the stack by one and places a value in the new memory cell (at the top). POP exactly reverses the process, i.e.. retrieves the last value written (the top) and decreases the size of the stack. PUSH followed by POP has exactly NO effect. And, as usual with Mac-1 most things are done through the accumulator (AC);

PUSH pushes the number in the AC, and POP retrieves the top of the stack into the AC.

PUSH operates as follows:

PUSH;sp <- sp - 1;SP decremented, NB. this INCREASES size of stack.

;m[sp] <- ac;put contents of AC into the memory cell that SP POINTS TO

POP:

POP;ac <- m[sp];get contents of cell pointed to by SP, into AC.

;sp <- sp + 1;decrease size of stack.

Note carefully again that the stack actually grows downwards, one word at a time - actually this is the case on a great many machines. Normally, in Mac-1 programmes, we will assume that SP starts off pointing at memory cell 4020.

STACK INSTRUCTIONS

Direct Accumulator-Stack Instructions

Push Push onto stack sp <- sp-1; m[sp] <- ac

Pop Pop off stack ac <- m[sp]; sp <- sp+1

Indirect Accumulator-Stack Instructions

Pshi Push indirect sp <- sp-1; m[sp]<-m[ac]

Popi Pop indirect m[ac] <- m[sp]; sp <- sp+1

Thus, the AC is used 'indirectly' - see indirect addressing mode, section 7.2; i.e. the value that is contents of the memory cell that is *pointed-to* by [ac] is pushed and popped.

Call and Return - CALL and RETN

CALL and RETN are used for CALLing subprograms (methods or functions in Java) and RETurning from them.

CALL

Call x Call procedure sp<-sp-1; m[sp] <- pc; pc <- x

Get stack (save pc) (put jump

Ready) address in pc)

CALL causes all of the following to happen:

- Decrement the stack pointer - so that we will not overwrite last thing put on stack,
- The contents of PC - which is pointing to NEXT instruction, the one just after the CALL - is pushed onto the stack, and,
- Jump to 'x', which is the address of the start of the subprogram is put in the PC register, this is all a jump does. Thus, we go off to the subprogram - just as in JUMP label, but the important difference is that we remember where we were in the calling programme, i.e. we must remember where we came from, so that we can get back there again.

Retn

Retn Return from proc. pc <- m[sp]; sp <- sp + 1
RETN causes all of the following to happen:

- Pops the stack, to yield an address/label; if correctly used, the top of the stack will contain the address of the next instruction after the call from which we are returning; it is this instruction with which we want to resume in the *calling* programme;
- Jump to the popped address, i.e. put the address into the PC register.

INPUT-OUTPUT INSTRUCTIONS

As stated earlier, there are no *direct* instructions for input-output; instead Mac-1a uses memory-mapped input-output, whereby some memory cells are mapped to input-output ports; for simplicity we assume that there are only two ports, one connected to a standard-input device, the other connected to a standard-output device:

- Input, mapped to 4092 (0FFCHex); status 4093 (0FFDHex).
- Output, mapped to 4094 (0FFEHex); status 4095 (0FFFHex).

Input from Standard-input Device

A read from address 0FFCHex yields a 16-bit word, with

the actual data byte in the lower or byte. There is no use in reading the input port until the connected device has put the data there: so 0FFDH is used to read the input status register; the top bit (sign) of 0FFDH is set when the input data is available (DAV).

Thus, a read routine should go into a tight loop, continuously reading 0FFDHex, until it goes negative; then 0FFCHex can be read to get the data. Reading 0FFC clears 0FFD again.

Output to the Standard-output Device

Output, to 0FFE, runs along the same lines as input. A write to 0FFE will send the lower order byte to the standard-output device. The sign bit of 0FFFH signifies that the device is in a ready to receive (RDY) state; again there is no use writing data to the output port until the device is ready to read it.

MORE ASSEMBLY LANGUAGE PROGRAMMING

This section further illustrates the use of assembly language with some simple examples.

Note: in none of the following examples have I tried to optimise the code or to be *clever;* assembly coding is difficult enough without that.

Multiply Two Numbers

Mac-1 has no multiply or divide - not even for integers - so we have to do it all with adds and subtracts.

Note. we will assume that the result will fit into 16-bits; Q. what general check on the two operands will ensure this? Ans. if the multiplication is z = x * y; then if x <= 127 and if y <= 127, the result will certainly be less than 32767, which is the largest positive number that can be stored in 16-bit twos complement.

Divide

Again, we assume that both numbers are positive, and that it is sensible to divide them - again we will leave out some of the bullet-proofing details.

z = x / y;

We use the algorithm in Figure , i.e. we count how many times we have to subtract 'y' from 'x' to get to a remainder less than 'y'.

At the end (end:) the result is in 'z'. Of course, the result is 'integer' divide, e.g. we could modify this code to give you per cent (modulo - or 'remainder after division').

Iterate Over an Array

Assume that a0, a1, a2,... a9 are stored contiguously in 500, 501,...509, and we want to treat them as an array arr[10]; we require to sum them and put the result in sum. We will assume that all the numbers are sensible, i.e. that overflow isn't a problem.

We *could* address each of them individually:

```
init loco 0
addd a0
addd a1
...
addd a9
stod sum
```

but that wouldn't be too clever for very long arrays.

Chapter 7

Binary Number Formats and Subroutines

VARIOUS SIZES OF INTEGERS AND THEIR RANGES

Table shows some commonly used integer formats and their ranges.

Table: Commonly Used Integer Formats

Size	Name in Java	Minimum	Maximum
8-bit signed	byte	-128	127
16-bit signed	short	-32768	32767
32-bit signed	int	-2,147,483,648	2,147,483,647

FLOATING POINT

IEEE single precision (32 bits): $\pm 1.2 \times 10 - 38$ to 3.4×10^{38}, 7 significant digits.

$$\text{Value} = (-1)^3 \times 1.f \times 2^{\text{exp}-127}$$

bit 31=sign, bits 30 to bit 23 = 8 bitexponent, bits 22 to bit0 = fraction

IEEE floating-point uses the hidden bit trick mentioned above.

BITWISE LOGICAL OPERATIONS

In most assembly languages, and in C and C++ there are binary operations which logical operations on each corresponding pair of bits.

AND

$$a = 0011\ 0000$$
$$a = 0101\ 0111$$
$$a \ \&\ b = 0001\ 0000$$

Masking

Let us say that we have two four bit numbers packed into a byte. How do we disentangle them.

Take the byte 1001 01111; the two four bit numbers are 7and 9. First, the lower four bits; here we mask with 0000 1111.

$$a = 1001\ 0111$$
$$a = 0000\ 0111$$
$$low\ Mask = 0000\ 0111$$
$$a \ \&\ low\ Mask = 0000\ 0111$$

For the higher four bits, we shift right by four bits and use the same mask.

OR

$$a = 0011\ 0000$$
$$b = 0101\ 0111$$
$$a \mid b = 0111\ 0111$$

SHIFT

$$a = 0011\ 0000\ (= 16 + 32 = 48_{10})$$
$$a \text{ shift left } 1 = 0110\ 0000\ (= 96_{10})\ \text{i.e. } 48 \times 2)$$
$$a \text{ shift right } 1 = 0001\ 1000\ (= 24_{10})\ \text{i.e. } \frac{48}{2}$$

Thus, you sometimes find assembly language programmers using shift for multiplying (shift left) and dividing (shift right) by powers of two.

ROTATE

$$a = 1011\ 0000$$
$$a \text{ rotate left } 1 = 0110\ 0001$$
$$a \text{ rotate right } 1 = 0001\ 1000$$

Rotate is like shift, only bits can wrap-around.

ALPHANUMERIC CODES

Text characters, as well as numbers must be binary coded to get them into a computer memory. A code that copes with alphabetic characters, {a...z, A...Z} as well as digits {0...9 } is called alphanumeric.

Up to recently, the most frequently used code was the ASCII (American Standard Code for Information Interchange) code; ASCII uses 7-bits, (0 to 127); this includes printable and control characters.

Table 2.6 gives some codes worth remembering.

Table: ASCII table

Name	Hex	if control
Bel	07	ctrl-G
line-feed	0a	ctrl-J
carriage-return	0d	ctrl-M
blank-space	20	
Digits		
0	30	
...		
9	39	
alphabetic upper-case		
A	41	
...		
Z	5a	
alphabetic lower-case		
A	61	
...		
Z	7a	

UNICODE

ASCII has proved adequate for English text. But what about languages with accents? And those with funny shaped characters? UNICODE is a new international standard, governed by the UNICODE consortium, aimed at allowing a richer character set. In fact, Java uses UNICODE a 16-bit code - so that Java char type is 16-bit, compared to 8 bit in C and C++. According to [Tanenbaum, 1999] the total of known characters in the world's languages number some 200,000 - thus, there is already pressure on UNICODE.

TYPES

41*H* could be 'A' or the number 41*H*. "AB" together in a 16-bit word could be part of a string, or the number 4142*H*, or part of an instruction, or.... The computer programme must know beforehand what each memory cell represents - thus, types.

ERROR DETECTION

When information is transferred between various parts of a computer system it is possible that errors may be introduced. These errors take the form of transmitted 0s inadvertently being received as 1s or vice-versa.

Parity provides single error detecting capability. The scheme involves appending an additional bit to the string of 1s and 0s - the parity bit. Depending on the chosen convention, the appended bit is chosen so that the total number of 1s in the string is always even even parity or always odd odd parity.

Bit 7 is often used - pure ASCII uses 7 bits, bits 0...6...

Example.. ASCII character 'A' using odd parity.

A = 41 = *P*100 0001 = 1100 0001with odd parity bit placed in bit 7.

SUBROUTINES

As mentioned above, CALL and RETN are used for CALLing subroutines and RETurNing from them. One objectives of subroutines is to avoid having to repeat large chunks of code. Side-Note: On modern machines and particularly when block-structured languages like Pascal, C, or Modula-2 are used, subroutines via a stack are essential. Older machines often used a JUMP-and-STORE type of call: the return address was stored in a memory address somewhere amongst the code of the subroutine.

Subprograms Without Arguments

That is, we use global variables to pass values to and from the subprogram.

Recall the multiplication programme above:

```
z = x * y;
```

using the following algorithm:

```
z = 0;
for(i=1; i<=x; i++){
z = z + y;}
```

This is fine, but have a look at the assembly code; it is not the sort of thing you want to be bothered with each time you want to multiply two numbers.

The code for the multiply will never change, only the names of the variables (x, y, z).

Say you wanted to do the following:

```
c = a * b;
d = e * f;
g = c + d;
```

A simplistic solution would be:

1. Load two operands (a, b) into variables x, y respectively;
2. Jump to 'mult';
3. 'Mult' will run and put the result in 'z'; thus, 'z' is a global variable - it has global scope;
4. Copy 'z' to 'c', i.e. lodd z; stod c;;
5. Then, similarly, compute 'd', etc.

```
startprog:
lodd a (assume at location 200)
stod x
lodd b
stod y
jump mult   204
** lodd z   205
 stod c   206
```

But, without subprograms, the is a major problem: the programme never gets to '**', because when it's finished the multiply programme it continues on to the next instruction after 'mult' (end: i.e. 115H), not 205H as desired.

Note, however, there is nothing to stop you (at 115H) JUMPing to 205 - but this means that 'mult' programme is only useful for this one multiply; later down at 20aH (say) when we want to multiply 'e' and 'f', we want to JUMP back to a different place.

This gets us to one of the crucial differences between JUMP and CALL (subprogram). With JUMP, it's a one way ticket, you don't ever come back! With CALL you can remember where you came from and JUMP back there (using RETN) when you're finished in the subprogram.

Figure shows how we can make the multiply programme into a a procedure 'mult' (just add RETN at the end) and how to use it.

There is no explicit use of the stack, all PUSHes and POPs are done implicitly by CALL, RETN.

SUBPROGRAMS WITH PARAMETERS

The procedure 'mult' above has no parameters; effectively we used global variables x, y, z for the parameters and return value. In C++ this would look like Figure.

This is alright, but I'm sure your Programming courses up to now have warned you against the evils of global variables.

So, we now write 'mult1' that looks like this:

```
int mult(int x, int y)
{
return x * y;
}
```

and is called like: c = mult(a, b);

To do this we need to make explicit use of the stack: we PUSH onto the stack the two values to be multiplied - the arguments, then CALL, finally when we RETN we retrieve (POP) the result from the stack. We can make the multiply programme into a proper procedure 'mult1' (just add RETN at the end) with parameters and return values, see Figure. We will also change 'mult' slightly to ensure that it uses only two local variables - the only reason for this is to make it a bit more like the one in [Tanenbaum, 1990].

SUBPROGRAMS WITH RETURN VALUES

Above, we used the trick of passing the result back in the

AC. This is alright for a single 16-bit result, but, if the result was more than one word (e.g. 32-bit floating point stored in two words, or a record), we would have to use the stack.

The usual solution is to allocate space for the return values just before the return address.

OTHER USES FOR THE STACK

Most computers (eg. 80X86, 680X0, VAX) have a multitude of general purpose CPU registers - just as if Mac-1 allowed the assembly programmer access to registers A, B,...F.

Therefore, as well as storing the return address - which we could term 'storing the callers PC', it may be necessary to store these registers as well before going off to a procedure. This is because, inevitably, the procedure will overwrite some or all of the registers and on return, we want to be able to 'restore' the registers and carry on where we left off. This pair of processes is called 'saving' and 'restoring' the 'environment'.

Alternatively, a more common practice is to leave it up to the procedure to save whatever registers it will overwrite - and restore them just before returning.

Here, of course, we are concentrating on subprograms; there is nothing to stop a programmer using the stack as a general temporary storage area, or for a purpose like the swapping mentioned above.

Stack Frame

In connection with procedures, there are four uses for the stack:

- Passing parameters:
  - Passing parameters to the subprogram;
  - Returning values from the subprogram.
- Storing the return address;
- Saving the environment (registers);
- Finally, all local variables are created on the stack.

Local Variables

```
int a, b, c;
a = 25;
```

```
b = 159;
c = mult1(a, b);
a = 0
(*...etc*)
```

See section 7.9.2 for 'mult1' in assembly:
int mult1(int i, j);

Analysis of 'Call' to mult1

The interesting action happens after 'b:=159;'.

- Assume SP starts off at 4020, and instruction corresponding to 'a = 0;' is at address 210; assume the first executable instruction in 'mult1' is at address 100;
- The value a (=25) is pushed: [sp]<-401f, [401f]<-25;
- The value b (=159) is pushed: [sp]<-401e, [401e]<-159;
- 210 - the return address is pushed: [sp]<-401d, [401d]<-210;
- Jump to 100 - start of 'mult1';
- Here, we could save the AC, just to make the general point of register saving, but to retain compatibility with [Tanenbaum, 1990], we'll leave it out. At this point the stack looks like:

Addr.	Contents
4020	?
401f25	
401e	159
401d	210 <— SP (SP now points at 401d)

But we're still not done. We must allocate space for the two local variables on the stack. We could do this by:

```
loco 0
push
push
```

i.e. push two zeros onto the stack, but a quicker way is

```
desp 2
```

i.e. decrement the SP by 2, in which case the stack looks like

Addr.	Contents
4020	?

401f25

401e 159

401d 210

401c?*

401b ?* <— SP (SP now points at 401b)

Note that the space for the local variables is now uninitialised, i.e. 401c and 401b contain whatever was last put in them. This is why you can never assume that a local variable is initialised to 0.

RECURSIVE SUBPROGRAMS

If you called the procedure mult1 recursively three times - or, indeed, there were three nested calls of different procedures - the situation would look like Figure

In this way a procedure can call itself again and again, without one call interfering with the other; the only limit is the size of the stack.

Earlier machines, and languages, like FORTRAN, did not use a stack. Parameter passing, return addresses and local storage was all mixed in with the procedure code area - and there was only one copy - so any recursive calls, if they were allowed, would have overwritten the local data area etc. of the previous call.

PARAMETERS PASSED BY VALUE

In the scheme mentioned in the previous two subsections, parameters are passed by by value, or by copy. Thus, procedure mult1 can do whatever it likes to the memory location that contains the 25 - the copy of a (the parameter) and a itself (the argument) are separate and so the argument a - in the caller - will never change.

MACROS

As indicated above, a non-procedure solution could have been used to repeat the mult code as many times as a multiply was required. As well as making the programme bigger, this would have introduced the greater problem of three pieces of code to debug/maintain, instead of just one.

Now, if we are content to accept the increase in programme size, use of a macro avoids the second problem (i.e. maintenance of separate copies of the same code).

Essentially, you declare a macro containing the working bits of the subroutine (no need for the housekeeping bits at the top and bottom) and then insert the macro code wherever the CALL appears.

Macros are used whenever you want to trade memory for speed - you waste no time PUSHing and POPping the stack; however, avoid if possible - they make a programme difficult to read, think about and, consequently, hard to test.

INTERRUPTS

The scheme of polled input and output is fine for many cases, especially if the computer is just reading data from a single source. However, consider the case of the keyboard and GUI interfaces with a mouse.

In Windows and other operating systems the keyboard is read even when the computer is away running another part of the programme. This is done with a special type of subroutine call - an interrupt. When you hit a key on the keyboard, something like the following happens:

Hardware Actions:

Invisible to programmer:

- The keyboard controller detects the key hit;
- It asserts an interrupt line on the system bus;
- As soon as the CPU is prepared to handle the interrupt, it sends an acknowledge signal to the controller;
- The kb. controller sends a small integer - and interrupt vector to identify itself; note that there could be many interrupting devices;
- The CPU reads and stores the interrupt vector;
- The CPU PUSHes the PC and the flags (N,Z) onto the stack;
- The CPU constructs the address of the interrupt service routine from the interrupt vector;

- The interrupt service routine i CALLed (but implicitly).

Software Actions:

- Save all registers on the stack;
- Read the input port - in the normal way; if things are designed properly the device will always be ready after it has generated an interrupt;
- Put the data in a buffer, and maintain the buffer pointer; all this means is 'put the input character somewhere where the programme can get at it';
- The interrupt service routine may need to tell the controller that you have completed servicing the interrupt;
- Restore (POP) all saved registers;
- Execute a return-from-interrupt (IRET on an 80x86); IRET restores flags and POPs return address.

A key factor is the transparency of the interrupt. The interrupt causes the service routine to run, but when that routine is finished, and IRET executed, the executing programme should be none the wiser - except, maybe, it notices that an instruction took 20 or 30 microsecs to run, instead of just 1 microsec; and, of course, there will be another character in the input buffer.

DIRECT MEMORY ACCESS (DMA)

Mass storage devices like disk or tape require very rapid data transfer of data from the device to memory and vice-versa. A typical hard disk transfers data at about 1 byte per 2 microsecs (1993); neither polled nor interrupt-initiated input-output could cope with this.

In addition, if you look at the system diagram in Figure, you will see that both the disk (for example) and memory are connected to the system bus. Hence, there may be little requirement for the CPU to get involved in a data transfer, except to initiate it.

Typically, a third device will be connected to the bus - a DMA controller - which mediates between the two data transfer devices and ensures an orderly use of the bus. In DMA, the only effect on the CPU and executing programme is slight slowing down, because the DMA must *steal* bus cycles — so called cycle-stealing — for the data transfer.

For example, recalling Mac-1a, and memory read/write: during a LODD, for example, Mac-1a would place the address to be read in MAR, and issue an RD; if a DMA byte transfer was happening, the DMA would have to be able to tell the CPU to wait for a cycle or two.

Chapter 8

Theory of Internet

This unit familiarizes you with the basics of Internet. It also highlights the key usages that the Internet is put to, the various options available to connect to the Internet, the common terms associated with the Internet and facilities available on the Internet. It also details how you could set up your own e-mail account for sending and receiving mails and use the Internet chat facility to keep in touch with your friends anywhere in the world.

OBJECTIVES

After studying this unit, you should be able to

- Identify the key usages of the Internet,
- Understand the various options available for Internet connectivity along with their merits and limitations,
- Identify the Internet protocol used for transmitting and receiving data over the Internet,
- Understand the common terminology used in context with the Internet,
- Use the search facility to search for, virtually, any information available on the Internet,
- Create and use your e-mail account to send and receive messages, and
- Use the Internet chat to communicate with people in other cities and countries.

INTERNET BASICS

In the past, computers were stand-alone systems. Transferring information from one computer to another required media like a floppy disk or tape. Resources like the CD-ROM drive and peripherals like printers and scanners could not be shared across computers.

Interconnecting the computers or networking came as a welcome solution resulting in a cost-effective way to share equipment across all connected computers thereby helping people work collectively.

A network can be as simple as linking two computers or may consist of hundreds and thousands of different types of computers and peripherals, connected directly or indirectly.

The Internet is simply a series of computers, linked to one another around the world, communicating almost instantaneously with one another. It comprises tens and thousands of computer networks (a single network may consist of all the computers of an office linked to each other. A larger network may be connecting all the computers within a university premises) communicating with each other like a big net or web! It can be termed as a 'network of networks'. These computer networks are physically linked with one another through telephone, radio, cable lines, satellite, or even fiber optic. The Internet has literally put a world of information at ones fingertips. The Internet is the best thing that could have happened to us. Computer Networks are available in different types:

Local Area Network (LAN)

LAN connects two or more communication devices (like computers and printers) over a relatively short distance. LANs usually work within an office premises, a factory or a campus where communication devices are connected through a cable, within a distance of 2000 feet. Most LAN networks are shared medium networks, where the workstations shares and waits for its turn to use a resource such as printer, plotter etc.

Newer terms like WLAN and Bluetooth Technology are also associated with LAN today.

Wireless Local Area Network (WLAN)

Wireless local area network provides LAN connectivity

within a small geographic area, normally within 150 meters, and is typically used where cabling is either not possible or would be very cumbersome, for instance, you may wish to provide LAN connectivity in an open air restaurant!

Bluetooth Technology

Bluetooth technology is a wireless medium for sharing information across computers and other electronic devices like mobile phones, Personal Digital Assistants (PDAs) etc., using low power radio frequency.

Wide Area Network (WAN)

WAN networks span larger areas than a single building or a campus. They are long-haul networks covering wide geographical areas and often require multiple communication connections like leased lines, satellites and microwave radio links to interconnect various LANs. LANs are usually measured in feet, while WANs are measured in miles.

Metropolitan Area Networks (MAN)

A group of LANs connected through a high-speed, seamless interconnection, within a 'metropolitan' area, is termed as a Metropolitan Area Network (MAN). The word 'metropolitan' does not necessarily mean a 'city' but can be any area that is spread out, but is treated as one entity, e.g. a company having its two buildings on the opposite sides of the road.

MAN connects users with computer resources in a geographic area that is larger than that covered by a LAN but smaller than the area covered by a WAN.

A recent trend includes installations of wireless MANs.

KEY USAGES

The key usages that the Internet is put to include:

Online Shopping

Online shopping is one of the biggest uses of the Net.

Internet has helped in removing all barriers of distance and nationality. Logging onto a web portal, you can buy products and services from across the globe and pay for the same using your international credit/debit cards. All without ever having to step away from your office or home computer!

Online shopping has evolved from simple purchase and sale transactions to sophisticated online bidding and auctioning. From purchasing of gum chewed by Britney Spears to buying a state-of-art car, can all be done using web portals like eBay.com, Bazee.com, etc.

Internet Telephony and Chatting

Till a few years ago chatting on the Internet was one of the fastest growing uses of the World Wide Web. In a typical chat session, two or more individuals (from anywhere in the world) would log in to a chat room and converse with each other by typing. The typed message was instantaneously relayed on the computers of the chat room individuals. Because of its ease of use and anonymity, this was a greatly favoured medium among students, businessmen and housewives alike.

Some years ago some smart geeks figured out that Internet grid does not care what you send over it. Whether it is data, voice or video its all the same for the Net pipe. So, it is no wonder that you can now call up any phone number in the world through a computer based Internet line at a fraction of a cost of a normal landline call. Improvements in connectivity speed and proliferation of broadband has ensured that the voice and picture quality of Internet telephony is not only as good, but sometimes even better than that of conventional phones.

It is just a matter of time when all calls will be local calls!

Distance Education

Because of its non-intrusive and flexible mechanism, the Internet provides a perfect medium for knowledge sharing and information dissemination. As with other things, Internet has removed the geographical barriers such that a professor delivering a lecture in California can be heard and seen in real-time in Hyderabad. Students, especially those who are working, need not now be physically present in a classroom. You can now pursue specialized higher studies in the comfort of your own office or home – all you need is a simple desktop and a reliable internet connection.

Sharing Music and Books

Napster.com pioneered the concept of sharing music between music lovers. Although Napster.com is now no longer a free music site, there are hundreds of other web clones with slight variations, who offer free download of music.

The publishing industry has also realised the immense potential of e-books (electronic books). No printing costs, no distribution costs, and no stocking costs! Simply convert your paperback book into an electronic one (most commonly an Adobe Acrobat file) and let web browsers download this by making online payment at considerably reduced rates.

Banking

The banking industry was the first one to use IT in a major way to automate operations and save costs. It was banks who pioneered the concept of ATMs which made the paradigm shift of outsourcing bank-office work back to the clients. In an ATM, the bank customer himself/herself feeds in his account details instead of a bank clerk, thereby saving the bank considerable time and money. This concept became the cornerstone for the BPO industry especially the ITES (IT Enabled Services). Internet provides the next logical step towards taking the bank to the doorstep of the customer. You can now view your account details, transfer money, make requests for cheque books and drafts, get information on new products and services, all by accessing the bank's website.

Travel

The travel industry has been another major gainer from the Internet boom. Whether it is the hotels, motels or inns, airlines, train companies, taxi or car rental companies all of these have gained tremendously, by offering their services through websites. The customers, on the other hand, have also greatly benefitted because they can now compare rates, make online bookings, avail rock-bottom discounts, make last minute iternary changes, and pay online without having to run around multiple offices. This convenience has not only made travel more comfortable, but because of easy access of information and bookings, expanded the travel market substantially, by reaching out to people who would not have traveled so often otherwise.

Bill Payments

Thanks to the government sector also for realizing the benefits of IT, it is now possible to make online payments of public utilities like electricity, phones, water etc. by using credit cards as a payment medium. Private sector companies were anyway ahead in the race and so you can virtually buy almost anything on the Net by making online payments.

INTERNET CONNECTIVITY OPTIONS

There are various options available to connect to the Internet. The commonly used ones are explained below.

Dial-Up

Dial-up provides connecting a device to a network using modem over the public telephone network. Dial-up access is really just like a phone connection, except that instead of two individuals on the two ends you have computer devices. Since the dial-up uses the regular telephone lines, the quality of connection is not always good. In the past, the maximum data transfer rate over a dial-up connection was limited to 56 kbps (56,000 bits per second). Newer technologies are providing better transfer rates.

Integrated Services Digital Network (ISDN)

ISDN, as the name suggests, is a digital communications line. It allows for transmission of data, voice, video and graphics, at very high speeds, over standard communication lines. ISDN lines can carry large amounts of data, while providing a single common interface to access digital communication services required for varying devices, while keeping it transparent to the end user. Owing to these features, ISDN applications have revolutionized the way businesses communicate. ISDN is not restricted to public telephone networks, but can use packet switched networks, CATV networks, telex etc.

Digital Subscriber Lines (DSL)

A DSL connection is a very high-speed connection that uses the same wires as a regular telephone line. Many local companies, in addition to their regular phone services, also provide Internet services (DSLs). DSLs are, therefore, available in some (not all) areas where regular phone services are available. A DSL connection has a much higher speed of connection than a regular dial-up connection (56 kbps) and the connection can be left open, while you use your phone line for voice calls!

The reliability and monthly rates for a DSL connection are comparable to that of the cable network service, but the connection speed is slower.

Leased Line

An alternative way to connect two computers is through a leased line. It is like a 'private circuit' between the two machines. A leased line can best be understood as a permanent dedicated communication link between two points and is reserved, exclusively for the leased line purchaser.

A leased line can be a twisted pair, coax cable, or (more recently) a fibre optic cable. Leased lines have varying data transfer rates, going up to a speed of 1.544 Mbps. Using multiplexing techniques, these transfer rates can be divided between voice and data. Large companies having high Internet usage, usually go in for leased lines since it is a more cost effective solution than the traditional one like ISDN.

Cable Internet Services

Now-a-day, in addition to the traditional cable services,

most of the cable TV companies also provide Internet services. These services come at reasonable monthly rates, are reliable and have high download transmission and upload rates. You could contact your local cable provider to get more information on services provided by them.

Internet Protocols

'Protocol' defines a set of rules or code of behaviour. In the context of networking, protocol defines a 'language' of conventions and rules that specify how the data will be packaged, sent and acknowledged.

Before we dwell more into the internet protocols, let us first discuss addressing.

The Internet consists of a large number of computers connected with each other and hence there is need of a proper addressing system. Each computer within this network (called a host) must be uniquely identifiable. This is done by attaching a number and a name to it.

IP Address

The Internet Protocol (IP) address is an unique number that defines the location of your computer, such that it is an identifiable machine within all the computers connected to the Internet. This is a 32-bit number and is divided into four octets. For readability purposes, humans represent these IP addresses in a decimal notation that use periods to separate each octet. For example, the IP address

00001010 00000000 00000000 00000010

in decimal notation separated with periods is represented as 10.0.0.2.

Since each byte is 8 bits in length, in each octet in an IP address ranges in value from a minimum of 0 to a maximum of 255. Thus, the full range of IP addresses is from 0.0.0.0 through 255.255.255.255 which is total of 4,294,967,296 possible IP addresses.

Domain Naming System (DNS)

In a network, computers and devices can be grouped

together and can be administered as a unit with common rules and procedures, sharing a common name. Such a group is referred to as a Domain.

Domain Naming System (or Service), commonly known as the DNS, is an Internet service that translates domain names to or from IP addresses, which is the actual basis of addressing on the Internet. Some examples of domain names include Microsoft.com, Yahoo.com etc. The last three letters of the address provides information about the kind of organization to which the address belongs.

Table: Commonly Used Abbreviations in Domain Names

Abbreviation	What It Represents
Com	Commercial organization
org	Non-profit organizations
net	Networking organizations
gov	Government agencies
edu	Educational institutions
in	Indian organization

Communication Protocol

When different computers, peripherals and devices are connected in a network they need to follow a set of standard rules for transmitting and receiving data to avoid data collision. These set of rules and conventions are called Protocols. The Internet uses a set of communication protocols called the Transmission Control Protocol/Internet Protocol (TCP/IP). This protocol enables information to be transferred between dissimilar computers and is, therefore, said to bind the Internet.

Technically speaking, Transmission Control Protocol (TCP) and Internet Protocol (IP) are two distinct network protocols. They are so commonly used together that TCP/IP has become a standard terminology to refer to either or both of the protocols.

TCP

When two computers wish to communicate with each other reliably, they establish a connection. This is analogous to making a phone call, say to a friend in California. A connection is established when you dial the number and get a response from the other side. TCP guarantees that when data is sent from one end of the connection, it reaches the other end in the same order. Otherwise, an error is reported.

IP

Information in a network is transmitted in the form of packets. It is the task of IP to send a packet from one computer to another. It, however, does not verify that the packet actually reaches its destination, or that it reaches error free and in the correct order.

Technically, IP corresponds to the Network layer (Layer 3) in the OSI model, whereas TCP corresponds to the Transport layer (Layer 4) in the OSI model (a discussion on the OSI layers is out of scope for this Unit).

1. State TRUE or FALSE
   - Internet is simply a series of computers linked to one another around the world.
   - LAN connects two or more computers over large areas like across the city.
   - Bluetooth technology is a wireless medium using low power radio frequency to share information across devices.
   - TCP/IP is a set of communication protocols used by the Internet.
2. What are the various connectivity options available to connect to the Internet?

STARTING THE INTERNET

Before you start using the Internet, it may prove useful to understand some common terminology used in context with the Internet.

World Wide Web (www)

Commonly known as the 'Web' it consists of Internet servers that are connected through hypertext. Related text, organized into units by the user, that can be activated using a link is termed as hypertext. The documents are formatted in a language called HTML (HyperText Markup Language) which supports links to other documents, as well as graphics, audio and video files. Such documents are associated with the hyperlink in such a way that when a user clicks on the link, information on that topic is displayed. Thus, hyperlinks allow the user to navigate from one document to another without having to worry about the actual location of the document (which could be the same or another server located miles away). Thus, the World Wide Web has made it possible to share information between disparate users, computers and operating systems.

Website

The web can be understood as a collection of thousands and millions of information locations connected to each other. Each such location is called a *website*. A website comprises *web pages* – an electronic page like any other computer document, created using HTML (HyperText Markup Language). Web pages can contain pictures, sound files, videos in addition to text, thus allowing multimedia applications.

A website can be created by an individual or an organization and is a virtual location on the web. An Uniform Resource Locator (URL) defines the address of a Website and is used to point to the Website's *homepage*. The homepage is the first page that is displayed when the website is accessed and serves as a reference point containing pointers or links to additional HTML pages or links to other websites.

HyperText Transfer Protocol (HTTP)

HTTP can be defined as a protocol (set of rules) for exchanging text, image, sound, video and other multimedia files across the Internet. It typically consists of a HTTP client programme at one end, and a HTTP server programme on the other. It is the most important protocol used in the World Wide Web.

Uniform Resource Locator (URL)

An URL defines the address of a site on the Internet. It is

an abbreviation of Uniform Resource Locator, and states the global address of documents and other resources on the World Wide Web. For example:

http://msoft.com/index.html

ftp://www.freesoft/loadsoft.exe

The first part of the address indicates the protocol to be used, and the second part specifies the IP address or the domain name where the resource is located. Above, the first URL specifies a web page to be fetched using the HTTP protocol, while the second URL specifies an executable file to be fetched using the FTP (File Transfer Protocol) protocol.

BROWSER FUNCTIONS

Learning a few basic things about browsing the Web, such as how to use the buttons on the Internet Explorer toolbar, will make it fast and easy for you to use the Web.

Toolbar (Internet Explorer)

The row of buttons on top of a web browser is known as the toolbar. It consists of various icons that can be used to execute functions. In fact, most of the options available through the menu bar are also available through the icons in the toolbar. Some commonly used icons are detailed below:

Back

The back button allows you to navigate to the page you viewed last. Similarly, the forward button on the toolbar navigates to the current page from the previous page. To see a list of the last few pages visited, click on the down arrow button beside the *Back* and *Forward* buttons.

Stop

The stop button can be used to terminate the loading of the current page. This is usually used when you typed the wrong URL by mistake and you want to stop the Web Page from loading or if the webpage takes too long to download.

Refresh

As the name suggests, the refresh or the reload button is used to load the current webpage again. In other words, it refreshes the contents of the current page by fetching a new copy of it.

Search

Search allows you to find information on the web. You can find information on the web in a variety of ways:

- Click the *Search* button on the toolbar to gain access to a number of search providers. Type a word or phrase in the *Search* box.
- Type *go, find,* or? followed by a word or phrase in the Address bar. Internet Explorer starts a search using its predetermined search provider.
- After you go to a Web page, you can search for specific text on that page by clicking the *Edit* menu, and then clicking *Find* (*on this page*).

Favourites

Favourites/Bookmarks is used to record addresses of frequently visited websites. Once a website or a web page is added to the favourites list, it can be revisited by simply clicking on the link in the list. This saves the effort of typing the URL, each time the user wishes to visit the same site.

As your list of favourite pages grows, you can organize it

by creating different folders. For example, you could create a folder named 'Technology' for storing information about sites from where you collect some Technology related information.

To organize your favourites into folders:

- Click Organize Favourites on the Favourites menu.
- Click on Create Folder and press ENTER.
- Drag the shortcuts in the list to the appropriate folders.

History

History is a record of all pages visited in the last few days, hours, or minutes. Clicking on the history button displays a list of all recently visited webpages and/or websites. To revisit any one of them, simply click on the address.

Print

Print button is used to print contents of the current webpage.

Net Surfing

Net surfing is a term associated with browsing or exploring a network or the World Wide Web to find places of interest, usually without any specific goal in mind. It is analogous to channel surfing with the TV's remote control.

SEARCHING

You can search for information on virtually any topic on the Internet. This is possible by using websites, that provide a Search engine. One of the most popular search engines is Google. Other commonly used search sites include Yahoo, Rediff, Alta Vista, Hot Bot, AskJeeves, and Khoj.

Google (www.google.com)

Yahoo (www.yahoo.com)

Since different search engines use different algorithms, it will give different results for the same search criterion. The user must, therefore, know which search engine is best suited for his/her specific query.

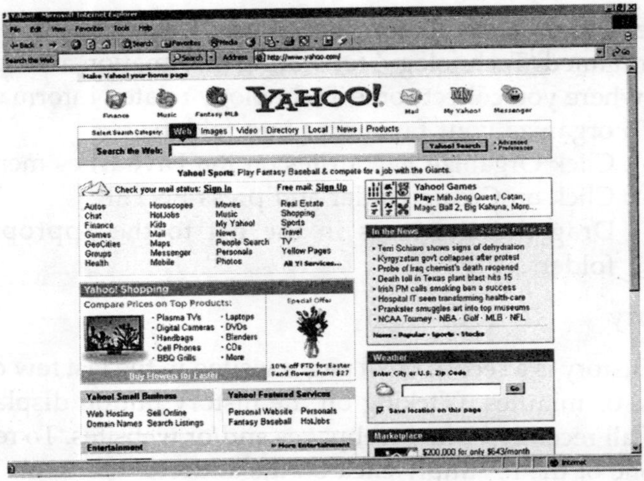

E-MAILING

E-mailing is one of the most common and popular uses of the Internet. You can send or receive mails from anywhere in the world, that too in a matter of seconds. Through e-mail, you can send and receive any type of file – image, video, sound, and, of course, plain text. It is a very versatile and open medium with the advantage of being a low cost one.

If you wish to send and receive e-mails, you will need to create an e-mail account for yourself, using a website that offers such services. Various sites provide this facility – some charge for it while others don't. Rediff.com is one of the sites that provide for free e-mail services. Other such sites include yahoo.com, hotmail.com, lycos.com and many more.

Since we are interested in learning how to use e-mail, let us use services provided by Rediff to do the same.

Creating an E-mail Account

The Internet explorer to visit the Rediff website. The homepage will be displayed as follows:

Since you are a new user at this time, you need to Sign Up as a new user.

Click on 'Sign Up 'to create yourself as a new user. A new page will be displayed that will allow you to select the kind of account you want – Free or paid (these differ in the storage space and additional facilities).

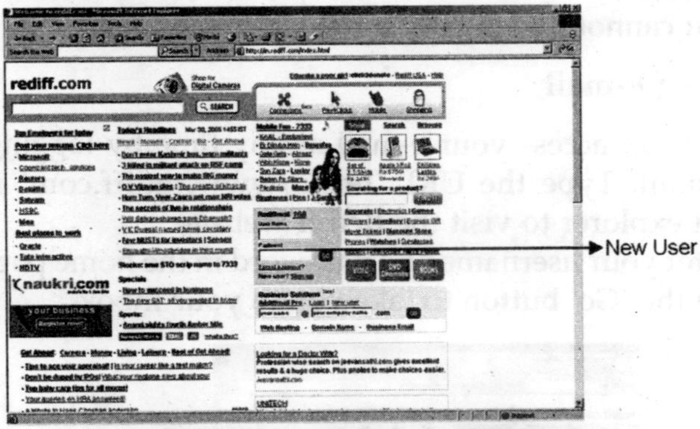

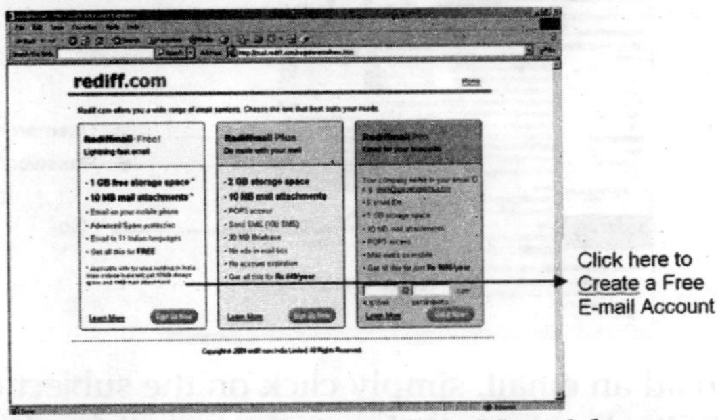

Once you click on the 'Sign Up Now' button, Rediff displays a registration form and requires you to fill some necessary details like a user ID, password, Name etc.

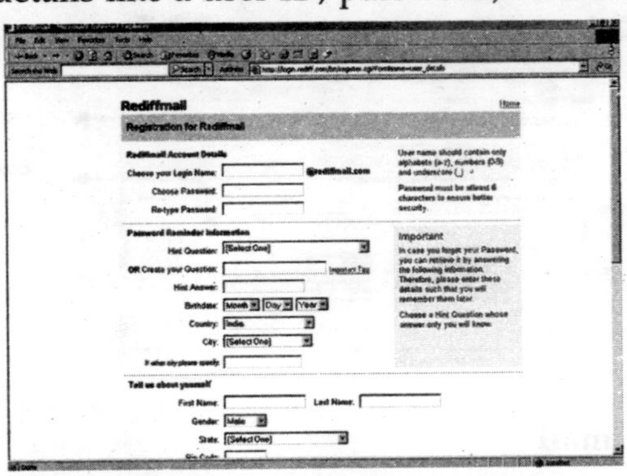

After you register yourself on a website, you become a member and can then simply log into your mail account using the username and password. It is, therefore, very important to remember your username and password because without that you cannot access your e-mail account.

Checking E-mail

You can access your e-mail at any time by logging into your email. Type the URL 'http://www.rediff.com' in the Internet explorer to visit the Rediff website.

Enter your username and password in the home page and click on the 'Go' button to take you to your Inbox.

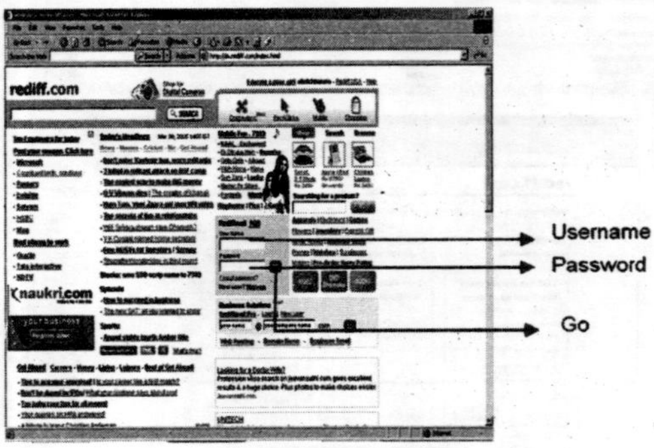

To read an email, simply click on the subject of the mail. This will display the actual text of the mail for you to read.

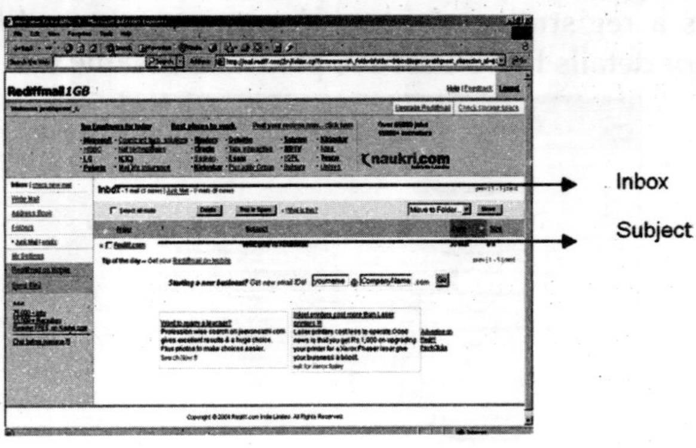

Sending E-mail

To send e-mail, click on Write Mail. The screen that follows would look like

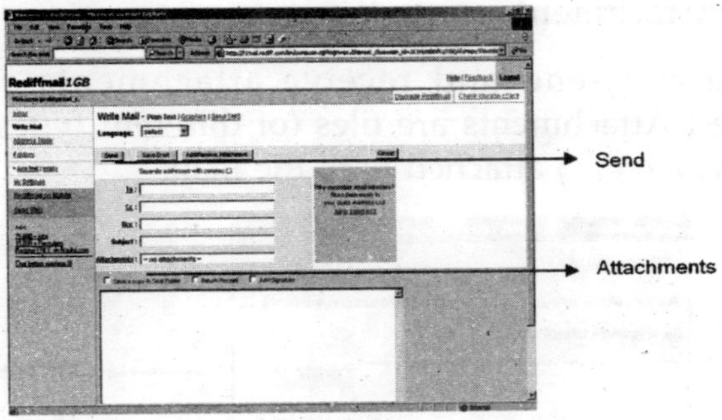

To

In the To box, type the name of the recipient of the form recipient@domain.com. You must enter the correct e-mail ID of the recipient else the message will return to you.

Cc

CC or Carbon Copy is used to send the message to more than one recipient at the same time. Type in the mail IDs of the additional recipients in this box (you can put more than one mail ID in this box by separating the list with commas).

Bcc

Bcc stands for 'Blind Carbon Copy' and is used when you wish to send the message to multiple recipients without them being able to see the names of other recipients. All the recipients' names will remain hidden. Only you would know the names of members to whom the mail has been sent.

Subject

The 'Subject' box is used to specify the subject of the mail. The recipient can get a fair idea about the mail contents by looking at the subject.

Message Box

It is the place provided for typing in your mail message.

Once you have typed in your message, simply click on the **Send** button to send the message to the recipient(s). You will get a message informing you that your mail has been sent.

E-mail Attachments

You can send and receive attachments with mail messages. Attachments are files (of different types like text, sound, video etc.) attached with the mail.

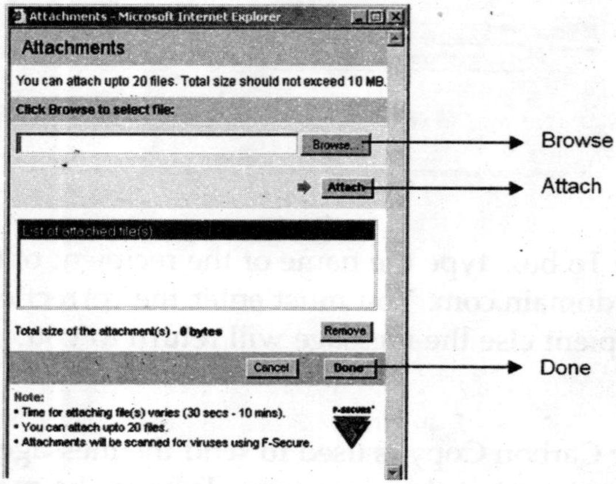

Sending Attachments

To send an attachment with your mail, click on the Attachments button while writing a new mail. A screen like below is displayed for you to attach the necessary files.

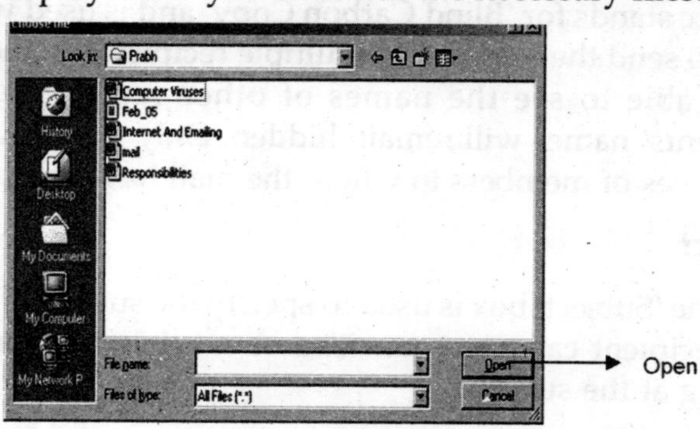

Clicking on the Browse button opens the standard files selection dialog box. It lets you browse through the files on your disks and select the file you want to attach.

Once you locate the file, click on it and then click on the Open button. You can repeat this process if you wish to attach more than one file with your message. Once you are done with the selection of files, click on Attach button to attach the file to your message. Finally, click on the Done button to return to your message. Now when you Send your message, it is sent along with the attachments (files).

Opening Attachments

If you receive an e-mail with attachment(s), you can view the attached files on-line and/or save these to your disk and view them later. While reading the received mail, clicking on the Go to Attachments button will display the following:

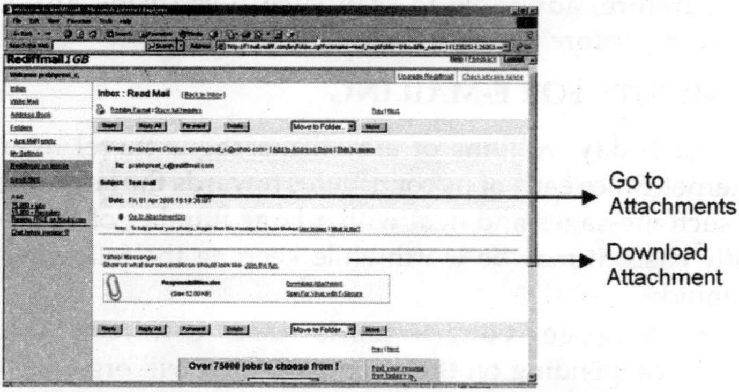

Clicking on Download Attachment will display the following screen:

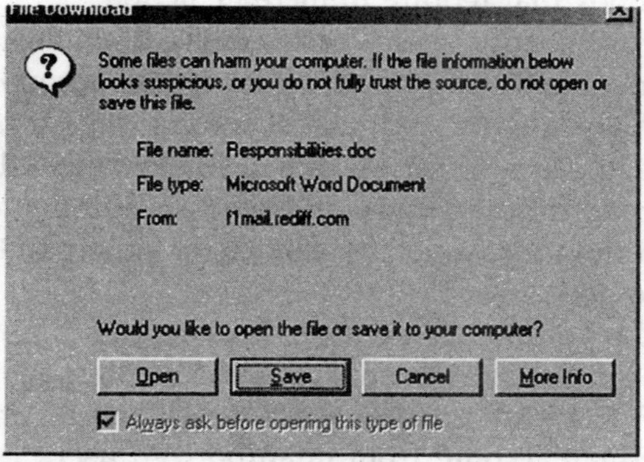

To view the file without saving it, click on the Open button. The file will open (provided your computer has the associated application installed, e.g. MS Word if the document is a word file, MS Excel in case it is an Excel file and so on) allowing you to view the file contents.

Alternatively, you could click on Save to save the file in the desired folder on your disk. You can then view this file(s), whenever you wish, at a later time.

A Word of Caution

Attachments can prove dangerous to your computer, because these can conceal dangerous viruses or other malicious programmes that may destroy the data on your computer. It is, therefore, advisable to scan such files (using anti-virus software) before opening them.

SOME TIPS FOR E-MAILING

Each day millions of e-mail messages travel over the Internet. Since each of us contributes towards the large volume of such messages and deal with a large number of them on a daily basis, it may be worthwhile keeping the following tips in mind:

- Arrange your e-mails into different folders (depending on their content). This will organize your mails into different categories, e.g. Travel, Education, Newsletters etc. while leaving only those in your Inbox that require immediate action.
- Periodically scan your messages to delete the old messages and preserve your e-mail account space.
- Always write meaningful subject in your mails.
- You can also set up e-mail filters to avoid cluttering your Inbox. Filters are used to automatically send certain messages (by sender for example) to separate folders.
- Zip your attachments if they are very big.
- Scan the attachments received before opening them.
- Periodically change your password to protect your e-mail account from unauthorized users.
- Do not forward junk mails or chain letters.
- Do not forget to log out of your e-mail account.

INTERNET CHAT

In the earlier days, the only medium of online communication with people residing in other cities and countries was a long distance call (STD or ISD). With the Internet gaining popularity, options like Internet Telephony, Internet Chat are also becoming the preferred medium of communication. Internet Telephony (or IPT) is characterized by transportation of telephone calls over the Internet. All you need is a microphone, earphone and special software on your PC to talk to anyone on the Internet. This makes the telephonic conversation very cheap and is being widely used amongst the Internet society.

Internet Chat (or IRC as it is popularly called) allows you to type in a message, and your friend (anywhere in the world, but logged on to the Net at the same time on the same chat site) would receive it almost instantaneously who can then respond in the same way. Other than the difference of having to type instead of speaking, chatting is almost as good as speaking to another person on the phone.

There are various free chat sites that you can use to communicate with other people – one of the most popular being Yahoo. You can log on to the free chat site, go to the specific chat room where you have agreed to meet the other person, and start chatting by typing your message.

You could go to the Yahoo site by typing the URL 'http://www.Yahoo.com'. Once you have done that, click on Chat from the Yahoo home page.

You can now type in your Yahoo ID and Password and then click on Sign in (in case you do not already have a Yahoo account, you can create one by clicking on 'Sign Up for Yahoo Chat' which will let you create a new Yahoo account).

Once you are logged in you can Enter Chat Room to start chatting.

Clicking on this will take you into a room called Chat Central where you can find many people chatting. You can simply jump in and start chatting. You can also change your chat room by clicking on Change Room to get a list of chat rooms to select from.

What is the Difference between Es-mail and Chat?

In this unit, you have studied the key usages of the Internet, the connectivity options available to connect over the Internet, the most common Internet protocol, and the common terminology used in context of the Internet. You have also learnt how to search the Internet using various search engines available.

This unit also familiarized you with E-mail and Chat, the two most common uses that the Internet is put to. It details, the steps required to create your own e-mail account, thereby being able to send and receive messages to people anywhere in the world.

Index

A

B

C

I

J

K

L

M

N

O

P

Encyclopaedia of

COMPUTERS APPLICATIONS IN MANAGEMENT

Encyclopaedia of COMPUTERS APPLICATIONS IN MANAGEMENT

Volume 3

Sumit Sethi

ANMOL PUBLICATIONS PVT. LTD.
NEW DELHI - 110 002 (INDIA)

ANMOL PUBLICATIONS PVT. LTD.
H.O.: 4374/4B, Ansari Road, Daryaganj,
New Delhi-110 002 (India)
Ph.: 23278000, 23261597
B.O.: No. 1015, Ist Main Road, BSK IIIrd Stage
IIIrd Phase, IIIrd Block,
Bangalore - 560 085 (India)
Visit us at: www.anmolpublications.com

Encyclopaedia of Computers Applications in Management

First Edition, 2009

ISBN 978-81-261-3912-5 (Set)

PRINTED IN INDIA

Printed at Mehra Offset Press, Delhi.

Contents

Preface

This Encyclopaedia is designed to provide a comprehensive introduction to the design and analysis of computer algorithms and data structures. In terms of the computer science and Computer Application, this encyclopaedia to be primarily focused on the Junior-Senior level Algorithms course.

This Encycloparedia owes its existence to the collaboration made possible by the Internet and the free software movement. Its author — a college professor, have yet to meet face to face, but we have been able to work closely together and have been aided by many wonderful folks who have donated their time and energy to helping make this encyclopaedia better.

Author

Chapter 1

Sentence Structure Determination

Syntactic analysis, better called parsing or sentence-structure determination (SSD), is one of the keys to ALDP, including MT. Although several plans have been programed, we have space to consider just two: a phrase-structure determination programme written (but not yet published) by John Cocke of IBM Research, and a dependency-structure determination programme written at

The RAND Corporation. Cocke's programme is designed to yield as many structures as possible for each sentence, revealing ambiguities if any exist. The RAND programme cannot yield more than one structure for a sentence, but it is intended to find the most plausible.

A PHRASE-STRUCTURE DETERMINATION PROGRAMME

The basic plan is to build all possible two-occurrence phrases, then all possible three-occurrence phrases, etc. The (several) structures of an n-occurrence sentence are the n-occurrence phrases.

Some occurrences have alternative grammatical types—they are *homographic*. Perhaps a sentence can be parsed if one grammatical type is chosen for a given homographic occurrence, and not if another is chosen; perhaps different structures are obtained. In any event, choice of grammatical type for a homograph influences SSD, so each type must be noted. Cocke's routine assumes that glossary look-up has assigned one or more grammar-code symbols to each occurrence. It takes these symbols as input.

Item Number	*Form*	*Grammar-code Symbol*
1	The	T
2	man	N
3	with	P
4	dark	A
5	hair	N
6	was	Vwas
7	wearing	Ving
8	a	T
9	trench	N
10	coat	N

Next, all consecutive pairs of occurrences are examined, with all possible grammatical interpretations. In the example, the first two occurrences must be examined as T–N and as T–V. Each pair is tested for agreement. Although there are many ways to make such tests, table look-up is simplest and as powerful as any (though perhaps less economical in operation than some). The table that Cocke requires is a list of ordered triples, X–Y = Z. These entries are, of course, just phrase-structure rules written in reverse.

Any pair that shows agreement (by matching the left-hand side of a table entry) is a phrase. The grammatical type of the phrase is the symbol on the right in the entry. A phrase is adequately described by its length, the sequence number of its first occurrence, and its grammatical type.

To form a phrase of length 3, it is necessary to use a 1-occurrence phrase and a 2-occurrence phrase in combination. The programme now proceeds to look over all such pairs, but taking only those in which the 1-occurrence phrase starts at location n, and the 2-occurrence phrase at location $n + 1$, and those in which the 2-occurrence phrase starts at n and the single occurrence at $n + 2$.

The programme iterates on the length of the phrases to be constructed, continuing until phrases as long as the sentence have been attempted. At each phrase length, say p, it looks at all phrases of length r, $r = 1, 2,..., p–1$, immediately followed by phrases of length $p–r$. The output of the programme is a list of all the phrases formed, at all lengths. Tracing backward through the listing, it is clear that the programme produced, for the illustrative sentence and using only the phrase-structure rules in Section.

Item	*Starting location*	*Length*	*Form*	*Grammar-code symbol*	*Constituent items*
1	1	1	The	T	
2	2	1	man	N	
3	3	1	with	P	
4	4	1	dark	A	
5	5	1	hair	N	
6	6	1	was	Vwas	
7	7	1	wearing	Ving	
8	8	1	a	T	
9	9	1	trench	N	
10	10	1	coat	N	
11	4	2	dark hair	NP?	4, 5
12	6	1	was wearing	V	6, 7
13	9	2	trench coat	NP?	9, 10
14	3	3	with dark hair	PP	3, 11
15	8	3	a trench coat	NP	8, 13
16	2	4	man with dark hair	NP?	2, 14
17	1	5	The man with dark hair	NP	1, 16
18	6	5	was wearing a trench coat	VP	12, 15
19	1	10	The man ... a trench coat	S	17, 18

Cocke's routine has been extended to deal with phrase-structure rules of the form X YZ, are used. If two kinds of phrases can be rewritten in the same way, it is impossible to know (until longer phrases are formed), which kind of phrase gave rise to a certain sequence. Cocke's table entries are therefore of the form

W – X-... Y–Z = R or S or... or T

Matching the sequence on the left yields (tentative) phrases of all the types shown on the right.

If discontinuous phrases have to be. handled, Cocke's routine must be extended still further in order to look at noncontiguous pairs or sequences of phrases. The logic that would be involved would lead us too far afield, however.

A DEPENDENCY-STRUCTURE DETERMINATION PROGRAMME.

The RAND programme relies on projectivity. An occurrence X is said to "precede" an occurrence Y if the two occurrences can be connected in a projective sentence. The general plan is to find occurrences that stand in the precedence relation, test them for agreement, connect them if they agree, and iterate. As more and more connections are made, new precedences are established. Let us see how the plan works out in some detail.

A *stage* in SSD ends when a dependency connection is made. At any stage, X precedes Y (written XpY) if and only if (1) X is to the left of Y; (2) X does not derive from (depend, directly or indirectly, on) Y, and Y does not derive from X; (3) either X is still independent, or Y is, or both are; and (4) every occurrence between X and Y derives from one or the other of them.

Condition 1 differentiates XpY from YpX, keeping word order in the notion of precedence. Condition 2 prevents multiple connections between any two occurrences. Condition 3 prevents further testing of a pair of occurrences, each of which already has a governor—no occurrence can have two governors in a dependency structure. Condition 4 guarantees projectivity in any structure formed. Graphically, every new connection line is *above* any intervening nodes.

A dependency connection is established, i.e., XdY is formed, when (1) XpY or YpX; (2) X is independent; and (3) X and Y agree, in the sense that X belongs to a grammatical type that can depend on an occurrence of type Y.

condition 1 ties together precedence and dependence. Condition 2 guarantees that no occurrence shall have two governors. Condition 3 is the obvious agreement requirement. Agreement can be tested here, as in Cocke's routine, with a table, but the entries have a different form. Each entry contains the grammar-code symbol of a governor, the grammarcode symbol of a dependent, and a *resultant* grammar-code symbol for each. The order of the two occurrences in text is reflected in the precedence relation and tested against the order of the two grammar-code symbols in the tabular entry to prevent, for example, connecting a noun to a following preposition that it could serve as object if their order were reversed. One more bit in each entry indicates which of the two occurrences is governor in the combination.

The need for resultant-code symbols is partially similar to the need for output symbols in a phrase-structure table. A noun governing an article is not equivalent to a noun with no dependents and can depend on different governors. In short, the resultant grammar-code symbol of the governor describes the whole *phrase* consisting of the governor and all its direct and indirect dependents as far as they have been attached.

But resultant symbols have another purpose. Since the sentence-building form of a dependency grammar attaches all its dependents to a governor by a single rule, whereas the SSD form connects them one by one, the resultant symbol must show what dependents have been attached and what can still be added. For example, after a verb and its object have been connected, a subject can still be made to depend on the verb, but not another object.

The RAND programme works from left to right through a sentence, going back as many times as necessary. In our illustrative sentence, however, this order would cause some trouble since the pair "a—trench" is tested before the pair "trench—coat." One more trick is needed, namely, a system of values. At any stage of SSD, more than one precedence pair is likely to be available. Each entry in the table of agreements has a value number assigned to it; the dependency connection with highest value is made first, and the one earliest in the sentence if several tie for highest value.

Dependency SSD is illustrated, stage by stage, The values that have been assumed are arbitrary to some extent, but not entirely. Modifiers of nouns must be handled early, and prepositional phrases must be assembled before subjects and verbs can be coupled—lest a preposition's object be regarded as a verb's subject, as might have happened here.

A NOTE OF CAUTION.

If the logic of SSD programmes is so simple, how can there be any doubt about their soundness and effectiveness? The answer is appallingly clear: by the end of 1960, no SSD routine had been tested on a large enough text, with a good enough agreement table, to prove its empirical validity. The principles of several systems are charmingly simple, and those systems are certainly economical. None of them work with near-perfect accuracy, but their errors can usually be

blamed on the dictionary or the agreement table. The table—or its surrogate—is the "grammar" of a natural language. When work on ALDP programmes began, there were no complete grammars or dictionaries, and no one was interested in constructing them. The exigencies of linguistic computation proved that complete descriptions of natural languages had to be constructed, and by empirical research: analysis of actual texts. But such research takes time, and it had not been completed by the end of 1960.

Only when empirical work has produced almost complete grammars will it be possible to judge current theories of syntactic structure and the SSD programmes they have inspired. If most sentences prove to have ambiguous structures, or if high accuracy can only be attained by far more complicated logic than is now envisaged, ALDP may be forgotten.

Encouragingly, the RAND programme is about 75 per cent accurate, and four errors out of five *seem* to be due to inadequacies in the agreement table or the grammar-code symbols stored in the dictionary. But the RAND programme has only been tested on Russian physics text, selected from well-edited journals.

SEMANTICS

The meaning of a word is either:

- The part of the world that it represents,
- The response that it evokes from a hearer, or
- What you will. According to Morris, semantics is concerned with the relationship between language and reality, whereas syntax has to do with the structure of the language itself. Many linguists restrict the definition of syntax even more strictly, referring (vaguely, I think) to the native speaker's belief that one "can" or "cannot" say certain things in his language as delimiting syntax. The limited view is that *absolute* rules are syntactic, *probabilistic* rules semantic. One broader view of syntax, based on Morris' position, considers any findings based on analysis of text syntactic, and any finding that uses other criteria non-syntactic.

Semantics and MT. Semantics and meaning, whatever they are, serve MT only by

- Helping with sentence-structure determination, or
- Helping to choose among multiple output-language equivalent of an input-language word. "Analysis of proteins in the liver" and "analysis of proteins in the laboratory" may convince some students—including Ida Rhodes that semantics can contribute to SSD, but others, such as

Chomsky, are convinced that it cannot. If pairs of phrases, like those quoted above, do have different structures, then *liver* and *laboratory* belong to different word classes. It is not yet certain that purely textual analysis can demonstrate the two structures, but it is certain that once the word classes have been established SSD procedures can be made to differentiate the phrases given the class memberships of the words involved.

Some multiple-equivalent words are said to be resolvable

if the field of discourse is known. A Russian word has one English equivalent in physics, another in chemistry, etc. In the RAND physics glossary, which contains only the English equivalents needed to translate Russian words as they occur in physics text, most words have only one equivalent apiece. Now, if these words have no other equivalents in other fields, the multiplemeaning problem is slight for Russian-English MT. If they do have other equivalents in other fields, then field of discourse is a powerful aid in reducing the problem. Of course, a human reader must decide what field a document falls into, but there is reason to believe that that decision can be made automatically. The clues might include the words in the title of the book or journal (*Journal of Experimental and Theoretical Physics*, for example), or the words in the text that appear more often in one field than another.

Even in the RAND glossary, some words have multiple English equivalents. Many of those are grammatical function words, such as prepositions, and are not translated—instead, the relations that they express are translated and put into English function words, word-order rules, etc. Then there are verbs that govern either infinitives or *that* clauses, and have different equivalents: "One should [plus infinitive]" or "It follows that...." And there are adjectives that mean one thing (*light*) with concrete nouns, and another with verbal nouns (*easy*).

Words like the adjective that is translated *light* or *easy* pose a delicate problem for the semantic-syntactic theoretician. If the distinction is syntactic, then *light* and *easy* are semantically identical: *easy* is to actions as *light* is to objects. Then the Russians are clever to use just one word, and our required word choice is redundant. On the other hand, if we speak of both colors and objects as *light*, whereas the Russians must use two different words, then we are the clever ones. We can decide how to translate one of these adjectives by looking at its governor and choosing the equivalent of the modifier according to the word class of the governor, but we are not learning very much about semantics in the process.

In short, decision procedures for most multiple equivalence problems apparently can be found by examining translations and comparing the translation wanted with the syntactically related occurrences. The governors of adjectives, the subjects and objects of verbs, the governors and modifiers of nouns, and so on, can frequently be classified in such a way that the translation of the adjective, verb, or noun depends only on the classes to which related words belong. But all of this amounts to a simpleminded kind of semantics.

SEMANTICS AND INFORMATION RETRIEVAL

Another kind of ALDP application is the retrieval from a library, or a file, of answers to questions or documents containing answers to questions. Some studies, such as Maron's or Luhn's, have concentrated on vocabulary disregarding syntax. Their general position is as follows: knowing what words are in a document generally provides sufficient information to determine what questions the document can answer. Some positive results have been obtained, but it might be claimed that the questions used to test these methods have all been too easy. Little has been done about using syntax in information retrieval.

The main idea behind retrieval by vocabulary is the same as the use of subject-field glossaries in MT: different scientific subjects use slightly different words. Therefore, having compiled a list of words that are used in a certain field more often than in others, documents that contain words on the list are likely to belong in the given field. A question also belongs in a field—the answer to the question is to be found by looking through documents with the right vocabulary. Another plan is to omit the field classification and go from a question to a list of words that should appear in any document containing its answer to documents containing all or most of those words.

Still another plan—as yet untried—would be to perform SSD on a proposed question, regarding it as an incomplete sentence. Then its answer would be located by comparing it with the complete structures of sentences in stored text. Unfortunately, a question like "What is the boiling point of hydrogen?" is not likely to be answered by a system that can only find the answer in a sentence that reads (literally), "The boiling point of hydrogen is...." The answer is more likely to be in a table, mentioned in text only by a sentence such as "The liquid-vapour phase-change temperatures of the elements are given in Table..."

This plan would require, therefore, a truly sophisticated syntactic theory, capable of recognizing similarities among quite varied sentences—as transformation theory hopes to do. Furthermore, if it did not require real semantics, it would at least require recognition of the fact that the *boiling point* of a substance is the *liquid-vapour phase-change temperature,* and that *hydrogen* is an *element.*

Semantics and Psychological Data Processing. Much of the raw material of social science consists of natural-language data obtained from interviews, interaction sessions, and the like. Osgood's work provides the key to automatic content analysis, at least in the rudimentary style appropriate to pioneers, and I have written on the subject. (Sebeok is working on automatic methods in analysis of folklore texts, but that branch of social science would lead us too far afield.) Osgood's method of evaluative assertion analysis is designed to estimate a speaker or writer's attitude toward an object—as overtly expressed—by summating or averaging the evaluative references that he makes to it. An evaluative assertion is a construction that links the object of unknown value with a word or phrase of widely known value, a common-meaning term.

SSD is required to make the detection of linkages automatic, and it probably has to be followed by transformational analysis, at least for convenience. Furthermore, in many cases, information about linking words must be stored in the dictionary. "He employs criminals" and "He pursues criminals" both link *him* with *criminality,* syntactically, but one sentence makes the connection positively, the other negatively. The evaluations of common-meaning terms also must be in the dictionary, where *criminal* is identified as *bad*. The goodness or badness of a word is certainly part of its meaning and therefore belongs in a semantic theory.

To detect expressions of affect, respect, or other attitudes in face-to-face conversation, to detect moods, needs, etc., in any utterance, or to find signs of neurosis or response to treatment in clinical interviews will presumably require more elaborate analysis than Osgood has contemplated. These applications—which have not yet been tried, or even thought through in a serious way—will probably require sentence-structure determination, as MT does.

They will also require semantic, or nearsemantic, analysis of the relationships among words and phrases in the vocabulary, as sophisticated information retrieval does. And they will no doubt require still more, including goodness-badness measurements on words, etc.

The psychologist who is anxious to see ALDP in his laboratory cannot claim that it will save him labour (Does the cyclotron save labour for the physicist?), but only that it will give him the power to analyse more material more thoroughly than he can do otherwise. He can expect MT, information retrieval, commercial applications, and the scientific interests of linguists to provide him, eventually, with much of what he needs, even including much of the semantic analysis. But finally social scientists themselves must investigate the use of language for psychological and social ends.

Chapter 2

Computer Music

Lejaren A. Hiller, Jr. earned his Ph.D. in chemistry in 1944 from Princeton University, where he also took extensive course work in music, primarily composition and theory with Roger Sessions, as well as considerable course work in electrical engineering.

He has since also obtained a M. Music from the University of Illinois. After several years of research work with E. I. duPont de Nemours, Inc., primarily in the fields of high polymer chemistry and reaction kinetics, he became a faculty member in the Department of Chemistry of the University of Illinois. Since 1958, he has worked in the School of Music, where he now directs research and teaching in experimental composition and acoustics.

While in the chemistry department, he did research on applications of computers to theoretical problems, particularly those of a statistical nature. He is the author of some twenty-five technical papers and books and has composed about thirty musical works—conventional as well as experimental compositions, such as those described in this article.

Robert Baker was born in Leavenworth, Kansas, in 1933. He received his B.A. degree from Washington University, St. Louis, in 1957, and the M.A. degree from there the following year. Since 1958, he has attended the University of Illinois to fulfill the requirements leading to the D.M.A. degree in composition.

He has held teaching assistantships at both Washington University and the University of Illinois; at present, he holds a research associateship to pursue studies of computer applications to musical problems. His compositions include both orchestral and chamber works, as well as smaller vocal and choral pieces.

Music is recognized to be an important communication medium because both composing and listening to music seem to have significance as components of a process for transmitting qualities of subjective human experience. Music, however, demands fewer referential meanings than other communication systems, notably language. In fact, it is possible, as every music listener knows, to achieve "musical sense" purely in terms of the elements of music itself. For this reason, the properties of music as communication attract the interest of investigators of language structure and decision making as well as of artists directly concerned with music as a means of artistic expression.

Especially today, with the recent development of high-speed electronic digital computers, the opportunity exists for precise and quantitative systematic studies of various musical structures on a scale that was not previously possible. It is the purpose of the present paper to demonstrate this point by describing an investigation performed late in 1960 with the aid of the ILLIAC, the electronic digital computer at the University of Illinois. We expect the results of this investigation to throw light on the nature of the compositional procedure and, perhaps, ultimately to yield some understanding of the way in which the logic of music may reflect the logic of thought in general.

We present the material even though some of it is still provisional and may be affected by anticipated results, because it illustrates the technique that permits one to interpret the procedures of one form of communication, music, in terms of another type of formal structure, machine programing.

Let us also note that, for composers, perhaps an even more important objective is the development of compositional procedures which yield musical structures that specifically exploit the logic of digital computer processes and exhibit forms unique to the method.

PREVIOUS EXPERIMENTS IN COMPUTER COMPOSITION

The use of an electronic digital computer for musical composition had its inception in 1955-56 in a series of experiments carried out by one of the present authors in collaboration with Leonard M. Isaacson, at that time a research associate at the University of Illinois. Since the idea of using computers for musical composition was then new, the primary objective was simply to evaluate as efficiently as possible a reasonably broad spectrum of various compositional techniques in terms of their suitability for computer programing.

No particular process was examined in detail; rather the objective was to achieve at least some semblance of a number of simple but characteristic musical structures. By the end of 1956, enough results were accumulated to form a twenty-minute composition which we named the *Illiac Suite for String Quartet,* after the University of Illinois' digital computer.

The score of this composition was subsequently published with statements that "the musical materials... were taken from a much larger body of material by unbiased sampling procedures so that a representative rather than a selectively chosen musically superior group of results would be included in the *Suite...* our primary aim *is not* the presentation of an aesthetic unity—a work of art. This music is meant to be a research record—a laboratory notebook." A more recent publication that presented a full account of this work, including all programing details, also gave references to other less extensive but nonetheless important experiments in computer analysis and synthesis of music carried out by other investigators through 1958.

Since that time, two other applications of computers to musical composition have come to our attention, though at the time of writing we have not been able to obtain the details of these experiments. Finally, we might mention two briefer recent articles written by one of the present authors, which review aspects of this earlier work. Because the studies contained in the *Illiac Suite* have already been so fully discussed, we propose now to review this work solely to introduce the new experiments we plan to outline here.

The process of generating computer music for the *Illiac Suite* was rationalized into a series of simple steps as follows: Initially, the computer was instructed to propagate random integers equated to notes of the musical scale, and later to other musical elements, such as rhythm and dynamics. These random integers were rapidly produced in the ILLIAC by a conventional random integer generating process. They were then subjected to various arithmetic tests derived from the particular "rules of composition" being employed in the various experiments.

These arithmetic tests were compiled into the testing programme which effected the acceptance or rejection of the sequence of random integers such that the "accepted" integers were employed to build up in the computer memory a short musical "composition" that did not violate the rules in effect. Further, it was necessary to include in the computing programme, a "try-again" subroutine which we entered whenever a random integer was rejected, so that a new integer might be propagated and tested. An "erase" procedure was also provided so that if an untenable situation developed in the process of composition such that no further composition was possible, i.e., that all subsequent notes were unacceptable, we could erase part or all of the composition thus far composed and start over again from some previous point.

This total procedure leads to a cyclic programme having a general form like that. Since this block diagram does not presuppose any particular musical form or style, to obtain a particular style we must specify, if we can, the particular rules which lead to that style. Once we do that, we produce a more specific block diagram for programing. Where the block diagram is given for producing first-species strict counterpoint, an academic form of composition based on sixteenth-century style. The detailed programing of this and similar block diagrams for composition is discussed fully elsewhere.

The *Illiac Suite* is made up of four Experiments, four movements that represent different research objectives. In

Experiment One, the primary purpose was simply to work out basic procedures that would enable the

ILLIAC to produce four-part writing suitable for string quartet performance. As a means of testing the various technical procedures, a limited number of first-species strict counterpoint rules were employed to produce a loose resemblance to sixteenth-century style. *Experiment Two* was produced to demonstrate that an accurate reproduction of this well-recognized compositional style could be achieved, because in this instance rules for producing that style were available in a form specific enough for translation into computer instructions.

In *Experiment Three,* attention was shifted to the problems of generating rhythms, dynamics, and dynamic changes, playing instructions, certain procedures for producing dissonant chromatic music and for producing twelve-tone rows. Finally, in *Experiment Four,* examples of "Markoff chain music" were generated in which successive note selection was made to depend on probability functions computed from tables of values arbitrarily derived from the overtone series and from a consideration of vertical interval lengths. In certain sections of *Experiment Four,* these probability functions were also made to depend on previous notes chosen and on their relation to the tonal centre of the movement, chosen arbitrarily to be C. The "coda" of this movement was developed to demonstrate how a simple complete closed musical structure might be produced in a computer. This coda is an extended generalized cadential structure which resolves on the tonic note, C.

All four movements of the Illiac Suite represent procedures which find formalization in the mathematical theory of communication, also called "information theory," developed by R. V. L. Hartley, C. E. Shannon, and numerous other investigators concerned with defining a quantitative rationale of the communication process. This theory has as its basis a definition of the word *information* that relates to the measure of randomness in a message. The more random is the choice of symbols making up a message, the higher the "information content" of a message is said to be. This statement finds quantitative expression in Shannon's equation: In which, Hn is the information content measured in bits per symbol (a bit is the basic unit of information) and pi are the probabilities associated with each of the symbols that might be employed in the message.* One great value of Equation (18.1)—and equations related to it—in musical studies is its provision of a quantitative measure of aspects of musical style that have not been precisely defined by other means. In studies recently completed at the University of Illinois,(1) it was shown that even the simplest application of this theory to the analysis of complex musical structures, specifically four sonata expositions by Mozart, Beethoven, Berg, and Hindemith, discloses wide divergences among these composers in terms of their respective styles; divergences that, in terms of information, appear to correlate well with the qualitative results of traditional musical analysis.

Because information theory says that maximum information occurs in a message when the message is made up of symbols chosen at random and that the information content can be reduced by reducing this randomness, it follows that the process for producing music in the *Illiac Suite* directly works on the principle of information content reduction. We start with random integers that, used as generated, produce random music.

In such random music, all elements of the musical structure under processing, such as pitch values, occur with statistically equal frequency in a sample of sufficient size. However, rules were inserted to make the choices unequal, often by forbidding certain choices, which is equivalent to setting certain *pi* = 0. In other instances, particularly in *Experiment Four*, certain choices were made more probable than others, thus also providing non-random selection of elements, but based on more complex sets of statistics. Actually, an interesting study would be the computation of the reduction in information afforded by the rules applied in the four movements of the *Illiac Suite*. Perhaps this will be the subject of a future reexamination of this music.

A GENERALIZED MODEL FOR MUSICAL COMPOSITION

After the *Illiac Suite* was completed, the most pressing problem became the formulation of a method for computer realization of more complete and varied musical structures that would begin to exhibit at least some real degree of aesthetic coherence. Obviously, a more generalized attack on the problem of describing the process of musical composition was required. As a point of departure, we organized this new study partly in terms of analysis and partly in terms of synthesis, because if we postulate some model of the compositional process, we must test its validity and effectiveness in terms of how well it yields recognizably musical results. In other words, we must devise a method of musical analysis that provides data for the compositional process so that it, in turn, provides the requisite musical output. We next proposed that compositional procedure be regarded as an exercise in decision making in which, for convenience, we distinguish between two basically different types of decisions that confront the composer:

- Procedural decisions, and
- Elemental decisions. The first of these are decisions concerning the *order* in which the various elements of a composition are to be chosen, regardless of what the specific choice of each successive element is to be. This order we call "procedural logic." By the second process, then, we mean the decisions concerning the specific choices of elements from among the many possible values these elements may take on.

Our general problem then may be stated as follows:

- To determine whether or not a general procedural logic exists, and if so, to formulate this procedural logic, and
- To determine which factors, on the elemental level, influence the choice of other factors and to attempt a quantitative description of the extent of this influence in terms of probability.

Our hypothesis is that a procedural logic does exist, at least for specific historical styles, and that this procedural logic *may even be independent of the specific historical style*. If this hypothesis seems to yield promising results in historical styles, it will also find application in *a priori* methods of composition and, more importantly, as the basis for self-generating processes of musical composition. Moreover, we can then set up a "dummy model" for the composer in which the procedure is independent of the elements to be chosen. Graphically, this can be represented by a scheme like that.

This model represents only one point in the music, so it would recycle for every such point until the composition under production is completed. Our present problem then is to find what to call E_1, E_2,..., etc. A not unreasonable conjecture as to what these might be is depicted for eighteenth-century homophonic music *not including* such things as thematic components and thematic form.

To see how this compositional model is being treated, we shall first consider how it can be used to set up an analytical method and, later, how it provides a basis for music synthesis. In this context, let us note that quantitative data concerning musical styles (which can be expressed, if one so desires, in terms of information contents) thus permit an alternative approach to the insertion of what amounts to *a priori* probabilities into computer programmes for musical composition. When the *Illiac Suite* was composed, such data were not available, so the only reasonable procedure was the use of *a priori* restrictions on randomness.

There is nothing wrong with this, but the other alternative now also becomes possible. In fact, one might now suggest three basic sources of "style" available to the programer of computer music, namely:

- A priori conditions chosen by the programer, on any basis that seems justified to him, including the use of completely arbitrary restrictions.
- Statistical conditions developed from the statistical analysis of styles or procedures; this is the primary basis of the present method.

- Self-generated styles developed by the computer itself as a logical consequence of a set of initial specifications that permit this freedom of development.

The last procedure is, of course, the most sophisticated form of computer programing of musical composition because it also incorporates techniques of coding learning processes. It would seem at present the logical goal toward which present experimentation should progress. Obviously, it is also inclusive of the first two sets of conditions.

THE STATISTICAL ANALYSIS OF STYLE

If we assume that the process of musical composition comprises a series of choices involving almost every aspect of music as we know it, we observe first that the choices are not normally random, but depend on At is to follow, if that choice has already been made. If we expect a computer to choose objectively, the computer must be programed to make two basic types of choices:

- Choose factor A independent of all other factors, and
- Given another factor, B, choose A dependent on B. (B may include several factors instead of only one.) To carry out this experiment we first must determine two thing:
- What is the most logical sequence in which to make the choices?
- Which elements are influential in the choice of one another?

The answer to would seem to provide the answer to, for if we regard all elements as possible variables and if at any point we can classify these variables as either independent or dependent, the "logical" sequence would be to choose the independent variables first in each case. But once having ascertained which elements influence others, and even assuming that some outcomes are ruled out because of a preceding choice, one is still left with a multitude of possible choices. Which of these then is the most "logical" to make? Or rather, which is the most "stylistic" to make? How can we define the term "stylistic" in a useful way? At this point we propose the following answer: If, after all influencing factors are taken into account, there are still a number of possible outcomes, then that outcome is most "stylistic" which is most statistically probable.

We adopt this statistical viewpoint because the methods of traditional musical analysis have been largely confined to an objective description of certain explicit aspects of music—its form, structure, vocabulary, effect, and so on. Little attempt has been made to describe music from the composer's point of view—the compositional process itself and the reasons for having chosen a specific "outcome" from among the large number of possible "outcomes." The difficulties in making such a study are indeed enormous. We are, after all, only presented with the *fait accompli*, the finished piece of music, a series of musical facts having form, structure, relationship to one another, and providing no explicit clues as to their motivational origin in the composer's mind.

At the very simplest level of composition, the composer is conscious of a *style* and chooses elements consistent with that style. The explanation for the style itself cannot be an entirely logical argument. Style is a historically evolving and constantly mutating collective conception of the propriety or impropriety of certain musical relationships. The composer consciously or unconsciously assimilates this style and makes use of it. For example, we cannot positively account for the reasons a harmonic progression, such as dominant to tonic, is so consistently used during certain historical periods, although many acoustical reasons may be advanced. Since much speculation has already been done at this level, we propose instead merely to accept style as an established fact and to look for the reasons behind the relationships of elements at a higher level, just as the composer himself accepts style, yet must fashion out of this basic material a composition having a higher form and structure.

Such a decision, however, does not relieve one of the responsibility of describing the style, for it is certainly possible and probable that the conception of style is responsible for many of the decisions at higher structural levels.

We are aware that many musicians may take exception to the probabilistic view of style proposed here, for the term "probability" seems to imply a certain amount of randomness inconsistent with the dialectical thought processes generally ascribed to the composer. That this need not be true is not always realized. Even the most logical of systems may be described in terms of probabilities, the probabilities so assigned being either 1 or 0, complete certainty of an event's occurring, or complete certainty of an event's not occurring. No randomness is necessarily implied. If musical composition were such a system of determinate logic ruled by certain laws of combination, then it would be the purpose of this inquiry to discover these "laws." Most musicians, ourselves included, would rather take the view that music is not such a completely rigid system of logic, and that few, if any, such general and always consistent laws exist. Indeterminacy is a common and probably vital aspect of music and, as such, suggests the need for further exploration of the relation between indeterminacy and subjective response.

As an analytical tool, therefore, the computer is being programed to compute two types of probability corresponding to the two choice types mentioned previously, namely:

$p\ (A)$, simple
$p\ (A \backslash B)$, conditional

Then, for two such elements, A and B, one can compute

$p\ (A)$
$p\ (A \backslash B)$
$p\ (B)$
$p\ (B \backslash A)$

such that, if

$p\ (A \backslash B) = p\ (A)$

then also

$p\ (B \backslash A) = p\ (\text{B})$

and A and B are independent. If this is true, the sequence of choices is immaterial. If this is not true, however, we are still faced with the decision of defining the dependent and independent variables in a functional relationship.

$A = f\ (B)$, or $B = f\ (A)$

Either way will do mathematically, but for purposes of computation, it is easier to regard the one with the fewest possible outcomes as the independent variable and to make the choices in that order. We believe the composer also takes this path of reasoning.

If, however, more elements are involved, say eight, many more computations would have to be made. Specifically, for each element, we would have to compute the probability of that element, given all possible combinations of the other seven elements. This would yield

$$1 + 7 + 21 + 35 + 35 + 21 + 7 + 1 = 2^7 = 128$$

computations for each element, and altogether, $2^7 \times 2^3 = 1024$ computations for all elements. Each one of these combinations would, in turn, have to be tested against each of the others for equivalent probabilities. Not only would the sample have to be enormously large to include a significant number of all of these possibilities, but the number of computations and the amount of storage space required in the memory for these data would require a programme so long that the prospect looks hopeless. And there are far more than only eight elements of music which might be taken into account.

For this reason, we have selected certain elements from among the many for a study of their own interrelations, disregarding the others.

Since our study is largely a probability study, we shall endeavor to pick a sample to be analyzed that is large enough such that each of the possible choices for the other ignored elements will occur with a frequency proportional to its frequency of occurrence within the total population from which our sample is drawn.

If so, we shall be calculating marginal probabilities. Indeed we should be doing this, even if we were to attempt a single complete study, for it is certainly doubtful if one could even formulate *all* factors which might influence the choice of an element. One would have to take into account each composer, his age, musical background, temperament, disposition that day, the weather, and so on, *ad absurdum*. In all events, such a study would be essentially useless, for theorists are primarily interested in a generalization based on a limited number of specific conditions which seem to recur often.

The value of our study lies then, not in the extent to which we shall have described all factors influencing a choice, but rather in the extent to which we shall have generalized a large set of specific circumstances into a smaller set of cases, each with a certain probable structure. For this reason, our present approach to the problem is one of marginal probabilities. We are limiting ourselves to a study of the marginal relationships between the following three aspects of musical structure: harmony, harmonic rhythm, and tonal structure. The samples of music chosen for analysis are from the so-called classic period of the late eighteenth and early nineteenth centuries, a style that is representative of common practice in compositional procedures. Specifically, we are analyzing a set of string quartet movements chosen from the compositions of Haydn, Mozart, and Beethoven.

Again, as in the earlier studies contained in the *Illiac Suite*, in which sixteenth-century style was employed as a check procedure, we have picked a well-known style as the first basis of testing the programing. It is our intention, as we did before, later to extend these studies to more novel styles and procedures once we have basic computer processes in operation. In this way, we expect to provide the link from the traditional and recognizable through currently employed techniques to the speculative and experimental.

THE ANALYTICAL METHOD

Let us now consider a particular example of the analytical method applied to specific musical structures. Let us note also that some of its logic bears considerable formal resemblance to certain modern methods of structural analysis of tonal music, notably processes first worked out by the analyst Heinrich Schenker. In the report of the earlier experiments incorporated in the *Illiac Suite*,(4) it was observed that Schenker's ideas of structural layers in music might provide "a working technique for structural assembly... that permits the assigning of a greater or lesser value to significant musical elements, particularly in relation to the time scale of the musical structure." Our present analytical scheme may yield *quantitative* data supporting the *qualitative* results of such earlier studies. So, for purposes of analysis, let us define three significant structural levels in music as follows:

- The detailed structure as it develops from measure to measure.
- The larger sectional structures.
- The over-all tonal structure.

Let us now briefly investigate the methods applied at each level.

18.5.1 THE DETAILED STRUCTURE.

We first seek to classify the variables as either independent or dependent. In order to isolate factors of harmony and harmonic rhythm, we delete from our sample of works all passages of a modulatory nature and transpose the remaining passages into a single key. We make the assumption that transposition of a passage into another key in no way affects the probabilities involved; i.e., that the relation of one element to another remains functionally the same regardless of key. We then separate passages in the major mode from those in the minor mode and run the experiment for both modes independently. We are left, then, with essentially three variables to investigate:

- The harmony at any point in the passage,
- The duration of the harmony, and (3) the position within the bar at which the harmony begins.To determine which of these factors is dependent on one or more of the others, we then compute probabilities as follows:First, we define the symbo

If the results of these computations demonstrate that L_i is dependent on previous durations back to, and including, L_{i-k}, and that H_i is dependent on previous harmonies back to, and including, H_{i-j}, it will then be possible to calculate the conditional probabilities: And if then, L_i may be chosen without regard to the values assumed by H_i.Or, if then H_i may be chosen without regard to the values assumed by L_i.

Furthermore, one of the above can be true without the other being true. If we use the notation $y = f(x)$ to mean that x is the independent variable upon which y depends, then there are four possibilities:

- The second is true but not the first: $H_i = f(H_i)$.
- The first is true but not the second: $H_i = f(L_i)$.
- Both are true: H_i, and L_i may be chosen independently.
- Neither is true: the intersection, $H_i L_i$, must be treated as a single variable dependent on others.

The writers believe, because of compositional experience, that b. will prove to be true for certain L_i, and c. true otherwise.

Third, it is also necessary to account for the position within the measure at which the progression takes place. If P_i denotes the eighth-note position at which H_i, (and L_i) commence (1 d" P_i d" 8), then P_i is certainly a function of the preceding durations, i.e., assuming common time,

$P_i = 1 + (L_i + L_2 + ... + L_{i-1}$, modulo 8) (18.10)

Since L_i is also a function of the preceding durations, there is a relationship between L_i and P_i. Clearly the choice of P_i precedes the choice of L_i, since P_i is uniquely determined by $L_i L_2 L_3 ... L_{i-1}$ and not by L_i.

Since the sequence $L_i -_k L_{i-k} + 1 ... L_{i-1}$ could have begun at any position within the measure, we shall also have to calculate to determine whether the probabilities of L_i and H_i are affected by P_i. Details of the programing of these computations are provided by the block. The method above should either confirm or refute the hypothesis that the variable with the fewest possible outcomes may be considered the independent variable. Generally speaking, there are far fewer possible durations than harmonies.

When considering harmonic rhythm, we generally do not consider durations below the eighth-note level at a moderate tempo. A harmony rarely lasts much beyond the length of a whole note. Consequently, Li is usually confined to the range 1d"Lid"8 eighth notes. Our hypothesis, then, is that $L_i = f(P_i)$, $H_i = f(L_i, P_i)$

In other words, the composer normally chooses first

duration, then harmony, thereby insuring a maximum amount of freedom in choosing the final variable.

Why might a composer wish to insure for himself this freedom? Because he thereby reduces his chances of having to reconsider his earlier decisions. If we imagine a composer faced with a choice of duration and harmony at some point in the music, we might further imagine him following both possible sequences: If he chooses first the harmony and then duration, and if some harmonies are mutually exclusive with certain durations, the choices for duration will become few and might interfere with a good harmonic rhythm. He might then have to reconsider his choice of harmony. On the other hand, if he chooses first the duration, even though this rules out certain harmonies, enough other possibilities remain to assure a smooth harmonic progression, so that his chances of having to reconsider the original decision are smaller.

LARGER HARMONIC STRUCTURES.

Once having described "style" in terms of probabilities, we shall want to investigate harmonic structures that exist between non-adjacent harmonies. Commonly in music, certain harmonic progressions involving a set of four or five chords are used as larger structures, other chords or chord progressions being inserted between the individual members of the main progression. For example, the common progression, I, V, VI, II, V, might be expanded by the insertion of secondary dominants between each of the chords as illustrated by the example. Such insertions need not be confined to secondary dominants, of course. If we denote by Xi a chord or a set of chords form-ing a progression between the members of the larger progression and , we may describe such a structure as with the parentheses indicating that the element enclosed may or may not be present. Several questions should be raised here:

- How are the probabilities of affected by these insertions?
- Which simple progressions are suitable for expansion into a larger structure? Are any new?

- Is X_i, dependent on or on or on both?
- Is there a larger rhythmic structure governing the larger harmonic structure?
- How is the larger structure made perceptually apparent?

Without going into the details of this analysis, it is apparent that many of the previous methods for analyzing style can be again used here to analyse larger harmonic structures. Thus, if a certain structure, *S*, is found to have frequency f and the total number of structures found in the sample is *n*, then Question b. then can be answered by a comparison of this with the progressions found to be frequently occurring in the previous section. (We consider "suitable" to mean "having the highest frequency of occurence.") The writers predict that many of the larger structures will prove to be identical with the smaller; however, there may well be new progressions found also.

Concerning Question c., we shall have to define some chord, Hm, between and , such that and. If Hm is also, we may call this the "pivot chord" analogous to the "pivot chord" of a modulation. All modulations do not contain pivot chords, but there is always a point between the two keys, and , at which the harmonies cease to be a function of the preceding key and become a function of the following key. The same may be said of larger harmonic structures not involving a modulation. Accordingly, we shall have to compute some further probabilities, i.e., the probability of H_m preceding H_{m+1}, and so on. It should be noted that the probability of A following B is *not* the same as the probability of B preceding A.

TONAL STRUCTURE.

Our hypothesis is that harmonic progressions form larger harmonic structures which, in turn, may form still larger harmonic structures. These larger harmonic structures eventually become a series of modulations from key to key, forming the key structure, and certain of the keys form the structure of the composition in the largest sense, the tonal structure. If such is true, tonal structure would in the largest sense be an ever-broadening form of the simplest harmonic progressions. All levels of structures must be investigated in order to determine not only the probabilities of the various elements, but also to determine whether the "procedural" logic of one level is also valid for higher or lower structural levels. We believe such will be the case, although the probabilities of specific elements may change somewhat from level to level. If the hypothesis is correct, the sequence of choices to be made for a structure, subject to prior choices of position and length in each case, would be indicated by the arrows. In such a procedure, the structural levels might be indicated as shown. It is toward this type of scheme that our programing of the "dummy model composer" is directed.

PROGRAMING FOR MUSIC SYNTHESIS

The present programmes for music synthesis by the ILLIAC already provide certain basic procedures later to be incorporated into the "dummy model" structure. These programmes generate tones, harmonies, rhythms, and so on, but without the incorporation of style data. Therefore, the output so far produced is highly random in structure; more so, in fact, than any of the samples of random music included in the Illiac Suite, because this time we have permitted a much wider range of choice of tones and rhythms.

First, we wrote a programme to generate random numbers within certain specified limits. This programme was tested for randomness and the maximum difference in the probabilities of any two outcomes was found to be less than 0.001. Either equal probabilities (to yield random music) or unequal probabilities (to yield non-random music) may be subsequently imposed by dividing 1000 into equal or unequal blocks dependent on the set of probabilities desired. For instance, for the situation of choosing among 88 *equally* probable tones, 1000 is divided by 88 (E" 11). A number is then generated randomly between I and 1000, and whichever block of 11 it falls into is the outcome. (In this particular instance, the left-over 32 integers are discarded.) If, however, we desire unequal probabilities of, say, 0.25 for one of the outcomes and the rest equal, then a block of 250 is provided for the element having a probability equal to 0.25 and a block of 750 ÷ 87 (E" 9) for each of the others. The numbers are associated in every instance with specific choices of elements being composed.

Second, a "dummy" programme has been written that generates melodic tones and rhythms for two voices for *n* bars. A flow chart for this programme. Since no interrelation between the two voices is intended at this time, the sequence of choosing events is quite simply Voice I, then Voice II, for one bar, then recycling until *n* bars are completed. This sequence of procedural logic will be altered, once tests for correlation of voices with one another are added. In other words, it is not reasonable to expect that one voice may be completed for a space of one bar before the next voice is written, unless we use a *cantus firmus* type of procedural logic. For testing the rhythm and note generation routines, however, this is a simple yet acceptable method of progressing.

Concerning the choice of rhythms available, we have thus far confined ourselves to the most usual subdivisions of the whole note and programed only for common time, i.e., meter. The subdivisions employed include all duple subdivisions down to, and including, the thirty-second note and all triple subdivisions down to, and including, the sixteenth note triplet or "twenty-fourth note". This provides eleven possible values, all of which can be combined in any way through the use of ties to provide additive durations.

In all, then, we have the possibility of forming all possible durations which can be expressed in the form: where i=1, 2, 3,..., 32 and j=1, 2, 3,..., 24 for one measure. Furthermore, these values can be tied over the bar line, which is primarily an indexing device rather than an indication of metrical stress. This provides, theoretically at least, a virtually unlimited number of combinations of duple and triple rhythms.

The generation of tones thus far is considerably less elaborate and amounts merely to random generation of integers between 0 and 87, corresponding to the 88 tempered tones of the ordinary chromatic scale. A sample of ILLIAC output combining these two schemes of rhythm and tone generation. This highly random material serves as "raw material" from which we expect to fashion more meaningful musical structures. Third, some studies have been completed on routines to generate harmonic rhythm and root tones. In a random situation, the generation of the harmonic root is simply a choice of an integer between 0 and 11, corresponding to the 12 tones of the tempered scale, and presents no more difficulties than the generation of melodic tones. The means of generating the harmonic rhythm is somewhat more difficult, however, in that we have classified harmonic rhythms into types and variations of these types. The types correspond to the number of roots present in a bar. The variations correspond to the placement within the bar of these roots and are classified into zero, first, second, or third order, depending on the correspondence or noncorrespondence of the positions of roots with the *a priori* positions of "strong" beats within a common time measure. The rhythm exhibiting the most syncopation is classified as third order; that exhibiting the least syncopation as zero order. Moreover, a third order structure is considered a variant of a zero order structure. For our present purposes, an exact description of these classifications is unnecessary, but to show that it provides useful results, we reproduce in Figure a sample of the rhythms and roots so generated.

All types and orders are considered equally probable in this example, so it is, consequently, once again quite random in nature. For harmonic rhythm we consider subdivisions down to the eighth note only, and do not include triple subdivisions. All durations here may be expressed as $i/8$, where i=1, 2,..., 8, for one measure. Ties across the bar line can occur only if the root generated for the beginning of one measure is the same as the last root generated in the preceding bar.

To be sure, then, these programmes represent some of the actual means of achieving a choice of the various elements required. What remains to be done at the time of writing is to combine these various routines into a sequence of events wherein each is entered at the most opportune time to produce the most accurately stylistic music. Both the determination of this compositional sequence and the reduction of randomness of choice by the introduction of appropriate subroutines await analytical results. We contemplate three types of tests of the validity of the synthesis:

- Subjective tests asking qualified musicians to discuss the synthesized music in terms of stylistic integrity, structural cohesiveness, and general musical interest.
- Analytical tests by the computer itself, having the computer regard its own music as the sample and compute the probablities involved. These probabilities would then be compared to the probabilities computed for the original sample.
- Specific choice tests. A section of a piece of music would be inserted into the computer and analyzed. The computer would be instructed to choose a succeeding element based on the probabilities found from the original sample. This choice would be compared with the actual choice made by the composer.

Dependent on the success of the noted investigation, future experiments are envisioned. One logical sequence of investigations is the following:

- An investigation of harmonic elements (including inversions of triads). This is the present study and includes the melodic aspect of the bass line.
- A study of melodic elements (monophonic music).
- A study of the combinations of a. and b. above (homophonic music).
- A study of melodic and harmonic combinations of four or more voices (polyphonic music).

The completion of these studies will enable us to programme large-scale musical structures in any "style" reasonably compatible with the "dummy model" structure. Provisionally, we think that the fugue and variations forms might well provide good tests of this kind of synthesis.

An inspection of the resultant musical structures should permit at least some inferences concerning the validity of the flow charts thus far set up as representations of the logical processes required by creative musical thought.

Chapter 3

Simulation of A Brain

WHAT IS "BRAINLIKE" BEHAVIOUR?

No better introduction to the topic has been given than that offered by Turing, one of the founders of modern computing. "The brain," he said, "has the consistency of cold porridge; therefore a bowl of cold porridge is a model of the brain, so far as it goes." Such a statement leads to the realization that to create a model which is to be more than a mere collection of gadgets, one must build from the foundations.

The subject of "models of the brain" has been totally changed in the last twenty years. In the 1930's, *any* machine that copied *any* function of the brain was of interest; since on the basis of the "null" hypothesis no function could be copied, every exception was significant. Then came the general purpose computer and a realization that mechanisms existed that could carry out *any* defined piece of behaviour. With the advent of the computer, the model was required to do more than merely demonstrate that it *could* perform some function, however high in behavioral level-the interest, if any, now lay elsewhere.

It does not seem to be widely appreciated that a somewhat similar change occurred when Pitts and McCulloch showed that a net with the simple properties that are found in all nerve nets could produce all behaviors. Today, however, demonstrating that a particular net can produce a particular behaviour seems less significant; interest has centered elsewhere.

THE TWO MEANINGS OF "BRAINLIKE"

The state of science has changed grossly in the last twenty years. Before World War II, our attitude toward the brain was partly superstitious; we considered the brain to be essentially miraculous in certain aspects, and we could put no bounds on the extent of its powers. We believed that "genius" could do everything, just as the elderly gentleman who saw sparks when Sam Weller's fist hit his nose felt that "electricity" could do everything. Today we know better. The logic of mechanism has forced us to conclude that the brain is remarkable in just two respects, and no more.The two respects are clearly distinguished by whether the brain's activity is or is not being considered in relation to a defined, and previously given, goal; more precisely, in relation to the "focal condition" defined by Sommerhoff. Note, for instance, the sentence from a newspaper: Despite these difficulties, the pilot landed the plane *safely*. (In this example, whether the pilot was human or automatic is irrelevant.) The criterion of the pilot's cleverness is the word *safely*. In the landing of aircraft, there is a well-understood goal or "focal condition" that is *given*. The pilot lands and shows his cleverness by whether he does (or does not) keep several essential variables within assigned limits:

- The shock to the landing gear not to exceed so much force
- The touchdown to occur within a certain area
- The aircraft not to turn over, etc.

A HIGHLY SELECTIVE SYSTEM

A vast amount of brainlike activity can be summed up as showing high selectivity for the focal condition. This is the activity of the automatic pilot, of the control mechanisms in the petroleum refinery, of the navigator who makes an exact landfall. By what route the focal condition is reached is often irrelevant; in fact, use of an unusual route is often regarded as emphasizing the braininess, as when a chess master in a tournament achieves his mate by a route that no bystander had thought of. Be that as it may, a system's behaviour is brainlike (in the first way) when it shows any remarkable power of achieving the focal condition in circumstances that make the achievement evidence of intense *selection*.19.2.2 A Sensitive-complex-active System. The other type of behaviour that can be called brainlike occurs when the brain demonstrates that it is almost unique on this earth as a system that is

- Extremely sensitive,
- Extremely complex and richly connected internally, and
- Extremely active.

Today, of course, we know that electronic and other networks can readily provide these properties. From the days of the Greeks until World War II the brain was the sole possessor of these properties; hence all properties belonging to the sensitive-complex-active system were regarded as brainlike. They are, however, sharply distinguishable from the first type because they are neither good nor bad in themselves; they are like oxidation —neither good nor bad in itself, just a natural or inevitable process under certain conditions, and capable of being used, or *suppressed*, according to the demands of any given focal condition.

SOME COMMENTS CONCERNING BRAINLIKE ACTIVITY

At the moment, little is known of these processes, though a start has been made. The Monte Carlo methods in the computer provide examples of various sensitive-complex-active processes, and much of statistical mechanics in the past has been of this type. The theory of epidemics provides another example; and the mechanism given by the author to show why habituation is so common is of the same type.

Since all brainlike activity can be examined within these two types, there is no room today for a merely superstitious attitude that accepts the brain (whether of a "genius" or not) as capable of anything. On the contrary, today the brain's capacity is recognized to be *strictly limited*. It is obviously limited in the second type of process, for as a material system, it is going along its physically and chemically determined trajectory, no more able to produce the magical in its impulse transmissions than it can produce the magical in its oxidations. The properties that it shows are those of any system that is increasing in entropy, and those of any Markoff process as it tends to equilibrium.

But the other type of activity, the goal-seeking, is equally bounded, though this is *par excellence* the behaviour that in moderate degrees is called "intelligent" and in extreme degrees "the work of genius." Yet the work of genius is ultimately one of selection, and for selection there is the axiom true for computer and brain alike: Any system that achieves appropriate selection (to a degree better than chance) does so as a consequence of information received.

Thus the living brain is as bounded as is the computer. The superstitious idea that a "genius" can do anything is in headlong collision with the *quantitative* limit expressed in the law of requisite variety and in Shan- non's *Tenth Theorem*. If the brain, especially the human brain, seems sometimes to transcend this limit, it is because *we* fail to appreciate that what the species has learned in 2 billion years of experiencing terrestrial problems, and what the individual has learned in the years of childhood, are together providing information relevant to the problem in hand. Human beings, for instance, are peculiarly gifted when dealing with problems in three-dimensional geometry (in which they and their ancestors have lived for aeons), but when they come to topologies that are very different—that of five-dimensional geometry, for example, or that of the partly ordered set—they show much less flair. Thus, brainlike activity is to be conceived in one of these two exact senses: either it refers to a process by which information received is transformed into an appropriate selection, or it refers to any process, subject to exact laws, that is unusually complex and active and also happens to be used by the living brain.

THE DISCIPLINE OF SIMULATION

A feature of attempting to simulate brainlike activity, commented on by all who have undertaken to do so, is the rigorous, but most salutary, discipline that it imposes on the thinking of the would-be designer. First, he must define his aims precisely. Does he wish to demonstrate "coordination between muscles"? Then he must define these concepts in terms of actual behaviour. It is of little practical use today to explain "coordination" in terms of "integration," the latter in terms of a "higher level," and "higher level" in terms of "consciousness," etc. It is necessary to keep to one *region of discourse,* and the substitution of one word for another offers no solution. Even if an attempt at simulation achieves nothing in hardware, it is usually a most instructive activity, leaving the worker with a far deeper insight into the nature of the proposed phenomenon than he previously had.

LOGICAL DEDUCTION.

Simulation has so displayed the essential features of logical deduction that today any complicated logical problem (e.g., that set up by an insurance policy with many highly conditional and interrelated clauses) can be solved directly by some mechanical process that carries out the necessary operations. Again, the problem of mechanical translation has resolved itself simply into a study of the mechanics of translation—of finding in what way the given language does actually possess structure and conditionalities internally. It is this information that must be given to a translator, whether to a machine being programed or to a child learning the language. The older idea that there was a *mystique* of translation must now be dismissed as a superstition based on ignorance.

PROBLEM SOLVING.

The same problem confronts the would-be programer of a machine to play chess, or to write music like Bach's. The real problem is not to assemble the hardware, but to find the constraints, the laws, short-term and long-term, that impose on the output something of the essential structure of chess playing or Bach writing. "What do I mean by music like Bach's?" is the essential problem to be solved. This is difficult; once the answer is known, making a machine to do it is today a mere matter of routine.

SIMULATION MODELS

This type of analysis *forced* a recognition that to model an organism that would adapt to an environment implied that one must also *model an environment*—the situation is meaningless, otherwise. Here the modelmaker must seriously consider what sort of an environment he is thinking of, whether it is properly representative of some biological environment, and if not, of exactly which set of environments it is representative. Hence, it is true to say that today we not only understand better what is meant by "brainlike," but we can also see more clearly the peculiar and pervading features of the world we live in—the world that has imposed so many special characteristics on the creatures that have evolved in it.

The same analysis forces an early recognition of the *essential* relation between the phenomenon of "memory" and the fact of non-observability of some of a system's parts. If not all of a system is observable, so that its behaviour is not wholly predictable (for lack of information about the states of the unobservable parts), then predictability may be restored if the observer takes into account what the observable parts have done earlier. Explaining what happens in the present by reference to what happened in the past is the core of the phenomenon of the objective (behavioristic) aspect of memory. The attempt to simulate "memory" brings these facts very quickly to the fore.

THE NEW DYNAMICS

The "logic of mechanism," or of mathematics, which has been developed, does not attempt to dogmatize about what the real world may or may not be; its aim is to provide an absolutely unambiguous and rigorous framework of concepts and theorems in which ideas about the real world may find their exact expression. A similar and well-known example is given by the calculus, which enables the trained student to discuss velocities, rates of change of velocities, rates of change of rates of change of velocities, etc., without the least confusion. With this conceptual machinery, the student can tackle problems in the real world (that involve, say, fluctuating acceleration) with a security that is quite inaccessible to the untrained. The aim of the new logic of mechanism is to give security in discussion, not merely when the discussion is between two workers, but also when the worker discusses matters with himself, i.e., in his own thinking processes about the matter.

We will now examine some of the elementary concepts relating thinking processes to the operation of a general purpose computer. Any particular machine is defined by a set *M* of states. A watch may have its mainspring in many degrees of being wound up and its balance and other wheels in various positions; all these states form the set *M*. On the other hand, the state in which the mainspring is in three pieces, lying between the wheels, is not (usually) included in *M*. So to define *M* means simply to define and put bounds on what we are going to talk about.

Under the drives of nature—gravitational, electrical, chemical, etc.-things change; i.e., go from state to state. Of outstanding importance are those systems with the characteristic that their next state is uniquely determined by their immediately preceding state. This postulate is true of the great majority of systems that are treated in physics, and it is slowly being made true for the systems studied in physiology and psychology. When it is true, a *machine* can then be defined as a system whose behaviour corresponds to a mapping of *M* into *M*. This definition has this advantage: it directly relates the essentially behavioristic concept of "machinelike behaviour" to one of the fundamental concepts of mathematics. Once joined in this way, the concept can be related, as Bourbaki has shown, to the whole rigorous world of mathematics.

If the machine has an input, then the mapping will have the form, essentially, of a table of double entry (though it may *look* very different if written in some other form). Thus if the machine *M* has states m_1, m_2... and its input has values i_1, i_2,..., the canonical representation will be of the form shown:

If the machine is at state m_1, and the input is at state i_1, then the machine will move to m_j (where m_j is some state in *M*), and so on.

Such a form can obviously be represented in a computer, and the computer can readily be programed so that if the store *I* contains value (number) i_1, and the number in store *M* is m_1, then the number in *M* shall be changed to m_j, which it will find in the block of stores that are carrying the canonical representation.

In general, in the fully arbitrary machine, the mapping must be carried simply as a table which is to be read. Often, however, the mapping has internal relations, so that the computer can find the next value of *M* by some process. Such would happen if the new value were always $i_j + m_k$. When the computer copies some machines in this way, it is usually said to be "solving a difference equation."

There is no room here to develop the logic of mechanism fully. *Eléments de Mathématiques* gives the principles; the mathematical details can be found in *Théorie des Ensembles, especially in Fascicule de Résultats.*

WHAT IS A MODEL?

The new logic of mechanism has made possible an unequivocal answer to this question. The concept of "similarity" is well understood and exactly defined in the mathematical world of mappings, for these problems have been studied long before they were thought to have applications to brain physiology and psychology. In general, simplifying means "applying an equivalence relation," so that the set M is reduced, by grouping of its states, to a smaller set (called the "quotient" set). But if the simplifying

is not to lead to mere nonsense, the simplified form must still be a machine, i.e., a mapping. So follows the consequence that a "model" must be *the quotient set of an equivalence relation that is compatible with the original mapping,* where *compatible* means "not losing the original property of being a machine."

This definition may seem somewhat distant from everyday practice, but it has the great value that it puts an absolute stop to vague disputes about whether something is a "proper" model of something else. It makes clear that all machines that resemble another machine in some well-defined way stand in the same fundamental "model" relationship to it. It also makes clear that all models (of a given system, such as a brain) can be related (by partial ordering) in their degree of closeness to the given system.

For example, a physicist may make a model, of jelly, shaped exactly like a brain, in order to study how concussion waves travel through it. In contrast, an electrician may use, as his model of the brain, a network of wires and hardware, to study how electrical impulses travel through it. Each model might be valid and yet the two might have no point at which they could be made comparable.

Not only has the new logic completely clarified the logical basis of what is meant by a "model"—it has also shown that there is no natural reason for restricting the concept to forms made in hardware. The quotient set may be in any, form, perhaps in states of hardware or other physical forms, and also in mathematical or other symbolic forms, extending eventually even to the purely verbal form (i.e., to plain English) *provided the latter behaves with the strictest rigor and discipline.* Thus, in answering the question, "Of what use is a model?" one must bear in mind that the world of models includes the mathematical and even the precisely defined conceptual.

Since every machine corresponds to a mapping, which can always be represented by a process in a computer, and since every model of the machine is another mapping, it follows that the general purpose computer can, in principle, behave as any model of the original machine.

Thus today, not only can the computer "model" the behaviour of an airplane wing in flutter, it can also "model" the computational procedures of another computer. (This use of simulation proves to be a valuable aid in checking a computer's reliability, when a second computer of proven reliability is available.) Computer II is performing, step by step, the processes that computer I will execute if it follows its programme correctly. The word "model" today means far more than it did twenty years ago!

With such facilities available, the research worker is challenged to use his imagination and then to use the facilities. Some of the ways in which models, in the general sense, can be of use in psychology, neurophysiology, and the social sciences will now be discussed.

VALUES OF SIMULATION MODELS

19.6.1 Simulation for Vividness. Simulation may be employed to emphasize and clarify some concept. Statements about machines in the abstract tend to be thin, unconvincing, and not provocative of further thinking. A model that shows a point vividly not only carries conviction, but stimulates the watcher into seeing all sorts of further consequences and developments. No worker in these subjects should deprive himself of the very strong stimulus of seeing a good model carry out some of these activities "before his very eyes."

A good teaching course today (to show the relations between mechanism and brainlike behaviour) should contain the following demonstrations, which I believe to be minimal.

As an introduction, the Tortoise of W. Grey Walter is ideal. Its principles are simple (if the engineering details are ignored), and it vividly demonstrates that a few primary rules, operating in a suitable environment, can lead to a remarkable complexity of goal-seeking behaviour. At one stroke, the Tortoise disposes of a vast number of pseudo-philosophical questions, leaving the observer well prepared to proceed further in the theory of the subject.

After the Tortoise has given its display of rich protozoon-like behaviour, a return to more disciplined thinking is desirable. The next step is to display what can be done by a formal "machine," as a mapping. It is easily made, using discreet states and steps in time, by a set of relays whose state (at time t) changes to a state (at time $t + 1$) that is a determinate function of what was the state at time t, and also what was the state of a set of "input" relays. The determinate function can be set up on a plugboard. The author built such a machine a few years ago, and it has proved invaluable for showing how various elementary types of behaviour can be analyzed into an exactly defined mapping, and how this mapping will lead to behaviour (on a row of lamps) that is obviously of the required type. This machine makes vivid the logic of mechanism, turning it into actual behaviour while relinquishing nothing of the basic rigor.

The student is now far removed from the vague and windy world of philosophy in which most beginners live when approaching the subject of mechanism and behaviour. The next step for him is to advance to more complex behaviour while still retaining a completely rigorous grasp of what is happening. One possible machine suitable for this step is the author's Homeostat, which shows how a second-order degree of complexity in goal-seeking is logically implicit in certain general functional relationships. Other models are certainly possible here and should be made; but at the time of writing, the author knows no other.

When the student is sufficiently familiar with these machines to be able to dismiss them and their lessons as obvious, he will be ready to proceed on his own. But he himself, when he develops new processes and tries to explain them to others, will almost certainly find himself impelled to "dress up" the presentation, till it appears as a little stagelike show. For often, only when the onlooker sees the process in that form can he suddenly say, "I see what you mean." Thus, "simulation for vividness" can be regarded as a proper and important method by which science can advance.

SIMULATION AS ARCHIVE.

A second use of the model is one that has not so far developed appreciably; yet it is bound to become important in time. I refer to the use of a constructed model as an archive and repository for collected knowledge. A good example is given by our knowledge of the mechanisms at the base of the brain. Year by year, the physiologists and psychologists are adding fragments to the accumulated knowledge, and it is becoming only too evident that the parts are interrelated in a fearfully complex way. The neuronic centres responsible for reflexes and instincts act on the centres for the vegetative nervous system and on the endocrines; these act on each other, on the cerebral cortex, and on the muscles; these interact and have effects on the emotional centres, and so on, through a number of parts whose list is being added to almost daily. To describe all these parts piecemeal in a textbook of physiology and to expect the student to work out the interactions in his head is to give him a quite impossible task. It seems likely that a model must be built, either as an analog or as a programme that can be added to, so that the student and advanced worker (and perhaps the diagnostician) will have available something that can answer the various questions that can arise. The model would then itself be both archive and computer.

Something of this type has happened in economics. Tustin shows how models can be used to represent economic theories and to answer questions about their consequences.

SIMULATION FOR DEDUCTION AND EXPLORATION

Perhaps the most compelling reason for making models, whether in hardware or by computation, is that in this way the actual performance of a proposed mechanism can be established beyond dispute. In the past (as exemplified in Newton *Principia*), questions about the behaviour of a proposed mechanism were either solved by mathematics or they were merely talked about. In practice, for two thousand years, *mathematics* has meant "such processes as can be carried out with simple writing materials on not more than a few square feet of material." So mathematics tended to confine itself to the linear cases, in which solutions are often readily obtainable. This restriction was not serious in the physical sciences, in which the linear is common, but it was almost fatal in the biological, in which the nonlinear is ubiquitous and important. As a result, many biological theories and models remained untested, and doubtless many bad ones survived longer than they should have.

Note, for instance, the idea that the molar functioning of the nervous system might be explained if every passage of a nervous impulse across a synapse left it increasingly ready to transmit a subsequent impulse. Such a property at the synapse must impose many striking properties on the organism's behaviour as a whole, yet for fifty years no opinion could be given on its validity, for no one could deduce how such a system would behave if the process went on for a long time; the terminal behaviour of such a system could only be guessed.

Today, such a process can readily be programed into a general purpose computer, and the ensuing behaviour actually displayed. We may fully expect in the next decade or two to witness first a thorough re-examination of the well-known hypotheses that have come to us from the past, then the rejection of some as being quite foolish, and finally the emergence of modified forms that are ready for further testing.

Another of the questions that requires thorough testing is just what would happen if an organism lived *strictly* according to the rules of the conditioned reflex. Would it not tend to sink into an invariable routine of selfreinforcing reflexes, leading to its ultimate destruction by inflexibility? Again, what are the dynamics of a system of conductors that affect each other through a "threshold"? Such a system is very like a forest dry enough to be on the verge of spreading a fire: if the threshold (of inflammability) is just below the critical value, any fire tends to peter out; if it is just over the value, any fire tends to increase without limit, till the whole forest is burned out.

This behaviour does not sound very brainlike, but the matter cannot be discussed rigorously, for the dynamics are grossly nonlinear and the mathematics too difficult for practical use. On a computer, however, such a process can be set in motion, and one can observe what actually happens.

Closely similar to this application of models is their use for exploration. There must be many new properties to be found in a system as unusual as a nerve network—and even more in a generalized dynamics—which is subject to enough constraint to give it structure (in the algebraic sense), yet free, as the brain is, from the constraint of energy conservation. In such systems, the trend toward equilibrium implies that the dynamic laws are acting selectively to the development of states that are *peculiarly selfpreserving in relation to those laws.* These and a host of other interesting possibilities still await investigation.

Among the possibilities is one that deserves special mention. Equilibria are fundamentally important in biological systems. Homeostasis is simply another name for it, as are survival and adaptation. But the ordinary system considered in physics is usually very poor in equilibria, either having only a few, or one, or (if it is ergodic) none at all—only a perpetual wandering.

Very little attention has been given to, and very little is known about, *systems with many states of equilibrium*. Yet such systems must be important in biological theory. To have much "memory" is to be able to keep traces of physical events *unchanging in time*; and this invariance is an essential component of the concept of equilibrium. At the present time, the only non-living systems we know of with this property are such trivialities as a dish of sand, whose grains can rest in any one of a great number of configurations. However, this system is too little dynamic to show much of interest. The computer is clearly the device of choice with which to explore this interesting topic.

DIGITAL OR ANALOG?

It must be admitted at once that today's digital computers are not well suited to carrying out a process that represents the behaviour of large numbers of parts, such as those in a nerve net, that in reality act simultaneously. The reason is that today's computers mostly act by finding what part 1 would do, then part 2, and so on. Only when *all* the parts' next values have been computed can the machine compute the next value of the whole.

As a result, if the net is, say, 1000 by 1000 in parts (i.e., a million in all) and if the computation for one part takes a millisecond, the whole will take over a quarter of an hour to advance by one step in time. If the system were made of relays able to act simultaneously, the steps could be achieved at about 10 per second, i.e., about ten thousands times as fast. True some computers are now being designed so that several computations can go on simultaneously, but those who wish to explore processes of this type would do well to conside whether some analog of parts that can all act simultaneously would not be preferable.Today's so-called general purpose computer is really very specialized: it can carry out an *arbitrary* process only after the programer has exercised some ingenuity. Thus, although it can carry out an operation, such as "multiplv two numbers," readily, the programer must impose on to it a very artificial and selected sequence if it is to carry out so simple an operation (on two strings of digits) as "in between the digits of the one insert the digits of the other," though this operation, on the digits, is much simpler than the multiplication.

The truly general computer, as the logic of mechanism shows, would be a machine on which could be represented any mapping of a product set into one of its components, of $I \times M$ into M, for instance. Changes on M here represent the process, and changes on I represent arbitrary changes, imposed by the operator, on the input. So far as I know, only one machine of this type has been made (and that almost a toy). The possibility that further developments in this direction might be of use in the behavioral sciences may be worth consideration.

Chapter 4

Nerve Net Theory

James T. Culbertson, Yale '34, majored in zoology while an undergraduate, then studied philosophy and taught logic and ethics at the University of Pennsylvania until 1937*when he returned to* Yale. *Since graduating from college, his main interest has always been the mind-brain problem, as evidenced by his doctor's thesis in the philosophy of science, The Place of the Sense World in Physical Theory, Yale University,* 1940. *He taught mathematics and physics in a Navy programme and then philosophy at* Michigan State. *He worked with nerve nets on the* Committee on Mathematical Biology at Chicago, 1947-49, *and taught philosophy at the* University of Southern California*until* 1951. *He was then on the "robots team" at The RAND Corporationas research associate for two years before coming to* California State Polytechnic College *where he now teaches philosophy and mathematics.*

The psychologist wishes to understand organic behaviour—the stimulusresponse or input-output properties of animals and human beings. Until recently there had been no psychologically interesting artificial behaviour. But now we have computers and automata. The behaviour of these manmade objects shows some interesting parallels to the behaviour of natural organisms, and the study of these stimulus-response machines has suggested many possible brain mechanisms to the psychologist.

But a much more basic behavioral study investigates the general principles of behaviour regardless of how they may happen to be exhibited in this organism or that machine. This general theory of automata, or nerve net theory, uses the neuron as a universal element.

Neurons, as herein defined, are called "universal elements" because any given behaviour (set of stimulus-response properties) can be mediated by some assemblage of them. For any specified behaviour, we can design some nerve net to exhibit that behaviour.

Thus human behaviour, whatever may be its mechanisms, has some place within this general theory, and the further the psychologist extends nerve net theory the more behavioral possibilities it will reveal.

There is a great variety of hardware in electronic computers and other digital "robots." But whatever their components, the logical structure of any such devices can be represented by "neurons," very simple conducting elements, all essentially similar. The theory of automata, which includes the study of computers as a special case, analyses robots into these logically primitive components.

Neurons can form nerve nets in an infinite number of ways. The receptor neurons receive stimuli so as to start impulses into the net, which may have any number of central neurons, while impulses from the net can leave through the effector neurons to cause responses.

An impulse starting from a neuron's entrance travels to each of its exits. The time it takes for an impulse to pass all the way through a neuron and then start an impulse in another neuron (or start a response if it is an effector neuron) is the same via all exits and is called the "action time" of the neuron. Customarily, this action time—specified as the same for all neurons—is taken as the unit for measuring time. For convenience, let the action time be 1 millisecond. Then an impulse starts in the next neuron 1 ms later; in the next, 2 ms later; and in the effector neuron, 3 ms later; then, this impulse starts a response 4 ms later.

In the nerve nets below, all impulse paths through a net traverse the same number of neurons, and there are no cyclic paths. Hence the time it takes for an impulse to go all the way through any given net is the same regardless of the path it takes. This is called the "reaction time" of the net. In Figure, the reaction time is 2 ms. The reaction time is 3 ms.

THE THREE KINDS OF NEURONS

The entrance to a receptor neuron is a receptor (□) and each exit is an endbulb (• or o). Endbulbs are either excitatory (•) or inhibitory (o), both kinds being shown, for example. Each excitatory bulb, when active, tends to start an impulse from the synapse it contacts, as will be explained later; each inhibitory bulb tends to prevent such an impulse from starting.

The entrance to a *central neuron* is a synapse and each exit is an endbulb.

The entrance to an *effector neuron* is a synapse and each exit is an effector.

NEURON ACTIVITY. THRESHOLDS. PULSE REGULATION

If an impulse starts from the entrance of a neuron, then that neuron is said to "fire." Also we may say that its entrance (receptor or synapse) fires, which is taken to mean the same thing. Receptors fire because of stimuli from the environment, whereas the firing of synapses is controlled by the endbulbs contacting them. When a neuron fires, the impulse proceeds to all its endbulbs (or effectors), making them active, and then the endbulbs (or effectors) cease their activity and "die."

This is merely a convenient term for whatever it is that happens in each endbulb. So, in regard to terms, receptors, and synapses *fire*, and endbulbs and effectors *die*. In this analysis, the actual physical nature of the endbulb activity is as logically irrelevant as the nature of the impulse that leads to it. The logically important statement is merely: *If a neuron fires at any time* t *then all its endbulbs (or effectors) die at* t + *1*. The time $t + 1$ is, of course, 1 ms after t since time is measured in milliseconds.

Whether a synapse fires is determined, in part, by its threshold. The threshold of any synapse is designated by θ and equals some integer. Roughly speaking, the higher its threshold the harder it is to make it fire. Thus e = 2 on the and θ = 2 on the central neuron in Figure, etc. If the value of θ is not indicated on a synapse, it is understood that θ = 1, for example, θ = 1 at each synapse.

Synapse-firing rule: *A synapse fires at any time if and only if* E - I Ý″ θ *where* E *is the number of excitatory bulbs contacting it which die at that time and* I *is the number of inhibitory bulbs contacting it which die at that time.*

At $t + 1$ and $I = 0$, since no inhibitory bulbs contact the synapse. Since $E - I$ is less than θ, the synapse does not fire at $t + 1$. The same is true, of course, if just r_2 fires. On the other hand, if both receptors fire at t, then $E - I = 2$ at $t + 1$, so the synapse fires at t + 1.

The influence of inhibitory bulbs on the synapse of the central neuron. For example, suppose all three receptors fire at t. Then at $t + 1$ we have $E = 3$ and $I = 2$. So this synapse does not fire at $t + 1$, since $E - I$ is less than θ. On the other hand, if just r_1 and r_2 fire at t, then $E - I > + \theta$ at $t + 1$, so it fires at $t + 1$.

It is assumed that the receptors in a net are *pulse regulated* in the sense that they can fire only at integer values of t. Thus the receptors can fire only when $t = 1$, or 2, or 3, or some other integer, time being measured in milliseconds from some time origin. They cannot fire when $t = 2\frac{1}{2}$ or $3\frac{1}{4}$ or any other non-integer. Obviously, with the receptors pulse regulated, the entire net becomes pulse regulated, because the action time of each neuron is 1 ms.

INPUT-OUTPUT PROPERTIES

In a nerve net, the receptors that fire cause impulses to start into the net, and which receptors fire determines which effectors the impulses ultimately reach. These stimulus-response properties of the net can be conveniently expressed by listing for each input the resulting output. Let the receptors be labeled $r_1, r_2, r_3, \ldots, r_k, \ldots, r_n$.

The set of receptors firing at any time is the *input* at that time. The input is represented by a binary number. The rightmost digit of this number is a 1 if r_1 fires and a 0 if r_1 does not fire. The second digit (from the right) is a 1 if r_2 fires and a 0 if r_2 does not fire. The third digit (from the right) is a 1 if r_3 fires and a 0 if r_3 does not fire, etc.

In general, the input is indicated by the binary number whose kth digit (from the right) is 1 if r_k fires, and 0 if r_k does not firë. Thus, Figure represents the input where r_1 fires and r_2 does not fire. The case where neither receptor fires is called the "null" input, 00. The net in Figure has four possible inputs: 00, 01, 10, and 11. The inputoutput properties of this net are therefore completely expressed by the table

in	00	01	10	11
out	0	0	0	1

In the output row we have a 0 or a 1, according as the effector is or is not activated. So the last column, for example, shows that when both receptors fire the effector is activated. (If we altered the net so as to make θ = 1 on the synapse, then the output row would read 0, 1, 1, and 1.)

Look now at Figure, which is an arbitrarily chosen illustration. There are three receptors, so there are the inputs shown in the following table where we see that only two inputs, 001 and 011, lead to a response.

In	000	001	010	011	100	101	110	111
Out	0	1	0	1	0	0	0	0

Raising the threshold decreases the number of inputs that cause a response: e.g., if we let θ = 3 on the central neuron, we would get the output row 0, 0, 0, 1, 0, 0, 0, 0. On the other hand, lowering the threshold gives more 1's in the output row. Thus if we let θ = 1 we would have 0, 1, 1, 1, 0, 0, 0, 1. And if we let θ = 0 we would have 1, 1, 1, 1, 0, 1, 0, 1. (Note that if θ < + 0, a synapse fires spontaneously every millisecond, except insofar as it may be prevented by inhibitory bulbs.) Suppose the threshold was still lower. If we let θ = -1 the output row would be 1, 1, 1, 1, 0, 1, 1, 1; and finally for θ = -2, *e* would respond for any input.

A COUNTING NET

We shall consider now a case involving several effectors. The counting net in Figure is so constructed that its response indicates the number of receptors that fire. We may think of effector e1 as causing a "1" to appear, e.g., lighting a light bulb with a "1" on it. Similarly a "2" appears if e_2 is activated and a "3" if e_3. Thus the number of receptors firing at *t* is indicated by the response at $t + 3$; e.g., if any two receptors fire, then only e_2 is activated, as shown by the fourth, sixth, and seventh columns of the in-out table.

In	000	001	010	011	100	101	110	111
Out	000	001	001	010	001	010	010	100

The reader should examine the net to see that it has the counting properties specified above. For instance, note that if r_2 and r_3 fire, then the first two central cells fire, and then just e_2 responds, as specified in the next to the last column.

LARGER COUNTING NETS

Using four receptor, four central, and four effector neurons we can construct a net for counting up to 4. Each receptor neuron will have an excitatory bulb on each central neuron, and the fourth central synapse will have $\theta = 4$. Using this method, nets can count any number of simultaneous receptor firings.

Note that the in-out table doubles for each receptor added to the net. For three receptors there are eight possible inputs, and hence eight columns as shown in the above table; for four receptors there are 16 possible inputs:

0000, 0001, 0010, 0011, 0100, 0101, 0110, 0111, 1000, 1001, 1010, 1011, 1100, 1101, 1110, 1111

namely, the first 16 binary numbers starting from 0000. For five receptors there are 32 possible inputs—the first 32 binary numbers starting with 00000. *In general, the number of possible inputs equals 2^n, *where n is the number of receptors. Hence as n increases, the table soon becomes unhandy.*

USING THE SIMPLEST COMPONENTS

We shall assume, however, some maximum number of endbulbs that a neuron can have and also a maximum number of bulbs that can contact one synapse. If the number of receptors exceeds these maxima, some question might arise as to whether the counting net could be constructed. But there is no difficulty: For any net (counting net or any other net) there is a net satisfying the same in-out table and containing no neuron with more than two endbulbs and no synapse contacted by more than two endbulbs. In other words, we never need neurons with more than two bulbs and we never need more than two bulbs at any synapse, provided, of course, that we may increase the reaction time and also the number of central neurons.

To prove that any neuron with more than two bulbs can be replaced by a plurality of neurons each with only one or two bulbs, let a two-bulb neuron, x, contact two different two-bulb neurons. Let these two neurons each contact two different two-bulb neurons, and then let these four neurons each contact two different two-bulb neurons, etc. We see that if x fires at t then 2^k bulbs die at $t + k$. Also, substituting one-bulb neurons for two-bulb neurons anywhere desired, it is obvious that if x fires at t then 2^k bulbs *or fewer* can be made to fire at $t + k$. Hence, for any net there is some net satisfying the same in-out table and using only one-bulb and two-bulb neurons. (It is understood that time delays are introduced wherever needed by inserting neurons so that the reaction time of the net is the same for all inputs.)

To prove that any neuron contacted by more than two bulbs can be replaced by a plurality of neurons each contacted by one or two bulbs involves a proof more lengthy than the above, but perfectly straightforward, and we leave it as an exercise for the reader.

How can one design a counting net in such a way that the complexity of the components does not increase with the number of receptors? To illustrate, let us use the simplest components possible: Each neuron has only one or two bulbs and only one or two bulbs contact any synapse.

Figure shows a method whereby we can count any number of receptor firings using only these simplest components. If $n = 6$, how many central neurons would be required using this method? Note that, in general, the simpler the components, the more central cells must be used and the longer the reaction time.

These simplest components can always suffice, but to illustrate the general principles of nerve net construction, we shall hereafter use neurons with as many branches as we wish and synapses as large as we wish.

SOME OTHER NERVE NETS

There are many kinds of counting nets. Instead of a different effector responding for each different number of receptor firings, the net may count directly in the binary system. In this case, the "readout" can appear in a register in which e_1 controls the first digit window (the rightmost) and e_2 controls the second digit window, etc. The first (rightmost) digit is a 1 if e_1 responds and a 0 if e_1 does not respond. The second digit is a 1 if e_2 responds and a 0 if e_2 does not. Similarly for e_3, etc. Thus, if any one receptor fires, then the register shows the number... 0001.

If two fire, it shows...0010, etc. If, for example, eleven receptors fire, the number...001011 appears in the register. The number of 0's at the left is determined, of course, by the size of the register. Let the number of receptors be three, i.e., $n = 3$. Then there are just two effectors e_1 and e_2. We can use a two-place register and the output row of the in-out table would read 00, 01, 01, 10, 01, 10, 10, 11.

The student should see how to construct this nerve net using three receptor neurons, three central neurons, and two effector neurons. The net is exactly like Figure until we come to the connections from the third central neuron to the effector neurons. This neuron has an excitatory bulb on each of the two effector neurons (remove the third effector neuron). Thus, if h receptors fire, then the number h (expressed in the binary system) occurs in the register. The reader should now diagram a binary counting net for $n = 4$, by putting in another receptor cell, another central cell, and another effector cell. Thus he will become more skilled in this game of small nerve nets, where general principles of in-out digital devices can be illustrated in miniature.

The effectors of the counting net could operate a register in which the readout was in the decimal system. This would obviously require more central neurons.

Counting nets can be used to discriminate lengths, areas, and intensities, or any other properties of the stimulus configuration that can be measured by a number. Also they can form parts of numerical nets for adding, subtracting, multiplying, and dividing. To illustrate, the student might design a subtracting net, say with two receptors labeled p_1 and p_2 and two receptors labeled q_1 and q_2. We want the response to indicate the number, *m*, of active *p*-receptors minus the number, *s*, of active *q*-receptors. The effectors can be labeled *e*-2, *e*-1, *e*0, *e*1, *e*2, the subscripts being the five possible values of *m* - *s*. He should construct the net so that if *mp*-receptors fire and *sq*-receptors fire then just e_m-*s* responds Δms later, where A is the reaction time. For instance, if two of the p-receptors and one of the *q*-receptors fire at *t*, then just e_1 responds at *t* + Δ. Should he find this miniature subtracting net interesting, he might design a multiplying nerve net: The response is to indicate the number of active p-receptors times the number of active *q*-receptors.

We have examined counting nets for counting simultaneous events but there are also nets for counting successive events and nets for any other numerical or logical operations. We have stressed the counting net only because it is an easily understood example for illustrating certain properties true of any net.

FORM PERCEIPTION

Let us see how a net can perceive shape or form. In the nets below, the form is not abstracted from its position, size, and rotation. This is a very serious restriction, because the shape the net is constructed to recognize can elicit the response only if it has some fixed position, size, and angular rotation. There are nets, larger than we can examine here, that can perceive the specified shape or shapes abstracted from the Gestalt transformations of position, size, and rotation. Thus a net can be designed to recognize, for instance, an F wherever it may fall on the retina (array of receptors over a surface) or whatever size it may be (within obvious limits) and however it may be tilted.

Effector e responds at *t* + 2 if, and only if, r_1, r_2, and r_4 fire at *t* and r_3 does not fire at *t*. This is a response to an extremely simple image, 1011. The method illustrated is completely general, however complex the image. It is required that effector neuron g fire only for some given subset S of the net's receptors. On g, let each receptor neuron have either an excitatory or an inhibitory bulb, according as either it is or is not a member of S, and let $\theta = m$ where m is the number of members of S. Then g fires only for S.

The student should design the following nerve net using the method described and illustrated above: Given seven receptor neurons and an effector neuron g, design a net such that g fires just for the image 1101101. Remember the right-to-left convention, whereby the state of r_1 is indicated by the rightmost digit.

Clearly we may have any number of effectors, each recognizing a different image: Given six receptor neurons and two effector neurons, g_1 and g_2, design a net such that g_1 fires just for the form 101110 and g_2 just for the form 110101. Here each receptor neuron will have two branches, one going to g_1 and the other going to g_2.

NETS TO SEE IMAGES RESEMBLING A GIVEN IMAGE

Certain images resemble each other more closely than do others. Thus 1001 resembles 1011 more closely than 0100 resembles 1011. Now we wish to alter the net so that it responds not only to this "just right" image, but to the four other forms that most closely resemble this just right image, namely, 0011, 1001, 1010, and 1111. (Each of these differs from 1011 in only *one* digit.) What change must we make in the net? Obviously, all we need to do is lower the threshold from 3 to 2. The resulting output is shown in the third row of the table. Furthermore, suppose we wish the net to respond not only to 1011 and to the four images that differ from 1011 in just one digit but also to the eleven that differ from 1011 in *two* digits. For this, we lower the threshold to 1, as shown in the fourth row.

In general, consider any net constructed so as to respond to one just right image where the net has n receptors and m of them are in S. Then, on g, $\theta = m$ as indicated. Now lower the threshold so $\theta = m\text{–}k$. Then the net will respond to exactly N

images each differing from the just right form in k digits or less, where

Here$_n$ C_i means the number of combinations of n things taken i at a time.

The little squares are receptors in a retina. Suppose the blacked squares indicate the particular image that the net (not shown) is to recognize. Following the method outlined in Section, we let each blacked receptor neuron have an excitatory bulb on the effector neuron g and each unblacked neuron have an inhibitory bulb on g. And we let $\theta = m$ where m is the number of blacked receptors. Then g will fire if, and only if, the F image falls on the retina precisely as shown in the figure. This is a very strict requirement. There is a response if, and only if, every blacked receptor fires and no other receptor fires. Only the specific image is adequate. Suppose we constructed this nerve net with all the accessories and environment of a bibliophile, lenses for focusing images, nerve nets for turning pages, etc. Still the probability of the just right F image hitting the retina might be very small.

Making $\theta = m - 1$ would be slightly more practical, since not only the just right image but any one of n other nearly right images could fire g; that is, any image resembling the just right image except that either one unblacked (background) receptor fires or else one blacked receptor fails to fire.

Making $\theta = m - 2$ would allow ${}_nC_2$ additional inputs to fire g, these resembling the just right image a little less closely. Making θ = m - 3 would allow nC3 more inputs to fire g, etc. As we lower the threshold, considerable image tolerance develops. The image can be wobbled around a little or be slightly deformed, small lacunae can occur within the figure and small islands outside it in the ground. There would be some optimum value of θ, depending in part on the size of the retina and on how much we would allow an image to differ from the standard F image and still be able to elicit a response.

This net recognizes a form in a particular position and size with as much tolerance as we want, as mentioned above. But it does not recognize the abstract form. That is, we cannot move the F sidewise or vertically, or change its size, or rotate it except within the limits of tolerance. There are, however, as we have already said, some very nice form abstractors, such that g would fire even though the F image was moved about on the retina, or changed in size, or rotated, or replaced by its mirror image. These nets have many central cells and would require a longer discussion than we can give here. But the above net is a very important accessory whereby we could get very good results with a very "cheap model" form abstractor. Of course, many different images can be run through the same form abstractor and then diverted to their different appropriate effectors.

NETS SATISFYING IN-OUT TABLES AND OTHER CONSTRAINTS

Given a net, it is easy, though perhaps tedious, to determine its in-out properties by examining thresholds and endbulbs at synapses. We can express these properties by an in-out table so that for any input we can read, from the table, the resulting output.

It is, however, the more interesting reverse problem that we wish to examine here. Given the in-out table, how can we construct a net that will satisfy that table? In addition to the in-out table there may be some other constraints, such as limiting the number of central neurons allowed or the reaction time.

We shall continue to use our miniature nerve nets as illustrations. A typical problem would be—using only two central neurons, design a net satisfying the in-out table:

In	000	001	010	011	100	101	110	111
Out	1000	1011	1000	1011	1000	0110	0110	0110

In working out this problem, we note first of all that there are three receptors, since each input is a three-place number, and there are four effectors. Draw in the receptor neurons r_1, r_2 and r_3 and the effector neurons with effectors e_1, e_2, e_3, and e_4, leaving enough room for the central neurons. Then figure out how to connect the receptor neurons to the two central neurons and then the central neurons to the effector neurons and the thresholds so that the above in-out table is satisfied.

The beginner may encounter difficulty in solving certain problems in this game of miniature nerve nets. (If the reader finds difficulty with the foregoing problem, he might try the simpler nets in the next paragraph first.) For any problem to be meaningful, it must, of course, present a bona fide in-out table; e.g., the outputs must all have the same number of digits and the number of columns must be 2^n where n is the number of digits in each input. For a solution to be possible, the constraints must be such that a net satisfying them can actually be designed. For each inout table, some minimum number of central neurons is required. We can use more than this minimum number of, neurons in designing the net, but of course we cannot use fewer.

Consider, for example, the problem: Without using any central neurons, design a net satisfying the in-out table whose output row is 0, 0, 0, 1.

Also consider the same problem except that the output row is to read 1, 1, 0, 1. Again the solution is very simple. But now consider the problem: Without using any central neurons, design a net satisfying the in-out table whose output row is 1, 0, 0, 1. This problem has no solution since two central neurons are needed for these inout specifications. The student should draw this net using two central neurons. Also he should do the same given the output row 0, 1, 1, 0.

Without using any central neurons, design a net satisfying the in-out table whose output row is 001, 000, 011, 010, 101, 100, 111, 100. Using no neurons with more than two endbulbs and no synapses contacted by more than two endbulbs, design a nerve net satisfying the in-out table whose output row is 000, 011, 000, 011, 000, 110, 110, 110.

In Section 20.13 we shall see that for any given in-out table it is theoretically possible to design a net that satisfies that table. By *theoretically possible* we mean that there is no uncertainty as to procedure. Of course, for a large net it might not be feasible to design the net, just as it would not be feasible to write down the first 10^{100} integers using paper and pencil, although this is theoretically possible; i.e., there is no uncertainty about the procedure.

THE NUMBER OF BEHAVIORALLY DIFFERENT NETS

To speak of the behaviour of a nerve net we shall suppose it is to be inserted in, and part of, a robot. The receptors are at fixed places on, or in, the robot, and the effectors contact output power devices of some kind (muscles, motors, etc.). The receptors differ in position and they may also be of different kinds (photoceptors, chemoceptors, tactile receptors, etc.), so the firing of one set of receptors is always a different input from the firing of any other set of receptors. Similarly, the effectors differ in position and perhaps also in kind, so the activity of one set of effectors is a different output from the activity of any other set of effectors.

Now let us consider a robot with n receptors and ì effectors and see how many behaviorally different ways the n receptors and ì effectors could be interconnected by a nerve net. We may think of the n receptors and ì effectors as already fixed in the robot, and now we wish to investigate the number of behaviorally different ways a net could interconnect them.

The input row in the table of any net is determined merely by how many receptors it has, and then the output row is filled in according to the in-out properties of the net. It is interesting to see how many different in-out tables there are for n receptors and ì effectors. It is interesting because the number of such in-out tables (for a fixed value of n and a fixed value of ì) is so much larger than one might at first suppose.

Consider, for example, nets with three receptors (n = 3) and three effectors (ì = 3).

How many behaviorally different nets are there? Two nets differ behaviorally if, and only if, their in-out tables differ. Here a little arithmetic shows us that there are 16,777,216 behaviorally different nets with three receptors and three effectors. Each of these is indicated by a different way of filling in the output row below.

in	000	001	010	011	100	101	110	111
Out								

There are eight ways to insert the output for the input 000 and eight ways to insert the output for the input 001, etc. Hence there are 8^8 behaviorally different nets having three receptors and three effectors. Each would give us a behaviorally different robot.

Of course, one robot is completely paralyzed (all 0's in the output row), and 195,840 of them are partially paralyzed (one or two effectors never respond), but the vast majority of them make use of all their effectors.

A small percentage of the robots are partly or completely paralyzed as just mentioned, and also the same small percentage have one or more continously active effectors, and likewise a few have only two or three responses. There are, however, 8! = 40,320 of them that give a different response to each input, while only eight give the same response to all inputs. It might be interesting to classify the behaviorally different cases, but that is not our purpose here. In this section, we merely wished to point out that if a nerve net has n receptors and ì effectors, then there are 2^{i2n} behaviorally different ways it could be constructed.

NETS SATISFYING ANY GIVEN IN-OUT TABLE

We were given in-out tables and then found nerve nets to satisfy them. In each case, we designed a net with behavioral properties satisfying the table. One might ask whether there is any in-out table for which no net can be designed. The answer is "no." Given any in-out table there is some net satisfying it. Moreover there is a general method for constructing the net. We wish to explain this general procedure here.

By this means, we can design a net having any in-out properties we want.All reaction times will be 3 ms, using this method, and the essential feature of the method is that there is a different central neuron for each input—each input causes its specific central neuron to fire. Only one central neuron can fire at a time, the one specific to the input that has occurred 1 ms before.Perhaps the easiest way to explain will be to take a simple example first and then give the completely general directions later. Let us construct the net satisfying the in-out table

in	00	01	10	11
out	011	010	100	110

The table shows two receptors (and hence $2^2 = 4$ inputs) and three effectors. We proceed as follows:

- Draw in the two receptors r_1, r_2, the three effectors e_1, e_2, e_3, and four central neurons.
- Label the central neurons with the input numbers.*
- On each central neuron let θ equal the number of 1's in its label.
- On each effector neuron let $\theta = 1$.
- Let r_k have one bulb on each central neuron. This bulb is excitatory or inhibitory, according as the kth digit in the neuron's label is a 1 or a 0.

The general method

- Let each central neuron, c, have an excitatory bulb on e_j, if, and only if, the jth digit in the output for the label of c is a 1.

Regarding step 5, note that r_1 has an inhibitory bulb on the first central cell because the first (rightmost) digit in the cell's label is a 0, and r_1 has an excitatory bulb on the second central cell because the first digit in that cell's label is a 1, etc. Similarly r_2 has an inhibitory bulb on the first central cell because the second digit in the cell's label is a 0, and r_2 has an inhibitory bulb on the second central cell because the second digit in its label is a 0, etc.

Regarding step 6, note that the first central cell contacts e1 and e2. This follows from the fact that input 00 is to have the output 011 according to the in-out table. Similarly step 6 indicates the other throughput to output contacts.

The student should check the net carefully to see that its behaviour is that specified by the in-out table. Also he should try one or two other examples to develop confidence that he can design a nerve net with any given in-out properties. The procedure is made general by substituting the following for step 1: Draw in the n receptors $r_1, r_2, \ldots, r_k, \ldots, r_n$, the ì effectors $e_1, e_2, \ldots, e_j, \ldots, e_ì$, and 2^n central neurons.

Use the general method to design a net satisfying the in-out table whose output row is 01, 01, 01, 00, 10, 11, 00, 10. Fill in the output row of an eight-column table in any way and then design the net having the indicated behavioral properties.

The general method always uses more central neurons than needed; i.e., no in-out table requires 2^n central neurons; however, it is a completely systematic method.

In this general method, each receptor neuron has n endbulbs, and n endbulbs contact each central neuron. But the general method can easily be modified so that no neuron has more than two endbulbs and no more than two endbulbs contact any synapse.

The general method can be applied to inputs over time so that the output at $t + 3$ can be a function of *all* the inputs before *t*. This gives a "complete" robot, able to respond in any desired way to any given circumstances and past history of experience. Though interesting in principle, the general method could not be applied in any actual case unless the number of receptors was quite small.

By means of nerve nets, we can design any prescribed artificial behaviour, including, for example, the simulation of human behaviour. Note, however, that nerve net theory, as part of the general theory of automata, is quite independent of animal and human neurophysiology. Nerve net theory merely says that if neurons (as herein defined) are put together in such and such ways, then certain behavioral properties will result, and if they are put together in such and such other ways, then other behavioral properties will result. Nerve net theory implies nothing at all about animal or human nervous systems. It is not an empirical investigation.

ARTIFICIAL SUBJECTIVE PHENOMENA

In the nerve net analysis of artificial behaviour, we saw how the state of the nerve net at any time was determined by the preceding state, and we traced these states through the nerve net from the receptors to the effectors. In the analysis of artificial behaviour, we were interested in showing how the structure of the net gave it certain in-out properties.

If, on the other hand, we examine the structure of the *impulses* passing through the net, we have a possible analysis of the mental events or subjective phenomena that accompany the net's activity. The impulses passing through the net join together at synapses and separate where neurons branch. Thus the impulses passing through a nerve net form a network of impulses in space-time. Consider, for example, the nerve net in Figure. The space-time network of impulses passing through this net is determined by the input and by the properties of the net. Suppose, for example, that r_1, r_2, and r_5 fire at some time *t*. In this space-time graph of neuron impulses, the point p_1 for instance, is the firing of r_1 at time *t*.

The network of impulses in Figure is a subspace of space-time in which it is embedded. Let us define this particular network or subspace, as the "psychological space" of the net for the input 10011. When distances are measured in this psychological space, they must be measured *along the impulse network*. For example, what is the psychological distance (as opposed to physical distance) between the firing of r_1 and the firing of r_2? Measuring along the network, we find that it is 2 ms. On the other hand, the distance between the firing of r_2 and the firing of r_5 is 4 ms.

Proceeding in this way, considering the network of impulses (a subspace of space-time) as a "psychological space," we can work out the rules of measurement in this space. This gives us, we believe, an analysis of artificial sense data.

Chapter 5

Advances in Biomedical Science and Diagnosis

THE NEED

Already there has been extensive use of computers in technology, business, and the physical sciences. But in the biomedical sciences their use has barely begun. In the future, however, perhaps the greatest utilization of computers will actually be in the biomedical sciences.* The problems that arise here characteristically involve large masses of data and many complicated interrelating factors, and it is just these types of problems for which computers are primarily suited. Also of great significance are the recent dynamic changes taking place in the biomedical fields themselves. For example, biological processes are now being examined in terms of atomic structures, energy levels, binding forces, molecular configurations, and the kinetic and thermodynamic details of biochemical reactions. Increasing quantization, with concurrent emphasis on the biophysical and physiochemical bases of biological systems, is rapidly bringing a large portion of biomedical science to a point where complicated mathematical manipulations and mass data reduction and analysis are absolute prerequisites to further progress.

At the present time, however, only about 5 per cent of digital computer time in university laboratories is devoted to biomedical research. For example, the Cooperating Colleges of New England, comprising some thirty universities and colleges which utilize the computer laboratory at the

Massachusetts Institute of Technology, report * that only 6.8 per cent of the computer time is spent in the biological sciences, and of this 1.7 per cent is used in crystallography, 0.8 per cent in agriculture, and 3.9 per cent in psychology, leaving only 0.4 per cent of the computer time for use in what might be called "pure" biomedical research. Hence the need arises for biomedical research workers to have a greater understanding of the capabilities and advantages of electronic computers and for a greater stimulation of the use of computers in biomedical research.

MAIN ADVANTAGE

Of course, currently many hundreds of applications of computers are being studied throughout the country in the biomedical sciences. Most of these are being made by relatively isolated research workers who, with only few exceptions, have extensive crossdisciplinary backgrounds. They include professors of anatomy who are also X-ray spectroscopists, physicians who were once electrical engineers, biophysicists and physiologists who were originally physicists, psychologists with extensive mathematical background, and others. As in any new field, the research workers involved are only recently becoming aware of each other's work.Many of these applications utilize the computer as a rapid calculator that can perform complex mathematical and logical operations more conveniently and often more economically than could be done by manual means.

However useful computers may be for such jobs, their greatest advantage does not derive merely from ability to calculate rapidly. Rather, electronic computers are significant because they *can make feasible the solutions to problems that could not otherwise be approached*. Thus computers can enable theories to be explored, experiments to be performed, and data to be collected which would otherwise be impracticable; thus, computers greatly extend the biomedical research worker's range of capabilities.21.1.3 Point of View. It is, of course, impracticable to review here those hundreds of applications already in progress, or the many more that are being proposed.

Hence, we shall mention only sufficient applications to indicate the immense potential of this powerful new tool. It is most convenient to consider the applications in four basic (but inevitably overlapping) categories:

- Numerical solution to equations of biological importance
- Simulation of biological systems
- Biomedical data processing
- Computer aids to medical diagnosis

After a general discussion of these categories, specific illustration's will be cited in order to give the reader a concrete idea of the role of the computer in advances in biomedical science and diagnosis.

NUMERICAL SOLUTION TO EQUATIONS OF BIOLOGICAL IMPORTANCE

BIOLOGICAL EQUATIONS

One method for studying a biological phenomenon is to make some hypothesis concerning its mechanism, write the corresponding (in general, differential) equations, and compare the solutions of the equations with experimental data. If the solutions do not agree with the data, the hypotheses are altered, and the process is repeated. This method has been used for centuries in the physical sciences. In many instances, it is not too difficult to write mathematical equations to describe a complex phenomenon reasonably; more often than not, however, such equations cannot be solved by conventional analytic methods. Yet with the utilization of electronic computers, they may frequently be solved numerically. Indeed, the numerical solution is often the most desirable, since it can be compared directly with the experimental data.

To illustrate the role of the computer in generating numerical solutions to biological equations, we shall briefly consider three examples:

- Analysis of the pupil servomechanism;
- Theory of neuron signal conduction; and
- Calculation of compartmental rate exchange

parameters. The first of these examples describes the work of L. Stark in quantitatively investigating a problem in biocontrol engineering (or analysis of reflex actions). The application of servo-control engineering to the analysis of reflexes by means of computers opens a new approach to a quantitative and unified understanding of reflex controls and interrelationships of the human nervous system. The second example is concerned with the now famous Hodgkin-Huxley equations, whose work was actually carried out by hand computation. The third example describes a development made important by the extensively used radioactive tracer techniques which are applied to diagnosis and clinical research.

PUPIL SERVOMECHANISM

The reflex under study was the change of size of the pupil with light intensity entering the eye. The changing size of the pupil was measured for various light intensities by means of a pupillometer. Critical experiments were performed by having the incident light intensity under the control of the pupil size by means of an external feedback loop. The reflex control loop under study is diagramed, where the goal was to find the precise mathematical expression for the "transfer function" $G(s)$ which describes in quantitative terms the relation between the incident light and the pupil adaptation as controlled by the brain's reflex mechanism. Of course, the method is to guess at certain forms for the function $G(s)$, and then check the computed result with the experiment. However, other experiments can assist in determining $G(s)$. For instance, by utilizing a small beam, the changing size of the pupil will not affect incident light intensity—this is called "opening the loop." By putting the beam of light on the edge of the pupil, a small change in pupil size will have a larger effect than normal—this is called instituting "high gain." The pupil response to such artificial stimuli was

used to aid in studying the function $G(s)$. In this way, Stark has shown that a reflex can be analyzed in a manner similar to that for an electronic feedback control or servomechanism, and in fact, the same mathematical methods employed by the servo-engineer and developed for feedback control analysis can be used for the biocontrol systems as well.

NEURON SIGNAL CONDUCTION.

A major advance in neurophysiology has been made by A. L. Hodgkin and A. F. Huxley by their mathematical formulation of equations for nerve membrane currents, which also may apply to muscle membrane. These equations have been extremely effective in predicting many phenomena of classical axon physiology, including thresholds, action potentials, and excitation changes (such as prolongation of action potentials) due to variation in temperature and drug effects. The equations themselves are based on a model, but the form of the functions, as well as constants that enter into the model, are essentially empirical and based on experimental curve fitting. In this sense, many questions are left unanswered concerning origins of the mechanisms described by the equations. On the other hand, the accuracy and range of predictions that can be produced by computations using these equations are great.

Thus the results of various numerical computations based on the equations can be an effective aid to the precise formulation of further investigations and analysis of future experimental results. The equations are sufficiently complicated to require the use of a computer for predictive or other numerical investigations.

The propagation of the action potential and the electrical circuit equivalent of an axon. To describe the mechanism of nerve conduction briefly, we can consider the nerve fibre as a long cylindrical tube with a surface membrane separating two aqueous solutions. In the outside medium, more than 90 per cent of the osmotic balance across the membrane is made up of sodium (Na) and chloride (CI) ions; while inside most of the osmotic balance is made up of potassium (K) and various organic anions, less than 10 per cent being accounted for by the Na and Cl ions. By using very fine micropipettes, it is possible to penetrate the membrane without serious mixing of the inside and outside aqueous fluids and to measure the potential difference between inside and outside. This difference is about 80 millivolts (mv) across the membrane, and there are no detectable potential differences within the interior. If the voltage is applied to the inside of the membrane by a microelectrode, the membrane potential inside is raised, and then dies out, unless the inside potential is raised above the threshold, in which case the complete action potential develops. After the action potential decays, the nerve fibre in that area becomes temporarily inexcitable.

The explanation of these phenomena—i.e., the model upon which the Hodgkin-Huxley equations are based—is roughly as follows: The Na permeability of the membrane is raised by the stimulating depolarization of the axon. If the threshold level is reached, the Na conductance of the membrane increases rapidly, and the interior of the fibre becomes positive. The Na permeability is then switched off, the membrane becomes permeable to K, and a large K conductance is developed, lowering once more the inside potential to its resting state. Note that the electrical return of the system is not brought about by a reversal of ionic movement, but rather by successive permeability changes, at first to Na and then K. The rate constants of these changes and their time course of decline have been determined experimentally by A. L. Hodgkin and A. F. Huxley. Although for one stimulation the total ion transfer is very small, it is clear that there must be a way to pump the Na out of the inside of the membrane and to replenish the K. These are evidently long-term phenomena that can be ignored during an action potential description.

We have included a membrane capacity C and a leakage aspect, as well as the K and Na conductances, which are $1/R_K$ and $1/R_{Na}$ respectively. Thus, if *V* is the inside potential difference from its resting value, a is the radius of the axon, *R* is the inside resistance per unit length, *x* is the distance along the axon, and *t* is time, then is a partial differential equation describing the function $V(x, t)$. Actually the situation is more complicated than this, since $1/R_K$, $1/R_{Na}$, and $1/R_{C1}$ are themselves each determined by differential equations, because they are time dependent.

COMPARTMENTAL RATE EXCHANGE

Radioactive tracer measurements require extensive computer-aided reduction if they are to be used quantitatively and accurately for diagnostic purposes. For example, a certain amount of radioactive iodine may be injected into the patient for an investigation of hyperthyroidism.

Then the amount of radioactive substance is measured as a function of time in such "compartments" as the blood iodide, thyroid gland, protein-bound iodine, feces, and the excreted urine.

Then, if $q,(t)$ represents the amount of radioactive material in compartment i at time t, the rates of change of radioactive material can be expressed by where the constant ëij is the fractional turnover rate of radioactive material from compartment j to compartment *i*. These are called "rate exchange equations." We have five compartments (where we have taken $\lambda_{12} = \lambda_{23} = \lambda_{31} = \lambda_{14} = \lambda_{35} = 0$). The computer problem is to fit the data measured from the patient to the solution of a set of such equations in order to determine the ëij for the patient.

Then, for example, $\lambda_{21}/\lambda_{41}$ or λ_{32} may be indexes of disease, i.e., symptoms. Many problems associated with such a technique—such as uniqueness of the computed results, consistency of redundant information, statistical variations, etc.—are still being worked out.

The method is not unique to thyroid dysfunction. Radioactive chromium and cobalt are traced in connection with the leukemias and anemias; radioactive iodine and copper are traced for kidney and liver dysfunction tests, pancreatic insufficiency, gall bladder disease, circulatory diseases; radioactive-carbontagged chemicals can be used for pinpointing specific metabolic pathway dysfunctions. Computer-aided quantitative tracer analysis opens up entire new fields of specific diagnostic analysis.

SIMULATION OF BIOMEDICAL SYSTEMS

BIOMEDICAL SYSTEMS

Complicated and highly involved phenomena, such as entire biological systems, can be analyzed by means of computer simulations. Usually a great deal is known about the localcomponent aspects of such a system, but a study of how these many complicated parts combine to make the whole has not heretofore been generally feasible because of the immense amount of calculation required.

These calculations can frequently be accomplished, however, if the functional equations of the component parts and their interaction rules are assembled on a digital computer. A computer simulation can advance:

- The study of a complicated system as an integrated result of many individual, interacting component parts,
- The evaluation of the relative influence of each small component in relation to the whole system,
- The testing of hypotheses about a part of a system for consistency with known data about the whole system, and
- The designing and planning of future, more critical experiments concerning still unknown components of the system. Unfortunately, although many large-scale system simulations have been carried out on digital computers in the military and business fields, few if any have been accomplished in the biomedical field.

We now present three examples of the simulation of biomedical systems. (Brain and neuron net simulations are discussed elsewhere in this book; hence we shall not consider these important simulations here.) The first simulation to be briefly described is that of the circulatory system; the second, that of "teaching" a rat; the third concerns word-frequency distributions.

In order to present the concepts involved, we have chosen to present stylized and grossly simplified versions of such research, containing the essence of the simulational technique and concepts utilized.

SIMULATION OF THE CIRCULATORY SYSTEM

H. Warner investigated a simulation of the heart and circulatory systems by means of an analog computer. The simulation itself consists of a hypothesis about the interrelationships between the heart and the rest of the circulatory system, in the form of simultaneous differential equations. Figure shows the division used of the heart and circulatory system into six compartments for the purposes of the simulation. These compartments are right ventricle, pulmonary arteries, pulmonary veins and left atrium, left ventricle, aorta and arterial bed, and body system veins and right atrium. The order in which these compartments are named is also the order in which the blood passes through them. Of prime interest in the simulation are the relationships between the blood pressure, P_i, and volume, V_i, within each compartment, and the flow, F_i, of blood from one compartment to the next.

The different roles played by the ventricles during systole and diastole (i.e., contraction and subsequent expansion of the heart, pumping blood out and being refilled, respectively) should be observed. During the systole, the blood flow between the right atrium and the right ventricle, F_i, and the flow between the left atrium and the left ventricle, F_4, both become zero; the ventricles are pumping blood into the pulmonary and sys-tem arteries. Analogously, during diastole, F_2 and F_5 both become zero; the ventricles are being refilled from the atria. The ventricles have been repeated, once for systole and once for diastole, since different sets of equations govern them at those times. The initial conditions at P_1 and V_1 for systole are the final values of P_1 and V_1 resulting from diastole; conversely, the initial conditions at P_1 and V_1 for diastole are the final values of P_1 and V_1, resulting from systole. Similar remarks apply to P_4 and V_4. These observations are indicated by the dashed lines in the figure.

A more complicated simulation might also include the

effects of the temperature, heart rate, blood chemistry, etc. Were its parts proved reasonably accurate, such a simulation could be applied directly for clinical use. For example, suppose the state of a patient's circulatory system, as measured by clinical and laboratory tests, was entered into a computer coded to simulate the circulatory system. The computer could then determine the future course of the patient's circulatory system. Were this course predicted to be unsatisfactory, various therapeutic measures could be evaluated by means of the simulation until some maximum effective measures were determined.

TEACHING A RAT

This study is concerned with the simulation of animal learning; it presents an excellent example of the Monte Carlo technique. The computed simulation-model results can be compared with data obtained from laboratory animals. By adjusting the ingredients of the model until it compares favorably with experiment, the learning process may be studied; when an "accurate" model has been obtained, the effect of varying parameter values may be investigated on the computer; based on this information, new and more critical experiments may be designed, and so forth.

The particular model to be described assumes that a rat is presented with a decision-making problem in order to obtain his food. The animal is repeatedly confronted with the same set of n alternatives, say n doors in different shapes. The rat is rewarded for a "correct" choice by food; it is punished for "incorrect" choices by a shock. To be specific, let us say there are four possible mutually exclusive and exhaustive choices (i.e., the rat chooses one and only one of the four doors), and let p_0, p_1, p_2, p_3 represent, respectively, the probabilities of the four outcomes of the "choosing event." These probabilities represent the random factors of the animal's actions in the choice. Associated with each choice, for example, the ith choice, is another event, the "learning event" which, say, has three possible mutually exclusive and exhaustive outcomes, with probabilities respectively (π_{i0}, π_{i1}, π_{i2}); these probabilities reflect the random factors associated with the learning effect of the "reward" or "punishment" following the ith choice. The outcome of the "learning event" in turn influences the "choice" probabilities.

This is taken into account by associating with each learning outcome, say the ikth outcome, a set of "reinforcement" values (β_{ik}, β_{ik}, β_{ik}, β_{ik}), which are then used to modify the choice probabilities (p_0, p_1, p_2, p_3) as follows: where p02, p12, p22, p32 are the new or reinforced-choice probabilities for the next round. In this way the choice probabilities become changed as the animal "learns"; in fact, the successive values of the probabilities on successive rounds of the teaching process represent the process of learning by the rat.

Summarizing, then, the procedure is as follows: A random number is chosen, and one of the choice-event outcomes is thereby determined according to the probabilities (p_0, p_1, p_2, p_3). Associated with each choice is another set of outcomes to the learning event, to which are also associated a set of probabilities, i.e.,

Choice outcomes	Probabilities.	Learning outcomes	0	1	2
0	p_0		π_{00}	π_{01}	π_{02}
1	p_1		π_{10}	π_{11}	π_{12}
2	p_2	π_{20}	π_{21}	π_{22}	
3	p_3	π_{30}	π_{31}	π_{32}	Probabilities

where for each of the 4 × 3 = 12 choice-learning-outcome combinations there is a set of reinforcement values (β_{ik}, β_{ik}, β_{ik}, β_{ik}) Thus, a second random number is chosen, and one of the learning events is thereby determined from the appropriate set of probabilities (π_{i0}, π_{i1}, π_{i2}). Having determined, therefore, a particular ikth choice-learning outcome for the rat's behaviour, the reinforcement values are utilized to determine the new set of choice probabilities for the next round.

Will such a process "settle down"; i.e., will the choice probabilities (p_0, p_1, p_2, p_3) approach limiting values, or will they tend to oscillate? What is the effect of the constant parameters π_{ik} and β_{ik} on the behaviour of the choice probabilities? Can variation of the parameters π_{ik}, and β_{ik} be produced experimentally by varying the value of the reward and punishment to the rat? What is the effect of increasing the number of choices? What is the minimum number of learning outcomes that must be obtained for the model to compare favorably with experiment? What is the effect on the model itself of varying the number of learning outcomes considered? These and many more interesting questions can be approached, but the project becomes feasible only because of the availability of the high-speed digital computer.

WORD-FREQUENCY DISTRIBUTIONS SIMULATIONS

Perhaps the most remarkable feature of the human brain is its ability to direct the process of speech. Each word must be precisely chosen and integrated into a flow of word sequences, with the purpose of expressing a thought. It is reasonable therefore to study the words uttered by an individual as perhaps providing a key to the mechanisms of the brain or to pathological disturbances. Let us suppose, for example, that we recorded 100,000 words spoken by an individual and counted the number of times each word was repeated, i.e., determined the *frequency,* f, with which each word was used. Next, let us *order* the words according to their frequency of use, and let the position of each word in this order be called its rank, r. If we now make a graph of f versus r, we shall obtain a graph similar to that. For example, ri words were used more than fi times, as shown in the figure. Zipf's law states that the f versus r curve is given by where c is a constant. Another form of Zipf's law can be obtained if we let n be the number of words at a given frequency; then, which means, for example, that four times as many words occur approximately 100 times as occur approximately 200 times. To see this, we note that the difference in rank between two words, Δr, is approximately equal to the number of words that have frequencies lying

between f and f + Δf; that is, Δr = n [(f + Δf) - f] = n Δf or, on taking limits, n = dr / df = d (c / f) / df = c / f^2 as desired.

The distribution described b by Zipf is the simplest first approximation to the word-frequency distribution law. It has been shown by many workers, however, that in the simple form given above, it does not fully explain all the details of the distributions. Significant further contributions have come from the work of Mandelrot, Howes, and others; however, consideration of these is beyond the scope of the present treatment.

Various theories can be proposed that might describe this phenomenon, but many of these theories must be tested by Monte Carlo simulations with a computer. For example, consider the theory that the probability of a word's being used is proportional to the frequency with which it has been used. To simulate this hypothesis on the computer, we might programme the computer to select words from a given list of k words, according to certain probabilities as follows: Initially, let the probability of any word being selected by the computer be 1/ k. When, say, the ith word is chosen, then the probability p_i of selecting that word in the future is increased by the computer by some amount Δq. Of course, all the probabilities will then have to be renormalized so that

This process is continued until a stationary distribution is obtained for frequency versus rank. This procedure has a great many variations: the initial distribution need not be uniform; the increment Δq might depend on various factors, such as the frequency itself; and so forth. Clearly, a computer is required for such experiments. Further experiments may study how the final distribution changes with a change in the parameters (that is, Δq, or the total number of words, k) under consideration; or it may be possible to simulate the frequency distribution obtained experimentally from aphasics or from persons with other mental disorders.

BIOMEDICAL DATA PROCESSING

DATA PROCESSING

There are a great many applications of computers in the straightforward statistical analysis of medical records, experimental results, and other data. Notable is the large variety and amount of psychological research being accomplished: the psychologists always seem to be among the first to take advantage of the computer in a newly established computing centre. Computers are aiding the statistical evaluation of new drugs, correlation of disease with various possible etiologies, studies of the effectiveness of new cures and preventives, etc.

Many special purpose clinical data processing computers have been introduced in the biomedical sciences. One of the most notable, described below, is the general anesthetic administrator machine that utilizes the patient's electroencephalograph to monitor the anesthetic administration. A different kind of data reduction problem is involved in connection with various continuous recordings—such as electrocardiograms, electroencephalograms, gastroenterograms, and electromyograms—obtained from living animals. Much work has been accomplished in applying the computer to the problems of electroencephalograms, and some of these studies will be briefly described below.

GENERAL ANESTHETIC MACHINE

Agents for general anesthesia can be gases, such as ether, nitrous oxide, etc., which are inhaled by the patient, or liquids, such as sodium pentothal, which are injected into the patient's blood stream. Sometimes combinations of agents are used. The drug is picked up by the circulation and transmitted to the brain. As the concentration in the brain increases, the patient goes through four successive stages of reaction: the induction or first stage, the excitement or second stage, the surgical or third stage, and the danger or fourth stage. Conventional methods for distinguishing these phases are by observation of certain physiologic indices, the four most important being

- Diameter of the eye pupil and reaction to light,
- Character and depth of respiration
- Rate and character of pulse, and
- Blood pressure. These and other indices are continually observed by the anesthetist during the induction of anesthesia and performance of the surgical operation. Figure roughly indicates the relationship of the four main indices with respect to the four stages of anesthesia. During the first stage, the patient loses consciousness; during the second, the patient has a tendency to be restless or even unruly; during the third, surgical procedures can be performed; the fourth stage is that of cardiac and respiratory paralysis and death.

Clearly, due to human error and individual variability of the patient, the successful administration of a general anesthetic is a difficult procedure. But the electrical activity of the brain as recorded by the electroencephalograph varies with the different stages of anesthesia.

By appropriately integrating the output of the electroencephalograph, properly filtered, etc., it is possible to determine automatically the stage and plane of the patient during anesthesia. The output of the integrator is translated into an electrical pulse, the time density of which is controlled by the brain activity. For example, during stage, a high electrical pulse density will be generated to bring the patient into stage. As the patient goes progressively deeper into stage, the density of the pulses will decrease due to decreased activity of the brain. Administration of the anesthetic agent can be directly controlled by the pulse density, the higher the density, the more being administered. Again, a control can be used to calibrate manually the depth of anesthesia desired. This procedure has been successfully utilized in the operating room for human anesthesia.

The technique has the advantage of minimizing the chance of human error and enabling the anesthetist to concentrate more fully on the individual-patient variability factor and on emergencies that may arise. Of greatest importance is the computer's smaller delay time in feedback control, as compared with that of the human anesthetist; this results in greater uniformity in the control of the depth of the anesthesia.

Another advantage is concerned with surgical techniques in situations such as heart surgery, where curarization of the patient has been increasingly employed. One result is that the anesthetist can have no information of the conventional kind even to estimate whether the patient is conscious or not. In fact, instances have been reported in the literature in which a curarized patient has undergone an operation and been conscious throughout. In such cases, the electroencephalographic control of anesthesia may be the only available method for monitoring curarized patients.

NEUROELECTRIC DATA PROCESSING

As illustrations of the use of computers in analyzing neuroelectric data we consider two approaches:

- Averaging evoked responses; and
- Studying patterns in the electroencephalogram.

Averaging Evoked Responses

An evoked response is the reaction to a controlled stimulus; this stimulus may be, for example, a clicking sound, a flash of light, or the turning on or off of a sound or light, etc. All these kinds of stimuli have one characteristic in common; there is a reference point in time that characterizes each repetition of the stimulus, e.g., when the click or the flash occurs, when the sound or light is turned on or off, etc. If we observe the neuroelectric potential waveforms from the time-reference point of the stimulus, the result is apparently random in nature; i.e., the evoked response, if it exists, is buried in the noise of the virtually random fluctuations from other sources. The problem is thus reduced to isolating the evoked response.

Let us consider a repetition of one such stimulus: a sound click. We shall assume that the neuroelectric response evoked by each click is invariant, i.e., remains approximately the same for each click, and that all other neuroelectric fluctuations are random in nature and therefore, of course, nonrepetitive. Then, if we measure the total response composed both of evoked response and random components and if we average the duration of many of these, using each stimulus as a reference point in time, the random component should average out, leaving only the desired estimate for the isolated, evoked response.

This method of isolating estimates of evoked responses can be applied to an awake human or animal subject with electrodes on the scalp. In this way, psychophysical and physiological responses can be studied. For example, for the clicking evoked response, m(ti) was obtained for clicks of differing intensity, and the subjects' threshold for response observed and compared with the subjective findings.

A computer is required to obtain these averages, because from 100 to 3,000 or more stimuli are required for the average to "converge," i.e., to remain relatively stable. It is clear that the electroencephalograph includes some composite function of all the specific responses of the brain to external stimuli; this function may be, but is not necessarily, basically additive. In this view, the total electroencephalogram is then composed of these composite responses, together with a similar function of all other, or internally stimulated, responses. Can the contributions of these stimuli be analyzed in such a way that they can then be resynthesized to predict an electroencephalographic record? The method of averaging evoked responses, together with the capabilities of a digital computer, makes an approach to such problems feasible.

Study of Patterns in the Electroencephalogram

This study represents an effort to have a digital computer carry out an analysis that is analogous to that of an electroencephalographer who visually examines an EEG (electroencephalogram) for various characteristic patterns as an aid to making a diagnosis.

The approach is empirical, based on a trialand-error procedure. The technique differs from that described in the last paragraph in that attention is focused on particular patterns in a waveform, without involving averaging or other mass processing of the EEG response. Such pattern-recognition research, however, must initially be made on a digital computer which can be logically programed in a flexible manner to use various criteria with respect to selected segments of the EEG.

A study based on recognizing the "a-bursts" of an EEG has been made.4 These α-bursts are one of the most striking properties of an EEG. It is frequently important to know the "alpha index," defined as the percentage of the record that contains alpha rhythm. In order to have the digital computer calculate this index, three criteria for recognizing an α-burst were set up.

First, a section of the record must have at least a certain minimum peak-to-peak amplitude in order to be considered at all. For a particular EEG being analyzed, this peak-to-peak amplitude factor, called the amplitude parameter or AP, is defined as the ratio of the minimum amplitude, or MA, and the median amplitude, or DA.

Thus (MA) = (AP) (DA). The greater the AP, the smaller will be the part of the EEG considered; the smaller the AP, the greater the part of the EEG considered.

If a section of the EEG meets the first criterion, then the second criterion is considered; namely, that the interval between two successive zero crossings, or the IZ of the curve, be less than some given length.

This factor was given by the median zero crossing interval, or MI, for the whole EEG record, plus or minus a certain fraction of the median length, this fraction being called the interval parameter, or IP. Thus (IZ) = (MI) ± (IP) (MI), as illustrated in Figure.

The third criterion requires that at least five consecutive zero-crossing waves meet both the first, or amplitude, criterion and the second, or interval, criterion. Those segments of the EEG record satisfying all three criteria are defined as segments of *rhythmic burst activity.*

Investigation techniques of this type open a whole new area in the quantitative evaluation of electroencephalograms and their relation to diagnosis.

LOGICAL REASONING IN MEDICAL DIAGNOSIS

SYMPTOM-DISEASE COMPLEX AND MEDICAL KNOWLEDGE

Mathematical logic (the propositional calculus) is employed in order to make a computer list diagnostic possibilities for the symptoms presented by a patient. The use of logic for this purpose is closely related to the concept of symptom-disease complexes (sdc's). A symptom complex is a list of the symptoms that a patient does and does not have; a disease complex is a similar list of diseases. A *symptom-disease complex* is a list of both symptoms *and* diseases that a patient does and does not have. For example, consider where, for simplicity, our attention is limited to two symptoms, *S*(1) and *S*(2), and two diseases, *D*(1) and *D*(2). Each column represents a symptom disease complex, where a unit in the row signifies that the patient has the corresponding symptom or disease, and a zero signifies that the patient does not have the symptom or disease. Thus the column in the rectangle of represents the symptom-disease complex of the patient having symptom *S*(1), not having *S*(2), having

D(1), and having *D*(2). The columns of Figure represent all conceivable sdc's that can be formed from two symptoms and two diseases. If p symptoms and q diseases are under consideration, then clearly there are 2^{p+q} conceivable sdc's. For our example, $p = 2$, $q = 2$, whence there are $2^{2+2} = 16$ columns.

We use the phrase "all *conceivable* sdc's," but not all of these are possible or actually occur. It is *medical knowledge* that informs us which sdc's do or do not occur. For example, suppose that for the particular symptoms and diseases under consideration, medical knowledge informs us that if a patient does not have *D*(1) and does not have *D*(2), then he cannot have *S*(1) and he cannot have *S*(2), and conversely. Such a statement can be symbolized in terms of mathematical logic as where the bar "—" represents NOT and the dot represents AND. The effect of such a statement of medical knowledge is to eliminate from consideration some of the conceivable sdc's which are not possible. For example, the following columns represent the sdc's that cannot happen according to our rule of medical knowledge; the left-most three columns represent sdc's where the patient has no diseases but does have the symptoms, and the right-most three columns represent sdc's where the patient has no symptoms but does have the diseases. These columns have been crossed off.

S(1)	110	000
S(2)	101	000
D(1)	000	110
D (2)	000	101

Suppose, for example, another assertion of medical knowledge is that if the patient has disease *D*(2), then he must have symptom *S*(1), which can be symbolized as *D*(2) *S*(1).

This means, in addition, that the sdc's represented by the following columns cannot occur for they are contrary to the assertion of medical knowledge. The logical effect of medical knowledge is to reduce the totality of all conceivable sdc's to those which are possible or compatible with the assertions embodied in medical knowledge. All possible sdc's for our illustrative situation. In general, medical knowledge is stated in the form of our second assertion: If the patient has a certain disease complex, then he can have the following symptom complexes. This is why most medical textbooks are organized by diseases and discuss symptoms associated with each disease.

S(1)	0	0
S(2)	1	1
D(1)	1	0
D (2)	1	1

Thus, the patient may have both *D*(1) and *D*(2), or else *D*(1) and not *D*(2), or else *D*(2) but not *D*(1). This means that the symptoms considered are insufficient in this case to distingwish between *D*(1), *D* (2), or both *D*(1) and *D*(2). Therefore, the logical analysis can result in a list of possible diagnoses consistent with the symptoms presented by the patient.

A more formal statement of our logical analysis is as follows: Let $D(1), D(2),..., D(n)$ be the diseases under consideration, and let $S(1), S(2),..., S(m)$ be the symptoms under consideration. Then medical knowledge appears as a Boolean function

$$E=E[D(1),..., D(n),S\ i(1),..., S(m)]$$

The symptom complex of the patient is the Boolean function

$$P=P[S(1),..., S(m)],$$

and the logical aspect of the medical diagnostic problem is to determine a function

$$f=f\ [D(1),..., D\ (n)]$$

of the list of diagnostic possibilities such that the following Boolean equation is satisfied:

$$E\ (P\ f)$$

DETERMINING FURTHER TESTS

The ease with which medical symptoms or test results can be obtained varies greatly with the complexity of the examination, cost, inconvenience to the patient, etc. Thus, in any particular medical specialty, the examinations could be classified using difficulty of execution as the criterion. For example, it is often a straightforward matter to obtain some aspects of the patient's medical history; some parts of a physical examination are more convenient to do than others; some blood tests and X-ray examinations are more costly than others; certain tests, such as biopsies or exploratory operations, are used when no other techniques provide needed information.

It becomes clear that it is not feasible first to make all possible tests on a patient and then to determine the diagnosis. The more realistic method uses iterated stages:

Making tests; determining how precise a diagnosis can be made from the results so far obtained; determining what further tests should be made; making these tests; determining how precise a diagnosis can be made from the additional results obtained; determining what further tests should be made; making these tests; and so forth, until a satisfactory diagnosis has been accomplished.

This problem can be formulated in terms of our logical considerations of the previous section. The formulation will be described by means of an illustration.

For this illustration, the symptoms have been classified into history, physical examination, laboratory blood tests, and bone marrow tests, arranged in order of increasing difficulty of performance.

Notice that *S*(1) actually contributes nothing to the diagnosis because, having a unit in every, column, it does not distinguish between any columns. Suppose, for illustration, that the patient has both *S*(2) and *S* (3). Then the diagnosis so far is that the patient has a disease complex associated with one of the left most eleven columns.

Thus, because of the patient's symptoms, we eliminate from consideration the rest of the columns,. Of the physical examination symptoms *S*(4), *S*(5), and *S*(6), only two are necessary, for all three cannot differentiate between the remaining columns better than can any two. Suppose *S*(4) and *S*(5) are taken, and the patient has *S*(4) and not *S*(5); then only seven columns remain as possible diagnoses, namely columns, 3, 4, 5, 6, 7, 8, and 9.

The choice among the blood tests *S*(7), *S*(8), *S*(9), *S*(10), *S*(11), and *S*(12) is not as easy to make. It can be shown that only three of these six tests need be made, namely, *S*(9), *S*(10), and *S*(12). Suppose the patient presents positive results for tests *S*(9) and *S*(12), and a negative result for test *S*(10). Then only a single column remains, namely column 5.

Thus the bone marrow tests need not be made, and the patient has a combination of both diseases *D*(4) and *D*(5) but none of the other diseases.

Suppose, on the other hand, that at the physical examination the patient had both *S*(4) and *S*(5). Then only columns 1 and 2 would remain; the blood tests will not distinguish between them, and bone marrow test *S*(13) would have to be made.

CALCULATING THE ALTERNATIVE DIAGNOSTIC PROBABILITIES

PROBABILITY IN MEDICAL DIAGNOSIS

Frequently it is not feasible, nor desirable, to make further tests to distinguish between alternative possible diagnoses. The problem then resolves itself into answering the question: In the light of the patient's present symptom complex, what is the probability that he has a particular disease complex? We are asking for a conditional probability: Given the patient's *symptom complex, sj,* what is the probability of his having a *disease complex, di*? This is frequently denoted by $p(di \backslash sj)$, where the symbol to the right of the slash is the condition, and the symbol to the left of the slash is the occurrence whose conditional probability is desired.

The well-known Bayes' formula offers important information concerning the composition of $p(di \backslash sj)$. where indicates a summation over all possible disease complexes dk under consideration. Let us focus our attention on the two terms in the numerator, namely, $p(di)p(si \backslash di)$ since the denominator merely acts as a normalization factor. The term $p(si \backslash di)$ is the probability of having the symptom complex *sj* when it is known that the patient has the particular disease complex *di*. This is precisely what is described in medical textbooks when a particular disease is under consideration. Of course, textbooks do not at the present time assign numerical values to $p(si \backslash di)$, but they do state that associated with a certain disease particular symptoms are common, frequent, rare, etc. The reason for discussing $p(si \backslash di)$ rather than p(di\si) is that the etiology of the symptoms is related to, or stems from, the disease. *Thus* $p(si \backslash di)$, i.e., the symptoms resulting from a disease, *is a constant for the particular disease complex under consideration, being relatively independent of other circumstantial factors*.

On the other hand, consider the term $p(di)$. This is the probability that, of the particular population of patients involved, any particular patient has this disease complex *di*. By "particular population of patients," we mean that population from which the patients can be considered as chosen at *random* in the technical sense. For example, the population may be that of the entire United States, or that of a particular clinic in a particular hospital, etc.; in each case, $p(di)$ will, in general, be different. *This term relates the influence of geographical, seasonal, epidemiological, social, and other such factors to the diagnosis*. Thus, in the tropics one is more apt to find tropical disease; during an Asian flu epidemic, the symptoms of a cold are more likely to be relegated to Asian flu; some diseases, like poliomyelitis, have a seasonal variation, etc. A little reflection indicates clearly that both these factors—the circumstantial or local, and the constant relating to the disease-symptom syndrome—influence the diagnosis.

PROBLEMS IN COMPUTING STATISTICS

As we have noted above, the statistics in which we are interested, i.e., $p(di \backslash si)$, reflect local changes in place and time, and therefore must be collected locally. In order to be valid, however, "sufficiently large" data must be used, which may not be available locally. Bayes' formula comes to our aid under such circumstances, for it is clearly not necessary to have as large a sample to determine $p(di)$ as to determine $p(di \backslash si)$. Thus, since $p(si \backslash di)$ is a constant, not dependent on local conditions and independent of time, nationwide statistics collected over a long period of time can be used for this purpose. Then, locally, only $p(di)$ need be derived from collected data, and Bayes' formula used as illustrated above to determine $p(di \backslash si)$. Notice also that the local collection of statistics to calculate simply $p(di)$, where no symptoms enter, is a much simpler process than that which we have just described. Thus, the use of Bayes' formula presents important practical advantages.

Another important problem arises in connection with *rare diseases*. If we had a clinic for rare diseases, then for the population of this clinic, the diseases would not be rare and the problem would be solved. Patients having rare diseases must be referred to this clinic, however; hence, the rare diseases must be diagnosed even under conditions of "rarity." The columns or sdc's corresponding to rare-disease complexes *cannot* be allowed to have a zero tally, for then they would be missed. Thus, a minimum but *greater than zero* tally must be kept for these rare sdc's at all times.

This minimum tally will give wrong probabilistic results, i.e., in general, too large results; but the minimum non-zero tally should be warning enough. Actually, when comparing non-rare diseases, the probabilities will not be misleading, but when comparing rare with non-rare diseases, the probabilities will have no meaning.

Finally, consider the problem of the delay with which our "current" statistics reflect time-dependent changes. Obviously, even though we are dropping old statistics at the same rate as receiving new statistics, the initiation of an epidemic, for example, will be observed with a finite delay, as will the end of an epidemic.

This is a practical problem that exists no matter how the statistics are taken, and it applies to all public health and other such fields, as well as to medical diagnosis.

It simply reflects the delay in current information gathering and processing. It might be observed that an "uncertainty principle" applies here, analogous to the well-known uncertainty principle that appears in quantum mechanics, namely, $(\Delta L)(\Delta t) > å$ For, if we wish to make our statistics more sensitive to time changes (i.e., decrease the delay time Δt), then we must accept more statistics per unit time (i.e., collect statistics from a larger area) thereby increasing ΔL, the geographical locality factor.

On the other hand, if we limit the area in which we collect statistics (i.e., decrease ΔL) we shall have to compensate for the smaller rate of incoming statistics by waiting a longer time (i.e., increase Δt). The situation is far from hopeless, however, for there are many techniques for handling such situations. For example, physicians are alerted at the time of the seasonal occurrence, say, of poliomyelitis. Similarly, the statistics can be tampered with by artificially raising certain tallies from previous epidemiological experience. In this way, the lead in incidence over statistical reflection can be reduced. After the initial priming, the usual tallies can then take over.

DISCUSSION OF COMPUTER AIDS TO MEDICAL DIAGNOSIS

It must be remembered that one cannot get out of a computer more than one puts into it; i.e., a computer can do no more than it is *programed* to do. If a certain disease-symptom relationship is not recorded in the computer memory, the relationship cannot enter into any computations. Incorrect data entered into the computer's memory can generate incorrect results. Incomplete history taking, incorrectly executed laboratory tests, incorrect interpretation of result of diagnostic procedures, etc., will all contribute to incorrect computer outputs.

These remarks, of course, apply to any method of making the diagnosis and formulating the treatment plan; the computer has no magical properties from this point of view.

Although it is important to understand the limitation of the computer, it is also unwise to underestimate its capabilities. For example, a computer can be made to:

- "check" the input information for logical inconsistencies,
- "learn" from the statistical experience of current data that may be continually fed into its memory,
- "organize" current information for coordinate retrieval,
- "read" an article and extract pertinent diagnostic information,
- carry out complicated "reasoning" processes,
- "evaluate" an optimum or near-optimum course of action for given circumstances, and so forth. Nevertheless, it is the scientific ingenuity of the human mind that "tells" the computer how to perform these remarkable feats.

There are other problems associated with the use of computers besides those of input data accuracy and data omission. First, standardization of nomenclature is a practical necessity. The computer can be made to recognize different words as denoting the same idea, but it obviously cannot distinguish between different idea denoted by the same word.

Second, standardization of the coding procedures is needed so that, for example, medical records from different hospitals will have directly compatible codes. Third, standardization of test interpretations is an everpresent problem. For example, at what point does the blood sugar level test indicate diabetes? No matter where the line is drawn, the test result will be positive for some patients who do not have diabetes and negative for some who do. The test results must be interpreted to minimize the errors, keeping in mind that such errors cannot be totally eliminated. Observe that these problems arise simply because the use of a computer requires logical self-consistency, together with the preliminary analysis of all possible relevant outcomes.

Although computers can setve the physician in many ways, we do not mean to imply that computers will make the physician's job easier. On the contrary, to utilize computer the physician must learn how to communicate with them and how to evaluate correctly the information obtained from them. But we believe that ability to make a more precise diagnosis and a more exact determination of the best possible treatment plan will more than offset these difficulties.

Chapter 6

Computer Simulation

THE PRESENT-DAY TRANSFORMATION OF THE SOCIAL FABRIC

The twentieth century is witnessing the effects of a threefold technological revolution, in production, transportation, and communication. These changes are perceptibly modifying the dynamics and structure of large social organizations.

The quantity of productive or destructive output per executive, the wide, often global distribution of a single organization's personnel, investments, and resources, and the far-flung network of rapid transportation and communication —these have intensified and accelerated the executive decision-making process.

This acceleration is producing what seems to be a radical, qualitative transformation in the entire fabric of our social existence, not solely in the military sphere but also in industry and government.

To understand these social phenomena, we are developing a conceptual framework to which we give the name "Leviathan." We shall describe one aspect of our approach, namely, the use of a large digital computer to cause artificial social structures and social processes to develop according to sets of rules that we can experimentally prescribe and control. An IBM 7090 is employed for a purely automatic mode of operating our simulation, and a Philco 2000 machine is used when we wish to experiment with a limited number of live subjects.

LARGE SOCIAL GROUPS

In turning to computer simulation for scientific knowledge, we abstract general features of social process, features that remain invariant as our attention passes from one real organization to another of the same kind, and from kind to kind of social organization.

We confine our attention to large social groups, including military organizations, that produce artifacts or services. In such large productive groups, much of the productive (or destructive) work is carried forward by means of one-way communications.

Often these communications are secondhand, i.e., via intermediaries. When more than perhaps a hundred or two hundred people are banded together in some common enterprise, it becomes physically impossible for every pair of members to meet and converse with each other face-to-face over any span of time.

In direct consequence, considerable numbers of members of a large organization are essentially faceless. Who files a letter or moves an article to its proper shelf in a warehouse is usually not significant, provided that the work gets done. Further, when face-to-face relationships are thus transcended, large groups generally exhibit more complex social structure than do small groups.

Although large groups include face-to-face constellations, these subordinate units are, to some degree, organized as if they themselves were individuals. Thus, a squad can be ordered to perform a given mission, and with respect to the order, it may be meaningless to ask for the contribution of each specific member.

A purely formal, structural property of large groups thus becomes apparent: large groups have system levels. Whereas on one level a group behaves as if plural, consisting of individual persons or of subordinate groups, for a higher level, the plural group can act socially as if it were a collective individual. In large social groups there can be "individuals" composed of individual groups.

THE TECHNOLOGICAL SYSTEM AND THE GOVERNING SYSTEM

Once we look within a large productive system like an industry or governmental bureau or a military command, we can distinguish two basic subsystems: the technological system and the governing system. We define the *technological system* to consist of all those machines, messages, and applications of human energy that apply directly in the creation of the product or service of the entire social system. In the technological system is included everything that gets the product manufactured or the service delivered. The *governing system* includes the messages, machines, and social energy of a second order, which are about the technological work or service. Thus, any message or data concerning how many men, months, and work are required during a given period of time in order to produce a product would be a message that belongs in the governing system. Equally, a command to reallocate manpower or to change production schedules would probably belong in that system.

Time flows in different ways through the two systems. In the technological system, the flow of time is linear. Raw materials enter at a given date and leave at a later date. We may think of the flow of time in the technological system as analogous to the advance of a wave front. In the governing system, on the other hand, time tends to have a cyclical character. Suppose some event occurs in the technological system, requiring the intervention of the governing system. Perhaps a machine breaks down and production (or destruction) stops, or perhaps the quality of the product being produced shows signs of falling below an acceptable level. This event occasions an intervention.

The executives in the governing system seek to diagnose the problem and to cope with it. Finally, a decision is made, and a change is effected in the production process. While this entire chain of events takes place, it is quite possible that the product that occasioned the chain has reached completion and has been delivered to the customer. Then the intervention, which actually changes the production system, is effected on a new generation of products. It takes effect at a much later time than the date of the event which occasioned the intervention. A cycle has been completed; if further intervention is required to produce further improvement in the process, the activity goes again around a similar cycle.

STRUCTURE AND CHANGE

It would be over simple to suppose that governing and technological processes are just two self-contained systems. A productive system can, of course, for some purposes, be viewed as a simple combination of subsystems, while the aggregate of subsystems comprises a simple net like a nerve net. Then we generate a larger system by flowing the output of one subsystem into the input of another. But a governing system, in contrast, rarely exhibits such aggregational simplicity. Myriad activities temporally proceed in parallel at diverse levels of organization. Novel syntheses of intelligence, of strategies, of norms, of responsibilities, and of spans of authority emerge and hold sway over and over again at successively higher levels of integration. Often they conflict with one another and partially nullify each other's effects. Each higher-level synthesis absorbs lower-level integrations, in analogy to the organization of molecules in cells, cells in organs, organs in animals.

In point of fact, then, technological and governing systems are mutually adaptive to one another, and thus become fused in a single total system. As a result, an entire system can be viewed from the two points of view of change and of structure.

One can consider the system as a maze of channels through which flow progressively completed products and messages. Both work and communications move from station to station. Operations on the work transform the product or service that is being formed or performed. Interpretations and decisions alter the content of communications. The social system from this point of view is social process or functioning.

An equally true view of a social system focuses on its formal structure. A social system is at least that which is represented in an organization chart. It also, of course, includes as part of its formal structure what a behavioral scientist would denominate its informal organization. By *informal organization* is meant the patterns of interaction that depend more on friendship and interpersonal associations than on publicly acknowledged standard operating rules. Another element is the *formal coordinative,* or *lateral, structure.* By this is meant the publicly approved rules and channels of communication between independent subordinate trees in the formal organizational chart. Thus a coordinating committee, socially established by the governing system, is an example of formal lateral structure. Formal line structure and informal and formal lateral structure combine with the technological system of any large productive organization to guarantee that structure be as essential to operations as are dynamic interactions.

The fusion of structure and dynamic interaction raises problems for behavioral scientists, because complex structure complicates the interrelationships between micro-operations. Even if a given activity is repeated identically in ten different channels, it makes a difference to the operations of the system through which channel the activity flows. Aside from the relationship of suitability between message and channel, the same message through different channels can have different meanings for the total system. A statement that drill press no. 3 is down will obtain assistance from the maintenance department if it flows through one channel, and it might occasion reprimand from a first-level supervisor. From a higher-level executive, the statement might initiate an investigation into the performance of the maintenance department. Finally, such a statement might be declared unsuitable for admission into the office of the president without prior filtering at an intermediate level.

COMPUTER SIMULATION

How should the complex interplay of structure and change in large social groups be studied? At the present stage of development of the social sciences, we lack scientific hypotheses sufficiently simple in consequences and sufficiently fecund in implications to reduce this complexity to propositions that would be encompassed by currently widespread analytic techniques. One innovation, the large digital computer, because of its high speed and large storage capacities, may possibly be the single instrument that will assist social scientists to achieve mastery over the complexity. We begin to construct our social group from the technological system and proceed upward. First, raw material is introduced; then the work of an organization gets done; then information is generated about the performance of the work; and finally the technological process is modulated and controlled.

THE COMPUTER PROGRAMMES

THE TECHNOLOGICAL TASK

We begin our simulation by inventing a perfectly concrete, particular, and brute or surd task for Leviathan to perform. What shall this task be? If we were writing in the nineteenth century, we would probably seek to represent some activity that could be performed by a factory with the aid of natural power, for example, the production of flour from grain in a mill. Or we might want to represent effects of bombarding a fortress during a siege. In the twentieth century, it is more interesting to construct a productive process that involves communication of symbolic material. In our initial computer programmes (which are reaching the operational stage as this is being written), we introduce encrypted messages coded by a special series of rules that we invent, and the task of the technological system is to restore these messages to their original clear form. The rules for decrypting, and the assembly lines that perform the decoding tasks, are held invariant through successive experimental investigations that employ Leviathan's programmes. What do undergo fluid and adaptive change are executive interactions, organizational structure, and deployment of manpower.

THE PROGRAMME SYSTEM

The first programmes (*input preparation*) receive messages that consist of words expressed in Latin letters. The letters of the words are converted to numerical values according to the Hollerith-like code:

A = 11, B = 12,..., Z = 36

Three sets of clues to the clear form of the original words are then generated; extra letters are supplied by a pseudorandom number generator until a total of eight letters occurs; and the resulting combinations of original letters and "random" letters in each word are scrambled by means of a second use of the "random" number generator.

The resulting disguised words, each word accompanied by its proper three sets of clues, are read out on magnetic tapes. In turn, the tapes constitute a library of pre-prepared inputs (or "stimuli") for the second, third, and fourth groups of programmes.

The second programmes (the *automatic processor*) decrypt the disguised words with the aid of their accompanying clues. We say that these programmes execute the technological tasks accomplished by the represented society.

They simulate what is accomplished in a productive (or destructive) social group by the hands and machines that contribute directly to the services or products issuing from the group.

The third programmes (*agent accounting*) attribute the simulated technological work of the represented social group to the directly productive energy in the technological system.

The automatic processor and the agent accounting programmes together symbolize the technological system of any social organization simulated by the entire set of programmes.

The fourth programmes (*governing system*) represent the governing pyramid of control and command. Here are represented the flow of internal messages about the underlying technological work, the interpretation of these messages, the evolution of strategies for accomplishing the missions of the represented social group, command and control decisions, and the production of directives or orders. Demands of the environment will be represented in future programmes.

Finally, the fifth programmes (*data reduction*) perform data reduction on intermediate developments within the second, third, and fourth programmes.

SIMULATION OF THE PRODUCTIVE PROCESS

THE AUTOMATIC PROCESSOR

The automatic processor can be viewed as a three-stage filter. In the first stage, parallel tests are made to determine whether each disguised word satisfies one of 25 possible versions of the first of the three clues that are provided for decrypting that word. In the second stage eight parallel tests seek to determine the form in which the second clue is satisfied. The third stage consists of eight similar parallel tests. Viewed as a filter, the three stages of the processor successively eliminate equivocation and ambiguity.

At the entrance into the processor, there is a waiting line or storage queue. From this queue, each disguised word goes to all 25 first-stage subprocesses, each subprocess accepting a disguised word only when it is ready to work on it.

After each subprocess has completed its work for a given disguised word, if the word does not meet the necessary conditions for the category under test by that subprocess, it is discarded from the subprocess. If it does meet the condition, however, it is passed along to the first intermediate storage queue.

There are 25 first intermediate queues, one associated with each subprocess. The words which survive the first-stage subprocess and enter the first intermediate storage queues fall into two groups:

- Those which satisfy the first necessary condition, because in their original clear form they happen to belong to the category with which the storage queue and subprocess is associated;
- Those which accidentally satisfy the necessary condition, but really are spurious identifications.

The 25 intermediate storage queues (Components III) feed into eight second-stage subprocesses (Components IV). In the second-stage subprocesses (Components IV), tests are again applied, this time based on the second set of clues generated by the input preparation encrypting programme. Words failing to meet the tests are discarded; partially identified words are delivered to the second intermediate storage queues, of which there are eight (Components V).

The eight second intermediate storage queues deliver their contents to the third and last subprocess (Component VI). These last-stage subprocesses correctly identify the original words.

THE CLUES PREPARED BY THE INPUT PREPARATION PROGRAMMES

How does the elaborate network of processing lines and storage queues that constitute the automatic processor operate? To answer this question, it is first necessary to explicate in finer detail the encrypting discipline of the input preparation programmes. These programmes generate clues as follows:

Gematric Number

The sums of the numerical values of the letters in the correct words are taken. We note that, in general, the least value that any such sum could possibly have in any word the Leviathan may receive is 11 (the value of the letter A) and the greatest value is 288 (8 times 36, or the sum of the letter values of ZZZZZZZZ).

We engender equivocation by dividing the range of possible gematrics, namely, 11 through 288, into the six subregions: 11-60, 61-110, 11-160, 161-210, 211-260, 261-288. We subtract 50 repeatedly from the gematric of the correct word until the resultant value lies between 11 and 60. This value we give Leviathan with the understanding that the correct value is this least gematric rood 50.

Suppose that the correct word given to the input preparation programmes is *SINGED*. The letter values of this word comprise the set [29, 19, 24, 17, 15, 14]. The sum of these letter values is 118. Subtracting 50 twice, we obtain the least gematric, G1 = 18. Then G_2 = 68, G_3 =118, G_4 =168, G_5 = 218, G_6 = 268.

Difference Value

The absolute value of the difference between the first and last letter of the correct word is also given to the simulated system. For the word SINGED, this is #"29 - 14#" = 15.

Pair Sums and Differences

As part of the encrypting discipline, the input preparation programmes add randomly generated letters so that all words contain just eight letters. (Words longer than eight letters are converted by this procrustean process into two words, the first of which contains eight letters. The combination of the original word and the added random letters is called the "canonical" word. In the example of SINGED, let us suppose B and Z were added by the generator. Then the canonical word is SINGEDBZ.

Canonical word:	*S*	*I*	*N*	*G*	*E*	*D*	*B*	*Z*
Letter values:	29	19	24	17	15	14	12	36
Unit values:	9	9	4	7	5	4	2	6
Sums of pairs:	18		11		09		08	
P_1:	68		61		59		08	
Tens values:	2	1	2	1	1	1	1	3
P_2:	3		3		2		4	
P_3:	0		3		1		4	

We now form three subsets of clues in the following fashion:

- Pairs of letters are taken together. The digits of their numerical equivalents in the tens position are stripped off and the sum of the remaining digits is taken. In SINGEDBZ, the first two letter values are 29 and 19 respectively. The 2 and 1 are stripped away from 29 and 19; and the remaining digits, 9 and 9, are added together to form 18. If the original pair of letters is in counter-alphabetical order, as they are in the SI of SINGEDBZ, 50 is added to this sum.

- The sums of the first digits are taken. For the SI of SINGEDBZ, these are 2 and 1, and the first sum is 3.
- The absolute values of the differences of the second digits are taken. For the SI of SINGEDBZ, we have #"9 - 9#" = 0.

The input preparation programme now scrambles the order of the letters in the canonical word, using the random number generator to do this. Thus the automatic processor would receive from the input preparation programmes an eight-letter word, say GDSBZEIN, or [17, 14, 29, 12, 36, 15, 19, 24], plus these clues: G_1 = 18, D = 15, P_1 = [68, 61, 59, 08], P_2 = [3, 3, 2, 4], P_s = [0, 3, 1, 4]. Its task is to restore the given word to its original clear form.

OPERATION OF THE AUTOMATIC PROCESSOR

Records containing words encrypted in the foregoing fashion enter the processor and are stored in the input storage queue. Each of the first-stage subprocesses tests whether the words in this queue or waiting line can be made to satisfy the gematric clues.

In the case of GDSBZEIN, or [17, 14, 29, 12, 36, 15, 19, 24], the sums of the letters in the following combinations satisfy this gematric test: [15, 17, 36], [15, 24, 29], and [17, 12, 15, 24] equal 68 or G_2; [17, 29, 12, 36, 24], [14, 29, 36, 15, 24], [17, 14, 29, 15, 19, 24] and [17, 14, 12, 36, 15, 24] equal 118, or G_3. The survivors of the gematric test are stored in the first intermediate storage queues until the individual second processing stages are ready to operate on them.

In these second stages, tests are made for satisfaction of the differences condition. In our example, two combinations survive this test: In [14, 29, 36, 15, 24] and [17, 14, 29, 15, 19, 24] occur 14 and 29; and #"14 - 29#" = 15, the given value of the difference clue. D and S are identified as the terminal letters of the correct word. The survivors of this test are placed in the second intermediate storage queues.

The third processing stages test for satisfaction of the pair sums and differences condition. In our example, D or 14 cannot be the first letter of the correct word. This is because the first pair sum is 68, and 68 - 50 = 18. Eighteen is the sum of the second digits of the first two letters of the correct word. The second digit of 14 is 4 but 18 - 4 = 14; and no second digit can be 14.

Hence the first letter of the correct word is 29, or S. Its second digit is 9; 18 - 9 = 9; the second letter must have a 9 for its second digit. This is the letter 19, or 1. The last letter of the correct word must be D. Since I, or 19, does not occur in [14, 29, 36, 15, 24], the correct word must contain [17, 14, 29, 15, 19, 24].

We now know the letters that comprise the correct word and the first, second and last letters of this word. What can we learn from the fact that the value of the last letter of the correct word is 14? We know that this letter occurs in the third pair of letters of the correct word. The third pair sum is 59. Stripping off 50, 09 remains. Deducting the second digit of 14, namely 4, we find that the second digit of the fifth letter of the correct word is 5. Hence this letter must be 15, or E.

The remaining two letters in the correct word are 17, or G, and 24, or N. These must occur in counter-alphabetical order, because the second pair sum, namely 61, includes the increment 50. Also in the given word occur two letters added to the correct word to form the canonical word, namely, B and Z. These must occur in alphabetical order because the fourth pair sum, 08, does not include the increment 50.

The processor has now retrieved the canonical word and identified the original correct word: SINGED; BZ or [29, 19, 24, 17, 15, 14; 12, 36]. It confirms its identification by testing whether this word meets the second and third subsets of pair clues. If it does, the correct word in canonical form is placed in the output storage queue.

SEQUENTIAL OPERATIONS AND THE CLOCK

The automatic processor consists of three stages of parallel operations. In the first stage are 25 subprocesses that operate in parallel, whereas in the second and third stages there are eight parallel processes. The computers we are employing are not parallel machines; their mode of operation is sequential.

Hence the programmes must scan out the various subprocesses in succession. Intuitively, we might think of a large productive organization stopped for an enduring instant in the flow of its activity. During this time, many pieces of many tasks are simultaneously executed. Perhaps a secretary says Hello, an executive dictates three words, and a drill press drills two holes in some work. For purposes of simulation, we say that one total scan through every action of the automatic processor represents all the work of an organization that takes place simultaneously during an extended moment. Now as the processor continues through scan after scan, the individual scans can be interpreted as successive moments of parallel operations. Sequential scans in the representing medium, the computer programmes, are interpreted as successive simultaneous durations in the life of the simulated organization. Sequential scanning then defines a clock for the simulated organization. *N* scans comprise a period (we can think of an hour); *M* periods, an epoch (perhaps a day); and *L* epochs an era.

Notice that we do not first specify intervals of time and then measure the duration of our simulated social events as if they were contained in some absolute temporal box. On the contrary, we first create our social events

and then measure time relatively, as one kind of relation among the absolutely existing events.

ANALOG SIMULATION

It is already possible to observe in what sense we assert that Leviathan's programmes constitute analog simulation on a digital computer. The automatic processor actually performs the work that would be performed in any real productive system. The programmes directly transform encrypted words into their original clear form; the programmes literally retrieve the original forms latent in the disguised words and their associated clues. The subsequent programmes—agent accounting and the governing system—also carry out this approach of directly performing operations in direct imitation of selected, important features of real social operations.

INTERMEDIATE BEHAVIORAL LANGUAGE

The analog character of our simulation becomes even clearer if we consider a powerful technique that we employ in formulating it. The entire formulation is stated in an intermediate behavioral language. A typical operation in this language is "026. Test whether there is room in storage queue. If yes, X. If no, Y." Two other examples are "050. Add X to Y" and "040. Test: Does X = Y? If yes, V. If no, W." These operations in the intermediate language can support three interpretations:

- The operations are directly translatable into the commands that cause the computer to operate. The computer operations really accomplish these activities, operating directly on the encrypted words that are being decoded.
- The operations are such that they can be stated completely in the notations of mathematics or of set theory.
- The operations can literally be accomplished by the overt behaviour of live persons. Hence the operations are invariant across human behaviour, mathematico-logical formulation, and computer operations.

For computer operations, this mode of formulation permits the designers. of Leviathan to think in terms of human behaviour, confident that the formulations can be performed by computing machinery.

Any formulation that can be made to operate by live subjects following prescribed rules without further interpretation and that is coherent in the intermediate formulation, can be translated into machine operations. Hence formulation can proceed in a language "sealed off" from any particular machine, that is, invariant to reprograming from one machine to another.

For social investigations, the intermediate behavioral language guarantees strict, operational formulation. If every significant overt action in an experiment can be literally duplicated by computing machinery, then the experiment refers without remainder to overt, operational behaviour.

Finally, because the intermediate language is exhaustively translatable into either mathematical or set-theoretic terms, we can be scientifically rigorous without being exclusively quantitative. We can express with precision many qualitative relationships essential to social structure and process. Also we guarantee an objective statement to any conclusions that we may derive from our formulations.

SIMULATION OF PRODUCTIVE AGENTS

Productive Energy and Social Energy. V

It is now time to introduce simulated agents. This we can do by extending our interpretation of the intermediate behavioral language. We designate the micro-operations in the language "atomic actions," and we arbitrarily assert that each micro-operation represents the expenditure of one unit of social energy. Ironically honoring the tradition that gave birth to therbligs, we call our units "taylors," after the industrial engineer, F. W. Taylor, who sought to rationalize human labour. Then each time an atomic action is executed in the automatic processor, one unit of human energy, 1 taylor, is said to have been expended. The atomic actions are thus shared between the productive and the social energy of the technological system.

Next we simply attribute the social energy to productive agents. At this point, a word of historical explanation is in order. In formulating the Leviathan technique for large-group analysis, we had two options. We could have either identified our agents with specific locations in the core storage of a computer or else built our agents around simple proper names. The first alternative seemed hardly suitable after Whitehead's strictures against misplaced concreteness and the fallacy of simple location. Any investigator possessing practical experience with organisms and adaptive systems is keenly aware that systems have a way of being neither simply where nor simply when. A system is excised from the total cosmological process by an act of abstraction. Autonomy is always relative. (Is the air we breathe, that is shared among people, part of the real internal constitution of a person?)

Hence we follow the second alternative. We begin by naming our agents, starting with "0001." Once we give these proper names to our agents, the names serve as cores of identity about which we can accumulate, in lawful ways, events or properties that are brought into existence by the rules of our simulation. Provided an event or property is one that we would associate with an agent, it can be at-

001	STORE	Store X at Y
002	RECEIVE	Receive X from Y
004	PURGE	Remove X from Y
006	ARRIVED?	Test: Has X arrived at Y?
007	LEFT?	Test: Has X left Y?
010	SET	Set X to Y and discard X from Z
011	LOOK UP	Obtain definition of X from Y
015	EXTRACT	Extract X from Y, leaving Y vacant
016	INSPECT	Extract X from Y, leaving X in Y
026	ROOM?	Test: Room at X?
031	SEND	Send X to Y
033	ASSOCIATE	Associate X with Y
036	CONTROL	Request X to take control
040	EQUAL?	Test: X = Y?
041	PRODUCT?	Test: Do all X equal Y?
044	GREATER?	Test: X greater than Y?
050	ADD	Add X to Y at Z
051	SUMMATE	Take sum of items at X
054	SUBTRACT	? X - Y?

tributed to any one of our agents, regardless of its date or location. We shall explain later the degree to which we accumulate concreteness and specificity about our executive decision makers. As for the productive agents, on the other hand, submerged as they are in the technological system and representing hoi polloi—the workers in industry, the civil service clerks in government, and the enlisted men in military systems: for these, we provide only a very limited degree of specificity or individuality. To these directly productive agents, we attribute skill profiles and affiliation with particular squads or teams that report to first-level supervisors in the governing system.

SKILL PROFILES

In the intermediate behavioral language, 19 items comprise the total set of atomic actions that occur in the technological system. These can be classified into six categories. Each category is said to be a class of skills. This is the interpretation of *skill class*: Each productive agent has a variety of skills. Depending on how much of each skill he has, he can contribute so much of that kind of effort during an epoch toward accomplishing Leviathan's work. From this definition, it follows that atomic actions and skills are closely associated. When an agent exercises a particular skill, he performs atomic actions associated with that skill. The table of skill classes defines for Leviathan what atomic actions can be performed, given any one of the six kinds of skills.

I. Queue-processing	II. Data-coordinating	III. Message-clerking
001 Store	006 Arrived?	002 Receive
015 Extract	007 Left?	004 Purge
016 Inspect		031 Send
026 Room		

IV. Data-processing	V. Testing	VI. Computation
010 Set	040 Equal?	050 Add
011 Look Up	041 Product?	051 Summate
033 Associate	044 Greater?	054 Subtract
036 Control		

Once skill classes have been defined, we can introduce the notion of a "standard skill profile." Suppose that an organization wished to hire a message clerk. Given that there are the six categories of skills specified in Figure, little contribution would be expected from a message clerk in categories I (queue processing), II (data coordinating), IV (data processing), V (testing or quality control), or VI (computation), but the contribution from category III, which includes receiving messages, removing messages from files, copying or repeating and sending messages, would be maximal. A data clerk would have a different profile of skills. Of course, it is not possible to tell a computer anything so general as that computational skills shall be "low" for one kind of newly hired person and "higher" for another. We need specificity. Fortunately, taylors give us what we need. For a given standard profile, we assign various amounts of taylors to each of the skill classes. It happens that up to 4096 taylors can be assigned to each skill class (212) or a maximum of 6 × 4096 = 24,576 taylors in all for any one productive agent. Thus standard skill profiles for typical message clerks and typical data clerks might resemble the values.

	Amount of skill	
	Message-clerking	**Data clerk**
I. Queue-processing	Low	Low
II. Data-coordinating	Low	Higher
III. Message-clerking	High	Low
IV. Data-processing	Low	Higher
V. Testing	Low	Low
VI. Computation	Low	Higher

Skill class

	I. Queue-process-ing	II. Data-coordi-nating	III. Mess age-clerk-ing	IV. Data-proces s-ing	V. Test-ing	VI. Compu-tation	Total
Mess age clerk	125	145	4000	550	150	75	5045
Data clerk	85	1550	1400	2525	150	850	6560

From the standard skill profiles, we derive individual skill profiles. Although our enlisted personnel (or workers or government clerks) are essentially faceless, we do give them this much individuality—their skill profiles vary from one to another. The variation is specified in terms of increments and decrements over the values of taylors in the standard profiles.

The result of our formulations of skill classes, standard skill profiles, and individual variations are individual skill profiles. To each proper name of a productive agent, we attribute a unique individual skill profile. Later, we shall see that this skill profile is known to the experimenter who establishes the conditions (boundary parameters) for a given investigation employing Leviathan, but it is withheld from the executives who know the standard skill profiles but must infer inductively what are individual variations among productive agents.

Given individual skill profiles, it is possible to define "learning" for the productive agents, even though, besides individual skill profiles, little else is specified for each productive agent. Learning on the part of productive agents consists in attaining changes in individual skill profiles. Thus such learning is simple to define, has relevance to qualitative differences among agents (namely, differences in the respective skill classes, which are interpreted to be qualitatively distinct), and yet remains precise and measurable.

THE TABLE OF ATOMIC ACTIONS AND THE AGENT ACCOUNTING TABLE

We have now explained the basic ingredients with which we simulate a technological system on a computer. What more is needed to set such a simulation into operation?For an actual run, we should first have to specify four kinds of information that can vary from investigation to investigation, even though the programmes remain the same:

- Number of agents. How many productive agents should be included in a given investigation? This number need not remain the same throughout an experimental run on the computer, for it is possible with Leviathan to study expanding and contracting organizations, and the change in number of personnel can be controlled in three, non-exclusive, ways. A pattern of change in size and composition of the productive force can be prearranged to occur according to a desired time-scale, as certain events specified by the investigators occur, or at the command of the executives in the governing system.

- Standard skill profiles. The next step would be determination of the standard skill profiles to be used during the progress of an investigation.
- Profiles assigned to agents. These standard skill profiles would then be assigned to individual agents by the investigators.
- Individual variations in profiles. From the standard skill profiles individual variations among the agents would be defined. The only limitations on individual variations are these:
  - That the result of combining standard skill profile and individual variations in every case result in positive values of taylors, and
  - That no skill class have a value exceeding 4095 taylors.

These four requirements are embodied in a table in the computer. The table consists of the proper name of each productive agent and his individual skill profile.

A fine adjustment can be added to the entries in the table. If an agent is absent, for example, on account of illness, operationally this means that during a particular period of simulated time the values of his individual skill profile are all zero; i.e., he can contribute no taylors to the productive or destructive work of the organization.

Absenteeism can be individually controlled by a probabilistic formula specified by the investigators. The pseudo-random generator supplies "random" numbers, and, depending on the values of these numbers and the pattern contained in the formula, the individual agents are occasionally absent. Obviously, if this is important for some investigation, we can introduce contingent absenteeism, in which an agent has a pattern of probable absence that depends on kinds of events in the history of the simulated organization.Now, once we have our table of individual productive agents and their skill profiles, we can interconnect the agent accounting programmes with the automatic processor.

This interconnection is the basic mechanism that permits us to simulate a technological system. How is the connection effected? By creating a second table in the following way:

- Name of atomic action. At each point in the automatic processor where the computer programme literally accomplishes the work specified by one of the atomic actions, we insert the name of the appropriate atomic action. Thus, if the atomic action happens to be "026" ("room?"), which tests whether a storage queue has room available to receive further work, "026" is inserted in the computer programme immediately following the set of computer instructions in the automatic processor that do test for room in a given storage queue.
- Skill class of action. For each atomic action listed in the automatic processor, the skill class to which the atomic action belongs is inserted in the computer code directly beside the respective atomic action.
- Name of agent. If now we add the name of the agent assigned to perform the given atomic action, the computer can charge this agent with responsibility for performing his appropriate work in the technological system of the organization being simulated (but see Section 22.5.2 for more precise statement).

We are now ready to interassociate the items on two lists. One list contains the atomic actions in the order in which they occur, together with their respective skill classes and an indication of the agent who will be said to have performed the atomic action. We call this list the "table of atomic actions." Another list is the table of individual skill profiles associated with the respective productive agents. We call this list the "agent accounting table."

THE OPERATION OF THE COMPUTER PROGRAMMES THAT SIMULATE THE TECHNOLOGICAL SYSTEM

The simulation of the technological system proceeds as follows: The automatic processor scans out the prescribed operations that constitute the technological work of the simulated organization. As each operation specified by an atomic action is completed by the automatic processor, the computer determines, from the table of atomic actions, which agent is responsible for performing the operation and what is the skill class of the operator. Control is passed in the computer to the agent accounting programmes. These programmes locate the proper individual productive agent in the agent accounting table, find the appropriate skill class for the atomic action being attributed to the agent, and subtract 1 taylor from the supply of taylors listed under the skill class. Then control is returned to the processor. Like an inexorable loom, the computer executes an atomic action, charges the appropriate agent, executes the next action, charges the next agent, and continues to swing back and forth between the automatic processor, with its table of atomic actions, and the agent accounting table.

At the end of an epoch, the loom is halted, the taylors remaining in each individual skill profile are totaled, these totals are recorded, and in the agent accounting table, the individual skill profiles are reset to their original values. If learning is postulated, new values for the number of taylors in each skill category are set into the skill profiles that make up the accounting tables. The differences between the original and the subsequent values are measures of the amount of learning that may be said to occur.

As a result of the weaving action between the automatic processor and the agent accounting programmes, the technological work of the simulated social organization is accomplished and the productive agents are charged with having made their proper contributions. The outcome of this activity is the simulation of a technological system.

THE GOVERNING SYSTEM

THE HIERARCHY OF DIRECT COMMAND

We begin our formulation of governing systems by building a skeleton. The skeleton represents the hierarchy of direct command or table of authority and responsibility, commonly shown as a tree on organization charts of productive social groups. We impose our skeleton on a governing system by incorporating it into the agent accounting table. This we do simply by grouping the agents represented in the table and interpreting each group of agents as a squad at the lowest level of command. Next the squads are grouped together in ever larger aggregations. Then, as the automatic processor grinds out the productive work of a simulated organization, each productive agent in each squad is charged with having performed a given atomic action. Because the squads are themselves grouped in ever more comprehensive groupings, each successively higher grouping of agents is *ipso facto* also charged with having performed that action

ORGANIZATIONAL RESPONSIBILITY FOR PERFORMANCE OF TECHNOLOGICAL WORK

Note that the responsibility for a given atomic action is not assigned to a specific individual as such, but rather to his organizational unit. In the table of atomic actions that we insert into the automatic processor, we specify (in addition to the skill class of each atomic action) the lowest-level organizational units to which the agents are assigned. Thus squads of agent, not individual agents, are assigned to specific tasks in the automatic processor. As a result, the programmes operate as follows:

- Work is accomplished in the processor.
- Control is passed to the accounting programme.
- The squad assigned responsibility for this work is located in the agent accounting table.

- The skill class of the atomic action is located in the table.
- The entire squad is scanned under this skill class.
- The agent within the squad with the largest number of taylors remaining in this skill class is located.
- This agent is charged with having performed the atomic action by the device of subtracting one taylor.
- Control is returned to the automatic processor.

OPTIONAL VARIETIES OF ORGANIZATION AND DYNAMIC REORGANIZATION

The hierarchy of direct command is incorporated into our computer programmes, as we have just seen, by imposing it as a skeletal structure on the table of productive agents. Now the list of atomic actions in the automatic processor specifies the flow of work in the technological system, whereas the agent accounting table specifies the formal structure of the organization. When the two tables are interconnected by the operation of the computer, the various organizational groups of executives in the hierarchical line organization are given responsibility for specific areas of productive work. How the line organization is associated with the production processes is completely at the control of the investigators.Almost any form of formal organization that we can specify can be simulated by means of properly specifying the connections between the table of atomic actions and the social groups in the agent table. In particular, we can readily organize our simulated social groups:

- By stage of completion of work, after analogy to an industrial combination with top-level divisions responsible respectively for obtaining raw materials, for example, from mines or oil wells, for intermediate processing into semifinished products, and for final processing for completed products.
- By subprocesses, in a structure that might be exemplified by processing tax returns from the northeastern region, from the middleeastern region, and so forth, until all regions are represented.

- By predominant skill required to accomplish the technological work, for example, organization in terms of a division of engineers, of training specialists, of computer programers, etc., all combined to design a large, nationwide system of command and control over the flow of economic intelligence.
- By allowing the pseudo-random number generator to provide a "random" organization for us.

The form of organization need not remain static during the operation of the programmes, for the simulated executives can be made to restructure their own hierarchy of command dynamically as the simulation proceeds on the computer. This can be made to happen contingently on the occurrence of selected kinds of simulated events, for example, when consumer demand results in reducing the total kinds of products or services supplied by the total simulated system. The costs and consequences of different techniques for phasing over from one concrete form of organization to another in large social groups provide a fertile field for the application of Leviathan.

INFORMATION GENERATED IN THE TECHNOLOGICAL SYSTEM

Two basic kinds of information are generated by the technological system and are supplied to the executives in the governing system: information relating to production and information relating to manpower or social energy of the productive agents.

In the production area, the executives have access to information concerning the capacity of storage queues, the degree to which they are filled, the rate of entry of items into the subprocessing lines, and the quantity of items entering per epoch.

Information about manpower is generated in this way. At the end of an epoch, the taylors expended by each agent are extracted from the agent accounting table and recorded. Also, the taylors expended in each skill class are aggregated for each entire squad. If we think of the individual workers occupying rows in the accounting tables, the sum of taylors taken across each row at the end of an epoch is the total taylors expended per worker during that epoch. The totals of the columns represent the taylors expended per skill class by the entire squad. The original values set in the table at the start of each epoch represent, when aggregated by columns, the skill resources of the respective squads. Further aggregations of the squads furnish the skill resources and the expenditure of taylors by entire groupings on the first and higher supervisory levels in the pyramid of command.

Unless the investigators or the simulated executives specify otherwise, all information to the higher echelons of command during a simulation automatically follows the formal chart. This is true for information relating both to production and manpower. With time lags specified by the investigators, such information is sent in aggregate form to the executive offices in the command pyramid. Each office has access to information in the area of production and in the cadres of agents under its command. Each office receives this information in two forms: aggregated for the total area under its command and differentiated with respect to the organizational groups reporting to it.

In the information available at the higher echelons of command, the clumps of information may be too gross for many purposes of control and command. To obtain finer-grained information, specific messages requesting such data can be sent, interpreted, and answered. Of course, all such communication is subject to routine lags, in times for delivery.

22.5.5 INFORMATION INTERPRETED AND ASSESSED ACCORDING TO CRITERIA

Some information is tested by criteria and evaluated in the light of such criteria, and only the result of evaluation is passed forward to other executive offices. Suppose that in the agent accounting tables, taylors are insufficient to complete the work assigned to a given organizational group during an epoch. Criteria (simple numbers) are available to the executives to determine whether the insufficiency is so great that an agent should simply be transferred out of one group into the lacking group. Other criteria support decisions to interchange productive agents between pairs of groups for better fit of skills to skill requirements. The data relate to insufficiencies of specific amounts and skill categories. The assessment can be: we need an additional man. Many similar criteria are formed and assessment are made at various points in the command echelon.

DECISION MAKING

DECISION MAKING AND THE DEVELOPMENT OF SOCIAL GROUPS

Decisions that significantly affect the operation of a social organization can conveniently be classified between two poles. One pole is that of control, tactics, administration, implementation; the other is that of command, strategy, and policy. Decisions of control are directed toward maintaining an organization within the direction of progress prescribed for it by decisions of command. For decisions of command, futurity is of the essence. These are choices that shape the future of an organization and open it to development, whereas decisions of control are far more closed in viewpoint, seeking to maintain an organization as prescribed by command. Because the interplay of structure and dynamics is of central concern for the Leviathan studies, the relationships between these two kinds of decisions become very important. Command prescribes new complexes of structure and function; control implements these prescriptions. But this is not all. Command transforms itself dynamically as an organization lives out its destiny. Very rarely can an executive or group of executives elect a future in a single act of choice and then realize that future with any precision. Like the headlamps of an automobile at night, command lights up the country that lies ahead, but does so for evervarying distances; control remains closely bound to the present, even when it delivers what command exhorts, for where the roads lie and how they interconnect deeply affects the progress of the vehicle. Thus, decisions of command shape the future of an organization, and decisions of control implement these; but on a higher level of synthesis, viable command is constantly tested, monitored, and itself reshaped in a healthy organization.

According to this view, decision in the governing system is the essence of the executive process, because it is the key instrument by which the social organization constantly recreates and reestablishes itself. Thus, a just formulation of the executive decision-making processes becomes of crucial concern to Leviathan. For the formulation will dictate how the computer programmes are written for Leviathan and how they enact or represent the command and control functions.

THE SIMULATED DECISION MAKERS

The governing system in any productive organization can be viewed as an elaborate set of transmission and decision nodes, connected by system links. In structuring such nets, we can attend to the links or to the nodes. What happens at the nodes?

In the computer programmes, the decision makers are given bit relationships to represent individual traits. Values for these traits are parameters specified by the investigators as pure, logical variables, scaled from one to seven, with neutral point at four. If a tendency of an executive to make

decisions leading to expansion of his situation be scaled, *one* would represent strong tendencies to contraction; *two,* moderate tendencies; *three,* slight tendencies; *four,* neutral; *five,* slightly toward expansion; *six,* moderate; and *seven,* strong. In similar fashion, pure scale variables can be associated with speed of decision making, alacrity in execution, proclivity to delegate responsibility for decision making, tendencies to consult line, staff, associates, or supervisors for information or for direction in which to decide, tendency to centralize, quantity of parallel decision processes, prefiltering demands for decisions by importance, quantity of prefiltering, degree to which associates are informally consulted, tolerance of ambiguity, self-protectiveness, tendency to elaborate channels, and the like.

Once such sets of tendencies are chosen for individual executives situated at decision nodes in the formal organization, modifiers are introduced. The modifiers have the effect of altering the foregoing tendencies differentially, depending on the subject matter decided upon.

			Tendency						
			-			N			+
Modifier			1	2	3	4	5	6	7
	-	1	1	1	2	2	3	3	4
		2	1	2	2	3	3	4	4
		3	2	2	3	3	4	4	5
	N	4	2	3	3	4	4	5	5
		5	3	3	4	4	5	5	6
		6	3	4	4	5	5	6	6
	+	7	4	4	5	5	6	6	7

Fig. Effect of modifiers on tendencies.

Thus some executives will realize their extreme tendencies (for example, a tendency to caution) more fully with respect to human relations than with respect to problems of production. Or they may realize them more fully in economic matters than in setting priorities. Among the modifiers are those which take effect with respect to efficiency of manpower, effectiveness of manpower, production rates, products, capital, small issues in general, and large issues. Given a tendency, a row is selected in the matrix depending on the place an individual executive is made to occupy in the scale of seven. His modifiers are values represented in the rows. Once a column and a row are specified—a tendency and a modifier—then a cell in the matrix is determined, and the value in the cell is the resulting tendency employed in the simulation for that executive under those circumstances.In addition to tendencies and modifiers, a further weighting factor is required before a given decision results. This is a relevance factor. The various tendencies are significant only to limited degrees, depending on the subject matter of the decision. In making decisions, men assess matters of semantic relevance. People fit their judgments to the objects concerning which judgments are made (while they always do this, they do not always do this well). Computers do not have this kind of semantic insight. Hence the investigators must build into the computer programmes a comprehensive scheme of relevance factors.22.6.3 The Decision Sequence. The remainder of the decision process is essentially a matter of behavioral mechanisms. This does not mean that the mechanisms will not result in very complicated sequences of interactions between executives. But complication can always be delegated to a computer, provided that the micro-operations are experimentally controlled. The investigator prescribes the stitches to be executed and the spools of variously dyed threads; the computer weaves out the social fabric. These are the stages in the individual decision processes as they will be incorporated in Leviathan's computer programmes:

- Filtering. When the time of decision making arrives for each simulated executive, many requests for decisions, originating both from other areas in the organization and from his inner driving interests, simultaneously press for satisfaction. Each executive initially filters these to select the objects about which his next decision will be concerned. Parameters that will be controllable include span of selection, rate of filtering, criteria for priority filtering.
- Elaboration. Often the decision will be that more information is required. The decision process will temporarily be arrested as requests issue from him for further data. Or he searches his own store of impressions to collect the basis for making the decision. The result of elaboration is a perception of alternative choices open to him. Parameters include direction of consultation (up, down, staff, associates), rate, amount, relevance.
- Evaluation. He next forms an estimate of the problem

to be solved and the data available. Parameters include relevance, rate, and the disciplines for establishing criteria.

- Determining objectives. Based on his perception of existing policy, he seeks to determine the answers to questions about the outcome of his process of deciding such as: To what end? What for? Parameters include relevance, rate, sources of objectives.
- Choice. He chooses among the alternatives available, forming an estimate of the relevance of the various alternatives to the problem to be solved and the objectives currently acknowledged.
- Implementation. He explores possibilities of implementation. Parameters are similar to those for elaboration.
- Command. He issues an order to execute. Parameters include rate and organizational location of recipients.
- Follow-up. He establishes within himself an intention to follow up to determine whether the command has been realized.

The outcome of the concerted activity of the executives will be the performance of the total organization. The executives, acting in concert, modulate the flow of work through the productive processes, the allocation of manpower, and the assignment of internal priorities. In short, they exercise control and command over the total system of which they comprise the governing complex.

Chapter 7

Business Simulation

R. Clay Sprowls is Associate Professor of Business Statistics and Assistant Director of the Western Data Processing Centre, the Graduate School of Business Administration, the University of California, Los Angeles. He received his Ph.D. in business statistics from the University of Chicago in 1951. His present research interest is in the use of electronic computers to simulate business operations. He is the author of a textbook, Elementary Statistics, and of papers on statistical methods.

DEFINITION AND EXAMPLES

"To simulate," according to Webster, is "to assume the appearance of, without the reality." This definition implies that simulation is concerned with the construction of models or prototypes of some part of reality. Models may be physical: for example, the model of an airplane which is flown in a wind tunnel to test the design and performance of the plane. They may be mathematical: for example, the set of equations describing the orbit of a satellite. They may be logical or input/output models: for example, the logistics of an air force described by a number of black boxes (including, perhaps, people) connected by rules of operations and decision making. Models need not be uniquely physical or mathematical or logical. They may involve elements of each of these classifications, especially the mathematical and logical.

The appearance of so much material in one book devoted to computer applications indicates that simulation is an important and interesting modern research tool of the behavioral sciences—as it has been in engineering and the physical sciences for a long, long time—and that a highspeed electronic computer is an integral part of many simulations.

This chapter is concerned with one attempt to simulate the complete operations of a small business firm, named the Task Manufacturing Corporation, on a high-speed electronic digital computer. *One may immediately ask: Why such a simulation? Is such a simulation justifiable? Can one reasonably construct a model which gives the appearance but not the reality of the business firm?

As one moves further and further away from the individual worker in, say, the warehouse, and up into management levels, his conception of, and dealings with, the firm become more and more a study of information flows. The employee in the warehouse may be concerned primarily with moving boxes of finished product from a location in the warehouse into a box car; this is his daily job. The boxes must be moved as a part of the business operation, but involvement with the physical movement falls almost exclusively to this one man. Employees of other departments who are concerned with these shipments—for example, inventory control, sales analysis, or accounting—deal with recorded data about this movement. Higher levels of management know about the movement, make decisions based upon it, and change policies as a result of it, but only on the basis of information contained in a report. The facts of the physical environment may not be at all important to them because the business system appears as an information processing system consisting of transactions (of which the warehouse movement is one), information about these transactions, and decisions and policies relating to these transactions. Simulating the complete operations of a business firm is the task of modeling the information processing system.

ASSUMPTIONS ABOUT THE TASK MANUFACTURING CORPORATION

The appearance of reality can be given in many ways. For example, a time series of random drawings from a probability distribution may give a reasonable representation of the sales of a firm. As a model of the market, it is a simple and rather unsophisticated representation. A more elaborate statistical model is a multiple regression equation relating sales of the firm to several independent variables. This kind of model is used in many of the so-called management games.The Task Manufacturing Corporation is based upon a different view of the nature of the models needed and is to be contrasted with management games in this as well as another way. The management game usually uses a simulated environment to study the behaviour of individuals or teams of players or to instruct such individuals or teams. These games always involve the presence of players. Simulations may also involve players and be used for instruction, but primarily they are directed toward studying the behaviour of the system either with the behaviour of individuals given, or without them entirely. As a result, the type of model needed for simulation may be quite different from one that will suffice for a management game. The Task Manufacturing Corporation especially takes a different view of the type of model needed.It starts with the premise that a business system is concerned with the origination of transactions (of many different kinds), with the recording of information in these transactions, and with the policies governing, and decisions based upon the processing of, the information in these transactions. The transactions in this simulation come from the subsystems of the firm.The most important subsystems which give rise to these transactions are

- Employees, or workers in the production process,
- Machines, or productive units,
- Customers, or buyers of the product,
- Vendors, or suppliers of raw materials, and
- Financial institutions, or sources of financing.

Models of the subsystems describe *individual units* of each, for example, individual employees, machines, customers, vendors, and financial institutions, rather than an over-all work force, or production system, or market place with merely mathematical equations relating gross economic and engineering variables. A main task in the simulation is developing models of these individuals from mathematical and logical relationships which reflect some understanding of basic mechanisms underlying each of them and give rise to transactions which are the source of information for operating and controlling the business firm.

The simulation is not complete when models of these five subsystems are finished. Certain information processing and bookkeeping procedures must be established. These include accounting for accounts receivable and payable, general accounting, cost accounting, inventory control, and other routine record keeping.

More important, the models must be linked together with company policies and plans in order to have a total system. It is these linkages that are the interesting and important things to study. There is no intent to make, for example, a model of a customer that can be used to predict what customers in the real world will do. The same is true for any of the other main subsystems. The intent is only to describe what they do for this firm in a manner that is consistent with whatever theory is available from the social and physical sciences and with empirical observations about the behaviour of their real-life counterparts. One important use of the simulation is to validate the individual models with respect to both the theory and the observations.

The most important part of this research effort is the study of the interrelationships among the different activities. Management science and data processing specialists are now talking about the whole business firm and integrated data processing. "Let's look at the business as a whole," is a slogan of the day. But the whole is more than the sum of its parts, and a great deal must be known about the performance, the activities, and the transactions of these parts in order to study the interrelations among them. The Task Manufacturing Corporation is an attempt to study these interrelations through the simulation of the business from subsystems composed of individual units.

A BRIEF DESCRIPTION OF TMC

In order to set TMC in perspective with respect to size

and scope, a very brief description is needed. The corporation employs about 400 people, 200 of whom are engaged in the direct labour activities of manufacturing a line of five related products in some combination of seven different operating departments. Four of these departments are machine shops: drill press, punch press, screw machine, and spot weld. The other three are finishing, assembly, and packaging. No single product uses all seven departments; only the packaging department deals with all five products. Final products are stocked in inventory in anticipation of sales which are made from a home office in Los Angeles to customers scattered geographically over the whole United States. Outside the immediate home office area, the sales outlets are generally large wholesalers or building-supply houses located in large cities. Near the home office, customers are also smaller wholesalers and both large and small retailers. At any one time, sales are made to between 150 and 200 customers.

Although the products have no real-life counterparts, they are thought of as items of the building-hardware type. The raw materials from which they are made are castings, steel strip, and steel bars. Both the strip and bars have different size specifications so that, altogether, eight different raw materials are carried in inventory and ordered from suppliers. The products do have manufacturing specifications, complete with blueprints, for use in production planning, tooling, and purchasing. The specifications for Product 2, a Stop Index Assembly, are shown on the drawing in Figure.

The products sell for around $1 each. Total annual sales volume for all products in the line is approximately $4 million. The corporation has $1 million of current assets and $1½million of total assets. It has 55,000 shares of $10 par stock outstanding and no bonded debt. Annual earnings are about $2 per share. It has at present no policy for paying dividends. This description makes the Task Manufacturing Corporation a small business firm by almost any definition.

EXAMPLE OF THE PRODUCTION PROCESS IN TMC

Limitation of space prevents a full discussion of all of the models used in TMC. The example given here in quite some detail is that of the production process.

The physical production of the products made by TMC involves the interaction of the employee and machine models. Individual employees work in each of the seven production departments. Individual machines are located in each of these departments. Employees are assigned to machines and scheduled to work on a particular product, and it is this combination of employee and machine that produces an output. Initially, company policy provides that one employee is assigned to one machine and there is no excess labour force. There is excess capacity in the sense that machines in some departments are idle and not in use because they are not needed to produce the scheduled production. At some future time, this company policy may change and an excess of employees over machines may be desirable or inevitable.

The basic time unit in which TMC operates is one week. Once an employee is scheduled to work on a particular product, a particular machine, and for a defined work week, none of these conditions can be changed until the next week. To be consistent with the time unit, new employees are hired to start at the beginning of the week, and employees quit or are fired at the end of the week. Machines that need overhaul are taken off the production line at the end of the week and scheduled back at the beginning of a week after the overhaul is completed. Further, an initial condition is that work in process normally moves from one department to another at the end of the week, but this condition can be changed to lessen work-in-process shortages when the previous department has a finished supply on hand from the current week's production.

THE MACHINE MODEL

Punch presses, drill presses, screw machines, and spot welders are machines. In the finishing, assembly, and packaging operations, the use of "machine" is meant only to convey the notion of a production unit of some sort. All machines used in TMC look alike; i.e., they all have the same general model. They differ from each other with respect to the parameters which describe their behaviour. The machine model reflects engineering design features and known data about machine operations. Parameters are selected that give realistic values to the simulated counterparts of real-life drill presses and punch presses working on products similar to those manufactured by TMC. The working tolerances are also realistic, as shown in Figure. Machine behaviour is described by a model which involves both mathematical and statistical relationships. The most important characteristics are described in some detail but without any exact relationships being given.

TMC machines can break down. The probability that a machine will break down is an exponential function increasing with the age of the machine, the time since its last overhaul, the number of overhauls, and the rate of machine breakdown. The latter is included on the assumption that a machine showing a propensity to break down will break down more often than one without this propensity. In other words, a machine's own behaviour modifies its future behaviour. If a machine breaks down, the length of down time is determined by a random drawing from a Poisson process. If a machine runs, its efficiency (a new machine is rated as 1.00) is an exponential function decreasing with the age of the machine and the number of overhauls.

A machine may be pulled off the production line for overhaul at any time, but built into the model is a company policy that an overhaul is ordered automatically when the productive efficiency reaches a certain level, say, 0.70. The value of this level may be changed.

The machine model is such that it implies company policies with respect not only to overhaul but also to replacement of old machines, to use of idle capacity (i.e., scheduling of idle machines with respect to age and operating efficiency), and to product assignment changes, which involve setup times.

One of the first uses of any model in TMC is its validation both with respect to theoretical considerations and known behaviour. Shows effective weekly operating hours of a single new machine with average parameter values for a period of eight years. The machine was scheduled for a standard day shift of 40 hours with no overtime.

The general shape of the curve is an exponential decreasing with time as was planned. The scale of the graph may be so small that minor variations are difficult to detect. Breakdowns occurred in the following weeks: 40, 64, 182, 249, 281, 295, 308, and 325.

The first overhaul took place automatically as a matter of policy in week 386 when the machine efficiency reached 0.70 or, on the graph, 28 effective hours. (Actually, 28.0 hours was first reported in week 383, but the efficiency was not down to exactly 0.70 and the reported 28.0 hours is a rounded value).

Immediately following the overhaul in week 388, effective hours are four hours less than expected because a setup time is involved. Then, the machine efficiency increased to 0.90 (36 hours) but not back to the level of a new machine. It is a characteristic of the model that the efficiency increases after an overhaul, but to a lower level after each succeeding overhaul. This characteristic implies that there will come a time when it no longer pays to overhaul.

The behaviour of this individual machine reflects both engineering features and known behaviour of actual machines of the kind simulated here. It is known to the operators of TMC. No attempt is made to predict the behaviour of real machines from this model.

The model is merely a device to originate production transactions from individual machines in order to study a production system. The simulated machine behaviour, at least in the author's opinion, appears to represent realistically actual machine behaviour.

THE EMPLOYEE MODEL

The individual employees who work in the TMC production departments have the same general characteristics. They, like the machines, differ with respect to the values of their parameters. In general, employees can quit, be absent, be injured, and vary in their efficiency (for which 1.00 is assumed a normal, or standard). Their behaviour is governed by mathematical and statistical functions of known characteristics.

For example, each new employee must learn to do his job. To reflect this, a learning curve is built into the model. The initial level of efficiency is primarily a function of the number of years of past experience. The average ultimate level an employee will reach is a function of accident and general health ratings. The rate at which he learns, i.e., proceeds from the initial level to the ultimate level, is a function of experience, education, and intelligence.

The parameter values of each of the characteristics mentioned—accident, health, experience, education, and intelligence are known from data recorded on an assumed employee application form. Some are a matter of record and entered by the applicant; others result from physical or psychological testing.

Once a new employee reaches his ultimate average efficiency level, his output is not constant at that level. The model is not deterministic in this sense. One examination given to employees is a psychological test for what is called "emotional stability." The value of this parameter causes an employee's efficiency to vary stochastically both in the amplitude and period of oscillation. An upper bound is placed on the efficiency. No fixed lower bound exists, but only a mechanism that forces employees to recover automatically from periods of very low efficiency if they do not quit or are not fired.

Years of experience	5	
Intelligence	100	(scaled from 70-160)
Education	12	(high school graduate)
Accident	5	(scaled from 1-10)
Health	5	(scaled from 1-10)
Emotional stability	0.25	(scaled from 0.1-0.5)

Figure the effective production hours for an average employee working a standard 40-hour work week on the day shift with no overtime for eight years. His ability to quit (and be fired) has been suppressed for this test in order to insure that the eight-year period will be completed. He has the following parameter values:

In this eight-year period, the employee had four absences—in weeks 40, 166, 235, and 319—each of one-day duration. He was injured for three hours in week 264. Had the "quit" or "be-fired" characteristics not been suppressed, he would not have quit nor would he have been fired. It took him five weeks to reach the standard efficiency of 1.00, and except for absences and injuries, his efficiency fluctuated between 39 and 43 effective work hours per 40-hour week.

Employees with different parameters will behave differently from the typical one illustrated. TMC has a cross section of workers ranging from very good to very poor, from very stable to very erratic, and from old to new.

RUNNING THE PRODUCTION MODEL

Individual employee and machine behaviour is known for typical units from a study of the outputs in Figures 23.1 and 23.2. In addition, standard production data for each operation are available as well as the schedule of operations for each product. Again, it is not possible to report here all the relevant data, but some examples can be given.

Figure illustrates data of a typical operation scheduling chart, that for Product 2, a Stop Index assembly for which the specifications are given in Figure. A similar chart is available for each of the five products. It shows the *physical* flow of raw materials and work in process from the time of ordering until the finished goods are sent to the shipping department. The lead times (in weeks) are firm once the material enters the first production department, because the basic time unit in the simulation is one week. The variable lead time indicated for the ordering of raw materials is determined by the vendor model and inventory policy. To give some idea of the complexity of even a simple production model for a small firm, a chart of the physical flow of all materials This figure is a composite of the separate product operation scheduling charges. Although Figure shows the punch press, screw machine, drill press, and spot weld departments at the same level with respect to this flow, they are drawn this way for convenience and not because work in process does not flow between some pair of them. Products 1 and 4, for example, move from the punch press to the drill press department. Neither is the flow necessarily directly through the departments as they are laid out here. One exception is the movement of Product 1 from assembly back to finishing and then on to packaging.

There are two parts to running the production process: planning and operation. Planning involves setting a production schedule based upon a sales forecast. This forecast may come from a computer model or from extensions of past sales data, or it may be given without any explanation. Operating results then come from a computer run with the employee and machine models scheduled to operate according to the plan. Reports are generated weekly to show the results and, in some instances, to explain or provide clues to the causes of seemingly exceptional behaviour. On the basis of a comparison of the results and the plans, changes can be made, a new set of plans instituted, and the production model run for another period, etc., in an alternating sequence of planning and operating.

At present, changes in plans are made by people. No provision is made (it will ultimately be provided) to change plans by a built-in scheduling process. The production process can be run for several weeks with the same set of plans, i.e., a fixed schedule.

Without other models, one can study only a part of the physical aspects of production. With inventory and vendor models and an accounting system added, one may study the interrelationships between planning and operations with respect to features such as alternative schedules, overtime versus new employees, machine assignments, second shifts, machine replacement versus overhaul, hiring and firing, etc. Routine reports may not always give clues to causes of abnormal behaviour. Because data are recorded on a transaction basis and kept in permanent files, special reports may be needed to explain a behaviour in more detail.

Ultimately, the firm will be run entirely on an exception principle, once enough is known to state rules that define exceptions and the actions to be taken.

People are brought into the simulation at an early stage not only because their presence simplifies the simulation in some hard areas (scheduling, for example), but to involve them in the use of simulation as an educational exercise.

EXTENSIONS AND ALTERNATIVE MODELS

The paper has discussed at some length employee and machine models. These represent one specification, but not the only one, for two basic subsystems of a business firm. With time, alternative models not only of these but of other subsystems should be available. In fact, a library of models is being planned from which one can pick and choose in order to simulate a complex system with desired characteristics.

The machine model described in this paper is rather uninteresting. Since it is a useful device for generating production transactions, a more elaborate specification of the same kind is probably not desirable. Alternatively, numerically controlled machine tools could be introduced. Such a model involves the design of an alternative plant with changes not only in the individual machine model, but also in the whole concept of the role of the individual employee and, therefore, in the employee model as well. One graduate student has already begun an investigation into this alternative, describing for a single product both the programme needed to control a machine to produce the product and some estimates of the cost and numbers of such tools needed.

The present model for an employee is useful but rather mechanical. It does not incorporate or recognize researches into human behaviour from the behavioral sciences. An alternative formulation which would take such research into account could be based upon the theory of employee behaviour developed by March and Simon. This model takes into account the motivations of satisfaction and dissatisfaction with the job, a search for alternatives, and the probability of finding such alternatives.

Even without going so far as to design a new employee model, additions to the present model may make it more interesting. Use can be made of the emotional stability characteristic that is already a part of employee behaviour to introduce a group effect so that individuals affect and are affected by the behaviour of the group. Such an effect could be on both a departmental and plant-wide basis, depending upon the design.

As the simulation proceeds, more and more extensions and alternatives will present themselves; ultimately, a library of models for each subsystem will be available.

Chapter 8

Simulation of International Relations and Diplomacy

Oliver Benson is Professor of Government, Chairman of the Department of Government, and Chairman of the International Studies Programme at the University of Oklahoma. He is a graduate of the Institute of International Studies of the University of Geneva, where he received the degree Docteur U+0OE8s sciences politiques in 1936. Author of a book on the diplomatic origins of World War II and of some thirty articles on current world politics, he served for six years as editor of the Southwestern Social Science Quarterly.

As an academic field, international relations is relatively new. Usually offered in American colleges and universities in departments of political science, it is for the most part a post-World War I discipline. The older specialties, diplomatic history and international law, were blended with the newer study of power to create a more realistic set of concepts. Though definitions vary widely, and disagreement is sometimes violent, most academic workers in the field would agree, with different emphasis, that the subject is concerned with the interaction of those societal conglomerates habitually holding ultimate loyalty of the constituent individuals, or as in Hans Morgenthau title, with *Politics among Nations*.

QUANTITATIVE METHODS IN INTERNATIONAL RELATIONS

Research patterns in international relations are as various as the definitions, although the reader interested in computers, but incidentally familiar with typical works on diplomacy. So too may the specialist in international relations. Nevertheless, quantitative elements have had at least a limited part in the work of many scholars, alongside the more traditional historical and legal studies, and the more modern analytical, socioeconomic, psychological, policy development, and problem-solving approaches.

Statistics

The average college textbook in international relations includes at least several tables of descriptive statistics on international trade, military establishments and costs, natural resources, and comparative data on various indicators of national strength. Such content is rarely given any inferential analysis or manipulation beyond the level of deriving percentages, but its inclusion suggests a continuing assumption that it is relevant. Outstanding among treatises using considerable quantities of statistics is Quincy Wright major work, *A Study of War*. Wright also suggests a number of tentative general hypotheses in simple mathematical models.

Capabilities Analysis

Measuring national power and war potential with a combination of statistical and analytical methods is a special field of research. The application of capabilities analysis has sharpened the long-standing concept of the balance of power, one of the timehonored "laws" of presumed universal applicability in diplomacy. Klaus Knorr's *War Potential of Nations* is an example. He suggests that major account should be taken of resources, motivation, and administrative skills—a good indication of how concrete and imponderable factors are combined. Political geographers, notably Stephen B. Jones, have contributed both information and ideas to the task of analysis of the strategic implications of power distribution. Jones, like Knorr, stresses the importance of both "quantity modifiers" and "quality modifiers" of national strength.

Decision-making Analysis

Application of the methods of sociologists and psychologists to international relations has greatly enriched its research equipment. The work of Richard C. Snyder and his colleagues on decision making as a focus, and that of Herbert Simon and his associates in the more generalized field of public administration, have forced a re-evaluation of methodology throughout the entire discipline of political science. Simon *Models of Man* is a more thoroughly mathematized treatment, employing formal models for the manipulation of social and psychological variables in the study of human and group behaviour.

MATHEMATICAL METHODS

More strictly mathematical treatment is rare, but is represented by a growing number of research workers in international relations. The newness of the field is indicated by the date (1939) of the first major mathematical monograph entirely concerned with international politics—that of Lewis F. Richardson.

Calculus of Armament Contests

Richardson concentrated his attention on the spiral of armament races, developing a system of equations meant to represent each state's desire to exceed its rivals. Such a system he showed to be unstable, since the equations are satisfied only if all war potentials increase indefinitely and exponentially. He introduced complications for parameters other than armament costs, expanded his calculus to provide for *n* states, and supplied empirical runs for the periods leading up to the two World Wars. Owing to the inclusion of two selections from his writing in the popular *The World of Mathematics*, his work is probably the purely mathematical treatment best known to the general reader.

Maurice Ash, in a suggestion bearing some similarity to marginal economic analysis, postulates a "constant power curve" of maximal security, which rises ever more steeply as reserves are exhausted. He suggests that a country's desperation increases as it approaches the end of its capacity to mobilize reserves: at a certain point, only war can redress the balance. Applications based on the Ash approach might indicate the probability of a war of desperation, such as (perhaps) the Israeli attack on Egypt in 1956.

Arthur Burns, of the Australian National University, develops a similar point by the use of "multiplier diagrams," verging on game theory but in an essentially subjective treatment. His system supplies hints as to changes which come with varying degrees of information about the rival and with the development of radically new weapons systems. The graphic "rectangle of greatest danger" is plausibly found to be in a period of secret armament with substantial forces, because of the uncertainty of information available to the rivals.

Game Theory

It is a tribute both to mathematicians and political analysts that they have shown the greatest caution in attempts to use game theory in the study of world politic, despite its superficially apparent applicability. Morton Kaplan, Thomas Schelling, and others, have done preliminary work with its methods, which offer promise for the investigation of situations where goals partly conflict and partly coincide and where cognizant choice is based on evaluation of the possible outcomes. Rapoport suggests that the study of large-scale human behaviour may eventually require theoretical methods between the two extremes of Richardson's differential equations of physical determinism, on the one hand, and game theory's allowance for human choice, on the other.

General Applications

Several scholars suggest more broadly based systems of analysis to connect mathematical-statistical methods and the more traditional approaches. Quincy Wright suggests that within the general field of international studies there be developed a small quantitatively oriented "discipline," parsimonious of assumptions, and so organized as to be self-correcting and self-improving. "The Form of a Discipline of International Relations," he suggests a semimathematical model, wherein the available data, both objective and subjective, are manipulated to locate elements of the various states in a sort of twelve-dimensional space, on axes of flexibility, energy, strength, cooperation, technical advance, and resource abundance (the "capability field"), and of abstractness, objectivity, liberality, situation-orientation, affirmation, and manipulation (in a "value field"). He draws on objective data for about half of these locators, including population, trade, literacy, government employees, ranking administrators, income, national budgets, exchange of mail, energy production and resources, land area, education, and participation in international organizations. The other half of his data is based entirely on subjective judgments. By spotting successive changes in location, he would hope to develop vectors for the various states with reference to the twelve axes.

Karl Deutsch, who has worked most energetically with actual data as applied to international relations, urges political scientists to give more time to processing and interpreting the great quantities of data they spend so much time acquiring. He has developed an analysis of international trade, using three 100 × 100 matrices processed on a computer, to detect trends of international interaction since World War II—a project which no tool less capable than the computer could perform, given the 30,000 matrix boxes involved. Deutsch has also suggested a variety of methods for establishing typologies of states, as well as of their interactions, by the arrangement of data deemed to bear on the stability and capabilities of governments. Some 75 categories of data, combined into 24 ratios, result in a tentative classification scheme which could serve as a starting point for examination of many hypotheses about international behaviour.

SIMULATION

The complicated problems of war have long been studied under certain patterns of simulation, but only in recent years has the general field of diplomacy received similar analysis. Simulation is an artificial model of (hopefully) the most significant features and operating principles of reality, or in the felicitous phrase applied by the editors of *Harper*'s to Simulmatics' electoral behaviour simulation for the 1960 presidential campaign, "make-believe on mathematical principles."

GUETZKOW'S INTER-NATION SIMULATION

In the Northwestern University International Relations Programme, Harold Guetzkow has conducted a series of carefully designed and imaginative experiments with human actors playing the roles of internal and external decision makers in a setting of inter-nation interaction.

The simulation was designed both for theoretical study and for instruction and contained patterns of internal pressures on decision makers as well as external problems.

Precise rules were worked out, but considerable freedom of decision was left to the role players, making possible a study of their "quasi-nation" actions. Guetzkow has worked out a series of scales for measurement of a number of variable influences found to bear on decision, but at this writing the quantitative findings are considered too tentative for definitive conclusions.

A "BALANCE OF POWER" GAME

At the Princeton Centre of International Studies, Morton Kaplan, Arthur Burns, and Richard Quandt devised a "possible set of rules" for a competitive game, intended to test a generalized model of a balance-of-power international system. Their theoretical analysis of the system postulated is rigorously abstract, so that exploration of the properties of the system could be carried out without qualitative influences from the real world.

Their simulation, like Guetzkow's, is deemed still experimental, and they expressly disclaim any belief that their game can turn up positive principles. At most, they think, it may be useful in ruling out traditional beliefs about the "balance of power."

Though not exhaustive, this brief survey indicates that mathematization and quantification in international analysis certainly have a fascination for many scholars, including some of the most eminent in the discipline.

It is clear that further research along the lines blocked out by these studies can be based only on some minimal command of mathematical and quantitative method. It is equally clear that such research, if not guaranteed to be fruitful, at least offers some promise of usefulness.

THE SIMULATION PROGRAMME: "A SIMPLE DIPLOMATIC GAME"

With the foregoing considerations in mind, the author has put together a somewhat crudely designed simulation programme meant to duplicate some of the obvious features of international politics. The reader is cautioned that the. project is more an experiment in the introduction of computer techniques to the field of international relations than a serious research project. It is hoped that eventually valuable results may come, not specifically from this particular programme, but from further applications of computer methods which it may suggest.

How the Simulation Is Organized

Development of the simulation programme required arbitrary decisions on a number of elements in international politics on which no general agreement exists. For example, the two most crucial indexes derived in the programme are those on "war potential" and "propensity to act" (a rough measure of aggressiveness). Although both concepts are common in international relations literature, quantification of them is certainly open to argument.

The author emphasizes that he is not committed to the particular quantification formulas he has adopted, nor even to the idea that any system of indexing these qualities can give a reliable indicator. They are used in the programme solely to find out whether yaluable results can be obtained by tentative assumptions. For an overview of the programme, there follows a listing of the major routines employed, with a suggestion as to the purpose of each.

The Storage Routine

This stores all data employed in the programme. These original data consist of nine war potential indicators (population, military age manpower, transportation, gross national product, gross national product *per capita,* energy production, steel production, literacy, and atomic capability) for each of nine major states; nine weights for gaging the relative importance of these factors; nine subjective indicators, for the same nine states, of "propensity to action" drawn from Quincy Wright's capability and analytical fields; weights for these; location of the nine states and of nine small target states in latitude and longitude; alliance membership of the eighteen states; information about overseas military bases maintained by the nine major states; information about the mutual trade between the nine major states and the nine target states; information about the total trade of each of the eighteen states; a special notation of whether each of the nine major states is a nuclear power; a table of haversines for use in the determination of distance; a table of intensities of action for use in selection of counteractions; and a variety of alphanumeric codes for the final printout.

The Preliminary Computation Routine

This derives the war potential indexes, the "propensity" indexes, a deduction factor for low propensity, and a "value of the international situation" for each of nine actor states.

The Action Routine

This constitutes the heart of the programme; it is initiated by an "action card," describing an action by one of the nine states against one of nine targets, and eventuates in a determination of a logical counteraction by each of the actors other than the one initiating action.

The three processes next described are involved in this determination. The Coalition Strength and Leadership routine selects the two strongest coalitions and their leaders, and defines the "nature of the universe" as "tight bipolar," "loose bipolar," or "balance of power."

The Selection of Counteractions routine consists of four sections. In the first, a distance routine yields an index of proximity. A trade index is computed as the average of total trade and mutual trade. Coalition status and presence of overseas bases are related to these in order to supply an "interest index," indicating the interest of each actor in the target.

This composite interest index becomes one of three factors (intensity of action and original war potential index being the other two), whose product determines the presumed loss to each state (or gain to initiator of action). Selection of counteractions is then made, the action selected being that needed to redress loss.

The counteractions chosen will range in intensity from.100 to.900, the index representing presumed percentage of effort required to carry them out. In the Revision of Counteractions routine, four revisions may occur:

- The index is lowered by the low propensity deduction.
- It is lowered to.800 should the logic lead to.900, and the actor not be a nuclear power (.900 is the index for maximum intensity and is coded HBOMB in our programme).
- It is lowered to.700 should the logic lead to any higher index, should the state be an ally of the initiator of action, and the universe polar (.800 is the index identified as war, and our rules exclude war against an ally in any but a balance of power world).
- "Nature of the universe" revisions complete this routine. In a loose or tight bipolar universe, the leaders of the two strongest coalitions counteract to recover relatively the same power they had before (i.e., the same percentage of total power); in a balance of power universe, all states counteract to recover relative power. In a tight bipolar world, only the two leaders act, their allies merely supporting them.

Finally, using the new strengths of the nine actor states, the programme recomputes indexes based on 100 per cent and assigns these as the new values for use in future runs, in either a "competitive" game or a "stochastic" game, at the option of the user.

Alliance Change on Loss Routine

This part of the programme maintains a count-box for each of the states. If the initiator of action is a leader of one of the two strongest coalitions, the routine is entered. If one of the leader's allies ends the cycle with a net loss, the ally's tally is increased by one. On three successive losses, an ally becomes a neutral, and a neutral joins the rival coalition. Losses resulting from the rival coalition leader's initiative restores the tally to zero. This feature of the programme makes the coalition alignments unpredictable should the user select the "stochastic" game at the outset; should he select the status quo game, original coalition data are used.

Competitive Game Routine and Printout

An "alternator" is used to determine which of two permissible players (or teams) is involved if the user has designated the run as a "competitive" game. Every second competitive run concludes by a comparison of the gain-loss ratio of the two initiators of action. If the first gained relatively more (or lost less) than the second, A is listed in the printout; if the second gained relatively more, B is indicated; if the gains (or losses) were equal, AB is the entry.

The printout reports the initial action, the counteractions selected by each of the other eight major states, the interest index, the new war potential index, the "value of the international situation," the new nature of the universe, and any alliance changes.

COMPUTER TECHNIQUES USED IN THE SIMULATION

Without attempting a complete analysis of the programme, it has seemed desirable to review a few of the more standard computer programing problems encountered in its preparati

Branching

Branch instructions are the computer's logic. On them depend some of the remarkable achievements so mystifying to the layman, as well as some of the purely "showy" demonstrations that have little relevance to the true purpose of the machine.

Most machines employ similar branching devices; most used are tests to detect a zero and tests for the sign.

The IBM 650 instructions BMI, NZU, and NZE, together with similar instructions for indexing registers, are typical. Upon receiving the instruction BMI (Branch on MInus), the programme tests the accumulator for a minus sign; if the accumulator is minus, the programme goes to one address for its next instruction; if not minus, it goes to another. The NZ instructions effect a similar branch by testing whether the accumulator is zero. By combining these two-way tests, the programer may achieve a complicated pattern of alternative branches.

As an example, in the branch for "nature of the universe," somewhat different principles of action should be applied depending on the relative distribution of strength among the nine major states, as well as within the two dominant coalitions.

For consistency with certain general theory about power politics, a distinction is made among the "balance of power," the "loose bipolar," and the "tight bipolar" distributions.

Having added together the war potential indexes of states in each coalition, and having arrayed the coalitions in order of strength, the programme proceeds, in the section portrayed, to test the combined strength of the two most powerful groups.

In addition to this test, a determination is made as to whether the strongest state in each coalition is dominant.

The reader will note that the programme fragment consists entirely of branches, denoted in flow chart convention by the oval boxes.Another device effective for multiple branching is used in the original storage routine. Space is provided on the data cards for two different items of input information:

- An instruction location
- The location in which to store the first of five data items contained sequentially in the first five spaces on the card. The multiple-multiple branch thus effected can handle any variety of categories and subcategories desired.Translating machine language into plain words, the programme to store a variety of data will be
- Read the card (results in storage of the eight "words" in a defined read region). in five successive storage locations beginning with the location specified in word seven of the read region.
- Read another card.

The sequence is terminated by a final "end of data" card coded as null except for the location of a terminating instruction in word eight. In our programme, this relatively simple device stores all the original data listed above in 24.4.1.1.

The Loop

The loop is the programing device most significant to the computer's great power. Essentially it consists of a fixed or conditional number of iterations of a sequence of arithmetic-logical steps with modification of factors on each iteration. Following each iteration, a test is necessary to determine whether the required number of passes has been made. The test is usually made by a count-box, if the number of passes is fixed, or by reference to a maximum satisfactory error factor, if conditional.

The count-box is actually a regular storage location, in which the programme had previously entered the number of passes required. Following each iteration, this number is reduced by one; the zero branch test is used to terminate the loop and send the programme to its next section. Most advanced computers provide special count-boxes, or "index registers," which make the programing of loops far simpler, though the basic logic remains the same.

Loops, and testing for their termination, occupy a special

place among programing hazards. The beginner is urged to ponder carefully these words of McCracken.

Depending on the nature of the loop and of the test, it is possible to make a truly remarkable variety of mistakes in testing. If the loop should be carried out n times, it is quite easy to make mistakes which will result in doing it:

- Not at all;
- n – 1 times;
- n + 1 times;
- 2n times;
- Until the power fails or the machine breaks down.

Most programmes of any complexity will have nested loops, i.e., loops within loops; it is not unusual to have as many as five layers of such nested loops, but programmes of that order are best left to the expert. The novice need only realize that such a programme, once perfected, offers no more intrinsic difficulty for the computer than the simple adding of one and one. This may seem a great labour for a small result, but it must be remembered that neither the complexity of the factors nor the variety of arithmetic steps involved presents any greater problem than the simple addition and multiplication here performed.

As an example of a loop concerned almost entirely with logical operations, at one point in the programme it is necessary to distinguish the leading power in each of the two strongest coalitions. The naked eye, observing written data, could accomplish this at a glance in the actual world of today. But our programme is generalized, our computer a moron, and our data numerous. It is therefore necessary to prepare instructions following somewhat the pattern of Figure. (The fragment above, with it sequel, has provided us with indexes of strength, and our original data tell us the coalition affiliation of each state.)

In this chart, C refers to the combined war potential indexes of the states in a given coalition; Cd, to the code number of the coalition (5 are provided for); Scd, to the same code numbers supplied in the original data to identify the coalition affiliation of the nine major states; Lcd, to the code number, determined in the programme, of the leading member of a given coalition; W, to the war potential indexes of the nine major states.

It may be noted that by substituting x for 4 in the first instruction of section B of the chart, the same routine could be used to arrange any given number of factors in an array in order of magnitude from largest to smallest, a device useful in many statistical applications.

Subroutines

For the beginning programer, the most welcome discovery is that much of his labour has already been performed. In any computer installation will be found a library of *subroutines,* expertly prepared programme sections which may be tied into any programme by suitable devices. Matrix multiplication, regression by least squares, chi-square tests, indeed any commonly used mathematical or statistical process, will be available, and more are being added daily. Moreover, by understanding the technique for including a subroutine in a programme, the beginner acquires a useful method for identifying fragments of his own programmes which are used over and over, and which may therefore become subroutines of his own devising.The subroutine is addressed each time entered by a fixed calling sequence. The calling sequence must include:

- The location of the instruction to which the programer wishes to exit when the subroutine is completed.
- The numerical data to be processed by the subroutine, or the location of that data. If tabular material is to be processed sequentially, first and last locations may be designated.
- The address of the first instruction of the subroutine.

The subroutine begins by storing the exit instruction. It proceeds to its efficient manipulation of the data indicated, places the answer or answers in locations promised in the writeup, and exits to the instruction prescribed by the user. Any process used often in a programme may usually be reduced to a subroutine by the programer himself. Though the result will lack the nicety of the experts, the technique is useful for a lengthy fragment even if used only twice. In using subroutines prepared by others, the programer must follow the instructions of the writeup meticulously, or he will find himself in immediate trouble.

In the diplomatic simulation programme, most repetitive patterns are handled by loops, but subroutines are used in several situations. Typical of a genuine mathematical manipulation is a sine routine employed as part of the process of determining distance between actor and target states, used in turn in the so-called interest index. On each action card, nine haversines are derived, i.e., the programme shown in the chart is contained within an outer loop set for nine iterations. Latitude and longitude for the eighteen states are supplied by the original data cards.

Another example is a programer's output subroutine, used to provide two sets of printouts: the original printout of nine lines descriptive of conditions at outset of action and the eventual printout of nine lines descriptive of counteractions and conditions resulting therefrom. Widely separated in the programme, they nevertheless follow the same logical sequences, since the basic job in a printout is filling the appropriate words of the printout band needed to prepare a single line of output.

Alternators

The alternator is a special form of branch, used when two parts of a programme are to be entered in regular alternation on successive passes. The programme fluctuates regularly between the initial instructions of the first and final printout routines. Since these two sets of output are always printed in the same order, the situation calls for an alternator. Many devices are possible, but the "flip-flop" illustrated is a trick often used for accomplishing the purpose. We set a "+ 1" initially in a location coded here as ALTNR.

In IBM's SOAP symbolic programing language, this alternation is done by three simple instructions:

RSL ALTNR
STL ALTNR
BMIFIRST FINAL

RSL is instruction I of the table; STL is instruction 2; BMI is the branch on minus.

Table Look-Up

The table look-up instruction is a feature of several machines, including the IBM 650, and where not provided can be programed.

Essentially, it results in counting the locations from a fixed base to the location containing a number equal to, or higher than, an indicated number.

This count is then entered in the accumulator, where it may be used as an address for any desired manipulation of the number sought. Often, table entries can be packed together with factors associated with each entry, so that when the desired entry is found, the factor associated with it can be used.

Instruction	Content of "ALTNR"	Content of accumulator
(First Pass)		
1. Clear accumulator; subtract contents of "ALTNR" from it.	+1	-1
2. Store accumulator in "ALTNR."	-1	-1
3. Is accumulator negative? (Yes; branch to first printout)		
(Second Pass)		
1. Clear accumulator; subtract contents of "ALTNR" from it.	-1	+1
2. Store accumulator in "ALTNR."	+1	+1
3. Is accumulator negative? (No; branch to final printout)		

Fig. Alternators

In the distance routine described above, the assumption is made that the interest index of a state declines with distance. Suitable ingredients for the interest index are therefore packed as descending numbers in a table of ascending haversines.

Location	Contents	
	Haversine table	Interest factor
1200	002447	1000
1201	009549	0900
1202	020611	0800
1203	034549	0700
1204	050000	0600
1205	065451	0500
1206	079389	0400
1207	090451	0300
1208	097553	0200
1209	999999	0100

Once the look-up instruction reports the location of the haversine equal to, or greater than, the one which denotes the great circle arc between our actor and target states, the contents of that location are brought to the accumulator.

By the simple "shift left six" instruction the six leading digits are discarded and the desired "interest" ingredient obtained.

The solid bank of 9's in location 1209 is designed to stop the search, regardless of a possible error in computation of the haversine.

Even safer would be a "stop" completely filled with 9's, since no higher factor would be possible, and thus the look-up instruction would certainly cease searching at this point. Depending on the exact purpose of the search, the 9's might serve to indicate an error, to switch the programme to another table, or to send the programme to another branch.

Another convenience of the table look-up is the possibility of storing associated factors in another table following the one searched. Since each entry in the associated table is separated by the same fixed number of locations from its corresponding entry in the base table, the count reported may be added to this fixed number to obtain the location of the desired factor. As an illustration, our simulation employs alphanumeric codes to indicate approximate intensity of diplomatic or military actions, and these are tabulated in sequence after the table of intensities.

If the table look-up instruction is entered as "1959" to search for intensity 859, it will nevertheless begin the search at location 1950 (only certain locations are possible as initial table search bases). Instead of location 1958 being reported for an action of maximum intensity, however, the count will be added to the instruction actually entered, so that location 1967 will be reported.

This is the location in which is stored a set of alphanumeric digits, translatable by a special feature of board wiring into the alphabetic code word "HBOMB," used in the programme printout to suggest maximum intensity of action (the other code words represent, respectively: diplomatic protest, UN action, severing diplomatic relations, subversion campaign, boycott or reprisals, troop movements, full mobilization, and limited war).

TRIAL RUNS AND FINDINGS

Since the simulation programme is intended mainly to suggest and to test hypotheses about international interaction of states (most cautiously, be it emphasized), the reader is entitled to a report on what has been done in this direction. The limited runs thus far are in no sense conclusive of anything, least of all of the adequacy of the programme, but with that warning, a few tentative principles seem to find certain support.

The method used in actual runs is to feed, as input, successive intensities of action by different major states against different target states and to record the effects on the actor, his rivals, and his allies.

The competitive feature of the game has been employed only for limited trials.

On the basis of this use of the model, we can say that *with its assumptions*, the conclusions described below appear valid.

The reader should consider them examples of the sort of work attempted, rather than as established conclusions.

TABLE OF ASSOCIATED FACTORS

Location	*Table of intensity*	
1950	0000000100	
1951	0000000200	
1952	0000000300	
1953	0000000400	
1954	0000000500	
1955	0000000600	
1956	0000000700	
1957	0000000800	
1958	9999999999	
	Table of alphanumeric codes	*Printout translation*
1959	7269637282	KICKS
1960	8475618775	UNAXN
1961	8265856579	SEVER
1962	8284628583	SUBVT
1963	7779698273	PRISL
1964	8379767677	TROOP
1965	7476628975	MOBZN
1966	8661797383	WARLT
1967	6862767462	HBOMB

Strength Attracts

There is a marked tendency for the strong to get stronger. This may be a direct result of a built-in bias, whereby the programme arbitrarily assigns an advantage (though not a certain one) to the initiator of action.

Even so, this bias is of less advantage to the second-rate powers than to the leaders.

Maintaining Neutrality

Even for strong powers, there is an apparent tendency toward coalition. The built-in pattern for computation of loss may be at fault and probably needs to be revised and refined with more subtle treatments. On the other hand, it may well be that no present possibility of precise measurement is reasonable for so subjective a set of attitudes as are bundled together in the isolationist syndrome.

Action/Loss

Moderate action yields less loss than does strong action. Logic might indicate that this is obvious, since complete inaction would lead to no loss whatever. But the programme assigns a gain to the actor proportionate to the intensity of his action.

Strong action should therefore bring greater gains. There seem to be just enough rules for revision of gains, assessment of costs, and penalties for evoking strong counteractions, so that uncertainty enters the picture. Indeed, at this stage of development of the simulation, the creation of this measure of uncertainty seems a considerable achievement. At least one feature of the real world is accurately portrayed!

ADVANTAGES AND LIMITATIONS OF THE SIMULATION

The reader who has traced through the foregoing fragments of the programme can recognize that its main complications are logical rather than mathematical.

The author claims no standing whatever in the mathematical guild and is aware that fundamental expansion of a project such as this will require close collaboration between mathematician and political scientist. Perhaps the most promising area for early inquiry is that of refining indicators for human factors of decision. In the programme, these are represented in the propensity index, and are acknowledged to be most dubious.

Even with simple tools, elementary mathematics, and inadequate measurements, the programme demonstrates what is possible in the way of data manipulation with the computer's aid. The speed and storage capacity of the machine are hardly taxed by the data thus far employed. In using the programme, one is constantly reminded that much more information could be handled.

There is an ever-present challenge to develop more sophisticated models for processing the extensive statistical compilations of relevant data available in such abundance today.

Chapter 9

Computer Based Instruction

What do evaluation studies say about computer-based instruction? It is not easy to give a simple answer to the question. The term *computer-based instruction* has been applied to too many different programmes, and the term *evaluation* has been used in too many different ways. Nonetheless, the question of what the research says cannot be ignored. Researchers want to know the answer, school administrators need to know, and the public deserves to know. How well has computerbased instruction worked?

Reviewers handle such questions in two different ways. Some reviewers are selective in their approach to evidence. They hold that evaluation questions are best answered by key experiments, and so they sift through piles of reports to find the studies with the most convincing results. These studies become the focus of their reviews. Other reviewers feel that evaluation results are inherently variable and that evaluation questions are seldom decided by the results of an experiment or two. Such reviewers put together a composite picture of all the findings on a topic, and they use statistical methods to identify representative results. Both approaches are valuable. The first shows what researchers and developers can accomplish in extraordinary circumstances; the second shows what is likely to be accomplished under typical conditions. We need both types of reviews in the area of computer-based instruction.

All of my reviews on the topic of computer-based instruction, however, have been of the second type. For more than 10 years, my colleagues and I have been organizing and summarizing the evaluation literature on computer-based instruction and trying to identify representative results. I believe that comprehensive reviews like ours provide a good context for discussing the more exceptional results in the area. Our reviews provide a background. They make discussions of exceptional results more meaningful because they put them into perspective.

METHOD

The review method that we use is called *meta-analysis,* and it was given its name by Gene Glass in 1976 in a classic synthesis of the literature on the effects of psychotherapy. Glass used *meta-analysis* to refer to the statistical analysis of a large collection of results from individual studies for the purpose of integrating the findings. Reviewers who carry out metaanalyses first locate studies of an issue by clearly specified procedures. They then characterize the outcomes and features of the studies in quantitative or quasi-quantitative terms. Finally, meta-analysts use multivariate techniques to relate characteristics of the studies to outcomes.

One of Glass' major innovations was his use of measures of *effect size* in research reviews. Researchers had used effect sizes in designing studies long before meta-analysis was developed, but they failed to see the contribution that effect sizes could make to research reviews. Glass saw that results from a variety of different studies could be expressed on a common scale of effect size a nd that with this transformation reviewers could carry out statistical analyses as sophisticated as those carried out by experimenters.

Size of effect can be measured in several ways, but the measure of effect size most often used is the standardized mean difference. Sometimes called Glass' effect size, this index gives the number of standard deviation units that separates outcome scores of experimental and control groups. It is calculated by subtracting the average score of the control group from the average score of the experimental group and then dividing the remainder by the standard deviation of the measure. For example, if a group that receives computer-based coaching on the Scholastic Aptitude Test (SAT) obtains an average score of 550 on the test, whereas a group that receives conventional teaching averages 500, the effect size for the coaching treatment is.5 because the standard deviation on the SAT is 100.

Methodologists have written at least five books on meta-analytic methods in recent years, and reviewers have conducted numerous meta-analyses of research findings. In a recent monograph, for example, we described results from more than 100 meta-analytic reports in education alone (J. A. Kulik & C.-L. C. Kulik, 1989). In addition, meta-analytic methodology has also been used extensively in psychology and the health sciences. Reviewers have used it to draw general conclusions on such diverse subjects as the effects of gender on learning and the effectiveness of coronary bypass surgery.

OVERVIEW

At least a dozen separate meta-analyses have been carried out to answer questions about the effectiveness of computer-based instruction. The analyses were conducted independently by research teams at eight different research centres. The research teams focused on different uses of the computer with different populations, and they also differed in the methods they used to find studies and analyse study results. Nonetheless, each of the analyses yielded the conclusion that programmes of computer-based instruction have a positive record in the evaluation literature.The following are the major points emerging from these meta-analyses:

- Students usually learn more in classes in which they receive computerbased instruction. The analyses produced slightly different estimates of the magnitude of the computer effect, but all the estimates were positive. At the low end of the estimates was an average effect size of.22 in 18 studies conducted in elementary and high school science courses. At the other end of the scale, Schmidt, Weinstein, Niemiec, and Walberg (1985) found an average effect size of.57 in 18 studies conducted in special education classes. The weighted average effect size in the 12 meta-analyses was.35. This means the average effect of computer-based instruction was to raise examination scores by.35 standard deviations, or from the 50th to the 64th percentile.

- Students learn their lessons in less time with computer-based instruction. The average reduction in instructional time was 34% in 17 studies of college instruction, and 24% in 15 studies in adult education.
- Students also like their classes more when they receive computer help in them. The average effect of computer-based instruction in 22 studies was to raise attitude-toward-instruction scores by.28 standard deviations.
- Students develop more positive attitudes toward computers when they receive help from them in school. The average effect size in 19 studies on attitude toward computers was.34.
- Computers do not, however, have positive effects in every area in which they were studied. The average effect of computer-based instruction in 34 studies of attitude toward subject matter was near zero.

This brief review shows that there is a good deal of agreement among metaanalysts on the basic facts about computer-based instruction. All the metaanalyses that I have been able to locate show that adding computer-based instruction to a school programme, on the average, improves the results of the programme. But the meta-analyses differ somewhat on the size of the gains to be expected. We need to look more closely at the studies to determine which factors might cause variation in meta-analytic results.

SPECIFIC FINDINGS

The computer was used in conceptually and procedurally different ways in studies examined in these meta-analyses. Did all the approaches produce the same result? It seems unlikely. It is more reasonable to expect different results from different approaches. A plausible hypothesis is that some computer approaches produce better than average results, whereas other approaches produce belowaverage results.

To examine this hypothesis, I used a set of 97 studies that were carried out in elementary school and high schools. Each of the studies was a controlled quantitative study, in which outcomes in a class taught with computerbased instruction were compared to outcomes in a class taught without computerbased instruction. Most of the 97 studies were included in earlier meta-analytic reports on the effectiveness of computer-based instruction.

There are a number of ways of dividing these studies into groups by computer use. Early taxonomies often distinguished between four uses of the computer in teaching: drill-and-practice, tutorial, dialogue, and management. Recent taxonomies collapse some of these categories and add others. Taylor (1980), for example, distinguished between three uses of the computer in schools: tutor, tool, and tutee. First, as a *tutor*, the computer presents material, evaluates student responses, determines what to present next, and keeps records of student progress. Most computer uses described in earlier taxonomies fall under this heading in Taylor's scheme. Second, the computer serves as a tool when students use it for statistical analysis, calculation, or word processing. Third, the computer serves as a *tutee* when students give it directions in a programming language that it understands, such as Basic or Logo.

Slavin (1989) advocated a different way of looking at instructional innova tions. He believed that innovations can be defined with different degrees of precision. At Level I, innovations are defined vaguely. According to Slavin, such grab-bag categories as open education and whole-language instruction suggest only fuzzy models for instructional practice. The terms are used for a variety of procedures that do not have a distinct conceptual basis. Level II innovations are more clearly specified. They usually have a conceptual basis that is easy to describe, but in practice Level II approaches are implemented in different ways. Slavin's examples are cooperative learning, direct instruction, mastery learning, and individualized instruction. Level III approaches are precisely defined. They include specific instructional materials, well-developed training procedures for teachers, and detailed prescriptive manuals. Slavin's examples are DISTAR and Man a Course of Study.

Computer-based instruction should probably be thought of as a Level I, or loose, category. The term refers to a variety of procedures with a variety of conceptual bases. Under this heading, however, fall several well-defined categories of computer use, which can be thought of as Level II categories. An important one is computer-based tutoring. Most programmes of computer tutoring derive their basic form from Skinner's work in programmed instruction.

Skinner's model emphasized division of instructional material into a sequence of small steps, or instructional frames; learner responses at each step; and immediate feedback after each response.

Level III innovations include common instructional materials, training procedures, and so on.

One example is the computer-based material developed under the direction of Suppes and Atkinson at Stanford and later disseminated through the Computer Curriculum Corporation.

It seems reasonable to suppose that results will be least consistent for the loose category of Level I innovations and results will be most consistent for Level II and Level III innovations. To examine this hypothesis, I carried out three separate analyses of the 97 studies of computer-based instruction in elementary and high schools. I first examined the effects in all 97 studies.

This Level I analysis was broad; it made no concession to the different uses of the computer in different studies. Next, I examined subgroups of studies, grouping the studies by major types of computer use. This analysis was of Level II categories of innovation. Finally, I examined effects in an especially homogeneous subgroup of studies. Each of the studies in this subgroup used similar materials in a similar way. This final analysis focused on a Level III category of innovation.

LEVEL I ANALYSIS

The distribution of the effect sizes is nearly normal in shape. The median of the effect sizes is slightly lower than the mean, however, indicating a slight degree of positive skew in the distribution. This skew is produced by several studies with unusually high effect sizes. Some analysts feel that unusually

high and low values are "outliers" that should be eliminated from a distribution. Others believe that extra-ordinary results merit careful scrutiny because they may provide valuable clues about improving instructional treatments.The average effect size in the total group of 97 studies, however, is.32. This implies that the average student receiving computer-based instruction performed at the 63rd percentile, whereas the average student in a conventional class was at the 50th percentile. Effect sizes can also be interpreted in terms of months on a grade-equivalent scale. Pupils in elementary schools gain approximately.1 standard deviations per month in their scores on most standardized tests. An effect size of.32 can thus be thought of as equivalent to a gain of about 3 months on a grade-equivalent scale.The standard deviation of the distribution of effect sizes is.39. This implies that approximately two thirds of all studies found effects between -.1 and.7 and that 95% of all results fell between -.4 and 1.1. Thus, there is a good deal of uncertainty about the effects of computer-based instruction in a specific setting. Effects of computer-based instruction may be generally positive but they are not totally predictable.

LEVEL II ANALYSIS

The 97 studies can be classified by computer-use into six types:

- *Tutoring:* The computer presents material, evaluates responses, determines what to present next, and keeps records of progress. Computer uses classified as drill-and-practice and tutorial instruction in earlier taxonomies are covered by this term. The category is therefore similar to Taylor's (1980) category of computer-as-tutor.

- *Managing:* The computer evaluates students either on-line or off-line, guides students to appropriate instructional resources, and keeps records.
- *Simulation:* The computer generates data that meets student specifications and presents it numerically or graphically to illustrate relations in models of social or physical reality.
- *Enrichment:* The computer provides relatively unstructured exercises of various types—games, simulations, tutoring, and so on—to enrich the classroom experience and stimulate and motivate students.
- *Programming:* Students write short programmes in such languages as Basic and Algol to solve mathematics problems. The expectation is that this experience in programming will have positive effects on students' problem-solving abilities and conceptual understanding of mathematics.
- *Logo:* Students give the computer Logo instructions and observe the results on computer screens. From this experience students are expected to gain in ability to solve problems, plan, foresee consequences, and so on.

The means and standard deviations of effect sizes for studies in each of these categories. The table shows that effect sizes differ as a function of category of computer use. Results for three categories of computer use are especially noteworthy: results for computer tutoring, results for Logo programming, and other results.

Tutoring. The distribution of effect sizes for studies of tutoring is normal in shape. The average effect size is.38; the median effect is.36; and the standard deviation is.34. Comparing this distribution to the distribution for all studies yields some potentially important information. The mean of the distribution for tutoring studies is slightly higher than the mean of the total distribution, and the standard deviation is slightly lower. Thus, if we know that a school system is employing its computers for tutoring, we would predict better than average results for a computer-based programme, and we would also know that our predictions would be slightly more accurate than predictions that did not take programme type into account.

Table: Effect Sizes for Six Categories of Computer-Based Instruction

		Effect Size	
Application	**Number of Studies**	**M**	**SE**
Tutoring	58	.38	.34
Managing	10	.14	.28
Simulation	6	.10	.34
Enrichment	5	.14	.35
Programming	9	.09	.38
Logo	9	.58	.56

Logo. The results for Logo programming are especially striking. The average effect size is high for the whole set of studies, but what is even more notable is the inconsistency in results. Some of the highest effect sizes in Table, for example, are associated with use of Logo. In a study by Rieber (1987), the scores on measures of problem solving of children who learned with Logo were 1.5 standard deviations higher than the scores of children who were taught by conventional procedures. But not all studies produce such positive results. Most studies, in fact, report very small effects from Logo programmes.

One difference between Logo studies reporting strong positive results and those reporting small effects is method of criterion measurement. In all the studies with strong positive results, the criterion test was individually administered. In all studies with weak results, criterion tests were group administered. These facts raise questions about the meaning of the average effect for Logo studies. The strong positive results may have been produced by unusual evaluator rapport with Logo students during testing or even by unconscious bias in administering and recording responses of the Logo group.

The fact is that Logo does not measure up on group tests, and these were the tests that were used in virtually all other studies of computer-based instruction. The case for strong benefits from Logo therefore seems unproven at this point.

OTHER USES OF THE COMPUTER

The record is also unimpressive for other approaches to computer-based instruction. Computer-managed instruction, for example, seldom produces significant positive gains in elementary and high schools. Its record of effectiveness seems similar to the record compiled by diagnostic and prescriptive systems that use only paper-and-pencil and printed materials in instructional delivery. Programming in Basic or Algol does not usually have positive effects on student learning in mathematics courses.

Learning of basic mathematical concepts, in fact, sometimes suffers with the introduction of computer programming into mathematics courses. Use of computer simulations in science courses also seems to have little effect on science learning in elementary and high school courses. More and better simulations may be needed to influence student examination performance.

LEVEL III ANALYSIS

The Stanford-CCC programme was evaluated in nearly two dozen controlled experiments during the past two decades. No other programme of computer-based instruction has been the object of so much scrutiny.

The accumulated studies on the Stanford-CCC programmes are a unique resource in the evaluation of computerbased programmes. We can use the studies to gauge the consistency of results from a Level III programme. It is only natural to expect these results to be less variable than those we have already reviewed. But is the reduction in variability large or small?

The distribution of effect sizes from evaluations of the Stanford-CCC programme is nearly normal in shape. The average effect size is.40; the median is.39; and the standard deviation is.23. The mean value is slightly higher and the dispersion is clearly smaller in this distribution than in the distributions in Figs. 1.1 and 1.2. Thus, knowledge that a school is using the Stanford-CCC materials allows us to make clear and accurate predictions about what to expect. Gains of 1.4 years on a grade-equivalent scale are likely with a year-long programme, whereas students who are conventionally instructed would gain only 1.0 year on the same scale. Gains of nearly 2.0 years are also quite possible, whereas gains of less than 1.0 years are highly unlikely.

Chapter 10

Information Technology and Software Adoption Policies

Zimra Peled Elad Peled Gad Alexander Ben-Gurion University of the NegevThis chapter reviews an approach that guided a 5-year research-oriented information technology innovation (Project Comptown) that extensively computerized school systems in two localities in Israel. The intervention, evaluation, and resulting software adoption policies all evolved from a single conceptual formulation that we call "ecological". This formulation treats the constituents of large-scale interventions and evaluations and combines their multisystemic and treatment-specific components into a model of educational change.The first part presents the ecological formulation and briefly describes the Comptown project. The second part elaborates principles, considerations, and procedures that are central for the evaluation of large-scale information technology interventions. This part presents a model that within the same evaluation handles two types of processes that are modeled by two types of fundamentally different paradigms:

- Cultural ecological processes that cannot be subjected to experimentation: The evaluation of these processes is based on paradigm modeling processes that evolve from complex cultural-ecological arrangements. The use of this paradigm prescribes longitudinal explorations, multiple ecological contrasts, identification of systemic interdependencies, and hypotheses generation.

- Treatment specific processes that are subjected to experimental manipulations: The evaluation of these processes is based on a paradigm that modeling processes evolve from mindful computer software manipulations (i.e., conscious manipulation of the elements of the software).

The use of this paradigm prescribes the use of experimental and quasiexperimental frameworks that make it possible to test causal hypotheses and treatment-specific effects. This part elaborates a paradigm that models information technology software adoption policy implied by the ecological approach.

THE MULTISYSTEMIC ECOLOGICAL FORMULATION

The leading concept in this chapter is presented by a multisystemic ecological formulation based on Bronfenbrenner's theory of nested ecological frameworks and on ecological notions of educational theories. This formulation perceives the ecology of the classroom as a concentric arrangement of four nested systems that act and interact.

The innermost and core construct of this arrangement is the classroom, containing learners and teachers. This system consists of three open-ended functional settings (physical, activity, content) in which instruction and learning occur. Next is the school, containing the school administrative staff. This system is the primary operational unit in which resources and policies are transformed into the classroom settings. The third ring comprises the community's political, administrative, business, and social systems, containing the community's key personalities as well as the learners' parents. All three systems express needs and expectations, and exercise pressures that may directly affect (advance or disrupt) learning and instruction.

Finally the outer ring includes educational policy-making institutions containing elected and appointed officials at the regional and national levels. Through laws, administrative regulations, and resource allocation this outer ring, markedly separated from the school and the classroom, may generate new sources of stimulation that either enhance or discourage new developments in the immediate educational system.The mapped arrangements are not merely structural. Their mapping is based on five assumptions:

- Each system consists of implicit cultural, and explicit functionalinstrumental components.
- All the ecological systems are interrelated by a common "cultural blueprint" that sets the pattern for the structures and processes that occur within and across the systems.
- Classrooms, schools, and social-political institutions are culturally dependent systems. To a large extent, their properties and activities are dominated by cultural traditions, and their cultural messages affect behaviors and have ripple effects in related systems.
- Ordinarily cultural functioning is implicit. Its reproduced patterns and processes remain unnoticed. Their effect becomes explicit, and their critical evaluation becomes possible, only through interventions that introduce enduring innovations into the ongoing activities of the existing systems.
- Enduring educational innovations are generated and carried on by two types of parallel and mutually stimulating change processes: cultural-ecological and treatment-specific. Cultural-ecological change processes result from combinations of acting and interacting factors, within and across the ecologically interconnected systems. Treatment-specific (mostly cognitive) change processes result from particular treatments that are applied within the ecologically specified educational settings. Information technology interventions and information technology policy decisions must therefore equally aim at the individual participants, the school and classroom, and their expanded ecological environment.

Project Comptown empirically implemented this formulation.

PROJECT COMPTOWN: AN ECOLOGICALLY ORIENTED INFORMATION TECHNOLOGY INTERVENTION

Comptown was designed to create an ecology in which the correspondence between cultural-ecological and individual changes could be identified; it was to be one in which the interplay between individual activities and environmental opportunities and constraints could be better understood and exploited.

The project was therefore carried out in two localities that differed greatly in their demographic, administrative, and political characteristics; in their educational agendas; and in their approach to educational issues.

Table: Demographic, Administrative, and Political Characteristics of the Two Comptown Sites

Characteristics	*Locality "A"*	*Locality "B"*
Demographic		
Population	13,000	54,000
Composition	homogeneous mainly middle class	heterogeneous
Administrative and Political	centralized	decentralized
Educational administration		
Interest groups	insignificant	pronounced
Political pressure	insignificant	dominant
Main educational issues	improvement and innovations of schools	provision of quality education to large groups of advantaged
and disadvantaged students		

In Locality A the entire educational system participated in the project. In the second locality (Locality B) only a subset of the elementary schools participated. The demographic factors—the political and administrative systems, along with other "situational" factors (that emerged throughout the intervention)-created contrastable ecological environments in which the project's premises, goals, and operational principles were implemented and its posited educational change expectations could be explored and evaluated.

Table: A Summary Description of the Educational Systems and the Scope of the Intervention in the Two Comptown Sites

Characteristics	Locality "A"	Locality "B"
General		
Scope of the experiment	the entire city	three neighborhoods
School structure		
elementary school	grades 1-6	grades 1-8
secondary school	junior high 7-9 senior high 10-12	grades 9-12
Scope of the Intervention		
Elementary schools		
Schools	6 (all)	9 (of 23)
Students	2,000	3,400
Teachers	200	260
Secondary Schools		
Schools	1,	none
Students	1,430	none
Teachers	125	none

COMPTOWN'S PREMISES, GOALS, OPERATIONAL 'RINCIPLE, AND CHANGE PERSPECTIVES

The project built on three universally applicable and cologically oriented premises: First, in the "information era" ıe computer is a "major cultural tool" that "defines and edefines man's role in relation to nature". Realizing ıformation technology potential in schools augments the ducational environment and narrows the gap between the "school culture" and the "real-world culture."Second, "sound" educational usages of information technology provide opportunities to generate educational innovations and activate unrealized learning and teaching potentials.Third, collaborative politicians, community leaders, and parents create a "supportive ecology" in which "information technology culture" (directly or indirectly affecting schools) can germinate.Following its premises the project's intervention goals were to:

- Create a computer culture in schools: that is, create a learning environment in which information technology redefines teachers' and students' roles in relation to teaching and learning processes.
- Utilize the computer's potential for innovative teaching and learning both in and outside school.
- Create a supportive ecology in which a "computer culture" can expand.

The following are seven operational principles that complementarily implemented the three goals in each Comptown site:

- "High density" allocation of computers enabling each student to have access to a computer for 2 to 3 hours a week in a computer laboratory as well as in the regular classroom.
- Integration of varied computer applications into as many subject matters as possible focusing on "open tools" rather than on "closed" and "structured" software.
- A system approach selecting ways and means aimed at the whole educational system (i.e., all the participants and all the activities), as well as its related environments.
- A multimedia approach where participants interacting with diverse representations of the same task could change the course of learning and instruction and develop exploratory processes.
- Use of computer tools in a mindful manner where students and teachers could be encouraged to reflec

on their work and develop new understanding of the learned task.

- Involvement of the classroom nesting systems (school, community, ministry) in the project's issues and implementing policies.
- Cultivation of positive attitudes and beliefs toward the project within and across the systems that create the ecological environment in which the innovation is designed to take place.

Comptown introduced these goals and principles to dramatically change the nature of the traditional print-and-book-dominated classroom. It assumed that the long-term intervention would have three additional educational (cognitive) consequences. First, repeated choices mindfully carried on, such as weighing the benefits and costs of information technology and traditional alternatives, will enhance teachers' and learners' awareness of two sets of relations: those prevailing in the old setting and its underlying culture, and those prevailing in the innovative setting and its underlying culture. Second, these cultural insights will enable learners and teachers to

- Test their old and new learning environments by comparison, and
- Mindfully change their course of learning and teaching as they progressively augment their higher order thinking skills (Salomon, 1985, 1990a; Salomon & Perkins, 1989; Salomon, Perkins, & Globerson, 1991). Third, understanding the links between information technology and older strategies may cultivate two properties that are critical to educational change:
- An intuitive understanding of the unique contributions of alternative learning environments to the ongoing cumulative learning process, and
- The use of multiple perspectives in a learned task.

The implementation of the ecological model in a complex ecological environment followed a multilevel-multisystemic design that

- Distinguished preparatory, implementation, and
- The use of multiple perspectives in a learned task.

The implementation of the ecological model in a complex ecological environment followed a multilevel-multisystemic design that, distinguished preparatory, implementation, and adoption phases of the innovation conditions and functions; and used specified intervention strategies in the classroom and in the nesting systems.

The evaluation of the project showed that, unlike the claim often made in "experimental" or "cultural" research literature, processes and outcomes that were demonstrated in information technology classrooms were neither specific nor holistic. Rather, they resulted from two types of interrelated developments:

- Continuous (often long-term) and complex ecological developments that were contingent on the specific nesting arrangements of the intervention and
- Treatment (often short-term) generated processes that were realized through interactions between learners and particular information technology devices (applied within an ecologically specified framework).

The assumptions and concerns that guided this evaluation were not specific to Comptown. They were conceptually rooted in the general ecological formulation.

MAJOR CONCERNS OF AN ECOLOGICALLY ORIENTED EVALUATION

In the systematically nested ecological formulation the basic structure components are dynamic classroom settings. The basic process components are intersystemic and intrasystemic interactions that create and carry on the culturalecological and treatment-specific innovations. An evaluation that is guided by these conditioning assumptions is consequently concerned with three issues that are ordinarily bypassed by conventional input-output evaluations and are central to the ecological evaluation.

The first issue involves the identification and study of

parallel and mutually stimulating cultural-ecological processes that are contingent on the intervention. These processes often act in complex and cyclical ways.

Accordingly, the evaluation is concerned with combinations of dynamic factors that contribute to particular results, although the relations among these factors and the unique effect of each single factor may remain unknown; and developments that need to be studied in cyclical ways, so that new knowledge gained leads to new hypotheses that refer to new and previously unanticipated combinations of factors that both affect and are affected by the intervention.

The second issue is the design of multiple ecological contrasts in which different combinations of structure and process constituents that are not given to experimentation can be studied and evaluated.

This design implies the construction of basic data structures that formally define the building blocks (facets) of contrasted ecologies, and translate these specifications into reproducible observations.

The third concern of an ecological evaluation is the understanding of the effects of specific treatments that are compatible with the ecological model and are part of the intervention.

These understandings, which are essential for further intervention manipulations, imply the design of an ecologically sensitive experi-mentation that is theory driven and that rules out counterinterpretations within the well-specified ecology.

The following examples from Comptown elaborate these concerns.

ECOLOGICAL CHANGE PROCESSES: THE COMPTOWN EXAMPLE

In Comptown, ecological processes that were repeatedly activated by interactions in each and all ecological systems were realized through interconnected classroom accommodations, school modifications, centralized policies, and beliefs and attitude-based behaviors.

Table: Indicative Physical, Activity, and Content Accommodations in Classroom 6, School Y, Locality A (1985, 1988)

Addommodation	*1985*	*1988*
Physical	Whole class : oriented	Group work = oriented
Instructional aids		
Table and chair organization	Facing classroom's front (facilitating frontal teaching)	Optionally organized in activity centers for group work
Activity		
Essential student learning activities	Attentive listening and imitating	Group and machine interactions; exploring and modeling
Classroom behavior	Essentially controlled and quiet; occasional misbehavior	Noisy and constantly moving; minimal misbehavior
Dominant teacher delivery modes	Lecturing and demonstrating	Tutoring and guiding group and student machine interactions; using computer-based activity as a main delivery channel
Content		
Curricular goals	Knowledge and basic skills acquisition	Development of new and enriched content areas such as handling of Information and use of multiple technologies and multiple knowledge sources

*The concept of "whole class" work has three components:

- The classroom is organized as a single whole with the teacher as a sole vehicle of instruction;
- The same instruction, conditions, and resources are available to all classroom students;
- The acquisition of basic skills and knowledge are the end goals to be achieved.

Accommodations promoting whole class work are demonstrated by physical, activity, and content indicators characterizing Classroom 6 in 1985. **The concept of "group work" has three components:

- The classroom is divided into simultaneously operating groups;
- Alternative systems for group work are maintained by alternative instructional provisions, conditions, and resources that are available to the different groups;
- Acquisitions of basic skills and knowledge is accompanied by the acquisition of higher order skills, use of multiple technologies, and multiple information resources. Accommodations promoting group work are demonstrated by physical, activity, and content indicators characterizing Classroom 6 in 1988. the indicative developments in the first 3 years of the intervention (1985-1988). Each of the four tables focuses on preproject and project-triggered characteristics that realize one of the four ecological change processes involved in the innovation.

Table focuses on accommodations (physical, activity, and subject matter content) observed in Classroom 6 (School Y, Locality A).

The developments in this classroom (managed by the same teacher, in the same school, and in same locality) accurately represent the changing trends in classrooms that actively and continuously tried to implement the project's goals. Furthermore, the analysis of the accommodations showed that:

- The contrasted characteristics realized inseparable aspects of interrelated classroom events.

- The emerging patterns could neither be understood nor valued in terms of isolated classroom settings.
- The observed accommodations were nested; that is, additional ecological processes that converged in the classroom were differently realized in the 1985 and the 1988 situations.

Table demonstrates some of the school's modifications that framed the classroom's "move" from one educational orientation (frontal teaching) to the other (interactive group work).

The listed administrative, social, and curricular modifications reveal a dynamic school policy that was fruitful both inside and outside the school. Inside the school it reshaped some of the prevailing principles, reinforced existing trends, and nurtured interactive relations between the school and its classrooms.

Outside the school it produced new ideas that activated local support systems and influenced centralized policy-making institutions.

The policy modifications of School Y and its generated internal and external interactions were typical processes in Locality A. In this locality involvement, support, and intervention actions progressively increased, moving in the same direction. These interdependencies did not develop in Locality B.

These examples show that the distinctive ecological arrangements of Localities A and B generated different ecological processes.

Furthermore, the examples that follow show that these processes interacted differently with the fourth type of ecological change processes: "belief-and attitude-based behaviors".

In Comptown, belief- and attitude-based behaviors operated across the ecological levels in two ways. First, at the introduction of the innovation, they provided a bridge between the intervention and its unknown results.Second, as the intervention evolved, they tested the initial promises of the intervention against its particular outcomes.

Although contradictory in their consequences, belief- and attitude-based behaviors played identical roles in the two localities.

They aimed at the project's promises and cultivated theoretical expectations that were not based on already existing experience.

In Locality A, realized expectations augmented positive attitudes toward the project. In Locality B, the real events contradicted expectations, nurtured critical attitude-based behaviors, and augmented the negative approach toward the project.

Taken together, the previous examples reveal

- Systematic relations between an implicit "community culture" and explicit school and classroom characteristics, and
- Cyclical progressions of dynamic multisystemic ecologies that cannot be modeled by conventional hypotheses-testing paradigms.

The evaluation of Comptown showed that classroom accommodations and school modifications demonstrated in Locality A did not develop in Locality B.

However, the evaluation could not determine, or experimentally show, whether the radically different project histories reviewed in this chapter resulted from different political and social constellations, different physical settings, different school cultures, different attitude-based behaviors, or a combination of these factors.

This experience implies that the evaluation of complex ecological arrangements should build on a paradigm that models multisystemic linear and nonlinear functioning and that emphasizes:

- An explorative, hypothesesgenerating approach that contrasts ecologies (rather than an hypothesis-testing approach that builds on randomized experiments), and
- A data structure that formally and empirically characterizes variations within the contrasted ecologies.

FORMALIZATION OF BASIC ECOLOGICAL DATA STRUCTURES

The nested systems formulation assumes that classroom occurrences reflect and permit the tracing of developments across the ecological levels. In ecologi cal evaluations the formal specification of basic data structures is based on this assumption. Furthermore, the proposed ecological paradigm treats within Guttman's facet theory structure and process components that:

Table: Beliefs and Attitude-Based Behaviors in the Two omptown Sites

System	*Belief and Attitude-Based Behavior*	
Locality A	***Locality B***	
Ministry	Positive attitude toward the	Lack of confidence in the local
1985	research project generates support in the project	authorities generates limited support in the project
1988	Positive field outcomes and current demands result in longtime commitments	Attitudes and support remain unchanged
Local, Political Authorities	Convinced that computer	Approach Comptown as one
1985	culture in schools serve local interests; participate in progress and difficulties	of the competing projects; make no effort to support
1988	Demonstrate consistent attitudes; increase involvement and commitment to the project's success	Approach and support remain unchanged
School Principals	Led to believe that the	Led to believe that the
1985	promised innovations can improve learning and teaching;	innovation can improve learning and teaching; express

	set priorities that match the project's operational principles	support in the project
1988	As the project moved toward promised targets augment involvement and express specific interests	Doubt and dispute the project's policies and disappointed by results
Teachers 1985	Convinced that additional work caused by the project is worthwhile; voluntarily praticipate in training	Internalize the project's objectives; voluntarily participate in training
1988	Gained success in work leads to interest and involvement in the achievement in specific goals	Difficulties in implementing Comptown's working principles result in no commitment while continuing to use the training offers of the project
Parents 1985	Believe the computers carry a promise for better education; they support and are involved in the project	
1988	Responding to enthusiastic reactions of children, parents' involvement is increased	

- Represent the classroom and delimit its ecology, and
- Translate ecological variations into reproducible observations that can be used in a contrast-based evaluation.

A two-stage design is required to achieve this type of data representation. The first stage involves the specification of three structure and four process components that are essential and necessary for the design of the ecological evaluation. The second stage elaborates specific properties and processes that characterize each specific phase of the intervention.

The structure components that are essential in a first-stage design are the physical, activity, and content settings, often discussed in ecological and educational literature. The physical setting accounts for technology, materials, and learning aids available in the classroom. The activity setting accounts for all management, delivery, learning, and misbehavior activities enacted in the classroom. The content setting accounts for instructional, social, and technical goals, and for curricular emphases and students' motivation generated emphases.

The process components that are essential in a first-stage design are four facets that enable characterization and contrast of the newly introduced culturaleducational frameworks, and the preproject old frameworks. These process facets are :

- The inventory of the items that distinguish the setting,
- The organization of the items within the setting,
- The intrasystemic accommodations that involve the setting, and
- The intersystemic relations that affect the settings.

Because any situation or event in the classroom can be characterized as a particular combination of these settings and facets, all three settings and four facets are considered essential and necessary for the design of the evaluation.

Tables can be taken as typical observations that built on these specifications.

The presented examples were derived from Comptown's longitudinal exploration of multiple ecologies that contrasted: same classroom within the same school, different classrooms within the same school, classrooms in different schools within the same locality, different schools within the same locality, different schools in different localities.

Local and regional policy-making institutions were represented by district and regional superintendents, who in turn represented the national policy formulated by the Ministry of Education and Culture.

The Comptown intervention was carried out in three phases:

- Ppreparation,
- Implementation, and
- Adoption of the innovation. Each phase had different foci and different characteristics that first-stage design could not capture. The second-stage design introduced detailed refinements that clarified specific objectives and referent systems and thereby operationalized first-stage specifications.

The ecological paradigm developed in this section has four distinguished characteristics:

- Properties and processes that have no effect on classroom occurrences and that cannot be traced through properties and processes in classroom settings are omitted from the evaluation design.
- The units of analysis are the natural systems. Behaviors included in the design are not separated from their natural settings and can be studied as culturally and ecologically dependent behaviors.
- The settings and facets that guide the construction of the observations remain intact across different ecological arrangements.

The two-stage design allows for additions, corrections, deletions, and accommodations that conceptually elaborate and empirically validate the ecological model.

ECOLOGICALLY SENSITIVE EXPERIMENTATION

The ecological assumption implies that information technology treatments cannot be separated from their ecological contexts, or from the cultural comparisons and educational activities they enhance. Accordingly information technology treatments should be defined in terms of

- Interactions between learners in an ecologically characterized classroom, and a particular type of educational software, and
- The alternating representations (conventional and computer-based) introduced.

The ecologically sensitive experimentation that we propose elaborates this formulation in four facets. These facets are:

- The type of information exchanged and processed in the interaction ;
- The cognitive demands set on the learner ;
- The proximity between processes generated throughout the interaction and processes that are encouraged by the already functioning educational frameworks ; and

Table: A Faceted Design for the Characterization of IT Software Ecologically Sensitive Experimentations

Facet	*Facet Element*
Type of information	1. Subject matter bound 2. Procedural
Cognitive demands	1. Low level (reactive) 2. Low level supplemented by a limited number of higher level demands 3. High level and interactive (reflecting on and constructing own learning processes)
Proximity to existing learning processes	1. "More of the same" (not augmenting "zone for proximal development") 2. "Different and complementary" (augmenting "zone for proximal development")
Control of alternating representations	1. Use of software in a nonselective manner 2. Use of software in a selective manner

- The control of alternating representations (i.e., alternating use of conventional and nonconventional software representations in a nonselective or a critical selective manner. Table presents the faceted design for the characterization of information technology software used in ecologically sensitive experimentations.

Because information technology treatments are nested within natural ecological settings, the generality and validity of the treatment cannot be routinely handled. They must be demonstrated in two ways. First, the treatment and the stimulated cognitive processes must be relevant to a variety of learning and teaching contexts. Second, the implementation of the treatment and control conditions must be equivalent and representative in relation to similar learning and instruction activities in regular classroom settings. A design that satisfies these conditions, and tests the implications of a mindful use of a particular type of software in natural classroom settings.

This design was repeatedly used in Comptown for the evaluation of the cognitive benefits of a mindful use of types of software that encourage the development of higher order cognitive skills and meet the ecological criteria of generality and validity. The "algebraic linear functions" and the "database" studies are two examples. The design of the experiments combined.

- A careful selection of an information technology treatment that involved formal thinking operations;
- The definition and the prediction of measurable outcomes; and
- The use of control and treatment groups with equivalent student distributions, equivalent classroom settings, and equivalent ecological environments.

The algebraic linear functions study evaluated the relation between a mindful use of computer-generated simulations and the users' ability to abstract the basic principles of these functions and apply these principles to new types of algebraic functions. This study was carried out over 6 months (teacher training included) with eighth- and ninth-grade students and concluded with three tests: a regular achievement test that evaluated learners' ability to apply familiar algebraic principles to familiar problems, a one-step inference test that evaluated learners' ability to apply familiar principles to new and unfamiliar problems, and a multiple inference test that evaluated learners' ability to use general abstractions for the generation of new principles and to apply the newly generated principles to new and unfamiliar problems. Interestingly, classrooms that selectively and critically used computer simulations coped best with multiple inference problems but did not score higher than their control groups on the regular achievement and the one-step inference tests.

The database study evaluated the relation between the mindful use of database software and the learners' ability to organize data, identify meaningful variables, and formulate and test hypotheses. This study was carried out over 6 months (teacher training included) with sixth-grade students and was concluded with a paper-and-pencil test that evaluated learners' ability to apply database inquiry procedures to new information that is not studied in schools. The results indicated that a mindful use of computer database software might help to realize IQ potentials. The correlations between IQ and database scores in the treatment classrooms were consistently and significantly higher (with low, medium, and high IQ students) as compared to the same correlations in the control classrooms.

Comptown's ecological sensitive experiments were carried out in natural classroom settings that were part of a complex multisystemic ecology. Using methods associated with quasi-experimental studies the Comptown experiments satisfied two needs:

- They enabled the identification relations between specific types of software and specific cognitive gains and thereby test theory-driven, cause-and-effect hypotheses.
- They created contexts in which systemic conditions in the treatment classrooms differed from their

controls. They thereby delimited systemic aspects (of a complex classroom ecology) that affect the specific intervention and deserve more attention. One paramount characteristic was the congruence between the generic properties of the instruments of learning and teaching and the teacher's pattern of instruction. This finding motivated the construction of a "taxonomy for information technology adoption policy" : an information technology software selection procedure guided by the ecological approach.

A TAXONOMY FOR INFORMATION TECHNOLOGY ADOPTION POLICY: AN INFORMATION TECHNOLOGY SOFTWARE SELECTION PROCEDURE IMPLIED BY THE ECOLOGICAL APPROACH

In the ecological model a pattern of instruction and the use of means and methods of instruction derive from a single conceptual framework that, to a large extent, is culturally and ecologically dominated. An intervention that introduces new instructional technologies may either disrupt an existing harmony and reveal the multifaceted nature of these implicit, ordinarily "hidden" connections, or lead to inadequate and fruitless use of the newly introduced technologies. Recognizing the vital importance of adequately matching teacher and technology, Comptown's ecologically sensitive experiments introduced information technology software while changing the teacher's pattern of instruction.

The "taxonomy for information technology adoption policy" tries to generalize the Comptown experience and reveals the possible correspondences between the generic properties of patterns of instruction and six types of information technology software ordinarily used in education (drill & practice, tutorials, games, simulation, open tools, and educational programming).

More specifically, the taxonomy consists of three components: one that characterizes instructional processes that determine teachers' patterns of instruction, one that specifies properties of software, and one that defines the range of congruence between instructional processes and software.

Instructional processes are further elaborated by five decision-making processes (facets) that delimit the diversity of patterns of instruction. Software properties are further elaborated by five facets that specify these properties in terms of their managerial and instructional qualities (i.e., elements of these facets reinforce elements of practiced patterns of instruction). Table presents the five instructional decision-making facets and their elements.

Table: presents the five software facets and classifies educational software accordingly.

The linear functions and database experiments are concrete examples that demonstrate the benefits of congruence. In these experiments congruent software properties augmented instructional methods. We use these studies as representative applications of the more general framework delimited by the taxonomy. The instructional goals emphasized by the linear functions treatment teachers (who internalized the project's operational principles and were trained to use the simulation software mindfully) were

- Derivation of a set of abstract principles (Facet A, Element 3) that permit each student to rediscover abstract sets of relations and construct new functions (Facet D, Element 3), and
- Development of computer skills that allow each student to systematically and mindfully manipulate computerized simulations (Facet A, Elements 1, 2). The learning activities enhanced by these teachers were either group directed or individualized and autonomous (Facet C, Elements 2, 3). To this end, the treatment classroom teachers were constantly engaged in curricular decisions (Facet B, Element 2) that involved
- mapping of elements of instructional patterns onto elements of the simulation software, and
- selection and integration of computer-based activities into the ongoing instruction and learning procedures.

The software's managerial properties enabled teachers to deliver some control responsibilities (Facet F, Element 2) to software users and act as facilitators (Facet E, Element 2).

The software's information-processing properties reinforced the teachers' tendency to enhance use of semistructured learning:

Table: Instructional Decision Making Facets and Their Elements

Facet	*Element*
A. Goals of instruction	1. Knowledge and comprehension
	2. Application
	3. Analysis and synthesis
	4. At least two of the above
b. Responsibility for the design of the content to be learned	1. Curriculum expert
	2. Teacher
	3. Student
(who decides?)	4. Two or all of the above
C. Type of learning activities that teacher decides to enhance	1. Teacher-directed activities
	2. Group-directed activities
	3. Individualized and autonomous activities
	4. At least two of the above activities
D. Enhanced learning styles	1. Reaction to uniform structured learning materials
	2. Interaction with peers and learning materials
	3. Rediscovery and construction of new knowledge
	4. Learning in more than one of the above modalities
E. Teachers" perception of their pedagogical role	1. Dominating
	2. Facilitating

Similar developments took place in the database study. The treatment teachers emphasized the acquisition of computerized database strategies and higher order information handling skills. Responsibility for the design of the content, to a large extent, devolved on software users. Teachers facilitated group-directed learning activities that were essential to new knowledge construction operations.

The database software information-processing requirements induced learners to supply information and use software's algorithm for the construction of new knowledge. These requirements intensified an already existing pattern of instruction developed by teachers who had internalized Comptown's operational principles. Hence, data construction procedures could be practiced in an enriched educational environment.

Both experiments spell out congruence in terms of fluid interdependencies between instructional patterns and instructional properties of software and demonstrate pedagogical, psychological, and administrative implications of software selection and use.

Furthermore, the experiments suggest that congruence rests on a dual verification process: examination of the elements that characterize a pattern of instruction and examination of the correspondence between a pattern of instruction and generic software properties. Table maps elements of patterns of instruction on elements of software properties and reveals optional software and instructional cross-classifications that support these processes.

Two arguments that are embedded in the proposed matrix further stress its educational implications. First, software instruction correspondences provide an immediate context in which instruction and knowledge construction reinforce each other. Second, a systematic and a reasoned choice among educational alternatives may enhance educational change.

However, it should be noted that the proposed theoretical classification leaves open practical constraints and opportunities that characterize each specific educational context and should be part of any change considerations.

Chapter 11

Assessment of Distance Learning Technology

The history of positive claims for distance learning technology and, on the other hand, a number of negative reports have led many to accept the need for a change in the way we evaluate new technologies for distance learning.

The number of new and complex technological devices that could be applied to distance learning is increasing. Cuban, in his history of technology use in schools, cautioned that "determining what levels of [technology] use now exist is like trying to snap a photograph of a speeding bicyclist".

With adequate evaluation in place, we may be able to "tune" existing technologies so that they meet our needs, anticipate new developments, and settle disputes, in time to plan and operate rational, cost-effective K-12 local, regional, and national distance learning systems.

Underlying all evaluation plans are beliefs about how we employ technology so that we enhance the delivery of instruction and the quality of learning experiences.

At the heart of every evaluation plan is a curiosity about how new technologies can increase students' access to quality instruction and thereby increase their academic achievement, motivation, and value for learning.

The purpose of this discussion is to:

- Discourage evaluation questions that have not proved useful in the past;

- Suggest that future evaluations distinguish between the effects of delivery and instructional technologies;
- Offer some generic evaluation plans, questions, and examples associated with delivery and instruction; and
- Discuss issues related to the cost-effectiveness of distance learning.

FORMING AND ASKING EVALUATION QUESTIONS

Evaluation is the process by which we judge the worthwhileness of something in order to make decisions (Baker, 1991). Technology assessment encompasses a number of analytic and measurement strategies that produce information that helps make worthwhileness judgments about technologically based educational programmes. Judgments made during the development of a programme are termed *formative*. Evaluation that seeks to describe the results of an operating programme is often referred to as *summative*. Because our values govern both formative and summative evaluation activities, we need to be clear about the kinds of distance learning evaluation questions that will meet the needs of our schools and communities.

The questions we decide to ask about distance learning and the evaluation instruments we employ will necessarily keep us ignorant about some matters while informing us about others.

Evaluation questions carry implicit assumptions and beliefs about the significance of different elements of distance learning and their impact on desired outcomes. For example, if we ask whether a new teaching medium produces more student achievement than traditional media, we have assumed that media are able to influence student achievement—an assumption that has been seriously questioned.

One of the most important recommendations underlying this discussion is that all evaluations should explicitly investigate the relative benefit of two different but compatible types of distance learning technologies found in every distance learning programme. One technology influences the delivery of schooling and another technology influences learning from instruction.

Delivery technology is characterized by the equipment, machines, and media that provide access to instruction. Familiar examples of delivery technology are books, computers, and teachers. Instructional technology seeks to influence the learning of students. Examples of instructional technology are ways to sequence and structure lessons, the use of examples, provisions for practice, and tests. Instructional technology is transported to the student by delivery technology. Any instructional technology can be provided to students by a variety of delivery technologies. For example, information, examples, practice, and tests can all be delivered to students by either books, computers, or teachers.

These two different technologies are typically confused in distance learning evaluations. Student achievement gains or losses influenced by instructional technology are most often attributed to delivery technologies. Reductions in the cost or time it takes to access special student populations (for example, rural or disadvantaged students) are incorrectly attributed to instructional technology. Confusion about technological benefits can lead to inappropriate and expensive policy mistakes. At the root of the confusion one finds many different definitions of technology.

WHICH TECHNOLOGY FOR WHAT PURPOSE?

In its most general sense, the term *technology* suggests the application of science and experience to solving problems. The major obstacle in our past struggle to understand the contribution of new technology in distance learning is that we have confused the contributions of these two different technologies.

One distinct class of technologies results from the application of various scientific and engineering principles to the development and use of equipment, materials, and procedures that record and transmit instruction. These educational media technologies are associated with the physical sciences that have produced the new electronic media (for example, fibre optics, interactive video disc, and computers). Delivery technologies increase student and teacher access to learning resources, which is one of the most important goals of distance learning.

A second type of technology applies various social science principles and past experience to develop teaching methods and curriculum choices. This instructional technology draws primarily on research in teaching, learning, and motivation to enhance student achievement. The "products" of an instructional technology are new instructional design theories, teaching methods, and motivational strategies that can be embedded in "courseware" (instructional materials) for distance learning. A primary goal of this chapter is to recommend that all evaluations of distance learning programmes attempt to provide reliable and valid determinations of the separate influences of delivery and instructional technologies.

SEPARATING DELIVERY AND INSTRUCTIONAL EVALUATION QUESTIONS

Support for a separate consideration of delivery and instructional technologies in evaluation is well established in the research literature but rare in evaluations or programme planning. Schramm (1977), historically the most established reviewer of media studies in education, concluded that "learning seems to be affected more by what is delivered than by the delivery medium".

More recently, analyses of media and technology research that compared the learning benefits of different media could be summarized with the analogy that media "do not influence learning any more than the truck that delivers groceries influences the nutrition of a community". Distance learning media are vehicles that transport instruction to students. The choice of vehicle influences the important outcomes of student access, and the speed or cost of the delivery but not the learning impact of the instruction that is delivered to the "consumer." Delivery vehicles indiscriminately carry helpful, hurtful, and neutral instruction.

CHOOSING CRITICAL INDICATORS FOR EVALUATION

Among the specific issues that must be addressed in future evaluations of local applications of distance learning technology are: What aspects of evaluation planning enhance the usefulness of information for decision makers? How might we collect information that will aid in our judgment about the different influences of the delivery and instructional features of the programme?. Whereas a number of evaluation concerns apply to some but not all programmes, three generalizations seem useful to all:

- Adopt an early concern for evaluation,
- Use a multilevel evaluation plan, and
- Conduct formal cost-effectiveness analyses.

ADOPT AN EARLY CONCERN FOR EVALUATION

Both evaluation specialists and administrative decision makers need to be involved early and actively in distance learning system design. Past experience suggests that waiting until a system is designed before thinking about evaluation has been a familiar but very wasteful pattern. It is critical to have early information about, for example, exactly what set of conditions are being replaced by new distance learning programmes. One way to accomplish this would be to spend an ample amount of time during the programme planning stages carefully describing the specific problems we wish the new approach to solve.

We should describe how we will measure the current conditions (e.g., a baseline measure of the existing situation, including the views and impressions of the stakeholders) and thoroughly discuss what we believe to be the *alternative* solutions to the problem.

If an evaluation plan is developed as the programme is planned and implemented, a number of advantages are realized. In the area of computer-assisted learning, Levin described eight exemplary costeffectiveness evaluation programmes. Each of these examples collected baseline measures of the problems they were trying to solve. Each of the eight programmes began their concern with evaluation at the start of their planning.

Early evaluation makes it possible to determine which aspects of a distance learning programme were positive and which were negative. Negative aspects can then be modified and the positive accentuated to achieve maximum benefit. For example, most distance learning programmes attempt to bring a much richer set of curriculum choices and quality teaching to K-12 school programmes.

Programme planners might begin with an analysis of options (the variety of media available to deliver new curricula) and their audience (for example, measure the number of students who would enroll in new courses). Early concern with evaluation results in the collection of information on both the need and the audience for distance learning as well as the existing alternatives. Another advantage of early evaluation involvement is that an ongoing evaluation plan can be developed. Too often programmes are developed and implemented, then at some later stage the programme planners remember that "we have to do some evaluation." As a result, very little is learned about the programme being studied that is useful either for the immediate programme or for other distance learning ventures.

Early evaluation planning most often yields useful information, yet it is a rare phenomenon. Levin noted that his search for adequate cost-effectiveness evaluations was difficult. He found that only one in six published reports was adequately designed. Because most reports are not published, one suspects that early evaluation is not our typical procedure at the moment. The second general direction that is useful for all distance learning programmes is to adopt a multilevel evaluation plan.

USE A MULTILEVEL EVALUATION PLAN

The two levels of evaluation that most often seem to give useful development information are measures of

- Participant reactions, and
- The achievement of programme objectives.

Participant reactions to distance learning programme effectiveness is the most common (and unfortunately, often the only) level of evaluation attempted by K12 school districts. Typically, this level of evaluation employs printed forms containing a combination of questions designed to inquire about the "feelings" and "impressions" of different groups involved in the programme.

A common question is "How would you rate the quality of the teaching in this programme?" (typically rated on a 5-point scale that ranges from exceptional through average to poor). Items such as "List what you think are the STRONG (or WEAK) points of the programme" permit the respondent to write in personal views and comments. Questionnaire forms are most often used for reactions because they protect the anonymity of respondents and therefore, we presume, increase the candor of the responses. Forms are often sent to all of the programme participants but are filled out and returned by only a small percentage of those who receive them. Participant reactions are useful provided they do not serve as the *only* level of evaluation data. They should be used primarily to uncover both informal participant impressions and *unanticipated* benefits and problems. Reaction items should be divided between those that deal with the medium (e.g., ease of access, reliability or technical quality of transmission or machines, space allocation issues) and those associated with the instruction (e.g., the quality of teaching, how things learned in the programme were used outside of class).

Collecting *participant reactions* has the advantage that programme managers get informal impressions of the programmes and often uncover unanticipated results. For example, the Northeastern Utah Telelearning project, which uses microcomputer-based instruction transmitted between remote schools over telephone lines, found an unexpected problem because they used open-ended reaction forms. Students complained that in the early stages of the programme it was very difficult to contact a teacher to get help when it was needed. On the other hand, the Interact Instructional Television Network in Houston, Texas , used a similar instrument and discovered an unexpected positive outcome of its project. It was observed that students in small television reception rooms tended to help each other a great deal during the instructional programme. They could help while the programme was continuing without disrupting the teacher or other students.

This "peer tutoring" seemed to be having a positive impact on student learning and motivation. On closer inspection, the tutoring activity seemed to be due to the fact that the microphone the students used to communicate with the teacher at another location had to be turned on to function. When the microphone was turned off, the students could consult among themselves before they turned it on to answer a question or discuss a point with the teacher. When following up on the peer tutoring finding, the Houston project uncovered the fact that some of the tutors hired to supervise the student television reception rooms were demanding that the students "keep quiet," which discouraged the peer tutoring. The tutors had assumed that talking indicated a "discipline problem" that had to be corrected. Once discovered, the peer tutoring might be encouraged and its barriers eliminated (e.g., through adjusting the training of tutors as in the Houston example).

The problem with participant reaction data is that it is most often collected in such a way that it is not a reliable or a valid indicator of programme effects. Yet, unreliable information might occasionally provide useful information as it did in the Houston project. Questionnaire data can be representative if evaluators select a random sample of participants large enough to engage a meaningful number of each group involved in the project. To increase participation evaluators have found it useful to send each randomly chosen participant a card telling them they have been selected, that their response is vital, and to expect the questionnaire soon. Follow-up notes to all those chosen can encourage laggards to send in their forms without violating anonymity. Depending on the numbers involved in the entire programme, a small (5% to 10%) random sample of participants can give a very accurate impression of the reactions of the entire group.

Questionnaires should be used at various stages in the programme development, including very early on. Unanticipated problems and benefits uncovered by questionnaires usually require much more careful study. For example, when students in most distance learning programmes are asked, a majority will typically state they would *not* continue to elect a distance learning option if they could choose a "traditional class" as they did in the Northeastern Utah Telelearning.

The fact that students would elect a traditional programme if one was offered does not indicate that the Utah project failed. On closer inspection it is often found, as is suspected in the Utah case, that students sometimes feel isolated in distance learning settings and would therefore select more traditional options for social and "nonacademic" reasons. This is particularly true of middle school and high school students. They typically have strong social needs that are not always met in distance learning programmes.

Other problems that can be spotted using the "early warning system" of reaction questionnaires are communication problems between participants, the extent and impact of technical difficulties, inappropriate implementation of plans, and opportunities to extend the programme into new areas. Yet in even the best of circumstances, reaction forms will not give solid information about the achievement of most delivery and instructional goals. For this purpose, programmes need to adopt a second level of evaluation.

Achievement of programme objectives is the second and most substantive evaluation goal. Formal measurement of objectives is usually considered by evaluation specialists to be the most crucial information to be gathered. Objectives should be divided into at least two categories: those associated with delivery and those associated with instruction. One category of outcome that is common to both types of' technology is cost-benefit and cost-effectiveness. In cost-benefit and cost-effectiveness evaluation, we attempt to measure "bang for the buck," that is, the cost of the impact obtained from various features of the programme.

The discussion turns next to outcomes specific to instructional technology, then to delivery technology outcomes and finally to cost-benefit and cost-effectiveness measurement.

Instructional technology objectives include changes in student learning, values, motivation, and the transfer of and application of knowledge outside of the classroom. These important goals are influenced by the "courseware" or instructional programmes that are developed and/or chosen and transmitted to distant learners. In some cases, instruction is designed by teachers. In other cases, already developed courseware is purchased and transmitted to remote sites. The instructional decisions embedded in each lesson influence student learning and motivation. Different teaching method and curriculum options have very different effects on student learning, which might be explored in evaluation. So, distance learning evaluation might include at least the following four types of questions related to instructional technology.

- Which of the curriculum and teaching method choices in a given distance learning programme impacted student achievement and subsequent ability to use (transfer) the knowledge acquired outside of the instructional setting?

Achievement can be tested with teacher-made or standardized achievement tests. Increasingly, schools are interested in the extent to which students transfer what they learn outside of school. Transfer might be estimated by open-ended questions on reaction forms. If the school district has other schools receiving similar curricula from different delivery forms, an obvious opportunity exists to check on any achievement or motivation differences between the options. When possible, alternative teaching methods and curriculum choices should be explored in order to maximize the learning of different kinds of students. For example, highly structured and supportive instruction might be contrasted with a more "learner-directed" and discovery approach to curriculum. Many programmes have found that students who are anxious or have learning problems profit a great deal from added structure and support, whereas students who are more independent are able tend to benefit more from a discovery approach.

- What impacted student and teacher motivation to learn and invest effort in making this programme a success?

Current theories of motivation have introduced a very counterintuitive element in distance learning programmes and evaluation. Formerly, it was thought that media choices greatly influenced both student and teacher motivation. Now it is understood that motivation is influenced by beliefs and expectations and is therefore due to individual differences in beliefs about media and not to the media per se. Yet a number of studies of media preferences agree with O'Neil, Anderson, and Freeman that "in general, students' attitudes are positive while instructors' attitudes are negative". There is recent but solid evidence that when students expect that a new medium will make learning easier and more "entertaining," they like it. However, there is good evidence that their liking does not lead them to work harder. Quite to the contrary, the more they think a medium makes learning "easy," the less effort they will invest to learn. This effect has been explained as a student misjudgment about the kind of effort required to learn based on our previous experience and expectations. For example, U.S. students typically assume that television is an "easier" medium than books or teachers, probably because of their use of the medium for entertainment. This reaction on the part of our students is quite different than that of Israeli students who, on the average, have been found to invest more effort in television because their early experiences with television have been less entertaining and more demanding intellectually.

There is additional evidence that students will not invest effort if they believe a medium to be very difficult. With U.S. children, this is sometimes the reason for their lack of willingness to read. So the greatest motivation is invested in media and instructional programmes that are perceived as being moderately difficult. This evidence would suggest that one way to influence student motivation would be to select "moderately difficult" media. However the evidence also suggests that student and teacher beliefs about media difficulty change over time, sometimes radically. The more stable predictor of motivation seems to be student beliefs about their own ability and the demands placed on them by different instructional tasks. This would suggest that we should evaluate the students' perceptions and beliefs about the *learning tasks* contained within the media employed by distance learning programmes and their own *self-efficacy* as learners. This form of evaluation could be embedded in reaction questionnaires:

- Which of the curriculum and teaching method choices in a given distance learning programme impacted:
- Student and teacher values for what was learned and,
- Subsequent motivation to teach and learn and to use what was learned outside of the instructional setting?

Reaction questionnaires that are carefully constructed and administered will give a good indication of student and teacher values related to the programme, teaching, and the curriculum. Negative value statements do not always reflect negatively on the programme (recall the students in the Utah project who liked traditional classrooms better than distance learning because of social opportunities). Generally, one hopes to foster a positive value for learning and new curriculum options with distance learning. Shifts in attitude that result from *changes* in the programme can be monitored *if* reaction forms are sent periodically (every few months) throughout the development stages.

- Which of the curriculum and teaching method choices in a given distance learning programme impacted the cultivation of different kinds of knowledge, including procedural skills *and* higher order thinking, learning-to-learn, and metacognitive skills?

Although higher order skill learning is more difficult to assess than ordinary "achievement," few programmes have been successful in this area. One current example of a technology-based thinking skills programme is the Higher

Order Thinking Skills (HOTS) programme, which focuses on Chapter (disadvantaged) students. The programme originates at the University of Arizona and is distributed to member schools in many states. Teachers in the programme use computer lessons, class exercises, and discussion to increase the thinking and study skills of students. HOTS evaluation involves the ongoing use of standardized tests, noting changes in the quality of questions students ask and analyses of their class assignments. Although a few formal measures of thinking and study skills exist (and more are being developed), programme managers might consult with evaluation specialists about selecting and developing tests to measure problem-solving and study skill development.

Whereas learning, values, and study skills are important instructional outcomes for distance learning, the delivery technology will influence yet another type of outcome.

Delivery technology transmits various forms of instruction to students. The recent introduction of computers to schools has resulted in more attention to technology delivery benefits. Evaluation questions associated with delivery technologies include attempts to assess the effect of medium on:

- Student *access* to a greater variety of curriculum choices,
- School or programme *utilization of resources*, and
- the reliability of delivery choices. Questions one typically finds in the evaluation of media include:
- Did the distance learning media maximize student access to new, and/or high-quality courses and teaching when compared with other choices?

Access to new or beneficial courses and instructional techniques or teachers is one of the primary objectives of most distance learning programmes. Collecting access data often involves comparisons between different ways to deliver courses or the size of enrollments in classes both before and during the implementation of the programme. For example, the Share-Ed programme in Beaver County, Oklahoma , used a new fibre optic network to provide new curriculum to rural schools. They collected participant reactions on the advantages of the increased curriculum choices offered to students who are allowed to take college credit courses in high school as a result of the new system. These reactions, when combined with baseline and process data on actual enrollments, provide good evidence of the extent of access provided by the innovation. Evaluators should carefully consider increased or enhanced access of minority, older, or widely dispersed student groups.

Although "access" usually suggests the availability of new curriculum options, it can also imply teacher access to students on a more personal level.

Teachers in the Houston, Texas, Interact Instructional Television systems report problems with their personal and immediate access to students during instruction in order to "check their reactions or mood" and adjust their teaching accordingly. On the other hand, teachers using computer-delivered courses often report increased "individualized" access to students and enjoy the opportunity to "watch them learn."

- Did the media influence the utilization of school and community educational resources (e.g., space, equipment, skilled teachers, new courseware developed at one site but not readily available at others)?

It is often the case that because distance learning programmes are recorded and distributed to many different sites, the best teachers are made available to many more students. Evaluators might track statistics about how the background and/or training of teachers in distance programmes compare with district averages. An instance of a different kind of utilization is to be found in the Beaver County, Oklahoma, Share-Ed programme. The local telephone company was installing fibre optic communication lines to improve local service. The system was capable of handling far greater transmission volume than the existing usage anticipated in the communities served.

The school systems' use of fibre optic lines for television and voice transmission for distance learning utilized unused space on the system. Because distance learning courses are often provided to fewer students per school than the average course, they often make use of underutilized rooms (e.g., storage spaces) and equipment.

- Are distance learning media more reliable than other alternatives?

ne of the primary concerns expressed by the critics of distance media is their technical reliability. In the Beaver County, Oklahoma, television system, for example, the reaction forms used in evaluation only picked up technical problems when the students were asked to describe "weak points" of the system. None of the administrators noticed technical problems, 11% of the teachers mentioned reliability, but 36% of the students responded to the reaction form by going into detail about microphone feedback, distracting equipment, out-offocus pictures, equipment noises, and colour problems. This difference in reporting reliability problems probably stems from the amount of experience each group had with the actual television transmission. However, programme evaluation should establish regular checks by technical staff on these problems in order to judge the severity of participant reactions and make repairs when necessary. When technical transmission problems are not solved, they can decrease achievement scores and reduce participant commitment to the system.

In successful distance learning programmes, delivery (media) technology and instructional technology must work together. The delivery features of new media must be employed so that they will eventually save precious educational resources. Curriculum and instructional design must be utilized so that they support the effective learning and transfer of important concepts. Instruction must be developed to reflect the special delivery characteristics of different media. In addition, however, communities and funding agencies are increasingly concerned not only with the effectiveness but also the *cost* of distance learning programmes. Cost is a "goal" or "outcome" of both delivery and instructional technologies.

COST-EFFECTIVENESS EVALUATION

During an evaluation of the separate delivery and instructional value of distance learning programme effectiveness, cost data should also be collected. This parallel activity allows us to combine "effectiveness" (i.e., delivery and instructional outcomes) with "cost" data to provide cost-effectiveness information to decision makers. Cost-effectiveness evaluation requires that the cost of two or more different alternative technology options are compared for the same outcome measures.

In many ways, cost-effectiveness ratios are the most interesting information we can supply to school officials, taxpayers, and their elected representatives. Limited educational resources will eventually require a much greater emphasis on both the monetary and time cost of new programmes.

Delivery Technology Cost

Evaluations that precede the introduction of new media should explore the costs of various alternatives. In many cases, older technologies (e.g., tutors, books, cassette television programmes, the mail system) are cheaper in monetary cost. Evaluations of costs should always consider trade-offs with cheaper and more traditional delivery options. There is evaluation data indicating, for example, that tutors who are trained and paid minimum wage are much cheaper than computers for many instructional tasks. An excellent discussion of cost-effectiveness analysis is provided by Fletcher (1990), who reviewed previous studies and presented cost data for interactive video disc programmes used in military training. He noted that some programmes divide costs into categories such as

- Initial investment,
- Technology support (maintenance and replacement), and
- Operating costs; other programmes lump all costs together. He advised that separation gives a better picture of the source of costs and helps cost containment. He noted that cost-effectiveness ratios vary widely in past reports. Some studies find huge cost

> benefits for technology-based distance learning. Other studies report large cost disadvantages. Clearly this question involves a number of factors, many of which have not yet been identified. Fletcher implied that cost-effectiveness analyses can be (and are) manipulated when he suggested that "basically, these cost ratios can be as low as we want, depending on the actual equipment being simulated".

Evaluations conducted during the introduction and maintenance of a distance learning programme are advised to adopt the "ingredients" costing approach described later. Instructional Technology Cost There are a great variety of different school and community goals that influence evaluation criteria under the general heading of instructional effectiveness costs. The cost required to increase student motivation, learning, and transfer is being questioned with greater frequency. School districts may wish to consider collecting cost data as a way to support the development of policy. The development of an instructional technology yields a variety of teaching, motivation, and transfer outcomes at very different monetary costs.

Besides monetary cost, schools are increasingly interested in the time costs associated with the mastery of different learning or performance goals. Some types of learning tasks consume much more "teaching time" and/or "learning time". For example, it takes much longer to teach a student study skills than to teach memorization of facts. It also takes longer for a student to learn procedural knowledge to the point where it becomes automatic-about 100 hrs of practice for even simple procedures is the current estimate. Fletcher (1990) reviewed a number of military applications of computer-based instruction and found time savings to average about 30% across many different sites. It is therefore likely that there will be more and more emphasis on the time costs of different instructional technology options.

In some applications, the cheapest and/or quickest options are not necessarily the best. Students who learn cheaper or faster do not necessarily learn better. The new "cognitive" learning theories provide the insight that it may be more important to know *how* students reach learning goals than to know that they get correct answers on examinations. It often takes longer for students to learn in such a way that their correct answer on a test reflects "deep cognitive processing" and the exercise of higher order cognitive learning skills, than to take a surface level shortcut. Educators need to be wary of focusing evaluations on time savings at the expense of the quality of learning.

Generally, once a distance learning team has worked out the list of goals associated with both monetary and time costs, an evaluation design can be chosen. One of the first issues to be confronted is the choice of how the data reflecting costs will be gathered. There are a number of methods, but Levin's *ingredients* method seems particularly applicable to both delivery and instructional technologies.

The Ingredients Method of Determining Costs. Although there are a number of emerging ways to determine local costs and efficiencies, one of the soundest and most comprehensive is the "ingredients method" developed by Levin at Stanford University. It "requires identification of all of the ingredients required for the distance learning intervention, a valuation or costing of these ingredients and a summation of the costs to determine the cost of the intervention". In the K-12 setting, cost is defined as the value of what is given up by using resources in one way rather than for its next best alternative use. For example, if teacher time is given up then it may not be used for other purposes. Therefore, the cost of teacher time is assessed by assigning a value to what is lost when teachers are assigned to distance learning technology programmes.

The ingredients method is implemented in two stages. In the first stage, all necessary programme ingredients are listed. The identification of ingredients requires that we list distance learning programme necessities associated with five categories:

- Personnel,
- Facilities,
- Equipment,
- Materials and supplies, and

- All other. In the second stage, each of the ingredients listed in each of the five categories is valued.

Space limitations preclude a complete description of the ingredients method but a review of Levin will provide most of the information needed to determine ingredient costs. Levin gave specific technology examples that are very relevant to the kinds of programmes now evolving in many schools, and he urged complete listings of ingredients. For example, he required that all "donated" time of volunteers and outside organizations be included as a personnel ingredient if it is necessary for the conduct of the programme. He reasoned that failure to cost donated time will give an unrealistic picture of the "replication" expense. He also claimed that, in the rare instance where one finds a complete costing of technology-based programmes, one often finds evidence that the organizational climate greatly influences costbenefit ratios. He presents evidence that when the same distance learning programme is presented in many different sites, the cost of implementation can vary by 400%. Some organizational designs seem much more efficient than others for technology-based, distance learning programme delivery.

Chapter 12

Evaluating Intelligent Tutoring Systems

The somewhat astounding way in which the functioning of the apparatus seems to fit in with the so-called "laws of learning" deserves mention in this connection. The "law of recency" operates to establish the correct answer in the mind of the subject, since it is always the *last* answer which is the right one. The "law of frequency" also cooperates; by chance the right response tends to be made most often, since it is the *only* response by which the subject can go on to the next question. Further, with the addition of a simple attachment the apparatus will present the subject with a piece of candy or other reward upon his making any given score for which the experiment may have set the device; that is the "law of effect" also can be made, automatically, to aid in the establishing of the right answer.

Pressey's ideas were probably viewed by some as quite promising, given their relationship to then-current learning theory, but they were never applied or even evaluated in any rigorous sense. Today, intelligent tutoring systems (ITS) epitomize the notion of theory-based, individualized, automated instruction. Many of us are just as excited about the potential of ITS as Pressey was about his teaching machine. Unfortunately, although ITS have been in existence for well over a decade, the degree to which they have been successful remains equivocal due to the relative dearth of controlled evaluations. Some of the more familiar ITS evaluations reported in the literature include the LISP tutor , instructing

LISP programming skills; Smithtown , a discovery world that teaches scientific inquiry skills in the context of microeconomics; Sherlock, a tutor for avionics troubleshooting; and Bridge teaching Pascal programming skills. Results from these evaluations show that the tutors can accelerate learning with, at the very least, no degradation in outcome performance compared to appropriate control groups.

How much can we make of these findings? As always, there is a selection bias for publication of unambiguous evidence for successful instructional interventions.

Thus, we do not know how many studies found disappointing results. We are personally familiar with other (unpublished) tutor-evaluation studies that were conducted but were "failures." We are also aware of a great many ITS that have been built but never evaluated. We believe that a consistently applied, systematic, and rigorous approach to evaluation would speed the emergence of ITS into applied settings.

The primary goals of this chapter are to outline a systematic approach to research and development of intelligent tutoring systems, and to present a set of steps to organize the design of evaluations for these systems.

RESEARCH AND DEVELOPMENT OF ITS: A GENERAL APPROACH

Our general approach has two main thrusts. First, in order to manage the tradeoff between internal and external validity, we believe ITS research and development should progress from laboratory studies of pedagogy in artificial tasks toward field studies of fully implemented ITS for real-world tasks. In other words, begin by identifying powerful instructional manipulations in controlled settings, and then work up to evaluating those manipulations in applied settings. Second, to maximize the efficiency of the research as well as the generality of the results, we believe ITS research and development should be driven by learning theory and constrained by evaluation data. In other words, if it should work, try it; if it doesn't work, change it.

Managing Experimental Validity

Experimental design involves arranging conditions to promote the validity of an experiment. If the causal link between independent manipulations and dependent measures is equivocal, the experiment is said to lack internal validity. If the ability to generalize from the experimental sample to the population of interest is equivocal, the experiment is said to lack external validity.

In pedagogical research, increases in external validity are generally accompanied by decreases in internal validity. As you increase your ability to generalize pedagogical findings to applied settings, you lose the level of experimental control afforded within the laboratory.

We believe the solution to this problem is to initially develop and test pedagogical principles in a laboratory setting with careful attention to experimental control. Promising approaches should then be tested in increasing fieldlike settings, and ultimately in applied settings with careful attention to external validity.

Figure depicts the posited tradeoff between internal and external validity; as internal validity decreases, external validity increases. This relationship is particularly true with regard to research on pedagogy. Research in laboratory settings is desirable because of the experiment control that is possible in the laboratory. One can control for prior knowledge, assign subjects to groups, counterbalance for teacher (experimenter) effects, and so on. On the other hand, research in field settings (e.g., high school classrooms) is desirable because all aspects of the target setting are present in the experiment.

Many of these aspects, however, are potential confounds to the experiment, making it difficult to relate outcome performance measures to the experimental manipulation. Field research on pedagogy, if done well, can have high external validity, but often at the expense of internal validity.

Our approach to managing the tradeoff between internal and external validity is to begin with laboratory research (high experimental control and internal validity) using carefully designed laboratory tasks. As we find instructional manipulations that are powerful, we attempt to replicate the effect with more realistic tasks, again within the laboratory. Eventually, we study the intervention in an applied instructional context (field setting) with real-world tasks. Figure depicts this flow, and places these stages of research on the validity vector. We believe that neither laboratory nor field research alone will give a complete and accurate picture of the instructional effectiveness of a particular intervention. Further, we believe the choice of target tasks used to study instructional interventions at the various stages deserves careful consideration.

Managing Experimenter Bias

We believe that ITS research and development can advance more rapidly if the process is both driven by learning theory and constrained by empirical data. By *learning theory,* we mean a coherent, plausible body of ideas about how people acquire, store, retrieve, and apply knowledge and skill. We find that instructional prescriptions (or "theories" of instruction) that fail to address mechanisms of human knowledge acquisition and representation, are inadequate for our purposes. However, even if the design of an ITS is carefully linked to wellestablished theory, its value can only be ascertained from empirical testing.

Theory is important in generating hypotheses about teaching and learning, and in driving generalizations about pedagogical effectiveness across instructional domains, but empirical testing is critical in order to judge how these ideas fare in reality. Only empirical data, with appropriate control conditions, can provide convincing documentation of the effectiveness of an intervention.

Figure shows this proposed cyclical relationship between theory and data, where research begins with theory that is progressively modified by empirical results.

In summary, empirical data about the effectiveness of theory-based instruction provides feedback about how well our implementation works, and may also lead to a revision of the original theory. We believe it is extremely important to evaluate systems rigorously and often in order to make progress in ITS effectiveness.

In the next section, we present examples of research that reside at each of three anchor points along the validity vector. Our intention is to give a sense of the kinds of studies that are possible, and to indicate how the results of such studies can influence subsequent ITS work. It is important to keep in mind, however, that we view these three stages of research as relatively arbitrary points along a continuum, rather than truly distinct categories. We present examples of

- Laboratory research employing artificial tasks,
- Laboratory research employing real-world tasks, and
- Field research using real-world tasks.

Laboratory Research With Artificial Tasks

Artificial, or laboratory, tasks do not exist (in their exact form) in the real world. Examples of artificial tasks that have been used over the years in psychological research include memorization of nonsense syllables, cryptarithmatic, forcedchoice reaction time tasks, and cursor-tracking tasks. Such tasks are devised to allow uncontaminated study of various phenomena of interest to the experimen ter. Artificial tasks are useful in pedagogical research because they allow us to eliminate or reduce the effects of prior knowledge on learning, isolate very specific components of real tasks of interest, and study knowledge/skill acquisition in shorter time frames than would be required for real tasks. Space Fortress *Research on Small-Group Pedagogy. Space Fortress* is an example of an artificial task that has a rich record as a research tool for studying issues of training and skill acquisition. This gamelike dynamic control task was originally developed at the University of Illinois under funding from the Defence Advanced Research Project Agency as part of the Learning Strategies project. We have developed an updated version of the programme to run in our laboratory, with more flexibility than the original for our research purposes. Shebilske and Regian, and Shebilske, Regian, Arthur, and Jordan report some of the research conducted in our laboratory using Space

Fortress. For instance, we have found that it is possible to train up to four subjects on a single computer while achieving individual performance levels equivalent to those attained by subjects trained in the same amount of time on four separate computers.

This is achieved by using a training protocol that involves a combination of whole-task practice, shared part-task practice, and observational learning among trainees. These findings are leading us to design prototype instructional systems that operate from the perspective of small-group pedagogy rather than individual pedagogy. In general, automated instruction is more cost-effective and sometimes more instructionally effective when designed for small groups rather than for individuals. When teaching multiple students simultaneously at a single computer, the hardware investment is reduced, as are demands on human instructor time. Also, students in small groups tend to teach one another, benefiting both the provider and the recipient of the instruction. Because students diagnose and remediate each other's performance, the difficult problems of automated diagnosis and natural language processing are avoided.

Space Fortress Research on Gender-Related Performance Differences. Another research area that we have been examining with Space Fortress involves the significant spatial component of the task. Typically, spatially loaded laboratory tasks yield robust gender effects with males outperforming females. This effect occurs on static spatial tasks (e.g., mental rotation, mental paper folding, form boards) as well as dynamic ones (e.g., collision estimation, dynamic control of moving figures). There has been a long-running argument over whether this gender difference in spatial performance is due to sex-related biological differences or differential developmental experiences.

There is clear evidence that at least some of the difference is related to differences in testosterone levels. Recently, we have been examining instructional interventions that may overcome the hypothesized experiential deficits. We were surprised to find a very simple intervention that seems to go a long way in this direction; namely, placing women in discussion groups with men. We had female subjects participate in brief but regularly occurring (and specifically structured) discussion groups with male subjects, to talk about *Space Fortress* strategy and tactics. This simple intervention dramatically increased women's *Space Fortress* performance. Short discussion groups following practice sessions produced a small positive effect on men's skill acquisition, but a significant positive effect on women's. The women under this treatment performed nearly as well as the men. This very inexpensive intervention may help reduce gender differences in skill acquisition for other kinds of tasks as well.

Loader *Research on Mental Models During Training.* A second example of an artificial task from our laboratory is *Loader*—a complex procedural task. It requires subjects to execute long sequences of consoleoperation actions (e.g., button presses, switch actuations, dial rotations) to accomplish specific goals. The task is based on a computer-simulated console that controls railroad cars, tracks, and cranes in a fictitious railroad yard. The task is designed to be a laboratory analog of procedural console operations and process control tasks, which are common in industrial and defence settings.

We hypothesized that acquisition of *Loader* performance skill would be supported by the development of a dynamic mental model linking console actions to events in the "railroad yard." That is, in the process of learning to carry out a specific sequence of actions to accomplish a goal, the operator would come to imagine the corresponding events in the railroad yard, even if she could not actually see the yard while operating the console.

We therefore conducted the following experiment. Forty subjects were shown a simple static diagram representing a bird's-eye view of the railroad yard. The diagram depicted the layout of tracks, the initial location of cars, and the locations of bins and the crane. Subjects were told they would learn to operate a console that would enable them to move the cars around on the tracks, and to use the crane to move canisters between bins and cars. Subjects were randomly divided into two groups (i.e., dynamic model vs. no model). During training, both groups received identical text-based instruction in an instructionalwindow above the *Loader* interface. One group, however, additionally saw a *dynamic* version of the bird's-eye view of the railroad yard. After training, both groups were tested under identical conditions. They were asked to perform the complete procedure without guidance and without access to either type of railroad yard representation. The results were striking. Rather than becoming dependent on the animated rail yard model, subjects in the dynamic model condition apparently internalized the model, as evidenced by their performance after the model was removed. Posttraining performance was 33% faster and 50% more accurate for subjects trained with a dynamic graphical model compared to the nomodel condition, even though the graphical model was not present during testing. This is an example of a very simple graphical aid that can be added to simulation-based ITS to produce significant and enduring performance enhancement.

Laboratory Research With Real Tasks

By real tasks, we mean tasks that constitute all or part of actual tasks that are performed in the world outside of the laboratory. In addition to having counterparts in the real world, they typically are more complex in structure than artificial tasks. Because real tasks tend to be more complex, they may take longer to acquire and performance may be more error-prone than artificial tasks.

Bridge Tutor. "Bridge" is the name of an ITS that teaches a subset of the Pascal programming language, which fits our criteria for being a real task. We conducted a study using this tutor prior to conducting a full field evaluation of Bridge. Approximately 200 subjects participated in the initial laboratory study.

Many of them, however, had significant problems learning the programming curriculum because they lacked or had forgotten prerequisite knowledge presumed by the system (e.g., not knowing what an integer or variable was). Findings from this study highlighted about 10 weak concepts in programming and math: integer, real number, string, data, sum, product, constant, variable, expression, and value assignment. As a result of this laboratory investigation, we built a "pretutor,"an approximately 2-hr computer-assisted instruction (CAI) module that instructed those 10 concepts. Subjects received on-line definitions of concepts, followed by a series of questions pertaining to the concept (e.g., Is 5.24 an example of an integer?).

After each response, feedback was provided on both the accuracy of the response and the item in question (e.g., "No, 5.24 is not an example of an integer because integers are positive or negative whole numbers without decimal points, and 5.24 contains a decimal"). This pretutor presented items in a learning-by-doing format with a strict mastery learning criterion. In the subsequent field study, once subjects encountered the Bridge tutor, they no longer had to ask, "What's a variable?" or "What's an integer?" The problem was solved, and learning Pascal programming skills was not confounded by inadequate knowledge of necessary concepts.

ELECTRICITY TUTOR

MHO is a tutor that teaches basic principles of electricity. In one laboratory study (Shute, in press-a), we tested about 400 subjects using two instructional environments created as slightly different versions of MHO. These two environments differed only in the computer-generated feedback. All other aspects of the tutor were identical. In the rule-application environment, the ITS told the learners what the relevant principles were, and in the rule-induction environment, learners had to induce principles on their own, only given information about what variables were relevant. One learner characteristic that was examined was "exploratory behaviour," a quantified measure of on-line tool usage (e.g., taking a meter reading from a circuit). Results from this laboratory study showed that learners with more exploratory behaviors learned significantly faster and scored significantly higher on outcome tests if they had been assigned to the inductive environment than the applied environment. On the other hand, less exploratory learners performed significantly better from the more structured, application environment compared to the inductive environment. It is interesting to note that there was no significant main effect due to learning environment on any of the many outcome or efficiency measures used in that study. Thus, neither of the instructional approaches was a clear "winner," overall. Instead, the study gave us critical information about how subsequent versions of the tutor should adapt to student behaviour.

FIELD RESEARCH WITH REAL TASKS

This section discusses studies that have employed real tasks tested in the field as opposed to in the laboratory. As noted earlier, the controls that are possible within laboratory environments may be more difficult, or impossible, to achieve during the conduct of field studies. For example, it may not be possible to randomly assign subjects to treatment conditions in a field study. However, with field research, the ability to generalize to the actual instructional context of interest is enhanced, increasing the study's external validity.

Smithtown

Shute and Glaser (1991) developed an ITS designed to improve an individual's scientific inquiry skills as well as provide a microworld environment for learning principles of basic microeconomics. Both of these foci constitute real knowledge and skills as they are applied outside of the laboratory in the real world. Shute, Glaser, and Raghavan (1989) reported that results from a field study comparing three groups of subjects: a group interacting with Smithtown, an introductory economics classroom, and a control group. The curriculum was identical in both treatment groups (i.e., laws of supply and demand).

Results showed that whereas all three groups performed equivalently on the pretest battery (around 50% correct), the classroom and the Smithtown groups showed the same gains from pretest to posttest (26.4% and 25.2%, respectively), significantly outperforming the control group. Although the classroom group received more than twice as much exposure to the subject matter as did the Smithtown group (11 vs. 5 hrs, respectively), the groups did not differ on their posttest scores. These findings are particularly interesting because the instructional focus of Smithtown was not on economic knowledge, but rather on general scientific inquiry skills, such as hypothesis testing.

LISP Tutor

Another example of an ITS field was conducted by Anderson and his colleagues at Carnegie-Mellon University. They developed a LISP tutor that provides students with a series of LISP programming exercises and tutorial assistance as needed during the solution process. In one study, Anderson, Boyle, and Reiser (1985) reported data from three groups of subjects: human-tutored, computer-tutored (LISP tutor), and traditional college instruction (subjects solving problems on their own). The time to complete identical exercises were 11.4, 15.0, and 26.5 hrs, respectively. Furthermore, all groups performed equally well on the outcome tests of LISP knowledge. A second evaluation study compared two groups of subjects: Students using the LISP tutor and students completing the exercises on their own. Both received the same lectures and reading materials. Findings showed that it took the group in the traditional instruction condition 30% longer to finish the exercises than the computer-tutored group. Furthermore, the computer-tutored group scored 43% higher on the final exam than the control group. So, in two different studies, the LISP tutor was successful in promoting faster learning with no degradation in outcome performance compared to traditional instruction.

In this section, we have provided examples of the types of studies we believe are useful at various stages in the development of ITS. We hoped to give a sense of the kinds of studies that are possible, and to indicate how the results of such studies can influence subsequent ITS work. In the following section, we turn to the goal of designing evaluation studies. We describe a set of steps that may be used to organize the design of ITS evaluation studies.

STEPS IN ITS EVALUATION

Outcomes of evaluation studies occasionally reflect the quality of an experimental design rather than the efficacy of the ITS. In our experience, we have seen evaluation studies fail due to poor experimental design, inadequately operationalized constructs and measures, and even deficient logistical planning and implementation. In the following sections, we present some general steps that may be followed to implement an effective ITS evaluation:

- Clearly delineate the goals and methods of the tutor,
- Clearly define the goals of the evaluation study;
- Select the appropriate design to meet the defined goals; and
- Instantiate the design with appropriate measures, subjects, and controls.

Clearly Delineate the Goals and Methods of the ITS

A careful review of the ITS goals and methods should be undertaken prior to designing an evaluation study. Occasionally, the instructional goals or methods may have shifted over the developmental life cycle of the ITS. In any event, if

the designer of the evaluation study is unfamiliar with the tutor's goals and methods, then designing a good evaluation study is almost impossible. We believe the evaluation designer should be very clear about the following critical issues.

What Instructional Approach Underlies the Tutor?

How, generally and specifically, does the system accomplish instruction? Is instruction guided or unguided, student directed or tutor directed? Is knowledge explicitly presented by the system or induced by the student? To what degree will all students have seen the same information or experienced the same interactions? Do students "complete" the tutor after a fixed time period or after reaching some performance criterion?

What Learning Theory Does It Assume?

What knowledge or skillacquisition theory motivates the instructional approach of the tutor? Which aspects of the tutor are directly theory-driven and which are arbitrary? How closely linked are the instructional approach and the learning theory? It is important to distinguish among a learning theory, a general instructional approach, and a specific instantiation of that instructional approach. Failure to do so can lead to over generalizations about evaluation results.

What Exactly Does It Teach?

It is important to be very clear about what students are expected to learn as a result of interacting with the tutor. First, in a concrete sense, what exactly will they know or be able to do after tutoring that they did not know or could not do before? Specific and measurable knowledge or skills should be clearly delineated as the expected learning outcomes. For example, one might hope that students will be able to solve differential equations, list the bones in the human hand, or diagnose faults in a specific electromechanical system. It is also useful to characterize the goals of instruction in a more abstract manner. For example, one might hope to teach procedural skills, declarative knowledge retrieval, or logical problem solving. The ability to generalize findings across or within instructional domains is dependent on some type of theoretical characterization of domain dimensions.

What Other Impacts Is It Expected to Have?

Are there other ways in which interacting with the tutor is expected to impact the student? For example, *Smithtown* explicitly instructed scientific inquiry behaviors, but it provided an environment that promoted learning about microeconomics. Less intentional side-effects of tutoring might include near or far transfer of skill, changes in perceived selfefficacy, or modification of attitudes about computers. If you believe such effects are probable and important, then appropriate and objective measures should be obtained to demonstrate the effect. So-called anecdotal evidence is usually the clearest indication of a missed opportunity during an evaluation.

In What Context Is It Supposed to Operate?

Is the system intended to supplement existing instruction or provide stand-alone instruction? Is the system targeted to individuals or small groups? What prior knowledge, training, or demographic characteristics are assumed of students? Is the tutor supposed to be used in an academic setting to support declarative knowledge acquisition, or in an industrial training environment to support acquisition of procedural skills? It is important to clearly specify the environment in which the tutor is intended to operate in order to give it a fair chance of succeeding in evaluation, and in deciding on appropriate control conditions.

Clearly Define the Goals of the Evaluation Study

Evaluation studies should not be fishing expeditions. A thoughtful consideration of what you want to know enables you to develop an experimental design that will unequivocally give you that information. You should also be realistic about the difficulties involved in implementing various designs, and adjust your goals at the outset to those that are realizable. Consider the following questions:

What Would You Like to Know After the Study is Completed?

What is the primary question you want answered, or alternatively, what is the most important claim you want to be able to make? You may want to know if the tutor is more effective, more efficient, or both, than some instructional alternative at producing criterion performance on some task. You may want to see how much students learn beyond their incoming knowledge and skills, or as a function of their incoming knowledge and skills. You may want to see how tutor effectiveness is influenced by students' individual learning style. You should clearly specify your research questions and hypotheses before you design the study.

How Will You Measure Success, and By What Standard Will You Judge It?

Think carefully about how to measure what is being taught, and how you will judge success. Suppose your instructional goal is to teach nine test-taking strategies, and you found that I week after students received 2 hrs of tutoring, they were able to state five of these strategies, on average. Was your tutor a success? What if you also learned that I week after students received 5 min of instruction using a simple mnemonic approach, they were able to state eight of the nine strategies. By comparison, your tutor would seem ineffective. But what if you found that students learning from your tutor could reliably apply five of the nine strategies, whereas students trained with the mnemonic approach can state, but not apply, eight strategies? Because any human performance is extremely sensitive to the methods used to measure it, your measures of learning should closely reflect the goals of instruction.

You may want to capture quantitative indices, protocols, and/or observational data. Because your subjects will be working at computers, it will be possible to plan for the online capture of quantitative measures of performance, such as latencies, accuracies, and behavioral counts. With considerably more effort and expense, protocol analyses can yield important information about learning that cannot be captured directly by the computer. Alternatively, trained observers may be employed to record aspects of learning and performance that are impossible to obtain otherwise.

Step 3: Select an Appropriate Design to Meet

Defined Goals

Only after reviewing the goals and methods of the tutor and clarifying the goals of the evaluation study is it appropriate to select an evaluation design. Researchers involved in the evaluation of automated instruction have sometimes chosen to distinguish between formative and summative evaluations of courseware. Generally speaking, formative evaluations have an *internal* control condition, and ask the question: How can the system be improved? Summative evaluations have an *external* control condition, and ask the question: How does the system compare to other systems or approaches?

Originally, the formative/summative distinction was used to distinguish between diagnostic (formative) evaluation during student learning versus outcome (summative) evaluation after student learning. This distinction was only later adapted to the purpose of categorizing evaluations of courseware during development versus after completion. However, we have found that distinction too restrictive for our purposes. Concerning types of evaluation studies, we prefer to think in terms of the continuum described earlier and a set of general evaluation categories. In particular, we present five broad design categories that may be used for evaluation studies. These include

- *Within-system designs* asking how two or more alternative versions of a single tutor compare to one another;
- *Between-system designs* addressing the effectiveness of one tutor in relation to another in terms of teaching the same subject matter;
- b*enchmark* designs asking how a tutor fares in relation to some standard instructional approach;
- Hybrid designs constituting combinations of the above options; and
- *Quasi-experimental designs* representing any of the previous categories, but without random assignment of subjects to conditions. Such an approach is often necessary for true field studies, but should be undertaken with some care. Although these five categories do not represent an exhaustive set, they are common and useful design types for evaluation studies.

Step 4: Instantiate Design With Proper Measures.

Subjects, and Controls

The next step is to carefully plan the details of the design. Carefully consider the selection of dependent and independent measures, the number and type of subjects, and the appropriate control conditions.

Dependent Measures

We have found that a common problem in failed evaluation is poor selection, design, or implementation of dependent measures to assess knowledge and skill acquisition. The dependent measures should directly reflect both the goals of the ITS and the goals of the evaluation study.

We prefer to obtain a variety of dependent measures. Because ITS instruction is done on computers, it is cheap and easy to capture data on virtually everything that happens during instruction. Given the expense and trouble involved in building an ITS and implementing a large-scale evaluation, we choose to err on the side of gathering too much data. Besides, it is the nature of learning and instructional research that the apparent effectiveness of an intervention will depend, in large part, on how you measure performance. If you measure performance in a variety of ways, you are more likely to pick up treatment effects if they exist. Possible dependent measures include performance latency, performance accuracy, declarative knowledge, procedural knowledge, procedural skill, automatic skill, secondary task performance, higher order knowledge, as well as measures of near transfer, far transfer, and skill retention or decay.

Independent Measures

It is likely that the effectiveness of an instructional intervention will vary with individual characteristics of students. Individuals come to any new learning situation with varying knowledge, skills, and abilities. Common individual difference measures include general intelligence, grade point average, standardized aptitude test scores, cognitive process measures (e.g., working memory capacity, information processing speed), personality measures (e.g., impulsivity, aggression, introversion), and demographic information (gender, age, years of school, experience with computers). Consider collecting these kinds of measures in order to control for potential confounds in your experimental design (e.g., two schools with different mean IQs for enrolled students).

Control Conditions.

One of the most common arguments in interpreting the results of evaluation studies is over the suitability of the control conditions. The choice of treatment condition

- As well as the proper control condition
- Must be principled, based on a reasonable consideration of the claims you hope to make. For example, if you choose only to include a no-treatment control, you may only be able to claim "My intervention is better than nothing."
  This assumes, of course, that data support the claim. Certain rules of thumb may be applied to help eliminate control-condition problems in ITS evaluation research.
  One problem that may arise in ITS research is the creation of Hawthorne effects (i.e., treatment differences due only to the fact that one group, usually the tutor-instructed group, receives special attention). Hawthorne effects, like placebo effects, are easily obtained, and thus must be carefully avoided. In the ideal case, the only difference between the control and treatment condition should be the treatment itself. Confounding difference you may want to avoid including differences in motivation, time-ontask, exposure to certain information, background characteristics, and so on.

Subjects

In addition to specifying rigorous control and experimental conditions, you will need to identify the right type and number of subjects that are needed in the study. In this regard, the most important considerations are the target population to which you would like to generalize, and the effect size that you expect to obtain.

For whom is the tutor intended? If the purpose of your ITS is to teach university graduate students a certain curriculum, and your test subjects come from an undergraduate population, you won't be able to accurately assess the effectiveness of your tutor on the target population.

As a rule of thumb, we believe evaluation studies looking for main effects of instructional treatments should use at least 30 subjects per condition. For aptitude-treatment variables (ATI) studies, using individual difference measures as independent variables, studies should use at least 100 subjects per treatment.

This estimate can be relaxed somewhat for sufficiently powerful designs involving extreme groups or matched cases. Most investigators in the ATI tradition before 1980 used 40 or fewer subjects per treatment, and may have lacked the power to pick up even moderate effects. Keep in mind the relationship between sample size and power. The ability to pick up a given treatment effect goes up as sample size increases. Most basic experimental design textbooks describe how to estimate the required sample size for picking up a treatment effect of some hypothesized magnitude. When performing these calculations, keep in mind the difference between statistical significance and real-world importance. With enough power, you can pick up very small treatment effects, even though the effect size may be too small to be of practical importance.

Chapter 13

Assessment of Intelligent Training Technology

IMMEDIATE EFFECTIVENESS VERSUS POTENTIAL

Technology assessment in the world of intelligent training systems must consider not only the effectiveness of a training system but also the likelihood that it can be assimilated by the organizations that could use it. This can be seen either superficially as a marketing problem or more deeply as a problem in changing schooling or training. In either case, though, it is not enough for a product to be effective; it also must either fit the existing organizational structure and available technology or be so attractive as to bring about adaptive changes that make it usable.

When a product is assessed for its immediate utility, evaluation is extremely straightforward. We try it and see how it works. Sometimes we can develop quantitative assessment approaches that allow us to rank alternate products.

For example, consumer testing laboratories have mechanical devices that simulate sitting in a chair and getting up. With such devices, we can count how many sitting/rising cycles it takes before a chair's springs fail. With a mixture of such tests, we can develop composite scores that assess the durability of chairs. In other cases, where more subjective judgments of adequacy are involved, we can ask potential consumers to rate properties of a product. So, we see ratings of orange juice, microwave popcorn, wine, and other food products by panels of tasters, either professional or from the lay public. For some products, the effect of using the product can be directly measured. For example, when testing razors, we can count the number of cuts received by a sample of razor users and perhaps even measure the lengths of hair roots left after shaving.

Instructional products are often evaluated the same way. We use the product and measure its positive and negative outcomes. Usually, this is done by testing students after their use of a product and seeing whether they do better on goalrelevant test items after using the product than after some alternative treatment. Costs, corresponding to the razor cuts of the preceding example, are also assessed. Often, there is an explicit comparison between requirements for the instructional treatment being tested and the resources available in some pool of representative schools. Other costs, such as teacher preparation time, student class time, and so on, are also considered.

User acceptance is also an important consideration when instructional products are evaluated. For example, certain textbook series are considered to have great instructional potential but to be market risks because teachers won't adopt them. Often, this occurs when a textbook series fails to match current curricular sequencing, requires significant teacher preparation time investment, or fails to provide certain aids to teaching that competitors make available. One of the costs likely to be associated with a technological aid to education is the investment of time teachers must make to learn how to use it. A particular problem for computer-based systems is whether the computer equipment it requires is broadly available.

In the case of computer-based consumer commodity products, assessment must consider user acceptance and installed platform base. Many a product has failed in the market, even though it was demonstrably better than its competitors, because it required a different operating system or more memory. More trivial sources of product failure include complex copy protection schemes, complexity in providing the right size of diskettes, and lack of compatibility of files with extant products in the marketplace. Clearly, from the standpoint of an educational product meant for use today, an assessment of the product must consider not only whether it is effective when used but also whether people are prepared and willing to use it.

When evaluating an educational product's potential for the future, these factors are harder to deal with. The computers that schools have today are primitive and characteristically inadequate for many of the most exciting educational technology possibilities. For example, one big advance in the computer world is simpler, smarter interfaces that are more forgiving. Even the better-equipped schools, however, tend to have underpowered machines that cannot run the larger programmes that are needed to provide easy-to-use information-processing tools. To restrict positive assessments to software that runs on underpowered machines is foolish, especially when schools show a continuing ability to upgrade their resources, albeit slowly and spasmodically, in response to technological change. However, it is difficult to predict when enabling conditions will arise in any market, including the school market. Fortunes have been made and lost in guessing whether DOS, Unix, Windows, or OS/2 will prevail, for example. Accordingly, it seems very important at least to understand what conditions will be required for a promising prototype system to be used and valued, and it would be extremely helpful to have means of assessing the likelihood of those conditions arising.

In the case of intelligent training systems, some information is available concerning the hardware platforms that will be prevalent in the future, and there are also development platforms that can be used to produce software that will run under several different operating systems. For example, it is clear that Microsoft Windows is a major force in the computer world. Combined with other forces previously evidenced, Windows assures that there will be a relatively large population of computers with 80386, 80486, or 80586 processors; four or more megabytes of memory; and decent (VGA or better) graphics in the business and industry world.

Recent market trends suggest that the Macintosh operating systems will have a long presence in the school world, the desktop publishing world, and perhaps other niches. Unix windowing systems such as X will also be supported by the next generation of multiple-platform operating systems.

On the software side, much of the research base in artificial intelligence depends on Common LISP running on large Unix™ work stations. Currently, delivered systems are often rewritten in C so they will run faster on standard work stations (major LISP vendors are working to complete adequate delivery systems for LISP that run efficiently on multiple platforms). Rather recently, Smalltalk has emerged as a programming language of choice for training system development, and it is what my team uses for its biggest and most applied project. Recent actions in the commercial software world suggest a move toward use of object-oriented languages such as Smalltalk (or C++ for teams with high programming skill levels) because they produce software that is more maintainable.

In the easy case, then, a decision maker can predict, with a high degree of confidence, that the hardware and the software architecture required to support a desirable prototype system will be in place. Often, however, given the requirements of development, there will be a gap between the hardware platform for a prototype system and the hardware broadly available in the short term.

A conservative view of the problem of assessing both software quality and the likelihood of a hardware plant to run the software would be that only software that makes a striking contribution will succeed in navigating the hardware gap. From this viewpoint, assessment means a search for evidence that a product not only is effective but further that it is so effective that it cannot easily be avoided.

A global finding of massive effect, though not particularly informative for product refinement, provides a basis for predicting that a product will be used, even if it requires improved hardware. More broadly, the bigger the infrastructural investment that would be needed to use a piece of software, the bigger the demonstration of general efficacy needs to be.

These observations are informed by our own experience with the "Sherlock Project," a long-term effort to shape a technology of coached practice environments for training complex problem-solving jobs in the Air Force (Lajoie & Lesgold, 1990; Lesgold, Lajoie, Bunzo et al., 1992; Lesgold, Lajoie, Logan et al., 1990). Our first "product," Sherlock I, needed many refinements but it did produce the massive effect needed to assure likely adoption, and it led to support for ambitious efforts to refine and generalize the system and move it to different platforms. Consequently, the way in which we evaluated it may be worthy of examination. Later, I discuss this project, especially our approach to assessing it. I conclude by reflecting on some issues critical to assessment of training technology that became apparent in the course of the development of Sherlock.

ASSESSMENT EXPERIENCES FROM THE SHERLOCK PROJECT

What Is Sherlock Like?

Since 1983, my associates and I have been developing a technology for training complex problem-solving expertise for the U.S. Air Force. The Sherlock Project has been an extended effort to develop improved approaches to the training of complex job skills, especially training that supports transfer to new but related jobs. After empirical studies of experts and trainees the work has revolved around a family of prototype training systems called coached intelligent apprenticeship systems.

The basic training approach of these systems is to present trainees with simulations of work problems that are among the most challenging that arise in real life. To help them through these problems, coaching is provided, that is, help of varying forms is available to the trainee on request. Artificial intelligence techniques are used to provide the work simulations and to provide coaching tailored to the trainee's capabilities. Two generations of coached intelligent apprenticeship environments have now been built. The first of these, Sherlock I, was evaluated extensively in the field. Its successor, Sherlock II, is largely a response to lessons we learned from the evaluations. Sherlock II includes a simulation of a very complex electronic device, a "test station" [4] with thousands of parts, simulated measurement devices for "testing" the simulated station, a problem selection scheme that presents fault diagnosis problems within the device simulation, a coach that provides assistance when help is requested in the course of diagnosis, and a reflective follow-up facility that permits a trainee to review his or her performance on a problem and compare it to that of an expert.

In developing the Sherlock systems, we had a number of psychological concerns. We wanted to afford opportunities for learning by doing, and this required simulation of complex job situations, not just of small devices. Also, we wanted to tailor the coaching provided by the system to the knowledge needs of the trainee. Ideally, trainees should be kept in the position of almost knowing what to do but having to stretch their knowledge just a little in order to keep going. Consequently, hints should be provided with some inertia. They should provide enough help to avoid total impasse but this help should come slowly enough so that it is easier to think a bit on one's own than to wait for the correct next step to be stated completely. This requires considerable modeling of student capability and may also require modeling of the course of trainee-machine interaction. Of course, it also requires expert modeling in order to know what advice to give.

During the course of difficult work, it is not likely that much extended learning can take place. Both psychological experimentation and theoretical models of casebased learning indicate that learning from task situations requires a lot of cognitive effort. For this reason, we have put much of the power of our training systems in postproblem reflective follow-up. After solving a problem, which requires about a half hour of effort, trainees can review their actions step by step, asking what an expert would do at any point along the way. Or, they can simply ask for a trace of an overall expert solution. At each step in either trace, they can receive background information on why the step is being taken. Also, colour diagrams at each step in the trace show what is known about different parts of the system being diagnosed (parts proven good in green; paths with incorrect information in them in red, etc.). Much of this capability rests on the same knowledge structures that support coaching during problem solution.

Sherlock I ran on a special artificial intelligence work station and was written in Interlisp and Loops, a proprietary object-based language for Interlisp. Trainees interacted with the system by pointing to screen-graphic renderings of the front panels of devices and to schematic diagrams of their innards. Sherlock II runs on a standard 80386 machine, requires around 8MB (depending on the version used and research requirements for data collection), about 20MB of hard disk, a processor speed of 20 MHz or higher, a videodisc player and interface, and a GENLOCK card to mix the video and computer graphics images.

Trainees interact with Sherlock II by making selections from menus and by pointing to video views of test station components. For example, to make a resistance measurement, trainees would click on a screen icon of the hand-held digital multimeter to access the front panel display of the meter in video, indicate knob settings on the video image with the mouse, select the component he or she wanted to test from a menu, and then indicate meter probe locations by pointing to a video image of the component. Coaching advice also is available via the menu system. Sherlock I, in spite of its more specialized artificial intelligence environment, was much less intelligent and more brittle in its knowledge than Sherlock II. In addition, it lacked the reflective follow-up capability that we now believe to be of great importance.

Basic Assessment Results for Sherlock I: The Massive Effect

Sherlock 11 has undergone multiple revisions, and major field tests were scheduled for Spring 1993. We do have field assessment data for Sherlock I. Overall, Sherlock I was excessively rigid but remarkably successful. Because the goal structures for each problem were hand coded and many hints were specific statements written in advance, the system was not very extensible, and the interaction between trainee and machine somewhat rigid. However, the bottom line is that 20-25 hrs of Sherlock I practice time for trainees in their first 4 years of duty produced improvements almost to the level of their more senior colleagues who had many more years on the job. In more practical terms, trainees could not generally troubleshoot test station failures before the Sherlock training, but they could afterward. Here is how this conclusion was established.

The goal of Sherlock I was to train the ability to diagnose test station faults, the hardest part of the F-15 manual test station job. So, we [8] used simulated test station diagnosis problems in the field evaluation. Virtually all of the job incumbents at two Air Force bases participated in the evaluation, a total of 32 airmen in their first 4-year term and 13 at more advanced levels. The 32 firsttermers were split into an experimental and a control group of 16 each. The experimental group had a mean experience of 28 months in the Air Force, whereas the control group had a mean of 37 months (the difference was not statistically significant and worked against the comparison of interest). The advanced group had about 6 more years of experience, a mean of 114 months. The simulated test station diagnosis problems were presented verbally. An example problem is the following:

While running a Video Control Panel unit, Test Step 3.e fails. The panel lamps do not illuminate. All previous test steps have passed.

In such a situation, the unit being tested is usually defective, but in this particular case, it turns out that a relay card in the test station is bad. This type of problem is one that is extremely difficult for novice technicians. In the evaluation study, technicians would hear the problem statement and then be asked two questions:

- *What would you do next?*

- *Why would you do that?* They would then be told the result of their action and the cycle of questioning would repeat until the problem was solved or an impasse was reached. Verbal protocols of these problem-solving interviews were then given to Air Force experts who scored them blind to the condition assignments of the subjects.

Scoring scales were derived from expert rankings of the problem-solving performances using "policy capturing" techniques. Given group standard deviations ranging from 12 to 29, the results show that the experimental and control group pretest means and the control group posttest mean are at one level and the experimental posttest mean and the advanced group mean are at a second, much higher and significantly different, level.

The data were also considered from a second viewpoint, the amount of on-the-job experience needed to produce gains equivalent to those produced by the Sherlock experience of 20-25 hrs of coached practice. The totality of the pretest data was used to generate a regression coefficient for predicting months of Air Force job experience from these test scores. Using the scale created by this regression, the gain shown by the experimental group from pretest to posttest is equivalent to about 4 years of job experience, using conservative estimates, although the confidence interval for this estimate is necessarily huge, given the small numbers of subjects. A follow-up testing 6 months after training (Pokorny, unpublished data) showed retention of over 90% of the gains made from pre- to posttesting.

Overall, then, Sherlock was very successful, in terms of producing the ability to do the specific job of manual F-15 test station diagnosis, which is not readily acquired from simple on-the-job experience or from the training now available prior to reporting for work.

Interpreting the Massive Effect

The massive effect of Sherlock is real, but it requires interpretation. Basically, Sherlock is effective because it has no competition. That is, it affords opportunities for learning that were not available before, either on the job or in the classroom.

A variety of logistic and other limitations make it very difficult for on-the-job training to be effective in teaching the hardest parts of the job. When those hard tasks appear, it is often an urgent situation, in which getting equipment back on-line takes precedence over providing training opportunities. Further, the specific events that would present good training opportunities with respect to our high threshold criterion (the hardest tasks in real-life work) are relatively rare. In the schoolhouse, it is even more difficult to create realistic situations in which the hardest diagnostic tasks can be practiced, and such practice seems to be critical to attaining high levels of skill.

When looking at high-end job performance, even in purely cognitive tasks like fault diagnosis, there often is no substitute for realistic practice. Abstract principles can be taught in the classroom, but it is rare for those principles to be applied automatically in the real world without some practice, especially in situations of great complexity and stress. Consequently, one interpretation of the massive effect of Sherlock I is that it provides practice, under simulated task conditions, that is sufficient for learning, whereas prior learning opportunities within on-the-job practice did not. Seen from this viewpoint, the assessment issues that are raised are somewhat different in character. We consider each of these, in the context of the Sherlock experience, in the next section.

ISSUES IN INTELLIGENT TRAINING TECHNOLOGY ASSESSMENT

REALITY AND NATURE OF THE MAIN EFFECT

The first issue is the reality of the main effect. If one is going to assert that a system accomplishes a major chore that is otherwise not readily accomplished, this needs to be backed up. It is necessary to show that the system produces levels of competence that are worth more than the levels of competence achieved without using the system. At one level, this was easy. We could document the costs of not having technicians who could troubleshoot test station failures, and we were able to show that after Sherlock training, technicians could handle problems that they could not handle before. Because the Air Force was hiring civilian experts to stand by to assist uniformed personnel when test station faults occurred, the costs could be documented. However, we feel it is important to have a quantitative documentation of the training outcome as well as of the monetary value of the training.

That is, we wanted to have quantitative scores of performance in the test station troubleshooting tasks whose value we had established.

To get this, we had two basic options. On the one hand, we could list a number of properties of good test station troubleshooting activity and then score troubleshooting episodes for the presence or absence of those properties. For example, one important property is making measurements instead of swapping components. We could decide arbitrarily to subject some number of points from a person's score for each action required to solve a problem, charging more for swapping than for testing. Further, we could almost certainly reduce the costs to dollars. Each action takes time, which has measurable cost, and swapping a good part generates a variety of measurable costs. Depleting an inventory has at least indirect costs, because the inventory must be kept higher if such depletions must be anticipated.

It is also important to note that Sherlock I was based on many design principles, some of which were enumerated earlier. Which design principles have what effect on the various possible outcome measures is difficult to establish. One implication of this difficulty in isolating the mapping of treatment parameters to effects is that once a main effect is established, detailed parametric research may be justified. In the case of Sherlock, the initial results have motivated support for such a programme of research, which continues in the context of Sherlock II.

TRANSFER

On the other hand, we could have experts evaluate the performances of those who did or did not use the system, and then compare their ratings. At first blush, this seems considerably less satisfactory than the quantitative approach just described, and it would be if we were concerned only with immediate costs and performances. However, if we want to predict transfer to systems that may not yet exist or that may not be available for testing, especially when predictive studies of transfer may not have been carried out for the knowledge domain, then it may be necessary to rely on expert appraisals of competence. Expert judgments have known shortcomings. In the military context, it is not unusual for staff who are cooperative to be valued over those who are not, independent of their expertise, for example. With respect to assessing changes that we expect a tutoring system to introduce, such social factors represent error variance in an evaluation design.

The Air Force worked with us to find ways to use expert judgments to derive scorable properties. The basic scheme is very straightforward. Difficult troubleshooting problems are posed verbally to the testee. Testees call for various actions to be performed in solving the problem. Results of each action are provided to the testee. A trace is kept of all the activity of each trainee in solving each criterion troubleshooting problem. Experts are asked to examine the traces and to rank order them. Then, they are questioned about the bases for their rankings. From this questioning, one derives a list of features that contribute to judgments of expertise. The next step is to assign point values to each of these features, so that they can be used to set a score for the trainee. Finally, the scoring scheme thus developed can be used to score additional performances by the same or other test subjects.

Setting the point values for each scoring feature can be done in several different ways. One approach is to set the point values to best predict the rank orderings assigned by experts to the whole performances. This is a common strategy and generally involves regression analyses. The strategy makes sense if we assume that the experts are making their holistic judgments solely with respect to issues of expertise we care about. Sometimes this is not the case. A second approach is to analyse the features cited by experts and to evaluate them. This can be done both empirically and theoretically. Empirically, it is possible to do clustering analyses of the scoring features. Once clusters are identified, some amount of theorizing is required to decide why certain features cluster. This may result in a decision that some features are good indicators of important job knowledge whereas others are mainly generic indicators of being "good airmen." For example, following recommended troubleshooting sequences religiously may be highly valued but may not correlate with indicators of deep domain knowledge.

When the policy capturing approach is used there is potential loss of explainability for scores. Saying that a trainee got a high score for doing things that experts value highly is not quite as satisfactory as saying that the high score was awarded for performance approximating that of an expert in identifiable ways.

For this reason, we are moving toward a modification of the pure policy capturing approach. We are now experimenting with an online evaluation scheme in which our expert model directly tallies various indications of expertlike and nonexpertlike actions. These tallies can then be used in two ways. First, they can be summarized in ways that match the abstractions that are implicit in the expert model's goal hierarchies for performance. Second, regression analyses [10] can be done to predict human expert judgments of overall performance from the more microscopic objective tallies.

Nichols et al. (in press) probed for data beyond problem-solving steps. Test subjects were asked to explain each step they were taking, to indicate expected outcomes of tests, and to comment on what was learned from each new piece of information (such as a measurement made on the circuit). This approach was useful in providing information about performances that had high face validity. People who offer principled explanations for their problem-solving actions and who solve the problems efficiently are certainly candidates for good transfer performance.

On the other hand, the very requirement of explaining steps that are being taken may produce performances that are more systematic, and even more generally expert, then otherwise would occur. The requirement to explain one's performances is a significant intrusion into task performances. So far, there is no indication that it distorts results, but further study seems advisable. Overall, it seems well advised to ground the evaluation of a training system in performances of difficult tasks from the target task domain.

MODE OF PRESENTATION

In the first field tests of Sherlock I, some people in our client organization objected to using computer-administered problems for assessment, because the training programme provided practice in using our computer system as well as jobspecific practice. For the most part, this objection is attenuated as the evaluation becomes more heavily grounded in details of expertlike performance. Still, it is surely possible that a testee unfamiliar with the interface might appear to be performing less optimally than would otherwise be the case. For example, it is possible to "miss" in making choices from a pop-up menu, and such a "miss" might result in a tally of a nonoptimal choice during problem solution. Of course, the verbal problem simulation approach we have used so far in field evaluations is also problematic, because it requires trainees not only to be able to solve problems but also to be able to articulate their decision processes. However, the biases due to verbal aptitude requirements when verbal simulations of problem solving are used apply to both experimental and control conditions, whereas the biases due to computer-administered simulated problems apply only to the experimental group. Accordingly, we recommend that posttesting not be done via computer unless both experimental and control subjects are well trained in the interface.

It can still be useful to use the computer for administering and scoring the problems, however. The experimenter can sit at the computer and enact each action of the trainee. Further, the system could be modified to accept annotations along with actions, so as to log the trainee's explanations along with the trace of actions. A major advantage of using the computer in this way is that testing need not be done by a domain expert. The system simulation in a training system like Sherlock contains a verified device model. It therefore can provide the result of every action the testee proposes. In earlier field work, testees occasionally called for an action whose results the tester could not determine. Because some of our testing was done on third shift (between 11:00 PM and 7:00 AM), an expert had to be phoned in the middle of the night to determine what result to report back to the testee in response to the action proposed.

Ideally, systems will be developed for multiple jobs in a "job family." Again, once testees are familiar with the basic interface conventions used for a family of training systems, the systems themselves make good testing and data logging systems. Transfer can be assessed by noting the trajectory of performance over training sessions for both original training on one system and transfer training on a second. Given proper counterbalancing of order of training, it is possible to quantify transfer in terms of time (and its monetary value) saved in learning the second system given training on the first. Again, there are objections to using the training system as an assessment vehicle if prior experience with the interface is not controlled, and again the systems may make good examiner stations even when testing is done via verbal interactions.

ASSESSMENT ADVANTAGES OF OBJECT-BASED APPROACHES

Object-based design has power that is making it the standard in the software development world. For the very same reasons, object-based design may be key both in training for transfer and in assessment of transfer potential. More generally, intelligent training systems offer a peculiarly good opportunity for achieving synthesis of learning and assessment, which has been widely advocated as a goal for education and training generally.

The expertise in systems like Sherlock II is represented in computational "objects." An object is an independent piece of computer programme that stores its own local data and can thus respond to various requests that other parts of the system might make of it. Components of the system being diagnosed are represented by objects. Knowledge about how to deal with a specific component is embedded in the object that represents that component. For example, component objects will have routines relevant for the objects they represent. The object for a given component, such as a particular type of printed circuit card, might "know" how to draw the component it represents on the screen. It also will likely know how to model its component as part of an electronic circuit, how to test that component, and how to coach trainees in their interactions with that component. Because most training systems will do some sort of student modeling, the object for a component also needs to know how to record the student's interactions with that object, how to score those interactions, and how to make the recorded information available to other parts of the system that might be generating more abstracted evaluations of the student.

Further, objects are generally arranged in an inheritance hierarchy to facilitate system development. General objects are defined that have basic capabilities. When more specialized capabilities are needed, new objects are created that inherit general capability from their "parents" but add to that some specific functionality. For example, all component objects may need to tally the time of each action taken by a trainee that involves the component within their "scope." The time tallying routine would, in a good object-oriented programming system, be defined only once, for a general component object, and the routine would be inherited by more specialized objects that also require it. At a higher level of expert function, a level that abstracts over specific components and even types of components, expertise is represented as a goal structure for problem solving. In our approach, a task analysis will lead directly to specifications for the computational objects to be used in training systems. The goals of training are represented by objects, and those objects, too, must be able to perform, coach, and illustrate their specific bits of expertise. Furthermore, they, too, can be readily modified to keep track of how well trainees approximate expertise in their performances.

A goal hierarchy represents one kind of abstraction of expertise, but there is also another kind. The concept of an inheritance hierarchy of knowledge, which is central to object-oriented programming (though lacking in some partial objectoriented programming languages!), also has potential for the prediction, training, and assessment of transfer, both potential and actual. This is especially the case when specialized objects do their work through a combination of a few specific actions combined with a "call" to a more generic routine. I currently believe that analyses of multiple jobs for transfer should result in products that specify inheritance hierarchies of knowledge components. Further, I believe that transfer can then be predicted by noting the relative amounts of knowledge that are shared, that require only minor specializations of what is already known, or that require major new learning. I am currently trying to refine such an approach to task analysis (a first effort is discussed in Lesgold, 1991).

Given the decision that task analyses will lead directly to specifications for the computational objects to be used in training systems, and given the scheme of having those objects able not only to simulate expertise and train, but also to assess trainee performance, it is a small step to systems that can assess transfer potential as well as job-specific learning as they train. The step entails objects' contributing to decisions about transfer. For example, if there are cases where performance from the viewpoint of a specific object is expertlike, whereas performance from a more general viewpoint is not, this may indicate that the trainee has learned a successful algorithm that does not adequately generalize. Such an indication would count against any claims that the system teaches for transfer.

For example, when technicians test a component by verifying its inputs and then verifying its outputs, or vice versa, they are exercising a general capability that should transfer to many components of many systems. If instead they trace those input-to-output paths that are relevant to a particular situation, they will still be able to decide whether the component is good, but their performance does not have the same guarantee of transferability.

Architectural aspects, and use of object-based approaches in particular, are considerations that should enter into assessments of software for integrated training and testing.

DURABILITY OF EFFECTS

For the effects of intelligent training systems to be worthwhile, competence must not only develop and transfer, it must also persist. Training that is durable is much more valuable than training that requires regular "maintenance." Although complex, time-sensitive performances inevitably require maintenance, basic competences generally should not, provided they have been adequately taught and learned. Still, the training world is replete with courses taught, exams passed, predictable and overrehearsed performances carried out, with minimal long-term effect. Consequently, we felt it important to do retention testing of the Sherlock I system. In fact, retention was extremely high, in excess of 90%. Further, it was relatively uniform—few trainees showed precipitous drops in performance. We think such demonstrations are important, given the cost of intelligent system research and development. Just as with transfer, it would be helpful to have predictors of retention.

However, the development cycle for intelligent training systems is long even without adding extra months to separate initial from retention testing. I propose that instead, once a particular technology for training system development is well established, it would be possible to predict retention from the many micromeasures of competence that are used for assessing competence and transfer potential. In the Sherlock work, for example, if retention rests on conceptual understanding, then those specific performance indicators that depend on understanding the device being diagnosed and the methods of diagnosis should be good predictors of retention. If understanding plus efficiency of certain basic cognitive processes is needed, then indicators of both should be good predictors of retention. We did not conduct the needed analyses to support this approach when we field tested Sherlock I, but we expect to be able to with Sherlock II.

Predicting retention is not the same as measuring actual retention, especially when prediction formulas from one training system's history are used to estimate likely retention for a different system, but it is a start. To the extent possible, predicted retention measures should be supplemented by actual retention measures, at least on an occasional audit basis. However, predicted retention is an important aspect of assessment, especially because of the increased emphasis on rapid prototyping and more efficient development of computer-based training. Just as with conventional training approaches, it is always possible to audit performance with the system already in place and in use. Predicted retention would allow first tryouts of the system to be more informative, so that sound deployment decisions could be made earlier in the development cycle.

BOUNDARY CONDITIONS

Like any treatment, intelligent training systems will work only within certain boundary conditions. However, assessments of training seldom attend to boundary conditions. It is common to provide background data on the sample that was used to assess system capability. However, users are generally left to make their own inferences about how and when results from that sample might generalize. Some improvement over that state of affairs is possible and important. Consider the field testing of Sherlock I, for example. It was tested at operational Air Force bases, not at the training school. As a result, it could be assumed that a variety of basic electronics principles and procedures had been mastered by the test sample. Otherwise, they would not have been allowed job site roles. On the other hand, because they were on the job, they had daily concrete experience with the artifacts being simulated. It is conceivable that Sherlock I might not work well in the tech school environment. On the other hand, the scheme in which coaching is always available, so that true performance impasses are unlikely, seems rather robust and might be sufficient to permit a much wider range of trainees to use the system effectively.

From a research-and-development point of view, it seems appropriate to con- duct, for each new design approach to intelligent training system design, specific studies of the boundary conditions under which the system works. This is not too unreasonable. It simply means keeping records and analyzing for data patterns as the first implementations of the approach are carried into broad use. Then, if boundary limitations emerge, they can be considered by future users. Related to boundary conditions are interactions between components of the instructional treatment and trainees' prior knowledge. Consider, for example, the range of treatment possibilities present in Sherlock II or being considered for future versions.

These include practice in solving problems presented according to a fixed progression, a student-model-determined progression, or a studentrequest-determined progression; opportunities to replay one's own or an expert solution to the problem just solved; opportunities or requirement to critique one's own, or a peer's, performance on a problem; and opportunities for any of the aforementioned activities as a member of a cooperating peer group. It is quite possible that some of these learning opportunities might work better for one type of student and others might work better for another. For example, there may be some threshold of domain knowledge that is required before one can frame effective questions about an expert performance. If so, then students yet to reach that threshold may not find opportunities to replay problem solutions and ask questions about them to be very helpful. A second possibility is that some students may have more successful practice with one or another of the approaches and therefore value it more.

Although much about the effectiveness of training approaches for trainees with differing prior knowledge remains to be elucidated, it seems appropriate for an assessment of a training system to consider what is known, and to take such information into account in interpreting the adequacy of the test samples used for evaluating the system. A further step is possible when a system records a detailed trace of system usage by the student. Then, it is possible, by examining the course of learning for specific members of the test sample, to use extant knowledge to make predictions about interactions of prior knowledge with treatment, and to proceed to partial verification of those predictions.

MAINTAINABILITY AND EXTENSIBILITY

In addition to its utility in promoting learning, an intelligent training system must also be evaluated as a technological artifact. Too often, the process whereby training software is procured results in systems that cannot be maintained or extended. Initially, it will seem to the system purchaser that if the system works, there is nothing else to worry about.

However, virtually all training systems require modifications over their lifetimes. Weaknesses in the training are discovered. Devices that are part of the task domain are modified or replaced. New duties are added to the job. New trainees, with different entering capabilities, become part of the training population. All of these things happen routinely in the training world.

The requirements for maintainable software are well known. The software must be modular, with each module carefully documented. Detailed explanations and specifications of how the system works, and why, should be available. Standard computer languages should be used and only standard hardware should be required. We have found that a deeply objectoriented approach helps greatly in maintaining and extending software; indeed, we have had to rewrite virtually all code that did not reflect deep understanding of object-oriented practices.

Good object-oriented designs make use of inheritance, so that each knowledge component of the system is defined only once. This facilitates repairs and changes. In the object-oriented paradigm, actions are taken by passing a message to the object that is to act. When, in contrast, actions are taken directly, whenever a change is required, each instance of such actions must be detected and modified. This is very costly. Good object-based design, therefore, enhances productivity immeasurably. For example, having developed software that could display electronic circuit diagrams, with colour coding of component states and explanation of components when their diagram representations are selected, our main software designer, Edward Hughes, was able to build a new system for inputting, displaying, and allowing interactions with troubleshooting flowcharts. He simply made a "flowchart editor object" that inherited most of its capabilities from the same "graphic editor object" that supports the "circuit editor object" he had programmed earlier.

At a more mundane level, when I wanted to build a database of hints generated by Sherlock, all I had to do was modify the "hint display object" to dump all text to a file in addition to sending it to the relevant text window pane object.

Just as with any system, the learning time it takes a user to use a software development approach must be considered. Experience to date has been that object-oriented programming skill takes a long time to train—3 to 6 months for a topnotch programmer with good formal computer science background (roughly master's degree level in computer science). However, even at that high cost, the approach pays.

From a software evaluation viewpoint, use of good objectoriented techniques, including the representation of core design principles and approaches in separable objects, makes a training system much more valuable, and makes changes in the system much more efficient. Moreover, user acceptability is very high. Our experience with several different object-based languages suggests that it would be difficult to wean software developers away from an object-based approach once they have practiced it.

Chapter 14

Explicit Instructional Strategies

The development, and evaluation of a set of domain-independent instructional strategies for teaching problem-solving outcomes in elementary algebra through Intelligent Computer-Aided Instruction (ICAI).

The elementary algebra course is one of the most important for all entry-level freshman students of any major at most universities and 2-year colleges in the United States. Many students have a difficult time understanding the facts, concepts, and principles of algebra. As a result, the procedural portion in subsequent problem solving becomes a difficult task. Many students eventually fail the course.

Our long-term goal was to develop a computer-based tutor that will be as effective in algebra instruction as a human tutor. The purpose of this chapter is an attempt to combine artificial intelligence technology with instructional theories of problem solving to achieve an effective teaching environment in algebra. The design implemented various instructional strategies from various design theories, and developed a set of transformations in the context of linear algebra to improve an existing ICAI system.

INTELLIGENT COMPUTER-ASSISTED INSTRUCTION

In recent years there has been increased emphasis on individualized instruction and computer technology specially applying intelligent learning systems that facilitate learning at all levels of education and training (O'Neil, 1981).

The intelligent learning systems are known as intelligent tutoring systems

(ITS) or intelligent computer-assisted instruction (ICAI). The integral components of any ICAI system may consist of

- The knowledge base: what the learner is to learn, that is, the expert model representing the relevant knowledge in the domain that solves problems like an expert (based on the domain);
- A student model, which may be constructed by comparing the student's performance to the computer-based expert's behaviour on the task; and
- A tutor, that is, a model that should be composed of the desirable properties of a human tutor. The research analytic evidence for ICAI has been reviewed by Littman and Soloway (1988) and Wenger (1987).

An example of such an ICAI programme is MicroSEARCH. MicroSEARCH, based on the work of Sleeman (1987), solves deductive-type problems using a heuristic search strategy. The programme allows selection of transformations and examination of the solution tree as the transformations are applied.

Any problem solving requires a certain amount of search. An integral part of AI today is the theory of heuristic search: search that departs from blind trial and error, which makes use of information drawn from the problem domain to guide itself selectively until it finds solutions or goals.

Algorithms in which arbitrary choice is required are known as nondeterministic algorithms. In general, beginning mathematics students react poorly to any use of nondeterministic algorithms.

They expect all tasks to be solvable by welldefined algorithms. In addition, the teaching system seldom discusses search as a necessary strategy for solving a whole range of tasks. Many tasks in high school and entry-level college mathematics involve nondeterministic searches such as in algebra. Nondeterministic algorithms are currently taught poorly. Students are not taught that search is a legitimate strategy. Sleeman (1987) suggested that students should be explicitly asked

- To state all the transformations they consider to be appropriate to the task, and
- To systematically explore the complete solution space. The major disadvantage of this approach is the potential size of the search space.

TSEARCH was built to solve tasks that involved nondeterministic searches. It provided a variety of support facilities for its users. TSEARCH had been implemented using Rutgers LISP on the DEC-10. TSEARCH is a shell for building a class of intelligent tutoring systems. It does not allow the student to type in the transformed expression but merely the number of the transformation to be applied. TSEARCH works only in a domain in which the set of operators are specified. The system presents a problem for the student to solve. The problem is generated by the system or retrieved from a list of problems.

The selection procedure of the problem is based on issues specified and the state of the student model. An issue, as stated by Kearsley (1988), is meant to be a method of transforming equations, whether a single transformation or the interaction of several transformations, and represents the skills to be acquired by the student.

The transformation is applied to the current expression and results in a new current expression. This generates a tree from the current expressions. The student can backtrack through the tree and pick up other branches. The system automatically redisplays the updated tree after each transformation and analyses the student's transformation choice. If the choice matches the system's preferred (system domain) choice, then it provides positive feedback. If the student's choice does not match the system's preferred choice, further analysis is required.

CRITIQUE OF TSEARCH

Sleeman (1987) stated that TSEARCH has four shortcomings:

- The major disadvantage of TSEARCH is its speed,
- TSEARCH allows students to be very passive in

learning because students can use the HELP facility for a prompt at each stage,

- The task selection algorithm should make use of the information in the transformation matrix to select (appropriate) tasks for the user, and
- The transformation matrix provides valuable information for the type of issue-based coach implemented in the WEST system. Such a coach could occasionally point out better solution paths than those chosen by the user.

THE DESIGN OF MICROSEARCH

MicroSEARCH is a version of TSEARCH implemented on an IBM PC using Pascal. The following design changes were made between the TSEARCH and MicroSEARCH versions.

- Instead of using all the rules for each type of task, only those known to be relevant are used.
- The system now has two phases: an offline phase that creates the "complete" solution space ("complete" up to some predefined cutoff point), and an online phase that accesses the solution and interacts with the student.

ISSUES AND CONCERNS RELATED TO MICROSEARCH

Of the issues raised by Sleeman in the last section, the only one addressed to date by MicroSEARCH has been that of speed. As of today application of *Micro*SEARCH is limited to a very specific domain, as in algebra, where only the *simplification section* was programmed and marketed by Park Row. MicroSEARCH encourages students to do a depth-first search of the task space like TSEARCH.

In ICAI the most common instructional strategies have been discovery learning and gaming. Obviously, one discovers error as well as truth.

Other approaches such as derived from Component Display Theory have not been implemented. More recently, there have been several systematic attempts to provide instructional information into the design of ICAI systems. Such attempts include the design of a new ICAI tutor and the design of instructional strategies to improve existing ICAI programmes. However, neither of these efforts systematically evaluated the resulting "improved" ICAI programmes.

We have chosen for the macrostrategy O'Neil et al.'s (1991) domain- independent instructional strategy to teach problem solving. *Domain* could legitimately refer to subject matter, application area, task, or performance outcome.

Independence can mean "other than" or "as well as" the target domain. *Domain-independent* instructional strategies could mean independent of the subject matter (i.e., strategies independent of math), or independent of the performance outcome (i.e., strategies appropriate both to concept learning and to problem solving), or both.

The problem of domain independence, in other words, is a problem of degree of transfer or generalizability. In this chapter, *independence* means independent of subject matter. Thus, domainindependent strategies are, in effect, strategies to teach particular performance outcomes, that is, problem solving in the particular domain of algebra.

The approach in this study was to synthesize and expand instructional strategies described from the following theoretical position: the domainindependent instructional strategies for problem solving provided by O'Neil et al. (1991) and component display theory by Merrill. Component display theory evolved from Merrill and Tennyson's earlier work on designing concept lessons and from their analysis and research to clarify the categories specified.

Using component display theory, a given presentation can be segmented into a series of discrete

Domain-Independent Instructional Strategies (Learning Conditions) to Teach Problem-Solving Outcomes

- Retrieval of relevant rules and concepts
- Successive presentaton of novel problem situations
- Demonstration of solutions by student

Domain-Independent Instructional Strategy to Teach Diagnostic Problem Solving:

- Define diagnostic problem-solving family to be taught by describing problem-solving characteristics or events pertaining to the family (e.g., "Electrical troubleshooting consists of checking current flow at input and output points.").
- Communicate a description of the appropriate example device(s)as whole system(s) and the necessary concepts and principles of operation in the order prescribed in Table.
- Confirm or teach subordinate skills (e.g., demonstrating how each check is made, how each exchange is done in the example device).
- Describe and demonstrate appropriate diagnostic problem-solving task strategies to be taught for this application (e.g., select component to test based on malfunction probability).
- Provide practice using a variety of novel problems requiring the strategies taught, and provide feedback and correction. displays.

Component display theory assumes that most cognitive instruction occurs through two modes, *telling or questioning,* and that these modes can be used with two instructional elements, generalities, or examples. In component display theory, learning outcomes are classified in two dimensions: the type of content involved (fact, concept, principle, procedure) and the task level (remember, use, find) required for that content. Nizamuddin (1988) provided extensive detail on the instructional design and its implementation in MicroSearch Plus.

Domain-Independent Instructional Strategy to Teach Diagnostic Problem Solving

Communicate a Description of the Appropriate Example Device (s) as Whole System (s) and the Necessary Concepts and Principles of Operation in the Order Prescribed Here:

- Present name and brief overall description of the device including operational controls of inputs and ways in which failures are indicated on the device with examples.
- Present concepts of causal media in system (e.g., current flow if electrical system, forces if mechanical, etc.).
- Present concepts of schematic representation and methods of illustrating physical/schematic mapping to be used with examples.
- Present concept of replaceable units. Present names, locations, and functions of replaceable units using diagrams as needed for examples. Require the student to identify the parts by pointing to them.
- Teach operation and function (how the system works in terms of inputs, controls, component functions, causal flows, and outputs) of major activating and intermediary components, with reference to schematics and physical layout diagrams, taught by tracing causal paths through components on schematics and referencing physical locations.

Domain-Independent Instructional Strategy to Teach Algebra Problem Solving as Implemented in Micro SEARCH Plus

- Define diagnostic problem-solving family to be taught by describing problem-solving characteristics or events pertaining to the family (e.g., "To solve 1st order linear equation," $ax + b = c$).
- Communicate a description of the appropriate example as a whole problem, and necessary concepts and principles of operation in algebra.
- Provide practice, using a variety of novel problems requiring strategies taught, and provide feedback and correction.

The instructional strategies were programmed in Pascal and integrated into the existing MicroSEARCH programme. The ICAI algebra programme MicroSEARCH was developed by Sleeman (1987) and was marketed by Park Row Software (1987).

This programme reflected the state of the art in cognitive science operating in a personal computer environment. Its predominant instructional strategy was that of a guided discovery approach.

The instructional effectiveness of adding our strategies to an existent ICAI shell programme was empirically tested.

AN EXPERIMENTAL STUDY

The altered ICAI programme was compared with the existing package, with three different formats. Students were randomly assigned to each format, that is, the MicroSEARCH test group with only 2 examples and 17 test items, the Micro-

Domain-Independent Instructional Strategy to Teach Algebra Problem-Solving as Implemented in MicroSEARCH Plus. Communicate a Description of the Appropriate Example as a Whole Problem, and Necessary Concepts and Principles of Operation in Algebra as Shown Here:

- Present name and brief overall description of the problem including order of operations (e.g., "We are going to solve a Ist order linear equation. For this problem-solving technique you need to separate the variables and constants of the given problem. That is, keep the variables on one side and constants on the other side, by the methods of combining the like terms, etc.").
- Present concepts and principles of causal information (e.g., equation, solve, addition property of zero, etc.).
- Present concepts and principles of symbolic representation with examples (e.g., $ax + b = c$, $x = c$, $5x = 10$, $x = 2$, $a + 0 = a$, etc.).
- Teach procedure (how to solve the problem, e.g., side change, reciprocal, etc.) of major activating and intermediary steps.

SEARCH group with 48 problems, and the enhanced instructional design group (MicroSEARCH plus).

It was expected that the experimental group

(MicroSEARCH Plus) would perform better than the other groups.

SELECTION OF THE SAMPLE

The sample was taken from a junior college in Southern California. The students were volunteered from beginning and intermediate algebra classes. We started with 140 subjects. For different reasons such as the student leaving early, computer problems, incomplete data, and so on, 37 students were dropped from the final analysis. A total of 103 valid subjects were entered into a computer that used a programme from the Statistical Package for Social Sciences to analyse the data.This sample (n = 103), with an average age of 25.5 years (SD = 7.79), included 31 males and 72 females. Ethnic distribution as 78 Whites, 7 African Americans, 8 Latinos, 4 Native Americans, 4 Asians, and 2 other students. To check the homogeneity of the age difference in all three groups a one-way analysis of variance (ANOVA) was performed. The ANOVA was not statistically significant. Thus the three groups were statistically equivalent on age.

MICROSEARCH

The original MicroSEARCH was developed by Sleeman (1987) for one section of elementary algebra, called the *simplification section*. The current state of our MicroSEARCH Plus is for *solving linear equations,* which is another domain of elementary algebra.Linear equations MicroSEARCH Plus has been created in different structures for different groups. The following are the brief descriptions for each group:

- Two practice problems and 17 test items: The first 2 problems were given for practice. They were similar to the 17 test problems, with no feedback or help. But each subject was assigned a proctor to provide clear understanding of the procedures in MicroSEARCH and the problem itself.

  After finishing the examples, then 17 test items were provided. During the test time, no proctorial help was given. Only two function keys were provided: F3

(NEXT)—leave the current problem and begin the next one; F9 (UNDO)-undo the previous transformation and return the problem to its most recent state.

- Forty-eight practice problems: This set also was divided into two parts.

  The first part had 13 problems with advice messages. The second part consisted of 35 problems with no advice messages. Five function keys were available: F1—help; F3 (NEXT)—leave the current problem and begin the next one; F4 (BACK)—Leave the current problem and return to the previous one; F8 (TREE)—show solution tree —undo the previous

Module 1. *Teach prerequisite concepts:*

- Equation.
- Solve an equation.

Module 2. Teach *prerequisite principle, the addition property of equation:*

- Teach prerequisite concept, additive inverse.
- Teach principle, the addition property of equations.

Module 3. Teach *procedure to solve an equation using the addition property of equations:*

- Teach procedure to solve an equation using the addition property of equations.

Module 4. Teach *prerequisite principle, the multiplication property of equations:*

- Teach prerequisite concept, reciprocal inverse.
- Teach principle, the multiplication property of equations.

Module 5. Teach *procedure, to solve an equation using the multiplication property of equations:*

- Teach prerequisite procedure, remove a coefficient.
- Teach procedure, to solve an equation using the multiplication property of equations.

Module 6. Teach *procedure, to solve an equation using both the addition and the multiplication properties of equations*:

Module 7. *Integrated practice*:

Here no advice messages were given. The following learner control keys were given: F1—help; F3 (NEXT)—leave the current problem and begin the next one; F4 (BACK)—Leave the current problem and return to the previous one; F8 (TREE)—Show solution tree; F9 (UNDO)—undo the previous transformation and return the problem to its most recent state, one step backward at a time.

Every participant in this research project was given an anxiety test before and after the instruction.

The following dependent variables were used: number of problems correctly answered on the test, total steps taken for the test, total time spent to take the test.

Seventeen equations were given to be solved. Any student starting from the initial state of a problem and reaching the goal state was considered to have the right answer. The right answer scored I point and the wrong scored 0 points. No partial credit scores were given. The programme kept track of the total time and counted the number of steps for each individual on each problem.

RESULTS

COMPUTATION SCORE

Out of 103 students, only 65 students' computation placement scores were found in the student record file; number of students in each group as follows:

Table: Performance Measures

Results of Cognitive Test Data (Number of correct test items)	
MicroSEARCH test group	(X=8.5; SD=4.8; n=32)
MicroSEARCH with multiple problem	(X=10.2; SD=4.7; n=36)
MicroSEARCH Plus with instructional enhancements	(X=12.3; SD=3.6; n=35)

MicroSEARCH test group N=22, MicroSEARCH with multiple problems group N = 22, and MicroSEARCH Plus with instructional enhancements group N = 21. The means for

Groups 1, 2, and 3 were 20.50, 20.55, and 20.24, and the standard deviations were 7.50, 5.37, and 5.47, respectively. The differences were not statistically different. Thus, the groups were matched on computational skills before the treatments were initiated.

NUMBER OF CORRECT PROBLEMS

The means for MicroSEARCH test group, MicroSEARCH with multiple problems group, and MicroSEARCH Plus with instructional enhancements group were 8.5, 10.2, and 12.3 respectively.

It was expected that the instructional design enhanced MicroSEARCH Plus group would exhibit significantly more correct answers than either the MicroSEARCH group with multiple problems and advice messages or the MicroSEARCH test group.

Groups were significantly different; $F(2, 102) = 6.26$, $p < 0.05$. The significant omnibus F-test was followed by the Newman-Keuls post hoc tests. A post hoc Newman-Keuls procedure concluded that the MicroSEARCH test only group and the instructional design enhanced MicroSEARCH Plus group, and the MicroSEARCH group with multiple problems and the instructional design enhanced MicroSEARCH Plus group all were significantly different at the.05 level. MicroSEARCH test only group and MicroSEARCH with multiple practice problems group were not significantly different. That means only advice messages with many problems did not significantly improve the problem-solving skills. On the other hand, instructional design enhanced MicroSEARCH Plus significantly improved problem-solving skills more than the other two groups.

STEPS

To complete the 17 test questions the means for MicroSEARCH test group, MicroSEARCH with multiple problems group, and MicroSEARCH Plus group were 203.03, 195.06, and 199.43, and the standard deviations were 131.80, 122,05, and 98.64, respectively.

TIME

The mean total times (in min) taken by the students in MicroSEARCH test group, MicroSEARCH with multiple problems group, and MicroSEARCH Plus group to complete the test were 46.10, 25.43, and 28.61, respectively. The standard deviations were 23.96, 11.53, and 19.90, respectively.

It was expected that the instructional design enhanced MicroSEARCH group would take less time than either the MicroSEARCH group with multiple problems and advice messages or a MicroSEARCH test group. Groups were significantly different; $F(2, 102) = 11.45$, $p < .05$. The significant F-test was followed by the Newman-Keuls post hoc tests. Results indicated that MicroSEARCH test only group was different from both MicroSEARCH with multiple problems group and MicroSEARCH Plus with instructional enhancements group. But MicroSEARCH with multiple problems group and MicroSEARCH Plus with instructional enhancements group did not differ significantly, which means both MicroSEARCH with multiple problems and MicroSEARCH Plus with instructional enhancements group took the same amount of time for the test.

It was expected that the instructional design enhanced MicroSEARCH group would generate significantly fewer steps than the MicroSEARCH group with multiple problems and advice messages or a MicroSEARCH test group. However the groups were not significantly different.

The following are important observations from the correlational studies. The total time to complete the test is directly related to the total steps required to finish the test ($r = .61$, $p = .01$). In other words, the total time depends on the number of steps required to finish the test, which is obvious— The more steps, the more time. Similar relationships also were found in total steps in examples and total time in examples ($r = .48$, $p = .01$).

A direct relationship also was discovered in students who took more steps and who consequently got more problems correct ($r = .43$, $p = .01$). Thus, it may be concluded that in a MicroSEARCH-style test, the more steps taken, the better chance there is to get the right answer; one reason may be the goal-oriented state of the system (i.e., variable = constant).

The outcomes of this experiment supported the major research assertion, that students in the enhanced Micro SEARCH Plus group would produce significantly more correct answers than either the MicroSEARCH with multiple problem and advice message or MicroSEARCH test only groups. It was expected that explicit training in problem solving would result in more efficient as well as effective learning.

The findings of this study suggest there is more room for improvements:

- The data from the study could be used formatively to improve the existing enhanced MicroSEARCH Plus programme, and
- A full set of design ideas including other concepts, principles, and procedures that were not implemented, and more emphasis on common errors, could be added. In addition, other facets of component display theory (for example, more extensive use of secondary presentation forms) can be extended.

Chapter 15

Hypercard Technology

Great interest in developing alternative, truer measures of student knowledge has stimulated national educational policy development , state testing innovation , and visions for local educational reform. Although research has explored the use of technology in an assessment role, it has focused on computers primarily as a surrogate , or as an expert scoring system. Yet the power of technology in an assessment role will be fully realized only if we can unlock its potential to improve the validity, not just the efficiency, of our inferences about student accomplishments. Validity was the main focus of our approach to the application of technology to assessment. An additional constraint was to develop a strategy that used existing software rather than invest in a costly, time-consuming software development effort.

A dual context informed our research. First, we attempted to develop technology-sensitive outcome measures that might be more sensitive to experimental uses of computers in classrooms. Second, we were interested in generating measures that would respond to calls for expanded validity standards. These new validity criteria, among others, include cognitive complexity, instructional sensitivity, transfer and generalizability, and fairness. The topic areas we selected for assessment were content in history and science; the cognitive task measured was the degree of understanding students possessed in these content areas. Although some research in our lab had used written explanations as direct measures of student knowledge , we wished to explore whether students could demonstrate their understanding in alternate ways,

ways that depended less on their language production skills. We wished to explore as directly as possible the way students represented their content knowledge.

KNOWLEDGE REPRESENTATION AS A COGNITIVE CONSTRUCT

Knowledge representation is a theoretical construct devised to help explain human competencies. Attributing cognitive representations to individuals is equivalent to describing classes of related competencies. Representing competencies with structured knowledge can help to illuminate extremely complex behaviour patterns associated with learning and problem solving.

Knowledge structures comprise organized relational knowledge. These structures, called *schemas,* are thought to provide organizing frameworks for interpretation and action. Schemas have been conceived as organizing and relating both declarative and procedural knowledge as well as strategic knowledge. Schemas constitute a framework for comprehending and interpreting objects and events. Researchers believe that schemas have a determining effect on the acquisition of new knowledge and guide knowledge storage and retrieval, generalization and interpretation of ideas, and the initiation and regulation of action.

In the last 15 years or so, there has been a trend in psychological and artificial intelligence research toward understanding the organization and structure of knowledge. In artificial intelligence (AI) research, this focus was necessitated by the inability of early AI programmes using search heuristics to outperform humans. Psychological theories based on search heuristics also failed to model human capabilities adequately. It became clear that search heuristics that did not use an organized knowledge structure were not very effective, so researchers shifted their efforts toward the development of theories that could account for the role of knowledge structures in cognition.

Many researchers in cognitive science have focused on the so-called noviceto-expert shift ; that is, they have tried to describe the difference between novice and expert knowledge structures in specific domains. To achieve such descriptions, knowledge structures must be assessed: A number of well-known techniques exist for evaluating knowledge structures involving, for example, various kinds of cognitive, conceptual semantic maps. Other methods have included the documentation of misconceptions, analyses of perceived similarities among elements in a domain , and information-processing analyses of problem-solving strategies. Although a plethora of evaluation techniques has been tested, there has been little systematic work on the question of what causes changes in knowledge structures.

In cognitive research, a common way to represent conceptual knowledge is in the form of nodes and links between them, nodes representing concepts or their attributes, and links the relations between concepts. Under this model, domain understanding develops by making connections (i.e., links) between ideas, facts, procedures, and other types of domain knowledge.

Views of memory suggest knowledge is organized in complex networks rather than in linear sequences. These semantic networks include conceptual, factual, and procedural knowledge components. In certain interpretive disciplines, such as the field of social studies and more particularly the area of history, there are fewer linear or unequivocal hierarchical relationships among relevant concepts, facts, and procedures.

Representing knowledge as a network of nodes and links is consistent with semantic mapping techniques and recent versions of schema theory , as well as related approaches to understanding that discuss the integration of skills and concepts.

The theoretical inspiration for the origins of cognitive structure can be traced back to the 1960s. Ausubel (1963) attributed success in the learning and retention of meaningful material to the cognitive structure that the learner possessed. The concepts contained in the learner's cognitive structure and the relationships between them are hypothesized to be primarily responsible for the integration of new material in the learner's existing cognitive structure—"an individual's organization, stability, and clarity of knowledge in a particular subject-matter field". Ausubel (1963) also stated that "the importance of cognitive structure variables has been generally underestimated in the past because preoccupation with noncognitive, rote, and motor types of learning has tended to focus attention on such current situational and interpersonal factors as practice, drive, incentive, and reinforcement variables. Cognitive structure is also, in its own right, the most significant independent variable influencing (facilitating, inhibiting, limiting) the learner's capacity for acquiring more new knowledge in the same field". Shavelson (1974) defined cognitive structure as "an assemblage of identifiable elements and the relationships between those elements" and as "the structure in a student's or teacher's mind, a hypothetical construct referring to the organization (relationships) of concepts in memory".

COGNITIVE MAPS

The cognitive map learning strategy approach is based on research on human memory. Early conceptual work was instrumental in advancing the notion that human memory may be organized as a network, comprising concepts (nodes) interconnected by different kinds of relationships (links). Quillian also offered the notion that there are certain types of nodes: *type* nodes, that lead directly to the meaning of its concept name, while interconnecting with other types of nodes, and *token* nodes, allowing for an indirect association with the concept. The physical representation of these nodes requires each type node to be placed in a different plane from the potentially many token nodes linked with it. The token nodes subsequently link to other token nodes located in the same plane. This memory model set forth by Quillian (1968) allows for various types of nodes to be used for eliciting content knowledge.

Dansereau and Holley stated: "Networking forms the basis for the primary strategies in the learning strategy system." In their research, students identified concepts and represented the relationships between them in the form of a concept map. Empirical research on the effects of concept mapping found that students using the concept mapping strategy performed significantly better on text processing tasks than students using their own method.

This early work also experimented with the categories and specific number of link labels used in concept maps. Initially, 13 links were provided, which proved to be somewhat unwieldy for students. Later work settled on a six-link system, consisting of hierarchical, chaining, and clustering link types. The six links in the system were:

- Is part of,
- Is a type of (an example of, a kind of),
- leads to (results in, causes),
- Is like (is similar to),
- Has (characterized by, is a property of), and
- Illustrates (supports, is evidence of).

Why should concept maps work? One argument relates to the use of cognitive resources. When constructing concept maps, the learner is free from tasks such as "writing everything down" and can concentrate on higher level cognitive processes. Keeping discourse to a minimum could potentially prove beneficial to student subpopulations with less language fluency. A second explanation for the potential power of concept maps is the focus they provide on spatial displays. Ault (1985) contended that "a concept map depicts hierarchy and relationships among concepts. It demands clarity of meaning and integration of details. Mapping exercises require one to think in multiple directions and to switch back and forth between different levels of abstraction". Novak, Gowin, and Johansen (1983) concluded that learning could be more meaningful if students "map" key concepts to reveal hierarchical levels and relationships. Jonassen (1984) went so far as to state that "the spatial distances between ideas (as measured by the number of intermittent links between ideas) are roughly equivalent to the semantic distances between concepts or schemata in memory".

Concept mapping research has been investigated as an instructional intervention in biology, general science , and geology. Previous research has shown significant differences in performance on main ideas, including close and essay measures, when students used concept mapping techniques to represent knowledge of a geology text. The inference stemming from that particular research study is that students constructing concept maps are acquiring and organizing main ideas and concepts.

In organizing or reorganizing semantic information, the grouping of concepts is almost always along the structural lines of superset, subset, similarity, part, proximity, consequence, and precedence. It is important to note that these relations can be applied in different ways to the same set of concepts. Collins and Quillian (1972) presented various types of relations between concepts, and possible links (in parentheses) have been categorized into their various relational categories:

- Superset (is a, is a member of),
- Subset (consists of, contains),
- Similarity (is like, is not like),
- Part (part of),
- Proximity (is adjacent to, is next to),
- Consequence (leads to, influences, causes), and
- Precedence (prior to).

There has been other research investigating students' interconnections of pairs of concepts (nodes) via the use of relational links. There has been a growing consensus that links should be named, modifiable, directional, and represented the following list of link categories:

- Hierarchy (type),
- Chain (leads to),
- Cluster (characteristic),
- procedural (next),
- influences, and
- part. Duncan (1989) offered the following set of link categories:
- Being (is a),
- Showing (is an example of),

- Causing (leads to, causes),
- Using (uses, can be used by),
- Having (has),
- Including (includes), and
- Similarity (is like).

CRESST EMPIRICAL RESEARCH

The intent of our research was to explore the utility of knowledge representation using a hypertext system as an alternative strategy to measure student understanding. The research we report is very much in progress. We describe our studies of expert representations in history topics and explorations in the assessment use of hypertext to measure history and science understanding of secondary school students. In these studies we used an adaptation of the Lambiotte et al. (1989) analysis. In a prior study (Baker, Niemi, Gearhart, & Herman, 1990) we used HyperCard as a vehicle for directly eliciting content knowledge representations from high school students.

In this study, 28 11th-grade history students were given an assessment of their understanding of the Great Depression historical period. The students were taught to use HyperCard to construct their knowledge representations of the Great Depression. Specific relational links were to be used in the knowledge representation task:

- Is prior to,
- Influences,
- leads to,
- Is like,
- Is not like,
- Is a type of,
- Is part of,
- Supports,
- Is an example,
- Is a property of, and
- Is used for. Prior knowledge, reading comprehension, and essays were administered. In an effort to explore construct validity, students completed additional

topic-related measures. The results of this study indicated that the technique was feasible.

We were also interested in the expert/novice paradigm in our context. What are the characteristics of expert knowledge structures, including structural patterns, structural elements, and content details of their direct knowledge representations? How similar are expert-constructed knowledge structures in terms of conceptual and structural attributes? Are there common declarative elements, relational links, and structural patterns that are found in the direct knowledge representations of experts?

Experts represent their knowledge at a deeper, more conceptual level than novices. Previous studies and research have shown that experts use principlebased conceptual entities whereas novices' knowledge structures are syntactically or surface-feature oriented, leading to more superficial relationships between concepts. The first hypothesis is that history experts will construct more cohesive direct knowledge structures about U.S. history knowledge than will students from the broad high school population.

Can expert performance be used as a basis for setting standards for students' knowledge representation in history? In order to use expert knowledge representations as criteria to rate student work, there must exist a degree of similarity between experts' representations. Components of similarity should include link relations, complexity, and semantic content of organization of the knowledge base.

When experts represent their subject matter knowledge, they perceive large meaningful patterns in their domain. Experts not only have more content knowledge in a given domain but also have a superior ability to organize their knowledge bases.

An expert study in content knowledge representation of U.S. history was conducted with three PhD history students. Each doctoral student wrote six essays over a 2-day period covering four content areas of U.S. history, including the Revolutionary War, the Civil War, immigration, and the Great Depression. Each expert read each historical debate (Paine-

Inglis, Henry-Inglis, LincolnDouglas, Pixley-Brooks, Simon-Graham, and Roosevelt-Long) and the respective writing prompts, and subsequently completed an explanation task for each prompt.

On the third day, the three doctoral students constructed HyperCard-stack concept maps for the Civil War and Great Depression topics. The HyperCard stacks contained the following relational links:

- Is prior to,
- Influences,
- Leads to,
- Is like,
- Is not like,
- Iis a type of,
- Is part of,
- Supports,
- Is an example,
- Is a property of, and
- Iused for.

The PhD students generated the nodes, noting them as concepts, facts, or procedures, and labeled the relationships between pairs of nodes using the set of relational links. Expert essays and concept maps were analyzed and some consistencies were discovered concerning both intra- and intertask comparisons. There was roughly 75% (50 out of 69) agreement between concepts used in the essay and nodes included in the concept map tasks. In both the Civil War and Great Depression topics, approximately the same number of nodes was used by the experts. The experts represented their views on the positions of the participants in the debates by relating concepts and principles to supporting facts. The experts used on average about 50% concept nodes and 50% fact nodes in their concept maps. The experts wove facts (Kansas-Nebraska Act, Missouri Compromise, and U.S. Constitution) and concepts (slavery, popular sovereignty, and states' rights) together by integrating both temporal and abstract aspects of their knowledge representations. One major difference between experts and novices was in the ability to correctly identify fact nodes and their relationships to more abstract ideas.

As with the expert studies, HyperCard provides a basic representational tool. Its basic unit consists of "a node, a link, and another node". Our work, related to Lambiotte et al. (1989) and Fischer (1989), requires the student to construct directly a structure in HyperCard. Thus the scoring of this open-ended task presents considerable challenge. Rather than developing totally arbitrary scoring schemes or using expert-novice comparisons, we have under- taken a series of research studies designed to explore the feasibility and validity of scoring dimensions using construct validity approaches.

CONSTRUCT VALIDITY STUDY

Subjects

Subjects for this study were 24 11th-grade and 21 12th-grade students in two classrooms participating in the Apple Classrooms of Tomorrow^{SM} (ACOT) project, an ongoing, multiyear investigation of the effects of high access to technology on educational outcomes and procedures. Most students had been enrolled in ACOT classrooms for at least 2 years. All had extensive experience with Macintosh computers and hypermedia environments.

Content Materials

Two topics in each subject area were tested:

- Primary texts from the pre-Civil War and Great Depression eras in U.S. history, and
- Descriptions of two types of analysis in chemistry, one involving tests to distinguish diet from regular soda[1] and the other a series of tests used to identify five different baking ingredients.

Tasks: Students were given texts to read as part of the assessment procedure (Baker et al., 1990, 1991). In this study we used the following texts: for the Civil War, the Lincoln-Douglas debates; for the Great Depression, speeches by Franklin D. Roosevelt and Huey Long; and for the two chemistry topics, descriptions of chemical analysis demonstrations performed by a high school teacher. The two chemistry texts were similar except for the structure of the analysis described. Each text took between 15 and 25 min to read. In the case of the chemical tests for sugar in sodas, any of the several tests described would be sufficient to identify the presence of sugar, that is, to distinguish diet from regular soda. In the case of quantitative tests to identify baking ingredients, results from several different chemical tests were needed to identify each of five different substances.

HyperCard Materials

Diskettes with specially modified HyperCard stacks were provided to students. These stacks contained built-in pull-down menus of link and node types. The link and node types were adapted for the science and history topics used in this study from semantic network and concept mapping literature. An example of a HyperCard screen is shown.

Individual HyperCard cards served as nodes in the concept maps students generated, and links were represented as buttons on the cards.

The node-type menu enabled students to label the cards as concepts, facts, or procedural nodes.

Tab le: Relational Links in 3 ExperimentalKnowledge Representation

Prior to
Influences
Leads to
Is like
Is not like
Is part of
Is used for
Supports
Is an example of
Is a property of
From Baker and Niemi (1991).

A menu of 10 relational links was also provided to help students identify relations among the concepts, facts, and events they included in their HyperCard knowledge representations. This menu did not include the "type of" links used in the graduate student study.

Each student completed a sequence of assessment tasks, including one history topic and one science topic. It took the 11th-graders who participated in the study 9 1/2 class periods, or about 6 1/3 hrs spread over 5 days, to complete all tasks. The 12th-graders spent 7 class periods, or about 4 2/3 hrs over 4 days, to complete all tasks except the history essay. All tests and questionnaires were administered by a member of our research team. Combining each history topic with each science topic yielded four topic sets. At the 11th-grade level, the order of the subject areas, history and science, was counterbalanced, and the four topic sets were also counterbalanced, producing eight possible topic orderings. Twelfth-graders took the science tests first, and topic orders were counterbalanced within the two subject areas. Thus, each topic set was given to about one-quarter of the students at each grade level.

TRAINING IN KNOWLEDGE REPRESENTATION

Prior to undertaking the assessment tasks, all students received training in HyperCard knowledge representation. Students were given about 30 min of training in the task of using HyperCard specifically for knowledge representation purposes. The trainer modeled the use of representation using the prespecified links but a different topic:

The area of music was chosen specifically because it was anticipated that students would have considerable background knowledge. Under-standing of the links was assessed by a criterion test in which students were given 16 node pairs and asked to generate as many different links as possible. All students demonstrated that they could use at least nine link types correctly. Understanding of node types was tested by requiring students to label five nodes correctly. After training, the following sequence of activities and time allocations were repeated for each subject area (science and history):

- 20-item prior knowledge test, 10 min;
- 5-item attitude measure, 5 min;
- Read texts, 20 min;
- Generate HyperCard stack, 40 min;
- 5-item attitude measure, 5 min;
- Write essay, 40 min;
- 20-item metacognitive measure, 10 min;
- 5-item attitude measure, 5 min;
- Debriefing questionnaire, 15 min. Because of the schedule constraints, l2th-grade students were unable to complete the essay task.

ESSAY DATA AND SCORING

Students completed relevant essays following each representation using word processing software. Two trained raters scored all essays on five validated dimensions: general impression of content quality, number of principles and concepts, prior knowledge, proportion of detail from texts, and misconceptions. Each dimension was scored on a 1-to-5point scale, with I representing the lowest performance level. Subject (history and science) order was counterbalanced across the two raters, and within each subject area, the order of the essays was independently randomized for each rater.

ANALYSES AND RESULTS

One way to explore the utility of HyperCard representations is to compare them to other indicators of student competence.

We posit that there should be some regular relationships between performance on our scored essays and elements of the HyperCard representation.

We expect reasonable relationships because our essay scoring scheme does not explicitly credit expression and other felicitous verbal skills, but instead attends to the extent to which the student is judged to have elaborated understanding of the topic area, a competence presumed measured by the representation. We also collected questionnaire and transcript data as additional measures of competence.

HYPERCARD ELEMENTS

Our computer programme automatically calculated the number of total nodes, node types, total links, and link types. Means and standard deviations are reported for history knowledge structure elements and for science knowledge structure elements in Table show that procedural nodes are rarely used in students' history maps, compared with their science maps. Also, patterns of link use are different across the two subject areas; for instance, the "example" link occurs more frequently in science than in history maps.

In this set of experiments we also provided a pull-down menu of node types: facts, concepts, procedural nodes, and other (uncodable) categories. Our findings suggest that students clearly differentiated the uses of nodes by subject matter area. Table displays the proportion of total nodes labeled by category for each of the task areas.

Facts are critical elements in all four tasks; however, they dominate in the history area. Concepts show relatively stronger frequency in the history area, but the major differences occur with the procedural node area where the science use averages more than four times the use in history. Such differences are expected, given the typical focus in history on declarative knowledge.

Different use patterns emerged as well for the types of links as a function of subject matter. Table presents the link categories for four tasks by topic.

Clearly, the links "part of," "example," and "used for" were found to be appropriate to the science tasks and links such as "influences" more appropriate for the history task.

Another set of relationships useful for analysis is the average number of links per node. Higher averages suggest a more elaborated view of the topic. The average links per node calculated by student. These data differ somewhat from the results obtained by dividing total links by total nodes.

Qualitative Review of Stacks; Inspection of the HyperCard stacks suggested that many students possessed a low level of prior knowledge. This was supported by the students' low performance on the prior knowledge tests.

Chapter 16

A Look Into The Future

Harold Borko's interest in electronic computers and their application to the behavioral sciences arises from his education and experience in mathematics and psychology. His studies in the field of mathematics and statistics led to an M.A. degree in psychometrics at the University of Southern California. A desire to apply as well as explore basic psychological principles was fulfilled by award of a Ph.D. in clinical psychology in 1952 at the same university. As a clinical psychologist he served in the United States Army until the latter part of 1956, when he resigned his commission to accept employment with The RAND Corporation. There, and later with System Development Corporation, he worked on problems involving the implementation of a system training programme for the Air Defence Command and used electronic computers to design and produce training exercises and to analyse the results of the training programme. At present, he is a member of the research staff where he is studying the application of computers to language-data processing and information retrieval, with emphasis on automatic machine abstracting and indexing of documents. In September 1959, he organized and taught a course called "The Use of Electronic Computers in Psychological Research" at the University of Southern California. This book had its origin in that course.

What lies ahead in the field of data processing and computing? Whatever they may be, the developments will affect the lives of all of us. We must be concerned with: What lies ahead? Without being prophets or seers, when we analyse the happenings of yesterday and today, it seems reasonable that we should be able to make predictions about tomorrow. All science is based on the assumption that future events are determined by past occurrences. Difficulties arise when we make predictions without full knowledge of the pertinent facts. To the extent that this knowledge is lacking, our predictions err. Although we recognize that we are on shaky ground, the need seems to justify the risk; let us move boldly and look into the future.

ADVANCES IN HARDWARE DESIGN

GREATER OPERATING SPEEDS

Undoubtedly there will be more computers tomorrow than there are today, but what will be their salient characteristics? There are general trends in computer design, and if we refer back to the chapter on the historical development and extend the trend line, we should be able to make some reasonable predictions. The desire for greater operating speeds dominates both the early history and the more recent developments in computer technology. As progress was made, speed of computation was reduced from hours to minutes and then seconds. Now we deal with milliseconds and microseconds, and we already have a new word in our vocabulary—the nanosecond, or onebillionth of a second. Unquestionably, the computers of the future will be faster than the machines presently available.

GREATER STORAGE CAPACITY

Concomitant with greater speeds, our extrapolated trend lines clearly indicate that the computers of the future will have greatly increased storage capacities. Progress is already being made in this direction.

Magnetic ferrite cores are being reduced in size, thus making it possible to package a greater storage capacity in a smaller physical area. Similarly, high density magnetic recording is being perfected so that more computer words can be stored in less space. Besides these improvements on the available hardware, a number of experimental memory devices are under development; one or more of these could lead to a greatly improved storage facility. One such system is a *diode-capacitor matrix* which stores words in a two-dimensional array and provides for parallel access. This system is more expensive than magnetic core memory, but it has many advantages, and as the price of components decreases, the system may become economically feasible. Also under development is a *ferroelectric storage system*. This device uses ferroelectric hysteresis in approximately the same manner as magnetic hysteresis is used by magnetic cores. The ferroelectric storage system is very compact, operates at a very fast rate, and uses very little power.

A prototype of a *thin film memory* has been designed and built at the Lincoln Laboratory of M.I.T. This experimental memory is constructed of inch circular spots, 600 angstroms * thick, and spaced ten to the inch. The memory contains 32 ten-bit words on two pieces of glass each holding a 16 × 16 array of spots. It is being installed in the control element of the TX-2 computer. Developmental work aimed at expanding the size of the unit is in progress.

A number of photographic storage systems are under development and these provide very interesting possibilities for future use. The Bell Telephone Laboratories are experimenting with the use of photographic plates as permanent memory stores for directory information and instructions for the telephone electronic switching system.

Data are stored in the form of thousands of tiny clear dots on an otherwise opaque photographic area 2 inches square. These spots of clear and opaque film are scanned by a beam which is generated by a cathode ray tube and focused by a system of lenses. The memory has random access and can locate and read a 68-bit word in 2.5 microseconds.

IBM, in the course of its work on language translation, has coded a Russian-English machine translation dictionary onto a 10-inch glass disc. The binary coded data are arranged in 700 concentric tracks which are photographically printed on the outer edge of the disc. By the use of photo reduction processes, 30 million bits are stored on this single 10-inch revolving disc. In all probability, this compact, high-density, high-speed storage system soon will be adapted to other scientific and business data processing problems.

CHARACTER READERS

Although progress has been made in increasing the internal operating speed and storage capacity of the computer, the methods of providing input data have remained relatively unchanged. Information is first coded and punched onto cards or paper tape. It may then be converted to a magnetic tape format or directly used as an input to the computer. In either case, converting information into a coded computer format is a slow and expensive process. The advent of character reader devices portends a major breakthrough in this area. In essence, a character reading device is designed to convert data—words or numerals—into a computer code without human intervention. A number of such devices are currently available. Many banks are using magnetic character readers. Using this machine requires that the original information be printed in magnetic ink and in a special type font. Another type of character reading device is employed by the major oil companies for use with their credit cards. This device does not require the use of magnetic ink, but it does specify specially designed characters. Obviously, the next stage will be the design of equipment capable of scanning a page of ordinary type and automatically converting the information thereon to a code suitable for computer processing. Prototypes of such equipment have in fact been developed, and commercial models will be available within the next few years.

GREATER RELIABILITY OF OPERATION

Currently, computers are used to process data which have been collected earlier. Thus two distinct steps are involved in the sequence of operations: first, the data are collected and coded; then, the data are processed. Since the two portions of the work are separated in time, the computer is always dealing with "old" data, such as yesterday's sales records. In most instances, this delay creates no hardship, because the results are still much more current than would have been possible without the use of the computer. There is, however, a growing trend to use the computer for "real-time" operational problems in which the data are processed as collected. The Air Defence SAGE System is an example of such use. In this application, the computer is used to monitor and update aircraft radar returns. But real-time operations are not limited to defence installations. The Remington-Rand UNIVAC 490 is a real-time system designed to provide business management with up-to-date operational information as it happens. This system is currently being used for airline reservation control, and it provides the airlines with accurate, instantaneous information of seat availability, cancellations, sales, and flight data.

The computer will be used to a greater extent than at present for realtime data processing. Before this prediction of future applications can come true, the computer must become a more reliable machine. In realtime operations, one cannot afford down time as a result of machine failure. This does not say that the present generation of computers is not reliable, but more time is spent on repairs and servicing than can be tolerated in economical real-time operations.

Today's answer to this problem is found in duplexing the computer facilities, but this is an expensive solution. Future generations of computers will be more reliable and less subject to machine failure.

Some steps are already being taken in this direction, as can be inferred from the widespread use of transistorized printed circuit cards. These components are less subject to failure than are vacuum tubes. In the future—and the process has already started—the printed circuits will be manufactured in automated factories under computer control. Not only will automation cut costs, but component variability will be reduced and system reliability increased.

CHANGE IN MACHINE LOGIC

The very term "computer" implies the ability to calculate, i.e., to perform the standard arithmetic functions of addition, subtraction, multiplication, division, etc. Historically, this is what the machines were designed to do. But computers can do more, and the trend is to increase and improve upon their logical decision-making capabilities. At present, these improvements are being made within the framework of the traditional machine logic. But electronic data processing systems in the broadest sense of the term are not calculators but are symbol manipulators. In the future, machine logic will be designed to process efficiently natural language and symbols rather than merely to add numbers.

The first faltering steps in this direction are being taken now. Computers are being used to translate languages, to compose music, to simulate social organizations, etc. This trend will be accelerated as new logical components make their appearance.

INCREASED DEVELOPMENT OF SPECIAL PURPOSE COMPUTERS

In this area, the trend lines are not nearly as clear and defined as in the preceding areas. Nevertheless, present trends indicate that future designs will deemphasize the large, expensive general purpose computers and will feature the smaller, more economical special purpose machines. These computers will be designed to do a particular job and to do it quickly, reliably, and economically.

In the early stages of development there is a great need for large, highly flexible machines. There is a need for experimentation in order to define the problem properly and to discover the means for solving it. There is a need for flexibility and the capability of doing many things—even though this capability is not exploited to its fullest. A high price is paid for these unused features. With maturity, the problems are defined and the operational procedures become standardized. Therefore, as the computer industry moves out of its early infancy to a more mature phase of development, there will be less need for general purpose machines. The data processing systems of the future will contain a number of compatible, special purpose computers, all integrated and operating with great efficiency.

ADVANCES IN PROGRAMING LANGUAGES

We have seen many advances in the design of computer hardware. Not the least of these is the proliferation of new computers that are appearing on the market at an increasing rate. This fact is of great significance to the programer. One can study, work hard, and become an expert programer on one machine. Then, for any one of a number of reasons (the programer takes a job with another company having a different machine, or his own company changes machines, etc.), he is no longer an expert. True, there is some transfer of training, but the programer must start again to learn new codes and a new machine language. Were only a single individual to find himself in this situation, it would be merely sad; but since this has been the common experience of many programers, the waste in manpower and money is tragic.

PROBLEM-ORIENTED LANGUAGES

A need exists for a compatible system in which programmes can be readily translatable from one machine to another. It is highly unlikely, and somewhat illogical, to expect competing manufacturers to design compatible hardware. It is logical, however, to standardize the programing language, and a great deal of effort is being spent in this direction. Standardization can be accomplished only by changing the emphasis from programing in machine language to programing in a problem-oriented language. This change of emphasis is beginning to occur and the trend will be accelerated in the future. ALGOL (*algo*rithmic programing *l*anguage), designed for scientific

numerical calculations, appeared in 1958. Concurrently, COBOL (*co*mmon *b*usiness *o*riented *l*anguage) was developed as an aid in the solution of business data processing problems. In addition, many manufacturers and some large user organizations are developing their own compilers specifically applicable to their own equipment and functions.

These problem-oriented languages are helpful, but they cannot be regarded as the panacea for all programing difficu-lties. They are costly to build and require many man-years of labour to perfect. The effort is worthwhile if the investment can be amortized over a number of years of operational use. But, occasionally, the computer becomes obsolete soon after the compiler for it has been designed. What is needed is an intermediate language—intermediate between the problem-oriented language and the machine language. (This concept was discussed in Section 7.3.) Some of the nation's most skilled programers are working in this area, and it is predicted that their efforts will soon bear fruit.

USE OF NATURAL LANGUAGE

Looking now to a distant future, we can glimpse some even more exciting developments. Programing codes are very precise, formal language structures by which the operator communicates with the computer. Codes are necessary because the computer and the programer do not speak the same language. Until now we have directed our effort toward teaching men the language of the machine; i.e., they learned to write the instructions in machine language. The problem-oriented language is a compromise approach by which both men and machine learn a third, or intermediate, language. Why not go the whole way and teach the machine to understand the natural language of man?

Before this can be accomplished, progress must be made toward the solution of two major problems. The first has to do with pattern recognition-i.e., the development of hardware capable of sensing and recognizing the different patterns which make up the numbers and letters of the alphabet. Some of the research in the field of perception and the use of the computer to generate and recognize patterns. Section pointed out that we already have a number of character-sensing devices that can "read" special type fonts, characters printed in magnetic ink, and even standard printed characters. Certainly progress is being made in this area. The second issue, and one more difficult to solve, involves programing the computer to interpret these sets of characters and to follow instructions or draw inferences. Eventually these and similar studies will result in the development of a computer programme which

(Institute of Radio Engineers) speaks for some engineers, the ACM (Association for Computing Machinery) speaks for a group of data processors and programers. But the breadth of the field of information processing extends beyond engineering and programing.

The diverse professional affiliations require an organization that will provide a common meeting ground and will help this expanding profession attain status. The critical shortage of qualified personnel has been emphasized; there is an equally great need for standards of competence and accreditation. A number of the leaders in the computer field have recognized the need. Daniel D. McCracken voiced similar views in *Datamation* early in 1960. Professional recognition of the information specialist can be the expected result of the creation and continued support of an organization that provides for the exchange of ideas and the establishment of standards for accreditation among information specialists.

Index